WORKS of ST. BONAVENTURE

COMMENTARY
ON THE GOSPEL OF JOHN

Bonaventure
Texts in Translation
Series

General Editor
Robert J. Karris, O.F.M.

Volume XI

Commentary
on the Gospel of John

Franciscan Institute Publications
Saint Bonaventure University
2007

WORKS of ST. BONAVENTURE

COMMENTARY

ON THE GOSPEL OF JOHN

Introduction, Translation and Notes
by Robert J. Karris, O.F.M.

Franciscan Institute Publications
The Franciscan Institute
Saint Bonaventure University
Saint Bonaventure, NY 14778
2007

Copyright © 2007
The Franciscan Institute
St. Bonaventure University
St. Bonaventure, New York

ISBN: 978-1-57659-143-7

Bonaventure, Saint, Cardinal, ca. 1217-1274.
  [Commentarius in Evangelium S. Ioannis. English]
  Commentary on the Gospel of John / St. Bonaventure ; edited
by Robert J. Karris.
    p. cm.—(Franciscan Institute publications)
  (Bonaventure texts in translation series ; v. 11)
  (Works of St. Bonaventure)

ISBN 978-1-57659-143-7 (alk. paper)
1. Bible. N.T. John--Commentaries. I. Karris, Robert J. II. Title.
BS2615.53B6613 2007
226.5'07—dc22
                    2007004937

Printed in the United States of America
Bookmasters, Inc.
Ashland, Ohio

TABLE OF CONTENTS

INTRODUCTION

HOW TO APPROACH BONAVENTURE'S COMMENTARY ON THE GOSPEL OF ST. JOHN

St. Bonaventure was like many a friar after him, for he never threw anything away. At the base of his Commentary on St. John is the exposition he had earlier created as a biblical bachelor. When he became a Master, Bonaventure gradually added 414 *quaestiones* that plumbed deeper into the meaning of a particular verse[1]

---

[1] I give one example. In his commentary on John 11:1 Bonaventure gives the literal interpretation: "So the condition of the sick person is given with a name, as the text says: *Now a certain man was sick, Lazarus*. From *the hometown*, as the text adds, *of Bethany*, to which place the Lord was accustomed to come. The text also mentions Lazarus' family when it says: *the village of Mary and Martha, his sisters*." In his *quaestio* 1 (John 11 n. 12) Bonaventure digs deeper into the meaning of this verse: "Question 1 deals with the very first verse where it is said: 'Lazarus was from the village of Mary and Martha, his sisters.' – Since 'the head of the woman should be the man,' the text should rather have put it differently: Martha and Mary were from the village of Lazarus. – It has to be maintained that it is not without reason that Mary and Martha are introduced as principal characters in this verse, since, although they are women by gender, nevertheless they exceeded Lazarus in strength of mind and in virtue. For it was by merit of their faith, as will become clear below, that Lazarus was resuscitated. So pay close attention that the Evangelist says two things. First, from the village of Mary and Martha, so that he gives a preference to the women instead of to Lazarus because of virtue. Second, his sisters, so that he might mention them last and thus delay mention of the fragility of their sex."

and some 26 non-literal interpretations to explore the polyvalence of a text[2] and to make his commentary more useful for preachers.[3] Further, he fashioned "a division of the text" or what we might prosaically call an "outline" to convey his overall interpretation of John's Gospel.[4] Finally, he articulated a "prooemium" or "Introduction" to lead his readers to the same mountain from which he was surveying John's Gospel. From this mountain Bonaventure was overwhelmed by the gracious and generous majesty of the Incarnate Word as he reveals himself in his life, death, and resurrection. From this mountain peak Bonaventure sees clearly that John's goal, which stems from his role as eye-witness to the Incarnate Word's revelation, is to lead his readers to faith.[5] So if readers immediately jump into Bonaventure's

---

[2] A suitable example occurs in John 19 n. 60 where Bonaventure explores the allegorical meaning of John 19:34 by asking why Christ's side was opened after his death and not before: "The allegorical reason is this: Just as Eve was formed from the side of Adam when he was asleep, so too the Church was formed from the side of Christ sleeping on the cross. For Augustine maintains: 'Because of this the second Adam slept on the cross, so that from there his wife might be formed, that flowed from his side.'"

[3] Perhaps this is one of the reasons for the popularity of Bonaventure's Commentary on John. See Dominic V. Monti, "Bonaventure's Interpretation of Scripture in his Exegetical Works," PhD thesis, The Divinity School, University of Chicago, 1979, p. 105 n. 1: "Stegmüller, n. 1778 (2: 211-12), counts some sixty-seven extant manuscripts. This is one of the most widely diffused of any Scholastic commentaries. The Commentary on John of Aquinas, for example, survives in only twenty-three."

[4] I invite readers to page ahead in this Introduction and to thumb through Bonaventure's Table of Contents or "division of the text" to get a feel for his reading strategy.

[5] See Prooemium 10: "Now regarding this question of certitude it must be said: 'The end imposes a necessity on those things that pertain to the end.' And since this teaching has as its goal to bring about faith, it ought not have the certitude of logical demonstration. It could not have internal certitude, because that flows from grace. It should not possess persuasive power. Therefore, the situation must be

Commentary at a particular passage, e.g., John 2:1-11, the wedding feast at Cana, they will surely derive some benefit from Bonaventure's exposition. But they would gain far more benefit if they would see this passage, as Bonaventure did in his "division of the text," as part of Christ the Word's manifestation to various groups and individuals, some of whom respond with sight and faith and others who do not. Further, because of their study of Bonaventure's "prooemium" readers would realize that through his narrative of Jesus' first sign John, the eye witness, endeavors to lead them to a deeper faith (see John 20:30-31). In brief, Bonaventure's Commentary on John is a hybrid, composed of various elements, all of which function very well together, and many of which will be the subject of further consideration in this Introduction.

CONTEMPORARY DIMENSIONS OF BONAVENTURE'S COMMENTARY

Context is everything. In the contemporary scholarly context Bonaventure's Commentary on John is unknown.[6] The leading Catholic commentators of our era, Raymond E.

---

that it has the certitude of authority. And this is the reason why all books of sacred scripture are handed down in the narrative mode, not by rational argumentation, for their purpose is to bring about faith, which occurs by means of free consent."

   [6] One can speculate on the reasons for this. Perhaps, one reason may stem from the overall scholarly prejudice towards medieval exegesis as "all allegory." Another reason, related to the first, may be scholarly lassitude or ignorance. A powerful reason may be the failure of the Franciscan Family to make this commentary available in an English translation. This failure is being remedied in this volume.

Brown,[7] Rudolf Schnackenburg,[8] and Francis J. Moloney,[9] make no mention of St. Bonaventure, even in their bibliographies. The very extensive bibliography in Ernst Haenchen's two-volume commentary in the Hermeneia series makes no reference to Bonaventure's Commentary on John.[10] The most recent commentary that I know of is a German handbook of 796 pages. Its bibliography of fifty-four pages has no entry for Bonaventure's *Commentary on the Gospel of St. John*.[11] So I have to start from scratch in presenting the contemporary dimensions of his commentary.

Willy-nilly many of my readers join me and bring to our reading of St. Bonaventure's *Commentary on the Gospel of St. John* eyes that have been trained to see things from the perspective of contemporary New Testament Studies. Our eyes will be disappointed, for they will not see Bonaventure engaging in questions about the historical background of John's Gospel. Thus, while Bonaventure cannot help but notice the hostility shown Jesus by the Jews in John's Gospel, his lack of historical critical methodology does not allow him to provide a consistently nuanced reading of the polemical passages in John.[12]

---

[7] See *The Gospel According to John (i-xii, xiii-xxi)*. Anchor Bible 29, 29A (Garden City: Doubleday, 1966, 1970).

[8] See *The Gospel According to St John, Volumes 1-2*. (New York: Seabury Press, 1980). *The Gospel According to St John, Volume 3*. (New York: Crossroad, 1982).

[9] See *The Gospel of John*. Sacra Pagina 4 (Collegeville: Liturgical Press, 1998).

[10] See *John 1: A Commentary on the Gospel of John Chapters 1-6, John 2: A Commentary on the Gospel of John Chapters 7-21*. Hermeneia (Philadelphia: Fortress, 1984). The bibliography is found in *John 2*, pp. 254-346.

[11] See Hartwig Thyen, *Das Johannesevangelium*. Handbuch zum Neuen Testament 6 (Tübingen: Mohr Siebeck, 2005). The bibliography is found on pp. 7-61.

[12] On medieval anti-Judaism in general and on Bonaventure's anti-Judaism in particular, cf. *Bonaventure on Luke, chapters 9-16*, pp. xiii-lvii.

Further, Bonaventure has no inkling that there may be Qumran or Nag Hammadi backgrounds for John's thought. While Bonaventure frequently addresses the problem of the discrepancies between the Synoptics and John, he does not broach the subject of whether the Synoptics or John are more historically reliable as sources for Jesus' life. As a matter of fact, the issue of the historical Jesus appears nowhere on Bonaventure's interpretive radar.

But before we relegate Bonaventure's Commentary on John to some medieval Parisian museum, we should be aware of those areas in which Bonaventure's exposition is very modern, even contemporary. Areas in which Bonaventure anticipates contemporary studies on John's Gospel are many. I mention a few. Bonaventure was astute enough to see straight off that bearing witness is an important theme in John's Gospel.[13] He, thereby, anticipated such studies as that of Andrew T. Lincoln.[14] While Raymond F. Collins may have coined the phrase, "The Representative Figures of the Fourth Gospel," Bonaventure remarkably anticipated Collins' insights.[15] For example, his expositions of the three passages in which Nicodemus occurs (3:1-15; 7:50-52; 19:38-42) are extraordinarily profound. Bonaventure's commentary on passages in John that concern women

---

[13] A careful reading of Bonaventure's interpretation of John 1:6-35 reveals that he appreciates The Fourth Gospel's portrayal of John as "the witnesser."

[14] *Truth on Trial: The Lawsuit Motif in the Fourth Gospel.* (Peabody, MA: Hendrickson, 2000).

[15] "The Representative Figures of the Fourth Gospel," *Downside Review* 94 (1976) 16-46. Now reprinted in his *These Things Have Been Written.* (Louvain: Peeters, 1990), pp. 2-45. Bonaventure, however, uses his Augustinian-based theology to interpret how the representative figure moves from non-belief to belief and by implication how a contemporary reader of the Fourth Gospel might move to a deeper faith. For more detail see Thomas J. Herbst, *The Road to Union: Johannine Dimensions of Bonaventure's Christology.* Pensiero Francescano 4 (Grottaferrata: Frati Editori di Quaracchi, 2005), esp. pp. 307-366.

is rich in depth and appreciation. What he says about the Samaritan woman, Martha and Mary, and Mary of Magdala is wondrously contemporary.[16] Bonaventure's analysis of John 13-17 may know nothing of Greek and Latin consolatory literature, but he anticipates contemporary studies by accentuating the consolatory, strengthening, and exhortatory functions of these chapters.[17]

BONAVENTURE AS A MEDIEVAL COMMENTATOR

THE DIVISION OF THE TEXT

Indeed, context is everything, and in order to understand Bonaventure's commentary on John we should place him in his own interpretive context. The extent to which we twenty- first century folks understand that context, the better able we will be to understand his achievement.[18] I give some examples. When most contemporary readers approach a commentary, they go immediately to what the commentator has to say about a particular passage.

---

[16] Bonaventure's interpretation of Jesus' words to Mary of Magdala, *Noli me tangere* ("don't be touching me"), in John 20:17 seems more satisfactory than many a contemporary interpretation. See Bonaventure's postill below and Harold W. Attridge, "'Don't Be Touching Me': Recent Scholarship on Mary Magdalene," in *A Feminist Companion to John, Volume II*. Edited by Amy-Jill Levine. (Cleveland: Pilgrim Press, 2003), pp. 140-166.

[17] See George L. Parsenios, *Departure and Consolation: The Johannine Farewell Discourse in Light of Greco-Roman Literature.* Supplements to Novum Testamentum 117 (Leiden: Brill, 2005); Paul A. Holloway, "Left Behind: Jesus' Consolation to His Disciples in John 13,31-17,26," *Zeitschrift für die neutestamentliche Wissenschaft* 96 (2005) 1-33.

[18] I refer interested readers to two fine works by Thomas Herbst, O.F.M.: "The Passion as paradoxical Exemplarism in Bonaventure's Commentary on the Gospel of John," *Antonianum* 78 (2003) 209-248; *The Road to Union.*

That is, they bypass the commentator's introduction to and outline of the biblical text. While such an approach may be expedient, it prevents the reader from benefiting from the great wisdom of the commentator. This approach especially lessens the reader's grasp of the insights of a medieval commentator, for Bonaventure, like his contemporary Thomas Aquinas, used the division of the text (*divisio textus*) as a means of interpretation.[19] Thus, whereas many contemporary commentators divide John's Gospel into two parts of almost equal length, The Book of Signs (chapters 1-12) and The Book of Glory (chapters 13-21), St. Bonaventure divides it into two parts of very unequal length: The Word in se (John 1:1-5) and the Word united to the flesh (John 1:6-21:25). This second part has three sections: The Incarnation (John 1:6-11:46), the Passion (John 11:47-19:42), and the Resurrection (John 20:1-21:25). A close reading of Bonaventure's exposition of John 1:6-11:46 (The Incarnation) will indicate that his dominant interpretive theme is christological and is Christ's "manifestation" or revelation to various individuals and groups. Thus, in his interpretation of John 4 Bonaventure finds a dual manifestation:

---

[19] See John F. Boyle, "Authorial Intent and the *Divisio textus*" in *Reading John with St. Thomas Aquinas: Theological Exegesis and Speculative Theology*. Edited by Michael Dauphinais and Matthew Levering. (Washington: CUA Press, 2005), pp. 3-8. See further John F. Boyle, "The Theological Character of the Scholastic 'Division of the Text' with Particular Reference to the Commentaries of Saint Thomas Aquinas," in *With Reverence for the Word: Medieval Scriptural Exegesis in Judaism, Christianity, and Islam*. Edited by Jane Dammen McAuliffe, Barry D. Walfish, and Joseph W. Goering. (Oxford: OUP, 2003), pp. 276-283. See also Bourgerol, "Introduzione," in *San Bonaventura, Commento al Vangelo di san Giovanni / 1 (1-10)*. Translation by Eliodoro Mariani. Introduction and Notes by Jacques Guy Bougerol. (Rome: Città Nuova, 1990), pp. 21-22.

Christ manifests himself to the Samaritans, especially the Samaritan woman, and then to the Galileans.[20]

QUAESTIONES

Bonaventure's use of *quaestiones* or "questions" might be usefully compared to the excursus in some contemporary commentaries such as those in the Hermeneia Series. Like the contemporary excursus these "questions" are meant to explore the meaning of a passage in greater depth. But the analogy of the contemporary excursus begins to limp when we realize the frequency of Bonaventure's "questions." I have counted 414 of them. They occur in every chapter. There is no chapter that has less than a dozen questions. Bonaventure devotes the most questions to two chapters: 38 on John 1 and 32 on John 6 [21]

I give a sample of the nature of these questions. As I just noted, many of Bonaventure's questions explore in some depth the literal sense of a verse. See, e.g., John 8 n. 14 which deals with John 8:6-8 and asks: What was the Lord writing on the ground when he pronounced his sentence concerning the woman taken in the act of adultery? See also John 8 n. 42 and the meaning of the word "beginning" in John 8:25. In John 14 n. 21 Bonaventure delves more profoundly into the meaning of John 14:12: "The person who believes in me, the works that I do that person will also do, and greater than these will he do."

---

[20] See Boyle, "The Theological Character," pp. 281-282 for the different division of the text Thomas Aquinas utilizes in his interpretation of John's Gospel.

[21] For Bonaventure's use of *quaestiones* in his Commentary on Ecclesiastes, see *Commentary on Ecclesiastes.* Translation and Notes by Campion Murray, O.F.M. and Robert J. Karris, O.F.M. Introduction by Robert J. Karris, O.F.M. WSB VII (St. Bonaventure, NY: Franciscan Institute Publications, 2005), pp. 11-23. For the 12 chapters of Ecclesiastes Bonaventure provides 34 *quaestiones*.

See further John 14 n. 36: What is the meaning of John 14:16: "The Father will give you another Paraclete"?

Some questions deal with a discrepancy between what John says and what the Synoptics (Matthew, Mark, and Luke) say. For example, John 1 n. 100 asks about the call of the disciples: "Chapter one of John's Gospel maintains that the disciples were called before John was delivered over. Matthew 4:12-22, however, states that Jesus called them after John had been delivered up." Very often Bonaventure draws upon the wisdom of St. Augustine to solve these discrepancies. See, e.g., John 20 n. 11: "Since other women had come with the Magdalene to the tomb, why does John speak only of her? Augustine responds in the third book of his *Harmony of the Gospels*: 'Mary Magdalene was more ardent than the other women who had ministered to the Lord. For this reason John not unfittingly mentioned her by herself and kept quiet about the others who were with her, as others bear witness.'"

At times Bonaventure devotes a question to an inconsistency within the text of John's Gospel itself. See John 3 n. 45 where Bonaventure solves the problem of the inconsistency between John 3:22 (Jesus is baptizing) and John 4:2 (Jesus does not baptize). See also John 7 n. 17: John 7:8 says: "I do not go up" while John 7:10 states: "Then he also went up." At times the Evangelist addresses the inconsistencies between John's Gospel and another passage in Sacred Scripture. See, e.g., John 15 n. 30: John 15:16 says one thing whereas Deuteronomy 26:17 says another.

Other questions deal with the erroneous conclusions that some heretics have drawn from John's Gospel. For example, John 1 n. 8 addresses the following issue: "But a heretic objects: If the Word proceeds from the speaker as a son from a father and the son is posterior to the father, then the Word was not in the beginning with God." A further example is found in John 14 n. 47: "Question 2 addresses John 14:28: 'You would indeed rejoice that I

am going to the Father, for the Father is greater than I.'
1. From this verse Arius argued that the Son is inferior
to the Father.... The answer to this problem is found in
Augustine's rule in Book I of *On the Trinity* that all things
that are said of the Son that indicate equality refer to the
divine nature and that all things that are said of the Son
that indicate inequality refer to the human nature. And
this verse should be understood accordingly." See also
John 18 n. 67: Some heretics have argued from John 18:36
("My kingdom is not of this world") that this world does
not pertain to the God of light, but to the god of darkness.

Sometimes tradition forces Bonaventure to tackle a
particular question. See John 2 n. 15 (The wedding at Cana
was that of John the evangelist); John 4 n. 86 (Gregory);
John 15 n. 16 (Augustine); John 15 n. 25 (Gregory).

Some questions have moral implications. See John 2
n. 16 (Why did the Lord go to a wedding? To show that
he was not against matrimony.); John 13 n. 25 (Why
did the Lord give his disciples an example of humility
rather than of some other virtue, since there are other
excellent virtues?) John 10 n. 28 asks how prelates and
indeed all Christians are bound to observe John 10:11:
"The good shepherd lays down his life for his sheep." John
19 n. 68 focuses on the loving devotion of Nicodemus and
asks whether he sinned in his superfluous prodigality.

Sometimes Bonaventure explains metaphors and
similes, e.g., John 4 n. 66 (How our salvation is Jesus'
food). Also in John 16 n. 40 he explains the meaning of
John 16:25: "I have spoken these things to you in proverbs."

At times some of Bonaventure's questions histori-
cize or psychologize components of a story. See, for instance, John 5:15-18 with its series of questions about
why Jesus didn't cure all the sick at the pool, etc.

Bonaventure's questions about women in John's
Gospel are surprisingly contemporary. For example, the
faith of Martha and Mary merited Jesus' resuscitation

of their brother Lazarus. See also John 11 n. 12 relative to the wording of John 11:1 and John 20 n. 26, which is a question without the name, on the meaning of John 20:17.

Sometimes a question is raised, not because of its intrinsic worth in the total exegetical project, but because of Bonaventure's position as a Friar Minor. See, e.g., John 12 n. 12 on John 12:6 and Judas carrying the money bag: "Finally, since the Lord lived in extreme poverty and commanded his disciples not to accept money, why is it that he had a purse?"

While some of Bonaventure's questions deal with weighty matters such as the three persons of the Trinity, some are small potatoes. See John 4 n. 46 (Why didn't the disciples question Jesus?) Also consult John 21 n. 13 about John 21:1: "Since Lake Gennesareth has sweet water and is tiny in comparison with a sea, why does the Evangelist call it a sea?"

A number of questions are taken up with Christological issues. For instance, John 5 n. 43 with respect to John 5:19: "The Son can do nothing by himself." Also see John 7 n. 15-16 which asks why persecution forced the Lord to leave Judea (John 7:1) when his persecutors could not act before the time determined by the Lord. See further John 13 n. 38-40 re: John 13:21: "He was disturbed in spirit."

Some questions, while theological, are not Trinitarian or Christological. For example, John 16 n. 9 ponders the meaning of John 16:2: "The hour is coming for everyone who kills you to think that he is offering worship to God." John 16 n. 36 deals with John 16:20, "You will weep and lament," and asks whether the apostles gained merit from their sorrow. John 21 n. 28 raises the question of what happened to the bread and fish that the risen Christ consumed. Bonaventure follows Augustine in answering: "So, then, the happiness of the body after the resurrection will be as incomplete if it needs food as it will be if it cannot take food."

In conclusion, there seems to be no unifying theme that surges through these 414 questions, for the biblical text of John's Gospel controls what questions will be raised.[22]

BONAVENTURE'S 26 NON-LITERAL INTERPRETATIONS

A third factor in Bonaventure's context was his practice of adding non-literal interpretations after he had explored the literal sense of a biblical passage. Bonaventure supplies far fewer non-literal interpretations in his Commentary on John than he did in his expansive Commentary on Luke. I offer these observations to help the reader assimilate the number and significance of the non-literal interpretations found in Bonaventure's Commentary on John. There are 26 non-literal interpretations: 7 allegorical; 7 spiritual; 6 *distinctiones*;[23] 5 moral; 1 mystical. Furthermore, chapters 1, 3, 7, 8, 10, 13, 16, 17 have no non-literal interpretations. With the exception of the three *distinctiones* in John 14 and 15, all the non-literal interpretations occur in narrative sections: 2 deal with the wedding feast of Cana in John 2:1-11; 1 concerns the cleansing of temple in John 2:13-22; 1 deals with the Samaritan woman of John 4:3-42; 1 deals with the second sign at Cana in John 4:43-54; 1 focuses on the man sick for 38 years in John 5:1-16; 3 are about the multiplication of barley loaves in John 6:1-15; 3 treat the man born blind in John 9:1-41; 4 concern

---

[22] See Monti, "Bonaventure's Interpretation of Scripture," p. 127: "It is also difficult to distill a systematic theology out of them, because the questions do not follow any logical order, but occur simply as they arise from a reading of the biblical text." But Monti, pp. 127-131 does go on to pursue the "Incarnate Word" as a special theme in the *quaestiones*.

[23] In his commentary on the 24 chapters that comprise the Gospel of Luke Bonaventure has 36 *distinctiones*. See my "St. Bonaventure's use of *Distinctiones*: His Independence of and Dependence on Hugh of St. Cher," *Franciscan Studies* 60 (2002) 209-250, esp. 209.

Martha and Mary and the resuscitation of Lazarus in John 11:1-44; 1 deals with the anointing at Bethany in John 12:1-8; 1 focuses on John 18:10 and Peter's cutting off the ear; 2 concern the seamless garment and opened side of crucified Jesus in John 19:23, 34; 1 is about the running of John and Peter in John 20:3; 2 concern John 21: the breaking of day in 21:4 and Peter and John in 21:15-23. Four of these non-literal interpretations are barely more than one sentence long: John 6 n. 21 (in a question); John 18:10 n. 18; John 21:4 n. 6; John 21 n. 51. The two most elaborate non-literal interpretations are: John 4:54 n. 82-83 and John 11:6 n. 8-11.

I quote extensively from John 4:54 n. 82-83 to give readers a sample of Bonaventure's non-literal interpretation: "The hours of this day are the different statuses of Christ. Through a consideration of these the soul is freed from different maladies.[24] – 83.The first hour is the incarnation. And this frees a person from pride by illuminating the soul towards humility, because he humbled himself in the incarnation. Philippians 2:7 reads: "He humbled himself, accepting the form of a slave." – The second is his nativity, and this frees us from avarice by illuminating the soul towards poverty, for the newly born Christ is poor, as Luke 2:7 says: "She brought forth her first born son and wrapped him in swaddling clothes and laid him in a manger, because there was no room for them in the inn." – The third is his circumcision, and this frees us from disobedience by illuminating us

---

[24] Hugh of St. Cher, p. 311m gives two lists for the seventh hour: "Or the seven hours can be said to be those seven, about which the Apostle speaks in 2 Cor 7:11: You were made sorry according to God. What earnestness it has wrought in you, what explanations, what indignation, what fear, what yearning, what zeal, what readiness to avenge. Or the seven hours are seven considerations of the world. The first is the consideration of its brevity, second its changeableness, third its infidelity, fourth its deceit, fifth its evil, sixth the things that fight against you, seventh the things that are inimical to you."

towards obedience. For although Christ was not subject to the Law, he, nonetheless, subjected himself to it. So of him it is fittingly said what the Apostle expresses in 1 Corinthians 9:19: "Although I am free in all things, I have made myself the slave of all...." – The fourth is his apparition, and this frees us from envy by illuminating us to communication of teaching, for he himself then made himself known to the Gentiles. Wisdom 7:12-13 has: "I rejoiced in all, for this wisdom went before me ... which I communicate without envy, and I do not hide her riches." – The fifth is the offering in the temple, and this frees us from ingratitude by illuminating us to prayer, since at that time the Lord himself was offered in the temple as a sign that human beings must offer themselves totally out of gratitude. Luke 2:22 states: "They brought the child Jesus to Jerusalem to present him to the Lord." – The sixth is his baptism, and this frees us from uncleanness by illuminating us to newness of life, for Christ was washed in the River Jordan. Matthew 3:13 states: "Jesus came from Galilee to the Jordan ... to be baptized by him." 1 Peter 3:21 says: "Baptism saves you, not the putting off of the filth of the flesh," etc. – The seventh is the temptation during his fasting, and this frees the son of the royal official from fever by illuminating him to the mortification of the flesh, since Christ afflicted the flesh through his fasting. Matthew 4:1-2 states: "Jesus was led into the desert by the Spirit to be tempted by the devil. And when he had fasted for forty days and forty nights, he was hungry." – The eighth is his passion, and this frees us from anger by illuminating us to patience, for Christ was most patient in his suffering. 1 Peter 2:21-22 says: "Christ suffered for us, leaving you an example that you may follow in his steps, who committed no sin nor was deceit found in his mouth." – The ninth is the descent into hell, and this frees us from hardness of heart by illuminating us to compassion, since the Lord was merciful to those who were "in darkness and the shadow of death."[25] Zechariah 9:11 reads: "You also by the blood of your covenant have led the vanquished out of the pit...." The greatest mercy is to shed one's blood for prisoners. – The tenth is the rest in the tomb, and this frees us from the pressures of the world by illuminating us to peace, because Christ rested in the sepulcher. Psalm 4:9 states: "In peace in the selfsame I will sleep and I will rest." And Psalm 75:3 reads: "His place is in peace." – The eleventh is the resurrection, and this frees us from the oldness of life by illuminating us to newness of life, since then Christ became the new man. Romans 6:4 says: "Just as Christ has arisen from the dead through the glory of the Father, so we also may walk in the newness of life." – The twelfth is the ascension, and this frees us from the love of earthly things by illuminating us to the desire for eternal things, whence Christ has preceded us. Colossians 3:1-2 has: "Seek the things that are above where Christ is seated at the right hand of God. Consider the things that are above, not the things that are on earth."

It seems to me that the majority of these non-literal interpretations are largely Bonaventure's own and not dependent upon previous commentators, even his contemporary Cardinal Hugh of St. Cher. These non-literal interpretations would be of benefit to preachers as they prepared their sermons, especially for the Sundays of Lent that might feature the Samaritan woman, the man born blind, and the raising of Lazarus at the insistent faith of his sisters, Mary and Martha.

---

[25] See Luke 1:79.

Sources behind Bonaventure's Commentary on the Gospel of St. John

It doesn't take long before a reader realizes that Bonaventure has two main acknowledged sources for his Commentary on John. John Chrysostom's 88 Homilies on John's Gospel are a key source, quoted some 132 times.[26] Another vital source is St. Augustine, who is cited some 230 times. Of these quotations some 150 stem from Augustine's *Tractates on John's Gospel*.[27] Significant, too, are some 60 citations from the Glossa Ordinaria and Glossa Interlinearis[28] Bonaventure quotes Gregory the Great, especially his Homilies on the Gospels, some 54 times[29] The enigmatic Bishop Victor of Capua is quoted four times: John 2:1; 18:10, 11, 15, 26.[30] Never cited by name, but influential, nonetheless, is Bonaventure's older contemporary, Cardinal Hugh of St. Cher.[31] It is the singular

---

[26] Jacques Guy Bougerol, "Introduzione," in *San Bonaventura, Commento al Vangelo di san Giovanni / 1 (1-10)*, p. 17.

[27] See Bougerol, "Introduzione," p. 15.

[28] See Bougerol, "Introduzione," p. 20.

[29] See Bougerol, "Introduzione," p. 20.

[30] See Bougerol, "Introduzione," pp. 19-20.

[31] The most notable instances are found in Bonaventure's exposition of John 10:6 n. 8, John 14:6 n. 7, John 18 n. 47 and 49. I give one example and refer readers to the appropriate footnotes on the other three passages. Bonaventure comments on John 10:6 (n. 8): "It should be noted that according to Chrysostom 'a *proverb* is a useful saying that openly gives practical advice, but also retains much meaning on a hidden level.' According to Basil 'a proverb is moral instruction, correction of vices, a proven way of life, directing human actions to a higher level.' According to common parlance a proverb is a saying that is general and concise that conveys something directly in its articulation, but also conveys something beyond the surface meaning of the words." Hugh of St. Cher, p. 350m interprets the same verse: "Jesus spoke this proverb to them, etc.] that is, this parable or this obscure saying or common saying about the shepherd. And note: a proverb is a saying that is general and concise that conveys something directly in its articulation, but also conveys something beyond the surface meaning of the words. Basil. A proverb is moral instruction

contribution of Thomas Herbst to have pointed out that Bonaventure is not only indebted to individual authors, but to an entire worldview which is presupposed in his exposition.[32] Furthermore, from time to time, especially in his *quaestiones* Bonaventure employs reason to interpret the Johannine text as he cites Aristotle. Finally, it almost goes without saying that Bonaventure's main source is the storehouse of Sacred Scripture, as he interprets the text written by John under the inspiration of the Holy Spirit by means of other biblical texts inspired by the same Spirit.

While Bonaventure is beholden to the tradition before him and to luminaries such as Augustine, John Chrysostom, and Gregory, his commentary is uniquely his own expert work. In this context it is helpful to recall what Beryl Smalley, the expert on medieval exegesis, wrote: "Much has been written on his (Bonaventure's) theories about the nature of Scripture and on his principles of exegesis, but very little on his actual surviving lectures on Ecclesiastes, St. Luke and St. John. Indeed it has been claimed that we should not look to them for his deeper thought; the school tradition hedged him into a narrow pathway. If this were the case it would reflect unfavourably both on the school tradition and on the lecturer who let it trammel the free run of his ideas. On the contrary, what surprised me on reading the Gospel commentaries was their originality and his refusal to be obstructed by current classroom methods."[33] It remains then for the reader to

---

and correction of vices, a proven way of life, directing human actions to a more safe level. And later he says: In ordinary speech the name of proverb is regularly given to human customs, that is, those things that are said with the voice of ancient tradition. But that is the common and unsophisticated meaning, but for us a proverb is a useful saying that openly provides practical advice, but also conveys much meaning on a hidden level."

[32] See *The Road to Union*, esp. pp 31-41.

[33] *Gospel in the Schools*, p. 203. See Herbst, *The Road to Union*, p. 34: "Bonaventure became a major contributor to the ongoing synthesis

dig down deeply into Bonaventure's creative thought in his Commentary on John. In this context I paraphrase what Gregory the Great said of John's Gospel and apply it to Bonaventure's Commentary: In this sea there's plenty of room for elephants to swim and for lambs to wade.[34]

Some correlations between Bonaventure's Commentaries on the Gospel of St. Luke and on the Gospel of St. John

For those who might wish to compare Bonaventure's *Commentary on the Gospel of St. Luke* and his *Commentary on the Gospel of St. John*, I propose four correlations.[35] Behind these commentaries stands the controversy over poverty that raged in Paris during Bonaventure's tenure there. Since I have written extensively about this issue elsewhere, I need not go into great detail here.[36] Of course, the Gospel of Luke provided many more opportunities for Bonaventure to sing the praises of poverty and condemn

---

of Augustinian thought, and this is evident in his exegesis of the Fourth Gospel. In a certain sense, Bonaventure is less of an 'Augustinian', in the strict sense of the term, than a 'synthesiser of Augustine'. In doing so he treads a well-worn path, but this does not detract from his originality. On the contrary and as with his predecessors, it marks him as a creative contributor to the development of Christian doctrine."

[34] See Prooemium n. 11.

[35] I invite interested readers and graduate students to find more correlations, both positive and negative.

[36] See my "St. Bonaventure's Christology and Teachings on the Evangelical Life in His Commentary on the Gospel of Luke" in *Franciscans and the Scriptures: Living in the Word of God*. Washington Theological Union Symposium Papers 2005. Edited by Elise Saggau. (St. Bonaventure, NY: Franciscan Institute Publications, 2006), pp. 33-59 and also "St. Bonaventure's Interpretation of the Evangelical Life in his *Commentary on the Gospel of St. John*," *Franciscan Studies* 64 (2006) 319-335.

the vice of avarice.[37] But a careful reading of Bonaventure's *Commentary on the Gospel of St. John* reveals that he champions the Lord's poverty and that of his disciples whenever he can. I give two examples. Bonaventure's exposition of Jesus' multiplication of loaves in John 6:5-9 is filled with references to Christ's poverty and that of his disciples. See what he says about John 6:7 (n. 8): "And they themselves were poor and didn't have even a little, for they had left everything." He comments about John 6:9 (n. 10): "In this, notice the wondrous poverty of the Lord and the disciples that they have just a few coarse loaves. So they frequently experienced hunger with the Lord." In his commentary on John 12:1-8 Bonaventure addresses a thorny problem in the poverty controversy and gives a traditional answer. In John 12 n. 12 he writes: "Finally, since the Lord lived in extreme poverty and commanded his disciples not to accept money, why is it that he has a purse? ... About this objection one has to follow the opinion of Jerome: The Lord had a moneybag, not for his personal use, but rather for the use of the poor."

Bonaventure's *Commentary on the Gospel of St. Luke* follows the lead of the evangelist and champions Jesus as Son of God.[38] In his *Commentary on the Gospel of St. John* he also follows the lead of the evangelist and is an extraordinary advocate of Jesus as Word of God.[39] I would caution readers from maintaining that one of these Christologies is more important to Bonaventure. What is

---

[37] Luke narrates the birth of Jesus in a manger (2:1-7), has Jesus indicate that he has come to proclaim good news to the poor (4:18; 7:22), and tells the parables of the rich fool (12:15-21) and of Dives and Lazarus (16:19-31), and presents Jesus challenging a ruler to sell all that he has, give the money to poor, and follow him (18:22). John's Gospel has none of these passages.

[38] See my "St. Bonaventure's Christology and Teachings on the Evangelical Life in His Commentary on the Gospel of Luke."

[39] See my earlier treatment of Bonaventure's "division of the text" and its significance in this Introduction.

important is that Bonaventure does not interpret either the Gospel of Luke or the Gospel of John as a contemporary historical critic would, but as the Trinitarian believer he is. The Second Person of the Blessed Trinity is both Son of God and Word of God,[40] and it is the task of Bonaventure the exegete, believer, and theologian to explore God's revelation on the pages of the Gospels of Luke and John.

While in both of these commentaries Bonaventure deals with the non-literal meanings of the text, he dedicates far more space to these meanings in his *Commentary on the Gospel of St. Luke*.[41] Unique to his *Commentary on the Gospel of St. John* are its 414 *quaestiones*. Many of the issues handled in these *quaestiones*, e.g., differences between the various Gospels, Bonaventure addresses during the course of his exposition in his *Commentary on the Gospel of St. Luke*.

Finally, both commentaries are written from the perspective of faith and are meant to nurture faith. In my third point above I alluded to this dimension of Bonaventure's Commentaries. While this dimension is more obvious in Bonaventure's *Commentary on the Gospel of St. Luke* because of its many non-literal interpretations which would benefit preachers, it is also present in his Johannine commentary. As Herbst sagaciously observes: "The application of doctrine within the Commentary harmonises with the Franciscan/Scholastic imperative

---

[40] It goes without saying, however, that God's revelation as Word provides Bonaventure with a rich theological mine for his thought. See Herbst, *The Road to Union,* esp. pp. 151-184 and Timothy J. Johnson, *Bonaventure: Mystic of God's Word*. Reprint edition. St. Bonaventure, NY: Franciscan Institute Publications, 2005, pp. 18-19.

[41] One of the reasons for this is that Bonaventure's *Commentary on the Gospel of St. Luke* had a longer gestation period and in its final rendition was largely intended for preachers who would greatly benefit from non-literal interpretations and *distinctiones*.

to evangelise, thus the Commentary is conceived of as an aid for preachers and a means of conversion."[42]

DATE

As I indicated earlier, Bonaventure's Commentary on John seems a hybrid. The vast majority of it is the simple exposition of the literal sense from Bonaventure's biblical bachelor days. The 414 questions and 26 non-literal interpretations are the work of Bonaventure as a master.[43] So I would tentatively date this work to ca. 1256.

A CLOSING IMAGE

Recently I finished reading *Food in Painting*.[44] It was one of those rare books that delighted, inspired, and informed me. It also humbled me, as I realized how little I knew and how much improvement my powers of observation needed. Why didn't I notice that in that gorgeous still life a fly and butterfly were present, symbols of *vanitas*? Why didn't it dawn on me that hunting dogs near a table heavily loaded with choice morsels were symbols of the possession of land on which the rich could hunt? Why was salt stored in vessels of precious metal on the tables of the rich? Of course, the answer is that salt cost the devil. Why were cooked lobsters laid on top of a pile of dead game in another still life? I learned that this painting not only contrasted radiant colors, but also revealed the medical science of the day, that is, a person

---

[42] *The Road to Union*, p. 18.

[43] See Bourgerol, "Introduzione," pp. 8, 11.

[44] Kenneth Bendiner, *Food in Painting: From the Renaissance to the Present*. (London: Reaktion Books, 2004).

had to balance wet and cold foods (lobsters) with dry and warm foods (hares) to maintain good health. My point is this. Bonaventure's *Commentary on the Gospel of St. John* is like a magnificent painting. In this Introduction and my translation and notes I have provided you with one set of eyes to see its beauty. It is the wondrous task of other experts to show you even more of its beauty, as they reveal how it fits into the entirety of Bonaventure's portfolio and how it resonates with the Parisian theological and cultural scene of the mid thirteenth century. May the Lord grant improved sight to all of us, so that we might see not only the beauty of Bonaventure's Johannine Commentary, but also and especially the beauty of the Gospel of St. John and the Incarnate Word.

OUTLINE OF BONAVENTURE'S COMMENTARY ON JOHN'S GOSPEL OR HIS *DIVISIO TEXTUS*

Whereas many contemporary commentators divide John's Gospel into two parts of almost equal length, The Book of Signs (chapters 1-12) and The Book of Glory (chapters 13-21), St. Bonaventure divides it into two parts of very unequal length: The Word in se (John 1:1-5) and the Word united to the flesh (John 1:6-21:25). This second part has three sections: The Incarnation (John 1:6-11:46), the Passion (John 11:47-19:42), and the Resurrection (John 20:1-21:25). Thus, Bonaventure's outline of John's Gospel will mess up, at times, the convenient separation of the gospel into neat chapters. Further, in an attempt to keep this outline as simple as possible, I give no indication that almost every sub-division is followed by one or more of the 414 *quaestiones* or "questions" that Bonaventure employs in his exposition of the text.

Prooemium

Part I: The Word in se: John 1:1-5

Part II: The Word united to the flesh: John 1:6-21:25

Section I: The Incarnation: John 1:6-11:46

John 1:14b-11:46: The manifestation of the Incarnation

John 1:14b-18: The manifestation of the incarnate Word in general

John 1:19-11:46: The manifestation of the incarnate Word in particular

John 1:19-42: The manifestation of the incarnate Word made by John

John 12:20-50: Second preliminary to the passion: Prediction of the passion

John 13:1-17:26: The Strengthening of the disciples

John 13:1-38: The Lord encourages his disciples by his example

John 14:1-16:33: Exhortation to steadfastness

John 14:1-14: The Lord exhorts his disciples to constant faith

John 14:15-24: The Lord exhorts his disciples to observance of his commandments

John 14:25-31: The Lord predicts the imminence of his departure

John 15:1-27: The Lord exhorts his disciples to constant love

John 15:1-11: The Lord exhorts his disciples to love of God

John 15:12-17: The Lord exhorts his disciples to love of their brothers and friends

John 15:18-16:4: The Lord exhorts his disciples to endure the persecution of their enemies

John 16:5-33: The Lord strengthens his disciples in the waiting of hope

John 17:1-26: The Lord strengthens his disciples by the aid of prayer

John 18:1-19:42: Events that occur alongside the passion

John 18:1-12: The arrest of Christ

John 18:13-19:16a: Christ's condemnation

John 19:16b-27: Christ's passion

ABBREVIATIONS AND SHORT TITLES

Bonaventure on Luke, chapters 1-8
> *St. Bonaventure's Commentary on the Gospel of Luke Chapters 1-8.* With an Introduction, Translation and Notes by Robert J. Karris. WSB VIII/1. St. Bonaventure, NY: Franciscan Institute Publications, 2001.

Bonaventure on Luke, chapters 9-16
> *St. Bonaventure's Commentary on the Gospel of Luke Chapters 9-16.* With an Introduction, Translation and Notes by Robert J. Karris. WSB VIII/2. St. Bonaventure, NY: Franciscan Institute Publications, 2003.

Bonaventure on Luke, chapters 17-24.
> *St. Bonaventure's Commentary on Luke Chapters 17-24.* With an Introduction, Translation and Notes by Robert J. Karris. WSB VIII/3. St. Bonaventure, NY: Franciscan Institute Publications, 2004.

Brown
> *The Gospel according to John (i-xii; xiii-xxi)* Introduction, Translation, and Notes by Raymond E. Brown. Anchor Bible 29/29A; Garden City, NY: Doubleday, 1966,1970.

CC	Corpus Christianorum
CFS	Cistercian Fathers Series
CSEL	Corpus Scriptorum Ecclesiasticorum Latinorum
CSS	Cistercian Studies Series
CCSL	Corpus Christianorum. Series Latina
CUA	Catholic University of America
Douay Version	*The Holy Bible Translated from the Latin Vulgate... The Douay Version of the Old Testament; The Confraternity Edition of The New Testament.* New York: P. J. Kenedy & Sons, 1950.
FC	Fathers of the Church
GGHG	Gregory the Great's Homilies on the Gospels
Hugh of St. Cher	*Hugonis de Sancto Charo ... Tomus Sextus in Evangelia secundum Matthaeum, Lucam, Marcum & Joannem.* Venice: Nicolas Pezzana, 1732.
Hurst	*Gregory the Great: Forty Gospel Homilies.* Translated from the Latin by Dom David Hurst. CSS 123; Kalamazoo, Michigan: Cistercian Publications, 1990.
LCL	Loeb Classical Library
NAB	New American Bible
NPNF1/2	Nicene and Post-Nicene Fathers, First or Second Series. Ed. Philip Schaff. Peabody, Massachusetts: Hendrickson,

	1994-95. Reprint of 1888/93 editions.
NRSV	New Revised Standard Version
Omnia Opera	*S. Bonaventurae Opera Omnia.* Studio et Cura PP.Collegii a S. Bonaventura (Ad Claras Aquas).Quaracchi: Collegium S. Bonaventurae, 1882-1902. There are nine volumes of text and one volume of indices. The volume number is first given and then the page number, e.g., 5:24.
PG	Patrologiae Cursus Completus. Series Graeca. Ed. J. P. Migne.
PL	Patrologiae Cursus Completus. Series Latina. Ed. J. P. Migne.
QuarEd	The editors who in 1893 produced the text and the notes of Bonaventure's Omnia Opera 6, which contains the text of Bonaventure's Commentary on John (*Commentarius in Evangelium S. Ioannis*) on pp. 237-530.
SBOp	*Sancti Bernardi Opera I-VIII* Ed. J. Leclercq and H. M. Rochais with the assistance of C. H. Talbot for Volumes I-II. Rome: Editiones Cisterciensis, 1957-77.
Vulgate	*Biblia Sacra Iuxta Vulgatam Versionem.* Adiuvantibus B. Fischer, I. Gribomont (†), H. F. D. Sparks, W. Thiele recensuit et brevi apparatu critico instruxit Robertus Weber (†) editionem quartam emendatam cum sociis

	B. Fischer, H. I. Frede, H. F. D. Sparks, W. Thiele praeparavit Roger Gryson. Stuttgart: Deutsche Bibelgesellschaft, 1969. 4th ed. 1994.
WSA	Works of Saint Augustine
WSB	Works of St. Bonaventure

A WORD ABOUT THIS TRANSLATION

My primary goals in translation have been readability and fidelity. I have not twisted the English language in attempts to match Bonaventure's playfulness with rhyme and alliteration, especially in his introductory sentences to a new exegetical section. Rather I have sometimes fashioned footnotes at such places to call attention to these displays of Bonaventure's art. In translation from the Vulgate I have not slavishly followed the Douay Version, but have adapted my translations to contemporary English usage and to the demands of Bonaventure's exposition. I know of only one contemporary translation of Bonaventure's Commentary on the Gospel of St. John. In 1990-1991 the Italian Conference of OFM Provincial Ministers in conjunction with Città Nuova Press published in its series on the Works of St. Bonaventure an Italian translation of all of Bonaventure's Commentary on the Gospel of St. John.[45]

---

[45] *San Bonaventura, Commento al Vangelo di san Giovanni/1 (1-10)*. Translation by Eliodoro Mariani. Introduction and Notes by Jacques Guy Bougerol. (Rome: Città Nuova, 1990). *San Bonaventura, Commento al Vangelo di san Giovanni/2 (11-21)*. Translation by Eliodoro Mariani and Notes and Indices by Jacques Guy Bougerol. (Rome: Città Nuova, 1991).

A WORD ABOUT THE INDICES

The indices are filled with treasures. The scripture index indicates Bonaventure's profound appreciation of God's wisdom and points to his methodology of interpreting Scripture by Scripture. His references to Augustine, Gregory the Great, and John Chrysostom manifest his dependence upon tradition. Careful perusal of this index will also reveal the extent to which Bonaventure was indebted to his older contemporary, Cardinal Hugh of St. Cher.

ACKNOWLEDGMENTS

The Franciscan Institute gratefully acknowledges generous funding from the Academy of American Franciscan History; the OFM Province of St. John the Baptist in Cincinnati; the OFM Province of the Sacred Heart in Saint Louis; and the OFM General Definitorium in Rome, Italy. The translator of this volume also owes a debt of gratitude to: Fr. Michael F. Cusato, OFM, director of the Franciscan Institute; Sr. Margaret Carney, OSF, president of St. Bonaventure University; Fr. Zachary Hayes, OFM, former general editor of the Bonaventure Text in Translation Series; Prof. Jean François Godet-Calogeras, managing editor of the BTTS; Sr. Roberta McKelvie, OSF, managing editor of Franciscan Institute Publications; Ms. Noel H. Riggs, executive administrative assistant; Mrs. Theresa Shaffer, Interlibrary Loan Librarian; and Sr. Daria Mitchell, OSF, editorial assistant.

This volume is dedicated in grateful appreciation to Sr. Margaret Carney, OSF, STD, President of St. Bonaventure University and former Director of the Franciscan Institute.

PROOEMIUM

1. *Behold, my servant will understand, and he will be exalted and extolled and will be exceedingly sublime.* Since the commendation of the author redounds upon the work and the commendation of the work reflects positively on the author, the scripture just quoted, which is taken from Isaiah 52:13, has been selected. In this citation Blessed John is praised for three things. That is, for his *holiness of life* where the text says: "Behold, my servant." For his *clarity of understanding* where the text reads: "will understand." For his *excellence in teaching* where the text states: "he will be exalted and extolled and will be exceedingly sublime." For this is the order in these matters: holiness of life merits the gift of understanding, and the gift of understanding disposes a person to excellence in teaching.

2. So he is commended for his *holiness of life* in this that the Lord calls him his servant. For none merit to be called servants of God except those who serve God in holiness all their days. Now the Lord calls him *his* servant. By reason of his service since he served God faithfully. Wherefore, what Numbers 12:7 says can fittingly be understood of him: "My servant Moses is the most faithful servant in my entire house."[1] Truly, Blessed John was most faithful in the entire house of Christ. In testimony of this fact the Lord committed to his care that most noble treasure,

---

[1] On p. 239 n. 3 QuarEd rightly note that the Vulgate reads: *At non talis servus meus Moyses, qui in omni*, etc. ("But it is not so with my servant Moses, who is, etc.").

namely, the virginity of his Mother.[2] – By reason of his office, which God bestowed upon him, and to which he had been predestined from eternity, according to what Isaiah 49:1-3 says: "The Lord has called me from the womb, from the womb of my mother the Lord has been mindful of my name." This is predestination. "And the Lord has made my mouth like a sharp sword. In the shadow of his hand the Lord has protected me and has made me like a select arrow. In his quiver the Lord has hidden me." This is the bestowal of the office of preaching. "And the Lord said to me: You are my servant, Israel, for in you will I glory." This is the reception of the office of servant, because he did not receive this office for his own glory, but for God's glory. – By reason of the graciousness which the Lord conferred upon him. For he was elected and chosen beforehand and beloved by God and gifted with a special bestowal of grace, according to what Isaiah 42:1 states: "Behold, my servant, I will sustain him, my elect. My soul delighted in him. I have spread the gift of my spirit upon him." Fittingly has the Lord's soul delighted in Blessed John, since he was that disciple – whom Jesus loved, according to the last chapter of John.[3] – Thus, Blessed John was Christ's servant because of fidelity, office, and God's graciousness.[4]

---

[2] See John 19:26-27.

[3] See John 21:7. The beloved disciple first appears in John 13:23. Most contemporary scholars do not immediately identify "the beloved disciple" with John the Evangelist. See, e.g., Raymond E. Brown, *An Introduction to the New Testament,* Anchor Bible Reference Library (New York: Doubleday, 1997) 371: "The evangelist, who wove the theologically reflected tradition into a work of unique literary skill, would presumably have been a disciple of the Beloved Disciple, about whom he writes in the third person."

[4] It is almost impossible to put into English Bonaventure's theological and verbal playfulness here. He writes *obsequ*ium, *offic*ium, *benefic*ium. In turn, *beneficium* means both graciousness and ecclesiastical benefice.

3. Now on account of his holiness of life he merited *the gift of understanding*, which was bestowed upon him in multiple ways. For his understanding arose from *the anointing* of the Holy Spirit, angelic *revelation, the teaching* of Christ. Through the anointing of the Holy Spirit he understood useful matters. Through angelic revelation he understood hidden matters. Though the teaching of Christ he understood sublime matters. And in these three, every striving and desire of our rational nature is encompassed and perfected.

So through the anointing of the Holy Spirit he understood useful matters since the Spirit of truth is the spirit of salvation. About this understanding Isaiah 28:9 reads: "Whom will he teach knowledge? And whom will he make to understand what is heard? Those who have been weaned from milk, drawn away from the breasts." Those who have been weaned and removed from the sweetness of present consolation merit to understand useful things, but others do not. For 1 Corinthians 2:14 says: "Sensual people do not perceive the things that are of the Spirit of God, for it is foolishness to them, and they are unable to understand because they are examined[5] spiritually." Now Blessed John had been weaned, because for the love of God he left father and mother and even the woman he had married.[6]

---

[5] On p. 240 n. 4 QuarEd accurately mention that the Vulgate reads *examinatur* ("is examined") while Bonaventure has *examinantur* ("are examined").

[6] See Matt 4:22: "And immediately they (James and John) left their nets and their father and followed him." See the very first line of Jerome's Prologue, which occurs after n. 11 below: "This is John the Evangelist, one of the disciples of the Lord, who as a virgin was chosen by God, whom God called on his wedding day when he was about to get married." See also Bonaventure's exegesis of John 2:1-11 below.

By means of angelic revelation he understood hidden things, which would come to be. Wherefore, what is said about Daniel himself in Daniel 1:17 is appropriately applied to him: "The Lord gave to Daniel understanding of all visions and dreams."[7] And this takes place through the ministry of angelic revelation, for in Daniel 8:16 one angel said to another: "Gabriel, make this man understand the vision." But an angel does not reveal as if the angel were the source of the revelation. A witness of this is found in Revelation 19:10 when John tried to worship the angel, who was showing these things to him. The angel forbade him, saying: "Look, you must not do that. For I am your fellow servant and that of your brothers and sisters." These instances show that the angel does not reveal in the same way as the Lord, but as a fellow servant.

He also understood sublime things by means of Christ's teaching. For even though Christ taught all his disciples, he, nonetheless, taught and gave special understanding to Blessed John, whom he loved more than the others. So it can fittingly be understood of him what the Lord said to Solomon in 1 Kings 3:12: "I have given you a wise and understanding heart, insomuch that there has been no one like you before you, nor will one arise after you." For there was no one before him nor did anyone follow after him, who reached so great knowledge of divinity.

4. Thus Blessed John understood useful and hidden and sublime matters, and by reason of this threefold understanding was exalted to *the triple dignity of instruction.* Therefore, the text says: He will be exalted, that is, to the *apostolic chair.* He will be extolled to *prophetic pronouncement.* And he will be exceedingly sublime through

---

[7] Bonaventure has introduced *Dominus* ("The Lord") into this quotation and carried over *dedit* ("gave") from Dan 1:17a.

his *evangelical teaching*. For this reason he produced three writings, namely, the canonical Epistles as authentic *preacher*; Revelation as illustrious *prophet*; and the Gospel, as most learned *author*.

So relative to the first point: He will be exalted to the apostolic chair. For this reason what is said in Psalm 106:32 fits him well: "Let them exalt him in the assembly of the people, and let them praise him in the chair of the elders." "The chair of the elders" is the chair of the Apostles, on which Blessed John did not sit idly. Rather he instructed those present with his words and those absent with his letters. Sirach 15:3-4 reads: "She will be made strong in him, and he will not be moved. And she will hold him fast, and he will not be confounded. And she will exalt him among his neighbors."[8]

He will be lifted up for *prophetic pronouncement*, according to what Ezekiel 8:3 states: "The spirit lifted me up between heaven and earth[9] and brought me into Jerusalem in the vision of God." By being lifted up in such a manner, Blessed John was extolled. Wherefore Revelation 21:10 has: "He took me up in spirit to a mountain, great and high, and showed me the holy city Jerusalem, coming from out of heaven." And indeed what he had seen he was to proclaim. So it was said to him in Revelation 1:19: "Write the things you have seen, and the things that are, and the things that are to come after these." For he was gifted with the three kinds of prophecy.[10]

---

[8] The "she" of this passage is Lady Wisdom.

[9] The Vulgate reads *inter terram et caelum* ("between earth and heaven") while Bonaventure has *inter caelum et terram* ("between heaven and earth").

[10] See Book I, Homily 1 n. 1 of Gregory the Great's *Homiliae in Hiezechihelem prophetam*, edited by Marcus Adriaen, CCSL cxlii (Turnhout: Brepols, 1971), p. 5. Gregory discusses the three time-

And he was exceedingly sublime through his *evangelical teaching*, in which he surpassed all others. Therefore, what is said in Genesis 7:17 can rightly be said of him: "The waters increased and lifted the ark up to a sublime height from the earth." This ark is Blessed John, in whom the seed of the divine word was preserved. These waters that have increased are the waters of saving wisdom, which have been multiplied in Blessed John, since, as Augustine says, "he drank the rivers of the gospel from the very fountain of the Lord's breast."[11] These waters of wisdom lifted him up to a sublime height, above all mountains, since in his Gospel he spoke in a more exalted way than everyone else. Thus, Augustine says: "If his gospel proclamation would have been more exalted, the entire world would have been unable to endure it."[12] Now since the sublime nature of the teacher is manifested in the

---

frames of prophecy: past, present, and future. While he believes that past and present prophecy do not fit the etymology of the word prophecy, he comes close to a contemporary understanding of prophecy as forth-telling God's word when he deals with 1 Cor 14:24-25.

[11] While this citation may have originated in Book I, c. 4 n. 7 of Augustine's *De Consensu Evangelistarum*, its wording here comes from the responsory to the second and eighth readings at Matins in the Roman Breviary for December 27, the Feast of St. John, Apostle and Evangelist. See *Sancti Avreli Avgvustini De Consensv Evangelistarvm Libri qvattvor*, CSEL xliii (Vienna: F. Tempsky, 2004), p. 7: "As if he were drinking in more fully and in a certain way more intimately the secret of his divinity from the breast of the Lord himself, upon which he was accustomed to recline during their banquets." See also *Breviarium Romanum*, Tomus prior (Ratisbon: Frederick Pustet, 1961), p. 92: *Fluenta Evangelii de ipso sacro Dominici pectoris fonte potavit* ("he drank the rivers of the gospel from the sacred fountain itself of the Lord's breast").

[12] On p. 241 n. 3 QuarEd give the negative results of their detective work to track down the source of this quotation from "Augustine." See *San Bonaventura Commento al Vangelo di san Giovanni / 1 (1-10)*, trans. by Eliodoro Mariani, introduction and notes by Jacques Guy Bougerol, *Sancti Bonaventurae Opera* VII/1 (Rome: Città Nuova, 1990), p. 41 n. 2 where Bougerol rightly suggests that the second part of Augustine's citation may come from Book IV, c. 8 n. 9 of Augustine's

sublimity of the teaching, he rightly seems to be exceedingly sublime, if an explanation is given for the sublimity of his Gospel.

5. Further, it should be understood that a teaching is considered sublime either because it deals with sublime matters or because it proceeds in a sublime manner or because it *leads* to sublime things. – The Gospel of John is sublime since it deals with sublime matters, namely, the incarnate Word according to two natures, which are exceedingly sublime, especially the divine nature. Ezekiel 17:22-23 expresses this well in a parabolic way: "The Lord God says this: I myself will take the finest part of the high and sublime cedar.... And I will plant it on a mountain high and eminent, on the high and sublime mountain of Israel...." "The finest part of the high and sublime cedar" is the hidden divinity of the Word. God the Father planted this "on the high and sublime mountain of Israel," since he united it to the human nature in Christ, who is "the stone cut out of the mountain without hands."[13] The Gospel of Blessed John flows from this finest part of the high and sublime cedar. Wherefore, in the same chapter[14] it is said: "The large eagle with great wings, long pinions, full of thick plumage of many colors, came to Lebanon and took away the finest cedar. He cropped off the summit of this cedar and carried it away into the land of Canaan." "The large eagle," through the breadth of charity. "With great wings," through the height of contemplation. "With long pinions," through the length of expectation. "Full of thick plumage of many colors," through a multitude of virtues. "It came to Lebanon," that is, to the mountain of

---

De Consensu Evangelistarum. See CSEL xliii, p. 404: "... the entire world would be unable to hold [those books]...."
   [13] See Dan 2:34 and 2:45.
   [14] Ez 17:3-4.

mountains, Christ.[15] "He took away the finest cedar," that is, the hidden divinity of the Word. "He cropped off the summit of this cedar," because he depicted the excellence of his divine works, such as his outstanding miracles and most exalted teaching, which the other Evangelists had not mentioned.[16] Now if "Lebanon" is a high mountain in the world and "the cedar" is the tall tree in Lebanon, and "the summit" is the tallest part of the cedar, it then follows that the one who "cropped off the summit of the cedar" wrote a treatise about sublime matters.

6. Not only does Blessed John treat sublime matters, but he also proceeds in a sublime manner. The sublime manner of proceeding is the manner of certitude. Those branches of knowledge, which are more certain, are called the more sublime. This sublime way of proceeding is described in Ezekiel 1:10 in the figure of the animals which are understood to be the Evangelists.[17] Ezekiel continues: "I heard the sound of their wings, like the sound of many waters, as it were the voice of the sublime God."[18] "The

---

[15] See Augustine's Commentary on Psalm 87 n. 10. See *Expositions of the Psalms 73-98*, translation and notes by Maria Boulding, WSA III/18 (Hyde Park, NY: New City Press, 2002), p. 267: "The same idiom is used when he is called the Mountain of mountains, as in the text, *in the last days the mountain of the Lord shall be manifested, established above all other mountains* (Is 2:2; Mic 4:1), or the Holy One of all holy ones."

[16] On p. 241 n. 5 QuarEd refer to Book XXXI, chapter 47 n. 94 of Gregory the Great's *Moralia in Iob* as a possible parallel to Bonaventure's explication of Ez 17:3-4. I have found no such parallel. See *S. Gregorii Magni Moralia in Iob Libri XXIII-XXXV*, ed. Marcus Adriaen, CCSL cxliiib (Turnhout: Brepols, 1985), pp. 1614-16. Bonaventure's interpretation may be unique to him. It is characteristic of him to group items in numbers of seven.

[17] Ez 1:10 reads: "As for the likeness of their faces: there was the face of a man, and the face of a lion on the right side of all four; and the face of an ox, on the left side of all four; and the face of an eagle over all four."

[18] Ez 1:24.

voice of the sublime God" is the voice of certitude, not of variableness, for "God is not as a human being that God would lie."[19] Thus, the Lord said this about himself in John 3:11: "We speak of what we know, and we bear witness to what we have seen." Blessed John spoke in this modality of certitude. For John 19:35 reads: "He who saw it has borne witness, and his witness is true. And he knows that he tells the truth." Wherefore, he himself says at the beginning of the first chapter of his first canonical Epistle: "What was from the beginning, what we have heard, what we have seen with our eyes, what we have looked upon and our hands have handled, of the Word of life ... we testify and announce to you."[20]

7. Not only does Blessed John proceed in a sublime manner, but he also leads to sublime things. Sublime things are eternal goods. For temporal goods are puny and momentary. For 2 Corinthians 4:17 states: "Our present light affliction, which is for the moment, prepares for us an eternal weight of glory that is beyond measure in sublimity." The teaching of John's Gospel leads to this "sublime weight of glory." For John 20:31 says: "These things have been written, so that you may believe that Jesus is ... the Son of God, and that believing you may have life in his name." That life is eternal and sublime, which "eye has not seen nor ear heard nor has it entered into the human heart."[21]

Therefore, the teaching of this Gospel is sublime. Moreover, it is fitting that its author is said to be sublime, not only sublime, but even exceedingly sublime, in the su-

---

[19] Num 23:19. On p. 241 n. 8 QuarEd correctly indicate that the Vulgate reads *quasi homo* ("like a human being") whereas Bonaventure has *ut homo* ("as a human being").

[20] 1 John 1:1-2.

[21] See 1 Cor 2:9.

perlative. For if the sacred scriptures are more excellent than other writings, and the Gospel than all the parts of sacred scripture,[22] and the Gospel of John than all the Gospels, then it follows that this book in an extraordinary way is more excellent than all other books.

8. From the aforesaid it is clear what the answers are to the questions that are customarily asked when one begins a study of a book of this nature. That is, its *efficient cause* is John the Evangelist. What he produced is holy, intelligent, exalted and extolled and more sublime than all the others. The *material cause* is the incarnate Word, especially with regard to the things that refer to his divinity. The *formal cause* or *manner of proceeding*, even if it assumes the form of a narrative, nevertheless, is that of certitude. Now the formal cause, as it pertains to *the divisions of the book*, will be treated subsequently, for the Evangelist proceeds in a very orderly way. Now the proximate *final cause* is faith whereas the ultimate final cause is eternal life, which is the most desirable end and goal.

Questions

9. But there are three questions relative to the three items, by means of which this teaching has been recommended, that is, its usefulness, certitude, and sublimity.

Question 1: What was the necessity behind the writing of this Gospel? It seems that there was none. – 1. For Gregory in his Commentary on Ezekiel says this about Ezekiel 1:6: "Each one had four faces': If you ask what John

---

[22] Augustine begins his *De Consensu Evangelistarum* with: "Among all divine authorities, which are contained in sacred writ, the Gospel rightly excels." See CSEL xliii, p. 1.

perceived, the answer is what Luke, Mark and Matthew perceived."[23] So according to this John did nothing but repeat what the other Evangelists had said. Therefore, if he had not written, nothing would have been lost. – 2. Furthermore, either Matthew wrote a Gospel that was sufficient or he didn't. If he didn't, then since he did not write by his own lights, but by the Holy Spirit, the Holy Spirit was inadequate. Now if Matthew handed down evangelical teaching in a sufficient manner, all other Gospels are superfluous, both that of John and the others. – 3. Moreover, if this Gospel were necessary for the Church, then why was this message so delayed, deferred, and refrained during the time of salvation?[24] So it seems that he acted negligently and sinned because he deferred so long.

I answer. It should be said that the Evangelists are the Lord's witnesses, and this not on account of a need for clarity on God's part, but on account of a need created by human weakness. So since our human weakness trusts more firmly and certainly in multiple witnesses than in a single witness, divine wisdom arranged that there would be many Evangelists. – Now if they said entirely different things, they would not bolster trust. For it is necessary that the testimony be solid and that the witnesses agree. But if they all together said the very same thing, certainly more than one would be superfluous. Therefore, so that the testimony would be certain and contain nothing superfluous, the Holy Spirit disposed that an Evangelist might be the only one to narrate something and that

---

[23] See Book I, homily 3 n. 1 in CCSL cxlii, p. 33. This objection cites Gregory the Great out of context, for Gregory's point is the unanimity of the four Evangelists, that is, they all proposed the same content. For example, he also says that if you ask what Luke proposed, it is the same thing that John, Matthew, and Mark proposed.

[24] See Sir 4:28: "And do not refrain from speaking in the time of salvation."

the Evangelists might narrate the same things, but in no way would they disagree among themselves.

1. With regard to the objection that what one perceives all perceive, it must be understood not that they say the entirely same thing, but that when they concur in narrating the same event, they do not disagree, as Augustine says in his *De Concordia Evangelistarum*.[25] – Or stress should be placed on the verb "they perceived," for they perceived the same thing since they were illumined by the one Spirit and faith. However, they did not express these things in writing in entirely the same way.

2. With regard to the question of whether Matthew's Gospel was a sufficient account this has to be said. Now there are two ways of treating a matter in a sufficient manner. First, the treatment must correspond to the nobility of the subject. Seen from this angle, it is impossible to treat of Christ in a sufficient way, not only for a single individual, but also for the entire world with all its languages, for all languages put together are impotent to tell his story. Wherefore, John 21:25 states: "Even if every one of the things that Jesus did should be written, not even the world itself, I think, could hold the books that would have to be written."[26] There is a second way of treating

---

[25] See Book I, chapter 35 n. 54 of *De Consensu Evangelistarum* and NPNF 1, Volume 6, p. 101: "For this reason let us now rather proceed to examine into the real character of those passages in which these critics suppose the evangelists to have given contradictory accounts (a thing which only those who fail to understand the matter aright can fancy to be the case); so that, when these problems are solved, it may also be made apparent that the members in that body have preserved a befitting harmony in the unity of the body itself, not only by identity in sentiment, but also by constructing records consonant with that identity."

[26] Bonaventure has adjusted the first part of this quotation. The Vulgate does not read *posse* ("could").

a subject in a sufficient manner. In this second way sufficient material should be provided to attain a goal. And thus each of the Evangelists provides the substance of the faith in a sufficient way. But none of the things are missing that bring about a clear explanation of the faith and lead to greater certitude and defense of the faith.

3. Relative to the question of why he waited so long before writing, the reason for this delay has to be found in the author, for he was a virgin and young. Therefore, out of modesty he didn't want to assume this task, until the bishops of Asia pleaded with him and the heretics shocked him. Thus, it is said in the Prologue[27] that he was the last to write a Gospel,[28] and this was as it ought to be for a virgin.[29] – Another reason stems from Scripture, since some scriptures focus on humanity and the active life while Blessed John focuses on Divinity and the contemplative life, as Augustine says in the Glossa.[30] Now since a person comes to invisible things through visible things[31] and to contemplation through apostolic activity, the others had to write first and then John as the last. – The third reason comes from divine dispensation. John observed the Gospel better than all the others. But if he had written first, he would have either written ev-

---

[27] This is Jerome's Prologue. See below after n. 11.3.

[28] See Jerome's *De Viris Illustribus*, chapter 9. See *Saint Jerome, On Illustrious Men*. Translated by Thomas P. Halton. (FC 100; Washington: CUA Press, 1999) 19: "John ... most recently of all, at the request of the bishops of Asia, wrote a *Gospel* against Cerinthus and other heretics, and especially against the then-arising doctrine of the Ebionites, who assert that Christ did not exist prior to Mary. On this account he was compelled to maintain His divine birth."

[29] Neither here nor in Jerome's Prologue is a reason given for this opinion.

[30] On p. 243 n. 2 QuarEd intimate that they have been unable to find this quotation in Augustine. It seems to be a distillation of Book I, c. 4, n. 7 of *De Consensu Evangelistarum*.

[31] Bonaventure is dependent here on Rom 1:20.

erything and left the others nothing to write or, if he had not written everything, the others were unable to supplement what he had written. Therefore, at the prompting of the Holy Spirit he allowed the others to write first, so that what they had omitted he himself might mention afterwards.[32] – The Greeks, however, set forth another reason, namely, John wrote in order to correct the others. But they are mistaken, for, if the same Spirit inspired the Evangelists to speak, it would be impossible for them to speak falsely. So some things were to be added, but nothing was to be corrected.

10. Question 2. Secondly, a question is raised about the certitude of this book. It seems that it proceeds in a faulty manner.

1. If it is true that the narrative mode is feeble and weak, since a person can contradict it, there is no firm basis by which the narrative can refute the alleged contradiction. And John proceeds in the narrative mode. Therefore, his Gospel is exceedingly feeble and weak.

2. Likewise, it seems that one should proceed in the way of certitude, for "nothing is more certain to human beings than their faith."[33] Therefore, no understanding or teach-

---

[32] This reason seems to be an abbreviation of Jerome, *On Illustrious Men*, 9. 2-3. See FC 100, p. 19: "But there is said to be yet another reason for this work, in that, when he had read the volume of Matthew, Mark, and Luke, he approved, indeed, the substance of the history and declared that the things they said were true, but that they had given the history of only one year, the one, that is, which follows the imprisonment of John and in which he was put to death. So, skipping this year, the events of which had been set forth by these, he related the events of the earlier period before John was shut up in prison...."

[33] On p. 243 n. 5 QuarEd state that this quotation is "according to" Book XIII, c. 1 n. 3 of Augustine's *De Trinitate*. But the exact quotation is not found there. The editors make a cross reference to Opera

ing should be handed on in a more certain way than those that generate faith. But the purpose of John's teaching is to generate faith, as is said in John 20:31. Therefore, his teaching must be most certain and must proceed in the way of certitude.

I answer that certitude is of four kinds, namely, certitude of logical demonstration, of authority, of interior illumination, and of external persuasion. The first certitude is of such a nature that it cannot be resisted. In this instance a human being is forced to assent, is unwilling to say no. And therefore, such certitude, when and where it obtains, eliminates faith. Another kind of certitude is that of authority, and this generates faith. Thus, Augustine says: "What we believe we owe to authority."[34] The third kind of certitude is that of interior illumination, and this perfects faith and brings it to consummation. The fourth is that of persuasion and occurs when believers formulate reasons of fittingness and efficacy, so that they might understand what they believe. This certitude, however, follows after faith, for rational explanations of this kind are most helpful and effective for believers, but for non-believers they are wholly useless and weak.

1.2. Now regarding this question of certitude it must be said: "The end imposes a necessity on those things that pertain to the end."[35] And since this teaching has as its goal to bring about faith, it ought not have the certitude of logical demonstration. It could not have internal certi-

---

Omnia 3.480 n. 3 where they state that Bonaventure's same quotation from Augustine is *sententialiter* ("according to the sense"). See *Sancti Avrelii Avgvstini De Trinitate Libri XV (Libri XIII-XV)*, ed. W.J. Mountain and Fr. Glorie, CCSL la (Turnhout: Brepols, 1968), p. 383.

[34] See *De Utilitate Credendi*, c. 11 n. 25.

[35] See Book II, c. 9 of Aristotle's *Physica*. Cf. WAE, volume 2, pp. 199b-200a.

tude, because that flows from grace. It should not possess persuasive power. Therefore, the situation must be that it has the certitude of authority. And this is the reason why all books of sacred scripture are handed down in the narrative mode, not by rational argumentation, for their purpose is to bring about faith, which occurs by means of free consent. The books of learned doctors, however, are conveyed by means of rational arguments since their goal is to engender understanding, which should nurture and bolster faith. But their reasons have no force, unless they are founded on faith.[36]

Now it must be admitted that the certitude of authority has little persuasive power in other branches of knowledge created by women and men, for they are often mistaken. But in Sacred Scripture, which has been given by the Holy Spirit, it has a firm foundation, for the Holy Spirit cannot lie or be mistaken. Wherefore, Augustine said in his *Commentary on Genesis*: "The authority of this scripture is greater than the perspicacity of all human ingenuity."[37]

---

[36] See n. 5.3 of the Prologue in *Breviloquium*, introduction, translation and notes by Dominic V. Monti, Works of St. Bonaventure IX (St. Bonaventure, NY: Franciscan Institute Publications, 2005), p. 18: "Now, these narrative modes cannot proceed by way of certitude based on reasoning, because particular facts do not admit of formal proof. Therefore, lest Scripture seem doubtful and consequently lose some of its power to move us, God has given it, in place of a certitude based on reasoning, a certitude based on authority, which is so great that it surpasses the keenest of human minds."

[37] See Book II, c. 5 in *Sancti Avreli Avgvstini De Genesi ad Litteram....* Edited by Joseph Zycha. CSEL XXVIII, 1; (Prague: F. Tempsky, 1894), p. 39. The original reads *capacitas* ("capacity") while Bonaventure has *perspicacitas* ("perspicacity").

11. Question 3. This question concerns the sublimity of the investigation and speech. And it seems that Blessed John, who investigated such sublime matters, did poorly.

1. For Sirach 3:22 reads: "Do not seek the things that are too high for you, and do not investigate matters above your ability." And again Proverbs 25:27 says: "The investigator of majesty will be overwhelmed by glory."[38] What is greater than the generation of the eternal Word? – Now if you say that he himself did not do the investigating, but narrated. I say against this what Isaiah 53:8 asks: "Who will narrate his generation?" And Jerome gives an exposition of the eternal generation.[39] – 2. Furthermore, the Apostle in 1 Corinthians 2:1 prides himself on the fact that when he first came to the Corinthians he did not come in sublimity of speech, but in humility.[40] So it seems that Blessed John is reprehensible because he begins his Gospel on too exalted a plane, one that he could not sustain throughout the rest of the Gospel.

I respond that it should be understood that an investigation of majesty and of sublime matters can be threefold, namely, it can be performed in a diabolical, human, or divine spirit. The first investigation stems from malice and is found among the heretics. Curiosity spurs the second type of investigation and is found among the philosophers. The third, however, issues from devoted love and is found among the apostles and prophets. The first is entirely to

---

[38] On p. 244 n. 1 QuarEd accurately indicate that the Vulgate reads *qui scrutator est maiestatis* ("the person who is the investigator of majesty") while Bonaventure has *perscrutator maiestatis* ("the investigator of majesty").

[39] See Jerome's comments on this passage in Book XIV of his *Commentary on Isaiah* in PL 24:528C-529B.

[40] The Vulgate reads *per sublimitatem sermonis* ("through sublimity of speech") while Bonaventure has *in sublimitate sermonis* ("in sublimity of speech").

be censured. The second is to be avoided while the third is to be embraced. The reason for this determination flows from the fact that the first and second type of investigation frequently lead to error, but the third does not, since the Spirit investigates the profound things of God, as 1 Corinthians 2:10 says.[41] Since John was inspired by the divine Spirit, he cannot be censured for his investigation and description of heavenly matters. And so the Holy Spirit, not a human being, told of the eternal generation.

2. Relative to the question about sublimity of speech, it has to be noted that sublimity of speech is sometimes censured because of an evil intention. An instance of this is a person speaking about sublime matters with the sole intention of drawing applause. Actions such as these are prohibited in 1 Samuel 2:3: "Do not multiply your boastful speech about sublime matters." – Sometimes it is censured because of its subject matter. An instance of this is when the subject matter is trivial and picayune and should not be blown out of proportion or obfuscated by pompous speech. About such matters Colossians 2:4 speaks: "Now I say this, so that no one may deceive you by sublime words." Subsequently, Colossians 2:8 says: "See to it that no one deceives you by philosophy and vain deceit." – Sometimes it is censured because its listeners do not have the capacity to understand it. Therefore, the Apostle said in 1 Corinthians 2:1: "I did not come to you in sublimity of speech." And the reason for this is that they were unable to understand.[42] On the contrary, Jerome says this about certain teachers: "Some with brows knit and bombastic words, balanced one against the other,

---

[41] On p. 244 n. 4 QuarEd accurately indicate that the Vulgate reads *Spiritus enim omnia scrutatur, etiam profunda Dei* ("For the Spirit investigates all things, even the profound things of God").

[42] See 1 Cor 3:2: "I fed you with milk, not with solid food, for you were not yet ready for it."

philosophize concerning the sacred writings among weak women."[43] – Now Blessed John had both subject matter that was lofty and a good intention and listeners who were advanced in the faith, for the Church had already flourished. For these reasons he rightly and fittingly spoke in a sublime manner. Nevertheless, it is wondrous, as Augustine says, that in John's words infants may suck milk for their nourishment while the perfect find solid food to sustain them.[44] Also what Gregory says is verified, namely, that while an elephant has room to swim there, a lamb wades.[45] Wherefore, the little ones, who cannot swim with the elephants, should wade with the sheep.

PROLOGUE OF ST. JEROME
ON THE GOSPEL ACCORDING TO JOHN

The author is John the Evangelist, one of the disciples of the Lord, who was a virgin chosen by God, whom God called when he had determined to get married. A double

---

[43] See Letter 53.7 and NPNF/2, Volume 6, p. 99.

[44] On p. 244 n. 8 QuarEd intimate that Augustine doesn't say this in so many words. See Tractatus 1 n. 12 in *Sancti Avrelii Avgvstini In Iohannis Evangelium Tractatvs CXXIV*, ed. D.R. Willems, CCSL xxxvi (Turnhout: Brepols, 1954), p. 7. See further *St. Augustine, Tractates on the Gospel of John 1-10*, trans. John W. Rettig, FC 78 (Washington: CUA Press, 1988), p. 51: "If, therefore, 'The Word was in the beginning, and the Word was with God, and the Word was God,' if you cannot imagine what it is, put it off so that you may grow up. That is solid food; take milk that you may be nourished, that you may be strong enough to take solid food."

[45] See Gregory the Great's "Letter to Leander," n. 4, which serves as an introduction to Gregory's *Moralia in Iob*. See *S. Gregorii Magni Moralia in Iob Libri I-X*, ed. Marcus Adriaen, CCSL cxliii (Turnhout: Brepols, 1979), p. 6: "In its public nature the divine word nourishes infants, while in private its nature is to suspend minds in admiration of its sublime matters. I would describe it in this way: It's like a river that is broad and deep and in which both a lamb may wade and an elephant swim."

witness to his virginity is given in this Gospel. First, he
was said to be beloved by the Lord above all the others.
Second, while he was hanging on the cross, the Lord commended his Mother into his care, so that a virgin might
take care of a virgin. – Briefly, he was the only one to
manifest in his Gospel, at the beginning of his work about
the incorruptible Word, that the Word became flesh and
that the light could not be comprehended by the darkness. Also at the Lord's first *sign*, which he performed at
a wedding, he showed that he was there, so that he might
demonstrate to his readers that where the Lord is invited, there the nuptial wine should never run out, and that,
the old things having been changed, all the new things
that Christ had instituted would appear.[46] – Further, he
wrote his Gospel in Asia, and afterwards he wrote his
book of Revelation on the island of Patmos, so that for
whom the incorruptible beginning is announced at the
beginning of the canon in Genesis,[47] to him also the incorruptible ending might be rendered through a virgin
in Revelation, when Christ said: "I am the alpha and the
omega."[48] – And this is the John, who, when he knew that
the day of his departure was drawing nigh, convened his
disciples in Ephesus and revealed Christ to them through
the experience of many signs. Having prayed, he went to
the place dug out for his grave and was placed with his
ancestors. He was found to be as untouched by the pain
of death as he was a stranger to the corruption of the
flesh. – So after all the others he wrote his Gospel, and
this was as it ought to be for a virgin. I do not give an exposition of the books he wrote nor of their chronology nor
of their order or table of contents, so that those seeking

---

[46] See John 2:1-12 where Jesus changes into wine the water that
was in six stone water jars, each holding twenty to thirty gallons, for
Jewish ritual purification.
[47] See Gen 1:1: "In the beginning God created heaven and earth."
[48] See Rev 1:17.

understanding of God's magisterial teaching may enjoy both their gift of the desire to know and the fruits of their labor. This is enough.

AN EXPOSITION OF JEROME'S PROLOGUE

12. Jerome wrote this Prologue for this Gospel and sets out many things.[49] For first he considers *the dignity* of the author. Second, *the mode of writing* where he says: "he was manifested in his Gospel." Third, *the time and the place of the writing* where he says: "he wrote his Gospel in Asia." Fourth, *the death of the author* where he writes: "And this is the John, who, when he knew that the day of his departure." Finally, *the relationship of this Gospel to the other Gospels* where he states: "after all the others he wrote his Gospel."

Thus, he expresses the dignity of the author when he says: "The virgin was called by the Lord during a wedding." Further, great and noble testimonies to his virginity are manifested in Christ's intimate love and the commission of his Mother.[50]

---

[49] On p. 245 n. 1 QuarEd state that although Bonaventure and others, e.g., Hugh of St. Cher, attribute this Prologue to Jerome, it is not found, as far as they know, among Jerome's works.

[50] On p. 245 n. 2 QuarEd write: "This twofold witness to John's virginity is commonly stated by the Fathers, even by Jerome.... But it is not Jerome, but Bede who states: 'The virgin was called by the Lord during a wedding.' The first part of this Prologue (Jerome's), with a few words changed, comes from Bede's Exposition of John 1:1." See PL 92:638A: "Now this John is one of the disciples of Christ whom the Lord called to virginity during the wave-tossed tempest of a wedding. A twofold witness to his virginity is given in this Gospel, for he is said to have been loved by God above all the others and God, from the throne of the cross, commended his mother to him, so that a virgin might take care of the Virgin."

Moreover, he shows that the manner of writing is in accord with the writer in this that the writer, incorrupt in his flesh, was also called at a wedding. So he first began his Gospel "with the generation of the incorruptible Word,"[51] and then presented Christ's changing of water into wine at a wedding as the first of his signs. From the words, "he showed that he himself was there," he provided his name.[52] And according to our common way of speaking, namely, "your actions reveal who you are," he showed in his own way who he was.

He says that the place of writing "was in Asia," while the time of writing was after he had completed writing Revelation. And so John's Gospel was the last book of sacred scripture. And so it was fitting that just as in that first book "the incorruptible beginning is announced at the beginning of the canon," so also in the last book written it says: "In the beginning was the Word." These words of John 1:1 correspond to Genesis 1:1, "In the beginning God created" and to what the Lord said in Revelation 1:8: "I am the alpha and the omega." Through this it is also determined who the speaker is in Revelation 1:8.[53] – Or

---

[51] See Book I, Homily 8 of Venerable Bede. This homily for the Feast of St. John the Evangelist is actually Homily 9. See *Bede the Venerable, Homilies on the Gospels.* Book One, trans. Lawrence T. Martin and David Hurst, CSS 110 (Kalamazoo: Cistercian Publications, 1991), p. 94: "... [John] disclosed all the hidden mysteries of divine truth and true divinity, to an extent that was permitted to no other mortals. And this privilege was properly kept for a virgin, so that he might put forth for consideration the mysteries of the incorruptible Word, having not only an incorrupt heart, but also an incorrupt body." See also *Bedae Venerabilis Opera*, Pars III/IV, ed. D. Hurst, CCSL cxxii (Turnhout: Brepols, 1955), p. 66.

[52] On p. 245 n. 4 QuarEd deal with the unnamed bridegroom of John 2:1-12 by giving four explanations of "he showed that he was there." The fourth one is that John showed that he himself was there and that the Lord had been invited to his wedding.

[53] Rev 1:13 reads: "One like to a Son of Man."

these words can be taken in this sense: "An incorruptible conclusion[54] is given by a virgin in Revelation," which is the last book of the canon, although not the very last book written. However, the first interpretation is more in accord with the literal meaning of the words.

He depicts the death of the author as miraculous, for he foresaw it. And after he had performed many miracles, he passed from this life without any pain. But there is doubt about this.[55]

He mentions its relationship to the other Gospels, for he wrote last. And this was fitting either for a modest virgin or for an incorrupt virgin or for a perfect virgin. Therefore, it was fitting that he might complete the Gospels. Nevertheless, he refused to give a full account of his relationship to them, so that he might leave to others a field worthy of labor.[56]

---

[54] The meaning here seems to be: Since Jesus Christ is the incorruptible Word and is the First (*alpha*) and the Last (*omega*), he is the incorruptible conclusion or ending to the entire Bible.

[55] See Jerome's *On Illustrious Men* 9.7: "John returned to Ephesus under Nerva, and, continuing there until the time of emperor Trajan, founded and built churches throughout all of Asia, and, worn out by old age, died in the sixty-eighth year after our Lord's passion and was buried in the same city." See Bede, Book I, Homily 9 in Martin/Hurst, p. 90: "For as we find in the writings of the fathers, when he had reached a ripe old age he knew that the day of his passing away was drawing near; his disciples were called together and, after advising them with exhortations and the celebration of mass, he said his last goodbyes to them. Then he descended into the place dug for his grave, and when the prayers had been performed, he was taken to his fathers, being found as free of the pain of death as he was a stranger to the corruption of the flesh."

[56] On p. 245 n. 8 QuarEd state that this Prologue, under the name of Jerome, but minus the elements that pertain strictly to the Gospel, also is found at the beginning of Revelation.

COMMENTARY ON THE GOSPEL
OF ST. JOHN

CHAPTER ONE

1. In the beginning was the Word, etc. This book, which deals with the incarnate Word, in whom a twofold nature, namely, divine and human, is considered, is divided into two parts. The first part concerns the Word *in se*, while the second deals with the Word in as far as it is united to flesh. That part commences with the words: *There was a man sent by God.*[57] Now since *word* refers to efficacious power, as Augustine says,[58] and indicates the speaker and that which is said by the word, the first part has two sections. The first section concerns the Word in relationship to the speaker. The second focuses on those things which

---

[57] John 1:6.

[58] See *Sancti Avrelii Avgvstini De Diversis Qvaestionibvs Octoginta Tribvs; De Octo Dvlcitii Qvaestionibvs*, ed. Almut Mutzenbecher, CCSL xliv a (Turnhout: Brepols, 1975), p. 136. See *Saint Augustine, Eighty-Three Different Questions*, trans. David L. Mosher, FC 70 (Washington: CUA Press, 1982), p. 127: "'In the beginning was the Word.' The Greek word *logos* signifies in Latin both 'reason' and 'word.' However, in this verse the better translation is 'word,' so that not only the relation to the Father is indicated, but also the efficacious power with respect to those things which are made by the Word. Reason, however, is correctly called reason even if nothing is made by it."

are spoken by the Word: *All things were made through him.*[59]

Part I: John 1:1-2
Concerning the Word *in se*:
First, in relationship with the speaker

In the first part there are four small sentences, which describe the incarnate Word relative to four qualities, which are: *unity* in essence; *dissimilarity* in person; *equality* in majesty; *co-eternity* in duration. And these qualities dash four errors against the stones.[60]

2. (Verse 1). Now the first quality is unity in essence and is noted in the first short sentence which says: *In the beginning was the Word.* As Augustine says: "There is the beginning without beginning, and this is the Father, and there is beginning from the beginning, and that is the Son."[61] Here by means of antonomasia the Father is considered the beginning.[62] So the meaning is: *In the beginning*, that is, in the Father, is the Son, not separated from the Father in essence. As John 14:11 says below: "I in the Father, and the Father in me," as undivided. For as it is said in John 10:30 below: "The Father and I are one."

---

[59] John 1:3.

[60] See Book II, d. 1. p. I. dub. 2 of Bonaventure's *Sentence Commentary*.

[61] This quotation is not found verbatim in Augustine. See Book II, chapter 17 n. 4 of his *Contra Maximinum Haereticum Arianorum Episcopum Libri Duo* in PL 42:784: *Pater ergo principium non de principio; Filius principium de principio* ("Therefore, the Father [is] the beginning without a beginning; the Son, the beginning from the beginning").

[62] *Random House Webster's College Dictionary* (New York: Random House, 1991) defines antonomasia: "1. the substitution of an epithet or appellative for an individual's name, as *his lordship*."

And by this *the infidelity of the pagans* is thwarted, who are indignant with us that we say three persons and not three gods, as Augustine says in *De Agone Christiano*.[63] And they do this since they do not understand how the Word was in the beginning.

3. The second quality is dissimilarity in persons, and this is mentioned in the second short sentence where it says: *The Word was with God*. For as Grammaticus says,[64] and also Victor,[65] prepositions are transitive. Therefore, the preposition *apud* ("with") implies a distinction whereby the preposition by reason of its special signification indicates that the source is in the Father and that a sub-source is in the Son. For it is said that the minor premise is contained along with the major premise and not the other way around, according to the ordinary way of speaking.[66] In this short sentence, even though a real minor and major premise are not found, nonetheless, the Father is the source and the Son is the sub-source. Through the

---

[63] See chapter 15 n. 17 of *Sancti Avreli Avgvstini De Fide et Symbolo ... De Agone Christiano ...,* ed. Joseph Zycha, CSEL xli (Prague: Tempsky, 1900), p. 119. See also *Saint Augustine, Christian Instruction ... The Christian Combat ...,* trans. by Robert P. Russell, FC 4 (New York: CIMA Publishing Co., 1947), p. 333: "Let us not heed those who are highly offended and indignant because we do not say that there are Gods to be adored. These heretics fail to understand a nature that is on[sic] and the selfsame."

[64] See Book XIV chapters 1-3 of *Prisciani Grammatici Institvtionvm Grammaticarvm Volvmen Maivs continens libros sedecim priores,* ed. August Krehl (Leipzig: Weidmann, 1819), pp. 581-601. I have been unable to find the exact place where Priscian Grammaticus treats of *apud* as transitive.

[65] On p. 246 n. 7 QuarEd mention that during the first six centuries there were some fifty-four people who were named Victor. This Victor, whose works are not extant, is probably Bishop Victor of Capua (d. 554).

[66] I use a simplistic example. All men are rational animals (major premise). John is a man (minor premise). Therefore, John is a rational animal.

noun *word* is understood the emanation of generation. And Sirach 24:5 mentions these three things: "I came out of the mouth of the Most High, the firstborn before all creatures." "The Most High" means origin and source. "Out of the mouth" means generation. "I came out" means distinction. And through this is refuted the heresy of the Sabellians, who maintain that the Father and the Son are one and the same, since they did not understand how "the Word was with God."[67]

4. The third quality is equality in majesty, which is mentioned in the third short sentence: *And the Word was God.* For if, as Anselm says, "God is that than which nothing greater can be thought,"[68] and if the Word was God, then he was that than which nothing greater can be thought and so was equal in majesty to the Father. In John 14:1 below he said to his disciples: "You believe in God; also believe in me." If the one God must be believed in as the supreme truth, then also the Word must be believed in. It follows that the Word was God. And this short sentence is a repudiation of the heresy of the Arians, who maintained that the Son was a creature and less than the Father, as

---

[67] See Theophylactus, *Enarratio in Evangelium Joannis* on John 1:2 in PG 1139BC: "So both Arius and Sabelius are refuted. Now Arius maintained that the Son of God was a creature and created. He is confounded by this passage when it says: 'He was in the beginning, and that Word was God.' Sabelius, who denied a trinity of persons, but insisted on their oneness, is refuted by these words: 'And that Word was with God.' For it is manifest in this passage that the Word is other and that John the Great declares that the Father is other."

[68] See *Proslogion*, chapter 4 in *S. Anselmi Opera Omnia I.* Edited by Francis Salesius Schmitt. (Edingurgh: Thomas Nelson & Sns, 1946), p. 111. See also *The Prayers and Meditations of Saint Anselm with the Proslogion,* trans. Benedicta Ward (London: Penguin, 1973), p. 246.

Augustine says.[69] For they did not understand how *the Word was God*.

5. (Verse 2). The fourth quality, which is co-eternity in duration, is indicated in this fourth short sentence: *He was in the beginning with God*. For God the Father was from eternity. If the Son were not co-eternal and if the Father was before the Son, then the Word would not have been in the beginning with God. But he was in the beginning, and therefore, he is co-eternal. For Proverbs 8:22-23 reads: "The Lord possessed me in the beginning of his ways, before he made anything from the beginning. I was ordained from eternity." And this provides a refutation of the heresy of the Photinians and Ebionites, who taught that Christ's beginning came entirely from Mary, as Augustine says in his *De Agone Christiano*.[70] For they did not understand how *the Word was in the beginning with God*.

QUESTIONS

6. In order to understand the aforementioned short sentences these questions can be asked:

---

[69] See Tractate 1.11 in FC 78, p. 50: "Let some one of the unbelieving Arians come forward now and say that the Word of God was made. How can it happen that the Word of God was made when God made all things through the Word?"

[70] See chapter 17 n. 19 in FC 4, p. 334: "And let us not heed those who say that Jesus Christ, the Son of God, is nothing more than a man, although He is so holy a man that He is deservedly called the Son of God. The discipline of the Catholic Church has cast out these heretics also, for, deceived by the desire for vain glory, they chose to engage in bitter controversy before understanding the true nature of the power and the wisdom of God, and the meaning of the words: 'in the beginning was the Word,' through whom 'all things have been made'; and how 'the Word was made flesh and dwelt among us.'"

Question 1. Since the term Son expresses a characteristic that is most distinctive, why does John describe the Son of God with the term *Word* rather than the term *Son?* For it seems that it should be the other way around.

I answer. It has to be said that the word Son only expresses a relationship with the Father while the term Word refers to relationships to the speaker, to what is being said by the word, to the voice that embodies the word, and to the teaching that is learned by another through the medium of the word. And since the Son of God had to be described in these sentences not only in relationship to the Father, from whom he proceeds, but also to creatures, which he made, and to the flesh which he took on, and to the teaching that he communicated, he had to be described in a most excellent and fitting manner with the term Word. For that term relates to all these matters, and a more appropriate term could not be found in the world.

7. Question 2. Furthermore, it is asked what is described by the word *was.* For if was refers to past time,[71] such a meaning is wholly contrary to eternity, because eternity has no past. Now if you say, as Augustine says in the Glossa,[72] that this verb sometimes expresses present

---

[71] Part of the question stems from the fact that *was* (in Latin: *erat*) is the imperfect past tense.

[72] On p. 247 n. 9 QuarEd state that this Glossa is found in Lyranus and that while Albert the Great and Hugh of St. Cher attribute it to Augustine, Thomas the Aquinas maintains that Origen is its author. See Tractate 99 n. 5.2 in *St. Augustine Tractates on the Gospel of John 55-111*, trans. John W. Rettig, FC 90 (Washington: CUA Press, 1994), p. 224: "Now, in that which is eternal, without beginning and without end, of whatever tense a verb is used, whether past, present, or future, it is not used falsely. For although the immutable and ineffable nature does not admit of *was* and *will be* but only *is* ... nevertheless, on account of the changeableness of the time in which our mortality and

time in analogy with similar verbs and further that here it does not express time, but designates essence without any hint of temporality, this does not solve the problem. For although the expressions of similar verbs ("The Son is generated" or "is begotten") do not express time, nonetheless it would be clearer if these expressions read: *Always begotten* and *always generated*. – Moreover, in John 8:58 the Lord expresses the matter in this way: "Before Abraham came to be, I am." He does not say I had been or I was. So in the verse in question he should have expressed himself by using the present tense or "The Word is."

I answer. It has to be said that the existence or *esse* of the Word is described here as permanent, immutable, and antecedent to everything else, for the verb *was* is of such a nature that it expresses these three things. Wherefore, he used the verb *was* in a most elegant manner. For since it occupies the middle position between present and past and since "the middle partakes of the nature of the extremes,"[73] it follows that it has permanence from the

---

our changeableness are involved, we do not falsely say *was* and *will be* and *is*. Was in past ages; is, in present ones; will be, in future ones. Was, because he was never lacking; will be, because he will never be lacking; is, because he always is."

[73] See Book III, text. 8 of the *Metaphysics* of Averroes. See further Controversy I, n. 5 of Anselm of Canterbury's "The Harmony of the Foreknowledge, the Predestination, and the Grace of God with Free Choice" in *Anselm of Canterbury*, volume 2, ed. and trans. Jasper Hopkins and Herbert Richardson (Toronto: Edwin Mellen Press, 1976), p. 190: "Thus, we can recognize that for lack of a verb [properly] signifying the eternal present, the apostle used verbs of past tense; for things which are temporally past are altogether immutable, after the fashion of the eternal present. Indeed, in this respect, things which are temporally past resemble the eternal present more than do things which are temporally present. For eternally present things are never able not to be present, just as temporally past things are never able not to be present. But all temporally present things which pass away do become not-present."

present, immutability from the past, and antecedence and origin from itself, namely, it is eternal with regard to time. Thus, the text justly says *was*.

8. But a heretic objects: If the Word proceeds from the speaker as a son from a father and the son is posterior to the father, then the Word was not in the beginning with God. If you say that this relationship is compared to that between the light and its brightness, another heretic objects: What if the light is far more radiant and more noble than the brightness that proceeds from it?[74] Therefore, the relationship between Father and Word is the same.

I respond: It has to be said that the use of a simile between God and creatures is never total since every creature is more dissimilar than similar to God. And therefore, there have been errors on the part of heretics who wanted the assimilation between God and creatures to be total. However, in many ways the similes are acceptable. For the Word is compared to a speaker as a son is compared to a father on account of a similar nature and equal perfection. The Word is compared as brightness to light on account of co-eternity. And so in all such arguments there is a limited conclusion.

---

[74] See Augustine's Sermon 117 n. 11 in *Sermons III/4 (94A-147A) on the New Testament* trans. and notes Edmund Hill, WSA III/4 (Hyde Park, NY: New City Press, 1992), p. 216: "If I wish to light a lamp, there is no fire there yet, nor yet any of that brightness; but as soon as I light it, simultaneously with the fire comes the brightness too. Give me here fire without brightness, and I will believe you that the Father can have existed without the Son."

PART I: JOHN 1:3-5
CONCERNING THE WORD *IN SE*:
SECOND, IN RELATIONSHIP WITH THE THINGS
THAT ARE SPOKEN THROUGH THE WORD

9. (Verse 3). *All things were made through him*, etc. In this verse the Word is described by the comparison with *what is spoken by the* Word and this with regard to four qualities, that is, as the *sufficient, unfailing, foreknowing* principle of creation that *bestows understanding* on others. And through these four qualities he repels many heresies.

So first the Word is said to be the sufficient principle, because he suffices to produce all things. Thus, the text says: *All things were made through him*, that is, by God the Father through the Word. For Sirach 18:1 reads: "He who lives forever created all things together," and did this through the Word. Thus, the Psalm says: "He spoke, and they were made."[75] Augustine in his book, *Confessions* says: "By the Word, co-eternal ... with you, you say whatever you say, and what you say comes to be.... You do not make in any other way than by saying."[76]

10. *And without him was made nothing*. These words indicate the second quality, that is, that the Word is an unfailing principle since no action occurs without him. For the Father does nothing without the Word. John 5:19 below says: "All things that the Father does, these things the Son also does in like manner."[77] In a like manner creatures do nothing without the cooperation of the Word.

---

[75] See Ps 32:9 or 148:5.

[76] Bonaventure adapts Book XI, c. 7 n. 9. See CCSL xxvii, p. 199.

[77] On p. 248 n. 8 QuarEd rightly indicate that the Vulgate reads *quaecumque enim ille fecerit* ("For whatever he does") while Bonaventure has *omnia quae Pater facit* ("all things that the Father does").

John 15:5 below states: "Without me you can do nothing."
And in this there is a complete repudiation of the heresy
of Manichees, who propound two principles, one proceeding from the God of light, the other from the God of darkness. For they did not understand how *all things were
made through the Word.*

11. (Verse 4). *What had been made in him was life.*[78] Here
the third quality is noted, that is, the foreknowing principle, for all things are in him, before they come to be,
and live in him, like a chest of drawers in the mind of
the cabinet maker.[79] Thus, Augustine maintains that the
Son is "knowledge ... full of all rational essences that have
life...."[80] Sirach 23:29 reads: "All things were known to the
Lord God before they were created. So after they were
perfected, he beholds all things." Therefore, the rational
essences live in him since they are not changed. James
1:17 states: "With the Father of lights there is no change,
no shadow of alteration." And every change is a small
death.[81]

12. *And the life was light for men and women.* The fourth
quality of the Word is that he bestows understanding
upon others. So he is said to be *light for men and women*

---

[78] On p. 249 n. 1 QuarEd accurately mention that the Vulgate concludes John 1:3 with *quod factum est* ("what had been made").

[79] See Tractate 1 n. 17 in FC 78, 57: "The chest in the product is
not life; the chest in the creative knowledge is life. For the soul of the
craftsman, in which exist all these things before they are produced,
has life. So therefore, dearest brothers, because the wisdom of God,
through which all things were made, contains all things in accordance
with his creative knowledge before he constructs all things, it follows
that whatever things are made through this creative knowledge are
not immediately life; but whatever has been made is life in him."

[80] See Book VI, c. 10 n. 11 in CCSL l, p. 241.

[81] See Book II, c. 9 n. 15 of *Saint Augustine: The Trinity*, trans.
Stephen McKenna, FC 45 (Washington: CUA Press, 1963), p. 69: "Mu-
tability itself is not inappropriately called mortality."

since the Word illumines men and women and makes them see. So Psalm 4:7 says: "The light of your countenance, O Lord, is imprinted upon us." Without this light there is no sight, as Augustine says, since, just as the eye does not see without being illumined by corporal light, so too the intellect does not see unless the most spiritual light shines upon it.[82] Although he bestows understanding upon all, he, nonetheless, does not bestow understanding of himself upon all since sinners understand through the light, but do not comprehend and understand the light. So the text continues:

13. (Verse 5). *And the light shines in the darkness*, since he makes sinners to understand true matters. *And the darkness did not comprehend it*, because those blinded by the darkness of infidelity do not understand. Genesis 1:2 says: "There was darkness over the face of the abyss," that is, infidelity on the face of the human heart. Thus, Ephesians 5:8 states: "You were once darkness, but now you are light in the Lord." 1 John 1:5-6 reads: "God is light, and there is no darkness in God. If we say that we have fellowship with God and walk in darkness, we are lying and not doing the truth." And this counters that error, which posited that all things occur by fate, there is no providence, and God does not know our actions.

QUESTIONS

14. Question 1. This question deals with John 1:3: "Without him was made nothing."

---

[82] To what writing is Bonaventure referring? A remote source is Book I, c. 8 n. 15 of Augustine's *Soliloquies*.

Against this is the fact that the person who steals is doing and making something. Therefore, what is stolen is something with the consequence that it is from God. Wherefore, sins and evil are from God and do not come into being without God. – If you say that sin is nothing since the sense of "without him was made nothing" is that "nothing" refers to sin since a negation resides in the term "nothing," that raises a further objection.[83] Since sin corrupts, and what corrupts performs an action, and what performs an action is a being that exists, and a being that exists is something, therefore, etc.

I answer. It must be answered that sometimes sin refers to an action that is a privation because of some due circumstance. Sometimes it refers to a deprivation of the due order towards which the good should tend. Sometimes it refers to the very deprivation of a good. In the first mode it is something. In the second it has an accidental existence. In the third it is nothing plain and simple. So by reason of the substratum of good that underlies the action it is from God, but by reason of its deformity it is not.

Now concerning the objection that sin is an agent. Such action takes place because of the nature of the substratum of good, as Dionysius says.[84]

---

[83] See Tractate 1 n. 13 in FC 78, p. 52: "For many are accustomed through a poor understanding of 'without him was made nothing' to think that nothing is something. Certainly sin was not made through him, and it is clear that sin is nothing and that men become nothing when they sin."

[84] There is no specific place where Dionysius says this. See chapter 4, n.19-35 of "De Divinis Nominibus" in *Pseudo-Dionysius: The Complete Works*, trans. Colm Luibheid, Classics of Western Spirituality (New York: Paulist, 1987), p. 84-96; e.g., n. 32 on page 94: "We have to assume that evil exists as an accident. It is there by means of something else. Its source does not lie within itself."

15. Question 2. Moreover, there is a question about the meaning of John1:3-4: "What has been made in him was life."

Contrary. All things were made in him. Therefore, all things are life. Psalm 103:24 says: "You have made all things in wisdom." So a stone is life.[85]

I answer. It should be mentioned that Chrysostom explains this sentence in this wise: *"That has been made"* is to be joined to the previous sentence, which then reads: *Without him was made nothing that has been made.* The word "that" is explanatory. And afterwards the text reads: *In him was life.* Thereby, the objection evaporates.[86] – Hilary puts the matter this way: *That has been made in him.* Thus, he stresses that the humanity, namely, incarnation, passion, and resurrection *was life* and takes "in him" causally, that is, the Word was the cause of our life and salvation.[87] – Ambrose makes this point: *That has been made in him, life,* that is, in him who is life. The

---

[85] See Tractate 1 n. 16 in FC 78, pp. 55-56, which also quotes Ps 103:24: "Then stone, too, is life. It is shameful to understand the sentence like this, lest that same most foul sect of Manichaeans should again steal upon us and say that a stone has life ... Let them not mislead you. Read it thus: 'That which was made' – punctuate here, and after that put – 'in him is life.'"

[86] See Homily 5 in *Saint John Chrysostom Commentary on Saint John the Apostle and Evangelist, Homilies 1-47*, trans. Sr. Thomas Aquinas Goggin, FC 33 (New York: Fathers of the Church, 1957), pp. 61-62: "... Let us proceed to the generally accepted reading and interpretation. And what is this? To finish the sentence at 'that has been made'; then to begin again from the following phrase, which reads: 'In him was life.' What he means is this: 'Without him was made nothing that has been made. No creatures that have been made,' he says, 'were made without him.' Do you not see how by this short addition all the absurd hurdles are surmounted?"

[87] See Book II, n. 20 of *De Trinitate Libri duodecim* in PL 10:63B: "For that which was made in him was also made through him."

the darkness did not comprehend it," that is, they adhered to the Word neither through faith nor love.

Part II: John 1:6-21:25
About the Word, united to flesh

17. *There was a man sent by God, whose name was John.* Earlier the Evangelist considered the Word according to *the excellence of his divinity*. In this part he deals with the Word's *assumption of humanity*. And since this assumption was done for the sake of our salvation, which was accomplished by his passion and consummated by his resurrection, this part has three sections. The first section focuses on *the incarnation*. The second on *the passion* at John 11:47 below: "The chief priests, therefore, gathered together." The third on *the resurrection* at 20:1 below: "Now on the first day of the week," etc.[93]

Section I: John 1:6-11:46
The Incarnation

And since the incarnation is useless for us unless it is revealed, the Evangelist first treats *the incarnation*, then its *revelatory manifestation* where 1:14 below says: "We have seen his glory." Now since the coming of Christ in the flesh was the coming of a King, he sent someone ahead to announce his coming, a precursor. Thus, the author first deals with the advent of *the precursor* and then the advent of *Christ* where 1:9 reads: "And it was the true light," etc.

---

nothing of you will at present escapes your notice, or you can take in the width of your ring at a glance" (translation modified).

[93] A common contemporary way of dividing John's Gospel is: Book of Signs (Chapters 1-12) and Book of Glory (Chapters 13-21).

JOHN 1:6-8
THE ADVENT OF THE PRECURSOR

18. (Verse 6). The Evangelist employs four characteristics to describe the coming of the precursor: nature, authority, name, office. He mentions nature when the text states: *There was a man*. The Glossa observes: "A human being, not an angel, as heretics are wont to say."[94] The heretics used to say this because of what Malachi 3:1 says: "Behold, I send my angel/messenger before your face, who will prepare the way before you."[95] But "in this passage the word *angelus* is the name of an office or function, not of the precursor's nature."[96] – His authority is conveyed in the words "sent by God," not from human beings, not on his own. Romans 10:15 says: "How will they preach, unless they are sent?" Contrariwise, Jeremiah 23:21 says of the false prophets: "They ran, and I did not send them."[97] – His name is found in the words, "his name was John."

---

[94] This is the Glossa Ordinaria. See Theophylactus's commentary on John 1:6 in PG 123:1147C: "When you hear the word *angelus* ("angel/messenger"), do not think that he had the nature of an angel or that he descended from heaven, but he is called angel/messenger because of his duty and ministry."

[95] On p. 150 n. 11 QuarEd rightly point out the christological variation between Bonaventure and the Vulgate. I translate the Vulgate: "Behold, I send my angel/messenger, and he will prepare the way before my face."

[96] I have adjusted this citation from Augustine to fit the context. See his Exposition 1 n. 15 in *Expositions of the Psalms ... 99-120*, trans. and notes by Maria Boulding, WSA III/19 (Hyde Park, NY: New City Press, 2003), p. 125: "We hold this firmly, and it would be wrong for us to doubt it. The angels are spirits. When they are simply spirits, they are not angels, but when they are sent, they become angels; for 'angel' is the name of a function, not of a nature."

[97] On p. 250 n. 13 QuarEd accurately indicate that the Vulgate reads *Non mittebam prophetas, et ipsi currebant* ("I did not send prophets, and they ran") while Bonaventure has *Currebant, et ego non mittebam eos* ("They ran, and I did not send them").

This name was authentic,[98] since human beings did not select it, but God did. In Luke 1:13 Zachariah is told: "Elizabeth, your wife, will bear you a son, and you will call his name John." – His office or function is the subject of the next verse.

19. (Verse 7). *This man came as a witness*. For his office was to give witness to the light, not on account of a defect in the light, but in believers. So the text states: *This man came as a witness, to bear witness concerning the light, that all might believe through him*. Acts 19:4 reads: "John baptized the people with a baptism of repentance, telling them to believe in him who was to come after him."[99] I stress: To believe through him, not *in him*. The Evangelist mentions the reason in the next verse.

20. (Verse 8). *He was not the light*, in whom they were to believe. But he came *to bear witness concerning the light*. And he did this. John 5:33 below states: "You have sent to John, and he[100] has borne witness to the truth."

Questions

21. Question 1 deals with John 1:7: "He came to bear witness."

Contrary. 1. John 5:34 below reads: "I do not accept human testimony."[101] So God should not have sent this man for this purpose. – 2. Furthermore, light does not need il-

---

[98] Literally, "authentic" means "from the author."

[99] The Vulgate reads *venturus esset* ("would come") whereas Bonaventure has *venturus erat* ("was to come").

[100] On p. 251 n. 1 QuarEd correctly indicate that the Vulgate does not read *ille* ("he").

[101] Jesus is the speaker.

lumination. Wherefore, the greatest Truth does not need a witness. So the precursor came for no purpose.

I respond. The issue has to be stated in this way: witness is given to someone and on account of someone. Thus, sometimes the reason for the witness stems from the person to whom witness is borne since his grasp of the truth is weak and he needs the testimony of another. Sometimes testimony is given for the sake of the person who has doubt about faith or is weak in faith. Now John did not come to give witness on account of a defect of the light in Christ, but because of the ineptitude in our eye.[102]

22. Question 2. Another question surfaces with regard to the meaning of John 1:7: "so that all might believe through him." If God sent him to accomplish this end, then both God and the precursor would be frustrated from attaining this necessary end. – I respond. It has to be remarked that an end is twofold: *in itself* and in another. For I say that an end may be frustrated in another, but be accomplished in itself, without any incompleteness or imperfection, as is obvious in the case of a speaker who persuades well, an angel guarding, Christ redeeming, and John testifying. For he has borne sufficient testimony, although not all have believed in him. Nevertheless, he has neglected nothing necessary.[103]

---

[102] Bonaventure's treatment puts into more logical format what John Chrysostom has in his sixth homily on John 1:6-8. For example, see FC 33, p. 72: "Therefore, just as He clad Himself in flesh lest, by advancing to the attack with His Godhead unrevealed, He might lose all men, so He sent a man as His forerunner in order that, since they would hear the words of a fellow human, the people might feel more at ease in coming to listen to him."

[103] See Theophylactus on John 1:7 in PG 123:1147D: "Now although some did not believe him, he is not to be blamed for that. For the sun shines for this purpose that it may illumine all, but if someone secludes himself in some darkened house and does not enjoy the bright light, what is this to the sun?" On p. 251 n. 8 QuarEd cite Saint

23. Question 3. Also what is the meaning of John 1:8: "He was not the light"?

Contrary. Ephesians 5:8 reads: "You were once darkness, but now you are light in the Lord." Therefore, all good people are the light. – The Glossa[104] responds that there is light that illuminates and light that is illuminated. John and other saints are not light that illuminates, but rather light that is illuminated by the prime light. – But contrary to this is what Matthew 5:16 states: "So let your light shine before men and women" and Philippians 2:15: "Among whom you shine like stars in the world."

I answer that light illumines effectively and derivatively. The light that illumines effectively is something that is light by its essence. Thus only God is the light that illumines. Derivative light is light by participation, and such is the case with the saints, who illumine by means of word and example.[105]

Albert's commentary on this passage, a commentary that shows how traditional Bonaventure's answer is: "It should be noted that this is 'an end in another,' and although he does not always accomplish his goal because of an impediment that resides in another, nonetheless, he has neglected nothing necessary and is not frustrated, but has arrived at his goal. An example is a doctor who doesn't always heal, a speaker who doesn't always persuade, an angel guarding who does not always guard effectively because of the one being guarded, and of Christ redeeming, by whom not all are redeemed."

[104] The Glossa Interlinearis reads: "Great, indeed, is he (John), but he does not shine by and of himself, for the saints are light that has been illuminated."

[105] See Tractate 2 n. 6 in FC 78, pp. 65-66: "So then John, too, was a light, but not the true light, because, not enlightened, [he was] darkness, but by enlightenment he became a light."

JOHN 1:9-14A
THE ADVENT OF CHRIST

24. *It was the true light*, etc. Now that he has stipulated the advent of the precursor, he now determines the advent of the *King* and does so by spelling out its characteristics and circumstances. So he describes the advent of Christ in this order. First, he notes *the reason for coming*. Second, *the disdain shown the one coming*. Third, *the usefulness* or fruit of *the coming itself*. Fourth, *the manner of coming*.

(Verse 9). So the reason for coming in the flesh is first mentioned. The reason is that God himself before the incarnation, although God was the greatest light present for all, was not being recognized by the world. Therefore, the visible effect was that he might be recognized and known. Thus, the text says: *It was the true light*, namely, in its essence. *That enlightens every person coming into this*[106] *world*. John 8:12 below reads: "I am the light of the world. The person who follows me does not walk in the darkness." This light was present to the world. Wherefore, the light was in the world by this presence. Wisdom 7:24 says: "He reaches everywhere by reason of his purity."[107]

25. (Verse 10). *He was in the world*, which was his effect. For the text continues: *And the world was made through him*. Thus, he could be known through the world. Wisdom 13:5 states: "By the greatness of the beauty and of the

---

[106] The Vulgate does not read *hunc* ("this").

[107] On p. 252 n. 1 QuarEd correctly indicate that Vulgate reads *suam munditiam* ("her/Wisdom's purity") whereas Bonaventure has *sui munditiam* ("his purity"). Does Bonaventure's identification of Christ with Light and with Wisdom stand behind this change?

creature the creator of these could be[108] seen so as to be known thereby." But nevertheless, *the world knew him not.* "The world," that is, people of the world, is metonymy. John 17:25 reads: "Just Father, the world has not known you." This is the reason why he came. Thus, Chrysostom comments: "Since he was not thought to exist in the world because he was not yet known, he deigned to take on flesh."[109]

26. (Verse 11). *He came unto his own.* Here the Evangelist mentions *the disdain shown the one coming,* and this especially from those who should honor him and from whose nation he assumed flesh.[110] *He came unto his own,* that is, he assumed flesh from the nation of the Jews whom he had chosen above all others. *And his own,* that is, the Jews, *received him not.* The text doesn't mean that no Jew received him, but that only a few did. Isaiah 1:2 says: "I have brought up children and exalted them, but they have disdained me." The Jews are said to be *his own,* because he was from their nation according to the flesh and because he was a descendant of David, who was king in Israel forever. – Another interpretation is: *His own* by special election, according to what Deuteronomy 26:18 has: "The Lord has chosen you as a special people."[111]

---

[108] On p. 252 n. 2 QuarEd accurately mention that the Vulgate reads *poterit* ("might be") while Bonaventure has *poterat* ("could be').

[109] See Homily 10 n. 2 in PG 59:75.

[110] See Tractate 2 n. 12 in FC 78, p. 70: "Who are they ('his own')? Human beings whom he made. The Jews whom he esteemed at first to be above all nations ... and were themselves especially his own since they were related to him through the flesh he deigned to assume."

[111] On p. 252 n. 6 QuarEd rightly indicate that the Vulgate reads *Dominus elegit te hodie ut sis ei populus peculiaris* ("The Lord has chosen you today that you may be a people special to him") whereas Bonaventure has *Elegit te Dominus in populum peculiarem* ("The Lord has chosen you as a special people").

27. (Verse 12). *But to as many.* This verse treats of the third point, namely, the fruit or benefit of his very coming, which is the reception of divine sonship. Since this benefit only extends to those who have received him and believed in him, the text continues: *But to as many as received him.* Thus, *his own* did not receive him, but *to as many as received him he gave them the power of becoming children of God.* And this is a great benefit. 1 John 3:1 states: "Behold what manner of love the Father has bestowed on us that we should be called children of God and such we are." And there is a great advantage in this, for Romans 8:17 reads: "If we are sons, we are heirs also: heirs indeed of God and joint heirs with Christ." So he gave this power of becoming sons of God *to those who received him.* And since this reception is through faith, he gives this further explication: *To those who believe in his name.* So *he gave to those who received, to those who believe in his name,* that is, in the reality behind his name. His name is Emmanuel, that is, God with us.[112] So the person who *believes in his name* is the one who believes that he is God and man and is a son of God. 1 John 5:1 says: "Everyone who believes that Jesus is the Son of God,[113] is born of God." Now since the children of God only come into existence through spiritual, not carnal, generation, the text continues:

28. (Verse 13). *Who not of blood,* that is, by the mingling of seminal fluids. *Nor of the will of the flesh,* that is, of a woman. *Nor of the will of a man,* that is, from pleasure and prurience. *But were born of God.* For John 3:6 below says: "That which is born of the flesh is flesh and that

---

[112] See Matt 1:23: "And they will call his name Emmanuel, that is interpreted, God with us."

[113] On p. 252 n. 9 QuarEd correctly notice that the Vulgate reads *Iesus est Christus* ("Jesus is the Christ') while Bonaventure has *Iesus est Filius Dei* ("Jesus is the Son of God").

which is born of the Spirit is spirit." And 1 Peter 1:23 states: "You have been reborn, not from corruptible seed but from incorruptible, through the word of God who lives and abides forever," that is, always.

29. (Verse 14a). *And the Word was made flesh.* In this fourth point the Evangelist touches upon the manner of his coming, which was through the assumption of flesh, in which there was the highest union. Therefore, the text states: *The Word became flesh,* that is, united to flesh. Philippians 2:7-8 reads: "He humbled himself, taking the form of a slave."[114] And since this union was without confusion, it was also without division. Therefore, the text continues: *And dwelt among us,* that is, in our nature. *He dwelt;* so he was not transformed. *He dwelt;* so he was not separated. About this dwelling Leviticus 26:11 says: "I will place my tabernacle in your midst, and my soul will not cast you off." And Psalm 75:2 states: "His place has been fashioned in peace and his dwelling in Zion."

QUESTIONS

30. Question 1 concerns John 1:9: "It was the true light, which enlightens every person coming, etc." For it was said above that some men and women are darkness.[115] Therefore, he doesn't enlighten all men and women. – If you say: In as far as he is considered as the light by him-

---

[114] On p. 252 n. 11 QuarEd rightly indicate that Bonaventure's citation is a combination of Phil 2:7-8: "but emptied himself, taking the form of slave and being made like unto men. And appearing in the form of man, he humbled himself...."

[115] See n. 13 and 16 above, e.g., n. 13: Those blinded by the darkness of infidelity do not understand.

self, then it is asked: If no one can resist God's will,[116] then it is necessary that all be enlightened.

To this Augustine responds thus: "He enlightens every person, namely, who is enlightened, because no one is enlightened except by him."[117] Take the example of the instructor teaching children. – Bede answers that this is understood of the light of nature, not of grace and whoever has been sealed with the light of the face of God.[118] – Chrysostom, however, comments: Since he is prepared to enlighten, but not all are enlightened. For they themselves have shut out the rays of light. Take the example of a blind man who walks under the sun.[119]

---

[116] On p. 253 n. 1 QuarEd correctly mention Gen 50:19: "Can we resist the will of God?" and Esther 13:9: "And there is no one who can resist your will, O Lord."

[117] See 27 n. 103 of *Sancti Avrelii Avgvstini ... Enchiridion ad Lavrentivm De Fide et Spe et Caritate...,* ed. E. Evans, CCSL xlvi (Turnhout: Brepols, 1969), pp. 104-105: "Not because there is no human being that is not enlightened, but because no one is enlightened except by him." Hugh of St. Cher, p. 283v, c quotes Augustine: "He enlightens every person, that is, no one is enlightened except by him. And he gives the example. If there were in a certain city one sole instructor who taught children, it would truly be said: He teaches all the children of the city, not that all are taught, but those who are taught, are taught by him."

[118] See Bede's exposition in PL 92:640C: "Namely [he enlightens] every person, who is enlightened, either by natural genius or by divine wisdom. For just as no one exists by his own efforts, so too no one can be wise of his own accord, but through the one who illumines, about whom it is written: *All wisdom comes from the Lord God* [Sir 1:1]." Obviously, Bonaventure is not quoting Bede directly.

[119] See Homily 8 n. 1 in PG 59:65: "So how does he enlighten every person? In as far as he is what he is. If those who close the eyes of their minds of their own accord, they do not want to see the rays of this light. It is not from the nature of the light that it happens that they remain in darkness, but out of their own iniquity and of their own accord they deprive themselves of this gift." Clearly Bonaventure is not citing Chrysostom directly.

Relative to your objection: If he wills it, he does it, it has to be said that absolutely he does not want to enlighten people unless they want to be enlightened. But he wants all people to be enlightened with his conditional will, as in the case of 1 Timothy 2:4: "God wills that all people be saved."

31. Question 2. What is the meaning of John 1:11: "He came unto his own"?[120]

1. For if note is taken of his advent, then note should be taken of his absence. But God is never absent. Therefore, he did not come. – 2. Furthermore, if God can be in all places at all times, why, then, does God need to come for some purpose? Therefore, if he had not come, he would have done the same thing.

To this Bede answers: "He was in the world through his divinity. He came into the world through his incarnation. Now to come and to be absent are characteristics of humanity, but to remain is a characteristic of divinity."[121] Wherefore, the sense of this text is: He came, that is, he appeared in a visible manner. – Relative to the question of why it was necessary for him to come, I answer: He did not come for his own sake, but for our sake. And the Evangelist makes this point well: Since the world did not recognize his sublimity, he appeared in the humility of humanity.

---

[120] John 1:11.

[121] Bonaventure seems to have rearranged Bede's text. See PL 92:640D: "Therefore, he was in the world, and he came into the world through his incarnation. Now to come and to be absent are characteristics of humanity; to remain and to be are characteristics of divinity. So although he was in the world through his divinity, the world did not know him. He deigned to come into the world through his humanity...."

32. Question 3. Moreover, what does John 1:12 mean: "He gave them power to become children of God, to those who believe in his name"?

Contrary. 1. Augustine states in his *De Praedestinatione Sanctorum*: "The possibility of believing is a property of nature."[122] Wherefore, they have this power from nature, and therefore, it is not a gift from Christ. – 2. Likewise, why does this text single out those who believe rather than those who love or do other things?

I respond. 1. It should be noted that there is potency that is perfect and active, and this is called active potency. And there is also potency that is imperfect and passive, and this is called mere possibility. The first potency exists only through grace, and it is that which is addressed in this verse. Therefore, the text says: 'He gave them power.' Augustine is speaking about the other type of potency. – 2. Concerning the question of why faith is singled out, I answer that faith is the first of the virtues and the foundation. So it is like a door that opens to the entire house.

33. Question 4 focuses on John 1:14: "And the Word became flesh." Why did the Evangelist use *word* rather than *light* since the Word is described both from the point of view of a word and of light? – If you say that light is common to the three persons of the Trinity, whereas word is only proper to the Son, who alone became incarnate, then the following question results: Why didn't the Evangelist say Son? And why did only the Son become incarnate,

---

[122] See c. 5 n. 10 in PL 44:968: "So the possibility of believing as well as the possibility of having charity is a property of human nature, but to actually have some form of faith or charity stems from God's grace to believers."

since divine goodness is absolutely communicated in each of the hypostases?

My response to this is that only the Son became incarnate. The reason for this is threefold. By reason of birth, since he was the son of the Virgin, and the word son should not be attributed to another person. By reason of work, because re-creation was effected through him who also effected creation.[123] By reason of effect. Since "he made us sons and co-heirs,"[124] we had to be led into our inheritance and adoption through the one who is Son by nature.

Now he used the expression word rather than son, so that he might preclude a carnal understanding and promote a spiritual one. For a son is carnally generated in creatures, but a word has a spiritual generation. A word manifests a spiritual generation, because, as Augustine says, a word is clothed in a sound and does not change into a sound.[125] Thus, the eternal Word took on flesh.

34. Question 5. Finally, what is the meaning of John 1:14: "He became flesh"? For either the sense is "he became flesh," that is, was changed into flesh or that he became, so that he might be flesh. But neither of these understandings makes sense. – If you say that this construc-

---

[123] See Part IV, c. 1 in *Breviloquium*. Introduction, translation and notes by Dominic V. Monti. WSB IX, pp. 131-32: "Thus, just as God [the Father] had created all things through the Uncreated Word, so he would restore all things through the Incarnate Word."

[124] See Rom 8:15, 17.

[125] See Book XV, c. 11 n. 20 of *De Trinitate* in FC 45, p. 477: "For just as our word in some way becomes a bodily sound by assuming that in which it may be manifested to the senses of men, so the Word of God was made flesh by assuming that in which He might also be manifested to the senses of men. And just as our word becomes a sound and is not changed into a sound, so the Word of God indeed becomes flesh, but far be it from us that it should be changed into flesh."

tion involves synecdoche and that the meaning of "flesh" here is "man" or "a human being" with the result that the meaning is that "he became man," then the question surfaces: Why does the Evangelist select flesh to represent humanity rather than the soul since the soul is the nobler part? – Further, why use this figurative way of speaking when one could use proper speech?

I answer. It should be remarked that this union took place for our instruction and our salvation. And it was instruction, because it was visible. And it was liberation, since it was capable of suffering. So ìfleshî signifies the visible part and the one especially capable of suffering. Therefore, etc.

JOHN 1:14B-11:46
THE MANIFESTATION OF THE INCARNATION

35. *And we saw his glory.* Earlier the incarnation of the Word was considered. Now comes a consideration of *the knowledge or manifestation of the incarnate Word.* This part has two sections. The first deals with his manifestation *in general.* The second with his manifestation *in particular* and commences with John 1:19: "And this is the witness of John."

JOHN 1:14B-18
THE MANIFESTATION OF THE INCARNATE WORD
IN GENERAL

This first section has two components, for the first concerns *knowledge* of the incarnate Word himself. The second focuses on the reason for this *knowledge* where verse 15 says: "John bore witness," etc.

Verse 14b. Now the knowledge of the incarnate Word that the Apostles and believers had, was of both natures. In their name the Evangelist says: *And we saw his glory*, that is, we recognized it: *glory*, relative to his divinity. Wherefore, the text continues: *Glory as of the only-begotten of the Father*. Of this glory 2 Peter 1:17 says: "He received[126] from God the Father honor and glory, when from out of the majestic glory a voice came down to him...: This is my beloved Son." – Now with regard to his humanity the text says *full of grace and truth*. One should supply "him" and then read: *we saw him full of grace and truth*. Now he was *full* since in him, as Colossians 2:9 reads, "dwells all the fullness of divinity in bodily form." *Full of grace*, to blot out sins. *Full of truth*, to fulfill the promises. Sirach 24:25 states: "In me is every grace of life and truth." Moreover, it should be noted that the words *as of* in *as of the only-begotten* do not connote a comparison or a likeness, but are a confirmation.[127]

36. (Verse 15). *The testimony of John*. After describing what was known, the Evangelist now shows the three ways in which that knowledge came about: testimony, a unique effect, and unique teaching. The first way was through authentic testimony, that is, the testimony of an authorized person, namely, John, who was holy from his

---

[126] The Vulgate reads *accipiens* ("receiving") while Bonaventure has *accepit* ("he received").

[127] See Chrysostom's Homily 12 n. 1 in PG 59:81-82 and FC 33, p. 112: "The word 'as' in this context does not express likeness or comparison, but affirms and unmistakably defines, as if he said: 'We saw glory such as it was fitting and probable for Him to have who is the only-begotten and true Son of God, the King of all things'.... Now, what is the custom of most men? Frequently, if they have seen a king most magnificently decked out and resplendent.... But when, having listed these details and others besides, they find it impossible to do justice to all the splendor by their words, they straightway add this: 'Why is it necessary to say many words? In brief, he was as a king.'"

mother's womb.[128] Therefore, the text says: "John bore testimony concerning him." Proverbs 14:5 reads: "A trustworthy witness does not lie." *And cried*, that is, John did so openly and confidently, according to what Isaiah 58:1 says: "Cry out. Do not stop. Lift up your voice like a trumpet." John said: "He who is to come after me has been set above me." Therefore, he has become more worthy than me according to human nature. Ephesians 1:22 has: "He made all things subject under his feet and gave him as head over all the Church." And the reason for this is *because he was before me*, namely, according to his divinity. John 8:58 below says: "Amen, amen, I say to you, before Abraham came to be, I am." And thus, he was prior to John.

37. (Verse 16). *And of his fullness*. These words point to the second cause of the knowledge that Christ was the Son of God, namely, because of a unique effect which was the gift of grace. Wherefore, the text states: *And of his fullness*, as if to say: We truly knew that he was *full*, because *of his fullness we have all received, grace for grace*. That is, the grace of reward for the grace of justification or, contrariwise, we have received the grace of justification for the sake of obtaining the grace of reward, which is rightly called *grace*, because, as Augustine says, "God crowns nothing in us beyond his gifts."[129] Romans 6:23 states: "The wages of sin is death, but the grace of God is life everlasting." Zachariah 4:7 reads: "The Lord will give

---

[128] Bonaventure seems to be alluding to Luke 1:15: "He will be filled with the Holy Spirit even from his mother's womb."

[129] See Tractate 3 n. 10 in CCSL xxxvi, p. 25 where Augustine uses *coronat* ("crowns") twice, but doesn't have the same words that Bonaventure quotes. See FC 78, p. 84: "Therefore, inasmuch as he afterwards bestows the reward of immortality, he crowns his own gifts, not your merits.... But God crowns the gifts of his mercy in us, but only if we should walk with perseverance in that grace which we first received."

equal grace for grace."[130] And the next verse shows that this effect is singularly Christ's.

38. (Verse 17). *For the Law was given through Moses.* The Law merely promised grace and truth and did not provide them, because Hebrews 7:19 says: "The Law led no one to perfection."[131] However, what the Law promised, Christ brought about. So the text continues: *Grace and truth came through Jesus Christ*, that is, were given. For this reason the Apostle cries out in Romans 7:24-25: "Unhappy man that I am! Who will deliver me from the body of this death? The grace of God through Jesus Christ," not the Law of Moses.

39. (Verse 18). *No one has at any time seen God.* This verse deals with the third cause of knowing which is singular teaching, because Christ, who alone is from God, could teach and has taught in an open manner and with certitude, since he alone saw God. So the text states: *No one has at any time seen God.* 1 Timothy 6:16 says: "The Lord dwells in inaccessible light."[132] Exodus 33:20 says: "No human being will see me and live."

40. *Except the only-begotten Son.*[133] Other sources read *but the only-begotten Son.* Both readings are acceptable. If "except" is the reading, then it goes with verse 18a and

---

[130] On p. 255 n. 1 QuarEd accurately mention that the Vulgate reads *exaequabit gratiam gratiae eius* ("The Lord will give equal grace for his grace"). Bonaventure does not have *eius* ("his").

[131] On p. 255 n. 2 QuarEd correctly notice that the Vulgate reads *Nihil enim ad perfectum adduxit lex* ("For the Law brought nothing to perfection") while Bonaventure has *Lex neminem ad perfectum duxit* ("The Law led no one to perfection").

[132] The Vulgate reads *habitans* ("dwelling") while Bonaventure has *habitat* ("dwells").

[133] *Nisi* ('except") is read by Hilary in Book VI, chapter 39 of his *De Trinitate*. See PL 10:189B.

reads: *No one has at any time seen God except the only-begotten*. If "but" is the reading, then it goes with verse 18b and reads: *But the only-begotten son, who is in the bosom of the Father, he has revealed him. In the bosom of the Father*, because having been born from him, he does not depart from him. John 3:13 says: "No one has ascended into heaven except him who has descended from heaven, the Son of Man, who is in heaven." *He has revealed* what he saw. John 3:11 states: "We speak of what we know, and we bear witness to what we have seen." Hebrews 1:2 reads: "Last of all in these days God has spoken to us by his Son, whom he appointed heir of all things, by whom also he made the world."

QUESTIONS

41. Question 1 asks about John 1:14: "Full of grace and truth." Is this said with regard to nature? If so, is it said about divine or human nature? It is not according to divine nature because whatever the Word has, he has by nature and not by grace. It also seems that it is not according to human nature since John 1:15 adds: "From his fullness we[134] have received grace for grace." But grace is given solely by God, not by human beings. Therefore, etc.

I respond. It has to be noted that in Christ there was the greatest singular grace possible for a human being. It was also the grace of union, a grace far greater than one could imagine. By reason of both of these graces he is said to have been full of grace. Further, by reason of this twofold grace he was the head of the Church. And since the grace of the head overflows into all the members, the text says: "From his fullness we have all received." – Relative

---

[134] The Vulgate reads *nos omnes* ("we have all").

to the question of whether it is divine or human nature, I answer that Christ is the head according to his human nature united to his divine nature. In this way the fullness of overflowing grace is to be understood.

42. Question 2 asks about John 1:16: "From his fullness we have all received." Against this statement is the fact that many predeceased Christ. Therefore, many lived before the fullness of Christ. Wherefore, not all have received. – I respond that it must be remarked that all have received, since Christ was the head of all the just from Abel to the very last just person. The members are united to this head by the bonds of faith and love.[135] For no one was saved without faith in Christ, as Blessed Augustine says.[136] No one was saved who had not received from the fullness of Christ. – As to the objection that he came later in time, it should be noted that through faith he was always present to everyone, although he came later in time in his corporeal presence.

---

[135] On p. 255 n. 10 QuarEd intimate that Bonaventure may be following the Glossa Ordinaria on a similarly rich Christological New Testament text. See the Glossa on Col 1:18 in PL 114:610C: "*Who is the beginning.* Of the Church according to divinity, that is, the founder of the Church, since he illumined with the gift of his mercy and by the power of his divinity all the just, who are born from Abel to the very last just person. According to his humanity he can also be said to be the beginning of the Church, for it was founded upon the faith of his humanity."

[136] See Tractate 109 n. 2 on John 17:20 in FC 90, pp. 285-286: "I omit these; for an answer can be made that prayer ought not to have been made for such dead persons who had gone away from here with their great merits and were received and were at rest; for this answer is similarly made about the just men of old. For who of them could have been saved from the damnation of the whole mass of perdition that was effected through one man, unless by the Spirit's revelation they had believed in the one Mediator of God and men who was to come in the flesh?"

43. Question 3 concerns John 1:18: "No one has at any time seen God."

Contrary 1. Numbers 12:8 reads: "I speak to him mouth to mouth, plainly, and not by riddles and figures does he see the Lord." This is said of Moses. Therefore, he has seen the Lord. – 2. Furthermore, Isaiah 6:1 states: "I saw the Lord sitting upon a throne high and elevated."

I answer by means of a distinction. One knows God as God is and through God's effects. Now to know God through effects is to see through a mirror, and seeing through a mirror is twofold. Either one sees through a mirror that is clear and is the eye, and this is the way the first human saw before sin. The other way is by means of a mirror that is obscure, and this is the way we see now since on account of sin our eyes are in darkness and all creatures have become darkened. So "we see now through a mirror in an obscure manner."[137] – God is known in another way, that is, as God is, and this in a twofold manner. The first way is in clarity, and this way pertains only to the Son and the blessed. The other way is in darkness, as Blessed Dionysius says in his *Mystical Theology*.[138] And in this manner Moses saw and those who contemplate sublime matters and in whose contemplation no creaturely image plays a part. And then these individuals more truly feel than know. Thus, Bernard says that when he sometimes

---

[137] 1 Cor 13:12.

[138] See c. 1, n. 3 in *Pseudo-Dionysius*, pp. 136-137: "... And who plunge into the darkness where, as scripture proclaims, there dwells the One who is beyond all things.... Here, being neither oneself nor someone else, one is supremely united by a completely unknowing inactivity of all knowledge, and knows beyond the mind by knowing nothing."

felt something in himself and then sought to see it, he immediately lost it.[139]

JOHN 1:19-11:46
THE MANIFESTATION OF THE INCARNATE WORD
IN PARTICULAR

44. *And this is the witness of John.* Above the Evangelist considered the manifestation of the incarnate Word *in general.* Now he treats this manifestation *in particular.* This section has two divisions, because the Word manifests *himself* and is manifested by *voice.* So the first division treats the manifestation made by John, who was *the voice* as precursor of the Word. The second division deals with the manifestation made by the Word himself and commences in 1:43: "The next day he was about to leave."

JOHN 1:19-42
THE MANIFESTATION OF THE INCARNATE WORD
MADE BY JOHN

This first division has three components that are distinguished from one another by John's threefold testimony. The first deals with the truth of the two natures. The second concerns the power of the one to be baptized. The

---

[139] Bernard doesn't say this in so many words. See his Homily 74, II n. 5 in *Bernard of Clairvaux On the Song of Songs IV*, trans. Irene Edmonds, CFS 40 (Kalamazoo: Cistercian Publications, 1980), pp. 89-90: "I admit that the Word has also come to me – I speak as a fool – and has come many times. But although he has come to me, I have never been conscious of the moment of his coming. I perceived his presence, I remembered afterwards that he had been with me; sometimes I had a presentiment that he would come, but I was never conscious of his coming or his going." See SBOp 2.242.

third treats holiness. – There is another way of providing headings for these components. John's first testimony is made to the Pharisees. The second to the crowds. The third to John's disciples. – There is yet a third way of treating this material. John gives his first testimony when Christ is absent; the second when Christ is coming to him; the third when Christ is walking away. The first testimony occurs in 1:19-28. The second commences in verse 29 where the text says: "The next day." The third begins with verse 35 which reads: "Again the next day."

Now the first part, in which John gives witness when Christ is absent, has two sections, for he first responds to those seeking the truth about himself and then about Christ where verse 24 has: "And those who had been sent were from among the Pharisees."

John 1:19-23
John speaks the truth about himself

Now this is the order the Evangelist follows in describing the answer that John gave to those seeking the truth about himself. First, he notes *the authority* inherent in those questioning him. Second, *the steadfastness* in John. Third, *the uneasiness* in the questioners. Finally, *the humble truth* in John.[140]

45. (Verse 19). The text hints at the authority of those questioning John, because they were authorized persons, sent by people in authority. John bore witness to them as the text says: "And this is the witness of John." John 1:15 above put it this way: "John bore witness." Now this

---

[140] Bonaventure's word play is obvious in the rhyme he employs: *auctoritat*em, *stabilitat*em, *importunitat*em, *humil*em *veritat*em.

verse specifies John's witness and gives the content of his testimony along with its circumstances. John gives this testimony *when the Jews sent from Jerusalem priests and Levites*. Note the authority of the persons, for they had been sent and were honorable. John 5:33 reads: "You have sent to John, and he[141] has borne witness to the truth." The text states: *They were sent to ask him: Who are you?* They asked this question in the person of all. In a similar way John sent his disciples in his person to ask Christ. Matthew 11:2-3 says: "John sent two of[142] his disciples to say to him: Are you he who is to come or shall we look for another?" The Jews wanted to ask this question by means of the Levites.

46. (Verse 20). *And he acknowledged*. This verse brings out the second point, namely, the steadfastness of John, who was not so intimidated by their authority that he would veer away from giving a true acknowledgment. So the text continues: *He acknowledged and did not deny*, that is, he made a true confession and stuck by it. 2 Corinthians 1:18 states: "But God is my witness that our message, which was[143] among you, is not 'Yes' and 'No,' but is 'Yes.'"[144] *And he acknowledged*, that is, the truth, *that I am not the Christ*. His answer does not so much address their question as their intention. About this type of faithful confession Matthew 10:32 says: "Everyone who acknowledges me before men and women, I will also acknowledge that person before my Father...." John gave the

---

[141] On p. 256 n. 8 QuarEd correctly indicate that the Vulgate does not read *ille* ("he").

[142] On p. 256 n. 9 QuarEd accurately mention that the Vulgate reads *de* ("of") while Bonaventure has *ex* ("of").

[143] The Vulgate reads *fit* ("occurred") while Bonaventure has *fuit* ("was").

[144] On p. 256 n. 10 QuaeEd rightly state that the Vulgate does not read *sed est in illo est* ("but is 'Yes'").

utmost acknowledgment, since, although he could have been regarded as the Christ, he refused to do so. Gregory comments: "When he chose not to grasp the name of Christ, he became a member of Christ."[145]

47. (Verse 21). *And they asked him.* Here the third point surfaces, namely, the uneasiness of the questioners, because they do not stop with a single question, but immediately ask others. So the text continues: *And they asked him: What then?* That is, what are you, if you are not the Christ? *Are you Elijah? And he said: I am not.* And still they persisted: *Are you a prophet?* That is, some minor one. And he answered: *No.* So they were questioning him in general about other prophets, especially about Elijah because they believed that Elijah would be the precursor of the Christ. Matthew 17:10 reads: "Why do the scribes say that Elijah must come first?"[146] But they still persisted.

48. (Verse 22). *They, therefore, said to him: Who are you?* They repeat their insistent question and give a rationale for their persistence: *That we may give an answer to those who sent us. What do you have to say about yourself?* It seemed foolish to them to return to those who sent them without a clear and certain answer, for it is characteristic of the wise messenger to bring back a clear and certain response. Proverbs 22:20-21 states: "Behold, I have de-

---

[145] See Homily 7 n. 1 of GGHG in CCSL cxli, p. 46 which reads *cum* ("when") whereas Bonaventure reads *dum* ("when"). I have adjusted the translation of Hurst, p. 21, who gives the number four to this homily.

[146] See Augustine's Tractate 4 n. 5 in FC 78, pp. 96-97 for Augustine's resolution of the discrepancy between John's statement that he is not Elijah and Jesus' statement in Matt 17:12 that he is.

scribed to you ... the wise way, so that ... you might respond from the words of truth to those who sent you."[147]

49. (Verse 23). *He said: I am the voice of one crying.* Here is the fourth point, namely, the response of humble truth. "Humble," because he did not bestow a dignity[148] on himself, when he was fulfilling a function. So he says: *I am the voice of one crying in the desert. Crying,* I say, this message: *Make straight the way of the Lord.* According to the letter of the text John was crying out in the desert.[149] Matthew 3 states: "John ... came preaching in the desert of Judea and ... crying: ... Make straight the way of the Lord."[150] For he preached penance, by which the way of the sinner is directed to the Lord. This way becomes twisted whenever a person sins, but the observance of the commandments provides directions. John 14:23 below reads: "If anyone loves me, that person will observe my word, and my Father will love that person, and we will come to that person." Thus the way of the Lord is directed towards the heart.[151] And John confirms his office

---

[147] On p. 257 n. 2 QuarEd correctly indicate how different and abbreviated Bonaventure's citation is from the original Vulgate, e.g., *sapientiam* ("the wise way") does not occur in the Vulgate.

[148] I have translated *dignitas* here with "dignity," for in n. 50 below Bonaventure will deal with the technical canonical terms, "ecclesiastical dignity" and "ecclesiastical person or personage."

[149] There seems to be a double reference here. One is to Isa 40:3, which is the text John quotes. Another is to Matt 3:1-3, which follows immediately in Bonaventure's text.

[150] Matthew 3:1-3 reads: "Now in those days John the Baptist came, preaching in the desert of Judea, and saying, 'Repent, for the kingdom of heaven is at hand.' For this is he who was spoken of through Isaiah the prophet, when he said: 'The voice of one crying in the desert, Make ready the way of the Lord, make straight his paths.'"

[151] See Homily 7 n. 2 of GGHG in CCSL cxli, pp. 47-48 and Hurst, p. 23: "The Lord's way to the heart is made straight when we order our lives in accordance with his precept. And so it is written: *With one who keeps my command my Father and I will come and make our home.*"

and function by the testimony of Isaiah when he says: *As Isaiah the prophet said.* Isaiah 40:3 says: "A voice crying in the desert: Prepare the way of the Lord."

QUESTIONS

50. Question 1. The first query deals with John 1:19: "Who are you?" For why did the Jews, who knew about John's origin and life, ask this question?

The answer is found in distinctions. Sometimes a person asks about the substantial basis behind a thing, as when one raises the question: Who did this or that? Sometimes a person asks about the proper name, as Priscian says.[152] "Who, father, is he who thus attends him on his way?"[153] Sometimes a special question addresses, among other qualities, a personís dignity, for persons of dignity and eminence are called ecclesiastical persons. Therefore, it has to be said about the Jews' question that although they knew John's origin, life, and name, they were, none-theless, in doubt about his dignity.

51. Question 2. Furthermore, there is a question about John 1:21 and John's response to the second interrogation that he was not Elijah.

---

[152] See Book XIII, c. 6 of *Prisciani Grammatici Institvtionvm Grammaticarvm Volvmen Maivs continens libros sedecim priores*, ed. August Krehl (Leipzig: Weidmann, 1819), pp. 576-80 and Book XVII, c. 5 of *Prisciani Grammatici Institvtionvm Grammaticarvm Volvmen Secvndvm continens libros dvos de constrvctione et reliqvos libellos omnes*, ed. August Krehl (Leipzig: Weidmann, 1820), pp. 24-29.

[153] See Book VI, line 863 of Vergil's *Aeneid* in *Virgil*, volume I, trans. H. Rushton Fairclough, LCL (Cambridge: Harvard University Press, 1967), pp. 566-68. Although QuarEd indented this sentence and printed it in smaller type, they gave no indication of its source

Contrary 1. Matthew 11:14 states: "If you are willing to understand it, he is Elijah."[154] Wherefore, either the Lord was lying or John was. – Contrary 2. Moreover, John himself says that he is not a prophet. Contrary to this is Luke 1:76: "You, child, will be called a prophet of the Most High."

I answer that John's response addressed the intention of his questioners rather than their actual questions. So it should be understood that when the Jews questioned about Elijah, they were asking about his corporeal presence and about that same person who was in the Old Testament. But John answers that he is not Elijah properly speaking, and the Lord says that John is Elijah in a figurative sense, for John was to the first coming what Elijah will be to the second coming.[155] Likewise, it should be mentioned that they were asking whether he was a prophet and performed the function of prophesying in the precise sense that a prophet predicts the future, but John was a prophet and more than a prophet,[156] because he revealed the present. So according to their intention he responded that he was not a prophet.

---

[154] On p. 257 n. 7 QuarEd rightly indicate that the Vulgate reads *vultis recipere* ("willing to accept it") whereas Bonaventure has *vultis scire* ("willing to understand it").

[155] See Tractate 4 n. 6 in FC 78, p. 97: "If you should look to the figure of forerunning, John himself is Elias; for what the former is to the First Coming, the latter will be to the Second." Presupposed in this material is Mal 4:5: "Behold, I will send you Elijah the prophet before the coming of the great and dreadful day of the Lord."

[156] See Matt 11:9: "But what did you go out to see? A prophet? Yes, I tell you, and more than a prophet." See also Homily 3 n. 3 of GGHG and Hurst, p. 6: "He is said to be more than a prophet because it is a prophet's task to foretell things to come, not to point them out as well. John is more than a prophet because with his finger he pointed to the one he spoke of." See CCSL cxli, p. 22.

52. Question 3. There is also a question about John's third response in John 1:23. 1.Why was John called a voice and what did he say that he was a voice? – 2. Furthermore, what is the meaning of "Make straight the way of the Lord," for Jeremiah 10:23 reads: "I know, O Lord, that the ways of human beings are not their own. Neither is it in a man ... to direct his own steps"? Thus, he is exhorted to do the impossible.

I answer. The point must be made that just as the Son of God is most fittingly called Word, so is his precursor most rightly called a voice. Voice has a fourfold property relative to the word, and because of this it is fittingly used. The voice precedes the word. So John precedes Christ. Luke 1:17 states: "He will go before him in the spirit and power of Elijah." The voice manifests the word. In the same way John manifests Christ.[157] John 1:7 above says: "He came as a witness, to bear witness concerning the light." The voice passes away, but the word remains. This is the same relationship between John and the Christ. John 3:30 below reads: "I must decrease, but he must increase."[158] The voice is useless without the word. So too is John's preaching without Christ. John 1:26 below has: "I baptize you[159] with water, but in your midst there has stood one whom you do not know."[160]

---

[157] See Homily 7 n. 2 of GGHG and Hurst, pp. 22-23: "From our own way of speaking you know that first the voice sounds, and then afterward the word can be heard. John declares that he is the voice because he comes before the Word. He is the forerunner of the Lord's coming and so he is called a voice, since the Father's Word is heard by humans through his ministry." See CCSL cxli, p. 47.

[158] On p. 258 n. 1 QuarEd accurately mention that the Vulgate has the reverse order: "He must increase, but I must decrease."

[159] On p. 258 n. 2 QuarEd correctly indicate that the Vulgate does not read *vos* ("you").

[160] See Augustine's Sermon 288 n. 2-3 where there is a long and complex discussion of word and voice.

2. Now concerning the objection that only God through grace and love makes straight the way, it must be said that we have to make the preparation to embark on the way according to our strength and lights. And this is what is commanded here. Thus, Gregory observes: "The Lord's way to the heart is made straight when we prepare our lives by obeying the Lord's precept."[161]

JOHN 1:24-28
JOHN SPEAKS THE TRUTH ABOUT CHRIST

53. (Verse 24.) *And those who had been sent.* John has just spoken the truth about himself. In this section he gives testimony *about Christ* in this order. First, he cites *the dishonesty of the questioners.* Second, *the truth of his testimony.* Third, *the public nature of his testimony.*[162]

The first point deals with the dishonesty of the questioners, for although they had heard the truth, they are seeking to discredit the teacher of truth. And the reason for this stemmed from their maliciousness. For the text says: *Those who had been sent were from among the Pharisees.* Therefore, they were malicious and spies. Chrysostom comments: "Those who had been sent did not know how to inquire after the truth, for envy motivated them."[163]

---

[161] See Homily 7 n. 2 in GGHG and CCSL cxli, p. 47. Bonaventure's quotation is verbatim.

[162] Bonaventure's verbal playfulness shines forth in his use of the number three and the rhyme present in *improbitas, veritas, celebritas.*

[163] While the thought may be that of Chrysostom, the wording is closer to Homily 7 n. 3 of GGHG in CCSL cxli, p. 48. See Hurst, p. 23: "The evangelist, when he told us just before this that *those who had been sent were from the Pharisees,* was silently informing us that they did not say this from any desire to know the truth, but maliciously, expressing their envy." See Chrysostom's Homily 16 n. 1 in FC 33,

So their questions were malicious and dishonest.[164] Thus, the text continues:

54. (Verse 25). *And they asked him and said to him*, as if they were accusing him: *Why, then, do you baptize, if you are not the Christ nor Elijah nor a prophet?* You are acting foolishly and without authorization. For Chrysostom says: "Since they were not able to win him over with flattery, they tried to assail him with accusations."[165] Therefore, Chrysostom exclaims: "What madness! What arrogance! What crooked investigation! You were sent, so that you might learn from him the answer to: *Who are you?* And are you desirous of pinning a crime against the Law on him?"[166] So this verse suggests the wickedness of the questioners.

55. (Verse 26). *John answered them.* Here the text introduces the second point, namely, the truth of John's witness. John emphasizes the truth of his office and by doing this the dignity of Christ. Thus, he says: *I baptize*

---

pp. 150-151: "A terrible thing is envy, beloved, terrible and ruinous to those who envy, but not to those who are envied. It harms and destroys them first, like some deep-seated and fatal poison within their souls."

[164] This harsh attack on the Pharisees does not seem motivated by the immediate context of John's Gospel and seems to stem from the anti-Judaism of medieval culture, to which Bonaventure was not immune. See my Introduction to *Gospel of Luke, Chapters 9-16*, pp. xiii-lvi.

[165] See Homily 16 n. 2 in PG 59:104. Bonaventure's citation is not verbatim. See FC 33, p. 155: "For, since they did not succeed in tripping him up by flattery, they hoped to be able to force him by accusation to say what was not true, but they were not strong enough."

[166] See Homily 16 n. 2 in PG 59:104. Bonaventure's citation is not verbatim. See FC 33, p. 155: "Oh, the madness! Oh, the arrogance and unbridled meddlesomeness! You were sent to learn from him who he was and whence, and surely you will not make rules for him?" See Hugh of St. Cher, p. 286v, g for a citation of Chrysostom that is more verbatim than Bonaventure's, but also has words in common with Bonaventure, e.g., *elatio* rather than *arrogantia* for "arrogance."

you with water, that is, with an external bath, not like the interior one that Christ gives. Rather I prepare for Christ. So Acts 19:4 reads: "John baptized ... with a baptism of repentance, telling them to believe in him who was to come...."[167] Then the text adds: *But in your midst has stood one whom you do not know*, that is, he is among you. *Whom you do not know*, according to what John 8:19 below says: "You know neither me nor my Father." I am preparing for him. So the text continues:

56. (Verse 27). *He it is who is to come after me*, for I go ahead of him as his precursor. *Who was before me*,[168] that is, who has greater dignity than I. John 3:30 below says: "I must decrease, but he must increase."[169] And he indicates to what extent he has greater dignity: *The strap of whose sandal I am not worthy to loose.* In the literal sense this is true, because no one, no matter how good, should think himself to be worthy to take off Christ's sandal. For the centurion in Matthew 8:8 said: "Lord, I am not worthy that you should come under my roof." – Now allegorically *the sandal* is Christ's humanity. The shod foot is divinity in human form. The strap of the sandal is the union of the two natures. Therefore, *to loosen the strap of the sandal* is to explicate the mystery of the union. John confesses that he is unworthy to do this, since Isaiah 53:8 says: "Who will declare his generation?"[170] As if he were saying: No one is worthy to do that.

---

[167] The Vulgate reads *venturus esset* ("would come") while Bonaventure has *venturus erat* ("was to come").

[168] These words are not found in the Greek text of the NT.

[169] The Vulgate has the reverse order.

[170] See Homily 7 n. 3 of GGHG in CCSL cxli, p. 50 and Hurst, pp. 24-25: "Our Lord came in the flesh; he appeared as if shod in sandals because he assumed in his divinity the dead flesh of our corrupt condition.... The sandal strap is the bond of a mystery. John is not able to undo the strap of his sandal because not even he who recognized the

57. (Verse 28). *These things took place in Bethany.* This verse touches on the third point, namely, the public nature of John's witness, which is clear from the fact that he bore his witness in a public place where many people congregated. Thus, the text states: *These things took place at Bethany, beyond the Jordan, where John was baptizing.* And thus many people came together. John 3:23 says: "Now John was also baptizing in Aenon near Salim, for there was abundant water there."

QUESTIONS

58. Question 1 asks about John 1:26: "I baptize with water." 1. For if John's baptism was merely an external washing of the flesh, it would seem that it was performed in vain and was useless. – 2. Also, John is more perfect than the Law. Therefore, the baptism of John was more perfect than the sacraments of the Law. So if circumcision gives grace, how much more does the baptism of John.[171]

I respond that it has to be said that John's baptism was not the remedy or medicine, but was the preparation for the remedy. Therefore, it does not follow that it was superfluous nor may the conclusion be drawn that it must confer grace.

Now John's baptism prepared for the remedy in a threefold manner. It led to a reformation of life. Thus, Matthew 3:6 says: "They were baptized by him ... confessing their sins." It led to their becoming accustomed to baptism, so

---

mystery of the Lord's incarnation through the spirit of prophecy can subject it to investigation."

[171] See Book IV, d. 2 n. 2 q. 2 of Bonaventure's *Sentence Commentary.*

that they were suitably prepared and did not reject the baptism of Christ. Thus, Gregory comments: "It was fitting that he whose birth foreshadowed Christ's future birth would also, by his baptizing, foreshadow the Lord who would baptize."[172] The third reason is that it led to Christ's manifestation. John 1:31 below states: "That he may be manifested in Israel is the reason I have come baptizing with water."

59. Question 2. There is a further question with regard to John 1:26: "in your midst." Why is it that the Lord always chooses the middle when he is the head? – Further it seems that he was not in the midst of them, for he is only in the midst of good people.[173]

It should be noted that according to the flesh he was in their midst, that is, in their midst as a middling human being. Now Christ is said to stand in the middle or even to specially chose the middle position, since being in the midst or in the middle is the position of humility. Luke 22:27 reads: "But I am in your midst as one who serves." Also Matthew 18:2-3.[174] – It is the position of community. Acts 10:34 states: "I know in truth that God is not a respecter of persons," etc. – It is the position of unity, since the extremes are united in the middle. Ephesians 2:14

---

[172] See Homily 7 n. 3 of GGHG in CCSL cxli, p. 49. Bonaventure has added the opening words of this quotation, "It was fitting that."

[173] There seem to be at least two presuppositions operative here. First, Bonaventure has already depicted the maliciousness of those who came to question him and among whom he stands. Second, Matt 18:20 may come into play: "For wherever two or three are gathered in my name, there am I in their midst." The two or three gathered are good and faithful disciples.

[174] Matt 18:2-3 says: "And Jesus called a little child to him, set him in their midst, and said: 'Amen I say to you, unless you turn and become like little children, you will not enter into the kingdom of heaven.'"

has: "He himself is our peace, who has made both one."
– It is the position of stability, because the middle of the earth is fixed. 1 Corinthians 3:11 says: "No one can lay another foundation except that which ... is Christ Jesus."
– It is the position of proximity, for it is close to all parts. Acts 17:27-28 reads: "If perhaps they might grope after him and find him, though he is not far from anyone of us. For in him we live and move and have our being."[175]

60. Question 3. Furthermore, what is the meaning of John 1:27: "Who is to come after me"? – Contrary: It is said in Matthew 11:2-3 that he sent two of his disciples to say to him: "Are you he who is to come or should we look for another?" In that instance John was in doubt. How is it that he is so certain in this passage?

The heretics provide their answer to this discrepancy by saying that John first believed and afterward doubted. But they are in error, for the Lord went on to commend John.[176] – Relative to this matter, it should be said that John knew with certainty that he was the Christ. More-over, he inquired through his disciples not because he was in doubt, but that he might remove the doubt of his disciples who did not believe in him.

---

[175] Bonaventure has five instances, for five is considered a perfect number when dealing with sense matters (there are five senses). Note the rhyme: *humili*tatis, *communi*tatis, *uni*tatis, *stabili*tatis, *proximi*-tatis.

[176] See Matt 11:9: "What did you go out to see? A prophet? Yes, I tell you, and more than a prophet."

John 1:29-34
John's witness to Christ as he approaches him

61. (Verse 29). *The next day John saw Jesus coming*, etc. Earlier Blessed John bore witness to *the absent* Christ. Now he bears witness to Christ *as he approaches him*. There are two parts to this section. The first describes *the giving of the testimony* whereas the second stresses *the certitude* or corroboration of the testimony where verse 31 states: "And I did not know him."

John 1:29-30
John's actual testimony about Christ

John's *witness* is described in this order. First is *the occasion* for the witness. Second is *the testimony*. Third is a *comparison with John's preceding testimony*.[177]

First, mention is made of the occasion for bearing witness, which was Jesus' coming to John to be baptized by him. So the text says: *The next day John saw Jesus coming to him*, namely, to be baptized. Matthew 3:13 states: "Jesus came from Galilee to John at the Jordan to be baptized by him."

62. *And he said*, that is, John. The second point, John's very testimony, occurs here. John's testimony is twofold and deals with the innocence of humanity and the power of divinity. For the sake of the innocence he says: *Behold, the Lamb of God*, that is, one who is innocent and undefiled. Isaiah 16:1 reads: "Send forth, O Lord, the lamb, the ruler of the earth, from Petra of the desert, to the mount of the daughter of Zion." With regard to the power

---

[177] See John 1:27.

of divinity the text states: *Behold ... who takes away the sins of the world*, which pertains solely to divine power. Isaiah 43:25 says: "I am, I am he who blots out your iniquities for my own sake." John says *Behold*, since the one whom others had foretold he himself points to with his finger. Therefore, Matthew 11:9 says this of John: "He is a prophet and more than a prophet."

63. (Verse 30). *This is he of whom I said* to you. Here is the third point or comparison with John's preceding witness. So he repeats the testimony that he had borne in Christ's absence and says: *This is he of whom I said*, namely, in my preceding testimony, *After me comes a man*, namely, in time of birth, for he was born six months after him. Concerning this man Jeremiah 31:22 says: "The Lord will create[178] a new thing upon the earth: a woman will compass a man." Who has been set above me, namely, in dignity, *because he was before me*, by his divinity. John 1:1 above said: "In the beginning was the Word."

A QUESTION

64. But a doubt surfaces here. 1. Since it is the responsibility of the less important individual to go to the more important individual and not vice versa, it seems that John should have gone to Christ. – 2. Moreover, since there was no blemish in Christ and baptism signifies the washing away of dirt, it follows that baptism would have had a false significance for him. So if the truthfulness of Christ does not tolerate falsehood, he should not have been baptized by John.

---

[178] On p. 260 n. 3 QuarEd rightly indicate that the Vulgate reads *creavit* ("has created") while Bonaventure has *faciet* ("will create").

My answer is that a distinction has to be made between something that occurs in a necessary manner and something that occurs in a voluntary manner. That a less important individual go to a more important individual is an obligation of necessity. Thus, John said to the Lord: "I ought to be baptized by you."[179] But that a more important person go to a less important one is a matter of perfection and supererogation. Thus the Lord went to John. So he himself said to John: "So it becomes us to fulfill all justice."[180] Wherefore, his act of coming to John was one of condescension and is a recommendation of humility.

2. Relative to the question of why he wanted to be baptized, I answer that just as something is said by means of a significant word about the head by referring to the members, so too through an action that is performed something is signified in the head for the sake of the members.[181] Thus John's baptism does not signify an interior cleansing in Christ, but only in the members. Now the reason why Christ wanted to be baptized is threefold: so that he might give an example of humility, so that he might confer regenerative power upon the waters, so that through John's baptism he might reveal himself to all. This latter is the principal reason and is the subject of the next verses.

---

[179] Matt 3:14.

[180] Matt 3:15.

[181] Is there some weak analogy in the words of a newly created cardinal, who says: "I accept this red hat on my head not for my own sake, but for the sake of the members of my diocese"?

JOHN 1:31-34
CERTITUDE OF JOHN'S TESTIMONY

65. (Verse 31). *And I did not know him*. After John has borne his witness, these verses describe his *corroboration* or certitude. The Evangelist follows this sequence. First, he considers *the manner* of arriving at certitude. Second, *the sign* that grants certitude. Finally, the certain *testimony*.

So first the Evangelist treats the manner of arriving at certitude, which happened through the act of baptizing. So he says: *I did not know him*, that is, I was not certain about him. *But that he might be manifested to Israel is the reason why I came baptizing with water*. The same thing is said in Mark 1:8: "I have baptized you with water, but he will baptize you with the Holy Spirit."

66. (Verse 32). *And John bore witness*. This verse touches upon the second point, namely, the sign that effects certitude, which was the descent of the Holy Spirit. So the text says: *And John bore witness*, as a witness that was certain, *saying: I beheld the Spirit descending as a dove from heaven*. Luke 3:22 reads: "The Holy Spirit descended upon him in bodily form as a dove." *And it abode upon him*, because it rested upon him. Isaiah 11:2 states: "The Spirit of the Lord will rest upon him." And this was the sign that effected certitude in him. So the text continues:

67. (Verse 33). *And I did not know him* beforehand, but I recognized him through this sign, because it was given to me by God. And so he adds: *But the one who sent me to baptize with water*, namely, God. John 1:6 above says: "There was a man sent by God." *I tell you, this one said to me: He upon whom you will see the Spirit descending*

and abiding upon him, he it is who baptizes with the Holy Spirit. For it is only in his name and power that baptism takes place. Acts 2:38 has: "Be baptized every one of you in the name of Christ."[182] Now a sign of this was the descent and abiding of the Holy Spirit. Thus Bede observes: "Only upon the Mediator ... did the Spirit remain ... perpetually ... from that time he began to become human, was conceived for his ministry and work."[183] And John arrived at certitude through this sign.

68. (Verse 34). *And I have seen*, etc. This verse deals with the third point, namely, certain testimony, for testimony is certain when people testify about what they have seen. Therefore, the text continues: *I have seen and have borne witness that this is the Son of God.* John 19:35 reads: "And he who has seen it has borne witness, and his witness is true."

QUESTIONS

69. Question 1. The first question revolves around the descent of the Holy Spirit. – For if the Holy Spirit is God and God is everywhere, then the Holy Spirit does not descend. – But if you say, that the Holy Spirit did not descend essentially, but effectually, this is the contrary point: No new effect was conferred on Christ because he lacked no gift of grace that he didn't have from his conception. Therefore, the Holy Spirit did not descend effectually.

---

[182] On p. 260 n. 9 QuarEd accurately mention that the Vulgate reads *Iesu Christi* ("Jesus Christ").

[183] See PL 92:650C. Bonaventure provides an abbreviated text that is less clear than the original.

Question 2. Furthermore, I ask why the Holy Spirit descended in that dove rather than in another? For either it was united to that dove or not. If yes, then the Holy Spirit assumed that creature. If not, then the Holy Spirit was equally in that dove as in another. Therefore, the Holy Spirit descended in any dove whatsoever.

Question 3. Moreover, why did the Holy Spirit descend in a dove rather than in something else?

I respond that God is said to be in creatures in four ways. In the first way God is in creatures solely by reason of their existence. And so God is in all and equally, neither descending nor moving nor departing. – The second is by reason of the creature's sign value. Thus God is said to be in creatures that are signs pointing to God, as on Mount Sinai and in the cloud.[184] – The third is by reason of bestowing grace and favor, as God is said to be in those whom God loves and who love God. – The fourth is by reason of union or assumption, as in Christ.

Now descending and ascending do not correspond to the first manner of existing, for it is universal and common, but they do correspond to the others ways of existing. Thus, God is sometimes said to descend, when God descends upon a creature that signifies God. Sometimes when God confers grace. At another time when God descends upon a nature that has been assumed. – So since this dove was set apart for this and manifested the Spirit in a special way, it was said to have descended upon it,

---

[184] See, e.g., Exod 19:9: "The Lord said to him (Moses): Now I will come to you in the darkness of a cloud." Exod 19:18: "Now all Mount Sinai was smoking, because the Lord had come down upon it in fire." Exod 34:5: "When the Lord had come down in a cloud, Moses stood with the Lord, calling upon the name of the Lord."

not upon another, not by reason of effect or union, but for the sake of manifestation.

70. As to the question of why the Spirit is manifested through a dove rather than some other creature, the answer rests in the properties of a dove, for it is a simple animal, meek, and fruitful. Now the Holy Spirit is gracious and fruitful and without guile.[185] "For the holy Spirit ... will flee from the deceitful."[186]

71. Question 4. What is the meaning of John 1:33: "I did not know him"? – Contrary to this statement is the testimony that John bore to Christ before he baptized him, as John 1:15 above states. Wherefore, either he knew him beforehand or he bore witness to someone he didn't know.

I follow Chrysostom's answer that he knew him in general, since he knew well that the Christ had come and that he himself was his precursor, but he did not know him personally and as a specific individual. The reason is that he had been in the desert from his infancy and had not seen him.[187]

But this answer is invalid, since John knew the Lord from his mother's womb.[188] How then it is said that he didn't know him when the only change was that he had grown

---

[185] See Bonaventure's *Commentary on Luke, 1-8*, pp. 270-71 on Luke 3:22 (n. 53): "Furthermore, he appeared over his disciples as *fire*, but over Christ as a *dove*, because as Gregory says: 'Christ came to gather us through his gentleness.'... And the apparition of the Holy Spirit as a *dove* is most fitting for baptism on account of the innocence, which baptism restores."

[186] See Wis 1:5.

[187] See Homily 17 n. 2 in PG 59:109 as a quasi-basis for Bonaventure's citation.

[188] See Luke 1:41-44.

up? – Also, Matthew 3:14 reads: "I should be baptized by you." – The answer is that he knew that he was the Christ, but did not know that the power of baptizing had been reserved to him. – But in this case the objection arises about whether it was the power to baptize externally or internally. That objection is false in either instance, for he should have known whether it was one or the other.

I respond. If the question deals with Christ's substance or nature, then John did not know Christ. However, it should be understood from this context that John knew Christ with certitude after he recognized the sign. Now concerning the power of baptizing, it must be granted that this power is fivefold: from authority, cooperation, invocation, excellence, ministry. – The first he gave to no one nor could he give it. He gave the last whereas he did not give the middle three. Now he could give the power of excellence and invocation, but he did not want to do so, lest the unity of the Church be ruptured. Concerning the power of cooperation the Master of the Sentences expressed his doubt, but nevertheless the opinion is commonly held that he could not give it. He had no doubt about the power from authority, but could express doubt about the third and fourth.[189]

---

[189] This is a very abbreviated discussion. See Book IV, d. V. c. 3 of *Magistri Petri Lombardi Sententiae in IV Libris Distinctae*, volume II/ Books III and IV, third edition, Spicilegium Bonaventurianum 5 (Grottaferrata: Collegium S. Bonaventurae, 1981), pp. 265-66. I summarize. The discussion deals with those who have the ministry of baptizing, but not the power of baptizing which Christ himself retains. John knew this when he saw the dove descending upon Christ. Peter Lombard quotes Augustine's Tractate 5 n. 11 on John's Gospel. See FC 78, p. 117: "And what did John know? The Lord. What did he not know? That the power of the Lord's baptism would pass from the Lord to no man, but that the ministry clearly would pass." In this section Peter Lombard says nothing about the other three powers, that is, cooperation, invocation, excellence.

John 1:35-42
John's testimony as Christ walked by

72. (Verse 35). *Again the next day John was standing there*, etc. John has already borne witness twice. This is his third testimony, and it occurs as *Christ is walking by*. And the Evangelist describes his testimony and then its fruitful results. This is the order. First is *the testimony* itself. Second is *the conversion* of the disciples. Third is *the acceptance* of the converted. Fourth is *the fruitful ministry* of those who had been accepted. Fifth is *the reception* of the fruitful preaching.

First is the testimony itself that is given in the presence of the Lord and the disciples of John. So the text says: *Again the next day John was standing there and two of his disciples*, namely, who were suitable to hear his testimony about Christ, for they were humble disciples, for they were followers of their master, for they also loved one another. Thus, they were disciples, who were with their master and were two in number. As Gregory comments: "There can be no love with less than two people."[190] For Luke 10:1 reads: "He sent them two by two before his face."

73. (Verse 36). *And looking upon Jesus as he walked by, he said: Behold the lamb of God.* He thus distinguishes him from the paschal lamb that was a type. He calls him *lamb*, so that his disciples might be attracted to him because of his meekness. Matthew 11:29 states: "Learn from me, for I am meek and humble of heart."

---

[190] See Homily 17 n. 1 of GGHG in CCSL cxli, p. 117. Bonaventure's citation is almost verbatim.

It should be noted that Christ was a man in the incarnation because of the perfection of wisdom. Zechariah 6:12 says: "Behold a man, Orient is his name." He was a lamb because of the meekness of patience. Isaiah 53:7 has: "He was led[191] like a sheep to the slaughter, and like a lamb before his shearer he will be silent, and he will not open his mouth." He was a lion in the resurrection because of the strength of his power. Revelation 5 reads: "Behold, the Lion from the tribe of Judah has conquered" (verse 5) and "the Lamb ... was slain" (verse 12).

74. (Verse 37). *And the two disciples heard him speak.* This verse treats the second point, namely, the conversion of the disciples that indicates the effectiveness of the testimony. The text continues: *And the two disciples heard him speak*, that is, bearing witness, *and they followed Jesus.* Thus, they took advantage of the sound counsel of their teacher. They followed the light since their works were good. For John 3:21 below says: "Those who do the truth come to the light, so their deeds may be manifested."

75. (Verse 38). *But Jesus turned around.* This verse considers the third point, that is, the acceptance of the converted disciples. For the Lord turned to them and spoke to them. So the text reads: *But Jesus turned around, and seeing them following him.* He turned around to those who had turned their lives around, according to what Zechariah 1:3 states: "Turn to me ... and I will turn to you. Having turned around to them, *he said to them: What is it you seek?* He didn't ask this question because he had any

---

[191] On p. 262 n. 4 QuarEd accurately indicate that the Vulgate reads *ducetur* ("will be led") while Bonaventure has *ductus est* ("was led").

doubt. Rather he wanted them to manifest their right intention through their response.[192]

76. *They said to him: Rabbi (which interpreted means Teacher) where do you dwell?* After the interpretive insertion the text continues: *Rabbi, where do you dwell?* as if they were saying: We are seeking you, your teaching, your dwelling. The soul that is in an earnest search for God raises this question. The Song of Songs 1:6 says: "You, whom my soul loves, show me where you are feeding, where you lie at midday." And since they are following him with the right intention, he admits them to his dwelling.

77. (Verse 39). *He said to them: Come and see. They came and saw where he was staying.* But Christ rejected those who were searching without a right and proper intention. In Matthew 8:19-20 a scribe said to him: "Master, I will follow you wherever you go. Jesus said to him: The foxes have dens, and the birds of the heaven have nests,[193] but the Son of Man has nowhere to lay his head." And since the person who does not stay converts in vain, the text continues: *And they stayed there that day.*[194] The Evangelist gives the reason: *It was about the tenth hour.* This sig-

---

[192] See John Chrysostom's Homily 18 n. 3 in PG 59:117-118 and FC 33, p. 181: "'What is it you seek?' What is this? Did He who knows the hearts of men, He who is intimately present to our thoughts, did He ask this? Yes, but not in order to learn (for how could that be?), but in order that by the question He might make them more at ease with Him, and might impart to them greater confidence and show them that they were worthy of listening to Him."

[193] The Vulgate reads *tabernacula* ("nests") while Bonaventure has *nidos* ("nests"). In this instance Bonaventure is following the text of Luke 9:58, which is parallel to Matt 8:20.

[194] On p. 262 n. 11 QuarEd accurately indicate that the Vulgate reads *apud eum* ("with him") whereas Bonaventure, as well as Thomas of Aquinas, has *ibi* ("there").

nifies the day of grace, which is the last day when people must stay and remain. 1 John 2:18 reads: "Now we know, dearly beloved, that it is the last hour."[195] During this last hour people must remain with the Lord Jesus. Luke 22:28 states: "You are the ones who have remained with me."

78. (Verse 40). *Now one of the disciples*, etc. This verse addresses the fourth point, namely, the fruitfulness of the disciples since immediately after they are converted, they call others. In this instance Andrew calls Peter. So the text says: *Now Andrew, the brother of Simon Peter, was one of the two who had heard John and had followed Jesus*.[196] So the Evangelist makes special notice of Andrew in order to show the fruit of his preaching, which is the subject of the next verse.

79. (Verse 41). *First he found his brother Simon* since he zealously sought him out in order to lead him to the treasure he had found. So the text reads: *And he said*[197] *to him: We have found the Messiah (which interpreted is the Christ)*. Like good merchants we have found the pearl, like good cultivators of the field we have found the hidden treasure. Matthew 13:44 states: "The kingdom of heaven is like treasure hidden in a field," etc.

80. (Verse 42). *And he led him to Jesus*. Revelation 22:17 reads: "And let the person who hears say: Come. And let the person who thirsts come." *But Jesus looked upon him*. This verse touches upon the fifth point, that is, the acceptance of the preaching of the disciples, since the Lord,

---

[195] On p. 262 n. 12 QuarEd rightly mention that the Vulgate has: "Dear children, it is the last hour."

[196] On p. 262 n. 13 QuarEd correctly notice that the Vulgate reads *eum* ("him") while Bonaventure has *Iesum* ("Jesus").

[197] On p. 262 n. 14 QuarEd accurately mention that the Vulgate reads *dicit* ("says") whereas Bonaventure has *dixit* ("said").

by receiving Peter, accepts the invitation or preaching of Andrew. For this reason he gives him a name as he would to his own disciple. Thus, the text continues: *But he looked upon him*, namely, Jesus looked upon Peter with a look of graciousness. About such a look Genesis 44:21 states: "Bring your brother[198] to me, and I will set my eyes upon him." *Jesus said: You are Simon, the son of John*. He speaks his name out loud, so that he might give him another name: *You will be called Cephas (which interpreted is Peter)*. Bede comments: "Readers should note that he is called *Cephas* in Syriac and *Peter* in Greek and Latin and that both languages derive the word from the word 'rock.'"[199] Wherefore, the Lord says to him in Matthew 16:18; "You are Peter, and upon this rock," namely, from which you have received your name, that is, upon me, "I will build my church." 1 Corinthians 10:4 says: "Now the rock was Christ." *You will be called Peter*, that is, from the solid rock of Christ, whom you will ardently love, you will receive your name.[200]

---

[198] The Vulgate reads *eum* ("him") while Bonaventure has *fratrem vestrum* ("your brother").

[199] See Bede's commentary on Mark 3:16 in CCSL cxx, p. 470. More to the point are the observations in Book I, Homily 16 of Bede's *Homilies on the Gospels* in CCS 110, pp. 162-163: "... we must know for certain that in Greek and Latin 'Peter' signifies the same thing as Cephas does in Syriac, and in both languages the name is derived from [the word for] rock. He was called Peter by reason of the firmness of his faith; he was called Peter by reason of the invincible toughness of his mind; he was called Peter because with single devotion he clung to that most solid rock, concerning whom the Apostle says: *The rock is Christ*.... So Peter received his name from the firm rock, namely Christ, whom he ardently loved."

[200] See Book I, c. 21 n. 1 of Augustine's *Retractions* in *Saint Augustine, The Retractions*, trans. Mary Inez Bogan, FC 60 (Washington: CUA Press, 1968), p. 90: "But I know that very frequently at a later time, I so explained what the Lord said: 'Thou art Peter, and upon this rock I will build my Church,' that it be understood as built upon Him whom Peter confessed saying: 'Thou art the Christ, the Son of the living God,' and so Peter, called after this rock, represented the person of

QUESTIONS

81. Question 1 treats John's last testimony in John 1:29: "Behold, the Lamb of God."

1. Since John adds nothing more to this testimony, it would seem to be an inadequate witness since the same could be said of any Saint, especially about the Apostles. Luke 10:3 reads: "Behold, I am sending you like lambs among wolves." – 2. Moreover, why does he choose lamb rather than another animal to describe him?

I answer that John said Lamb because according to Exodus 12 he was prefigured[201] and according to Isaiah 16:1 he was foretold by the prophets.[202] And since the gospel had to agree with the Law, John used Lamb to point to Christ.

82. But there is still another question: Why was he prefigured by the name of lamb or in a lamb? The response to this is multiple. By reason of its innocence. Thus, Exodus 12:5 states: "It will be without blemish, a male, one year old."[203] By reason of its patience. Isaiah 53:7 has: "He was silent as a lamb before its shearer." By reason of its great usefulness, for it is totally useful, giving milk for drink, meat for food, wool for clothing, pelt for adornment.

---

the Church which is built upon this rock, and has received 'the keys of the kingdom of heaven.' For, 'Thou art Peter' and not 'Thou art the rock' was said to him. But 'the rock was Christ,' in confessing whom, as also the whole Church confesses, Simon was called Peter."

[201] See Exod 12:3-28 about the paschal lamb.

[202] Isaiah 16:1 reads: "Send forth, O Lord, the lamb, the ruler of the earth, from Petra of the desert, to the mount of the daughter of Zion."

[203] On p. 263 n. 7 QuarEd rightly notice that the Vulgate of Exod 12:5 is slightly different: *Erit autem agnus absque macula* ... ("Now it will be a lamb lacking blemish").

Now relative to the objection that there are other lambs, it has to be maintained that Christ's innocence differs from that of others, for he was without blemish in that there never was any blemish in him. Now other Saints are without blemish, but their blemishes have been blotted out by grace.

83. Question 2 asks about the very giving of John's witness, since it is said in John 1:35 that "John was standing" and gave his witness before "two disciples."

Contrary. 1. John had been sent to announce Christ. Therefore, it would seem that he should not be standing, but traveling about and proclaiming the name of Christ. – 2. Furthermore, he would seem to be promoting envy by giving his witness to only two of his disciples, when he should be bearing witness to all, "so that all might believe through him."[204]

It has to be said that in order for John's testimony to be believed it had to authentic, acceptable or accepted and not suspect. Since his witness was authentic, he was standing and not moving about. Since his testimony had to be accepted, he gave it not to just anybody, but to those seeking it and willing to understand it. Because it was not suspect, he did not busy himself with proclaiming it about. Thus, Chrysostom comments: "His witness would have been suspect if he had so busied himself with its proclamation that the Jews would have been provoked to contradict it."[205]

---

[204] John 1:7.

[205] John Chrysostom doesn't say this in so many words. See Homily 18 n. 3 in PG 59:117 and FC 35, pp. 178-179: "Why in the world, then, did he not travel everywhere in Judea proclaiming Him, instead of taking up his stand beside the river, waiting for Him to come and waiting to point Him out when He did come? Because he wished Him

84. Question 3 concerns John 1:38: "Rabbi, where do you dwell?" And the Lord showed them his dwelling. – Contrary to this is what Matthew 8:20 states: "Foxes have dens, and the birds of the heaven have nests, but the Son of Man has nowhere to lay his head." Thus, this text states that Jesus did not have a dwelling.

I respond by stating that there are two ways of having a dwelling. The first is through the possession of ownership. Rich people have this type of dwelling. The second is through being at rest and occupying a place. All people have this type of dwelling and repair to some house to dwell. As a poor person, Christ did not have a dwelling in the first sense. But as a stable person, he did have a dwelling in the second sense, for he was not a gyrovague.[206]

85. Question 4. There is a further question about John 1:40: "One of the two disciples was Andrew." – Why did he provide the name of Andrew, but not of the other disciple? And if he was silent about the other disciple, why not about Andrew, too? – I respond that the reason for expressly naming Andrew and not the other disciple is

---

to be proclaimed through His works. His own endeavor, meanwhile, was merely to make Him known and to persuade at least some men to hear about eternal life."

[206] The "gyrovagus" is someone who just roams about. See Jesus' admonition to the seventy-two in Luke 10:7: "Do not move from house to house." Bonaventure may be echoing a monastic critique. See chapter I n. 13-16 of *The Rule of the Master*, trans. Luke Eberele, CSS 6 (Kalamazoo: Cistercian Publications, 1977), p. 106: "The fourth kind of monks, who should not even be called that and about whom I would do better to keep silent than to say anything, are called gyrovagues. They spend their whole life as guests for three or four days at a time at various cells and monasteries of others in various provinces. Taking advantage of hospitality, they want to be received every day anew in different places. They oblige their successive hosts, who rejoice at the arrival of a guest, to prepare choice dishes for them and to put the axe to poultry because of their coming ñ this, every day by different hosts."

twofold. The first reason is that Andrew was the lesser, as Chrysostom observes, and in order to show that Peter was called by Andrew.[207] And there is a wondrous dispensation in this, for he wanted to call the greater[208] and more senior people through lesser people, and the wise through the simple. Wherefore, he calls Peter by means of Andrew, and Nathanael the wise by means of Philip the rustic.

86. Question 5 focuses on John 1:42: "You will be called Cephas." Was this name given him at this time? – It would seem not: 1. The interlinear Glossa states: "The name was not yet given him, but presignified." – 2. Furthermore, Mark 3:14-16 says that the Lord called twelve. And at that time "he gave Simon the name of Peter." – 3. Also, Matthew 16:16-19 states that he changed Simon's name when he made his confession.

I give a common answer to these observations. In John the name Peter was presignified. In Mark it was giv-

---

[207] Bonaventure's response does not seem to stem directly from Chrysostom. See Hugh of St. Cher, p. 288b, u: "But the question is raised: Why is Andrew named, but not the other disciple? Chrysostom answers that Andrew is named because Peter was called by him, and the Evangelist will immediately mention Peter's call. But the other disciple is not named, perhaps because that other disciple was John, and out of humility he kept his name quiet. Or it may be that the other disciple was one of the minor disciples, and not comparable to Andrew, who was an Apostle." See Chrysostom's Homily 18 n. 3 in PG 59:117 and FC 33, p. 180: "For what reason, then, did the Evangelist not also make known the name of the other person? Some say it was because the writer was the other follower, but others deny this and say that the latter was not one of the chosen [disciples]. Therefore, it was not necessary to mention more than the bare facts about him. What use in learning his name, when the Evangelist did not even mention the names of the seventy-two?"

[208] Bonaventure seems to be invoking a medieval distinction between *maiores* and *minores*.

en. In Matthew it was confirmed.[209] – But Augustine speaks against this interpretation and states that Christ changed Peter's name when Andrew led him to Christ.[210] And Bede says something similar in his commentary on Mark 3, that is, the name was not given at that time, but beforehand.[211]

Because of these observations it should be stated that although his new name was given him now, it was not public knowledge, because from this time on others were not calling him Peter, but by his prior name. But afterwards, at the time indicated by Mark 3:16, he wanted him to be called by the name of Peter. Further, Matthew 16:18 indicates how this name change was celebrated with a dignity befitting the name.

87. Question 6 queries: Why did the Lord give a name to Peter when he was called rather than to others? – He would seem to be respecter of persons, since he conferred the dignity of a name on Peter who had no merit.[212]

---

[209] See Hugh of St. Cher, p. 288b, g: "Further, his name is not changed to Peter here, but the change is foretold. But Mark 3:16 deals with actual change of Peter's name whereas Matt 16:18 concerns the confirmation of the name change."

[210] See Book II, chapter 17 n. 34 of *Harmony of the Gospels* in NPNC 1, volume 6, p. 121: "Thus the Lord could address him at that later period by this very name, when he said, 'You are Peter' (Matt 16:18). For he does not say then, 'You will be called Peter,' but 'You are Peter' because on a previous occasion he had already been spoken to in this manner, 'You will be called' (John 1:42)."

[211] See Bede's comment on Mark 3:16 in CCSL cxx, p. 470: "Now this is not the first time that he gave Simon the name of Peter, but long before when seeing him brought to him by his brother Andrew, he said to him: *You are Simon, son of John. You will be called Cephas (which interpreted is Peter)*."

[212] On p. 264 n. 11 QuarEd cite Bede's comment on John 1:42: "Peter had not yet done anything, and already he merited to have his name changed. Had he believed more than Andrew?"

To this problematic Pelagius responds that Christ made the name change because of the greater natural strength that he saw in Peter. Thus, John 1:42 says: "Jesus looked at him." And Pelagius states that he happened to merit the name change because of his natural characteristics.[213]

It has to be remarked that God sees not only the exterior, but also the interior; not only the things that are, but also the things that will be. So as a sign that he would be the future shepherd of the Church, he gave him a new name. – Now relative to Pelagius' interpretation of "Jesus looked at the strength of Peter's natural characteristics," Victor[214] reproves this viewpoint: "He did not build the house of virtue upon the greater foundation of Peter's natural strengths, as Pelagius mistakenly says, thereby stoking the fires of error. Rather Christ looked upon Peter with the eyes of mercy and graciousness."

88. Question 7 inquires: Why aren't names changed now for those who enter a religious institute or even for those who are converted to Christ? Chrysostom answers that a name change was an inducement to pursue virtue. However, since we now have a single name, which is the great incentive to virtue, we should be content with that name.[215] And that is the name of Christianity, since all

---

[213] See Book I, chapter 41 n. 45 of Augustine's *The Grace of Christ and Original Sin* in *Answer to the Pelagians*, introduction, translation, and notes by Roland J. Teske, WSA I/23 (Hyde Park, NY: New City Press, 1997), p. 426: "He (Pelagius) claims, nonetheless, that the way itself can also be found by nature alone, but that it is found most easily, if grace helps us."

[214] This is Victor of Capua. See Bonaventure's comment on John 1:1 (n. 3) above with the note there.

[215] See Homily 19 n. 3 on John's Gospel in PG 59:122 and FC 33, p. 191: "At that time, however, each one received a different name, while now we all have the same one: that which is greater than all, namely,

of us are called *Christians*. – Nonetheless, the Roman Church still preserves a name change for the person of the Supreme Pontiff.

JOHN 1:43-11:46
THE MANIFESTATION OF THE WORD THROUGH HIMSELF

89. *The next day*, etc. This first part of John's Gospel, which commenced with "This is the witness of John," (John 1:19), deals with the manifestation of the Word and is divided into two sections. The first section considered the manifestation of the Word made through John's witness and voice and runs to John 1:42. But from John 1:43 to the end of John 11 the Evangelist treats the manifestation made by *the Word himself*. And since the manifestation has two aspects, namely, to whom and by whom it was made, this section has two components. The first focuses on the situation and circumstances of those *to whom* the manifestation is given. The second treats the situation and circumstances of *the Word that has been manifested* and commences at John 5:1: "After this there was a feast."

JOHN 1:43-4:54
THE MANIFESTATION OF THE WORD TO VARIOUS PERSONS AND THEIR RESPONSES

The first section has four parts in accordance with the types of persons to whom the Word manifests himself. In the first he manifests himself to his *disciples*. In the sec-

---

to be called Christians and sons of God, His friends and His body. This name can stir us more than all those famous ones and make us more desirous of the practice of virtue."

ond he manifests himself to *the Jews* where John 2:12 reads: "After this he went down." In the third he manifests himself to *the Samaritans* where John 4:1 says: "When, therefore, Jesus knew," etc. In the fourth he manifests himself to *the Galileans* where John 4:43 states: "After two days he departed."

John 1:43-2:11
The Word's first manifestation, which is given to his disciples

Now the Word's manifestation to the disciples has two sections. The first concerns *the call of the disciples* whereas the second treats *the manifestation* made to the disciples who had been called where John 2:1 reads: "And on the third day a marriage took place."

John 1:43-51
The call of the disciples

So the Evangelist describes *the call* of the disciples in this order. First, there is mention of *the call of the simple*. Second, *the call of the wise*. Third, why those called *are attracted to the Word*. Finally, *the confirmation of those who are attracted*. – Thus, the Lord's *call of the simple*, namely, of Philip, is described first, since he was called by the Lord himself from Galilee. So the text continues:

90. (Verse 43). *The next day*, that is, after the conversion of Andrew and Peter, *he was about to leave for Galilee, and he found Philip*, not in a haphazard way. Rather it was his intention to find what was lost. Thus the Lord found his disciples, who had been previously lost, since he rescued them from perdition. Luke 15:8 says: "The woman, who lost one drachma, searched carefully until

she found it."[216] *And he[217] said to him: Follow me*, as a servant his master, as a disciple his teacher, so that you may attain. Philippians 3:12 reads: "But I follow that I may attain that for which I have been laid hold of...."[218] The Evangelist mentions the place from which Philip came to make a further manifestation. So he continues:

91. (Verse 44). *Now Philip was from Bethsaida, the town of Andrew and Peter.* And so it is to be understood that he followed their initiative as he saw them following Jesus. For curtain follows curtain, according to what is signified in Exodus 26 about the composition of the tabernacle.[219] – According to the moral sense Philip means "mouth of the lamp."[220] Bethsaida means "house of hunters."[221] *Mouth* points to eloquent wisdom. About this Luke 21:15 has: ìI myself will give you wise eloquence that all your adversaries will be unable to resist or gainsay." *Lamp* means "honest way of life." Matthew 5:16 says: "Let your light shine before men and women, so that they may see," etc. *Hunters* means "preachers." Jeremiah 16:16 states: "I will send them many hunters, and they will hunt them."[222] So the call of Philip of Bethsaida signifies that the person who assumes the office of preaching must have eloquent

---

[216] Bonaventure turns the parable's question into a statement.

[217] On p. 265 n. 8 QuarEd correctly mention that the Vulgate reads *Iesus* ("Jesus").

[218] Phil 3:12 concludes with: "by Christ Jesus."

[219] Exod 26:1-3 reads: "And you shall make the tabernacle in this manner. You shall make ten curtains of fine twisted linen, and violet and purple, and scarlet twice dyed, diversified with embroidery.... Five curtains shall be joined one to another, and the other five shall be coupled together in like manner."

[220] See CCSL lxxii, p. 140: "Philip, mouth of the lamp, or mouth of the hands."

[221] See CCSL lxxii, p. 135: "Bethsaida, house of fruit or house of hunters."

[222] Hugh of St. Cher, p. 288b, q also cites Jer 16:16, but in its entirety.

wisdom and live honestly, "for the principle holds that they contemn the preaching of the one whose life they despise."[223]

92. (Verse 45). *Philip found Nathanael*, etc. This verse deals with the second point, namely, the call of the wise, which was done through the mediation of the simple. So the text says: *Philip found Nathanael*. Just as he himself had been found by Christ, so he also finds Nathanael. Bede observes: "Take a look at that hunter: How intent he is on capturing souls."[224] So the text continues: *And said to him: Him of whom Moses wrote in the Law and the Prophets*. Supply here: the prophets "wrote." Other texts read *and in the Prophets*.[225] In this case the text would read: *Him of whom Moses wrote in the Law* and it was written *in the Prophets. We have found Jesus, the son of Joseph of Nazareth*. This one was the Christ, who had been foretold in the Law and the Prophets. Deuteronomy 18:15 states: "The Lord will raise up for you from your people a prophet," etc. Isaiah 7:14 has: "Behold, a virgin will conceive and will bear a son," etc. He said that he was "the son of Joseph" by reputation. Luke 3:23 reads: "Jesus himself, when he began his work, was about thirty

---

[223] See Homily 12 n. 1 of GGHG in CCSL cxli, p. 82. Bonaventure's quotation is almost verbatim. This is a favorite text of Bonaventure. See, for example, *Commentary on Luke 1-8*, p. 134 on Luke 1:80 (n. 144). See also *Commentary on Luke 1-8*, pp. 488 on Luke 6:14 (n. 37): '*Philip*, whose name means *mouth of the lamp*. This means that episcopal teaching must be *lucid* and correspond to *the understanding of its audience*, so that 'their appearance may be like that of lamps,' as Ezekiel 1:13 says."

[224] This is a summary of what Bede says in his commentary on John 1:44. See PL 92:654A: "And this hunter, who before he was ordained to the office of preaching by the Lord, quickly and spontaneously showed by preaching to Nathanael how intent he would be in capturing souls and bringing them to life."

[225] On p. 266 n. 7 QuarEd say that Thomas Aquinas, in his commentary on this passage, follows these texts.

years old, being, as supposed, the son of Joseph." And indeed this is what he told Nathanael, as to one who was an expert in the Law and the Prophets. And this is evident from Nathanael's response.

93. (Verse 46). *And Nathanael said to him: Can anything good come out of Nazareth? Philip said: Come and see.* This text can be read as an assertion and yields the sense that something good can come from Nazareth. For this reason Matthew 2:23 states: "What was spoken by the prophet was fulfilled that he shall be called a Nazarene." And this is accepted from Isaiah 11:1 according to the truth of the Hebrew text. Where we read in the Latin: "A flower shall rise up out of his root," the Hebrew text has: "Nazarene."[226] Thus, understanding these matters as an expert, Nathanael uttered an assertion. – Others read this text as a question as if a doubt lies behind Nathanael's question: "Can anything good come out of Nazareth?" namely, such a great good. For, as Micah 5:2 says: "And you, Bethlehem Ephrata, are a little one," etc., the Christ was to be born in Bethlehem. Wherefore, the Jews ask in John 7:42 below: "Does the Christ come from Galilee?" Whether one reads the text as an assertion or as a question,[227] Philip stands firm and exhorts Nathanael to come. So the text continues: *Philip said to him: Come and see.* Chrysostom comments: "Philip, unable to convince his

---

[226] In his commentary on Luke 1:26 (n. 43) Bonaventure is clearer. See *Commentary on Luke 1-8*, pp. 58-59: "Whence Jerome says that according to the Hebrew meaning, the text should read: 'A Nazarene shall rise up from the root of Jesse.' Therefore, from Nazareth something of good can come – indeed, the flower of all good."

[227] See Augustine's Tractate 7 n. 15 in FC 78, p. 169: "But that phrase can follow both expressions, whether you express it as if asserting ... or whether [you express it] thus, as if in doubt and wholly questioning." See Hugh of St. Cher, p. 289k for a consideration of whether Nathanael's words are to taken as an assertion or a question of doubt.

brother by words of the treasure he has found, leads him to the treasure he has found."[228] And it is understood that he followed Philip.

94. (Verse 47). *Jesus saw Nathanael*, etc. The Evangelist makes his third point in this verse, that is, what attracts the person called. He is attracted by recommendation and by the revelation of secrets. Thus, the text states: *Jesus saw Nathanael coming to him*, namely, because of the admonition of Philip the simple. *And he said of him: Behold, a true Israelite, in whom there is no guile*. The reason he had no guile is that, although he was wise, he was not embarrassed to follow a simple person. Thus, Nathanael expressed in words what he believed in his heart, for he was not coming to Jesus with a desire to tempt him, but out of a desire to make progress in virtue. Proverbs 12:20 complains of a different sort of person: "Guile and deceit are in the hearts of those who think evil things." However, Nathanael does not believe Jesusí commendation until he has some certitude about what heís hearing, because men and women should not be eager to believe the good things that are said about them. This leads to the next verse.

95. (Verse 48). *Nathanael said to him: How do you come to know me?* Why are you commending me in such terms? The Lord draws him closer to himself through a revelation of secret matters. So these words follow: *Before Philip called you, when you were under the fig tree, I saw you*. On a literal level: he himself was in that secret place, perhaps a garden, where Philip called him. Or: *the fig tree* means

---

[228] Bonaventure cites the gist of Chrysostom's point. See Homily 20 n. 1 in PG 59:125 and FC 33, pp. 195-196: "When Andrew was not able to show forth the riches he had discovered, because he could not do justice to his treasure in words, he led his brother to what he had found."

the habit of sinning, as the first parents clothed themselves with fig leaves according to Genesis 3:7.[229] So it was the Lord who saw him and sought after him instead of him being the one who was searching after the Lord. This revelation attracted Nathanael. Thus, his faithful confession follows.

96. (Verse 49). *Nathanael answered and said to him: Rabbi, you are the Son of God*, with regard to your divinity, since you know the secrets of the heart. Jeremiah 17:10 reads: "I am the Lord who searches the heart and ... innards." *You are the king of Israel*, with regard to your humanity. The crowd confessed something similar in John 12:13 below: "Blessed is he who comes in the name of the Lord, the king of Israel."

97. (Verse 50). *Jesus answered*, etc. The fourth point occurs here, that is, the confirmation of the person attracted, for he confirms him by means of the promise of showing him greater things. Thus the text continues: *Jesus answered and said to him: Because I said to you that I saw you under the fig tree, you believe.* And so a little matter has drawn you to faith. *Greater things than these will you see.* John 5:20 says: "Greater works than these he will show

---

[229] Gen 3:7 states: "And the eyes of both were opened. And when they perceived themselves to be naked, they sewed together fig leaves and made themselves aprons." See Augustine's Tractate 7 n. 21 on John in FC 78, p. 174: "In the beginning of the human race Adam and Eve, when they had sinned, made coverings for themselves from fig leaves; thus fig leaves are understood as sins. Now Nathanael was under the fig tree, as under the shadow of death. The Lord saw him about whom it was said, 'A light has arisen for those who were sitting under the shadow of death.'" See also PL 92:655C where Bede comments on John 1:48 by means of Gen 3:7: "... this tree ... can fittingly signify the human race's habit of sinning."

him that you may wonder."[230] And he specifies what he means by greater.

98. (Verse 51). *And he said to him: Amen, amen, I say to you that*[231] *you will see heaven opened*, according to Matthew 3:16 John saw that the heavens were opened over him.[232] *And the angels of God ascending and descending upon the Son of Man.* In the literal sense angels did descend upon him according to Matthew 4:11: "Angels came near to him and ministered to him." According to the spiritual sense, in Augustine's viewpoint,[233] what had been said to Nathanael is now fulfilled in Christians, for, after the God-man ascended, entry into heaven is opened in him for believers. And they see the angels, that is, the preachers, *ascending*, while they consider the secrets of his deity, and *descending*, as they preach about his humanity. This vision was signaled in Genesis 28 where it is said that Jacob saw that the Lord was leaning on the ladder and the angels ascending and descending.[234]

---

[230] It is the Father showing the greater works to the Son.

[231] On p. 267 n. 5 QuarEd accurately indicate that the Vulgate does not read *quia* ("that").

[232] Matt 3:16 says: "And behold the heavens were opened to him."

[233] See Tractate 7 n. 23 on John in FC 78, p. 176: "But what did he see that time on the ladder? Angels ascending and descending. So also is the Church, brothers: the angels of God, good preachers, preaching Christ; that is, they ascend and descend upon the Son of man."

[234] Gen 28:12-13 reads: "And Jacob saw in his sleep a ladder standing upon the earth with its top touching heaven; the angels also of God ascending and descending by it. And the Lord, leaning upon the ladder, saying to him: I am the Lord God of Abraham your father, and the God of Isaac...."

QUESTIONS

99. Question 1. The first question deals with the Lordís coming into Galilee. Why does John 1:43 say that after John's testimony the Lord came into Galilee "on the next day"?

Contrary: 1. The other Evangelists state that he was immediately "led into the desert by the Spirit." See Matthew 4:1 and Mark 1:12. ñ 2. Furthermore, Mark 1:14 says: "After John had been delivered up, Jesus came into Galilee." But John 3:23-24 below gives clear indication that John had not been delivered up and had been baptizing for a considerable time after Jesus had come into Galilee.[235]

In the second book of his *Harmony of the Gospels* Augustine responds to these matters by stating that the Lord's coming into Galilee was twofold.[236] The first was after John's testimony, but before he had been cast into prison. And about this coming all the other Evangelists are silent. The second occurred after John had been imprisoned. About this coming John 4 makes mention.[237] During his first trip to Galilee he performed the miracle of changing water into wine at a wedding.[238] During the second he healed the son of the royal official.[239] – So relative to the first objection that he was led into the desert, it should be understood that John's testimony was given after the Lord returned from the desert.

---

[235] John 3:23-24 reads: "Now John was also baptizing in Aenon near Salim, for there was much water there. And the people came and were baptized. For John had not yet been put into prison."

[236] See Book II, c. 18 n. 42.

[237] John 4:3 states: "Jesus left Judea and went again into Galilee." John 4:43 has: "Now after two days he departed from that place and went into Galilee."

[238] See John 2:1-11.

[239] See John 4:46-54.

100. Question 2. There is a similar doubt about the call of the disciples. – 1. Chapter one of John's Gospel maintains that the disciples were called before John was delivered over. Matthew 4:12-22, however, states that Jesus called them after John had been delivered up. – 2. Moreover, Matthew 4:18-22 narrates that the Lord called Peter and Andrew while they were fishing from a boat, but John states that first Andrew, then Peter came to him at the testimony of John.

I base my response on Augustine who says that John preserved the historical order of the time of the call of the disciples while Matthew narrated the call by means of recapitulation.[240] – 2. Now relative to the manner and time of the disciples" call it has to be said that the disciples of the Lord are called in a twofold manner. The first is to faith while the second is to perfection. Peter and Andrew were called in the first manner when they recognized the Lord and believed in him upon the witness of John. In the second manner they were called while they were fishing from their boats, so that they might leave everything and follow Christ. In this section John is speaking of this first type of call. Matthew speaks of the second type of call.[241]

---

[240] See Book II, c. 17 n. 39 in *Harmony of the Gospels* in NPNF 1, Volume 6, p. 122: "Now it may be the case that Matthew has but gone over here something he had omitted in its proper order. For he does not say, 'After this, walking by the sea of Galilee, He saw two brethren,' but, without any indication of the strict consecution of time, simply, 'And walking by the sea of Galilee, He saw two brethren,' and so forth: consequently it is quite possible that he has recorded at this later period not something which took place actually at that later time, but only something which he had omitted to introduce before; so that the men may be understood in this way to have come along with Him to Capharnaum, to which place John states that He did come...."

[241] Bonaventure seems to have conflated Matthew and Luke. Matt 4:22 says: "And immediately they left their nets and their father and followed him." Luke 5:11 states: "And when they had brought their boats to land, they left *everything* and followed him."

101. Question 3 is a further question about the place of origin of those called. Chrysostom asks why the Lord called disciples from Galilee when the Judeans were more skilled in the Law.[242] Yes, why is it that he didn't chose people from Jerusalem? – Another question follows closely behind this one: Why did he call Nathanael by means of Philip? – And again, if Nathanael were such a holy person, as the Lord said, and also most expert in the Law, it seems that the Lord should have made him an apostle.[243] – If you say that he wanted to chose the simple, then by means of the principle that "every action of Christ is for our instruction"[244] it would seem that we must chose as prelates those who are simple and uneducated.

The Apostle in 1 Corinthians 1:26-28 teaches us the answer: "There were not many wise according to the flesh, not many mighty, not many noble, but God has chosen the foolish things of the world ... and the things that are not."[245] And God's reason for this is to confound the exalted of the world, and "lest any flesh should pride itself be-

---

[242] See PG 59:124 and FC 33, pp. 194-195: "The truly remarkable thing was with regard to Peter and James and Philip – not only that they believed in Him before witnessing His miracles, but also that they believed even though they were from Galilee, whence no prophet came, nor was it possible for any good to come, for the people of Galilee were somewhat boorish and rustic and dull. Indeed, Christ also showed His power from the very circumstance that He took the select group of His disciples from this unpromising place."

[243] Bonaventure gets into this quandary because he presupposes that John's Gospel narrates Jesus' choice of twelve disciples as his apostles. It does not. John 21:2 indicates that Nathanael is still in the company of the first disciples called and will receive a revelation of the risen Lord.

[244] This seems to have been a common axiom. See, e.g., chapter 1 of Alan de Insulis, *Summa de Arte Praedicatoria* in PL 210:113C and Opera Omnia 4:83.

[245] Bonaventure seems to presuppose the opening words of 1 Cor 1:26: "For consider your own call, brothers and sisters, that there...."

fore him"[246] and to show that everything that the Apostles accomplish is through divine power and not by human wisdom. This is the reason why the Lord chose Galileans, who were fishermen and simple rustics as Apostles. As Chrysostom observes: Galilee had rustic inhabitants.[247] This is also the reason why he called Philip the simple, and through him his wise brother. Moreover, this is the reason why he did not make Nathanael, a great teacher of the Law, an Apostle. Finally, this is the reason why he didn't call Paul among the first Apostles, but "as last of all, as one born out of due time, he was seen also by him,"[248] so that he might be humbled. – With regard to your objection that we should chose simple people as prelates I respond that the Lord chose simple people in order to make them wise. But since it does not lie in our power to make people wise, we must place those in charge who are already wise.

102. Question 4 concerns the obedience of the disciples, for they immediately followed the Lord before they had seen any miracles. It would seem that they acted foolishly, as is said here of Philip and the others. Whence the heretics find Matthew repulsive.[249]

The possible responses are the following. They were illumined interiorly. Or it can be said that they were led exteriorly. Some by means of testimony, as Andrew and his companion. Some by means of a miracle, as it said of Peter in Luke 5:1-11. Some by means of an example as is the case with Philip, who was following the example of

---

[246] 1 Cor 1:29.

[247] See note 242 above.

[248] 1 Cor 15:8. The Vulgate reads *mihi* ("to me") whereas Bonaventure has *ei* ("to him").

[249] On p. 268 n. 12 QuarEd refer to "Porphyrius and Julianus Augustus."

Peter and Andrew, his fellow townspeople, whom he knew were good.

103. Bede raises the fifth and final question: Why does Nathanael in John 1:49 call Christ *the Son of God* when in John 1:51 he himself says that he is the Son of Man?

Bede's answer is that "this has been done by the just determination of the divine dispensation, so that, as both natures are mentioned, he might profess his humanity while Nathanael might profess his exalted status."[250] In this way the two natures in Christ are made known and an example of humility is given, so that men and women might always acknowledge and say humble things about themselves. This is especially mentioned against those who have some noble blood, and when asked about their origin, do not give their father's name, but that of an uncle or some other famous relative. Our Lord Jesus Christ, although he was noble on God's side, but lowly on his mother's side, often refers to himself as Son of Man, but rarely as Son of God and only does so when he is compelled to. Note his difference from others in that these others, who are born from a mingling of seeds, are called children of men and women. But Christ, who had but one parent, fittingly calls himself a son of a human being.

---

[250] See PL 92:656C. Bonaventure's "citation" is an abbreviation of Bede's christologically richer statement.

Chapter Two

John 2:1-11
Manifestation of the Word Incarnate
to his disciples[1]

1. (Verse 1). *And on the third day*, etc. After he has described the call of the disciples, the Evangelist now depicts the *manifestation* made by the Word and about the Word Incarnate. Thus, the Glossa observes that after John had made revelations about the Lord, the Lord himself revealed himself by a miracle.[2] – Now the Evangelist narrates this manifestation in the following order. First, he posits *the occasion* for the miracle. Second, *the petition* for a miracle. Third, the miraculous *transformation* of water into wine. Fourth, *the acknowledgment* of the miracle. Fifth, *the manifestation* of Christ and *the edification* of the disciples, to whom Christ, through this miracle, deigned to make himself manifest.[3]

So first, the Evangelist notes the occasion for the miracle, which occurred when the Lord was present with his

---

[1] See Luca M. di Girolamo, "L 'Esegesi scritturistica di S. Bonaventura ed il suo commento all' episodio delle nozze di Cana (*Gv 2, 1-11*)," *Miscellanea Francescana* 103 (2003): 489-549.

[2] Glossa Ordinaria says that this comment derives from Augustine. See PL 114:363D: "After the revelation of Christ through John's testimony, he himself reveals himself through a miracle."

[3] Bonaventure himself manifests a six-fold word play: *manifestat*io, *impetrat*io, *convers*io, *approbat*io, *manifestat*io, *edificat*io.

disciples at a wedding. So the text says: *And on the third day*, that is, after the call of the disciples, *a wedding took place in Cana of Galilee.* Thus, the place is also mentioned. *And the mother of Jesus was there.* The text does not say that she had been invited, because she had come by reason of kinship and quasi-obligation, just as she had also gone into the mountains to assist Elizabeth as Luke 1:39 states.[4] This is the reason why the Lord was also invited. Therefore, the text continues:

2. (Verse 2). *Now Jesus was also invited to the wedding and his disciples.* Chrysostom observes: "He was invited to the wedding, not as someone great, but as a relative, and he, being humble, did not spurn the invitation, but went,"[5] according to what he teaches in Luke 14:10: "When you are invited to a wedding, go and recline in the last place."

3. (Verse 3). *And the wine ran short.* The stage is set for the second point, namely, the petition for a miracle, which is made by Jesus' mother, who commiserates with the poverty of the bridegroom. So the text reads: *And the wine ran short, and the mother of Jesus said to him: They have no wine.* It is as if she were saying: Use your abundance to relieve their poverty, for she knew that he would be "rich in mercy"[6] and power, although he might appear poor and weak. 2 Corinthians 8:9 says: "Although he was rich in all things, he became poor for our sakes."[7] But the

---

[4] Equally important to Bonaventure's argument is Luke 1:36: "And behold, Elizabeth, your *kinswoman*, also has conceived a son in her old age.... "

[5] See Homily 21 n. 1 in PG 59:129. Bonaventure's "citation" is a summary of what Chrysostom says.

[6] Eph 2:4.

[7] 2 Cor 8:9 reads: "For you know the graciousness of our Lord Jesus Christ – how, being rich, he became poor for your sakes, that by

Lord indicates to his mother that she could not command him inasmuch as she was his mother nor could he do this insofar as he was her son, for he had to refrain from acting until the proper time had come. So the Evangelist continues:

4. (Verse 4). *And Jesus said to her: What is it to me and you, woman?* The Glossa remarks: "That is, what does your nature and mine have in common that I should do this?"[8] He calls her *woman*, not because of weakness, but because of her nature and gender. For she was that woman, about whom Proverbs 31:10 speaks: "Who will find a valiant woman?" As if to say: As a holy woman, you have power to ask this. But as my mother, you may not command it. It was still not the time to perform this work. *My hour has not yet come*, that is, the hour of my glorification and passion, about which John 17:1 says: "Father, the hour has come. Glorify your son." But his mother, knowing that his response did not stem from indignation, but out of humility and for the purpose of instruction, confidently issues a command. So the text adds:

5. (Verse 5). *His mother said to the attendants: Do whatever he tells you.* For she knew that he could. She also knew that he knew. She knew that he would, because he was always obedient to her. For Luke 2:51 says: "He went down with them and came to Nazareth and was subject to them," namely, Jesus to his parents. And from this she was certain that we would do it. So she said: *Do whatever he tells you*, as good ministers, so that you may

---

his poverty you might become rich." Hugh of St. Cher, p. 290a quotes this entire passage in his moral interpretation.

    [8] This is the Glossa Interlinearis. See Augustine's Tractate 8 n. 9 in FC 78, p. 190: "Because, therefore, she was not the mother of [his] divinity and what she sought would be a miracle through [his] divinity, he answered her, 'What is it to me and to you, woman?'"

help bring about the miracle, just like the ministers did for Naaman, in 2 Kings 5:13: "Father, even if the prophet had told you to do some great thing, you would have done it."[9] *Do whatever he tells you.* Do not be diffident. John 11:10 below reads: "If you believe, you will see the glory of God."[10]

6. (Verse 6). *Now six stone water jars*, etc. This introduces the third point or the actual miracle. And since God makes all things in a certain "weight, number, and measure,"[11] the text provides the measure involved in the working of this miracle. For this reason the text has: *Now there were six stone water jars. Jars* are receptacles for holding water.[12] Genesis 24:17 reads: "Give me a little water from your jar."[13] These jars *were placed there according to the purification of the Jews*, that is, according to the custom of the Jews in purifying themselves. About this custom Mark 7:4 states: "And when they come from the market, they do not eat without washing first. And there have been handed down to them many other things to observe: washing of cups and pots...." *Each holding two or three measures.* "Metreta" comes from "metron," which means measure, and what is used here is the common and customary measure, which we in Paris call a sixth of

---

[9] On p. 269 n. 11 QuarEd accurately indicate that the Vulgate reads *certe* ("certainly"): "You would certainly have done it." The Vulgate reads *si* ("if") whereas Bonaventure has *etsi* ("if"). The Vulgate has *debueras* ("would have") while Bonaventure reads *debuisses* ("would have").

[10] See John 2:11: "... and he manifested his glory, and his disciples believed in him."

[11] See Wis 11:21. The Vulgate reads *mensura et numero et pondere* ("measure and number and weight").

[12] See Bede in PL 92:658B: "Vases fashioned to receive water are called jars."

[13] Gen 24:17 reads: "Give me a little water to drink from your jar."

wine.[14] So the Lord's command performed a miracle upon these measures. Therefore, the text adds:

7. (Verse 7). *And Jesus said to them: Fill the jars with water. And they filled them to the brim.* Now it should be understood that when they were filled, the water was changed into wine by the Lord's power. Therefore, he commanded that they be filled, so that he might perform a complete and perfect work, according to what happened at the beginning of things where Genesis 1:31 says: "God saw all the things that he had made, and they were very good." And Deuteronomy 32:4 reads: "The works of God are perfect."

8. (Verse 8). *And Jesus said to them.*[15] This verse addresses the fourth point, that is, the acknowledgment of the miracle, as the chief steward, who was responsible for testing the wine's quality, gives testimony to and acknowledges the wine. So the text states: *And Jesus said to them*, that is, the attendants, *Draw out now and take to the chief steward. And they took it*, according to Jesus' directive, namely, to the person he had determined, for the chief steward was in charge of the wedding and made decisions about such matters. "That is, a triclinium consists of three ranks of those reclining, separated by height."[16] Therefore, a chief steward is mentioned, because he is in charge of the banquet that is arranged in three

---

[14] Apparently tradition gave Bonaventure no real help in figuring out how many gallons or liters each stone water jar contained. So he refers to something well known to his readers. Is he talking about a sixth of a cask? A "metreta" is nine gallons.

[15] On p. 270 n. 4 QuarEd rightly indicate that the Vulgate reads *dicit* ("says") while Bonaventure has *dixit* ("said").

[16] Bonaventure, like tradition before him, engages in an interpretation of the Latin word for "chief steward." *Architriclinis* can be derived from *arch-* ("chief") and *triclin-* ("three"). He quotes Bede verbatim. See PL 92:661D where Bede's full argument is to see the

tables. Another interpretation is that the chief steward is in charge of three rooms. Yet another interpretation is that he is over the attendants, as Chrysostom maintains.[17] He commanded that the wine be brought to him, so that he might make a determination about it. Therefore, the text proceeds:

9. (Verse 9). *Now when the chief steward had tasted the water after it had become wine*, that is, the wine made from water, *not knowing whence it had come (though the attendants who had drawn the water knew), the chief steward called the bridegroom*, so that he might reprove him and commend and praise the wine.

10. (Verse 10). *And he said to him: Every person at first sets forth the good wine. At first*, that is, at the beginning. *And when they have drunk freely, then that which is inferior*, since by that time they are unable to distinguish one wine from another, but will say that any wine is a good wine. *But you have kept the good wine until now.* That is, until the end, and so you have acted inordinately and contrary to custom. This was an evil custom, since it was against the truth and against sobriety. For Ephesians 5:18-19 reads: "Do not be drunk with wine, for in that is voluptuousness, but be filled with the Spirit, speaking," etc.[18]

---

wedding as a figure of the sacraments of Christ and the Church and the three ranks as the married, the continent, and the teachers.

[17] It is not clear that Chrysostom says this in any one place, but see his Homily 22 n. 2 in PG 59:135 and FC 33, p. 217: "All of you, of course, know this, that it is those who have been entrusted with the management of such banquets who, above all, remain sober, since it is their sole responsibility to manage all the details of the feast in a seemly and orderly fashion."

[18] Eph 5:19 concludes: "speaking to one another in psalms and hymns and spiritual songs, singing and making melody in your hearts to the Lord."

11. (Verse 11). *This first of his signs.* This verse accentuates the fifth point, that is, the manifestation of divine glory and the building up of the faith of the disciples. He says this of his manifestation: *This first of his signs Jesus worked at Cana in Galilee, and he manifested his glory.* The Glossa[19] comments: "That is, his hidden divinity." John 14:21 below states: "I will love him and manifest myself to him." – He says this of the edification of the disciples: *And his disciples believed in him*, that is, they believed more strongly. Bede observes: "While the Lord was reclining at the wedding, the wine ran out, so that, after he had produced a superior wine by a miracle, the glory of God hidden in him might be manifested and the faith of those who believed in him might increase and flourish."[20]

12. According to the allegorical interpretation the third day is to be reckoned according to the threefold nature of time, that is, of nature, of the Law, and of grace.[21] On this third day there was a wedding between Christ and the Church through the assumption of the human condition. About these matters Matthew 22:2 says: "The kingdom of the heavens is[22] like a king, who made a wedding feast for his son." During this wedding feast the six jars of water that is vapid and without nutritive value are turned into flavorful and joyful wine, for the shadow of the Law has

---

[19] This is the Glossa Interlinearis which is dependent upon Bede's commentary. See the next note.

[20] See Bede's commentary on John 2:1 in PL 92:657B where the original reads *manifestaretur gloria latentis in homine Dei* ("so that the glory of God hidden in a human being might be manifested") whereas Bonaventure has *manifestaretur in illo latentis gloria Dei* ("so that the glory of God hidden in him might be manifested").

[21] See Bede in PL 92:657A where he distinguishes three periods: before the Law, under the Law, and under grace.

[22] On p. 270 n. 10 QuarEd accurately indicate that the Vulgate reads *factum est* ("is") while Bonaventure has *est* ("is").

become reality. Hebrews 10:1 says: "The Law, having but a shadow of the good things to come," etc. – The diversity of sacrifices are turned into one. Hebrews 10:11-12: "Every priest indeed stands daily ministering, and often offering the same sacrifices, which can never take away sins. But he,[23] having offered one sacrifice for sins," etc.[24] – Harsh punishments are turned into lenient ones. Acts 15:10 reads: "Why are you testing God by putting on the neck of the disciples a yoke," etc.[25] – Things hidden are brought to light. 2 Corinthians 3:15-18 says: "Down to this very day ... the veil covers their hearts ... but we ... with faces unveiled, reflecting as in a mirror the glory of the Lord," etc.[26] – Fear is changed into love. Romans 8:15 reads: "You have not received a spirit of bondage so as to be again in fear, but you have received a spirit of adoption as sons," etc.[27] – Promises are transformed into their fulfillment. In the Canticle of Zechariah Luke 1:68 has the prayer: "Blessed be the Lord God of Israel because he has visited and wrought redemption for his people."[28] – And these things took place because of the intercessory prayers of the Virgin. Luke 1:20 says: "Do not fear, Mary, for you have found favor with God."[29]

---

[23] The "he" is Christ.

[24] Hebr 10:12 concludes: "has taken his seat forever at the right hand of God."

[25] Acts 15:10 concludes: "which neither our ancestors nor we have been able to bear."

[26] 2 Cor 3:18 concludes: "are being transformed into his very image from glory to glory, as through the Spirit of the Lord."

[27] Rom 8:15 concludes: "by virtue of which we cry, 'Abba! Father.'"

[28] Bede, a possible source for Bonaventure, takes the six water jars as the six ages of the world. See PL 92:659A-661B. See Augustine, Tractate 9 n. 6 in FC 78, p. 200: "And so those six water jars signify the six eras in which prophecy was not lacking. Now these six eras, separated and distinguished by high points, so to speak, would be as empty vessels unless they were filled by Christ."

[29] Hugh of St. Cher, p. 290c interprets the six water jars as the six causes of sadness that stem from sin.

13. According to the moral interpretation the wedding is between God and the soul in the soul's reconciliation to God. About this Hosea 2:20 says: "I will espouse you to me in faith, and you will know that I am the Lord."[30] – The Lord Jesus came to celebrate this wedding, and had been invited. Revelation 3:20 reads: "Behold, I stand at the door and knock. If anyone listens to my voice and opens the door for me, I will come in to him and dine with him." – During the course of the wedding the wine ran out. This wine is interior devotion, about which Psalm 103:15 says: "Wine cheers the human heart." And Matthew 9:17 reads: "No one places new wine in old wineskins." This wine runs out when men and women become arid and lacking in devotion, as the holy soul says in Psalm 142:6: "My soul is like earth without water in your regard." – But at the petition of the Virgin who commiserates with those in misery, God filled the water jars with the water of compunction, which is changed into the sweetness of devotion. Thus, it is said in Exodus 15:25 that the waters of Meribah "were changed into sweet water."[31]

So note that the jar from which water is drawn is consideration. An empty jar is the consideration of something that is defective and vacuous, which people engage in when they sin. This jar is filled with water when people are overcome by tears at such a consideration. – So the first jar is a consideration that is defective in

---

[30] Hugh of St. Cher, p. 290c writes in his moral interpretation: "The third wedding is between God and the soul and is celebrated daily in the conversion of sinners." Hosea 2:19-20 reads: "I will espouse you to myself in justice and judgment and in mercy and commiserations, and I will espouse you to myself in faith, that is, faithfully."

[31] The Vulgate reads *versae sunt* ("were changed") whereas Bonaventure has *conversae sunt* ("were changed"). Exod 15:25 reads: "But he (Moses) cried out to the Lord, and the Lord showed him a tree, which, when he had cast it into the waters, they were turned into sweet water...."

recognition. Tobit 5:12 reads: "What joy can it be for me,[32] who sit in darkness and do not see the light of heaven?" – The second jar is a consideration that is defective in weighing the strength of the enemy. 2 Corinthians 11:3 states: "But I fear lest, as the serpent seduced Eve by his guile, so your minds may be corrupted and fall from the single-mindedness which is in Christ." – The third jar is a consideration that is defective in interior consolation. Jeremiah 2:19 reads: "See what[33] an evil and bitter thing it is for you to have left the Lord your God." – The fourth jar is a consideration that is defective in the power to resist. Psalm 37:11 says: "My power has abandoned me, and the very light of my eyes is not with me." – The fifth jar is a consideration that is defective in stability and permanence. Genesis 8:21 states: "The imagination and thought of men and women[34] are prone to evil from their youth." – The sixth jar is a consideration that is defective in secure hope. Qoheleth 9:1 has: "Human beings do not know whether they be worthy of love or hatred."[35]

---

[32] On p. 271 n. 7 QuarEd rightly indicate that the Vulgate reads *erit* ("will be") while Bonaventure has *esse potest* ("can it be").

[33] The Vulgate reads *quia* ("that") while Bonaventure has *quam* ("what").

[34] On p. 271 n. 11 QuarEd accurately mention that the Vulgate reads *cogitatio humani cordis* ("thought of the human heart") while Bonaventure has *cogitatio hominis* ("the thought of men and women").

[35] Hugh of St. Cher, pp. 290-290v, c may have been a source for Bonaventure's interpretation. The closest parallels are in the interpretations of the third and fourth jars and the conclusion. On p. 290v* Hugh of St. Cher writes: "The third jar is the uncertainty of good health. Qoh 9:1 says: Human beings do not know whether they be worthy of love or hatred.... The fourth jar is the debilitation of the mind both in doing good and in enduring adversity. Ps 37:11 states: My power has abandoned me.... These six jars must be filled with water of tears, which is immediately changed into the wine of spiritual joy."

Then these jars are filled to the brim with water, when the repentant soul, reflecting upon these considerations, waters her bed every night.[36] And from this water issues the best wine of devotion. About this wine Zechariah 9:17 says: "What is the[37] good thing and his beautiful thing, but the grain of the elect and the wine that brings forth virgins?" Into this the water of compunction is changed. Wherefore, the holy soul says in Psalm 29:12: "You have changed my mourning into joy."

QUESTIONS

14. This story occasions questions among the commentators:

Question 1. First, with regard to *the time* of the wedding. For some say that it took place on the same day on which the Lord was baptized. But how can this be, since it is said that it took place on the third day, after the Lord had come from Judea? – They answer that it was on the same day, but a year later.[38] – But then the following text is

---

[36] See Ps 6:7: "I have labored in my groanings; every night I will wash my bed. I will water my couch with my tears."

[37] On p. 271 n. 10 QuarEd correctly indicate that the Vulgate reads *eius* ("his"), that is, "his good thing."

[38] See Peter Comestor, *Historia Scholastica*, In Evangelia XXXVII in PL 198:1558AB: "Some say that about the time of the Passover that was celebrated after his baptism the Lord changed water into wine. That is why John follows this miracle in his narrative with his account of the Lord going up to Jerusalem and casting the buyers and sellers from the temple (John 2). They say that he would only have done this at Passover. But the custom of the Church stands in the way of these interpreters. This custom maintains that this took place at Epiphany and annually commemorates this event in a solemn manner. There are also those who say that he performed this miracle the same day on which he was baptized. But Matthew 4 ('Then Jesus was led into the desert') and Mark 1 ('Immediately the Spirit drove him into the

against this, for John 2:12-13 states that he went down to Capernaum and that he didn't remain there long, because Passover was near.[39] Therefore, this wedding took place near Passover, and thus not at Epiphany. – Now if this is conceded, this interpretation is contrary to the custom of the Church, for the Church celebrates three feasts on the same day.[40]

I respond that, as it has been indicated above, there are diverse interpretations. Two are probable and can be upheld. For if we want to maintain that this miracle took place after the Lord's baptism and his return from the desert and his coming into Galilee, we will say that it occurred near Passover. – The Church's custom does not stand in the way of this view. The Church celebrates the three events of the star and the dove and the transformed wine at the same time, since during these three the Lord first made himself known or since the changing of water signifies the regenerative power conferred on water because of the Lord's baptism.[41] – Now if we want to maintain the second opinion, then we will respond that

---

desert') stand against this view. For the Church maintains that these three things happened on the same day, but during different years." Hugh of St. Cher, p. 290a writes: "On the thirteenth day after Christ's nativity the three Magi adored the Lord. On the same day thirty years later Christ was baptized. On the same day one year later he changed water into wine."

[39] John 2:12-13 says: "After this he went down to Capernaum, he and his mother and his brethren and his disciples. And they stayed there but a few days. Now the Passover of the Jews was at hand, and Jesus went up to Jerusalem."

[40] The three feasts are the adoration of the Magi, Jesus' baptism, and Jesus' changing of water into wine.

[41] See John 1 n. 64 above: "Now the reason why Christ wanted to be baptized is threefold ... so that he might confer regenerative power upon the waters.... "

when the text states: *after these things*[42] *he went down to Capernaum*, one must not interpret the words "after these things" as meaning immediately. Although the time for Passover was approaching, it was not just around the corner.

15. Question 2: Whose wedding was this? – In the Prologue above it was said that the wedding was that of John,[43] and Augustine says something similar in the Glossa on the beginning of the Gospel.[44] – But Victor argues against this viewpoint: "Since virginity consists of a foretaste of eternal incorruptibility, it is incredible that John, about whose virginity testimony was given, would ever have consented to a carnal deed."[45] – The answer is that since great authorities concur in this matter, it should be maintained that the wedding was John's. Further, an indication of this can be inferred from the text, namely, since the Lord and his mother were invited to the wedding, John was the Lord's relative.[46]

There is a twofold solution to Victor's objection. First, he did not consent to carnal activity or sexual intercourse in an absolute sense, but, like the Virgin Mary, he placed

---

[42] On p. 272 n. 3 QuarEd rightly mention that the Vulgate reads *post hoc* ("after this") while Bonaventure has *post haec* ("after these things").

[43] See Jerome's Prologue n. 12 in the chapter on John 1 above.

[44] This Glossa is attributed to Augustine and may be found in Hugh of St. Cher, pp. 279-279v

[45] This quotation is from Victor of Capua (d. 554). See c. 13 n. 13 of Augustine's *Holy Virginity* in *Marriage and Virginity,* trans. Ray Kearney, WSA I/9 (Hyde Park, NY: New City Press, 1999), p. 74: "Virginal integrity ... in corruptible flesh ... is a foretaste of eternal incorruptibility."

[46] See Peter Comestor in PL 198:1559A: "Some assert that this wedding was that of John the Evangelist, and therefore Mary was invited, for she was his maternal aunt, and the Lord was invited, since he was his cousin."

himself at the disposition of the Holy Spirit, so that in this way the virgin, who was to serve the Virgin, would fittingly remain a virgin with the Virgin. – Second, even if he gave his consent in an absolute manner, his virtue was not blemished since his consent was licit. The same may be said of the dignity of virginity, because, as virginity means incorruption of mind and flesh, it can be lost in a threefold way. The incorruption of both is lost, and then it is lost eternally and temporally. Solely the incorruption of the mind is lost, and then its loss may be recovered. *Solely* the incorruption of *the body* is lost, and then it is lost temporally, but not eternally since the person will have the glory of virginity. Nonetheless, as Pope Leo says: They should not be counted among the holy virgins.[47] Therefore, John remained incorrupt in the flesh, even though his mind had consented. Afterwards he returned to his virginal state.

16. Question 3 raises the issue of why the Lord wanted to go to a wedding. – It seems that he should not have done so. For if a wedding is a place for reveling and the Lord himself must flee from all reveling, it follows that he should not have gone there. – I answer that it has to be noted that he went to build up faith and to stamp out heresy. Through the miracle he strengthened the faith of the disciples he had called, and he also brought about the

---

[47] See his Letter 12 in *St. Leo the Great, Letters*, trans. Edmund Hunt, FC 34 (New York: Fathers of the Church, 1957), p. 56: "Concerning those who were living the holy state of virginity, as we said above, but were violated by barbarians and lost the perfection of their chastity, not in their minds but in their bodies, it seems best to us that the following middle course should be observed. Let them not be lowered to the rank of widows, and yet let them not be considered among the number of holy virgins still undefiled." See Hugh of St. Cher, p. 278b: John had both [the integrity of mind and flesh], although he might have at one time or another lost the integrity of mind. But that was afterwards restored through penitence."

faith of the bridegroom. He extirpated heresy, that is, that of Julian, who condemned marriage.[48] On the contrary, the Lord wanted to be present at the wedding and to affirm and approve marriage with a miracle.[49] Further, if the Lord, once invited, had refused to go, then it would have seemed that he was in favor of this heresy and had condemned matrimony.

17. Question 4 deals with the Lord's answer to his mother in John 2:4: "What is it to me and you, woman? My hour has not yet come."

1. For either the divine Virgin asked for something that should be asked for or for something that should not be asked for. If she petitioned for something that should be asked for, he need not have given her such a sharp answer. If she was asking for something that should not be asked for, then he need not have listened to her and her petition. – 2. Moreover, what is the meaning of: "The hour has not yet come"? For either it has come, and then he is speaking falsely. Or it has not come, and so he does poorly what he does before the hour. – 3. Furthermore, from this the heretics argue that the Lord was subject to fate and the stars.[50]

---

[48] See Book I, c. 2 n. 4 of Augustine's *Answer to Julian* in *Answer to the Pelagians II*, introduction, translation, and notes by Roland J. Teske, WSA I/24 (Hyde Park, NY: New City Press, 1998), p. 269: "But you claim that marriage is undoubtedly condemned if what is born from it is not free from every debt of original sin." See Bede's Homily 14 on the Second Sunday after Epiphany in CSS 110, p. 134: "... even according to the literal sense this confirms the faith of right believers. Besides, it suggests how damnable is the lack of faith of Tatian, Marcion, and the rest who disparage marriage."

[49] Hugh of St. Cher, p. 290v, b also gives this reason: "To approve of marriage, against the Manichees who would impugn matrimony."

[50] See Augustine's Tractate 8 n. 10 in FC 78, pp. 190-191: "It is amazing that the astrologers, while believing the words of Christ, try to convince Christians that Christ lived under a fated hour. Let them,

I answer. 1. The Lord's response was not insulting, but instructive. For he shows the reason why he heard the request of his mother. Thus, there are three things to be noted in her petition. The one petitioning, and this is the Lord's mother. The persons for whom she is petitioning, and they are relatives who are poor. The content of her petition, and it is a miracle. The Lord shows in his answer that she should not petition this as mother since he could not do this with the nature he had received from her.[51] Therefore, he calls her woman, and not mother. She should not ask this for relatives, as one having concern for carnal parents. So he says: "What is it to me and you?" He also shows that a miracle should not be performed to relieve need, but to manifest his glory, for which there was no necessity at the moment. So he says: "My hour has not yet come." Nevertheless, since the woman making the petition was holy, since those, for whom she was petitioning, were poor, and since his glory was about to be manifested to his disciples, he listened to her.

2. Concerning the objection about the hour, it has to be understood that the hour of complete manifestation, which would come at the time of death, had not yet come. About this hour, Augustine says, he was not forced to die at this hour, but deigned to be killed at that hour in accordance with what John 10:18 states: "I have the power to lay down my life, and no one takes it away from me."[52]

---

then, believe Christ when he says, 'I have the power to lay down my life, and to take it up again. No one takes it away from me, but I lay it down of myself, and I take it up again.' Is this the power subject to fate, then?"

[51] Hugh of St. Cher, p. 290v, g also comments: "... but I do not have from you the wherewithal to perform the miracle."

[52] John 10:18 reads: "No one takes it (my life) from me, but I lay it down of myself. I have the power to lay it down, and I have the power to take it up again...." See Augustine, Tractate 31 n. 5 for this passage,

JOHN 2:12-3:36
THE SECOND MANIFESTATION IS MADE TO THE JEWS

18. *After these things he went down*, etc. In the passage above the Lord manifested himself to his disciples. From here to the beginning of John 4 the topic is his manifestation to the Jews, to whom he manifested himself in three ways, namely, by *sign, word* and *sacrament*. So this section has three parts. The first part concerns a manifestation given through a *sign* of power. The second focuses on a manifestation through the *word* of teaching where John 3:1 reads: "There was a certain[53] man from the Pharisees." In the third part the manifestation occurs by means of the *sacrament* of regeneration where John 3:22 says: "After these things Jesus came into Judea."

JOHN 2:12-25
THE MANIFESTATION MADE TO THE JEWS BY A SIGN

The first part has two sections. In the first he manifests himself by means of a sign of *authority*. In the second by means of a sign of *power and strength* where verse 18 states: "The Jews answered and said to him."

---

which Bonaventure also cites in his commentary on John 7:30 (n. 41) below.

[53] On p. 273 n. 4 QuarEd correctly mention that the Vulgate does not read *quidam* ("a certain").

John 2:12-17
The manifestation made to the Jews
by a sign of authority

19. (Verse 12). The sign of authority was in the powerful correction of the transgressors and is described in this order. First, the text suggests the Lord's *expedition to make the correction*. Second is the obvious *transgression of the Jews*. Third is the *correction of the transgressors*. Finally, there is *approbation of the correction*.

The Lord's *expedition to make a correction* is noted in this that he went down to Capernaum, so that he might leave his mother and brothers there. Therefore, the text says: *After these things*, namely, which had just been narrated, *he went down to Capernaum, he and his mother and his brothers and his disciples*. He went down with everyone, for he went there to live. Matthew 4:13 has: "Leaving the town of Nazareth, he came and dwelt in Capernaum." So he went down with everyone, so that he might more expeditiously go back up. For this reason the text continues: *And they did not remain there for many days*. And the reason for this is added:

20. (Verse 13). *Now the Passover of the Jews was at hand, and Jesus went up to Jerusalem*. And so he went down to prepare himself. Chrysostom comments: "Thus, he went down, before he would shortly afterwards go up to Jerusalem, so that he might not have to drag his brothers and mother everywhere."[54] Now he was going up according to Jewish custom and the mandate of the Law. Deuteronomy 16:16 reads: "Three times a year every one

---

[54] See Homily 23 n. 1 in PG 59:139. Bonaventure's citation is almost verbatim. Hugh of St. Cher, p. 291v, m gives a paraphrase of Chrysostom and highlights Jesus' respect for his mother.

of your males shall appear before[55] the Lord." Although the Lord was not subject to the Law, he, nevertheless, observed it, lest he might appear to be acting against it.

21. (Verse 14). *And he found in the temple.* This verse indicates the second point, that is, the obvious transgression of the Jews since they had made the temple a marketplace. So the text continues: *He found in the temple men selling oxen and sheep and doves.* For the avarice of the priests had introduced this practice, so that those who wanted to make a sacrifice would have one at hand. *And the money changers sitting.* Supply: He found. And the priests had introduced these, so that those who wanted to make an offering would not lack the money. And in this manner they were totally subservient to avarice. So the Lord complained about this situation in the words of Jeremiah 6:13: "From the greatest to the least all are given to avarice."[56]

22. (Verse 15). *After he had made a kind of whip.* This verse mentions the third point, that is, the Lord's powerful correction, since he not only corrects in word, but also in *deed.* So the text reads: *And after he had made a kind of whip out of cords*, namely, for striking, *he drove them all out of the temple, also the sheep and the oxen*, as unfitting to be in the temple. As the Lord said to Shebna, who was in charge of the temple, in Isaiah 22:19: "I will drive you from your position, and I will depose you from your ministry." *And he poured out the money of the money changers and overturned their tables.* And so he sharply corrected them

---

[55] On p. 273 n. 8 QuarEd accurately indicate that the Vulgate reads *in conspectu* ("before") while Bonaventure has *coram* ("before").

[56] On p. 273 n. 9 QuarEd rightly mention that the Vulgate reads: "From the smallest to the greatest all are given over to avarice."

through a deed. He also corrected by means of a word, and this to the sellers of doves. Thus, the text adds:

23. (Verse 16). *And to those who were selling the doves, he said: Take these things away, and do not make the house of my Father a house of business.* Psalm 92:5 says of this house: "Holiness befits your house, O Lord," not business. Augustine observes: "If he forbids such things in the place of prayer, how much more drinking and drunkenness and all things similar to these?"[57] Therefore, Augustine commanded in his Rule that "in the oratory nothing should take place except that for which it had been established."[58]

24. (Verse 17). *The disciples remembered.* This is the fourth point, namely, the approval of the correction which Scripture gives. So the text says: *And his disciples remembered*, not at this time, but after the resurrection, when they understood the Scriptures.[59] At that time, I say,

---

[57] Augustine doesn't say this in so many words. See his Tractate 10 n. 4 in CCSL xxxvi, p. 102 where he does mention "drunkards" and "drinking" and FC 78, p. 215: "What if he found drunkards there, what would the Lord do, if he nevertheless drove out those selling what was lawful and not contrary to justice...?" Hugh of St. Cher, p. 293 writes: "Note that as Augustine says: If God forbids such things to happen in the place of prayer, how much more drinking and all things of a weightier nature."

[58] See c. 2 n. 2 of *The Rule of Saint Augustine: Masculine and Feminine Versions,* trans. Raymond Canning, CSS 138 (Kalamazoo: Cistercian Publications, 1996), pp. 13 and 27: "The place of prayer should not be used for any purpose other than that for which it is intended and from which it takes its name." Hugh of St. Cher, p. 293a comments: "Augustine: In the oratory no one should do anything except that for which it has been made."

[59] On p. 274 n. 4 QuarEd cite Blessed Albert's commentary on this verse: "'His disciples remembered.' Supply: After his resurrection, when, as it is said in Luke 24:45 'he opened their minds that they might understand the Scriptures.'" See Rupert of Deutz, *Commentaria in Evangelium Sancti Iohannii,* edited by Rhabanus Haacke. CCCM

they remembered *that it is written: Zeal for your house has consumed me*. This is taken from verse 10 of Psalm 68, which begins with: "Save me, O God." Augustine writes this about being consumed by such zeal: "Those persons are consumed by zeal for the house of God who desire to correct all the perverse things they see there and do not rest in making changes. If they cannot make changes, they suffer and weep."[60]

25. According to the mystical sense the reader should note three things: the coming of the Lord into the temple; the finding of the transgressors; their being driven out. – About the coming Jerome comments: "According to the mystical sense Jesus daily enters the temple of the Father and drives out all ... from the Church who are guilty of the crime of both buying and selling. For it is written in Matthew 10:8: 'Freely you have received. Freely give.'"[61] – *He found those selling oxen*. Bede observes: "The oxen are the preachers, by whom the Lord's earth is plowed and sown with the seed of the word."[62] 1 Corinthians 9:9 reads: "You shall not muzzle the ox that treads the grain." Bede also comments: "The sellers of oxen are those who, not out of divine love, but with an eye toward gain blunt

---

ix, (Turnhout: Brepols, 1969), p. 127: "They remembered that this had been written about him at that time when he opened their minds to understand the Scriptures."

[60] Tractate 10 n. 9. Bonaventure's citation is not verbatim. For example, he has turned an opening question into a declarative sentence. See CCSL xxxvi, p. 105.

[61] See Jerome's commentary on Matthew 21:12-13 in PL 26:157A where Jerome specifies "the all" as "bishops and priests and deacons and laity and the entire crowd."

[62] Bede doesn't really say this. See PL 92:664B: "Now the oxen designate the teaching of heavenly life, the sheep works of chastity and mercy, the doves the gifts of the Holy Spirit, because by the help of a team of oxen the fields are readied. Now the field is the heart cultivated by heavenly teaching and ritually prepared to receive the seeds of the word of God."

the word of preaching for their listeners."[63] – *He also found those selling sheep.* As Bede says: "Sheep are the works of piety and mercy. Those who sell them are people who engage in works of piety for the sake of human praise like the hypocrites."[64] *He found those selling doves.* "Doves are the gifts of the Holy Spirit,"[65] because the Holy Spirit appeared over Christ in the form of a dove, as Matthew 3:16 says. "The persons who sell these doves are those who give for a price the freely received grace of the Holy Spirit, who impose hands, by which the Holy Spirit is received, even if not for monetary gain, then to win the favor of the crowd, who bestow sacred orders not in accordance with a meritorious life, but for the sake of a favor."[66] – *He found moneychangers.* Bede notes: "Those who exchange coins in the temple are those who do not make a pretense of pursuing heavenly matters, but who openly pursue earthly matters in the Church. They seek their own interests and not those of Jesus Christ."[67] Philippians 2:21 states: "They all seek their own interests." – *He drove out the sellers of sheep and oxen*, as Bede observes, "because he shows that both the life and the teaching of such people were rejected."[68] – *He poured out the money of the moneychangers and overturned the tables*, "since at the end when the reprobates are condemned, he will remove even the figure of the very things which they had loved, according to what is written in 1 John 2:17: 'The world with its concupiscence will pass away.'"[69] Also

---

[63] See PL 92:664C. Bonaventure's citation is almost verbatim.

[64] See PL 92:664C. Bede does not say "like the hypocrites," but cites Matt 6:5 (see Matt 6:18).

[65] See note 62 above.

[66] See PL 92:664C. Bonaventure's quotation is fairly accurate.

[67] See PL 92:664CD. Bonaventure's citation is verbatim.

[68] See PL 92:664D reads: "He also drove out the sheep and the oxen, since he showed that the life of such were rejected."

[69] See PL 92:665A. Bonaventure's quotation is almost verbatim. On p. 274 n. 13 QuarEd accurately indicate the Vulgate reads *tran-*

1 Corinthians 7:31 states: "The figure of this world is passing away." – He commanded that *the doves be taken away*. Jerome in his *Commentary on Matthew* notes: "*He overturned their seats or cathedras*, for he destroyed the business of such priests."[70] From this it follows that the sacred canons condemn the heresy of simony and prescribe that those be deprived of the priesthood who seek to purchase ordination to the priesthood.[71]

QUESTIONS

26. Question 1 concerns the timing of this event. For John says that this event took place immediately after the first miracle. But Matthew 21:1-13 narrates that it occurred around the time of his passion after he had ridden on the donkey. – Augustine answers this question in his *Harmony of the Gospels* by saying that this event took place twice.[72] John tells of its first occurrence while the other Evangelists treat the second occurrence. – And

---

sit ("is passing away") while Bonaventure has *transibit* ("will pass away").

[70] See PL 26:157AB. Bonaventure cites a greatly abbreviated version of Jerome's comments on Matt 21:12. I have retained the word *cathedra*, which occurs in Matt 21:12. Matt 23:1 uses it as the "teaching chair" of Moses. The Glossa Ordinaria on Matt 21:12 handles the problem of having the sellers of doves sitting on a chair of learning in this way in PL 114:153B: "And the seats of those selling. These seats are those of teachers, that is, he destroyed the priesthood of those who received money for the imposition of hands through which the Holy Spirit was conferred. From this it follows that the heresy of Simon is condemned. However, it is absurd to take this verse to mean that the sellers of doves were actually sitting in the chairs of learning."

[71] See Book IV, d. 25 a. 1. q. 3 and 4 of Bonaventure's *Sentence Commentary* for citations from these sacred canons.

[72] See Book II, c. 67 n. 129 in NPNF 1, Volume 6, p. 160: "This makes it evident that this act was performed by the Lord not on a single occasion, but twice over; but that only the first instance is put on record by John and the last by the other three." Hugh of St.

this solution also resolves the inconsistencies to which one might point, because on that latter occasion he made his correction in a more severe way and utilized different words than those he used here.[73]

27. Question 2 focuses on the finding of sheep in the temple. The priests did not tolerate the entrance of unclean men and women into the temple. So would they be less tolerant of the coming of sheep and oxen that would pollute the temple? It would seem probable that they would be much less tolerant. – My answer calls attention to the four courts in the temple. The first was for priests. The second for men who were clean. The third for women who were clean. The fourth was for unclean men and women and Gentiles. And "temple" was the word generally given to each one of these courts. It is in this fourth court that he found animals of this type.[74]

28. Question 3 addresses Jesus' correction, for Matthew 15:14 says: "Let them alone. They are blind guides of blind men and women." It does not seem that the Jews would be cured by a correction. So why does he rebuke them so harshly now when they were incorrigible? – I respond that, even though he knew that they were incorrigible,

---

Cher, pp. 292v, h-293 also cites Augustine and then goes on to quote Chrysostom. See the next note.

[73] See Homily 23 n. 2 of Chrysostom in PG 59:139 and FC 33, 225: "Further, it is clear that both expressions did not refer to the same occasion, and that He did this once at the beginning and again as He was going to His very Passion. And that is why, employing very vehement words on the latter occasion, He used the term 'den,' whereas at the beginning of His miracles He did not do so, but preferred to use a mild rebuke. Hence, it seems likely that He cleansed the Temple twice."

[74] See Peter Comestor, *Historia Scholastica* in PL 198:1362A who, in a commentary on III Kings, places the selling of the animals and the tables of the moneychangers in the second court.

he, nonetheless, wanted to manifest his zeal for the house of God. He also wanted, thereby, to give an example to prelates and to reveal that he was in harmony with the Father and a friend of the Law, "which he did not come to abolish, but to fulfill."[75]

29. Question 4 is: Why did he correct with a mere word those who were selling doves, but took action against the others? It seems that they should have been taken to task more sternly, for they designate those who practice simony. – I answer that on the literal level doves generate minor pollution in the temple. But on the mystical level they are to be understood as simoniacs, who are to be corrected not with a tiny punishment, but are to be driven from the Church by a judge's sentence.[76] Another interpretation is that the dove means the gift of the Holy Spirit, which is not to be driven out.

30. Question 5 raises the issue: Since the Jews were many and angry and Christ was by himself and unarmed, why didn't they rise up against him and kill him when he was driving them and their goods out in this manner? – Some answer that although they were evil, they were hypocrites. So in order not to show their avarice and malice, they appeared undisturbed and did not harm him. – Jerome provides a different answer: "there was a fiery and brilliant look in his eyes, and divine majesty was shining on his face,"[77] which immobilized them, so that they didn't

---

[75] See Matt 5:17: "Do not think that I have come to abolish the Law or the Prophets. I have not come to abolish, but to fulfill."

[76] The word, *sententialiter*, that Bonaventure employs here is canonical. See Leo F. Stelten, *Dictionary of Ecclesiastical Latin* (Peabody: Hendrickson, 1995), p. 324: "Sentence; a legitimate and definitive pronouncement by which a judge settles a question or a case that was proposed by litigants and tried judicially."

[77] See his commentary on Matt 21:15 in PL 26:158A. Bonaventure's citation is verbatim.

dare lay a hand on him. Therefore, Jerome judges this sign greater than the raising of Lazarus, because here one person all by himself and unarmed fearlessly drove out so many.[78]

31. Question 6 asks about the zeal that was in Christ. For if zeal implies anger, and anger perturbation, and in Christ there could be no perturbation, it follows that there was no zeal in him. – Victor answers that zeal has two meanings.[79] In the first meaning it does imply a perturbation of soul and anger, and such was not in Christ. Isaiah 42:4 reads: "He will not be sad nor perturbed." The second meaning of zeal is that of fervent love, and such was in Christ. Thus, the Glossa from Augustine comments: "Good zeal is a fervor of the soul, by which the mind, having cast aside human fear, is inflamed to defend the truth."[80]

JOHN 2:18-25
THE LORD MANIFESTS HIMSELF BY A SIGN OF POWER

32. *The Jews answered*, etc. The Lord had just manifested himself by means of a sign of his authority. Now he manifests himself by a *sign of power*, not presently

---

[78] See PL 26:157D-158A for Jerome's more extensive words, which conclude with "and did other things that an infinite army would not have accomplished."

[79] Bonaventure again quotes Bishop Victor of Capua (d. 554). On p. 275 n. 11 QuarEd give evidence that Alcuin also knows of this Victor, whose works are not extant.

[80] See PL 114:365:B for this Glossa Ordinaria. Hugh of St. Cher, p. 293e also cites this Glossa and discusses the question of whether Christ was angry or perturbed in his zeal. On pp. 276-277 n. 11 QuarEd give the results of their search of the works of Augustine. A weak parallel may be found in Book II, question 2 n. 3 of *Sancti Avrelii Avgvstini, De Diversis Qvaestionibvs ad Simplicianvm*, ed. Almut Mutzenbecher, CCSL xliv (Turnhout: Brepols, 1970), p. 79.

shown, but asked for and promised. And this sign was his wondrous rising from the dead. The Evangelist follows this order. First comes *the petition* for a sign. Second *the offering*[81] of what was petitioned. Third *the exposition* of what was offered. Fourth the subsequent *edification* of the faith of the Jews and through this the manifestation of Christ.[82]

Verse 18. First is a description of the petition for a sign, made by the Jews who saw with what authority Jesus had manifested himself. So the text says: *The Jews, therefore, answered* the Lord as the one who was doing the correcting, *and said to him: What sign do you show us why you are doing these things*? They are seeking for a sign of power. 1 Corinthians 1:22 reads: "The Jews seek signs." They said something similar in Matthew 21:23: "Tell us by what authority you are doing these things."[83] And they were asking a foolish question, because what he had just done was a great sign. Chrysostom remarks: "What insanity! Was it necessary for him to perform a sign to stop the evil things they were doing? Was not his manifestation of such zeal for the house of God the greatest sign of his power?"[84]

33. (Verse 19). *Jesus answered and said to them.* This verse touches on the second point, that is, the offer of the sign asked for. And he also offers them the sign of his

---

[81] Bonaventure uses *oblatio* which means "the offering of a response," but also "the offering of a sacrifice." See his comment on John 2:19 (n. 33) below.

[82] Note Bonaventure's word play: *postula*tio *obla*tio, *exposi*tio, *edificatio*.

[83] On p. 276 n. 1 QuarEd accurately indicate that the Vulgate begins with *dicentes* ("saying") while Bonaventure reads *dic nobis* ("tell us").

[84] See Homily 23 n. 2 in PG 59:140. Bonaventure's citation is a paraphrase.

greatest power in his rising from the dead. So he says: *Destroy this temple*, that is, by killing. *Destroy*, that is, you will destroy, *and in three days I will raise it up*, that is, I will rise up as if from sleep. For in Scripture death is called sleep, and resurrection rising up. Psalm 3:6 states: "I have slept and have taken my rest," etc.[85] *In three days* is to be taken as synecdoche. Hosea 6:3 says: "He will revive us after two days, and on the third day he will raise us up," namely, by the head.

34. (Verse 20). *The Jews, therefore, said to him.*[86] The next three verses deal with the third point, that is, the explanation of the sign offered, since he was not talking about the physical temple, but of the temple of his body whereas the Jews understood him to be speaking about the physical temple. So the text continues: *Therefore, the Jews said: It took forty-six years for this temple to be built, and you will raise it up in three days?* As if to say: This is entirely incredible and impossible for you. Understand that the construction of the first temple took seven years,[87] but because of wars and obstacles the building of the second one under Zerubbabel took forty-six years.[88]

---

[85] Psalm 3:6 concludes: "and I have risen up, because the Lord has protected me."

[86] On p. 276 n. 5 QuarEd rightly indicate that the Vulgate does not read *ei* ("to him').

[87] See 1 Kgs 6:38: "... and he (Solomon) was seven years in building it."

[88] See Ezra 3-6 and Philip J. King and Lawrence E. Stager, *Life in Biblical Israel* (Louisville: Westminster John Knox, 2001), p. 385: "Cyrus (in 538 B.C.E.) also granted the returnees permission to rebuild the Temple in Jerusalem.... Work on the Temple in Jerusalem, however, began in earnest after 520 B.C.E., when another wave of Jewish returnees arrived with Zerubbabel, a 'governor of Judah' and the last descendant of the Davidic dynasty mentioned in the Bible ... the Second Temple was completed in five years (by 515 B.C.E.)."

The Lord did not have in mind this temple.[89] So the text adds:

35. (Verse 21). *But he was speaking of the temple of his body*. For if our bodies "are the temples of the Holy Spirit," as 1 Corinthians 6:19, how much more the body of Christ, "in whom dwells the Godhead in bodily form," as Colossians 2:9 says.[90] Neither the Jews nor the carnally minded disciples possess this spiritual understanding, but after the resurrection they will. So the text continues:

36. (Verse 22). *When, therefore, he had risen from the dead, his disciples remembered that he had said this* about his body. For at that time he opened their minds to understand. Luke 24:45 states: "And he opened their minds to understand the Scriptures." *And* from that time on *they believed the Scripture*, for in it was prefigured Christ's resurrection as that of Jonah.[91] *And they also believed the word that Jesus had spoken*, because through his word he had foretold it. John 14:29 below reads: "Now I have told you before it comes to pass that when it has come to pass, you may believe."

37. (Verse 23). *Now when he was in Jerusalem*. This verse conveys the fourth point, that is, the building up of the faith of the Jews, who had seen his powerful signs. For one has to presume that he performed many signs, although the Evangelist did not mention them, as

---

[89] On p. 276 n. 6 QuarEd write: "Some ... are of the opinion that the temple mentioned here is the one that Herod had restored."

[90] Col 2:9 reads: "In him dwells all the fullness of the Godhead in bodily form."

[91] Jonah 2:1 says: "Now the Lord prepared a great fish to swallow up Jonah, and Jonah was in the belly of the fish three days and three nights."

Chrysostom observes.[92] So the text adds: *Now when he was at Jerusalem for the feast of Passover*, for which he had gone up, *many believed in his name, seeing the signs that he was performing*. Their faith was based on signs. John 7:31 says: "Many of the crowd, however, believed in him, seeing the signs he was performing."[93] And since they were basing their faith on signs, their faith was weak. So the text continues:

38. (Verse 24). *But Jesus did not trust himself to them*, not because he was afraid, but because he knew their weakness. And he showed how he knew this, since he knew people, not by exterior relationships as humans do, but by vision of the interior as God does: *In that he knew all men and women*. 1 Samuel 16:7 states: "Human beings see the exterior appearance, but God beholds the heart."[94]

39. (Verse 25). *And since there was no need that anyone should bear witness to him*[95] *concerning human beings, for he himself knew what was in them*. Jeremiah 17:10 states:

---

[92] See Homily 17 n. 3 in PG 59:111-112 and FC 33, p. 169: "From this it is reasonable to conclude that both these details, and many more besides, have been omitted, and this our Evangelist himself has plainly said at the end of his Gospel.... As for His miracles, they conceded some of them to certain Evangelists to relate, others to others, and they were all silent about still others."

[93] John 7:31 reads: "Many of the crowd, however, believed in him, and they kept saying: When the Christ comes, will he perform more signs than this man performs?"

[94] On p. 277 n. 2 QuarEd accurately indicate that the Vulgate reads *homo* ("a human being") while Bonaventure has *homines* ("human beings"). Further, the Vulgate reads *Dominus* ("the Lord") while Bonaventure has *Deus* ("God").

[95] On p. 277 n. 3 QuarEd rightly mention that the Vulgate places *ei* ("to/for him") in the "since" clause whereas Bonaventure puts it in the second clause. The Vulgate goes: "And since he had no need that anyone should bear witness concerning human beings.... "

"I am the Lord who searches the heart and ... innards." Hebrews 4:12 says: "The word of the Lord is living and efficacious and keener than any two-edged sword, and extending even to the division of soul and spirit, of joints also and of marrow, and a discerner of the thoughts and intentions of the heart."

QUESTIONS

40. Question 1 deals with the Lord's statement to the Jews in John 1:19: "Destroy." It seems that he commanded them to kill him. – My answer is that Scripture sometimes uses the imperative as an imperative. See Qoheleth 12:13: "Fear God and observe Godís commandments." Sometimes in a predictive way as here. The Glossa comments: "*Destroy*, that is, you will destroy."[96] At other times as a counsel as in Matthew 19:21: "Go and sell all that you have and give to the poor." Also as a permission; see Matthew 8:31: "If you cast us out, send us into the pigs."[97] Finally, as irony. John 13:27 has these words of the Lord to Judas about his betrayal: "Do quickly what you are doing."

41. Question 2 comes from Chrysostom and concerns the sign of his resurrection that the Lord always gives to the Jews.[98] For example, it is said in Matthew 12:39 and 16:4

---

[96] This is the Glossa Interlinearis.

[97] On p. 277 n. 6 QuarEd correctly notice that the Vulgate reads *gregem porcorum* ("herd of pigs").

[98] See Homily 23 n. 2 in PG 59:140-141. I have modified the translation of FC 33, "Therefore, he did not give them a sign and when, before this also, they had come and asked for one, he gave the same answer: 'An evil and adulterous generation demands a sign, and no sign will be given it but the sign of Jonah.' Then, however, he answered more clearly, but now more ambiguously; and this he did because of their extreme folly."

that "no sign will be given them,[99] but the sign of Jonah the prophet." Now since they would not understand the sign, why was he giving it to them? And if he were giving it to them, why didn't he do it in such a way that they would understand it?

I answer that he gave this sign to them, since it was the greatest and because it was secret. It was the greatest, since to be able to liberate oneself from death even after death is the most new, most noble, and most wondrous of all new things. It was also secret in that he gave it to them and spoke about it enigmatically, for through his just judgment he was manifesting himself in such a way that he remained hidden, until he would manifest himself after the resurrection. If he had completely manifested himself, he would never have died. Therefore, he points them to the time of his resurrection. So he was speaking enigmatically to them and also to his disciples, since, even if they would have understood at that time, they were about to understand more dearly[100] later on.[101]

42. Question 3 inquires: Why did the Lord say that he was a temple and compare himself to a temple? – Augustine answers that he said this not only because of the indwelling of Divinity, but also because of his similarity

---

[99] The Vulgate in both Matt 12:39 and 16:4 reads *ei* ("to it," which refers to "generation") while Bonaventure has *eis* ("to them").

[100] On p. 277 n. 9 QuarEd make special mention that the reading is *carius* ("more dearly") and not *clarius* ("more clearly"). Obviously, *carius* is the *lectio difficilior*.

[101] See Chrysostom's Homily 23 n. 2 in PG 59:141 and FC 33, p. 228: "What, then, did Christ reply? 'Destroy this temple, and in three days I will raise it up.' Many such things He said which were not clear to those who heard them at the time, but would be to others afterwards. And why did He do this? That when the fulfillment of the prophecy came He might be proved to have foreseen beforehand events to happen later."

to the temple. Thus, just as the temple was built in forty-six years, so too the conceived fetus is formed for forty-six days,[102] and forty-six times six days later, is born.[103] – But it seems that this is not a valid position, since the body of Christ was perfect from the instant of conception, as well as his soul. Also he had the use of free will. – For this reason it has to be said that the body becomes perfect in two ways: either by organization or by strength. Bodies other than the body of Christ before that time or during that time were built up and became perfect, that is, grew to perfection in organization and strength. But the body of Christ only in strength, not in distinctness of his members.[104]

---

[102] See Hugh of St. Cher, p. 294a: "Just as the temple in forty-six years, so too the body of Christ in forty-six days.... "

[103] I quote Question 56 (On the Forty-Six Years for the Building of the Temple) in its entirety from FC 70, p. 98: "The numbers 6 + 9 + 12 + 10 + 8 make 45. Therefore I add 1 and they make 46. This times 6 makes 276. Now it is said that human fetal development reaches completion in the following way. In the first six days [the fetus] is similar to a kind of milk, in the following nine days it is changed to blood, then in the following twelve days it becomes solid, in the remaining ten and eight days the features of all its members achieve complete formation, and in the remaining time until birth it grows in size. Therefore to forty-five days add 1, which signifies the sum (because 6, 9, 12, 10, and 8 brought together into one sum make 45); add 1, as was said, and the result is 46. When this number is multiplied by 6, which stands at the head of the series, 276 results, i.e., nine months and six days.... Therefore, it is not absurd to say that the temple, which signified his body, was built in forty-six years, so that there were as many years in the construction of the temple as there were days in the completing of the Lord's body."

[104] See Book III, d. 3. p. II. n. 3 of Bonaventure's *Sentence Commentary*.

CHAPTER THREE

1. *Now there was a certain[1] man*, etc. Earlier in this chapter the Lord manifested himself to the Jews by a sign of power, here in a second instance he manifests himself through a *word of teaching*, instructing all Jews through the person of Nicodemus, a ruler of the Jews. And since the word of teaching requires an attentive ear for it to be grasped, the first point to be noted is *Nicodemus's diligence*. Second comes the *Lord's teaching* where verse 3 says: "Jesus answered and said to him."

JOHN 3:1-2
THE DILIGENCE OF NICODEMUS

So four characteristics describe Nicodemus and show that he was a suitable learner: *the goodness of his life, the dignity of his office, his desire to learn, his aptitude to learn.*

2. (Verse 1). So first he is described from his goodness of life. The text says: *There was a man among the Pharisees, Nicodemus by name. From the Pharisees*, which was the

---

[1] The Vulgate does not read *quidam* ("a certain").

best and most respectable sect of all the Jewish sects. Thus, the Apostle, in Philippians 3:5, glories that he was "with regard to the Law, a Pharisee."[2] – The dignity of his office also helps to describe him, as the text reads: *A ruler of the Jews.* In this capacity he tried to quell the furor of the Jews in John 7:51 below: "Does our Law judge a person without first giving him a hearing?" – His desire for learning also characterizes him, since it is said of him:

3. (Verse 2). *This man came to Jesus at night.* So he came at night, so that he might be instructed and taught at a more leisurely pace, since things were quiet during the night hours. So Psalm 118:62 says: "I rose at midnight to give praise to you." – The Evangelist depicts his aptitude for learning when he says: *And said to him,* namely, to Jesus: *Rabbi, we know that you have come as a teacher from God.* For he was eager to be taught, because he had come to be taught and believed that Christ was the perfect teacher, and he wanted to become his disciple. For this reason he calls him *teacher,* as disciples are wont to call their instructors. John 13:13 below reads: "You call me teacher and Lord." And he states the reason behind his statements: *No one can perform the signs that you are doing unless God is with him.*[3] So it is obvious that he was among those, about whom it was said in John 2:23 above: "Many believed in his name, seeing the signs[4] that he was performing." The signs were his reason for believing that

---

[2] See Augustine's Sermon 106 n. 2 in *Sermons* III/4, p. 107: "These Pharisees were Jews, the cream of the Jews, you could say; at that time, you see, the Pharisees were considered to be the more respectable and learned among them."

[3] On p. 278 n. 7 QuarEd rightly notice that the Vulgate reads *enim* ("for") as the second word of this sentence. Bonaventure does not have *enim.*

[4] On p. 278 n. 7 QuarEd rightly indicate that the Vulgate reads *signa eius* ("his signs").

he was from God. Therefore, the blind man says in 9:33 below: "If this man were not from God, he would be able to do nothing."[5]

QUESTIONS

4. Question 1 focuses on what John 3:1 says about Nicodemus that "he was a ruler of the Jews" and about his belief in Jesus which is inferred from John 7:48 below: "Has anyone from the rulers believed in him...?"[6] As if to say, No. – I answer that Nicodemus believed and was from the rulers. And John 7:48 stems from the Pharisees, who were deceived. For Nicodemus believed, although not openly, but secretly.[7]

5. Question 2 asks about the hour, since that hour was the hour for evildoers and those "who do evil and hate the light."[8] How is it that Nicodemus wanted to come at night? It seems that he came for some inordinate purpose. – I answer that in this situation there was a certain embarrassment, weakness, and diligence. With regard to embarrassment Victor comments: "He came at night, because a teacher in Israel was embarrassed to

---

[5] On p. 278 n. 8 QuarEd accurately mention that the Vulgate simply reads *hic* ("this one") while Bonaventure has *hic homo* ("this man") and that the Vulgate reads *non poterat facere* ("could do nothing") while Bonaventure has *non posset facere* ("would not be able to do").

[6] John 7:48 concludes: "or of the Pharisees."

[7] See Bede's commentary on John 7:48 in PL 92:734BC: "For the learned Pharisees have become blind, while the people, who did not know the Law, have become enlightened and believed in the author of the Law. Nicodemus, however, one of the Pharisees ... and he himself was not an unbeliever, but was timid (that is why he came at night to the light, since he wanted to be enlightened and was afraid of being found out). He responded to the Jews: 'Does our law judge....'"

[8] See John 3:20.

learn in public."[9] With respect to weakness Chrysostom remarks: "Jewish weakness still held him fast. Therefore, he came at night, in fear and trembling to do this during the day."[10] Concerning diligence Bede observes: "He came at night, wishing through Christ's secret address to him to grasp the mysteries of faith, whose rudiments he had already at times glimpsed."[11]

6. The third question concerns John 3:2: "No one can perform these things that you are doing unless God were with him." – Against this is what Matthew 7:22 states: "Many will say to me on that day: Lord, in your name we cast out demons," etc.[12] – Some answer this question by stressing the words: "unless God were with him." For there is a difference between saying "God is with a person" and "a person is with God." And it seems that this is what Augustine wants to say in his *Confessions*: "You were with me, yet I was not with you."[13] Thus, the statement, "a person is with God," means that the person

---

[9] This quotation is from Bishop Victor of Capua. See the Glossa Ordinaria in PL 114:366A: "Night signifies the letter of the law, or ignorance of the heart, or fear. And so he comes at night, perhaps because as a teacher in Israel he was embarrassed to speak in public, or on account of fear of the Jews." The Glossa reads *dicere* ("to speak") while Victor has *discere* ("to learn").

[10] See Homily 24 n. 1 in PG 59:144. Bonaventure's quotation is not verbatim.

[11] See Bede's commentary on John 3:1 in PL 92:667D: "The ruler of the Jews came to Jesus at night, wishing to learn more fully through his secret address to him the mysteries of faith, whose rudiments he had already at times perceived through the public manifestation of signs."

[12] Hugh of St. Cher, p. 294v, k has his own way of addressing this same question and also cites Matt 7:22.

[13] See Book X, c. 27. n. 38. See *Saint Augustine, Confessions*, trans. Vernon J. Bourke, FC 21 (New York: Fathers of the Church, 1953), p. 297: "Late have I loved you, O Beauty so ancient and so new, late have I loved you! And behold, you were within and I was without. I was looking for you out there, and I threw myself, deformed as I was, upon

has love, by which he is joined to God. God is with a person, however, when God produces some special effect or gift in that person. Thus God is with those to whom he bestows the power of performing miracles. – But this discussion does not solve the problem, since Nicodemus did not intend to say this. Rather his point was that Jesus was from God.[14]

So the case has to be made that even though good and evil people perform miracles, the good are to be distinguished from the evil in manner and purpose. In manner, since the good perform miracles through public righteousness, whereas the evil perform them through ensigns of public righteousness. In purpose, for the good perform miracles to edify while evil people perform them for their own glory. Now Nicodemus distinguished miracles according to manner and purpose.[15] And he was led to his knowledge about Christ especially through the fact that Christ did not perform his miracles by invocation.[16]

---

those well-formed things which you have made. You were with me, yet I was not with you."

[14] See John 3:2: "We know that you have come a teacher from God."

[15] Bonaventure borrows this distinction from Augustine's answer to the question, "Why did Pharaoh's magicians perform certain miracles in the manner of Moses the servant of God." See Question 79 n. 4 in FC 70, p. 203: "When, therefore, magicians do things of a kind which the saints sometimes do, indeed their deeds appear to the eye to be alike, but they are done for a different purpose and under a different law. For the former act seeking their own glory; the latter, the glory of God.... Consequently, it is one thing for magicians to perform miracles, another for good Christians, and another for evil Christians. Magicians do so through private contracts, good Christians through a public righteousness, and evil Christians through the 'ensigns' or symbols of this public righteousness."

[16] See Bede's commentary on Luke 5:13 in CCSL cxx, p. 117: "*I will it. Be cleansed.* And immediately the leprosy left him. There is no intermediary between the work of God and the command, because in the command is the work."

John 3:3-21
Christ's teaching to Nicodemus

7. *Jesus answered and said to him*, etc. Having described Nicodemus's diligence, the Evangelist now depicts *Christ's teaching*, through which he instructs Nicodemus how he can come to salvation, for he had come to seek this. And this part has three sections according to the three things that Christ teaches him. First he teaches him *the way of salvation*. Second he teaches *the beginning of salvation* where verse 13 says: "No one has ascended into heaven." Third he teaches what is *an impediment to salvation* where verse 17 reads: "For God did not send his Son," etc.

John 3:3-12
Christ teaches Nicodemus the way of salvation

8. (Verse 3). So first he teaches what the way of salvation is: The sacrament of regeneration. In giving this instruction, he proceeds in the following order. First, he expresses *the necessity of regeneration*. Second, *the manner of regeneration*. Third, *the way of understanding*.

So Christ expresses the necessity of rebirth to Nicodemus who was desirous of learning. So the text goes: *Jesus answered and said to him*, that is, to Nicodemus who had come seeking at night, *Amen, amen I say to you: Unless a person be born again*, that is, regenerated, *that person cannot see the kingdom of God*. From this it is obvious that regeneration is necessary for salvation.

There is a birth of nature. John 16:21 says: "A woman about to give birth has sorrow ... but when she has brought forth ... she does not remember ... her anguish for her joy that a human being has been born into the world." – There is a birth of sin. Ephesians 2:3 reads: "We were by nature children of wrath." By nature, that is, by the corruption of nature. Thus Job 3:3 states: "Let the day perish on which I was born." – There is a birth of grace. I John 5:18 has: "No one, who is born of God, commits sin, but the grace[17] of God preserves him." And this happens through the sacrament. – There is a birth of glory. Job 11:17 says: "When you think that you have been consumed, you will rise like the daystar." – So this passage treats of the necessary birth from sacrament and grace.

9. (Verse 4). *Nicodemus said to him*. This verse introduces the second consideration, that is, the manner of regeneration, which is spiritual. But Nicodemus, thinking that this regeneration is carnal, has doubts and asks: *How can a person be born when he is old*? As if: This is impossible that an old person become a youth. Job 7:6 says: "My days have passed more swiftly than the web is cut by a weaver and are consumed without any hope." It is also impossible on the part of the generating. So the text continues: *Can a person enter a second time into his mother's womb and be born again*? He was still carnal, and therefore was thinking in a carnal manner. 1 Corinthians 2:14 reads: "The sensual person does not perceive the things that are of the Spirit." But the Lord is drawing him from a carnal understanding to a spiritual one. For this reason he says:

10. (Verse 5). *Jesus answered: Amen, amen I say to you: Unless a person be born again of water and the Holy Spirit,*

---

[17] On p. 279 n. 10 QuarEd correctly mention that the Vulgate reads *generatio* ("generation") while Bonaventure has *gratia* ("grace").

he cannot enter into the kingdom of God.[18] As if he were saying: I do not mean the birth that issues from the womb, but that which issues from water. I do not mean the birth that issues from semen, but what issues from the Holy Spirit. For the first is carnal and manifest, whereas the second is spiritual and secret. Therefore, he adds:

11. (Verse 6). *That which is born of the flesh is flesh, and that which is born of the Spirit is spirit.* So just as generation from the flesh is carnal, so too is generation from the Spirit spiritual. John 1:13 above says: "Who were born not of blood, nor of the will of the flesh, nor of the will of men and women, but of God." Not only is this birth spiritual, but is also hidden. And wherefore, sensual Nicodemus should not marvel that he does not understand it. So the text continues:

12. (Verse 7). *Do not wonder that I said to you: You must be born again*, although you may not understand.

13. (Verse 8). *The Spirit blows where it wills. Where it wills*, bestowing grace. Romans 9:18 states: "God has mercy upon whom he wills, and he hardens whom he wills." *And you hear his voice*, in the preachers. Matthew 10:20 reads: "For it is not you who are speaking, but the Spirit of your Father who is speaking in you." *And you do not know where it comes from or where it goes.* Job 9:11 has: "If he comes to me, I will not see him. And if he departs, I will not understand." *So is everyone who is born of the Spirit*, namely, spiritual and hidden. Romans 6:4 says: "For we were buried with him by means of baptism into his death, in order that, just as Christ has risen from the dead through the glory of the Father, so we too may

---

[18] The Vulgate reads *Spiritu* ("Spirit") while Bonaventure has *Spiritu sancto* ("Holy Spirit").

walk in newness of life." Just as burial and death and life are spiritual, so too is generation.

14. (Verse 9). *Nicodemus answered.* The third point occurs here, that is, the way of understanding this spiritual regeneration. Since Nicodemus lacks it, he is in doubt and searching. Thus, the text continues: *Nicodemus answered and said to him: How can these things be?* Nicodemus's question indicates his diligence, for he did not stop searching until he understood. Chrysostom observes: "If the Jews had heard this, they would have immediately derided him and departed."[19] And so the person who is captivated by intellect and faith merits the Lord's more complete instruction.[20] So he humiliates him. For this reason the text adds:

15. (Verse 10). *Jesus answered and said to him: Are you a teacher in Israel and do not know these things?* As if he were saying: You regard yourself as a learned teacher, but don't know the elementary things about faith. Hebrews 5:12 reads: "Although by this time you ought to be masters, you need to be taught again the rudiments of the words of God." As if he were saying: If you want to understand, you must humble yourself and believe since, if you do not believe this, you will be unable to understand the greater things. So the text continues:

---

[19] See Homily 24 n. 2 in PG 59:145-146. The main variation between Bonaventure's citation and Chrysostom's text is Bonaventure's addition of *statim* ("immediately").

[20] On p. 280 n. 5 QuarEd rightly suggest that Bonaventure may be alluding to 2 Cor 10:5: "... bringing every mind into captivity to the obedience of Christ."

16. (Verse 11). *Amen, amen I say to you that we ourselves*[21] *speak of what we know.* "We ourselves, that is, my apostles and I," as the Glossa remarks.[22] Another interpretation is to take we as a plural that intimates the mystery of the Trinity. *And we bear witness to what we have seen.* John 8:38 below states: "What I have seen with the Father, this I speak about."[23] And therefore, people should believe me. But nonetheless, you do not believe. So the text adds: *And our witness you do not receive.* John 5:43 below says: "I came in the name of my Father, and you did not receive me." And if you did not receive and accept the small things I said to you and did not believe, how much less will you accept and believe with regard to weighty matters. So the text continues:

17. (Verse 12). *If I have spoken of earthly things to you and you do not believe, how will you believe if I speak to you of heavenly things?* As if he were saying: You will not. So the way to understanding is to believe through faith the lesser matters before being led to the sublime. 1 Corinthians 3:1-2 reads: "As little ones in Christ I fed you with milk, not with solid food." But if they could not take milk, how could they take solid food? – Therefore, from the aforementioned it is clear that regeneration is necessary, spiritual, hidden and that no one can understand it without faith.

---

[21] On p. 280 n. 7 QuarEd accurately indicate that the Vulgate does not read *nos* ("we ourselves").

[22] See the Glossa Interlinearis: "We ourselves, namely, with the prophets and apostles."

[23] On p. 280 n. 8 QuarEd correctly mention that the Vulgate does not read *hoc* ("this").

Questions

18. Question 1 deals with John 3:3: "Unless a person be born again, he cannot see the kingdom of God." – Contra. 1. If this were a precept, then it follows that only those baptized by water and the Holy Spirit can be saved. But against this interpretation is the fact that there were many martyrs who had not been baptized. Furthermore, there are many who had faith, but died an unexpected death. Yet it says in John 3:15 below that "all who believe in the Son of God do not perish."[24] Consequently, even though a person is not baptized, that person will still be saved. – 2. Now if this statement is not a precept, then he is speaking poorly when he says in John 3:5, "the person cannot enter into the kingdom of God," for in John 3:3 "to see" is equivalent to a vision of the heavenly homeland.[25]

I respond that one has to bear in mind that there is a baptism of flood, flame, and flowing blood.[26] Therefore, one has to admit that by common law all are bound to be baptized, for it is a precept. Now if an impossibility occurs, either the grace of baptism of flame or blood is present or not. If it is, then it supplies for the baptism of water whose administration is impossible. But if all three are absent, this impossibility does not provide an excusing cause nor bring about salvation, not because of the transgression of the precept, but because of the stain of original sin, which has not been wiped away by grace.

---

[24] Bonaventure's citation of John 3:15 makes his point about the power of faith without baptism. John 3:15 reads: "that all who believe in him (Son of Man) may not perish, but may have life everlasting."

[25] Bonaventure is addressing the similarities and dissimilarities between the wording of John 3:3 and 3:5.

[26] This is my attempt to capture into English Bonaventure's mnemonic *baptismus fluminis, flaminis, sanguinis*. Hugh of St. Cher, p. 296b also has these three types of baptism.

– And so it is clear that those who have a formed faith are saved, even though they are prevented from being baptized by an unexpected death.[27]

19. Question 2 asks whether John 3:5 is the basis for the necessity of baptism. It seems that it is: 1. Since the pronouncement is promulgated here that without it there was no salvation. – 2. Moreover, if it was not instituted here, then when was baptism instituted?

Master Hugh answers by distinguishing between three times of grace.[28] In one period there was only circumcision, and that was before the coming of Christ. There is another period in which there is only baptism, and that was after the manifestation of the Gospel. There is a period, a kind of middle time, in which both exist mixed. Circumcision then was having its effect, and at that time there was no necessity to be baptized. Nor had the Lord promulgated by decree the necessity of regeneration, but he revealed to a friend that he was about to do this.[29]

2. Relative to the question about when baptism was instituted, this should be the answer. Materially when Christ was baptized. *Formally* when he rose and gave

---

[27] See Book IV. d. 4. p. II. a. 1. q. 1 and 2 of Bonaventure's *Sentence Commentary*.

[28] Bonaventure or tradition before him summarizes Book II, Part 6, c. 4 of Hugh of St. Victor's *De Sacramentis Fidei Christianae*. See PL 176:449D-450C. Hugh of St. Cher, p. 296b gives an even briefer summary of Hugh of St. Victor.

[29] See Book II, Part 6, c. 5 in PL 176:451A for this last section of Bonaventure's citation of Victor: "a counsel was revealed to a friend." The "friend" here is Nicodemus, as Victor's quotation of John 3:5 makes clear. Hugh of St. Cher, p. 296b speaks of Christ's revelation of the future of baptism to "his disciple who was searching as a friend."

it its form in Matthew 28:19.[30] Effectively when he suffered, since from his suffering it derived its efficacy. But purposefully in this passage when he predicted its necessity and utility when he said: "Unless a person is reborn of water and the Holy Spirit," etc.[31]

20. Question 3 concerns the meaning of John 3:6: "What is born of the flesh is flesh." – 1. So "what is born of the Spirit is spirit."[32] Therefore, what is born of the holy, is holy. Wherefore, a holy person begets a holy person, namely, a son. This is obviously false. The child is not holy, but a sinner. – 2. Furthermore, if what is born of the Spirit is spirit, it follows that what is born of God is God. But all of us are born of God, as 1 John 5:1-4 says.[33] Therefore, all of us are gods.

I answer that these things have to be understood according to their own nature and essence.[34] Thus, what is born through the generation of the flesh, that is, in as far as it is flesh, is flesh. The same holds with regard to what is generated by the Spirit. It is spiritual. – 1. With respect to the objection about the holy man, this is the response. He is generating in a fleshly manner and therefore generates something that is fleshly. Wherefore, even though he is cleansed with regard to his person, he

---

[30] Matt 28:19 reads: "Go, therefore, and make disciples of all nations, baptizing them in the name of the Father, and of the Son, and of the Holy Spirit."

[31] Bonaventure employs the four causes to explain baptism's institution.

[32] See John 3:6.

[33] 1 John 5:1-4 states: "Everyone who believes that Jesus is the Christ is born of God. And everyone who loves him who begot, loves also the one begotten of him.... Because all that is born of God overcomes the world; and this is the victory that overcomes the world, our faith."

[34] The Latin is *per se*.

is, nevertheless, not cleansed with regard to the principle of generation. Augustine gives the example of the grain of wheat that has been cleansed of its chaff and yet produces a grain that has chaff.[35] – 2. What is said about the Spirit is not meant essentially, but by means of conformity or adherence. 1 Corinthians 6:17 states: "The person who adheres to God is one spirit."[36]

21. Question 4 concerns John 3:8: "The Spirit[37] blows where it wills ... and you do not know where it comes from." – To the contrary is what Bernard says in his work on The Song of Songs: Every person has to recognize the time of spiritual visitation.[38]

Chrysostom answers that he said this about the wind since human beings do not comprehend it, much less where it

---

[35] See Book III, c. 8 n. 16 of Augustine's *Answers to the Pelagians: The Punishment and Forgiveness of Sins and the Baptism of Little Ones*, ..., introduction, translation, and notes by Roland J. Teske, WSA I/23 (Hyde Park, NY: New City Press, 1997), p. 130: "Since it bothers them that a sin which is washed away in baptism is present in those whom the baptized parents generate, how do they themselves explain that the foreskin that is removed by circumcision is present in those whom circumcised parents generate? How too is the chaff which is so carefully removed by human labor still found in grain which grows from wheat that has been threshed?"

[36] On p. 281 n. 8 QuarEd rightly intimate that the Vulgate reads *Domino* ("to the Lord") while Bonaventure has *Deo* ("to God").

[37] In this question Bonaventure deals with the dual meaning of *spiritus* ("Spirit" or "wind").

[38] Bonaventure seems to refer to Homily 57 n. 2. See *Bernard of Clairvaux On the Song of Songs III*, trans. Kilian Walsh and Irene M. Edmonds, CFS 31 (Kalamazoo: Cistercian Publications, 1979), p. 96: "Nor is she one of those who are rightly blamed by the Lord for not knowing how to judge the look of the sky while being unaware of the time of his coming. So sagacious is she, so experienced, so keenly vigilant, that she espied him coming a long way off, she heeded him leaping as he sped along, bounding over the proud, that through lowliness he might draw near to her lowly person." See SBOp 2.120.

comes from.[39] – But Augustine rejects this interpretation because human beings are well acquainted with the nature of winds, that the south wind comes from the south and tends to blow north. Therefore, he interprets *spiritus* as a reference to the Holy Spirit.[40]

One has to take the words at face value when the text says: "You do not know where it comes from." The text does not say: "You do not know when it comes," for a person can know quite well when it comes because of fervor and tepidity. But you do not know where it comes from, whether in the present as a reward for good deeds that a person has performed or to increase merits. You do not know where it is going, whether faraway, never to return again or nearby, from which it will quickly return. Therefore, Bernard says that a person must always be fearful: "Fear," he says, "when it smiles on you. Fear, when it departs, and when it returns again."[41]

---

[39] See Homily 26 n. 2 in PG 59:155 and FC 33, 254: "Accordingly, the expression 'blows where it will' is that of one showing the impossibility of restraining the wind, and that it streams forth everywhere, and that there is no one who can prevent it from being carried here and there; but it is dispersed very freely, and no one is strong enough to turn aside its onset."

[40] See Tractate 12 n. 7 in *St. Augustine Tractates on the Gospel of John 11-27*, trans. John W. Rettig, FC 79 (Washington: CUA Press, 1988), p. 35: "'The Spirit breathes where he will and you hear his voice but do not know where he comes from and where he goes.' Is [that] an earthly thing? Yes, if he was speaking about that wind which you know, as some have understood, when it was asked of them what earthly thing the Lord spoke when he said, 'If I have spoken earthly things to you, and you do not believe, how will you believe if I shall speak to you heavenly things?'"

[41] See Homily 54 n. 9 on The Song of Songs in SBOp 2.108. Bonaventure's citation has purposely omitted Bernard's key word *gratia* ("grace"), so that "it" may refer to the Holy Spirit.

22. Question 5 refers to John 3:12: "If I have spoken of earthly things," etc. What are these earthly things, for he has been speaking entirely about spiritual matters and has said nothing about earthly matters? – Chrysostom gives the answer that the earthly things, which he mentioned, are those things he said about *"spiritus,"* that is, about the wind.[42] But Augustine interprets them to refer to the raising up of the temple, which he had foretold in the preceding chapter, namely, with respect to its origin from the earth, whether this is understood of the material temple or of Christ's body, which was assumed from our earth.[43] – There can be yet another answer: He calls those things about which he had already spoken earthly not in an absolute sense, but since they were down to earth in comparison to the things about which he was going to speak.

John 3:13-16
The beginning and source of salvation

23. (Verse 13). *And no one has ascended into heaven.* Earlier he had determined the way of salvation. Now he determines *the source of salvation*, so that he might fully satisfy Nicodemus's questions about how these things

---

[42] See Homily 27 n. 1 in PG 59:157 and FC 33, 260: "Now, the phrase 'earthly things' here refers to the wind, according to the opinion of some."

[43] See Tractate 12 n. 7 in FC 79, pp. 35-36: "Can it be that which he had said about raising up the temple again? For he had received his body from the earth and he was preparing to raise up the very earth taken from earthly body. For it was not believed that he was going to raise up earth. He said, 'If I have spoken earthly things to you, and you do not believe, how will you believe if I shall speak to you heavenly things?' That is, if you do not believe that I can raise up the temple thrown down by you, how will you believe that men can be reborn through the Spirit?"

can happen. He follows this order in describing the source of salvation. First he determines who and what are *the saving source*. Second, what *the manner of saving* is. Finally, what *reason urges salvation*.

The source that saves us is he who alone can enter heaven by himself and all others through him. And this one is Christ the Lord. Therefore, the text says: *And no one has ascended into heaven*, that is, no one has the power to ascend there, *except the one who has descended from heaven*, through the assumption of humanity. *The Son of Man, who is in heaven*, through the presence and immensity of divinity. Therefore, everyone who ascends and is saved, ascends through him. About this power of ascending and descending Ephesians 4:10 speaks: "The one who descended is the one who also ascended above all the heavens, that he might fill all things." About his existence in heaven John 1:18 above says: "The Only-Begotten Son, who is in the bosom of the Father, he has revealed him." He is the one who made him ascend from death to life. John 8:36 below reads: "If the Son makes you free, you will be free indeed."

24. (Verse 14). *And as Moses lifted up*, etc. This verse touches upon the second point, that is, how the Son of God saves through his passion. Therefore, the text continues: *As Moses lifted up the serpent in the desert*. Numbers 21:9 reads: "Moses made a bronze serpent and set it up as a sign which those who had been bitten looked upon and were healed."[44] *In this way must the Son of Man be lifted*

---

[44] On p. 282 n. 4 QuarEd rightly intimate that Bonaventur's text is different from the Vulgate which I translate: "Moses, therefore, made a bronze serpent and set it up as a sign, which when those who had been bitten looked upon, they were healed."

up, namely, on the ignominious cross, so that all who look upon him in faith may be healed. So the text continues:

25. (Verse 15). *So that everyone who believes in him*[45] *may not perish, but have eternal life.* John 11:25-26 below reads: "Those who believe in me, even if they die, will live. And everyone, who lives and believes in me, will never die." He does a superb job of describing the passion in relationship to its figure, so that it might be more credible. And this is an outstanding figure since, just as in the desert they were not cured by the serpent unless they looked upon it, so too neither are they healed by Christ unless they believe in him.

26. (Verse 16). *For God so loved*, etc. The third point occurs here, that is, the reason that motivates to save in such a way. And this was the immensity of divine love towards lost men and women. For this reason the text states: *For God so loved the world*, that is, human beings who are of the world and sinners, *that he gave his only begotten Son.* Ephesians 2:4-5 says: "God, who is rich in mercy, by reason of his very great love wherewith he has loved us, even when we were dead by reason of our sins, brought us to life together with Christ." It is "very great love," since he gave far more than he should. Romans 8:32 states: "And who did not spare his very own Son,[46] but delivered him for us all." *He gave*, I say, for all with respect to sufficiency, but with respect to efficacy for the chosen and believers.[47] Wherefore, the text adds: *So that*

---

[45] The Vulgate reads *in ipso* ("in him") while Bonaventure has *in eum* ("in him").

[46] The Vulgate of this opening clause is *Qui etiam Filio suo non pepercit* ("Who did not spare even his own Son"). Bonaventure's text omits *etiam* ("even") and adds *proprio* ("very own").

[47] On p. 282 n. 8 QuarEd cite Book III, d. 20 c. 5 of Peter Lombard's *Sentences*: "[Christ] offered himself for all with regard to the

everyone who believes in him may not perish, but may have eternal life. The passion has no power for others, solely for believers, because, as is said in Hebrews 11:6: "Without faith it is impossible to please God."

QUESTIONS

27. Question 1 focuses on John 3:13: "No one has ascended into heaven except him who has descended from heaven." – Contrary. 1. All the saints have ascended, but not one has descended. – 2. Moreover, the body of Christ ascended into heaven, but did not descend from heaven. – 3. Furthermore, if this is understood of Christ, either it is understood about his divine or human nature. It should not be understood of his human nature, because that did not descend from heaven. Therefore, concerning the time under discussion in this verse it was not in heaven. Nor could it be understood of his divine nature, since it does not ascend, because there could be no greater being nor could he change his location.

Some answer that the exception noted here not only includes Christ, who is the head, but also the entire body of Christ. And all those and only those, who pertain to his body, ascend.[48] – But this interpretation cannot stand, since a body does not descend from heaven.[49] – Therefore,

---

sufficiency of the price, but for the chosen only with respect to efficacy, since he effected salvation only for the predestined."

[48] See chapter 39 of Peter Comestor's *Historia Evangelica* in PL 198:1560B: "The sense is: No one ascends except Christ with his body. Or according to the figure of speech by which we say: The Lord did what we do through him. And the sense is: No one ascends except the person God makes ascend."

[49] See Bonaventure's *Gospel of Luke 1-8*, p. 269 on Luke 3:21 (n. 52): "Because 'no one has ascended into heaven except him who has descended from heaven' (John 3:13), that is, unless one is a member of

it has to be understood that the meaning of to ascend in this passage is "by one's own power," and not by a power given from some other source. And thus only Christ could ascend.

2. Relative to the objection about the body, Augustine answers that it is a not an obstacle, for the body is like a garment. So if someone descends from the mountain naked and ascends clothed, nobody ascended except the one who descended.[50] And this is the point. – 3. The answer to the question about what nature was involved is this: in this prayer three things are being said about one hypostasis.[51] To ascend is fitting for it by reason of human nature. To descend is fitting by reason of the relationship of the divine nature to the human, for the divine nature

---

Christ who descended. And this happens only through the sacrament of regeneration." See Thomas Aquinas's commentary on John 3:13 (n. 471) in *Commentary on the Gospel of St. John.* Translated by James A. Weisheipl and Fabian R. Larcher, Aquinas Scripture Series 4 (Albany: Magi Books, 1980), p. 198: "I answer that no one goes up into heaven except Christ and his members, i.e., those believers who are just. Accordingly, the Son of God came down from heaven in order that, by making us his members, he might prepare us to ascend into heaven; now, indeed, in hope, but later in reality. 'He has raised us up, and has given us a place in heaven in Christ' (Eph 2:6)." See Bede in PL 92:670D: "No one ascended into heaven, except Christ in his body, which is the Church."

[50] See Sermon 263A n. 3 in *Sermons*, translation and notes by Edmund Hill, WSA III/7 (Hyde Park, NY: New City Press, 1993), p. 224: "As though he had said, 'Nothing has gone up to heaven except what has come down from heaven.' But what he actually said was, *Nobody has gone up except the one who came down.* This, I mean, referred to the person, not to anything the person had. He descended without the garment of a body, he ascended with the garment of a body; and yet nobody ascended except the one who descended.... After all, if someone climbs a mountain, or a wall, or any high place, with clothes on after coming down without any clothes ... would anybody say it wasn't only the one who came down that went up?"

[51] In this context hypostasis is equivalent to "person." There are two natures, divine and human, in one person or hypostasis.

humbled itself in assuming flesh. But to be in heaven, as then, is according to divine nature pure and simple. And thus everything cannot be twisted to fit one nature, but pertain to one hypostasis.

28. Question 2 stems from Chrysostom and concerns the words "Just as Moses lifted up, etc." in John 3:14: Why, since he is talking about the passion, didn't he say "hanging on the cross" and thereby speak more clearly?[52]

I answer that the Lord was revealing the mystery of the passion to Nicodemus as something honorable, credible, and secret. It was honorable, lest any person who was still carnal might find it despicable and horrific. So he said "lifted up," and not "suspended." It was credible, so that it might lead to faith. Therefore, through the wondrous earlier figure he hinted at the wondrous effect of the passion. It was also secret, so that he would cherish it more lovingly. And so he did not explain it, but left him with space for meditation, so that through that he might make progress and arrive at the gift of understanding.

29. Question 3 treats John 3:15: "So that everyone, who believes in him, may not perish." Therefore, no one, who has faith, will be condemned, not matter how evil the person is. – But if you say, that this verse is to be understood of faith formed by charity, then according to this interpretation no one, who has formed faith, can be

---

[52] See Homily 27 n. 2 in PG 59:158: "Now why didn't he say clearly that he would be crucified rather than leave his readers with an ancient figure?" Chrysostom goes on to give three reasons. See FC 33, p. 262: "In the first place, that they might learn that the old order was akin to the new, and not foreign to the latter; next, that you might know that not unwillingly did He go to His Passion; and, besides, that you might learn that no lasting harm was His as a result of it, and salvation for many was brought forth from it."

condemned. – My answer is that one should recall that this verse refers to true and genuine faith. Now genuine faith excludes fiction and duplicity. For faith is fictitious when a person believes, but does not love or when a person believes and loves, but does not persevere. So true and genuine faith believes, loves, and perseveres, and all such believers will be saved.[53]

John 3:17-21
Impediment to salvation

30. (Verse 17). *For God did not send.* He has already determined what the way and the source of salvation are. Now the Evangelist arrives at the third consideration: the impediment to salvation. First he shows that the impediment to our salvation *is not from God's side.* Second that *it stems from a defect of faith.* Third that *it stems from a lack of good deeds.*

So first he shows that our condemnation does not come from God's side, when he says: *For God did not send,* etc. This verse has to be read as a continuation of the preceding one where I truly said that God gave his Son, *so that everyone, who believes in him, may have eternal life,* not, I say, that believers be condemned. *For God did not send his Son into the world in order to judge the world,* namely, by condemning it, *but the world might be saved through him.* 1 John 3 reads: "In this we have come to know the love of God ... that he has first loved us and sent

---

[53] See Matt 10:22: "Now the person who perseveres to the end will be saved."

his Son as a propitiation for our sins."[54] Therefore, he was sent for propitiation, not for condemnation.

31. (Verse 18). *The person who believes in him is not judged.* This verse introduces the second point that condemnation and judgment issue from *a defect of faith.* And he shows this through the statement that the person who believes will not be judged, but the person who does not believe has already been judged. For this reason the text continues: *The person who believes in me,* namely, in the Son of God, *is not judged.* John 5:24 below states: "He will not come to judgment, but will pass from death to life."[55] *But the person who does not believe has already been judged,* that is, he is considered already condemned. *Because he does not believe in the name of the only begotten Son of God.* For, as it has been said in Acts 4:12, "There is no other name under heaven given to men and women by which we must be saved." And therefore, those who do not believe in his name are rightly condemned.

32. (Verse 19). *And this is the judgment,* etc.[56] The third observation occurs here, that is, the impediment to salvation and the reason for condemnation and judgment issue from a lack of good deeds. Because of this deficiency a human being flees from salvation. Therefore, the text says: *And this is the judgment.* The Glossa comments: "It is the cause of condemnation."[57] *Because the light has come into the world,* that is, the incarnate Word. John

---

[54] Bonaventure's citation is a combination of 1 John 3:16 and 4:10.

[55] On p. 283 n. 10 QuarEd correctly indicate that the Vulgate reads *non venit* ("does not come") while Bonaventure has *non veniet* ("will not come"). Also the Vulgate reads *transit* ("has passed") while Bonaventure has *transiet* ("will pass").

[56] On p. 284 n. 2 QuarEd rightly note that the Vulgate reads *Hoc est autem iudicium* ("Now this is the judgment").

[57] This is the Glossa Interlinearis.

12:46 below reads: "I have come a light into the world that whoever believes in me may not remain in the darkness." *And men and women have loved the darkness,* namely, of error, *rather than the light,* of truth. Job 24:13 states: "They have been rebellious to the light." And the reason for this blindness is the lack of good deeds. For this reason he continues: *For their works were evil.* And he shows that evil deeds are the reason for fleeing away from the light.

33. (Verse 20). *For everyone who does evil hates the light.* Job 24:25 reads: "The eye of the adulterer observes darkness." *And does not come to the light that his deeds may not be exposed,* that is, revealed to be evil. Ephesians 5:11-13: "Have no fellowship with the unfruitful works of darkness, but rather expose them....[58] But all things that are exposed are made manifest by the light." But the contrary is true, that is, that good deeds lead to light. So the text follows:

34. (Verse 21). *But the person who does the truth comes to the light.* Matthew 5:15 says: "No one hides a lamp under a measure, but puts it upon the lamp stand," for good deeds are light. So he also adds: *So that his deeds may be made manifest, for they have been performed in God.* They have been done in God, because they were performed out of love. 1 John 4:16 has: "The person who remains in love remains in God, and God in him." God is the supreme light, and therefore, these deeds have been revealed for God's honor. Matthew 5:16 reads: "So let your light shine before men and women, so that they may see your good deeds and glorify your Father in heaven."

---

[58] On p. 284 n. 4 QuarEd accurately indicate that the Vulgate does not explicitly mention *illa* ("them"); Bonaventure does.

QUESTIONS

35. Question 1 treats John 3:17: "God did not send his Son into the world to judge it." – Contrary to this is what John 5:22 below states: "The Father has given all judgment to the Son." – I respond that there is a twofold coming. The first is one of mercy while the second is one of justice. In the first he came for the sake of propitiation, not for judgment. However, in the second he will come for judgment.

36. Question 2 concerns the meaning of John 3:18: "The person who does not believe is already judged." – Contrary. If "God does not judge twice with regard to the same matter"[59] and unbelievers are already judged, it follows that they will not be judged on the day of judgment. – If you say that they are fittingly judged, the same holds true of evil Christians.

I respond that there is the judgment of present punishment, and all evildoers are subject to this judgment – for "there is no ugliness of sin without the beauty of justice"[60] – especially unbelievers, for unbelief is a great punishment by itself. There is also the judgment of minute examination, and non-believers are not subject to it. Further, there is the judgment of future retribution. First, all evildoers are judged. Second, those who are lukewarm, either in doing evil or doing good. Finally, all good and all evil people. So it is said that the unbeliever

---

[59] The reference is to the LXX of Nah 1:9: "He will not judge twice about the same matter and bring affliction." I translate the Vulgate: "a double affliction will not arise."

[60] See Book III, c. 15 n. 44 of Augustine's *De Libero Arbitrio* in *Sancti Avrelii Avgvstini Contra Academicos ... De Libero Arbitrio*, ed. W.M. Green, CCSL xxix (Turnhout: Brepols, 1970), p. 301: "so that the ugliness of sin may not exist without the beauty of punishment."

has already been judged either on account of blindness or because he will not be subject to a minute judgment, as Gregory states.[61]

37. Question 3 deals with John 3:20: "Everyone who does evil hates the light." – Contrary is the dictum: "All men and women by nature desire to know."[62] And also *to be happy*. But the evil nature of a deed does not lead to hatred of happiness. Therefore, neither does it lead to hatred of light.

My answer is that light can be understood in a twofold manner. If light is viewed from the angle of its prime effect, according to which it is the source of understanding, no one hates it. If light, however, is viewed from the angle of its secondary effect, which is to highlight turpitude, then since all evildoers abhor this situation they also abhor light since it has this effect. But happiness does not have an effect in the soul contrary to some natural desire, as Augustine has shown.[63]

---

[61] See Book XXVI, c. 27 n. 50 of *Moralia in Iob* in CCSL cxliiib, p. 1304: "So all unbelievers also rise, but for torment, not for judgment. For their case will not be judged at that time, since they proceed before the presence of the sitting judge already with the condemnation for their non-belief." Hugh of St. Cher, p. 298v, l-299 quotes the Glossa of Gregory relative to the four orders of men and women who appear before the judge.

[62] See Book I, c. 1 of Aristotle's *Metaphysica* in WAE, vol. 8, n. 980a.

[63] See, e.g., Sermon 306 n. 3 in *Sermons*, translation and notes Edmund Hill, WSA III/9 (Hyde Park, NY: New City Press, 1994), p. 18: "Every human being, though, of whatever kind or quality, wishes to be happy. There isn't anybody who doesn't want that, and want it in such a way to want it above everything else; or rather, in such a way, that whoever wants other things wants them for the sake of this one thing."

38. Question 4 also concerns John 3:20: If "the person who does evil does not come to the light," then is a sinner ever converted to faith? – It has to be answered that as long as a person continues performing an evil deed, that person does not come to the light. But if the person begins to hate evil, then he can come to the light. And in this manner sinners come to contrition.[64]

JOHN 3:22-36
CHRIST MANIFESTS HIMSELF
THROUGH THE SACRAMENT OF REGENERATION

39. *After these things Jesus came,* etc. The Lord had manifested himself to the Jews by a sign of power and a word of instruction. Now he manifests himself through *the sacrament of regeneration,* by accepting the Jews for baptism. And since both the Lord and John were baptizing, but only the Lord was regenerating, the Evangelist first introduces *the purification* of Christ and John. In second place occurs the excellent *question* that rises in verse 25: "Therefore, a question arose." Third comes *the concluding answer to this question* in verse 27: "John answered."

---

[64] See Augustine's Tractate 12 n. 3 in FC 79, pp. 41-42: "But you come to the light that your works may be made manifest, because they have been done in God, because also this very thing which displeases you, your sin, would not displease you unless God were shedding his light upon you and his truth showing it to you. But he, who even though admonished, loves his own sins, hates the admonishing light and flees it that his evil works which he loves may not be revealed."

John 3:22-24
The purification of Christ and John

40. (Verse 22). So *Christ's purification* by means of baptism is described first. Through this purification he is manifesting himself to the Jews, and so the text says: *After these things*, that is, after the aforementioned manifestations, *Jesus and his disciples came into the land of Judea*, in order that he might manifest himself to the Jews through baptism. So the text adds: *And he stayed there with them*,[65] namely, his disciples, *and was baptizing*. This is according to the testimony that John had borne him in John 1:33 above: "The person upon whom you will see the Spirit descending ... he it is who baptizes...."[66] But he himself was not the only one baptizing, but also his precursor. For this reason the text continues:

41. (Verse 23). *Now John was baptizing in Aenon near Salim.*[67] Now this is the Salem, which was the camp of Melchisedech, about whom Hebrews 7:1 speaks.[68] And the reason follows: *For there was much water there.* This is a good reason since John baptized only with water. Mark 1:8 says of John: "I baptized you with water." *And they came* to him *and were baptized*, even Christ who was baptizing. Matthew 3:5-6 reads: "Jerusalem and all Judea

---

[65] On p. 285 n. 2 QuarEd accurately indicate that the Vulgate reads *eis* ("them") while Bonaventure has *illis* ("them").

[66] John 1:33 reads in full: "And I did not know him, but he who sent me to baptize with water said to me, 'The person upon whom you will see the Spirit descending and abiding upon him, he it is who baptizes with the Holy Spirit.'"

[67] On p. 285 n. 3 QuarEd rightly indicate that the Vulgate reads *Erat autem et Ioannes* ("Now John was also baptizing") whereas Bonaventure does not have *et* ("also").

[68] Hebr 7:1 reads: "For this Melchisedech was king of Salem, priest of the most high God, who met Abraham returning from the slaughter of the kings and blessed him."

and all the region about the Jordan went out to him and were baptized my him."

42. (Verse 24). *For John had not yet been put into prison,*[69] since then his baptism would have ceased with the teacher gone. For it was temporal. Concerning the imprisonment of John Matthew 14:3 states: "Herod had taken John and bound him and sent him to prison," etc.[70]

JOHN 3:25-26
THE QUESTION ABOUT PURIFICATION

43. *So there arose a question*, etc. This verse introduces the question that surfaces from the twofold purification and has its specific origin in the fact that the disciples of John were falsely accusing the Jews of abandoning John's baptism and going over to Christ. Therefore, the text adds:

Verse 25. *So a question arose between the disciples of John*, as if finding its roots in them, *and the Jews*, dissenting among themselves about purification, namely, whether there was a greater purification accomplished by the baptism of John or that of Christ. And the disciples of John were maintaining that John's was greater while the Jews were stating the contrary. For this reason, seeing that they could not prevail, they invidiously blamed Christ himself. So the text continues:

---

[69] On p. 285 n. 5 QuarEd correctly mention that the Vulgate reads *fuerat* ("had") while Bonaventure has *erat* ("had").

[70] On p. 285 n. 5 QuarEd accurately notice that the Vulgate reads *posuit* ("put") while Bonaventure has *misit* ("sent").

44. (Verse 26). *And they came to John and said to him: Rabbi, he who was with you beyond the Jordan*, was with you as a lesser one, because you baptized him, whom you also exalted. Thus, they continue: *To whom you have borne witness.* John 1:15 above says: "John bore witness concerning him," etc. *Behold, he is baptizing*, as if, he is usurping your office. And in order to provoke him to envy, they add: *And all are coming to him*, as if not caring about you any longer. They were moved by envy. Joshua did something similar. Concerning the men who were prophesying he said to Moses in Numbers 11:28-29: "My Lord ... forbid them. And Moses answered: Why are you envious for me? Would that all the people be granted to prophesy and the Lord give them his spirit."[71]

QUESTIONS

45. Question 1 deals with John 3:22 which states that Jesus baptized. Contrary to this is what John 4:2 states: "Jesus did not baptize, but his disciples." So there is a contradiction. – I answer that it is said that a person, in whose authority one acts, is performing the action. So the expression, to do something, has a twofold meaning, that is, by means of authority or by means of ministry. Christ baptized with authority, but his disciples did so ministerially.[72] Or he baptized interiorly whereas his disciples did so exteriorly.

---

[71] On p. 285 n. 8 QuarEd intimate that there are some minor variations between the Vulgate and Bonaventure's text, e.g., the Vulgate reads *ille* ("he") while Bonaventure has *Moyses* ("Moses"). Hugh of St. Cher, p. 300v, I also cites Num 11:28-29.

[72] Bonaventure applied a variation of this distinction in his response to the fourth question at John 1 #71 above. See Augustine, Tractate 15 n. 3 in FC 79, pp. 79-80: "Perhaps it may also disturb you why it was said, 'Jesus was baptizing more than John,' and after it was said, 'He was baptizing,' it was added, 'although Jesus was not

46. Question 2 surfaces the question of why the Lord, in his own person, did not baptize exteriorly. And it seems that he should have in order to give others an example and to show the form and manner of baptism. – My answer is that he himself gave and taught others the manner of baptism, but did not baptize in order to avoid error and presumption. Error, because men and women would believe that those, who had not been baptized by him, were not truly baptized. Presumption, lest those baptized by him might be puffed up and despise those who had been baptized by the disciples and thereby belittle the baptism of the disciples.

47. Question 3 deals with John's baptism. Since the baptism of John was preparatory to Christ's baptism, the shadow should disappear once the reality had come. It seems, then, that he should have stopped baptizing once Christ began. – I respond that he did stop, but not immediately. And the reason for this is fourfold. He didn't want to seem to be against him. He didn't want to appear to be unstable. He didn't want to appear to have left the scene in an angry manner. He didn't want to spur his disciples to envy and jealousy.[73]

---

baptizing but his disciples.' What is this? Had a falsehood been told and then corrected by the addition, 'although Jesus was not baptizing, but his disciples'? Or is each statement true, that Jesus was baptizing and was not baptizing? For he was baptizing because he himself was cleansing; he was not baptizing because he himself was not doing the immersion. His disciples provided the ministry of the body; he provided the aid of his majesty."

[73] See Homily 29 n. 1 of Chrysostom in PG 59:167 and FC 33, p. 279: "He continued to do so (baptize) that he might not rouse his own disciples to greater resentment and make them more contentious.... Indeed, if he ceased baptizing he might, contrariwise, have seemed to do so because of envy or anger, but by continuing to preach he made his testimony stronger."

48. Question 4 asks: Whose baptism is more powerful, that of Christ or that of John? It would seem that John's is more powerful: – 1. Since Christ was baptized by John's baptism and since just as the priesthood of Melchisedech was more noble than that of Levi, since Levi gave a tithe to Melchisedech, so for the same reason it seems that John's baptism was more noble than Christ's.[74] – 2. Likewise, "Christ did not baptize, but his disciples."[75] But the disciples of Christ were not greater than John. Therefore, neither was the baptism of Christ's disciples greater than John's baptism. – 3. Furthermore, the question arises whether the disciples' baptism would grant grace. And it seems that it would not since it is said in John 7:39 below: "The Spirit had not yet been given, since Jesus had not yet been glorified." And if anyone, who had been baptized before the passion, died, that person would not have entered into the kingdom of God.

I respond that according to Chrysostom the baptism of Christ's disciples before the passion was only preparatory, just like John's baptism. Therefore, neither conferred grace.[76] – However, Bede[77] and Augustine[78] maintain that

---

[74] Behind this argument stands Hebr 7:1-10, esp. 7:4 and 9: "Now consider how great this man (Melchisedech) is, to whom even Abraham the patriarch gave tithes out of the best portions of the spoils.... And even Levi, the receiver of tithes, was also, so to speak, through Abraham made subject to tithes."

[75] See John 4:2: "Although Jesus himself did not baptize, but his disciples."

[76] See Homily 29 n. 1 in FC 33, p. 280: "Now, if someone should inquire what greater effect the baptism of the disciples had than that of John, we reply that it had no greater power. For, each one alike was without the grace of the Spirit, and all had a single purpose in baptizing: to bring the baptized to Christ."

[77] As far as I can tell, it is Augustine, not Bede, who is responsible for the quotation that follows.

[78] See Tractate 5 n. 18 in FC 78, p. 126: "... and if it was given by Judas, it was Christ's. Judas gave it, and baptism was not adminis-

"John baptized, and a person had to be re-baptized. Judas baptized, and a person did not have to be re-baptized." Wherefore, they state that the disciples' baptism conferred grace, and therefore was more noble because of its more noble efficacy.

1. Relative to the objection that Christ was baptized, it has to be maintained that John's baptism had no effect whatsoever on Christ.[79] – 2. With respect to the objection that the disciples were baptizing, this is true on the *external level*. But in that very baptism Christ was baptizing interiorly. But this is not the case with regard to John's baptism. – 3. Concerning the objection that the Spirit had not yet been given, it has to be understood that the text is speaking of a *visible* and manifest giving of the Spirit, how it was given through the imposition of hands, not about an invisible giving.

About the objection that the baptized person would not escape death, it has to be said that this did not occur because of a defect of grace in baptism, but because his price had not yet been paid. – And if a person objects that baptism receives its efficacy from the passion,[80] it has to be understood that it has the efficacy of grace given by reason of the divine power invisibly operating there and from the passion itself in as far as the opening of the door is concerned.[81] Another exposition: If he had not yet suffered, nonetheless faith in the passion was present. By

---

tered after Judas. John gave it, and baptism was administered after John. For, if baptism was given by Judas, it was Christ's; but that which was given by John was John's."

[79] See Bonaventure's answers to the question he raises at John 1 n. 64 above.

[80] See John 2 n. 19 above.

[81] See Book III, d. 18 a. 2 q. 3 of Bonaventure's *Sentence Commentary* in Opera Omnia 3:391-393: Through his death Christ merited for us the opening of the door of the heavenly paradise.

reason of this faith it had efficacy, although not in opening the door, but in bestowing grace.[82]

John 3:27-36
John resolves the question

49. (Verse 27) *John answered and said.* Having earlier presented the purification effected by the baptisms of Christ and John and the doubt arising from it, the Evangelist now describes John's *resolution of the question* which the disciples had raised. Thus, he determines that Christ, not he, is the one who regenerates. The Evangelist proceeds in this fashion. First John humbles himself and puts himself after Christ by means of a *consideration of human frailty*. Second he presents Christ as before him because of *the power of his baptism*. Third, in *wisdom of preaching*. Fourth, in *excellence of every grace*.

50. So first he humbles himself by means of a consideration of human frailty against his disciples who wanted him to exalt himself and his baptism. So the text says: *No one can receive anything unless it is given him from heaven.* James 1:17 reads: "Every good gift and every perfect gift is from above, coming down from the Father of lights."[83] And so although I am pure, I can attribute nothing to myself except what has been given to me. And therefore, I do not appropriate to myself Christ's office, but that of his precursor. 1 Corinthians 4:7 says: "What do you have that you have not received?"

---

[82] See Bonaventure's answer in John 1 n. 42 above: "The members are united to this head by the bonds of faith and love. For no one was saved without faith in Christ, as Blessed Augustine says."
[83] Hugh of St. Cher, p. 301a also cites James 1:17.

51. (Verse 28). *You yourselves bear me witness that I said: I am not the Christ.* John 1:20 above states: "And he acknowledged, I am not the Christ." *But that I have been sent before him,*[84] as the voice before the word. John 1:23 reads: "I am the voice of one crying in the wilderness: Make straight," etc.

52. (Verse 29). *He who has the bride,* etc. Here in a second place he shows that Christ is set above him relative to the power of baptizing. For the one who *regenerates* has the right to *baptize.* And the one who regenerates is the one who has the bride, from whom he generates. So the text continues: *He who has the bride is the bridegroom,* from whom he can generate and baptize. Ephesians 5:25-26 says: "Husbands, love your wives, just as Christ loved the Church and delivered himself up for her, that he might sanctify her, cleansing her[85] in the bath of water by means of the word of life."[86] Bede comments: "Christ is the bridegroom. The bride is the Church, fathered from the Gentiles. 2 Corinthians 11:2 says: 'I have betrothed you to one husband, to present a chaste virgin to Christ.'"[87] Therefore, it is his responsibility to regenerate, while it is mine not to regenerate nor to be envious, but rather to rejoice as a friend. So the text adds: *But the friend of the bridegroom, who stands,* through grace, *and hears him,* through internal inspiration, *rejoices exceedingly at the voice of the bridegroom. He rejoices exceedingly,* that is, he fully rejoices, since he wants to rejoice with him.

---

[84] On p. 287 n. 2 QuarEd rightly mention that the Vulgate reads *quia* ("that") while Bonaventure has *quoniam* ("that").

[85] On p. 287 n. 3 QuarEd correctly indicate the Vulgate does not read *eam* ("her").

[86] The Vulgate does not read *vitae* ("of life"). Hugh of St. Cher, p. 301d cites Eph 5:25-26a.

[87] See Bede's exposition of John 3:29 in PL 92:675B. Bonaventure's citation is fairly accurate.

Friend: John 15:14 below states: "You are my friends," etc. *Stands*. Romans 14:4 reads: "He stands or falls to his own Lord." Psalm 84:9 confesses: "I will hear what the Lord God is saying in me." *He rejoices exceedingly*. Philippians 4:4 says: "Rejoice in the Lord always," etc. And in this way John rejoiced as a friend and was not downcast like an envious person. So he says: *Therefore, this my joy is full*, that is, perfect, namely, his joy would be full when he had what he desired. John 16:24 below states: "Ask, and you will receive that your joy may be full."

53. (Verse 30). *He must increase, but I must decrease*. This is the greatest sign[88] that someone would rejoice at the exaltation of another even if it means his own demise. *He must increase*, in death, when he is exalted on the cross. *But I must decrease*, when his head is severed. Another exposition: *He must increase*, in reputation,[89] so that Christ may be believed. *But I must decrease*, so that although I was thought to be Christ, I should be considered his precursor. Still another interpretation: *He must increase*, in baptizing and in the number of his disciples. *I must decrease*, because John's baptism and his gathering of disciples must soon cease, while on the other hand those of Christ must expand. Concerning this expansion of his ministry the Apostle rejoiced in Philippians 1:18: "Whether in pretense or truth, Christ is proclaimed; in this I rejoice, and I will rejoice." Now he provides the reason why Christ must increase in that he is *the one who comes from above*, and so the text continues:

---

[88] On p. 287 n. 8 QuarEd state that many manuscripts read *signum verae dilectionis* ("sign of true love").

[89] Hugh of St. Cher, p. 301v, c also has this interpretation.

54. (Verse 31). *The one who comes from above is over all.*
The Glossa observes: "Therefore, he rightly increases,"[90]
and therefore, he has been exalted above all. Psalm 8:8
reads: "You have subjected all things under his feet," etc.

The one who is from the earth ... speaks of the earth.[91]
Here in a third point John states that Christ is above
him in the wisdom of preaching, since John, as an earthly
person, could speak of earthly matters whereas Christ of
heavenly matters. So the text states: *The one who is from
the earth ... speaks of the earth.* John is such a person,
who was conceived in sin. *The one who comes down from
heaven is over all*, in the dignity of his teaching. Christ
came from heaven. 1 Corinthians 15:47 reads: "The first
man was from the earth, earthy; the second[92] was from
heaven, heavenly." Wherefore, he is *from heaven*, since
he is spiritual, because he is sublimely divine. John 8:23
below says: "You are from below, but I am from above."
And since he is from above, he speaks with certitude
about heavenly matters. So the text adds:

55. (Verse 32). *And he bears witness to what he has seen
and heard*, as certain. *He has seen*, as the wisdom of
God, since he saw by himself. *He has heard*, as the Son
accepting it from the Father. John 15:15 below says:
"Everything that I have heard from my Father, I have
made known to you." And although his teaching was most
excellent, nevertheless, it was spurned by those who were
carnal. For this reason the text adds: *And no one accepts
his testimony*, that is, no worldly person. John 15:24 below
reads: "And they have seen and they have hated both me

---

[90] This is the Glossa Interlinearis.

[91] It is unclear whether Bonaventure is abbreviating the Vulgate:
qui est de terra de terra est et de terra loquitur ("the one who is from
the earth belongs to the earth and speaks of the earth").

[92] The Vulgate reads *secundus homo* ("the second man").

and my Father." But spiritual persons, who accept his testimony, have become certain of his teaching. So the text continues:

56. (Verse 33). *But the person who might receive his witness has set his seal of this that God is true,*[93] that is, it impresses itself on the heart with certitude like a seal.

57. (Verse 34). *For the one whom God has sent speaks the words of God*, and so is truthful as God is truthful. John 7:17 states: "If anyone desires to do God's[94] will, he will know of the teaching whether it is from God or whether I speak on my own authority."

For not by measure, etc. Here he touches on the fourth point, namely, that Christ is superior to him in excellence of grace, since he excels all in grace, and this excellence is the reason for the aforementioned observations. So the text states: *For not by measure*. I have truly said that *he is the bridegroom, he speaks of heavenly matters* and *is above all. For not by measure does God give the Spirit*, namely, to Christ. Not *according to a certain measure*, as God does to others. And he provides the reason:

58. (Verse 35). *For the Father loves the Son and has given all things into his hands*. Matthew 11:27 says: "All things have been delivered to me by my Father." And therefore, no one is saved except through the Son. Therefore, the text adds:

---

[93] On p. 288 n. 2 QuarEd accurately mention that the Vulgate reads *accipit* ("receives") while Bonaventure has *acceperit* ("might receive"). Hugh of St. Cher, p. 302f also reads *acceperit*.

[94] The Vulgate reads *eius* ("his") while Bonaventure has *Dei* ("God's").

59. (Verse 36). *The one who believes in the Son has eternal life*, that is, in merit. *But the one who is unbelieving towards the Son will not see life*; will not have glory, but punishment. So he says: *But the wrath of God rests upon him.* John 12:48 below says: "The person who rejects me and does not accept my words has one to condemn him," namely, the wrath of punishment. About this wrath Proverbs 6:34 states: "The jealousy and rage of the husband will not spare on the day of revenge," etc Another interpretation is to view wrath as stemming from original sin, by means of which an individual is a child of wrath according to Ephesians 2:3: "We were by nature children of wrath."

QUESTIONS

60. Question 1 is raised by Chrysostom who observes that in John 3:29 John the Baptist calls himself "the friend of the bridegroom" whereas in John 1:27 above John did not dare to say that he was worthy to be his servant: "The strap of whose sandal I am not worthy to loose." – Chrysostom himself responds that Christ adapted his answers to what was asked. In John 1:25-27 John's interrogators were trying to incite him to ambition, and therefore, he humbled himself and called himself an unworthy servant. In John 3:29, however, he is incited to imitation, and so he calls himself the bridegroom's friend and says that he rejoices in the bridegroom's good fortune.[95]

---

[95] See Homily 29 n. 2 in PG 59:169 and FC 33, pp. 283-284: "Now, how is it that he who said: 'I am not worthy to loose the strap of His sandal,' now declared that he was His friend? It was not to exalt or praise himself that he said this, but out of a desire to show that he himself also was especially promoting this, and that these things were taking place, neither against his will nor to his distress, but with his whole-hearted cooperation." It is obvious that Bonaventure has adapt-

61. Question 2 deals with John 3:31: "The one who is from the earth speaks of the earth." He said this on his own behalf, and it seems that he said this in an unfitting manner, for he was not speaking of earthly matters, but of heavenly. – Chrysostom answers by noting that he did not say this in an absolute manner, but in a comparative manner. Thus he was not speaking of earthly matters in and of themselves, but because he was comparing the earthly matters to Christ's teaching.[96] – Augustine's answer is that this sentence has to be understood either in itself or as a repetition: *The one who is from the earth*, in as far as he is earthly, *speaks of the earth*. But if he is speaking of heavenly matters, this is in as far as he is imbued with the Spirit and has come from above.[97]

62. Question 3 addresses the words of John 3:31: "He who comes from heaven," etc. – It seems from this that Christ would not have assumed human flesh, but heavenly. Or if he had assumed human flesh, why doesn't the text say that he came from the earth like other human beings? –

---

ed Chrysostom's response. Hugh of St. Cher, p. 301v, b also quotes Chrysostom's question and adapts his response: "Here he says that he is the friend of the bridegroom in response to those who thought he was being eaten up by jealousy towards Jesus. In John 1 when they thought he was the Christ, he said that he was unworthy to loosen the strap of his sandal. In both instances he was coming to the aid of those who were in danger."

[96] See Homily 30 n. 1 in PG 59:171-172 and FC 33, pp. 288-89: "So also in this context, when John said that he was speaking of the earth, he was comparing his teaching with that of Christ. For, 'speaking of the earth' means nothing else than 'My teachings are small and of little account, and of little value, compared with His, and are such as are suitable for earthly nature to receive.'"

[97] See Tractate 14 n. 6 in FC 79, 68: "How then of the earth does he (John) speak? But he said it about man. As far as pertains to man himself, he is of the earth, and of the earth he speaks; but if he speaks any divine things, he has been enlightened by God. For if he were not enlightened, earth would be speaking earth. And so the grace of God stands to one side, the nature of man stands to another."

Augustine responds: *"From heaven* or from above means from the height of human nature before the sin of the first parent.[98] – But this viewpoint seems to agree with that heresy that maintains that some particles remained incorrupt in Adam and that these particles were handed down through generations to the Virgin and that the flesh of Christ was fashioned from them.[99]

For this reason it is sound to maintain that this text is talking about a certain assimilation: since, just as flesh in Adam before sin was pure and without stain, so too Christ

---

[98] On p. 288 n. 11 QuarEd quote the Glossa Ordinaria, which attributes this citation to Alcuin: *"Who from above,* that is, from the height of human nature before the sin of the first parent, since from that height the Word of God assumed human nature and did not assume sin, although he assumed its penalty. For the one who *came from heaven*, that is, from the Father, is *above all things* in two ways: first, above all humanity, for he came from humanity before it sinned; second, according to the height of the Father, with whom he is equal." See Augustine, Sermon 362 chapter 14 n. 16 in *Sermons*, translation and notes Edmund Hill, WSA III/10 (Hyde Park, NY: New City Press, 1995), p. 252: "But if you ask why he said the second man was not in heaven but from heaven, whereas the Lord himself took his body from earth, because of course Mary was descended from Adam and Eve; you should understand that the earthly man was called so with reference to earthly desire.... All the same he is not an earthly, but a heavenly man, and is said to be from heaven. After all, if he has granted this to his faithful by grace, so that the apostle can rightly say, *For our domicile is not in heaven* (Phil 3:20), how much more is he himself a heavenly man, and justly said to be from heaven, seeing that no sin was ever to be found in him? It was because of sin, after all, that the man was told, *Earth you are, and into earth you shall go* (Gn 3:19). So that heavenly man is most rightly said to be from heaven, since his domicile never moved from heaven, although the Son of God also became Son of man by taking a body from earth, taking, that is, *the form of a servant* (Phil 2:7). For it was only the one that had descended who also ascended."

[99] See Book III, d. 3. p. II. a. 2 q. 1 of Bonaventure's *Sentence Commentary* in Opera Omnia 3:86 where Bonaventure says that this interpretation is "not only against the veracious sayings of the Saints, but also against the teaching of the true faith."

assumed immaculate flesh.[100] And it has to be noted that earth in this passage does not refer to a passible nature, but to a corrupt nature generated by the corruption of sin. Christ was not born according to this nature, but was conceived by the divine power of the Holy Spirit. Therefore, the text says "from above."

63. Question 4 concerns the meaning of John 3:34: "God does not by measure give the Spirit." – Either one understands this passage to speak of Christ according to his divine nature or according to his human nature. According to his divine nature this is not possible, since he himself does not receive the Spirit. Rather the Spirit proceeds from him. If a person maintains that this means according to his human nature, this stands against such an interpretation: The grace of Christ the man was created, but God creates all things according to a certain weight, number and measure.[101] Wherefore, nothing that is created is infinite. Therefore, it is according to measure.

I respond that one has to make a distinction between a measure of limitation and one of division. I call a measure of limitation that by which each and every finite creature is

---

[100] See Omnia Opera 3:86: "So it is plain that according to catholic teaching the flesh of Christ in the loins of the first parents, in whom he was materially, was not distinct from the flesh of other human beings in a qualitative manner, but in a formal manner in as far as once it was united to the Word, it had the distinction of not being the flesh of sin, but similar to sinful flesh. And for this reason Augustine holds that 'the flesh of Christ came from the height of human nature,' not that it was in the first parents without pollution, but because it was so purified and clean in his assumption of it that it was similar to the flesh in the state of innocence."

[101] See Wis 11:21: "But you have ordered all things in measure, and number, and weight." Hugh of St. Cher, p. 302v, c also cites Wis 11:21 and addresses, in his own way, the same issue that Bonaventure treats.

limited in its substance and power. By measure of division
I mean the determination of some being to some action,
according to what 1 Corinthians 12:4 states: "There are
divisions of gifts, but the same Spirit." That is, when a gift
or grace is given to someone for some determined effect,
as the Apostle says. Christ possessed grace in measure
according to the first sense, for his grace was not infinite.
In the second sense he did not possess grace in measure,
since it was not restricted in him to some operation, but
was available for all operations just as the head controls
all the senses. Thus, Chrysostom comments: "Here he says
Spirit for *an action of the Spirit*, for this action is what is
divided."[102] Therefore, it is obvious that he is speaking of
measure according to the division of gifts.

64. Question 5 focuses on the meaning of John 3:36: "The
person who believes has eternal life," since if the person
has eternal life, he does not believe. I respond that the
possession of spiritual matters happens through love. And
when they are loved completely, then they are possessed
completely.[103]

---

[102] See Homily 30 n. 2 in PG 59:173-174 and FC 33, pp. 292-293:
"But what is the meaning of the words: 'Not by measure does God give
the Spirit'? He wished to point out that we all have received the operation of the Spirit in measure, for here 'Spirit' means His operation,
since it is this which is imparted. But He possesses the entire operation of the Spirit, without measure and in its fullness."

[103] It seems that in the background is 1 Cor 13, esp. 13:13: "So
there abide faith, hope and love, these three. But the greatest of these
is love."

CHAPTER FOUR

JOHN 4:1-42
CHRIST MANIFESTS HIMSELF TO THE SAMARITANS

1. *When, therefore, Jesus knew*, etc. The Lord has already manifested himself to his disciples and to the Jews. In this part he manifests himself to the Samaritans, both by his preaching and announcing to them the word of salvation. Now this part has two sections. The first section describes *the opportunity for preaching* whereas the second provides *the form of the preaching* where verse 7 reads: "A Samaritan woman came" and where the Lord began to preach to this Samaritan woman. – Now the opportunity stemmed from the *place*, and this opportunity was twofold, that is, that of *passing through* and that of *resting*.

JOHN 4:1-6
THE OPPORTUNITY GIVEN CHRIST FOR PREACHING

2. (Verse 1). This verse touches about the first perspective of the opportunity of place, namely, that of passing through. So since he wanted to travel from Judea to Galilee, he had to pass through Samaria. So the text says: *When, therefore, Jesus knew that the Pharisees had*

heard.[1] They had heard, I venture, from John's disciples, who were related as envious and detractors. John 3:26 above says: "They said: All are coming to him." They had heard, I say, *that Jesus made and baptized more disciples than John.* And from this it had become clear to them that he was greater and more famous than John, and had already been manifested to them. They had heard this since it had been told them so.

3. (Verse 2). *Although Jesus himself was not baptizing, but his disciples*, lest they be provoked to jealousy.

4. (Verse 3). *He left Judea and went again into Galilee.* He had already left there once before, as John 1:43 states. Chrysostom observes: "The Lord left not out of fear, but to avoid their envy and jealousy."[2] So John 7:1 reads: "Jesus went about in Galilee, for he did not wish to go about in Judea because the Jews were seeking to put him to death." So after he had preached to the Jews, the opportunity presented itself for him to preach to the Samaritans. So the text continues:

5. (Verse 4). *Now he had to pass through the middle of Samaria.*[3] And so the opportunity of place came about because of his passing through. Luke 17:11 says: "... when Jesus was traveling to Jerusalem, he passed through the

---

[1] On p. 289 n. 9 QuarEd correctly indicate that the Vulgate reads *audierunt* ("heard") while Bonaventure has *audierant* ("had heard").

[2] See Homily 31 n. 1 in PG 59:176-77: "Why, you may ask, did he leave? Not because he was fearful, but he didn't want to give them a reason for envy and wanted to guard against jealousy." Hugh of St. Cher, p. 303k comments: "So Jesus departed from them, not out of fear, as Chrysostom states, but he wanted to avoid their envy and to guard against jealousy."

[3] On p. 289 n. 12 QuarEd accurately mention that the Vulgate does not read *medium* ("the middle").

middle of Samaria...." Just as he had passed through on his way up, so he had to pass through on his way back.

6. (Verse 5). *He came accordingly.* This verse introduces the opportunity of the place for resting, because he was exhausted and the place was pleasant. Thus he describes the place from the vantage point of the town and states: *He came accordingly to a town of Samaria called Sychar. Sychar* in the Chaldean language, and *Shechem* in Hebrew.[4] This is the town where Simeon and Levi killed the men in retaliation for the rape of their sister in Genesis 34:25-29.[5] And this town was. Supply: *near the field that Jacob gave to his son Joseph.* Genesis 48:22 says: "I give you a portion more than your brothers, the one that I took out of the hand of the Amorites with my sword and bow."[6] And this place was just right for resting since it was pleasant. So the text continues:

7. (Verse 6). *Now Jacob's well was there*, that is, which Jacob had found, according to what John 4:12 below says. And Christ needed rest. Thus the text states: *Jesus,[7] exhausted as he was from the journey, was sitting above*

---

[4] See CCSL lxxii, p. 52: *"I have given you Sicima as a special gift above your brothers* (more than your brothers) *which I received from the hands of the Amorites with my sword and spear.* Sicima, according to Greek and Latin practice, is declined. Hebrew, however, reads it as Shechem, as John the Evangelist also bears witness, although he wrongly reads it as Sychar and perpetuates this mistake. And now it is called Neapolis, a town of the Samaritans."

[5] The Vulgate, Septuagint, and Hebrew of Gen 33:18 say that the city/town was "Salem." Their sister's name was Dinah.

[6] See note 4 above. NAB translates the Hebrew of Gen 48:22: "As for me, I give to you, as to the one above his brothers, Shechem, which I captured from the Amorites with my sword and bow." Obviously there is confusion in the biblical manuscript traditions. Hugh of St. Cher, p. 303v, e and g also refers to Gen 34:25-29 and 48:22.

[7] The Vulgate reads *Iesus ergo* ("Jesus, therefore").

the well,[8] for the place was cool, and it was already hot. Thus the text adds: *Now it was about the sixth hour.*[9] And so he was exhausted from the long journey, hunger, and heat. Thus, the Lord himself says in Psalm 87:16: "I am poor and in labors from my youth. And being exalted, I have been humbled and troubled."

8. The allegorical interpretation. Having left Judea, "Jesus passed through the middle of Samaria towards Galilee," since, after the Jews had become blind, Christ migrated to the Father. For Galilee is interpreted as transmigration.[10] Romans 11:25 reads: "Blindness has befallen Israel, so that the fullness of the Gentiles might enter."[11] And Acts 13:46 states: "Paul and Barnabas spoke to the Jews: It was necessary that the word of God should be spoken to you first, but since you have rejected[12] it and have judged yourselves unworthy of eternal life, behold, we now turn to the Gentiles."[13] – *Jesus, exhausted from the journey, was sitting at the sixth hour,* for the Son of God assumed our flesh with its punishments during the sixth age, as Augustine says.[14] Jeremiah 14:8 says: "Why will you be

---

[8] In n. 9 below Bonaventure will interpret *supra* ("above") allegorically. The more common translation of *supra* would be "at."

[9] On p. 290 n. 4 QuarEd accurately indicate that the Vulgate does not read *autem* ("Now"). Hugh of St. Cher, p. 303 also reads *autem*.

[10] See CCSL lxxii, p. 140: "Galilee means subject to restlessness or transmigration accomplished."

[11] I translate the Vulgate of Rom 11:25: "For a partial blindness has befallen Israel until the fullness of the Gentiles might enter."

[12] On p. 290 n. 5 QuarEd rightly mention that the Vulgate reads *repellitis* ("you are rejecting") while Bonaventure has *repulistis* ("you have rejected").

[13] Hugh of St. Cher, p. 303v, b also cites Acts 13:46 and Rom 11:25, erroneously saying it is Rom 9f.

[14] See Tractate 15 n. 9 in FC 79, p. 83: "Why, then, at the sixth hour? Because in the sixth age of the world. In the gospel, count as one hour the one age from Adam to Noah, the second from Noah to Abraham, the third from Abraham to David, the fourth from David to

as a stranger in the land and as a wayfarer turning in to lodge?" – *He was sitting* above a well of water, because he was resting above the rivers of grace, so that he might pour them into those who believe in him. John 7:38 below says: "The person who believes in me, as the Scripture says, from within him rivers of living water will flow."

9. It should be noted that the text says that *Christ was sitting above the fountain*,[15] because he is the one in whom rests the fountain of all grace. Wherefore, he is rightly understood to be that fountain. Genesis 2:6 reads: "A fountain rose out of the earth and watered[16] all the surface of the earth." This fountain is Christ, from whom proceeds a fourfold river or flow of water. – The water of cleanness. About this water Ezekiel 36:25 says: "I will pour over you clean water," etc.[17] And thus Christ is said to be the fountain of cleanness. This is baptism. Zechariah 13:1 reads: "There will be a fountain open to the house of David and to the inhabitants of Jerusalem for the cleansing of the sinner and the unclean woman." For baptism cleans the sinner and the unclean woman, for it destroys original and actual sin. – The water of wisdom. Sirach 15:3 says: "She has given[18] him the water of saving wisdom to drink." And this is sacred doctrine.

---

the banishment to Babylon, the fifth from the banishment to Babylon to the baptism of John; the sixth is in progress from then on. Why are you amazed? Jesus came; and, humbling himself, he came to the well. He came wearied, because he carried weak flesh."

[15] Bonaventure is playing on a twofold meaning of *fons* as "well" and "fountain."

[16] On p. 290 n. 8 QuarEd rightly note that the Vulgate reads *irrigans* ("watering") while Bonaventure has *et irrigabat* ("and watered").

[17] Ez 36:25 reads in full: "I will pour over you clean water, and you shall be cleansed from all your filthiness, and I will cleanse you from all your idols."

[18] On p. 290 n. 10 QuarEd accurately mention that the Vulgate reads *potabit* ("will give to drink") while Bonaventure has *potavit* ("has given to drink").

And so Christ is said to be the fountain of wisdom. Sirach 1:5 states: "The word of God on high is the fountain of wisdom." This waters the hearts of teachers. Proverbs 5:16 has: "Let your fountains be conveyed abroad," etc.[19] – The water of grace. About this water John 7:38 says: "The person who believes in me ... from within him rivers of living water will flow." And thus Christ is called the fountain of grace. John 4:13-14 below states: "The person who drinks of the water that I will give him ... it will become in him a fountain of water, springing up into life everlasting." This is grace, as Jeremiah 2 says.[20] – The water of life. About this John 4:13 says: "The person who drinks from the water that I will give him will never thirst." And thus Christ is said to be the fountain of life. Psalm 35:10 reads: "With you is the fountain of life, and in your light we will see light." And Revelation 7:17 says: "The Lamb ... will guide them to the fountains of waters of life."[21]

All the waters from these fountains flow from Christ. For Isaiah 12:3 says: "You will draw waters with joy from the fountains of the Savior." But they flow only towards the humble and the valleys. Psalm 103:10 reads: "Who sends fountains into the valleys," that is, upon the humble.[22]

---

[19] Prov 5:16 concludes: "... and in the streets divide your waters."

[20] It seems that Bonaventure is referring to Jer 2:13: "For my people have done two evils. They have forsaken me, the fountain of living water. ..."

[21] Hugh of St. Cher, p. 304f provides a remote parallel to Bonaventure's four fountains: "For the fountain is Sacred Scripture. Joel 3d: A fountain shall flow from the house of the Lord, that is, from the cloister, for all the great Doctors and expositors of Sacred Scripture were religious such as Jerome, Augustine, Gregory, Ambrose and many others. And it will water the brook of thorns, for they have made the entire world of thorns fecund by their teaching."

[22] See Augustine's Exposition 2 n. 10 of Psalm 103:10 in *Expositions of the Psalms (Enarrationes in Psalmos) 99-120*, trans. and notes by Maria Boulding, WSA III/19 (Hyde Park, NY: New City Press, 2003),

10. Note that the devil sits above the fountain of uncleanness. About him Leviticus 20:18 says: "If he lies with a woman during her menstrual flow and uncovers her nakedness, and she opens the fountain of her blood, both shall be killed in the midst of their people." A woman in her menstrual period and unclean is our flesh. The man who satisfies his desires is the one who has sexual intercourse with her. – The fountain of perverse imitation. Proverbs 25:26 reads: "A just man falling down before the wicked is like a fountain that has been agitated by one's foot and like a polluted spring." For the wicked, when he sees that there is both evil and good in the just person, shoves the good aside and imitates the evil. – The fountain of vain curiosity. Sirach 26:15 says of the curious soul: "Like a thirsty traveler she will open her mouth for every fountain and will drink from every water."[23] For the curious want to know everything and to be excited by every wise teaching. – Fountain of eternal damnation. Revelation 8:10-11 states: "A great burning star fell ... into the fountains of waters, and the name of the star is called wormwood," for the devil fell from the highest heaven into the greatest calamity of punishments, to which he draws all those who drink of his waters.

---

p. 135: "Valleys and ravines are the opposite of hills and mountains. Hills and mountains are like swollen ground; valleys and ravines are humble, lowly areas. But do not underrate these lowly places, for *you unseal springs in the valleys.*"

[23] On p. 291 n. 3 QuarEd accurately intimate the three differences between the Vulgate and Bonaventure's text. The Vulgate does not read *omnem* ("every [fountain]"). The Vulgate reads *ab* ("from") while Bonaventure has *ex* ("from"). The Vulgate reads *omni aqua proxima* ("from every water nearby") while Bonaventure has *omni aqua* ("every water").

QUESTIONS

11. Question 1 deals with the very first verse. John 4:1 says: "When Jesus knew." – Either this refers to knowledge according to his divinity or according to his humanity. No matter from what perspective he says this, it seems to be false, since Christ knew everything from his birth. Therefore, he didn't begin to learn anything afterwards. – The answer to this is that just as Christ is said not to know, for example, about the day of judgment,[24] because he didn't want us to know, so too it is said that he knew something for the first time, because he showed himself as knowing it for the first time. – Another interpretation is that Christ knew beforehand by foreknowledge, but afterwards he knew through relationships. And this was not incongruent to human nature.[25]

12. Question 2 focuses on John 4:3: "The Lord left Judea" because the Pharisees already recognized him. – It seems that he was afraid and fled. To this Chrysostom replies that he left Judea not out of fear but to avoid giving them scandal and jealousy and envy.[26]

---

[24] See Mark 13:32: "But of that day or hour no one knows, neither the angels in heaven, nor the Son, but the Father only." Consult the parallel in Matt 24:35 which lacks "nor the Son."

[25] See Book III d. 14 a. 3. q. 2 of Bonaventure's *Sentence Commentary*. Hugh of St. Cher, p. 303k also addresses the question of Jesus' knowledge and, in dependence upon Augustine and John Damascene, comes to an answer that is longer, is based on Christ's two natures, and is similar to Bonaventure's.

[26] See Homily 31 n. 1 in PG 59:176-177: "Why, you may ask, did he leave? Not because he was fearful, but he didn't want to give them a reason for envy and wanted to guard against jealousy." See John 4:3 n. 4 and n. 2 above.

But then objections are raised. 1. Since "the truth of one's teaching is not to be swept away because of scandal,"[27] why did he continue to speak the truth, even though it created scandal, on many occasions such as Matthew 15:12-14, and now why did he shut up to avoid scandal?[28] – 2. Furthermore, if he left to avoid envy, I ask: Why were they more envious of Christ than of John, since John also was baptizing?

I answer that he left Judea for a threefold reason, that is, to avoid giving scandal, to garner more fruit, to give an example.[29] Relative to scandal, lest the Jews become worse through the heating up of their jealousy, but this was not the total reason. He also left to garner more fruit since he had made little progress there and would accomplish more in another place. Then once he had discontinued preaching because of scandal, he could garner more fruit by going to another place. He also left to give an example, as Augustine observes, so that he might show us that it is permissible to step away from the furor of persecutors.[30] –

[27] On p. 291 n. 8 QuarEd state: "Cap. *Qui scandalizaverit*, X. (lib. I. tit 44. c. 3) de Regulis iuris: One should not omit speaking the truth to avoid scandal (according to Bede's commentary on Mark 9:41)."

[28] Matt 15:12-14 reads: "Then his disciples came up and said to him: Do you know that the Pharisees have been scandalized at hearing this saying? But he answered and said, Every plant that my heavenly Father has not planted will be rooted up. Let them alone; they are blind guides of blind men and women. But if a blind person guides a blind person, both fall into a pit."

[29] Hugh of St. Cher, p. 303k provides four reasons. Only Hugh's third is similar to one (the third) of Bonaventure's reasons: "The third reason is that he fled into the temple to teach us to flee and not give in to the fury when the persecution is personal."

[30] See Tractate 15 n. 2 in FC 79, p.79: "But because in everything he did as a man he provided an example for the men who would believe in him (for each servant of God does not sin if he departs to another place when perhaps he sees the fury of those persecuting him or seeking his soul for evil; but the servant of God might seem to himself to sin if he

2. Relative to the question of why they persecuted Christ more than John, the answer is that John did not baptize in his own name, but in the name of the Christ who was to come, whereas Christ baptized in his own name. For he was teaching and baptizing as one who had authority.[31] So since the envious Pharisees didn't want to have anyone superior to them, they were more jealous of him.

13. Question 3 is Augustine's question: Why does the Evangelist say "Jacob's well" in John 4:6 and "well" in John 4:12?[32] – Augustine responds: "Every well is a spring, but not vice versa. For where the water flows out of the ground on the surface, it is only a spring. Where it has depth, it is then called both a well and a spring."[33]

JOHN 4:7-42
JESUS PREACHES TO THE SAMARITANS

14. *A Samaritan woman came.* Having set up the opportunity for preaching, the Evangelist now presents *the manifestation* accomplished through preaching. And since this manifestation was first made in a *special way* and secondly in a *common way*, this section first considers the preaching made to *the woman* and then that given

---

were to do this, had not the Lord preceded him in doing it), that good teacher did this to teach, not because he was afraid."

[31] See Matt 7:29: "For he was teaching them as one having authority."

[32] John 4:6 reads *fons* whereas John 4:12 has *puteus*. Both Latin words mean "well."

[33] See Tractate 15 n. 5. Bonaventure's citation is considerably shortened. See CCSL xxxvi, p. 152 for the full text. Hugh of St. Cher, p. 304a resolves the problem between *fons* and *puteus* (see n. 33) in much the same way as Bonaventure does, but does so by referring to the Glossa, not Augustine.

to *the Samaritans* where verse 28 reads: "The woman, therefore, left her water jar," etc.

JOHN 4:7-27
JESUS' SPECIAL PREACHING TO THE SAMARITAN WOMAN

And since preaching does not bring about faith without the consent of the will and the will does not give its consent unless God kindles a spark in it, the Lord first *kindles a spark* in the woman.[34] Then once the spark has been kindled in her, the Lord *announces the truth of faith* to her as she gives her consent where verse 15 reads: "The woman said to him: Sir, give me this water," etc. – So the Lord kindles a spark in the woman in this order, namely, by *asking that she render a service to him*; second by *promising* or offering *a gift*; third by *explaining the benefit offered*.

JOHN 4:7-14
THE LORD KINDLES A SPARK WITHIN THE SAMARITAN WOMAN

15. (Verse 7). First, he enkindles a spark in her by asking her to serve him by giving him a drink of water. This is something that the woman could minister to him since she had come to draw water. So the text says: *A Samaritan woman came to draw water.* And so she could give him a drink, and Christ was needy and therefore asked for a

---

[34] See Book V, c. 3 n. 5 of Bonaventure's *Breviloquium* in WSB IX, p. 181: "Now, it is not the nature of grace to compel free choice but anticipate it, so that both of them pass into act together. And so, in the process of justification the acts of free will and grace concur in a harmonious and orderly manner. First, 'gratuitously given grace' stirs up free will, and free will must either give or refuse consent to such arousal."

drink. Thus the text continues: *Jesus said to her: Give me to drink*. Indeed he needed a drink since there was no one present who might minister to him. For the text adds:

16. (Verse 8). *Now[35] his disciples had gone away into the town to buy food*. Rightly does the text say "to buy," for they were not asking that someone give them food free of charge, since there was no one there who might do so. Luke 9:52-53 reads: "The disciples[36] entered a Samaritan town to make ready for him, and they did not receive him, because his face was set for Jerusalem."

17. (Verse 9). *Therefore, the woman said to him*. Here the Lord continues to kindle a spark in the woman by promising or offering her a gift. For her part the woman was weighing the fact that he was a Jew and was reluctant to offer him this service and resorted to asking him a question. So the text continues: *The Samaritan woman, therefore, said to him*, that is, the one from whom he had requested a drink. *How is it that you, although you are a Jew, are asking a drink from me who am a Samaritan woman?* As the Glossa says: "She knew he was a Jew from the way he was dressed."[37] The Evangelist adds the reason behind her question: *For Jews do not associate with Samaritans*, viewing them as unclean since they

---

[35] On p. 292 n. 2 QuarEd rightly indicate that the Vulgate reads *enim* ("for") while Bonaventure has *autem* ("now").

[36] The Vulgate indicates that these were actually *nuntii* ("messengers"), not "disciples."

[37] This is the Glossa Interlinearis. The Latin *habitus*, which stands behind my translation "the way he was dressed," can also mean "bearing." See Chrysostom's Homily 31 n. 4 in PG 59:180: "And how did she know that he was a Jew? Perhaps, because of his manner of dressing or because of the way he talked." Hugh of St. Cher, p. 305a quotes a dictum: "They discern that Israelites are different from other peoples because of language, homeland, feast days, clothing, circumcision, cult, and food."

were Gentiles. For Genesis 43:32 reads: "It is unlawful for the Egyptians to eat with Jews, and they think such a feast profane." So since the woman had not been moved to grant his request, the Lord attracted her by promising her a gift. So the text says:

18. (Verse 10). *Jesus answered and said to her: If you did know the gift of God.* "The gift of God" is the Holy Spirit, about whom Acts 2:38 says: "Repent[38] and be baptized every one of you ... and you will receive the gift of the Holy Spirit." The Holy Spirit is said to be a gift since it must not be sold. Acts 8:20 states: "May your money go to destruction with you, since you thought that the gift of God could be purchased with money." If, I say, you knew *and who it is who is saying to you: Give me to drink,* that is, that he himself is the giver of the Holy Spirit, you would not have raised a question but asked for the gift. So the text continues: *You, perhaps, would have asked of him.* The adverb, "perhaps," is not a sign of doubt, but of free will.[39] And he would have satisfied your request. Thus, the text adds: *And he would have given you living water. You,* who are asking, *he would have given.* Matthew 7:8 states: "Everyone who asks receives, and the person who seeks finds, and to the person who knocks it will be opened." He calls the grace of faith *living water* which gives life. Habakkuk 2:4 reads: "My just one lives by faith."[40]

---

[38] On p. 292 n. 5 QuarEd accurately mention that the Vulgate reads *Poenitentiam inquit agite* ("He [Peter] said: Repent") while Bonaventure has *Poenitemini* ("Repent").

[39] On p. 292 n. 6 QuarEd cite Blessed Albert's commentary on this verse: "*You, perhaps*: This is not said in doubt, but on account of the movement of the woman's free will, which God does not compel in anyone...." Hugh of St. Cher, p. 305g comments: "You perhaps] since you are not compelled. In this the freedom of will is noted."

[40] On p. 292 n. 7 QuarEd correctly indicate that the Vulgate reads: *Iustus autem in fide sua vivet* ("But the just person will live by his

19. (Verse 11). *The woman said to him.* The third point surfaces here, that is, the explanation of the gift or the benefit offered. For the woman was thinking carnally of a temporal gift, and therefore was in doubt and sought an explanation. So the text says: *The woman said to him: Sir, you have nothing to draw with, and the well is deep.* And therefore, you cannot give water from this well. Further, how can you have water from some other source? So the text adds: *From what source, then, do you have living water?* That is, water that has a more noble ancestry than this.

20. (Verse 12). *Are you greater than our father Jacob?* Something similar is asked in John 8:53 below: "Are you greater than our father Abraham?" *Who gave us the well.* So he gave it because he found it. Concerning this well Genesis 29:1-2 says: "Jacob went on his journey and came into the east country, and he saw a well there[41] ... whose mouth was closed with a great stone." Not only did he give it to others, but he also kept it for his own use, as if he had no better well. Therefore, the text continues: *And he himself drank from it and his children and his flocks.* Genesis 29:11 states that Jacob watered his flocks there. So the woman, understanding in a carnal fashion and not knowing the Lord's power, was not attracted. So Christ explains the gift. The text adds:

21. (Verse 13). *In answer Jesus said to her: Everyone who drinks of this water,* that is, this visible and material water, *will thirst again.* And so it is no great thing to give this water, nor for me to promise to give it. *But the person*

---

faith"). Bonaventure's citation is closer to Rom 1:16: *Iustus autem ex fide vivit* ("But the just person lives by faith").

[41] The Vulgate reads *in agro* ("in the field") while Bonaventure has *ibi* ("there").

who drinks of the water that I will give him will never thirst. John 6:35 below states: "The person who believes in me will not thirst forever."[42] The reason follows why that person will not thirst:

22. (Verse 14). *But the water that I will give him will become in him a fountain of water, springing up unto life everlasting.* "Springing up," since it gushes forth from the place where there is an unending fountain. Psalm 35:10 says: "With you is the fountain of life," etc. It is also a fountain that refreshes completely. For Psalm 35:9 states: "They will be inebriated with the abundance of your house, and you will make them drink from the torrent of your pleasure." To this water the Lord invites in Isaiah 55:1: "All who are thirsty, come to the waters. And the person who does not have money," etc.[43] – So, then, he enkindled a spark in the women by asking for a favor, offering a gift, explaining the gift proffered.

QUESTIONS

23. Question 1 is this: Since the Lord commanded his disciples not to enter the towns of the Samaritans nor to go in the direction of the Gentiles according to Matthew 10:5[44] and since he also said in Matthew 15:24: "I was not sent except to the lost sheep of the house of Israel," how is

---

[42] On p. 292 n. 10 QuarEd accurately mention that the Vulgate reads *umquam* ("never") while Bonaventure has *in aeternum* ("forever").

[43] On p. 292 n. 11 QuarEd rightly note that the Vulgate reads *qui non habetis argentum* ("you who do not have money") while Bonaventure has *qui non habet argentums* ("the person who does not have money").

[44] Matt 10:5 reads: "These twelve Jesus sent forth, having instructed them in this way: Do not go in the direction of the Gentiles, nor enter the towns of Samaritans."

it that the Lord is now preaching to the Samaritans? For he seems to go against his own precept, and thereby to give a bad example. – I respond that the Lord forbade his disciples not because it would be evil, but lest he would scandalize the Jews for whom he had come in the first place. Therefore, the Lord commanded that they not go to Samaritans and Gentiles as their primary purpose. Nor did the Lord himself go to them. However, since "he wishes that all men and women be saved,"[45] and an opportunity presented itself and the woman came to him, only then did he begin preaching the word.[46]

24. Question 2 asks: 1. Since Jews regard Samaritans as unclean and the Lord observed the Law, how is it that he asked a drink from a Samaritan woman? – 2. Furthermore, he himself knew her response before he asked. Also he knew that she would not give him a drink. Therefore, he was asking in vain and as a fool. – Chrysostom answers that the Lord taught that the observance of regulations of this kind was an indifferent matter.[47] As he says in

---

[45] See 1 Tim 2:3-4: "This is good and agreeable in the sight of God our Savior, who wishes all men and women to be saved and to come to the knowledge of the truth."

[46] See Chrysostom, Homily 31 n. 4 in FC 33, p. 306: "Do you see how he made it clear that the Samaritan woman also came there for another purpose, always forestalling as he was, the impudent attack of the Jews: that no one might say that in speaking to Samaritans He was transgressing His own precept bidding [His disciples] not to enter a Samaritan city." Hugh of St. Cher, p. 303v,a solves this question thus: "To this it can be said that he gave that precept [Matt 10:5] so that they not out of set purpose and will go to the Gentiles or Samaritans to live there. Here, however, they arrived on the scene by sheer accident."

[47] See Homily 31 n. 4 in PG 59:180 and FC 33, p. 307: "That it was now a matter of indifference to Him to cast aside such observances as these. Indeed, He who encouraged others to break them would much more readily transgress them Himself. For it is not that which goes into the mouth which defiles a man, but that which comes out." Hugh of St. Cher, p. 304v,a addresses this same issue, quotes Chrysostom

Matthew 15, no external thing defiles a person.[48] And therefore, he did not put aside asking her, although she was a Samaritan. – 2. With regard to the objection that he knew that she would not give him a drink, it has to be noted that he knew that she would respond to him in a prudent manner and that from her answer he would have an occasion to teach. Because of these reasons he asked her.

25. Question 3 deals with John 4:8: "The disciples had gone into the town to buy food." – Contrary. 1. The disciples were Jews. Therefore, they should not associate with Samaritans. 2. Moreover, the Lord forbade them to have money in Matthew 10:9.[49] So how did they go to buy if they had no money?

My answer is that the Lord had taught the disciples that nothing is unclean or common.[50] – Another interpretation is that some foods were indifferent to both Jews and Samaritans such as bread and apples. And they went to buy such foods.[51] – 2. Relative to the objection that they did not have the wherewithal to purchase food, it has to

---

and Matt 15:11, and comes to much the same conclusion as Bonaventure.

[48] See Matt 15:11: "What goes into the mouth does not defile a person, but it is what comes out of the mouth that defiles a person." Matt 15:29-20 reads: "For out of the heart come evil thoughts, murders, adulteries, immorality, thefts, false witness, blasphemies. These are the things that defile a person."

[49] Matt 10:9 says: "Do not possess gold or silver," etc.

[50] See Acts 10:14: "But Peter said: Far be it from me, Lord, for never did I eat anything common or unclean."

[51] Hugh of St. Cher, p. 304v,b comments: "No foods were illicit for them when the Lord of the Law was present and dispensing them and especially in necessity. Nonetheless, I don't think that they bought illicit foods, for perhaps they purchased bread and fruit or such light fare as this, that was permitted travelers to eat, no matter among whatever Gentiles they were."

be remarked that they still had not been sent to perform miracles and to preach. – Also they were in unknown territory where they did not find bread and other food free of charge. Therefore, they were carrying money for the times of necessity.

26. Question 4 refers to what the woman says in John 4:12: "Are you greater than our father Jacob?" – Contrary. From this she seems to imply that Jacob was the father of the Samaritans, but this is false since the king of the Assyrians sent them.[52] – I answer that the word father sometimes refers to longevity of time, as we call old men fathers. Sometimes it refers to authority, as we call prelates and men in office fathers. Sometimes we call fathers those who have given us the gifts of benefices or education. Sometimes we call fathers those who have begotten us. The woman called Jacob father for the aforementioned three reasons.[53]

27. Question 5 deals with John 4:13: "The person who drinks of the water that I will give him will never thirst." – Contrary. Either this means bodily thirst or spiritual thirst. If it refers to bodily thirst, it is false because those who possess grace are thirsty. If, however, it refers to spiritual thirst, it still seems to be wrong. Sirach 24:29 reads: "Those who drink will still be thirsty."[54]

---

[52] See 2 Kings 17:24: "And the king of the Assyrians brought people from Babylon, Cuthah, Avva, Hamath, and Sepharvaim and placed them in the cities of Samaria instead of the children of Israel. And they possessed Samaria and dwelt in its cities."

[53] It is understandable why some MSS read: "the first three reasons."

[54] On p. 293 n. 8 QuarEd correctly notice that the Vulgate reads *Qui bibunt me* ("Those who drink of me").

I answer that the passage is speaking of spiritual thirst. For there is a thirst of a person who does not have something that he may have it. There is a thirst of a person who has something, that he may have more. There is a thirst of a person who has something completely, that he may continue to have it. The first is the case of concupiscence; the second of grace; the third of glory. This passage is speaking of the first type of thirst. Therefore, etc. For the thirst for grace is not for a thing that a person does not have because, as Augustine observes, the person who has the eternal gift, has it by loving, although that person does not have it completely.[55]

JOHN 4:15-27
THE SAMARITAN WOMAN GIVES HER CONSENT

28. *The woman said to him*, etc. The Lord has enkindled a spark in the heart of the woman to the point of consent. In this passage he *proposes the word of faith for belief* to the woman who is already giving her consent and asking. For the woman, although her heart had been enkindled, was not yet illumined. For this reason the Lord does not immediately propose the word of faith to her, but proceeds in the following order. First, *Christ reveals a secret*. Second, the woman *manifests a doubt*. Third, Christ *opens up the sacrament of faith*.

---

[55] There is no place where Augustine says this in so many words. See, for example, c. 15 n. 33 of *De Utilitate Credendi* in FC 4, p. 436: "Since no one can attain the surest and most supreme Good, without loving it perfectly and completely (and this is not possible as long as there persists any fear of bodily or chance ills), He won our love by His wondrous birth and His miracles, and He banished fear by His death and resurrection."

29. (Verse 15). So Christ reveals a secret to the woman who is already asking for the promised water and through this showing her consent. Thus, the Evangelist presents the woman's request: *The woman said to him*, etc.[56] The Lord had already promised her unfailing water. The woman was asking for this water: *Sir, give me this water, so that I may not thirst or come here to draw water*. And thirst and the labor of drawing water were punishments for her, and so she requested the gift of God, for, as Gregory comments, "the evils that oppress us here compel us to go to God."[57] For this reason the Lord invites those who are burdened in Matthew 11:28: "Come to me, all who labor and are burdened, and I will refresh you." So the Lord tells a secret to the woman who is petitioning in this manner, but doesn't do it immediately, lest she be offended, because the secret was insulting. But he waited for an opportunity to tell her. So the text continues:

30. (Verse 16). *Jesus said to her: Call your husband*, not by marriage, but by the abuse of marriage. *And come here*. He did not say this because he thought she had a husband, but to reveal the secret about her husband when she did respond. Thus:

[56] On p. 294 n. 1 QuarEd rightly mention that the Vulgate reads *ad eum* ("to him") while Bonaventure has *ei* ("to him").

[57] See Homily 36 n. 9 of GGHG in CCSL cxli, p. 341 where Gregory is commenting on Luke 14:23. See Hurst, pp. 321-322: "What is happening to those overcome by the adversities of this world who return to the love of God, who are led away from the desires of the present life, dearly beloved, except that they are being compelled to come in?" See Augustine's Tractate 15 n. 17 in FC 79, p. 87: "Her need forced her to work, and her weakness objected to the work. Would that she had heard, 'Come to me, all you who labor and are burdened, and I shall refresh you.' For Jesus was saying this to her, that she might labor no longer but she did not yet understand." Hugh of St. Cher, p. 306n cites this passage from Augustine, but without its reference to Matt 11:28.

31. (Verse 17). *The woman answered and said: I have no husband.* From her true answer the Lord took the opportunity of revealing her secret. So the text adds: *Jesus said to her: You have said well: I have no husband,* for she had made a true confession.

32. (Verse 18). *For you have had five husbands.* Behold, he is revealing her past. *And he whom you have is not your husband.*[58] By interchanging the accusative *hunc* for the nominative *hic,* the Evangelist is using the grammatical figure of an antithesis. He is revealing the present, and in order that she be not offended, he commends the truth of her statement: *In this you have spoken truly.* In this verse a principle is passed on for preachers that if they want to say harsh things to their audiences, they should also mix in some pleasant matters. For Paul followed this principle in 1 Corinthians 11:22: "Am I to commend you? In this I do not commend you." For he did not entirely censure them.

33. The mystical interpretation. The woman is the inferior part of reason. Her natural and legitimate husband is the superior part, which makes right decisions. 1 Corinthians 11:7 reads: "Man ... is the image and glory of the Lord,[59] but woman is the glory of man." – This woman is censured because she had five husbands when she devoutly served from her infancy the five carnal senses, who ruled over her like a husband.[60] The children are those who follow

---

[58] On p. 294 n. 3 QuarEd accurately note that the Vulgate reads *nunc* ("now") while Bonaventure has *hunc,* which is the accusative of *hic* ("this one") and is grammatically strange.

[59] On p. 294 n. 5 QuarEd correctly indicate that the Vulgate reads *Dei* ("of God") whereas Bonaventure has *Domini* ("of the Lord").

[60] See Augustine's Tractate 15 n. 21-22 in FC 79, p. 91: "... it seems to me that we could more easily take the five earlier husbands of the soul to be the five senses of the body. For when each man is born,

the cravings of youth. So the Apostle says in 2 Timothy 2:22: "Flee the cravings of youth." These youthful cravings, although they seem to be pleasurable, are in reality bitter. Therefore, they are signified by the five yoke of oxen. Luke 14:19 says: "I have bought five yoke of oxen," that is, the five heavy cravings of the senses.[61] – The first husband is taste. The gluttonous serve this husband. In their person Qoheleth 2:24 says: "It is better to eat and drink and to show good things to one's soul."[62] Isaiah 22:13 states: "Let us eat and drink." – The second husband is touch. The voluptuous serve this husband. In their person Wisdom 2:8 says: "Let no meadow escape our voluptuousness. Let none of us be deprived of our voluptuousness."[63] – Third, smell. Those searching after pleasures serve this husband. In their person Wisdom 2:7-8 says: "Let us fill ourselves ... with ointments, and let not the flow of the time pass us by. Let us crown ourselves with roses," etc. – Fourth, sight. The avaricious serve this husband. Sirach 14:9 reads: "The eye of the avaricious man is insatiable in his portion of iniquity.[64] He will not be satisfied until he consumes his own soul after drying it up." – Fifth, hearing. The curious serve this husband.

---

before he can use his mind and reason, he is ruled only by the senses of the flesh."

[61] See Bonaventure's commentary on Luke 14:19 (n. 42) in *Commentary on Luke, chapters 9-16*, p. 1362: "And there are said to be *five yoke of oxen* on account of the five senses oriented towards these earthly concerns." See also Homily 36 n. 4 of GGHG in CCSL cxli, p. 335: "What do we take the meaning of the five yoke of oxen to be except the five senses of the body?" See further Hugh of St. Cher, p. 306v,b: "You have succumbed to the love of the five senses."

[62] On p. 294 n. 8 QuarEd rightly indicate that Bonaventure has turned a question into a statement.

[63] The Vulgate does not read the second sentence of Wis 2:8. It is a textual variant. See Vulgate, p. 1004.

[64] On p. 294 n. 11 QuarEd accurately mention that the Vulgate reads *in parte* ("in his portion") whereas Bonaventure has *in partem* ("in his portion").

Acts 17:21 has: "The Athenians ... used to spend all their leisure telling or listening to something new."

She is rebuked for having a sixth husband who is *not her own*. This husband is error, which seduces and leads the soul astray. So once this error has been rejected, the Lord exhorts her to call her *husband*, that is, the natural judgment of reason, so that she can receive the sacrament of faith and not be "like the horse and the mule which have no understanding."[65] To such a soul the Lord gives "water springing up unto life everlasting."[66] This is the water of grace, which comes down from God. Therefore, it makes the water spring up to God, for the property of this water is that as much as goes up just as much comes down.[67]

34. (Verse 19). *The woman said to him*. This verse introduces the second consideration. For after Christ has revealed her secret, she manifested her doubt. For the woman, recognizing that the Lord was someone who penetrated into oneís secrets, proposes that he resolve her doubt. So the text continues: *The woman said to him: Sir, I see that you are a prophet* since you know secrets. Therefore, you can resolve my doubt.

35. (Verse 20). *Our fathers worshipped on this mountain*, namely, Abraham and Jacob. *But you say that at Jerusalem is the place where one ought to worship*. So if the fathers

---

[65] See Ps 31:9.

[66] See John 4:14.

[67] See Augustine's Tractate 15 n. 22 in FC 79, p. 92: "For when the soul begins to be capable of reason, it is either ruled by a wise mind or by error.... Therefore after these five senses, that woman was still erring and error was bandying her about. But this error was not a licit husband, but an adulterer.... 'Call' therefore, not the adulterer, but 'your husband,' that you comprehend me with your understanding and not perceive something false about me by error."

are to be imitated, how then do you teach this as if you were contemning the custom of the fathers? The Jews said this because of what Deuteronomy 12:13-14 states: "Beware, lest you offer ... to the Lord in every place ... but in the place[68] which the Lord will chose...." The Lord resolved the doubt behind this question by showing that neither here nor in Judea was their perfect worship. So the text adds:

36. (Verse 21). *Jesus said to her: Woman, believe me, the hour will come[69] when neither on this mountain nor in Jerusalem will you worship the Father.* This hour is the time of grace, during which the error of the Gentiles and the shadow of legal commandments must be left behind. Concerning this hour Romans 13:11-12 says: "It is now the hour for us to rise from sleep.... The night is far advanced; the day is at hand," etc. This hour determines that the place of prayer is not some place, but everywhere. 1 Timothy 2:8 reads: "I wish that the men pray everywhere, lifting up pure hands," etc. And although there is now no perfect worship either here or in Jerusalem, worshipping at Jerusalem is better. Therefore, the text adds:

37. (Verse 22). *You worship what you do not know*, since you do not have the Law. Furthermore, you worship both God and idols and believe that God is a local deity. 2 Kings 17 says of the Samaritans that they served the God of the earth and their idols.[70] *We worship what we know. We,*

---

[68] On p. 295 n. 5 QuarEd correctly indicate that the Vulgate reads *in eo* ("in that") while Bonaventure has *in loco* ("in the place").

[69] On p. 295 n. 6 QuarEd rightly note that the Vulgate reads *venit* ("is coming") while Bonaventure has *veniet* ("will come"). Hugh of St. Cher, p. 306v,i also reads *veniet*.

[70] 2 Kings 17:33 and 41 read: "And when they worshipped the Lord, they served also their own gods according to the custom of the nations out of which they were brought to Samaria.... So these nations feared the Lord, but nevertheless also served their idols. Their chil-

namely, the Jews. *For salvation is from the Jews*, that is, Christ the Savior. Galatians 3:16 reads: "The promises were made to Abraham and his descendants." Therefore, since perfect worship does not take place at Jerusalem, he teaches the woman when and how perfect worship will come about, lest he keep her in suspense. So the text continues:

38. (Verse 23). *But the hour is coming.* I told you that you do not worship perfectly since you believe that God is local. Nor do the Jews worship perfectly, for they worship under figures. *But the hour is coming*, namely, the hour of grace, *and now is*, for the Christ has already come. *When the true worshippers will worship the Father in spirit and in truth.* "In spirit" as opposed to locality and corporeity. "In truth," once the shadow has been cast off, according to what the Apostle said in 2 Corinthians 3:18: "We ... with faces unveiled, beholding the glory of the Lord, are being transformed into his very image from glory to glory," etc.[71] He shows who these true worshippers are: *For the Father also seeks such to worship him.* Supply: As it has been said, *in spirit and in truth.*

39. (Verse 24). *God is spirit*, not a body, so that you may believe. Isaiah 40:18 says: "To whom did you reckon[72] God is similar? Or what image will you make for God?" *And those who worship him must worship in spirit and in truth*, so that thus they might conform to him and be in spirit, not in the flesh. Romans 8:8 reads: "Those who are in the flesh cannot please God." So that they may be

---

dren also and grandchildren, as their fathers did, so do they unto this day." Hugh of St. Cher, p. 307a also refers to 2 Kings 17.

[71] 2 Cor 3:18 concludes: "... as through the Spirit of the Lord."

[72] On p. 295 n. 10 QuarEd correctly mention that the Vulgate reads *fecistis* ("have you made") whereas Bonaventure has *existimastis* ("did you reckon").

in truth, not in fiction. Wisdom 1:5 states: "The holy spirit of discipline will flee from anything feigned."

40. (Verse 25). *The woman said to him*. After she had indicated her doubt, here in a third point Christ opens up the sacrament of faith. For the woman, instructed by the Lord, lifts up the eye of her consideration to Christ and to the time of grace. So the text continues: *The woman said to him: I know that the Messiah is coming, who is called Christ. And when he comes, he will tell us all things*. The woman knew this since the Samaritans accepted the Law, were believers, especially that the Christ promised in the Law was not only for the Jews, but also for the Gentiles. Genesis 49:10 reads: "The scepter will not be taken away from Judah nor the ruler from his thigh, until the one comes that is to be sent, and he will be the expectation of the Gentiles."[73] So from this expectation the woman was led to Christ and had already been prepared to believe in him. Now what was there left to do except that the Lord be completely open to her? So the text proceeds:

41. (Verse 26). *Jesus said to her: I am who is speaking with you*. The Lord responded to the blind man in a similar way in John 9:37 below. When the blind man asked whether he were the Son of God, in whom he ought to believe, the Lord answered: "You have seen him, and it is he who is speaking with you." Once the faith has been proclaimed, he concludes his preaching and conversation, for his disciples are returning. So the text adds:

42. (Verse 27). *And at this point his disciples returned and were wondering that he was speaking with a woman*. They were in admiration of his clemency and graciousness. Augustine comments: "They were in admiration of a good

---

[73] Hugh of St. Cher, p. 307v,d also cites Gen 49:10.

and not suspicious about an evil."[74] And their admiration did not lead to a question, but to reverence and respect. So the text continues: *Yet no one said: What do you seek? or Why are you speaking with her? What do you seek?* as if they were saying: What is the necessity of this human communication? *Why are you speaking with her?* That is, what is the usefulness of this human communication? As Gregory observes: "For the word, which has no basis in a just necessity or a pious usefulness, is otiose."[75]

QUESTIONS

43. Question 1 explores the meaning of John 4:21: "The hour is coming when neither on this mountain nor in Jerusalem will you worship the Father." – 1. If this is true, then temples should not be constructed for prayer. – 2. Likewise, if those who worship must do so in spirit, then those sin who make bodily images for prayer.

I answer that certain conditions for prayer are essential such as a right intention and a righteous petition. Certain conditions are accidental such as time and place. I say, therefore, that the Lord did not say that a set place is to

---

[74] See Tractate 15 n. 29 in FC 79, p. 96: "That he was seeking a lost woman, he who had come to seek what had been lost, at this they wondered. For they were wondering at a good thing; they were not suspecting evil." Hugh of St. Cher, p. 308b comments: "Augustine says the same thing: that they [the disciples] were not suspicious of an evil, but were in wonder at the clemency by which he was teaching a Gentile woman who was in error."

[75] See Book VII, chapter 37 n. 58 of *S. Gregorii Magni Moralia in Iob Libri I-IX*, ed. Marcus Adriaen, CCSL cxliii (Turnhout: Brepols, 1979), p. 379: "Thus, otiose is the word that either has no basis in just necessity or in the intention of pious usefulness." In n. 58 Gregory cites seven passages from Scripture, e.g., James 1:19, to support his dictum.

be eliminated from genuine prayer as superfluous. Rather people should recognize that a set place is not essential for prayer, since true worshippers worship God everywhere. And although a set place is not necessary, nonetheless it is not superfluous. For it is effective in bringing back memories, arousing devotion, preserving unity, bringing about fellowship with the angels, since "princes went before joined with singers."[76] – As to the objection about images, it has to be said that they now present no obstacle, for no one believes that there is anything divine in them, nor that God is present there corporeally. Rather their purpose is merely one of signification.

44. Question 2 asks why the Lord says of himself and of the Jews in John 4:22: "We worship what we know." – Contrary. In John 8:19 below the Lord Jesus says to the Jews: "You know neither me nor my Father." – I respond that in John 8 he is speaking of non-believers, who were Jews in name only. In John 4 he is speaking of genuine Jews, who in reality merited to be called Jews.[77]

45. Question 3 notes this inconsistency: If "the Lord made his word brief upon the earth,"[78] how is it that his words with the Samaritan woman were so prolix? – Chrysostom

---

[76] See Ps 67:26.

[77] See the Glossa Ordinaria in PL 114:373D: "You Samaritans worship what you do not know, but we Jews, but not all, just the elect, worship what we know." See Augustine, Tractate 15 n. 26 in FC 79, p. 95: "Therefore, according to this, it was said, 'We worship what we know.' It was said, about the role of the Jews but not of all the Jews.... For God has not cast off his people whom he foreknew."

[78] See Rom 9:28 and c. 9 n. 3-4 of the 1223 Rule of the Friars Minor: "I also admonish and exhort the same friars that in their preaching their words be well chosen and to the point for the benefit and edification of the people. They should announce to them vices and virtues, punishment and glory with brevity of speech, for the Lord made his word brief upon the earth."

answers that if the Lord had blurted out to the woman: I am the Christ, he would have seemed to be talking nonsense.[79] So little by little, like a good teacher, he led her. He also gave us an example that we should not refuse to preach to just a few people, when he himself preached such a long sermon for one old lady.

46. Question 4 focuses on John 4:27: Why didn't the disciples, and especially Peter who habitually and audaciously interrogated the Lord, question him about his conversation with the Samaritan woman? – The response to this is that if they had questioned, they would have already seemed to be suspicious of his activity. Thus, they were afraid of being rebuked for asking a foolish question and of being undisciplined. And so they did not dare to question him.

JOHN 4:28-42
THE LORD PREACHES TO THE SAMARITANS COMMUNALLY

47. *The woman, therefore, left her water jar*, etc. The third part has been concluded, during which the Lord preached and revealed himself to the Samaritan woman all by herself and in private. Now the second part commences, in which the Lord preaches to *the Samaritans communally* and manifests himself to them. And since the preaching of the woman brings about this manifestation in part and Christ's words bring it about in part in the hearing of the disciples, who should be solicitous about this same matter, the Evangelist deals with this manifestation in

---

[79] See Homily 33 n. 2 in PG 59:191 and FC 33, p. 327: "If he had said this to the woman at the beginning, when she was not looking for it, He would have seemed foolish to her and to be talking nonsense. But now, by gradually leading her to recall the Messiah, He revealed Himself opportunely."

the following order. First, he mentions *the diligence of the woman* in proclaiming the name of Christ. Second, *the readiness and desire of Christ* to accept those called.[80] Third, *his inspiring of the disciples* to preach. Fourth, *the fervor with which the Samaritans believed*. Everything in this section is ordained to highlight their fervor.

48. (Verse 28). So the first point is the vigor and diligence the woman expended on manifesting Christ's name and the conversion of her people, since she immediately departed to proclaim the truth that she had grasped. So the text says: *The woman, therefore, left her water jar.* Having heard the word of faith, she left her water jar, so that she might more quickly run and proclaim the truth, lest perhaps the Lord might depart. Or in her zeal she forgot the reason why she had come and wanted to proclaim Christ. Thus, Chrysostom comments: "This woman instructs us that when listening to spiritual matters we have to spurn all temporal matters."[81] *And went away into the town*, namely, to make Christ's name known. So the text continues: *And said to the people.*

49. (Verse 29). *Come and see a man, who has told me whatever I have done.*[82] She was drawing them by means of the fact that he knew and had revealed her secrets to her. She did not say: Come and see a prophet. Rather she shared her life's story, so that she might grab their attention and attract them to Christ. *Is he the Christ?*

---

[80] I have supplied *vocatos* ("those called") from Bonaventure's commentary on John 4:31 (n. 51) below.

[81] See Homily 34 n. 1 in PG 59:193 and FC 33, p. 332: "This was intended to teach us – if only by a trifling example – when listening to spiritual things to put aside all material things and to make no account of them."

[82] On p. 297 n. 2 QuarEd rightly mention that the Vulgate reads *omnia* ("all"): "all that I have ever done."

She did not assert this truth, lest she seem to have been deceived. She did not assert it, but proposed it as something she doubted, so that they likewise might entertain this doubt and through it arrive at certitude. Chrysostom observes: "She did not want to lead them into belief by her own exhortation, but from listening to him."[83] Therefore, once they were excited, they went forth. So the text adds:

50. (Verse 30). *They went forth from the town and came to meet him*, since Christ was outside the gate of the town like someone unknown and suffered outside the gate. For Hebrews 13:12-13 states: "Christ[84] ... suffered outside the gate. Therefore, let us go forth to him outside the camp, enduring his reproach." This suggests that those who want to be taught by Christ must leave the tumult of the town. Jeremiah 48:28 reads: "Leave the towns and dwell in the rock, you who dwell in Moab." For Psalm 62:3 says: "As in a desert land, where there is no road and no water, so in the sanctuary I have come before you."[85]

51. (Verse 31). *Meanwhile, his disciples besought him*, etc. The second point occurs here, namely, the desire of Christ to receive those called. Since he desires their salvation as food, even more so than he might desire bodily food when he was in need and famished, the text reads: *Meanwhile*, that is, after the woman departed and before the Samaritans arrived, *his disciples besought him*,[86] as

---

[83] See Homily 34 n. 1 in PG 59:193 and FC 33, pp. 332-333: "She desired, not to persuade them by her own conviction, but to make them share in her opinion of Him by hearing Him themselves, since this would make her words more convincing."

[84] The Vulgate reads *Iesus* ("Jesus").

[85] Ps 62:3 concludes: "... to see your power and your glory."

[86] On p. 297 n. 6 QuarEd correctly mention that the Vulgate does not read *eius* ("his").

people solicitous about their teacher's welfare, *saying, Rabbi, eat.* For they had brought food, and it was past the time for eating. Chrysostom observes: "Seeing him exhausted from the journey, heat, and fasting, they were beseeching him to eat."[87] But the Lord preferred spiritual food to corporal food and refused to eat. So the text adds:

52. (Verse 32). *But he said to them: I have food to eat, of which you do not know.* I prefer this food to what you have brought. The disciples did not understand him, because he was spiritual while they were carnal. 1 Corinthians 2:14 states: "The sensual person does not perceive the things that are of the Spirit of God." So it is obvious that they did not know what he was talking about, because they were thinking on a carnal level. So the text proceeds:

53. (Verse 33). *Therefore, the disciples said to one another: Has someone brought him*[88] *something to eat?* Augustine comments: "Is there any wonder? First, the woman misunderstood what Jesus was saying about *water*. Then his disciples misunderstand what he means by *food*."[89] And since it is the task of teachers to instruct disciples who lack comprehension, the explanation follows.

54. (Verse 34). *Jesus said to them: my food is,* namely, the food about which you know nothing, *is to do the will*

---

[87] See Homily 34 n. 1 in PG 59:194: "For seeing him exhausted by the journey and the heat, they were exhorting him." Hugh of St. Cher, p. 308v,d paraphrases Chrysostom and stresses exhaustion from the journey and the heat.

[88] On p. 297 QuarEd accurately notice that the Vulgate reads *ei* ("him") while Bonaventure has *illi* ("him").

[89] See Tractate 15 n. 31. See CCSL xxxvi, p. 162: "Is there any wonder? The woman misunderstood what Jesus was saying about water. His disciples do not yet understand about food." Hugh of St. Cher, p. 308v,f also cites Augustine and reads: "... his disciples do not yet understand about food."

of the one who sent me. The will of God is our salvation. John 6:40 below says: "This is the will of my Father who sent me that whoever beholds the Son and believes in him, will have eternal life." The Lord wanted to fulfill this will through the work of redemption. So he says: *To accomplish his work.* The work of God is called a work because of the outstanding nature of his most merciful reconciliation. For Psalm 144:9 proclaims: "His mercies are above all his works." Therefore, the work of God is our conversion through faith to God. John 6:29 reads: "The work of God is that you believe in him whom God has sent."[90]

55. (Verse 35). *Do you not say*, etc.? The third point occurs here, namely, Christ's kindling in the disciples a desire to preach for the sake of the Samaritans' salvation. And he employs two considerations in animating them: the Samaritans' readiness to believe and the reward for the preachers.

Christ uses a parable to spur his disciples to a consideration of the Samaritans' *readiness to believe*: *Do you not say: There are yet four months and then comes the harvest?* On a literal level this means that summer is near. And indeed people say this, when they see that the time of harvest has arrived, a time they have been waiting for all year. *Well, I say to you, Lift up eyes*,[91] that is, consider this. *And see that the fields*, that is, the multitudes of the Gentiles, *are white for the harvest*,[92] that is, close to faith, since they are ready to believe, if there is someone

---

[90] On p. 297 n. 11 QuarEd rightly note that the Vulgate reads *Hoc est opus Dei* ("This is the work of God").

[91] On p. 298 n. 1 QuarEd correctly indicate that the Vulgate reads *oculos vestros* ("your eyes").

[92] The Vulgate reads *albae sunt iam ad messem* ("are already white for the harvest").

to preach to them. Matthew 9:37-38 says: "The harvest indeed is great, but the laborers are few. Therefore, pray the Lord of the harvest to send forth laborers into his harvest." So Christ is animating his disciples through a consideration of the Samaritans' readiness to believe. He also enkindles their zeal through a consideration of the fruits the harvesters receive. So the text continues:

56. (Verse 36). *And the person who reaps receives a wage,* not a temporal one, but an eternal one. So the text says: *and gathers fruit unto eternal life,* where, as Matthew 6:20 says, "neither rust nor moth consume, and thieves neither break in nor steal." About the wage of this reward Luke 6:23 states: "Rejoice ... and exult, for behold, your reward is great in heaven." And this reward is common to both reapers and sowers. Therefore, the text adds: *So that the sower,* etc. I say that it is good that one who reaps gathers fruit not only for the sower, but also for himself: *so that the sower and the reaper may rejoice together.* Psalm 125:6-7 reads: "Going, they went and wept, casting their seeds. But coming, they will come with joyfulness," etc.[93] And he gives the reason why both the reapers and the sowers should rejoice, since according to the proverb the other groups are distinct. So the text continues:

57. (Verse 37). *Herein is the word true,*[94] that is, the proverb: *One sows, another reaps.*[95] For the prophets have sown,[96] but afterwards the Apostles have reaped, and

---

[93] Ps 125:7 concludes: "... carrying their sheaves."

[94] On p. 298 n. 5 QuarEd accurately mention that the Vulgate reads *In hoc enim* ("For herein").

[95] Is there a basis for this proverb in Mic 6:15: "You will sow, but will not reap. You shall tread the olives, but will not be anointed with the oil. And the new wine, but will not drink the wine."

[96] See Augustine, Tractate 15 n. 32 in FC 79, p. 98: "Where, therefore, were reapers to be sent? Where the prophets had already preached; for they were the sowers."

this indeed because of the gift and command of the Lord, whose harvest it is. So the text adds:

58. (Verse 38). *I have sent you to reap that upon which you have not labored.* About this harvest and mission Matthew 9:38 says: "Therefore, ask the lord of the harvest to send laborers into his harvest." *Others have labored, and you have entered into their labors*, since you have garnered the fruits of their preaching. 1 Peter 1:12 reads: "It was revealed" to the prophets "that not for themselves" were they prophesying,[97] "but they were declaring to you those things that have now been declared to you."

59. (Verse 39). *Now of that town.* Here the text treats of the eagerness of the Samaritans to believe, an eagerness the message of the woman had instilled in them. So the text continues: *Now many of the Samaritans of that town believed in him.* And the reason follows: *Because of the word of the woman who bore witness* to his divinity: *He told me whatever I had done.*[98] The Samaritans believed because of the testimony of the woman, but the Jews refused to believe John. Wherefore, the Lord said to the Jews in Matthew 21:31: "Amen, I say to you that the tax collectors and the prostitutes are entering the kingdom of God ahead of you." And although their faith might not be strong, it was ardent. So the text adds:

60. (Verse 40). *So when the Samaritans had come to him,*[99] *they besought him to stay there.* Luke 24:29 states: "Stay

---

[97] On p. 298 n. 6 QuarEd rightly mention that the Vulgate reads *ministrabant* ("were ministering") while Bonaventure has *annuntibant* ("were declaring").

[98] On p. 298 n. 7 QuarEd accurately indicate that the Vulgate reads *omnia quaecumque feci* ("everything that I had ever done").

[99] On p. 298 n. 8 QuarEd correctly note that the Vulgate reads *illum* while Bonaventure has *eum* ("him").

with us, for it is getting towards evening." In contrast the Jews expelled him. Chrysostom remarks: "The Pharisees, although they had seen many signs, not only did not believe, but cast him out of their territory."[100] Thus, Matthew 8:34 states: "The entire town of the Gerasenes[101] came out to meet Jesus, and upon seeing him, they entreated him to depart from their territory." And the Lord acquiesced to the entreaties of the Samaritans. So the text continues: *And he stayed there for two days*, to confirm and strengthen their faith, which he did. Thus, the text adds:

61. (Verse 41). *And many more believed because of his word*. One should not be amazed at this, for, as Peter told him in John 6:69 below: "Lord, to whom will we go? You have the words of eternal life." Not only did he increase the number of Samaritan believers, but he also strengthened their faith. So the text continues:

62. (Verse 42). *And they said to the woman: We no longer believe because of what you said to us*, as if we were begging for human reassurance. *For we have heard for ourselves and know that this is in truth the Savior of the world*, namely, in listening, we have come to know, since, as Romans 10:17 states: "Faith depends on hearing, and hearing on the word of God."[102] *In truth the Savior of the world*, not only of the Jews. For John 3:16 above reads: "God so loved the world, that he sent his only begotten Son," etc. Thus, 1 John 2:2 reads: "He is a propitiation for our sins, not only for ours, but also for those of the whole

---

[100] See Homily 35 n. 1 in PG 59:198: "But the Jews, having also seen miracles, not only did not keep him among themselves, but also expelled him...."

[101] Bonaventure has supplied "Gerasenes" from Matt 8:28.

[102] On p. 298 n. 11 QuarEd rightly notice that the Vulgate reads *Christi* ("of Christ") while Bonaventure has *Dei* ("of God").

world." This was signified by Joseph, about whom Genesis 41:45 says: "Pharaoh changed his name and called him in the Egyptian tongue *the savior of the world*."[103]

QUESTIONS

63. Question 1 begins our questioning with a citation from Psalm 92:5: "Your testimonies have become exceedingly credible." Now the testimony of a woman is unreliable and flimsy, as that of the weaker sex. It seems that the Lord should not have manifested himself to the Samaritans through a woman. – I answer that Christ did not accept human testimony because of his own need, but because of the need of his listeners.[104] So since the witness of a woman would be least suspect to the Samaritans, the Lord wanted to make himself known to them through a woman, not because her witness would carry any weight, but because it would be credible to the Samaritans. – Another reason was to condemn the hardness of the Jews during the judgment, for they did not believe John the Baptist, but the Samaritans believed a mite of a woman. As the Lord himself told them in Matthew 12:41-42: The queen of the South and the Ninevites will arise in judgment against the Jews.[105]

64. Question 2 probes the testimony of the woman some more and focuses on John 4:29: "Come and see the man who told me everything that I have ever done." – Contrary. He only talked to her about the husbands she had had.

---

[103] Bonaventure added *Pharao* ("Pharaoh") to the Vulgate to specify the subject of the verb. See Gen 41:44.
[104] Bonaventure addresses this same type of question in John 1 n. 21.
[105] Bonaventure abbreviates Matt 12:41-42. Luke 11:31-32 provides a parallel to Matt 12:41-42.

So either the woman didn't do many other things, which is false. Or she was lying, and what she said was false. – I answer that the woman, when she heard him say this, did not merely look to the words of the speaker, but to the wisdom with which he spoke. And just as he had told her one secret, he could by the same power tell her "everything that she had done." Therefore, the woman, wishing to express Christ's power, expressed herself in universal terms, etc.

65. Question 3 raises the objection that since the evangelical law does not consist of shadows or figures, but rather of manifest truth, how is it that the Lord spoke to his disciples in parables? – It seems that he should not speak in this manner, but openly.

I answer that there is a twofold speaking in figures. In the first instance the truth is closed off and may not be explained to one's listeners. This is to speak in shadows and obscurely and pertains to the old law, not the new law. Another way is to speak in similitudes in such a way that that similitude may be explained and made clear. And this mode is to speak not in shadows, but rather in the light. And the Lord speaks in this way, so that a thing proposed obscurely in a figure may be clearly understood by his exposition. Through this way human understanding is humbled and the truth is more ardently loved and more firmly retained. For the truth, which is slightly hidden, becomes more acceptable, once it becomes clear.[106]

---

[106] See Chrysostom's Homily 34 n. 1 in PG 59:194 and FC 33, p. 334: "And notice how He frequently did not reveal all the details at once, but first cast the listener into uncertainty, in order that, having begun to inquire into what was meant, then because of being confused and growing weary, the latter might receive with more eagerness the explanation of the difficulty, and might be better disposed to listen attentively.... He did so because He wished first to make them more

66. Question 4 concerns the Lord's statement in John 4:34 where he calls our salvation his food. In a similar way in John 4:10 above he calls our faith his drink. – This does not seem like an appropriate way of speaking. For food preserves the person who is fed, but Christ preserves us, not us Christ. Wherefore, we are not the food of Christ.

My response is that food has a threefold property. The first is that it is eagerly desired. The second is that it refreshes the person who is fed by it. The third is that it is transformed into the body. – By reason of the first property Christ is our food, because we desire him, and we are his food, since he himself desires our salvation.[107] By reason of the second property Christ is our food, because he nourishes and refreshes us, and not vice versa. By reason of the third property we are Christ's food, because he transforms us into his body. Therefore, Augustine says that he fed the thief on the cross.[108]

67. Question 5 focuses on John 4:40: When the Lord perceived that they were on the brink of believing, why is it that he only wanted to stay two days with them? – It would seem that he should have been with them for a longer period of time. – I answer that he did this to avoid

---

attentive, as I have said, as a result of their perplexity, and to dispose them to listen carefully to His words, by reason of such enigmatic statements." Hugh of St. Cher, p. 309e uses Chrysostom to explain why Christ used similitudes.

[107] See Chrysostom's Homily 34 n. 1 in PG 59:194 and FC 33, pp. 333-334: "In this place He called the salvation of men 'food' to show how great a desire He has to take care of us. Indeed, our salvation is as much an object of desire to Him as eating is to us."

[108] See Sermon 1 n. 9 on Psalm 68 in *Expositions of the Psalms 51-72*, trans. and notes Maria Boulding, WSA III/17 (Hyde Park, NY: New City Press, 2001). p. 374: "His punishment was not undeserved, but he poured out the corrupt matter from within him by his confession, and fitted himself to eat the Lord's food."

giving scandal to the Jews, lest they be offended that he had abandoned them and gone over to foreigners.[109]

68. Question 6 deals with John 4:37 where the Lord told his disciples: "One sows, another reaps." So he is calling the apostles reapers and not sowers. – But contrary. 1. "The seed is the word of God."[110] Therefore, the person who preaches sows. But the apostles were preachers. Therefore, etc. – 2. Furthermore, 2 Corinthians 9:6 reads: "The person who sows sparingly will also reap sparingly." Wherefore, the person who sows nothing reaps nothing. – 3. Moreover, it seems that the apostles are not reapers. Rather this is the responsibility of the angels. Thus Matthew 13:39 states: "The harvest is the end of the world; the reapers are the angels." Therefore, the reapers are not the apostles.

I answer that there are three times, and they have this order: the times of the Mosaic Law, grace, and glory. The time of grace is like fruit with respect to the time of the Mosaic Law. The time of glory is like fruit with regard to the time of grace. – Accordingly, since harvest refers to the gathering of fruits, there is a twofold harvest. The first occurs during the time of grace, and its reapers are the apostles while its sowers are the prophets, who foretold this grace and made the people hope for it.[111] The other harvest occurs during the time of glory, and its reapers are the angels while its sowers are the apostles with regard to some and all with regard to themselves. – And

---

[109] See Hugh of St. Cher, p. 309v,g: "He stayed there for two days] only, lest the Jews might have something to say against him: that he contaminated himself with foreigners."

[110] See Luke 8:11.

[111] Hugh of St. Cher, p. 309k comments: "The prophets have sown; the apostles have reaped."

the objections go off in tangents, for the Lord is speaking of the harvest of grace.

JOHN 4:43-54
CHRIST MANIFESTS HIMSELF TO THE GALILEANS

69. (Verse 43). *Now after two days*, etc. The Lord has already manifested himself to his disciples, the Jews, and the Samaritans. This verse begins the fourth part of this section, in which he will manifest himself to *the Galileans*, from his own homeland, who were most resistant to belief. The Evangelist uses the following order in describing this manifestation that was made through a miracle. First, he intimates that among the Galileans there is *a lack of reverence* to give honor. Second, there is *a lack of faith* to believe. Third, there is *the request for a miracle*. Finally, from this arises *edification of faith*.

So first, the Evangelist suggests that there is a lack of reverence to honor Christ, for there were fellow countrymen. Therefore, Christ came to remove their irreverence by manifesting himself to them through miracles. So the text states: *Now after two days*, namely, the two days he spent with the Samaritans, *he departed from that place and went into Galilee*, that is, his own native land, so that he might convert those who were so resistant. So the text adds:

70. (Verse 44). *For Jesus himself bore witness*, that is, as underlining the point, *that a prophet receives no honor in his own country*. Luke 4:24 states: "No prophet is acceptable in his own country." The Glossa observes that since he had received no honor when he first came to Galilee, he returned there a second time, so that they

might at least believe in him because of his signs.[112] For in some way they had already been predisposed because of the signs that they had seen him perform in Jerusalem. So the text continues:

71. (Verse 45). *Therefore, when he had come into Galilee, the Galileans received him*, as if they had begun to honor him for a little while. Philippians 2:29 says: "Welcome Ephaphroditus with all joy in the Lord and show honor to people like him." The reason for their welcome follows: *Since they had seen all that he had done in Jerusalem during the feast.* I stress *they had seen. For they also had gone up to the feast.*[113] For all these things that they had seen were signs and miracles. John 2:23 above states: ìwhen he was at Jerusalem for the feast ... many believed in him, seeing the signs that he was performing."

72. (Verse 46). *So he came again to Cana in Galilee*, that is, so that they might perhaps believe, *where he had made the water into wine.* This was the first of his signs by which he made himself known to his disciples. For the Glossa notes: "A few believed this miracle, that is, the disciples."[114] John 2:11 states: "This first of his signs Jesus performed in Cana of Galilee, and his disciples believed in him."

73. *And there was a certain royal official.* This verse introduces the second point, that is, a defect in faith to believe. Just as they were honoring him in a certain way

---

[112] This is the Glossa Ordinaria on John 4:43-44.

[113] On p. 300 n. 5 QuarEd correctly indicate that the Vulgate reads *venerant* ("had gone") while Bonaventure has *ascenderant* ("had gone up").

[114] The Glossa Ordinaria on John 4:43 in PL 114:375C: "... only a few believed in him, for having seen the sign, his disciples believed in him, but not others."

and in a certain dishonoring him, so too they were believing in a certain way and in a certain way disbelieving. And this vacillation is evident in the fact that the royal official did not believe that he could cure his son unless he were present. So the text says: *There was a certain royal official,* namely, from a small territory in the kingdom,[115] *whose son was lying sick at Capernaum* where the Lord was not present.

74. (Verse 47). *When he heard that Jesus had come*[116] *from Judea into Galilee,* because word of his arrival had spread abroad. Mark 1:28 reads: "Rumor concerning him went forth immediately into all the region round about Galilee." *He came to him,* to implore him. Matthew 8:5 says: "A centurion came to him and entreated him," etc.[117] *And besought him to come down* and be bodily present.[118] John 2:12 above states: "He and his mother went down to Capernaum," etc. *And cure his son* through his miraculous power. Luke 6:19 reads: "Power went out from him and cured all." *For he was the point of death* through the powerlessness of human nature. In 2 Kings 20:1 it is said to Hezekiah: "You will die and will not live," namely, because he was sick unto death. And since this royal official, although he was beseeching the Lord,

---

[115] The Glossa Interlinearis plays on the Latin *regulus* ("royal official") as a diminutive of *rex / regis* ("king/of the king"): "*Royal official* because of the smallness either of kingdom or of faith."

[116] On p. 300 n. 8 QuarEd rightly mention that the Vulgate reads *adveniret* ("had arrived") while Bonaventure has *venit* ("had come").

[117] See Chrysostom's Homily 35 n. 2 in PG 59:201 and FC 33, p. 347: "Some think, then, that he is the one found in Matthew, but the latter appears to be another person, not only by reason of his rank, but also because of his faith."

[118] Hugh of St. Cher, p. 310v,a comments: "Bodily, because he did not believe that he would be everywhere according to the presence of the deity, for he did not believe that Jesus was God."

did not have robust faith, the Lord rebuked him for his incredulity. So the text adds:

75. (Verse 48). *Therefore, Jesus said to him: Unless you see signs and wonders, you do not believe.* And so it is hard for you to believe. Signs are minor miracles whereas wonders are major miracles.[119] About this hardness in the Jews John 12:37 below says: "Although he had worked so many signs in their presence, they did not believe in him." In contrast, the Samaritans had believed solely because of his word, a point that has already been shown above.

76. (Verse 49). *The royal official said*[120] *to him.* In this verse the third point surfaces, namely, the plea for a miracle. This petition, although it does issue from a faith that is perfect, nevertheless bears the insistence of a parent. So the royal official again pleads: *Lord, come down, before my child dies.* Since he is persistent in his petition, he obtains what he asked for. Matthew 7:8 reads: "Everyone who asks, receives, and the person who seeks, finds. And to the person who knocks, it will be opened." And Luke 11:8 says: "And although he will not ... give to him because he is his friend, yet because of his persistence he will get up and give him all he needs," that is, loaves of bread. So the text continues:

77. (Verse 50). *Jesus said to him: Go. Your son lives,* that is, he has been cured. So he said: *He lives,* since he had recovered from his mortal malady. And the man indeed merited this, because, although he did not yet believe in Christ, he did believe in the word of Christ. So the text states: *The man believed the word that Jesus had*

---

[119] Hugh of St. Cher, p. 310v,e says the same thing.

[120] On p. 301 n. 3 QuarEd accurately mention that the Vulgate reads *dicit* ("says") while Bonaventure has *dixit* ("said").

spoken to him, and departed. The Glossa observes: "Thus he merited a cure for his son."[121] For in Mark 9:22 the Lord said to the man asking for a cure for his son: "If you can believe, all things are possible for the person who believes," that is, the believer can ask for them.

78. (Verse 51). *But even as he was now going down.* The fourth point occurs in this verse, namely, the building up of faith that came about from the recognition through his servants' report of Christ's miraculous power. So the text says: *But even as he was now going down, his servants met him.* Since they had good news, they did not wait until he had arrived home. *They met* him, as they traveled with haste and joy, as servants meet their master. Matthew 25:6 reads: "Behold, the bridegroom is coming. Let us go out to meet him." *And brought word, saying that his son was alive,* that is, he had been cured.

79. (Verse 52). *Therefore, he asked about the hour, at which he had gotten better,*[122] so that he might acknowledge by means of that hour Christ's power on behalf of his son. *And they said to him: Yesterday, at the seventh hour, the*

---

[121] This is the Glossa Interlinearis. See Bede's comment on John 50 in PL 92:690A: "For he began to have faith in Jesus' word, and therefore, he merited a cure for his son. And the man who came with some doubt departed a believer. And so he merited the cure of his son." Hugh of St. Cher, p. 311c comments: "He already began to believe, as the Glossa says, that he cures by a word, and so he merited a cure for his son. Chrysostom and Augustine are of the opinion that he did not yet possess the certitude of faith, since afterwards he asked about the hour of the cure in his effort to ascertain whether the cure happened by chance or was performed by Jesus himself."

[122] On p. 301 n. 7 QuarEd correctly indicate that the Vulgate reads *Interrogabat ergo horam ab eis, in qua melius habuerit* ("Therefore, he asked them about the hour, in which he would have gotten better") while Bonaventure has *Interrogabat ergo horam qua melius habuerat* ("Therefore, he asked about the hour, at which he had gotten better").

fever left him. And from this he recognized Christ's power. Thus the text adds:

80. (Verse 53). *Then the father knew that it was at that very hour in which Jesus had said to him: Your son lives,* and so that he had been cured by Jesus' powerful word. This is according to what Wisdom 16:12 says: "It was not[123] herb nor mollifying plaster that cured them, but your word, O Lord." And from this recognition followed *the building up of faith.* So the text states: *And he himself believed, and his whole household.* So although he had not believed on account of the first sign, his faith was now perfect since he believed in this second sign. So the Evangelist continues:

81. (Verse 54). *This was the second sign that Jesus worked.* That is, it was second in relationship to the one he had performed at the wedding feast.[124] *When coming from Judea into Galilee,* so that, since they had not believed because of the first sign, they might believe on account of the second one. In Exodus 4:8 the Lord said to Moses: "If they will not believe ... nor listen to the word of the former sign, they will believe the word of the next sign."

82. The moral interpretation. Here consideration is given to who is the royal official, who is the son of the royal official, what sickness has taken hold of him, and at what hour he was restored to health. – The king is said to be the superior part of reason, to which is committed the total governance of the soul in the area of judgment. For Psalm 2:10 states: "And now, you kings, understand." This part

---

[123] On p. 301 n. 8 QuarEd accurately note that the Vulgate reads *neque* ("neither") while Bonaventure has *non* ("not").

[124] See John 2:11: "This first of his signs Jesus worked at Cana in Galilee."

of the soul is called a little king or royal official because of the smallness of justice it exercises when it rules the soul in an evil or puerile manner. Qoheleth 10:16 says: "Woe to the land,[125] whose king is a child, and whose princes dine in the morning." – The son of this king is called the inferior part of reason, which has the same nature and is to be instructed by the king. Sirach 30:2 reads: "The man who instructs his son will be praised." – The son of the king is sick with a fever, when reason pursues concupiscence, which is like a high fever which lays one low. Sirach 23:22 states: "A hot soul is like a burning fire. It will not be quenched until it devours something." Like this fever concupiscence makes a person restless. First there is boiling heat, then freezing chills. Isaiah 57:20 reads: "The wicked are like the raging sea that cannot rest, and its waves cast up dirt and mire."[126] – The son was freed at the seventh hour of the day. *The day* can refer to Christ, because he is the light shining upon the earth. John 8:12 below says: "I am the light of the world." – The hours of this day are the different statuses of Christ. Through a consideration of these the soul is freed from different maladies.[127]

---

[125] On p. 301 n. 16 QuarEd rightly mention that the Vulgate reads *Vae tibi, terra* ("Woe to you, O land") while Bonaventure has *Vae terrae* ("Woe to the land").

[126] Hugh of St. Cher, p. 311m provides a parallel for Bonaventure's third moral interpretation, although Hugh views the fever as avarice and cites Sir 23:22: "But the greedy person does not sense this heat, because he does not acknowledge his avarice. But he is frigid exteriorly, for he always believes he's dying of hunger and always believes that he has little and that he is going to lose those things that he has. So, too, he has cold hands, which have almost shriveled up with regard to alms. Likewise with regard to the other members of his body.... Sir 23:22 says...."

[127] Hugh of St. Cher, p. 311m gives two lists for the seventh hour: "Or the seven hours can be said to be those seven, about which the Apostle speaks in 2 Cor 7:11: You were made sorry according to God. What earnestness it has wrought in you, what explanations, what

83. The first hour is the incarnation.[128] And this frees a person from pride by illuminating the soul towards humility, because he humbled himself in the incarnation. Philippians 2:7 reads: "He humbled himself, accepting the form of a slave." – The second is his nativity, and this frees us from avarice by illuminating the soul towards poverty, for the newly born Christ is poor, as Luke 2:7 says: "She brought forth her first born son and wrapped him in swaddling clothes and laid him in a manger, because there was no room for them in the inn." – The third is his circumcision, and this frees us from disobedience by illuminating us towards obedience. For although Christ was not subject to the Law, he, nonetheless, subjected himself to it. So of him it is fittingly said what the Apostle expresses in 1 Corinthians 9:19: "Although I am free in all things, I have made myself the slave of all...." – The fourth is his apparition,[129] and this frees us from envy by illuminating us to communication of teaching, for he himself then made himself known to the Gentiles. Wisdom 7:12-13 has: "I rejoiced in all, for this wisdom went before me ... which I communicate without envy, and I do not hide her riches." – The fifth is the offering in the temple, and this frees us from ingratitude by illuminating us to prayer, since at that time the Lord himself was offered in the temple as a sign that human beings must offer

---

indignation, what fear, what yearning, what zeal, what readiness to avenge. Or the seven hours are seven considerations of the world. The first is the consideration of its brevity, second its changeableness, third its infidelity, fourth its deceit, fifth its evil, sixth the things that fight against you, seventh the things that are inimical to you."

[128] Except for the second hour, *nativitas*, Bonaventure employs words ending in "io" to denote the first and third through twelfth hours: *incarnatio, circumcisio, apparitio, oblatio, baptizatio, tentatio, passio, descensio, requietio, resurrectio, ascensio.*

[129] Bonaventure seems to be referring to the apparition of the star to the Magi, non-believers, who came from the East to worship the Christ. See Matt 2:1-11, esp. 2:7.

themselves totally out of gratitude. Luke 2:22 states: "They brought the child Jesus to Jerusalem to present him to the Lord." – The sixth is his baptism, and this frees us from uncleanness by illuminating us to newness of life, for Christ was washed in the River Jordan. Matthew 3:13 states: "Jesus came from Galilee to the Jordan ... to be baptized by him." 1 Peter 3:21 says: "Baptism saves you, not the putting off of the filth of the flesh,"etc. – The seventh is the temptation during his fasting, and this frees the son of the royal official from fever by illuminating him to the mortification of the flesh, since Christ afflicted the flesh through his fasting. Matthew 4:1-2 states: "Jesus was led into the desert by the Spirit to be tempted by the devil. And when he had fasted for forty days and forty nights, he was hungry." – The eighth is his passion, and this frees us from anger by illuminating us to patience, for Christ was most patient in his suffering. 1 Peter 2:21-22 says: "Christ suffered for us,[130] leaving you an example that you may follow in his steps, who committed no sin nor was deceit found in his mouth."[131] – The ninth is the descent into hell, and this frees us from hardness of heart by illuminating us to compassion, since the Lord was merciful to those who were "in darkness and the shadow of death."[132] Zechariah 9:11 reads: "You also by the blood of your covenant have led[133] the[134] vanquished out of the pit...." The greatest mercy is to shed one's blood for prisoners. – The tenth is the rest in the tomb, and this frees us from the pressures of the world by illuminating

---

[130] The Vulgate reads *vobis* ("for you") whereas Bonaventure has *nobis* ("for us").

[131] The Vulgate reads *in ore ipsius* ("in his mouth") while Bonaventure has *in ore eius* ("in his mouth").

[132] See Luke 1:79.

[133] The Vulgate reads *emisisti* ("you have sent forth") while Bonaventure has *eduxisti* ("you have led forth").

[134] The Vulgate reads *tuos* ("your").

us to peace, because Christ rested in the sepulcher. Psalm 4:9 states: "In peace in the selfsame I will sleep and I will rest." And Psalm 75:3 reads: "His place is in peace." – The eleventh is the resurrection, and this frees us from the oldness of life by illuminating us to newness of life, since then Christ became the new man. Romans 6:4 says: "Just as Christ has arisen from the dead through the glory of the Father, so we also may walk in the newness of life." – The twelfth is the ascension, and this frees us from the love of earthly things by illuminating us to the desire for eternal things, whence Christ has preceded us. Colossians 3:1-2 has: "Seek the things that are above where Christ is seated at the right hand of God. Consider the things that are above, not the things that are on earth."[135]

QUESTIONS

84. Question 1 deals with John 4:44: "A prophet does not have honor in his own country." – Contrary. 1. Since a person is honored only where that person is known and since a person is known among those of his own country and not among foreigners, it would seem that he will be more highly honored in his own country than in a foreign land. – 2. Likewise we see that David the prophet received the honor of kingship in his own country. – It also seems that Christ would have been honored. For John 4:45 says "the Galileans received him." Therefore, they honored him.

I respond that there is a twofold reason why a prophet is not honored in his own country: by reason of carnal generation and by reason of familiarity. By reason of

---

[135] See Bonaventure's commentary on John 11:19 below where he provides other explanations for the twelve hours of a day.

carnal generation. For since Christ is believed to have had a mother and father who were ignoble and common and poor, he is despised because of them. By reason of familiarity, since familiarity breeds contempt. So since they knew that Christ's parents and his education were poor, they did not believe that there was anything divine in him.

1. With regard to the objection that knowledge of a person makes people honor him, I have to say that a knowledge of a person's power helps, but not knowledge of a person's origin and weaknesses. – 2. With regard to the objection from the situation of David and other prophets, the response is that "from things that happen rarely one should not draw a general principle."[136] And since this type of honoring occurred rarely, therefore, etc. – As to the objection that the Galileans received him, Augustine answers that they received him externally and bodily, but not interiorly by faith. But the Lord does not require this type of honor.[137] For the Lord did not put great stock in external celebrations,[138] but in a mind of faith.

---

[136] See Chrysostom's Homily 35 n. 2 in PG 59:200 and FC 33, p. 345: "'What is this, then,' you may say; 'do we not see many men admired even by their countrymen?' It is particularly necessary not to judge such matters from rare examples. And if there are some men who are held in honor in their own country, they would be much more so in a strange country, since familiarity breeds contempt." Bonaventure's citation of Chrysostom is not verbatim. Hugh of St. Cher, p. 310c quotes Chrysostom: "But this rarely occurs, and from things that rarely occur one must not make a general statement."

[137] See Tractate 16 n. 3 and FC 79, p. 102: "And there, when he turned water into wine, as John himself writes, his disciples believed in him; and certainly the house was filled with crowds of guests. So great a miracle was performed and only his disciples believed in him."

[138] I have translated *in festo brachiali* by "in external celebrations." During a "brachial feast" there is a surcease of labor performed by human arms.

85. Question 2 is that of Gregory: Did this royal official believe or not?[139] – It seems that he didn't: – 1. For the Lord rebuked him in John 4:48: "Unless you see signs and wonders, you do not believe." – 2. The text itself supports this observation, since he asked that the Lord come down, as if he could not heal unless he was present. – But against this: If he didn't believe, why did he ask the Lord for the salvation of his son?

I answer that he believed, but half-heartedly. He believed that Christ had the power to cure and save his son, but he did not believe that divinity was present in Christ, by which he could be everywhere. Wherefore, there was faith when he petitioned for the cure, but there was a deficiency in his faith when he required Christ's physical presence.

86. Question 3 is also Gregory's: Why is it that the Lord offered to go to the centurion's servant,[140] whereas, when the royal official asked him, he refused to go?[141] – I respond

---

[139] See Homily 28 n. 1 of GGHG in CCSL cxli, p. 240 and Hurst, p. 222: "He had little faith in one he thought could not heal unless he was physically present. If he had believed completely he would have known that there was no place where God was not present. He was considerably distrustful, then, since it was not the Lord's greatness he esteemed but his physical presence. He sought a cure for his son even though his faith was in doubt, since he believed that the one he had approached had the power to cure, and yet he thought he was not with his dying son."

[140] See Matt 8:5-13 and Luke 7:1-10.

[141] See Homily 28 n. 2 of GGHG in CCSL cxli, pp. 240-241 and Hurst, p. 222-223: "Why is it that when the ruler asked him to come to his son he refused to go there in person, but he promised to go in person the servant, when the centurion had not asked him to do so?... Why was this, except to check our pride? We do not respect in people their nature, made in God's image, but their riches and reputation.... Certainly, if someone's servant asked us, [saying that] we should come to him, our pride would immediately suggest to our minds, You

that this took place to build up faith and morals. Faith, since when he offered to go to the centurion's house, he manifested to us the ardent nature of the centurion's faith. When he held himself back from going to the son of the royal official and cured him, even though he was not physically present, he invited the royal official to believe in his divinity. Now with regard to building up morals, the Lord offered to go to the servant of a centurion and refused to go to the son of a royal official, in order to curb our pride, for we bow before the mighty and scorn the lowly.[142]

---

shouldn't go because you would be lowering yourself; you would be risking your reputation and cheapen your position."

[142] Hugh of St. Cher, p. 311d has much the same interpretation in dependence upon Chrysostom and the Glossa.

CHAPTER FIVE

JOHN 5:1-11:56
THE SON OF GOD MANIFESTS HIMSELF AS HEALER, CONSERVER, DIRECTOR, AND VIVIFIER[1]

1. *After this there was*, etc. The Evangelist has completed his first main section in which he dealt with the manifestations of the Word incarnate from the perspective of the nature of the people encountering these manifestations. He now commences his second principal section about the manifestations of the Word incarnate and does so according to the nature of the Word who is manifesting himself. For he shows that the Son of God, who is the Word of the Father, manifests himself as *healer, conserver, director*, and *vivifier*.

The present chapter treats the first point of the Word as *healer*. The sixth chapter considers the Word as *conserver*. Chapters 7-10 present the Word as *director*. The Evangelist dedicates the eleventh chapter to the Word as perfect *restorer* in the resuscitation of Lazarus.

---

[1] This is my attempt to capture Bonaventure's rhyme: *curator, conservator, director, vivificator.*

John 5:1-47
The Word as healer

2. So the present chapter, in which the Word manifests himself as *healer* through the miraculous liberation of the paralytic, has four points, according to its four constituent components. The first component is *the miraculous cure*. The second is *false criticism of the cure* where verse 9 reads: "Now that day was a Sabbath." The third is *the refutation of the false criticism* where verse 18 says: "Therefore, in answer Jesus said to them."[2] The fourth is *the corroboration of the refutation* through many witnesses where verse 31 states: "If I bear witness," etc.

John 5:1-8
The miraculous cure

3. (Verse 1). So the Evangelist depicts this wondrous cure on the literal level from four angles: *the fittingness of the time*; *the layout of the site*; *the needy nature of the sick person*; *the power of the person who cures*.

So he first describes the fittingness of the time, since it was a festival time and during such times the Lord was wont to bestow gifts. Thus the text says: *After this*, that is, after the events narrated above, *there was a feast of the Jews*. Chrysostom comments that this festival day was Pentecost, which was midway between Passover and Scenopegia, that is, the solemnity of Tabernacles.[3] *And Jesus went up to Jerusalem*, according to the custom

---

[2] The Vulgate assigns these words to John 5:18. The Greek and most translations assign them to John 5:19.

[3] See Homily 36 n. 1 in PG 59:203: "What feast is this? It seems to me that it was Pentecost." Hugh of St. Cher, p. 311v argues that the feast is Pentecost in his Introduction and n. a.

followed by all Jews. Luke 2:42 says: "They went up[4] to Jerusalem according to the custom of the feast."

4. (Verse 2). *Now there is at Jerusalem*. This verse addresses the layout of the site where the cure took place. Since the cure occurred at the sheep pool, the verse reads: *Now there is at Jerusalem a sheep pool*, that is, a pool for cattle, since there the sacrificial animals were washed. And this pool was near the temple and got its name from its function. Thus, the text continues: *Called in Hebrew Bethsaida*, that is, house of cattle, because that was its task.[5] This pool was also decorated, as the text indicates: *Having five porticoes*. The next verse gives the reason for these:

5. (Verse 3). *In these were lying a great multitude of the sick*, who were incurable by the forces of nature. The text adds: *Blind, lame, and those with shriveled limbs, waiting for the moving of the water*, that is, so that they might be cured by the gift of divine grace, which was dispensed at the descent of an angel. So the text says:

6. (Verse 4).[6] *For an angel of the Lord used to come down at certain times into the pool*, that is, for the purpose of healing. The text adds the sign of the angel's descent:

---

[4] On p. 303 n. 11 QuarEd rightly note that the Vulgate reads *ascendentibus illis* ("They went up") while Bonaventure has *ascenderunt* ("They went up").

[5] On p. 304 n. 1 QuarEd cite Jerome's section on the Gospels from his *Liber de situ et nominibus locorum Hebraicorum*, a text I have not found: "*Bethsaida*, a pool in Jerusalem, which was called *probatike*, and can be interpreted by us to mean for cattle.... The priests were accustomed to wash the sacrificial animals in it. Thus the derivation of its name." In CCSL lxxii, p. 135 Jerome interprets Bethsaida as "house of fruit or house of hunters."

[6] This verse is not in the Greek. See Vulgate, p. 1665 where the text of John 5:4 occurs in the notes.

And the water was troubled, so that those who could not see the angel would see the water. The text then gives the divine effect: *And the first to go down into the pool after the troubling of the water*, as the most diligent, *was cured of whatever infirmity he had*, without distinction, since Acts 10:34 states: "God is not a respecter of persons."

7. (Verse 5). *Now a certain man was there*, etc. This verse introduces point three, that is, the neediness of the sick person, because he had been sick for a long time and had no *assistance*. Since he had been *sick for a long time*, the text reads: *Now a certain man was there. A certain man*, who[7] in his singular misery *had spent thirty-eight years in his infirmity*. Look at the length of the man's sickness which moved the Lord to have mercy on him and ask him a question and to speak with him. So the text continues:

8. (Verse 6). *When Jesus saw him lying there*, weighed down with his illness, *and knew that he had already been in this condition for a length of time*,[8] in the punishment of misery, *he said to him*, on account of his gracious compassion. *Do you want to get well?* through the strength of divine power. He said this not because he doubted the man's desire to get better, but so that the sick man might indicate his neediness. And he did so by his response. The text adds:

9. (Verse 7). *The sick man answered him: Sir, I have no one to put me into the pool once the water is stirred*. I am so poor that I have no one to help me. Psalm 21:12 cries out: "Tribulation is very near, and there is no one to help

---

[7] On p. 304 n. 3 QuarEd indicate the variations in the manuscripts, e.g., *qui* ("who") or *quia* ("since").

[8] On p. 304 n. 4 QuarEd accurately mention that the Vulgate reads *multum tempus* ("a long time") while Bonaventure has *multum temporis* ("a length of time").

me."⁹ And by myself I am powerless. So the text adds: *While I am coming, another steps down before me.*¹⁰ And so I am unable to be cured, since only one is cured and thatís the one who steps down first. Through his words the sick man indicates his neediness.

10. (Verse 8). *Jesus said to him.* The fourth point emerges here, that is, the power of the healer, since he cures by a mere command. Thus the text continues: *Rise, take up your pallet and walk. Rise*, because you are well. *Take up your pallet*, because you have gotten your strength back. *And walk*, because the cure is certain. And this took place. So the text adds:

11. (Verse 9). *And at once the man was cured.* Behold his good health. *And took up his pallet.* Behold his strength. *And began to walk.* Behold the certitude of his cure. And all this came about through Christís word. Psalm 148:5 says: "He spoke, and they came about." In Esther 13:9 Mordecai said: "Lord, almighty king, all things are in your power," etc.

12. The moral interpretation. The considerations here are: What is the pool that has five porticoes? Who are the sick? And how are they cured? – The pool, which is formed from rainwater, is repentance, during which there is an effusion of tears over the loss of heavenly goods. About this rain Jeremiah 5:24 reads: "They did not say...:

---

⁹ On p. 304 n. 5 QuarEd correctly indicate that the Vulgate reads *quoniam non* ("for there is no one") while Bonaventure has *et non* ("and there is no one").

¹⁰ On p. 304 n. 5 QuarEd rightly notice that the Vulgate reads *dum venio enim* ("for while I am coming") whereas Bonaventure has *dum venio* ("while I am coming").

Let us fear our God,[11] who gives us the early rains," that is, compunction for the evils we have committed, and the latter rain, for the good deeds we have omitted. This rain falls into the valleys, and is not found on the mountains and with the proud. 2 Samuel 1:21 states: "Mountains of Gilboa, let neither dew nor rain come upon you." – This pool of repentance has five porticoes, in which rest a multitude of sick, for there are five considerations that should make human beings remain in a penitent state.

13. The first consideration is the guilt of sin, by which people obligate themselves to suffer punishment.[12] Psalm 37:18 reads: "For I am ready for scourges, and my sorrow in continually before my eyes." – The second consideration is the severity of the judgment. Sirach 2:22 states: "If we do not do penance, we will fall into the hands of the Lord." Hebrews 10:31 has: "It is a horrific thing to fall into the hands of the living God."[13] – The third consideration is the present opportunity, for afterwards there will be opportunity to repent. Qoheleth 9:10 reads: "Whatsoever your hand is able to do, do it earnestly. For neither work, nor reasons, nor wisdom, nor knowledge will be in hell, whither you are hastening."[14] – The fourth consideration

---

[11] The Vulgate reads *Dominum Deum nostrum* ("the Lord our God").

[12] See Hugh of St. Cher, p. 312b where he notes that the five porticoes are the means by which the sinner comes to the recognition that he must embark on the road of repentance. Through the first portico of repentance the sinner provides restitution for all that he has stolen.

[13] See Hugh of St. Cher, p. 312b where the second portico is the realization that unless the sinner repents in the present, he will suffer eternal punishments in the future for all his sins. Hugh quotes Hebr 10:31.

[14] See Hugh of St. Cher, p. 312b where the third portico is the realization that after death there is no opportunity for repentance. Hugh cites Qoh 9:10.

is the uncertainty of the last day.[15] Qoheleth 9:12 states: "Men and women do not know their own end, but as fish are taken with the hook and as birds are caught with the snare, so men and women are taken in the evil time, when it will suddenly come upon them." – The fifth consideration is the uncertainty of one's own status, since people do not know whether they are doing something that is pleasing to God.[16] Therefore, Psalm 76:11 says: "And I said: Now I have begun." Sirach 10:11 has: "All power is of short life."[17]

14. The sick are: The blind sin out of ignorance.[18] Matthew 15:14 reads: "They are blind guides of blind people. But if a blind person guides a blind person, both fall into the pit." – They are the lame, who sin on account of powerlessness. Hebrews 12:13 says: "Make straight paths for your feet, so that you may not be lame."[19] – They are those with shriveled limbs, who sin out of malice or hardness of heart.[20] Sirach 3:27 states: "A hard heart will fear evil on the last day." Sirach 37:3 reads: "O wicked presumption!

---

[15] See Hugh of St. Cher, p. 312b where the fourth portico is the recognition that it is more fruitful and easier to do penance immediately rather than at the end of one's life or in purgatory.

[16] See Hugh of St. Cher, p. 312b where the fifth portico is the realization that repentance prolongs temporal life while continual sinning shortens it.

[17] On p. 305 n. 3 QuarEd indicate that some manuscripts cite Qoh 9:1: "Human beings do not know whether they are worthy of love or hatred."

[18] Hugh of St. Cher, p. 312f comments that the blind are blind because of ignorance and supports his case by two citations from Isaiah.

[19] The Vulgate reads *ut non claudicans erret* ("that no one who is lame may go out of the way") while Bonaventure has *ut non claudicetis* ("that you may not be lame").

[20] Hugh of St. Cher, p. 312h observes that those with shriveled limbs are those who are hard of heart.

Why have you shriveled up the earth and covered it with your malice and deceitfulness?"

These are cured when the angel comes, that is, at the divine visitation. Job 33:19 says: "He rebuked by sorrow while he was in his bed," etc. – After the stirring of the water, that is, internal tears.[21] Lamentations 2:19 has: "Pour out your heart like water before the face of the Lord." – By coming down into the pool of water, that is, the humility of repentance. Isaiah 47:1 reads: "Come down. Sit in the dust, O virgin daughter of Babylon. Sit on the ground. There is no throne for the daughter of the Chaldeans."

QUESTIONS

15. Question 1 concerns the power of this pool. – 1. How did the pool get this power, and why did this pool continuously have such power? – 2. Furthermore, since its power was so great, why is it that the Scriptures made no mention of it? It seems that the writers of Sacred Scripture were negligent. – If you say that this power first appeared near the passion of Christ, the question then arises: Why did it appear about the time of the passion and why, once the passion took place, did it cease?

Some answer that the wood of the cross was in that pool and that it began to appear at that time and float on the surface of the pool. So the Lord wanted to perform this miracle to make known the triumph of his passion. It

---

[21] Hugh of St. Cher, p. 313b comments: "Those who want to be cured must, after the moving of the water, descend into the pool, that is, after devotion and the shedding of tears they should take the next step of humbling themselves in repentance."

was near the time of his passion that the wood began to surface and float. It ceased functioning after the passion, because the wood had been taken out of the pool. – But this interpretation lacks scriptural authority, and since it is proposed without any authority, it is to be dismissed.[22] – Because of this others are of the opinion that the water had no power, but that the angel, who descended at a certain time, conveyed to the water the power that the Lord had given him. – Therefore, the observation should be made that the power given to the angel for the water is a figure of baptism, in which there is cleansing through the water and healing through the Spirit.[23] And this power was set forth near the time of baptism, and when baptism arrived, it ceased. Therefore, since its existence is first mentioned during the Lord's life and since it existed for so short a time, Scripture made no note of it.[24] – These are the answers to every objection.

---

[22] See Peter Comestor, *Historia scholastica, in Evangelia*, c. 81 in PL 198:1579BC: "Some have handed down the tradition that the Queen of Sheba in the spirit saw in the house of the forest (1 Kings 7:2), which was called Nethota, the wood of the Lord's cross, and announced to Solomon, after she had already departed from him, that some man would die on it and that because of his murder the Jews would perish and they would destroy their sacred place and people. Solomon was in dread at this news and buried the wood in the ground, where afterwards a pool was made. Now when the time of Christ's passion drew near, the wood floated to the surface, as if announcing Christ beforehand, and its surfacing caused the aforementioned moving of the water. But this is not authentic." Hugh of St. Cher, p. 312v,a cites the tradition, found in Peter Comestor, and determines that "it is not authentic."

[23] See Chrysostom's Homily 36 n. 1 in PG 59:203 and FC 33, p. 352: "He was on the point of giving baptism, which has much power and is a very great gift, baptism which cleanses of all sin and brings men to life, when they have been dead. These effects were foreshadowed as if in figure by the pool and by many of the other details of the event."

[24] Hugh of St. Cher, p. 312v,a explores three answers to what he calls question 3: Did the cure take place because of something existing in the water or because of the descent of the angel?

16. Question 2 asks: 1. Since it is just as easy for the Lord to cure all as it is one person and since the Lord is most generous, why didn't he give that water the effect of curing all? – 2. Likewise, a similar question is asked of the Lord himself: Why did he cure only one person, when he could as easily cure all the sick rather than just a single sick person?

I answer that this bodily healing was performed more for its sign value than as a gift to the person healed. For it was ordained to the healing of the soul. Since it was ordained to designate and prefigure that, it had to be performed in such a way that it would give optimal signification. And since healing in the Church only occurs in the unity of faith and charity, only one person was healed.[25]

Since this cure was not only for the sick person's benefit, but was also a sign, there is no valid objection to it.[26]

17. Question 3 raises another question about the miracle: If it is the nature of mercy to be merciful to those in misery,[27] it follows that where there is greater misery, there greater mercy must be exercised. Wherefore, the

---

[25] See Augustine's Sermon 125 n. 6 in *Sermons*, Trans. and notes Edmund Hill, WSA III/4 (Hyde Park, NY: New City Press, 1992), p. 258: "And why only one man? It is because there is only one Church throughout the whole world that unity is restored to health. So where only one man is restored to health, unity is signified. By 'one man' you must understand unity. So don't withdraw from the unity, if you don't want to be exempt from this saving restoration to health."

[26] On p. 306 n. 1 QuarEd comment on this sentence: "We have supplied this response from the codices."

[27] This principle is artfully constructed: Si *misericordiae est misereri miseriae*. See Book XX, c. 32. n. 63 of *S. Gregorii Magni Moralia in Iob Libri XI-XXII*, ed. Marcus Adriaen. CCSL cxliiia (Turnhout: Brepols, 1979), p. 1049: "Now mercy is called forth from a heart that is touched by misery, in that each person sees some person in misery and feels compassionate towards that person. For he is touched with a sorrow of

person who descended first should not be cured, but the person in greater need. – In answer I point to what has already been said, that is, that the miracle was a sign of the healing of the soul. Further, since God heals the soul according to the soul's disposition to receive grace and not according to the gravity of sins on the soul, it follows that the person who was more diligent and went into the water first was the first to obtain healing.

18. Question 4 deals with the Lord's other healings. When the Lord encouraged the paralytic in Matthew 9:2 to have courage[28] and demanded a confession of faith from others whom he healed,[29] how does it happen here that he asks nothing whatsoever from the man? – I answer that we should understand that when the Lord healed anyone, he healed the person not only in body, but also in soul. He healed the entire person. – For this reason one should note that there were some who had fallen into sickness because of sin. And since these must be healed in soul and the soul is only healed by faith in Christ, the Lord required a confession of faith from such people. – There were others, who were sick in order to manifest the glory of God, such as the man born blind in John 9 below and the deceased Lazarus in John 11 below. From such people the Lord did not require a confession of faith. Rather he gave them health out of sheer liberality. And John highlights the miraculous cure of such individuals. So since this sick person falls into this category, the Lord

---

soul, which makes his heart compassionate to free the person he sees from his misery."

[28] See Matt 9:2: "And behold, they brought to him a paralytic lying on a pallet. And Jesus, seeing their faith, said to the paralytic: Take courage, son. Your sins are forgiven."

[29] See Matt 9:28: "And when Jesus had reached the house, the blind men came to him. And Jesus said to them: Do you believe that I can do this for you? They answered him: Yes, Lord."

did not require faith from him. – But since this solution to the query runs counter to the Glossa,[30] it should be said that he only required faith from those who ask for restoration to health.

John 5:9-18b
THE FALSE CRITICISM OF THE HEALING

19. *Now that day was a Sabbath*. After the description of the miraculous cure of the paralytic, the Evangelist comes to his second point: *the defamatory attack against the cure* and proceeds in this fashion. First is *the rebuke of the person cured*. Second is *the developing calumny against the healer*. Third is *the manifestation of the healer*. Fourth is *the persecution of the one manifested*. Fifth is *the stubbornness in persecution*.

20. (Verse 9). So the Evangelist suggests his first point, the rebuke of the person cured, in that he notes that it was on the Sabbath that Christ healed the man and that the man took up his pallet. For this reason the Evangelist intimates the occasion for the defamatory attack when he says: *Now that day was a Sabbath*, that is, on which he had been healed and had taken up his pallet. The Jews

---

[30] See the Glossa Ordinaria on John 5:14 in PL 114:377c: "He intimates that he had been sick because of his sins." See Chrysostom's Homily 37 n. 2 in PG 59:209 and FC 33, p. 362: "Now, why did He not require faith of this man as He did in the case of the blind men, when He said: 'Do you believe that I can do this for you?' Because this man did not yet know clearly who He was. It was not before His miracles, but after them, that He appeared to seek this prerequisite [of faith].... Therefore, it is not at the beginning of His miracles that Matthew refers to Christ as making this stipulation, but only to the two blind men, at the time when He had worked many miracles." Hugh of St. Cher, p. 314a seems to follow Chrysostom's opinion.

seized upon this circumstance to rebuke him. So the text adds:

21. (Verse 10). *Therefore, the Jews said to the person who had been made healthy,*[31] accusing him: *It is the Sabbath: You are not permitted to take up your pallet.* For *to take up one's pallet* was seen as servile labor and had been prohibited on the Sabbath. Leviticus 23:8 reads: "The seventh day will be more celebrative and more holy. You shall do no servile labor on it."

22. (Verse 11). *He answered them.* This verse introduces the second point, that is, the development of a defamatory attack against the healer, because the sick man who had been healed defended his behavior by referring to the command of the healer. So the text continues: *He who made me well said to me: Take up your pallet and walk,* thereby commanding me by his own authority. And certainly the person who had such power for good also had the authority to issue so great a command. For Matthew 9:6 says: "But that you may know that the Son of Man has power on earth to forgive sins; he said to the paralytic: Arise, take up your pallet and go to your house." If he could forgive sins, it follows that he could dispense from the precept of the Sabbath. But the Jews, who turned a deaf ear to his words, asked about the healer, so that they could accuse him. Therefore, the text adds:

23. (Verse 12). *So they asked him: Who is this man,* who is a sick person, not God Almighty, *who said to you: Take up your pallet and walk?* He was sick because he commanded

---

[31] On p. 306 n. 9 QuarEd accurately notice that the Vulgate reads *illi qui sanatus fuerat* ("to the person who had been healed") while Bonaventure has *ei qui sanus factus fuerat* ("to the person who had been made healthy").

someone to act against the Law. The Jews ignored the fact that he had the power to cure. They stressed what was wrong and were silent about the good. Proverbs 11:27 states: "The person who seeks good things does well to rise early. The seeker after evil things will be oppressed by them."[32]

24. (Verse 13). *But the man who had been healed did not know who it was.* So their inquiry of necessity had to come up short. Psalm 63:7 says: "They have failed in their search." So it was said to the Jews in John 7:36 below: "You will seek me and will not find me," because they were not seeking to have knowledge, but to persecute.

25. *But[33] Jesus had quietly gone away.* The third point occurs here, namely, the manifestation of the Christ sought, but not found. This manifestation occurred not in the crowd, but in the church. So the text continues: *But Jesus had quietly gone away, since there was a crowd in the place,* that is, Jesus had gone away from the multitude that was in the place of the cure. Therefore, the healed man did not know him, since he had remained in and with the crowd.

26. (Verse 14). *Afterwards Jesus found him in the temple,* that is, when he had gotten away from the crowd. Augustine comments: "When he was in the crowd, he did not recognize Jesus, but afterwards he did in the temple."[34]

---

[32] On p. 306 n. 11 QuarEd correctly indicate that the Vulgate reads *consurgit* ("to rise") while Bonaventure has *surgit* ("to rise"). Further, the Vulgate reads *qui autem investigator* ("the person who seeks after") whereas Bonaventure has *investigator* ("the seeker").

[33] On p. 307 n. 1 QuarEd rightly notice that the Vulgate reads *enim* ("for") while Bonaventure has *autem* ("but"). Hugh of St. Cher, p. 313i also reads *autem*.

[34] See Tractate 17 n. 11 in CCSL xxxvi, p. 176.

Through this we are taught that whoever desires to come to a vision of God should flee the crowd of his affections and the wickedness of human beings and proceed to the temple of internal prayer.[35] For in the resuscitation of the little girl in Matthew 9:24 he commanded that the tumultuous crowd be cast out.[36] And since the Lord's mercy anticipates our actions, the text does not say that the healed man found Jesus, but that Jesus found him.[37] For he would not have recognized Jesus if Jesus had not first approached him. Therefore, the text adds: *Jesus said to him*, giving him instructions like a good physician: *Behold, you are cured*, as he reminds him of the gift of his healing. *Sin no more*, as he dissuades him from future sin. *Lest something worse befall you*, as he threatens with danger.[38] Luke 11:26 states: "The last state of that man has become worse than the first."[39]

27. (Verse 15). *The man went away*. This verse treats the fourth point, that is, the persecution of Christ who has been manifested. For the Jews realized, after the man

---

[35] For a more developed spiritual interpretation along these lines see Bede's commentary on John 5:10 in PL 92:693BC: "Now the fact that the man who had been healed did not recognize Jesus while he was still in the crowd, but afterwards in the temple, instructs us mystically that if we truly desire to recognize the grace of our Creator, to be confirmed by his love, and to come to a vision of him, we must diligently flee the crowd, not only of tumultuous thoughts and evil affections, but also of men and women who can block what we sincerely propose or teach us evil ways by bad example, or mock or even forbid our good works."

[36] Matt 9:24 reads: "Be gone, the girl is asleep, not dead."

[37] Hugh of St. Cher, p. 314v,a comments: "It should be noted that the text does not say that he found Jesus, but that Jesus found him. For Jesus is most diligent in seeking us and calling us back."

[38] Hugh of St. Cher, p. 314v,b observes: "He mentions three things: He recalls the preceding gift. He forbids sin. He threatens punishment."

[39] The Vulgate reads *sunt* ("are") whereas Bonaventure reads *facta sunt* ("have become").

had informed them, that Christ had made him well. Thus, the text continues: *The man went away and told the Jews*, who had earlier asked him, *that it was Jesus who had healed him*. He did not say this by way of detraction or accusation, but by way of proclaiming the name of Christ. For the Glossa observes: "That man proclaimed salvation to the Jews, so that they might follow him. But on the contrary they began to persecute him."[40] So the text adds:

28. (Verse 16). *And this is why the Jews kept persecuting Jesus, because he kept doing these things on the Sabbath.* For he seemed to have as his purpose to destroy their Law and to act contrary to the Lord who had given them the commandment of observing the Sabbath. John 9:16 below states: "This man is not from God, for he does not keep the Sabbath." Luke 6:7 reads: "The scribes and the Pharisees were watching Jesus whether he would heal on the Sabbath."

29. (Verse 17). *But Jesus answered.* The fifth observation surfaces here, that is, their stubbornness in persecution, which followed upon the Lord's response in which he showed that he did not break the Sabbath. So the text continues: *But Jesus said to them*, the Jews who are persecuting him: *My Father works even unto now*, even on the Sabbath and doesn't violate the Sabbath. *And I work*, namely, by working together with the Father, even on the Sabbath. So if God doesn't break the Sabbath, neither do I. Matthew 12:8 says: "The Son of Man is Lord even of

---

[40] This is the Glossa Interlinearis. See Augustine's Tractate 17 n. 12 in FC 79, p. 119: "He brought the news and they raged. He made known his salvation; they did not seek their own salvation." Hugh of St. Cher, p. 314v,h comments: "He told the Jews] not as an accuser, but as a preacher who wanted them to be converted to that very same gift."

the Sabbath." And since he is Lord, he can work on the Sabbath without any rebuke. Because of this response the Jews have become obdurate in their malice when they should have found peace in it. So the text adds, that is, because of Jesus' answer:

30. (Verse 18). *So this is why the Jews were seeking to put him to death.* Since they could not contradict his answer, they were seeking to kill him. John 7:20 below states: "Why are you seeking to kill me, a man, who has spoken true things to you?"[41] *Because he not only broke the Sabbath*, in their opinion, *but also called God his own Father. His own* in a unique sense. *Making himself equal to God*, which they regarded as blasphemy. John 10:33 below reads: "Not for a good work do we stone you, but for blasphemy and because you, although you are a human being, make yourself God." *Making*, as if he weren't, but was making himself God.

QUESTIONS

31. Question 1 asks: Since the commandment about the Sabbath is a commandment from the first table of the Law, from which, as Bernard says, God cannot dispense, it seems that the Lord did wrong when he broke the Sabbath.[42] – If you say that in this commandment there is a moral dimension and a ceremonial dimension and that

---

[41] It seems that Bonaventure has combined John 7:20 and 8:40. John 7:20 reads: "Why do you seek to kill me?" John 8:40 says: "But as it is, you are seeking to kill me, a man who has spoken the truth to you...."

[42] See c. 3 n. 6-7 of *Liber de Praecepto et Dispensatione* in SBOp 3.257-258 from which Bonaventure infers the opinion he attributes to Bernard. See Ex 20:1-17 and Deut 5:6-21 for the Decalogue. The first three commandments concern one's dealings with God; the remaining seven pertain to one's dealings with one's neighbor.

its moral dimension pertains to the first table and Christ did not break it whereas he did break the ceremonial dimension that does not pertain to the Decalogue....

But then there are two additional questions. 1. What are the moral and the ceremonial components of this third commandment? – 2. Moroever, why does this third commandment have more ceremonial observance connected with it than any other commandment of the Decalogue? – It seems that these components should not be intermingled, just as shadow does not mix with reality.

I answer that, as was mentioned, the commandment about the Sabbath has a moral as well as a ceremonial component. And therefore, in the Law it occurs not only among the moral, but also among the ceremonial. – 1. So if anyone asks what is moral and what is ceremonial in the third commandment, I respond that in this commandment human beings are commanded to be at rest for God's sake, so that they may be God's temples through love. This is the moral component. Beyond this there is the signification of the day[43] and in addition the cessation from all servile labor.[44] And these two items comprise the ceremonial component. – 2. With regard to the question why the third commandment has ceremonials intermixed with it, Augustine responds in

---

[43] Deut 5:15 states: "Remember that you also did serve in Egypt, and the Lord your God brought you out from there with a strong hand and an outstretched arm. Therefore, he has commanded you that you should observe the Sabbath day."

[44] Deut 5:14 says: "The seventh is the day of the Sabbath, that is, the rest of the Lord your God. You shall not do any work thereon, you nor your son nor your daughter, nor your manservant nor your maidservant, nor your ox nor your ass nor any of your beasts, nor the stranger that is within your gates: that your manservant and your maidservant may rest, even as you yourself."

his Letter to Januarius that it is the commandment of love, for the third commandment looks to the third person in the Trinity, and that love is commanded there. So in order to show that all ceremonials must have reference to the love of God and neighbor and must be interpreted according to this purpose, he intermingled the observance of ceremonials with the commandment of love.[45] – Another reason can be proffered: To the commandment of love all the other commandments are directed and in it they are fulfilled.[46] – Furthermore, in being at rest with God and by considering the divine law, a person is made loving in the observance of the same law. So since this commandment prescribes love and rest for God, the observance of all the commandments hangs from it. And therefore, when this is neglected and delivered to oblivion, all the other commandments are neglected. Wherefore, lest it be handed over to oblivion, the Lord signified the day. And lest it might be neglected on account of other things, he commanded cessation from all other things. And this is the ceremonial component.

---

[45] See Letter 55, c. 11, n. 20 and *Saint Augustine Letters, Volume I (1-82)*, trans.Wilfrid Parsons, FC 12 (New York: Fathers of the Church, 1951), p. 276: "The Holy Spirit, through whom that rest is granted to us, which we universally crave but do not find except by loving God, since 'His charity is poured forth in our hearts by the Holy Spirit Who is given to us,' because God sanctified the seventh day in which He rested, has enjoined on us in the third commandment, which is written about the observance of the Sabbath, not that we are to expect to rest now, in this life, but that all good works which we perform should have no other intention but that eternal rest to come." – The astute reader begins to grasp Bonaventure's logic: the third commandment is the commandment of the Holy Spirit, who will give us eternal rest, foreseen in the third commandment and who has already poured forth his love into our hearts; therefore, the third commandment is the commandment of love, empowered by the Holy Spirit; finally, any and all ceremonial aspects in the third commandment must be oriented to love.

[46] See Rom 13:8-10.

32. Question 2 asks further whether the Lord broke the commandment about ceremonial observance on the Sabbath. – It seems not since the only thing prohibited on the Sabbath was servile work, and the Lord performed no servile work on the Sabbath. For in Luke 14:3-6 the Lord showed that he did not break the Sabbath.[47] – But it seems that he did break the Sabbath, for the Jews were persecuting him because of it.

I answer that the Lord's observance of the ceremonial aspect of the Sabbath was threefold: spiritual, literal, and customary. He did not break nor could he break the spiritual. Rather he fulfilled it. He could break the literal, but he did not, for he performed no servile labor. He did break what was customary and commanded that it be broken. He broke it when "he made clay from spittle."[48] He commanded that it be broken when he commanded the man to take up his pallet. For such actions were not against the literal observance, but against the customary and the later interpretations of the commandment.

33. Question 3 raises an objection about John 5:16: "The Jews kept persecuting Jesus, because he did these things on the Sabbath." If the Lord could have done what he did on the Sabbath equally well on other days, it seems that the Lord himself brought the persecution of the Jews upon himself without any fitting reason.

---

[47] That is, the Lord's healing was not servile work. See Luke 14:3-4: "And Jesus asked the lawyers and the Pharisees, saying: Is it lawful to cure on the Sabbath? But they remained silent. And he took and healed him and let him go."

[48] See John 9:6.

I answer that the reason for this lies in the truth of teaching.[49] For since ceremonial observances had to cease with the coming of Christ, he, who was the teacher of the truth, had to teach this and show it through his behavior, so that the truth of the Gospel might remain with us. – The second reason was the severity of divine judgment, since, as John 9:39 below says: "For judgment I have come into this world," etc. So since from this action the wicked were blinded to procure Christ's death, which was our salvation, and the good were illumined to believe in him who had given the Law and could break it, therefore, etc. – The third reason is common necessity, since at that time the poor and the simple were accustomed to gather in the synagogues on the Sabbath, and the Lord had to attract them through miracles.

34. Question 4 deals with the Lord's answer to the Jews in John 5:17: "My Father works even until now, and I work." – Contrary to this is Genesis 2:2: "God rested ... from all the work[50] God had done." It seems that there is a contradiction here. – I answer that what is described in Genesis is the work of the first creation, and this consists in the creation of those things that pertain to the completion of the world and include within themselves creation, division, and ornamentation. And this was completed in six days. From this work God rested. There is another work, that of conservation. And since things could not be conserved in and by themselves, since they have been brought forth to be corrupted by nature, this work consists in the transmutation and propagation and creation of souls. And God is engaged in this work and

---

[49] On p. 308 n. 7 QuarEd indicate that many witnesses read *doctrinae necessitas* ("the necessity of teaching").

[50] The Vulgate reads *ab universo opere* ("from all the work") while Bonaventure has *ab omni opere* ("from all the work").

works together with nature. And this passage deals with this type of work, from which God does not cease on the Sabbath.[51]

John 5:18c-30
Christ's refutation of the Jews' defamatory attack

35. *Therefore, Jesus answered*, etc. The Evangelist has just described the miraculous cure and the defamatory attack against it. This verse commences the third section of this chapter, which lays out a *refutation of this calumny*. For the Lord refutes the Jews who are calumniating him for his work of healing and does so by demonstrating his omnipotent power to perform works. – This section has two parts. The first indicates and declares his power *in general*. The second concentrates on his power *in particular* where verse 24 reads: "Amen, amen I say to you: The person who hears my word."

John 5:18c-23
Christ's omnipotent power in general

36. (Verses 18c-19). So the power of the Son of God is declared and manifested in this order. First *the origin*

---

[51] Bonaventure's understanding of *conservation* may ultimately go back to Book IV, c. 12 n. 22-23 of Augustine's "The Literal Meaning of Genesis." See *On Genesis*, p. 253: "But he (God) rested like this in such a way as to continue from then on and up till now to operate the management of the things that were then set in place, not as though at least on that seventh day his power was withheld from the government of heaven and earth and of all the things he had established; if that had been done, they would forthwith have collapsed into nothingness.... Indeed, the very expression employed by the Lord, *My Father is working until now*, points to the continuousness of his work, by which he holds together and manages the whole of creation."

of the power is mentioned. Second *the magnitude of the power*. Third *the declaration of the magnitude*. Fourth *the reason for the declaration*.

So first the origin of the power of the Son of God is stated. For the Son of God says that he does not have the power of working from himself, but from the Father. Therefore, the text states: *Therefore, Jesus answered and said to them*, that is, to the Jews who were persecuting and calumniating him: *Amen, amen I say to you*, that is, truly and with certitude, *the Son can do nothing by himself*. For just as he does not have existence by himself, but from the Father, so neither does he work by himself, but from the Father. John 8:28 below states: "I do nothing by myself." *But only what he sees the Father doing*, that is, he can only do what the Father has given him power to do. John 8:38 below reads: "I speak about what I have seen with my Father."[52] And so whatever he can do, he can do from the Father, and he can do nothing other than what he has received from the Father.

37. *For whatever he does*, etc. The Evangelist introduces his second point here, that is, the magnitude of the power, for although the Son is receiving power from the Father, nevertheless he has power as great as the Father. So the text continues: *For whatever*. I just mentioned the excellent passage that the Son "does what he sees the Father doing."[53] *For whatever he does*,[54] *this the Son also does in like manner. In like manner*, uniformly and harmoniously. *In like manner*, since there is equal power. For it is said of the Son in Colossians 1:16: "All things

---

[52] The Vulgate does not read *meum* ("my").

[53] See John 8:28 and n. 36 above.

[54] On p. 309 n. 2 QuarEd accurately indicate that the Vulgate reads *fecerit* ("he does") while Bonaventure has *facit* ("he does").

were created through him and in him," for as John 1:3 above says: "Without him was made nothing." And the reason for this non-division in work is the non-division in essence and in love. Therefore, the text adds:

38. (Verse 20). *For the Father loves the Son.* I have made the good point that the Son can do everything that the Father also does. *For the Father loves the Son.* Therefore, *he loves* to the supreme extent, because they are supremely one. John 10:30 states: "The Father and I are one." And since they are supremely one, he communicates everything to the Son. So the text continues: *And shows him all that he himself does. He shows him,* that is, he communicates the power for every work. And the reason for this communication is unity and love. John 3:35 above says: "The Father loves the Son and has given all things into his hand."

39. *And greater works than these,* etc. The third observation occurs here: The declaration of the magnitude of the power that takes place through the magnitude of the works that the Lord has shown the Jews through the Son. So the text states: *And greater works than these,* supply: that have been shown you, *works he will show him,* that is, he will show you through him, *so that you may wonder,* on account of their magnitude. Supply what John 10:32 reads: "I have shown you many good works." And he shows what these works are, namely, raising of the dead. Thus, the text continues:

40. (Verse 21). *For as the Father raises the dead and gives them life,* through almighty power, *even so the Son also gives life to whom he wills,* through the power equal to that of the Father. John 11:44 below treats the raising of Lazarus in body, and John 11:25 deals with the raising of his soul: "I am the resurrection and the life. The person

who believes in me, even if he dies, will live." A similar example to this bodily raising up occurs in Luke 7:15.[55]

41. (Verse 22). *For the Father does not judge anyone.* The fourth point surfaces here, that is, the reason for the declaration of this power, that is, why God declares that his power is in and through the Son. So that he may show that he is equal to him and equally to be honored. And therefore, he has given judgment to the Son. For this reason the text reads: *For the Father.* John 5:20 puts the matter well: "Greater works than these he will show him, so that you may wonder," for he thereby also gave him the judgment. So the text states: *For the Father does not judge anyone,* namely, by appearing in judgment, *but has given all judgment to the Son.* Acts 10:42 says: "He has been constituted by God as judge of the living and the dead." And the reason for this is the honoring of the Son. Thus, the text adds:

42. (Verse 23). *So that all may honor the Son as they honor the Father.* About this Proverbs 7:1 states: "Son, honor the Lord, and you will be well. Do not fear a foreign god in addition to him."[56] The Son of God is to be honored and feared because of his judiciary power, since as Matthew 10:28 states: "He is able to destroy both soul and body in hell." And the reason why the Father wants the Son to be honored is that the honor of the Son is the Father's honor. So the text continues: *The person who does not honor the Son does not honor the Father who sent him.* John 8:49 below says: "I honor my Father, and you dishonor me." Augustine observes: "If the Son is believed in less than

---

[55] Luke 7:15 concludes the story of Jesus' raising of the only son of the widow of Nain: "And he who was dead sat up and began to speak."

[56] On p. 309 n. 8 QuarEd rightly indicate that the Vulgate does not have this verse, which is from the LXX.

the Father, the Father is dishonored, for either in his envy he did not want to beget an equal or being weak, he could not."[57]

Questions

43. Question 1 concerns John 5:19: "The Son can do nothing by himself." – Contrary. The individual who can do things by himself is more powerful than the individual who does things through another. But the Father can do things by himself whereas the Son from another. Wherefore, the Father is more powerful than the Son. – But if you say: The vast majority of power consists in actual strength and not in having power, and to have power by oneself refers solely to the manner of having power and not to actual power, then the conclusion follows that the Father is not more powerful than the Son. However, the objection arises that the more noble way of having power is to have it from oneself and not from another. Therefore, if the Father has power from himself, he has it in a nobler manner than the Son, who possesses his power from another.

The answer to this problem lies in the observation that to have from another occurs in two ways, namely, through participation and through emanation alone. To have from another through participation is the less noble manner, for the manner of participation is not equal to the manner of having by essence. The other manner of having is *to* have from another solely through emanation, with the result

---

[57] See Tractate 19 n. 6 in FC 79, p. 144: "I want, you say, to give greater honor to the Father, less to the Son. There you take honor away from the Father where you give less to the Son. For what else do you think when you reflect in that way except that the Father did not want or could not beget a Son equal to himself? If he did not want to, he was envious; if he could not, he lacked the ability."

that that which emanates has by essence the same as that which is giving. And this has no trace whatsoever of an ignoble nature. Rather there is entire equality. For to have from the Father is a characteristic of nobility in the Son, just as to beget is in the Father. And so the answer is clear and obvious.[58]

44. Question 2 focuses on John 5:19: "The Son can do only what he sees the Father doing" and John 5:20: "The Father shows the Son whatever he does."[59] – 1. Therefore, if something exists by nature prior to its being seen, the Father works beforehand, and afterwards the Son does his work as if following an exemplar. – 2. Likewise, if the Father can do nothing whatsoever without the Son, how does the Evangelist say that the Son works just as he sees the Father working?

I respond. It has to be maintained that the following two expressions, "The Father shows the Son" and "The Son sees the Father working," are the same. They differ with regard to their purposes. Now it should be understood that these words are being transferred from creatures to God. Further, the word shows and the characteristic feature of seeing both are twofold. That is, there is the emanation of understanding. Since I see you working in such a manner, an understanding of working is left in me. There is also the exemplarity of the antecedent. In such a way, your working and its showing precede, as an exemplar, my understanding. Wherefore, I say that by reason of the first instance, that is, by reason of emanation and not by reason of the antecedent, that

---

[58] See Book I, d. 19. p. 1 q. 2 in Bonaventure's *Sentence Commentary*.

[59] Bonaventure has slightly adjusted John 5:20: "For the Father loves the Son and shows him all that he himself does."

these human words are transferred to the divine. Thus, the words, "the Father shows the Son," do not mean that the Father has knowledge before the Son, but that the Father gives to the Son. Furthermore, the words, "the Son sees the Father working," do not mean that the Father works beforehand, but that the Son possesses what he has from the Father.[60]

45. Question 3 concerns John 5:19: "Whatever the Father does, this the Son also does in like manner." – Contrary. 1. The Father begets the Son. Therefore, the Son begets a Son. – If you say that the word "to beget" does not indicate a work, but a relationship, then there is this objection that "to send the Son" does indicate a work. Wherefore, if whatever work the Father does, that also the Son does, then it follows that if the Father sends the Son, then also the Son sends the Son. – 2. Moreover, if the Trinity is entirely undivided in substance and operation and further, since manifestation and appearance are effected through an operation, how can the Trinity appear or manifest themselves in a determinate way in one of their hypostases? This seems in no way possible.

---

[60] Bonaventure has taken Augustine's answer to this problem and translated into his own categories of emanation and exemplarity. See Tractate 21 n. 3-4 in FC 79, p. 183: "But not, at any time, was he not born and later born, just as not, at any time, did he not see and later see; but in that which for him is 'to see,' in the same way is for him 'to be'.... Therefore let us not interpret carnally that the Father sits and does work and shows it to the Son, and that the Son sees the work which the Father does and does that in another place or from another material. For 'all things were made through him, and without him was made nothing.' The Word of the Father is the Son; God has said nothing that he has not said in the Son. For by saying in the Son what he was going to do through the Son, he begot the Son himself through whom he might do all things."

With regard to these objections the point should be made that certain words applied to God indicate solely a relationship such as "to beget." Others indicate solely an action such as "to create." Others indicate action and relationship such as "to send." Others indicate action and signification such as "to appear." – Therefore, I maintain that when the text says "Whatever the Father does," it should be understood on the level of an operation that is both communal and essential. Wherefore, if the verb is inferred to signify solely an action, that inference is sound. However, if the verb is taken to signify solely a relationship, then that inference is rank sophistry and a playing with words. Now if the verb is taken to indicate both action and relationship, this is, nonetheless, invalid because it includes relationship, even though the inference relative to action was valid such as in the cases of "to send" and "to become flesh." It is similar if one combines action and signification, for the inference is invalid on account of signification. For just as Augustine says: Even though every action and appearance is effected by the three, nevertheless, one signifies the Father in a special way, another the Son.[61] – An example of this occurs in the word "understanding" that results from the operation of three powers, namely, memory, understanding, and will, but yet signifies just one of the three. This is what is happening in the point at issue here, and the objections are patently false.

---

[61] See *Contra Sermonem Arianorum*, c. 16 in PL 42:695 where Augustine comments on Gen 1:26: "Let us make human beings in our image" and says that this most fittingly applies to the Trinity. He goes on to reflect upon the three components of the human soul: memory, understanding, and will: "Therefore, all action of ours issues from these three, for there is nothing that we do that these three do not do together. So when we speak of one of them and an action seems to pertain to one of them, that action is done by all three."

46. Question 4 concerns the reason behind John 5:20: "The Father shows all to the Son," because "he loves the Son."[62] Augustine says that "to show to the Son" is to beget the Son.[63] So "to love" is either taken here in a notional or in an essential sense. If in a notional sense, then it is false, because common spiration is not the reason for emanation by generation, since generation according to this explanation is prior.[64] If in *an* essential sense, it is still false, for essence is not the reason of emanation or relation. For then the Son would beget.

I answer. When the text says, "The Father shows all to the Son," the words to be stressed are "shows" and "all." So I maintain that the reason for showing all things is love. The accent is not on showing, but on showing all. For love is taken in an essential manner here and refers to the supreme unity of the Father toward the Son. And since supreme unity is in essence, it follows that there is absolutely no division in operation. And so it is necessary that in all things the Son works together with the Father. Wherefore, the text says well "he shows all," for he loves in a supreme manner.

---

[62] John 5:20 reads: "For the Father loves the Son and shows him all that he himself does."

[63] See Tractate 23.9 in FC 79, p. 222: "The Father shows the Son what he is doing and by showing begets the Son." See also Tractate 21.4 in FC 79, pp. 182-83: "So, therefore, the Father shows to the Son the thing which he does, so that the Son sees all things in the Father and the Son is all things in the Father. For by seeing he was born and by being born he sees."

[64] Bonaventure's explanation here of the Trinity is even briefer than what he provides in Part I, c. 3 of his *Breviloquium* where the emanation of generation precedes that of spiration.

JOHN 5:24-30
CHRIST'S OMNIPOTENT POWER IN PARTICULAR

47. *Amen, Amen I say to you*, etc. The Lord has just finished declaring his power in general. Here he begins to declare it *in particular*, moving from *the power to give life* to *the power to judge*. So this section has two parts. In the first he declares his power *to give life*. In the second, his *power to judge* where 5:27 reads: *And he gave him power to render judgment*. The power of giving life manifests *the benignity of mercy* whereas the power of judging *the severity of justice*.

JOHN 5:24-26
CHRIST'S POWER TO GIVE LIFE

The Evangelist describes *the power to give life* in this order. First, *those* to whom he gives life. Second, *how* he gives life. Third, *by what power* he gives life. So the first point deals with *the object*. The second with *the action*. The third with *the power*. Perfect understanding of power encompasses these three, that is, power, deed, and object.

48. (Verse 24). So the first point to be determined is *those to whom he gives life*, namely, the life of the soul, but not to all, but to believers. These are the ones who heard the word of God and believe what they have heard.[65] Therefore, he says: *Amen, Amen I say to you*. That is, I truly say to you. *That the person who hears my word*, which disposes that person to faith, since as Romans 10:17 says, "faith comes from hearing," *and believes him who sent me*, by

---

[65] Bonaventure seems to be referring to Jesus' parable of the sower. See, e.g., Matt 13:18-23.

giving his consent to what he has heard. See John 12:44 below: "The person who believes in me, does not believe in me, but in the one who sent me." Indeed, that person has eternal life. John 3:36 above states: "The person who believes in the Son of God has eternal life," eternal life, not eternal punishment. Wherefore, he also adds: *And does not come to judgment*, namely, the judgment of death. *But has passed from death to life. From death*, that is, from the present life, which is death, has passed to eternal life without the judgment of condemnation. John 3:18 reads: "The person who believes in him is not judged." Now the present life is said to be death, because as Romans 8:10 states: "The body ... is dead because of sin." From this death they pass to the life of the just. For these temporal death is their passing. John 13:1 below says this of Christ the Head: "Knowing that the hour had come for him to pass from this world to the Father." The just glory in this as Psalm 5:12-13 says: "Let all those be glad who hope in you. They will rejoice forever, and you will dwell in them. And all those who love your name will glory in you, because you will bless the just."

49. (Verse 25). *Amen, Amen I say to you.* In this verse he touches upon the second point, that is, how he gives life. He gives life through internal inspiration that gives life to the person who hears. Thus, the text reads: *The hour is coming and now is here*, namely, the hour of grace that is now here. About this Romans 13:11 states: "It is now the hour for us to rise from sleep," that is, from the sleep of sin and death. *When those who are dead* by sin *will hear the voice of the Son of God*, through internal inspiration. Ephesians 5:14 says: "Awake, sleeper, and arise from the dead, and Christ will enlighten you." *And those who hear will live* by grace, since his word gives life to those who hear. John 10:27-28 reads: "My sheep hear my voice ... and I give them eternal life." And I give and preserve it

by word. Deuteronomy 8:3 states: "Human beings do not live by bread alone, but by every word that proceeds from the mouth of God."

50. (Verse 26). *For as the Father*, etc. This verse treats the third point, that is, by what power he gives life. He gives life by the power that is his according to the divinity given to him by the Father through being begotten. Thus the text says: *For as*, etc. I have spoken soundly that the Son gives life. *For just as the Father has life in himself*, that is, in an essential manner, *so too he has given to the Son also to have life in himself*, that is, in an essential manner, and not by participation. And since that which is life in an essential manner causes life to flow in all things, as Dionysius says,[66] the Son has the power of himself to give life. Wherefore, John 11:25 below reads: "I am the resurrection and the life. The person who believes in me, even if he dies, will live." In a similar way John 14:6 says: "I am the way, the truth, and the life." I am not living by means of the life of another. Rather I am the life that gives life to others.

---

[66] See *The Divine Names*, Chapter Six in *Pseudo-Dionysius: The Complete Works*, trans. Colm Luibheid (New York: Paulist Press, 1987), pp. 103-105, esp. pp. 103-104: "Let us now praise Eternal Life, since from it comes life itself and all life and by it life is appropriately distributed to all who in any way partake of life.... Just as when talking of Being I said it is an eternity of absolute being, so now I say that the divine Life beyond life is the giver and creator of life itself. All life and living movement comes from a Life which is above every life and is beyond the source of life. From this Life souls have their indestructibility, and every living being and plant, down to the last echo of life, has life.... It gives to life itself the capacity to be life, and it gives to everything alive and to every form of life the existence appropriate to it." See also PG 3:855-858.

John 5:27-30
Christ's power to render judgment

51. (Verse 27). *And he has granted him power*. He has just declared his power to give life. Now he declares his power to *judge*. He proceeds in this sequence. First he considers *the power* by which he judges. Second *those* he judges. Third *how* he judges. These are the same three points used in the description of his power to give life.

So first he determines by what power he judges, that is, by the power granted him by the Father in his humanity. So the text reads: *And he has granted him power*, namely, the Father has granted to the Son, *to render judgment, because he is the Son of Man*. So this power comes to him in his humanity, so that the wicked, who are unable to see God, can see him at the judgment. Revelation 1:7 states: "Every eye will see him, and those who have pierced him." This occurs in his humanity, since he was judged in his humanity. Job 36:17 says: "Your cause has been judged as that of the wicked. You will receive cause and judgment."

52. (Verse 28). *Do not wonder at this*. This verse introduces the second point, that is, those he judges. Although all must rise up, nonetheless, he will not judge everyone, but only the evil. So the text reads: *Do not wonder at this*, that is, at what has been said, "he has granted him power to render judgment because he is the Son of Man," *for the hour is coming*, namely, the end of the world. Job 14:12 states: "A human being, when he has fallen asleep, will not rise again till the heavens be broken." *In which all who are in the tombs will hear the voice of the Son of God*. If the dead will hear, it follows that they will rise at his voice. 1 Thessalonians 4:16 says: "The Lord himself with command, with the voice of archangel, and with the trumpet of God will descend from heaven. And the dead,

who are in Christ, will rise up first." And although all rise up, not all will be judged. So the text continues.

53. (Verse 29). *And those who have done good will come forth unto resurrection of life*, for they have been resurrected to life. *But those who have done evil unto resurrection of judgment*, that is, of damnation. That is, the Lord will judge them. 2 Maccabees 7:14 reads: "It is better, being put to death by human beings, to look for hope from God, to be raised up again by him. But there will be no resurrection to life for you." These are the words the fourth son addressed to Antiochus whose resurrection will not be to life, but to judgment. 1 Corinthians 5:13 says: "Those who are outside God will judge." They are outside because of their evil lives. Daniel 12:2 reads: "Many of those who sleep in the dust of the earth will awaken. Some to eternal life, and others to opprobrium."

54. (Verse 30). *Of myself I can do nothing*. This verse addresses the third point, namely, how he judges. For he judges justly, not according to his own will and a will bent away from God like human beings who pervert just judgment. Therefore he says: *Of myself I can do nothing*, and so I cannot judge. But *as I hear, I judge*, that is, as I receive from the Father, and so it follows that he judges justly. Thus the text continues: *And my judgment is just*, since he does not bend the rule of justice through a discordant will. The text says: *Because I seek not my own will*, namely, in rendering judgment, *but the will of him who sent me*, that is, God the Father who is just. So John 8:26-29 says: "The one who sent me is true.... I always do the things that are pleasing to him." And therefore, he acts justly, for as Deuteronomy 32:4 states: "God is faithful and without any iniquity, just and right." Psalm 144:17 proclaims: "The Lord is just in all his ways," etc.

Questions

55. Question 1 asks: According to what nature is the Son given the power to judge? – It would seem that it was according to his human nature. – 1. The actual wording of John 5:27 supports this: "And he granted him power to render judgment, because he is the Son of Man." – 2. Likewise, Augustine says: "He granted him the power of judgment by sending him in the flesh."[67]

But contrary. 1. Deuteronomy 32:35 states: "Revenge is mine, and I will repay," says the Lord. So revenging punishment pertains to God alone. Therefore, if judgment is revenging punishment, then it pertains to the Son according to his divine nature. – 2. And this is shown by what John 5:22-23 says: "The Father has given all judgment to the Son, so that all people may honor the Son just as they honor the Father." But the Son should not be honored as the Father is according to his human nature, but only according to his divine nature. Therefore, etc.

I answer. It has to be said that the power of judging is twofold, namely, the power of authority and the power of ministry. The first pertains to the entire Trinity whereas the power of ministry pertains to the Son sitting and appearing in judgment according to his human nature. Here are the responses to the objections.[68] – 1. The divine prerogative of revenge does not exclude the incarnate Son, but only someone who is purely human. – 2. With regard to the objection about honor, it has to be said that the person of the Son, on account of the humiliation

---

[67] See Tractate 22.11 in FC 79, p. 207: "And then, because he was made man, what did he give him? 'And he has given him power to do judgment, because he is the Son of man.'"

[68] See also Book IV d. 13 a. 1. q. 1 of Bonaventure's *Sentence Commentary*.

of the incarnation, seemed to have decreased in honor. Therefore, the Father wished that in the same humanity, in which he humbly appeared, he would judge, so that no one would scorn him as incarnate, but would fear him as they fear the Father whose inviolable sentence endures. Wherefore, the judgment he renders through his humanity makes him to be feared on account of his divinity.

56. Question 2 asks whether judgment will pertain solely to the Son. – This seems to be the case from John 5:22: "The Father has given all judgment to the Son." And Acts 10:42 states: "He it is who has been appointed by God as judge of the living and of the dead." And 1 Corinthians 4:4 reads: "The one who judges me is the Lord." Therefore, if he alone is our Lord, then he alone is the one to judge.

Contrary. 1. 1 Corinthians 11:31 states: "If we would judge ourselves, we should not thus be judged." Wherefore, it pertains to us to judge ourselves. – 2. Furthermore, Matthew 19:28 seems to indicate that judgment pertains to others, for it says: "You will sit upon twelve seats," etc. This was addressed to the Apostles.[69] Likewise, 1 Corinthians 6:3 reads: "Do you not know that we will judge angels?"

With regard to these points it has to be said that judgment consists of three elements, that is, examination, approbation, and determination or the pronouncement of sentence. – The first action, namely, of examination pertains to all, and because of this the Apostle says that

---

[69] Matt 19:28 says: "And Jesus said to them (the disciples): Amen I say to you that you who have followed me, in the regeneration when the Son of Man will sit on the throne of his glory, will also sit on twelve thrones, judging the twelve tribes of Israel."

we must prove ourselves, that is, examine ourselves.[70] – The second action, to approve or to reprove pertains to the perfect, for they will approve and reprove, and evildoers will be reproved by comparing them to the perfect. But this does not happen in the present, but in the future. Thus, the Apostle says that such a judgment in the present time would be judgment before the time. 1 Corinthians 4:5 states: "Do not judge before the time." – The third action, that of determination pertains solely to the Son, for he himself will promulgate the sentence. If another person were to perform this action, he would recklessly usurp the Son's right. Whence the Lord's prohibition in Matthew 7:1: "Do not judge." And the Apostle warns in Romans 14:4: "Who are you to judge anotherís servant?" – So when the text says that "the Father has granted all judgment to the Son," this is to be understood of the judgment of determination, not that of examination or of approbation.

57. Question 3 also concerns those to be judged and asks: Who will be judged? – From John 5:24 it seems that only evildoers will be judged: "The one who believes the one who sent me has eternal life and does not come to judgment, but has passed from death to life." Also John 3:18 above reads: "The person who believes in him is not judged." – Contrary. 2 Corinthians 5:10 states: "All of us will stand before the tribunal of Christ."[71]

I answer. It should be said that the judgment of determination is taken in a comprehensive way and thus includes the sentence of salvation and of punishment.

---

[70] See 1 Cor 11:28: "But let a person prove himself, and so let him eat of that bread and drink of the cup."
[71] 2 Cor 5:10 reads: "For all of us must be made manifest before the tribunal of Christ."

From this perspective all will be judged. Judgment is also taken in a proper sense for damnation, and that is the meaning here. "Those who have done evil will go forth unto resurrection of judgment," that is, damnation. A similar understanding applies to John 3:18.

58. Question 4 is a query about the mode of judgment. – 1. He judges according to what he hears. – Contrary is what Isaiah 11:3 says: "He will not reprove according to what he hears." – 2. Furthermore, John 5:30 says that he does not seek his own will, but God's will. Wherefore, his will is in disagreement with God's will.

I respond to the first that he does not judge according to what he hears externally and in reports, but according to what he hears internally from the illumination of the Father. – About the second point this must be said. Truth is twofold in John 5:30. "I do not seek my own will" either because he has his own will, but does not seek to follow it or because he does not have his own will and does not seek to follow it. Christ is speaking in this latter sense whereas the objection is dealing with the first sense.[72]

JOHN 5:31-47
CORROBORATION OF CHRIST'S REFUTATION OF THE JEWS

JOHN 5:31-39
CERTITUDE OF THE TESTIMONY

59. *If I bear witness*, etc. This is the fourth section of this chapter and deals with *the corroboration* of the

---

[72] On p. 313 n. 16 QuarEd indicate a solution: "Either because he has his own will, but does not seek to follow it solely or because the Father neither has nor seeks anything contrary to it."

aforementioned refutation and consists of the multiple witnesses that approve of what the Lord has spoken above. This section has two parts. The first lays out *the certitude of the testimony* whereas the second treats *the censure* of the Jews who do not believe where verse 40 has: "Yet you are not willing to come to me."

Now the first part has two components. In the first the Lord, even though he could produce his own testimony, declines to do so. In the second the Lord adduces the testimony of others where verse 33 reads: "You have sent to John," etc.

John 5:31-32
Christ declines from giving testimony about himself

Verse 31. So Christ declines from giving his own testimony, since they would consider it uncertain and unbelievable. So the text reads: *If I bear witness concerning myself, my witness is not true*, that is, it is not efficacious in effecting belief, especially if I bear witness only by myself. John 8:13 below states: "The Pharisees said to him: You are bearing witness to yourself. Your witness is not true." Nevertheless, there is no lack of true witnesses to me. So he adds:

60.(Verse 32). *There is another who bears witness concerning me*, namely, the Father or even John. Concerning these two the following text is rightly understood: *And I know that the witness that he bears concerning me is true*, since he bears witness as one who has certitude. For the Father bears true witness, since, as it is said in John 8:26, "the one who sent me is true." John also is a person who has certitude. Thus, in John 1:34 above John said: "I have seen and have borne witness that this is the Son of God."

Proverbs 12:17 reads: "The person who speaks what he knows about is a judge of justice,[73] but the person who lies is a false witness."

JOHN 5:33-39
WITNESS OF OTHERS TO CHRIST

61. *You have sent to John*, etc. The Lord declined from giving testimony about himself. In a second point he adduces *the witness of others*. And since testimony is firm when it comes from the mouths of many witnesses,[74] this part has four elements according to the four testimonies that Jesus adduces. The first witness is *John*. The second consists of Christ's *works*. The third witness is *divine*. The final witness is that of *the scriptures*. These witnesses are further distinguished because the first is *declared*. The second is *displayed*. The third is *inspired*. The fourth is *written*.

Verse 33. So he first presents the testimony of John that was given to them at their own request. Thus the text continues: *You have sent to John*. He did not intrude himself, but responded to your request. John 1:19 above states: "And this is the witness of John when the Jews sent to him," etc. *And he has borne witness to the truth*, as a faithful witness. Proverbs 14:5 reads: "A faithful witness does not lie." And lest the Lord be seen as begging for human testimony,[75] he adds:

---

[73] The Vulgate reads *index iustitiae* ("an index of justice") while Bonaventure has *iudex iustitiae* ("judge of justice").

[74] See Deut 19:15: "In the mouth of two or three witnesses every word will stand."

[75] Hugh of St. Cher, p. 319v,h comments: "He does not need human testimony."

62. (Verse 34). *I, however, do not accept human testimony.* Supply: because of my need for it. Psalm 15:2 reads: "I said to the Lord: You are my God, since you have no need for my goods." But I consider these things on account of your salvation. So he also says: *But I say these things, so that you may be saved*, namely, that you may believe in me because of his witness, for as it is said in Mark 16:16: "Those who believe and are baptized will be saved." And truly they should have believed the testimony of John. So the text continues:

63. (Verse 35). *He was the lamp burning*, through grace, *and shining*, through teaching. Another interpretation is: *burning*, through interior love, and *shining*, through external goodness of life. Bernard comments: "To burn is too little by itself, and to shine is useless by itself, but to burn and shine together is perfect."[76] Therefore, Elijah best signifies John. Sirach 48:1 states: "Elijah ... rose up like a fire, and his word burnt like a torch."[77] Now faith had to be added to such a light burning so perfectly. This the Jews did not do. Thus the text continues: *But you desired to rejoice for a while in his light*, a light that shone so that you might believe in his teaching and witness and imitate his life which you had seen for a while. Matthew 11:18 states: "John came neither eating nor drinking, and they say: He has a demon." Matthew 21:32 reads: "John came

---

[76] See *Sermo in Nativitate Sancti Ioannis Baptistae* n. 3. Bonaventure's citation inverts the first two clauses. See SBOp 5.178: "For to shine is useless by itself, and to burn is too little by itself. To burn and shine together is perfect." In his commentary on John 5:35 Hugh of St. Cher, p. 320b cites a different passage from Bernard: "If a person has not been set on fire, he doesn't burn. You never light other pieces of charcoal from burnt out charcoal." Hugh of St. Cher, p. 320v,1 gives a moral interpretation of John 5:35 and quotes Bernard: "To shine is useless. To burn is holy. To shine and burn together is perfect."

[77] Hugh of St. Cher, p. 320b also cites Sirach 48:1.

to you in the way of justice, and you did not believe him. But the toll collectors and prostitutes believed him."

64. (Verse 36). *But the witness I have.* This verse introduces the second witness, namely, that of Christ's works, that is greater than preaching. So the text continues: *But the witness I have is greater than John,* because it has a great motivating force for belief in me. *For the works themselves*[78] *that the Father has given me,* for I have accepted being and action from him, *to accomplish,* that is, that I may perform them perfectly. For Deuteronomy 32:4 says: "The works of God are perfect." *These very works that I do* by means of my own power *bear witness to me that the Father has sent me.* As the Father, so the Son, for the Father has communicated such great works to the Son. John 15:22-24 says: "If I have not come ... and done among them works that no one else has done, they would have no sin." Through these works one must believe that the Father sent him. John 14:10 reads: "The Father dwelling in me, it is he who does the works." And John 10:38 states: "If you do not believe me, believe the works."

65. (Verse 37). *And the Father who sent me,* etc. The third witness surfaces here, that is, the divine witness, that he calls paternal. So he says: *And the Father who has sent me,* through the incarnation, *has borne witness to me,* through interior inspiration, for as John 6:44 states: "No one comes to me unless the Father ... draws him." So through an intelligible voice he reveals and bears witness, but the carnal Jews cannot hear him nor see him speaking. Therefore, the text continues: *But you have never heard*

---

[78] On p. 314 n. 8 QuarEd correctly mention that the Vulgate reads *Opera enim* ("For the works") while Bonaventure has *Ipsa enim opera* ("For the works themselves").

his voice, through a revelation to the mind as Peter heard according to Matthew 16:17: "Blessed are you, Simon Bar Jonah, for flesh and blood has not revealed [this] to you, but my Father, who is in the heavens." *Or seen the face*,[79] in clear and open sight. Exodus 33:20 reads: "No human will see me and live." John 1:18 above says: "No one has even seen God."

66. (Verse 38). *And you do not have his word abiding in you*, namely, through faith. And he provides the reason for this: *Since you do not believe him whom he has sent*. And the one whom he has sent is the Word and is the one abiding in your hearts through faith. Ephesians 3:17 states: "that Christ may dwell in your hearts through faith." Isaiah 9:8 says: "The Lord sent his word into Jacob, and it has fallen upon Israel." It did not remain in Jacob, because "his own received him not."[80]

67. (Verse 39). *You search the Scriptures*. The fourth witness appears here, namely, that of the Scriptures. The Lord admonishes and exhorts to a diligent study of their spiritual understanding. Thus, the text continues: *You search the Scriptures*, that is, plumb interior meaning, for, as the Apostle says in 2 Corinthians 3:6, "the letter kills, but the Spirit gives life." As to the reason why they must search them, he adds: *In which you think that you have eternal life*.[81] That is, through them you think that you know and through this knowledge have eternal life, since through them you know God, who is eternal life.

---

[79] On p. 315 n. 1 QuarEd rightly notice that the Vulgate reads *neque speciem eius vidistis* ("Or seen his face").

[80] John 1:11.

[81] On p. 315 n. 3 QuarEd rightly notice that the Vulgate reads *quia* ("because") which Bonaventure does not have. Further, the Vulgate reads *in ipsis* ("in them") while Bonaventure has *in quibus* ("in which").

Wisdom 15:3 reads: "To know you is consummate justice, and to know your justice and your power is the root of immortality.' Christ says that these Scriptures bear witness to him. So the text adds: *It is they who bear witness to me*, namely, all the Scriptures of the Old Testament. In Luke 24:44 the Lord Jesus said: "All things must be fulfilled that are written about me in the Law of Moses and the Prophets and the Psalms." Acts 18:28 says about Apollos: "He vigorously refuted the Jews in public and showed from the Scriptures that Jesus is the Christ."

QUESTIONS

68. Question 1 concerns John 5:31: "If I bear witness concerning myself, my witness is not true." – Contrary. 1. Numbers 23:19 reads: "God is not like a human that he would lie." Therefore, since Christ is God, etc. – 2. Further, John 8:14 says: "Even if I bear witness to myself, my witness is true."[82] But he says in John 5:31 that his "witness is not true." Therefore, etc.

A threefold response is in order. The first answer emphasizes the subject of the sentence: If I, in my human nature, bear witness to myself, my witness is not true, but it is true according to my divine nature. – But this solution is not cogent, since just as he does not deceive according to his divine nature, so too he does not deceive according to his human nature. – Another answer accentuates the adjective: My witness is not true, that is, it is not efficacious and is not accepted as true. Nonetheless, it is true, because I speak the truth. And so the point is taken

---

[82] John 8:14 reads: "Even if I bear witness to myself, my witness is true, because I know where I came from and where I go. But you do not know where I came from or where I go."

that he is speaking the truth about reality, but what he says is not accepted as true by the Jews.[83] – A further answer is to take the statement in an absolute sense: If I, all by myself, bear witness to myself, then my witness is not efficacious. But if I bear witness, alongside others, then it is efficacious. Therefore, he says in John 8:16 below: "Because I am not alone." Wherefore, since he had earlier commended himself by the witness of his power in effecting a miracle, he adduces other witnesses here to corroborate it.

69. Question 2 focuses on the witness of the works. John 5:36 says: "The works that I do bear witness to me." – But the prophets did the same works as miracles.[84] The apostles, who followed him, did the same and even greater.[85] Therefore, if he could be known sufficiently through his works that he was the Christ, the same could be said of the prophets and apostles.

I respond and maintain that the miracles of good people and evil people can be distinguished, as Augustine says.[86] So they could recognize that Christ's miracles and works

---

[83] See Hugh of St. Cher, p. 319v,c: "For even though I bear witness to myself, it is still true, although not according to your evil suspicions. And that this is the way the passage should be read is clear from John 8:14 below: If I bear witness to myself, my witness is true. For in 8:14 he is pointing to the truth of the reality whereas in 5:31 he refers to the suspicions of the Jews who are listening to him."

[84] See Sir 48:1-10 about Elijah, who, for example, raised a dead man from below by the word of the Lord God (48:5).

[85] See John 14:12: "The person who believes in me, the works that I do he also will do, and greater than these he will do, because I am going to the Father" and 2 Cor 12:12: "Indeed, the signs of the apostle were wrought among you in all patience, in miracles and wonders and deeds of power."

[86] This seems to be a general reference to "Question 79" of Augustine's *Eighty-Three Different Questions*. See John 3 n. 6 above where Bonaventure also refers to Question 79: "Why did Pharaoh's

were those of a good and holy man. But Christ said that he was God. However, no good person, who remained good, can make himself equal to God. If he did, he would be a thief. Therefore, if they could recognize that Christ was holy because of his works and through his words that he was the Christ, the works would be sufficient witness that Christ was speaking the truth and through this that he was the Christ. This applies in a similar manner to other good persons that say that they are speaking what is true. But they were not saying this about themselves, but about Christ, as the apostles did.[87]

Another solution is to say that the works did not provide a cogent witness, but one that might influence one to believe. This would apply also to the witnesses of John and of Scripture. But the testimony of the Father through revelation is compelling.

70. Question 3 deals with the witness of the Father. Christ tells the Jews in John 5:37: "You have never heard his voice or seen his face."

Contrary. Weren't many Jews present when, as Luke 3:22 says, a voice from heaven sounded in an understandable manner: "You are my beloved Son"? – Furthermore, Deuteronomy 5:26 reads: "We heard his voice from the midst of the fire."[88] – Likewise, Exodus 20:22 states: "You have seen that I have spoken to you from heaven."

---

magicians perform certain miracles in the manner of Moses the servant of God?"

[87] Hugh of St. Cher, p. 320v,f comments succinctly: "For the saints do not perform miracles on their own account, but they are done by God on account of their merits."

[88] Bonaventure summarizes Deut 5:26: "What is all flesh that it should hear the voice of the living God, who speaks from the midst of the fire, as we have heard, and be able to live?"

I answer and contend that God speaks in a twofold way and appears in a twofold manner. In the first way God speaks and appears in himself and through himself. And so God speaks through an interior revelation of the mind in a certain unspeakable, but nevertheless understandable manner. God does not speak thus with evil people. God speaks in another manner through a subject creature, and God spoke in this way in giving the Law. According to this second way they saw God in a subject creature and heard God through their ears, but they did not see or hear God in the first manner. And it is about this that John 5:37 speaks. Augustine comments on the words, "the Father bears witness" in John 5:37: "The one, who has borne witness externally to me who is visible to human eyes, internally burns the hearts of men and women to acknowledge me."[89]

71. Question 4 raises the issue of the sufficiency and order of these witnesses. – It should be noted that the first witness, that of John, was influential. The second, that of the works, is promotive. The third, that of the Father, is compelling. The fourth, that of Scripture, roots one in the truth. And from these four one complete and perfect witness issues forth, and they are ordained in a gradual way according to the aforementioned conditions.

---

[89] This quotation occurs without attribution in Glossa Ordinaria on John 5:35. See PL 114:380A. The Glossa continues: "Further, all the prophets and apostles were lamps, but Christ was the light, *who illumines everyone coming into this world.*"

John 5:40-47
Rebuke of the unbelieving Jews

72. (Verse 40). *Yet you are not willing to come to me*, etc. Now that the certitude of the witnesses has been set forth, the Evangelist next presents *the rebuke of the unbelieving Jews*. The Lord censures the Jews on four counts. First, for *lack of divine love*. Second, for *the blindness of false love*. Third, for *the desire for vain honor*. Fourth, for *lack of faith*.

So first he censures them for lack of divine love, whose sign is that they do not come to the one whom God has sent. So the text says: *Yet you are not willing to come to me, so that you may have life.* Although there is sufficient testimony on my behalf, you do not want to come to me. Rather you hate me and flee. John 8:43 states: "Why do you not understand my speech? Because you cannot listen to my word." He also reproves them for not giving him glory. Thus, the text continues:

73. (Verse 41). *I do not receive glory from men and women*, but from the Father. John 17:1 below says: "Father, glorify your Son." So I do not rebuke you for your love of your own glory, but on account of your lack of divine love. So the text states:

74. (Verse 42). *But I know that you do not have the love of God in you.* Rather hatred resides in you. John 15:24 reads: "Now they have seen and have hated both me and my Father." And such people are worthy of rebuke, because they lack a wedding garment. Matthew 22:12 says: "Friend, how did you come in here without a wedding garment?"

75. (Verse 43). *I have come in the name*, etc. This is the second point, that is, the blindness of false love, since they did not receive the humble person, but will receive the proud person. Thus the text states: *I have come in the name of my Father*, whose glory I seek and not my own. John 8:50 below says: "I do not seek my own glory." *And you do not receive me*, that is, *me* who is humble. John 1:11 reads: "He came unto his own, and his own received him not." *If another person comes in his own name*, as the antichrist, who seeks his own glory, because 2 Thessalonians 2:4 states: "He is exalted above all that is called God or that is worshiped, so that he sits in the temple of God," *you will receive him*, that is, you have been blinded to the just judgment of God. 2 Thessalonians 2:10 says: "God will send them into a work of error,[90] so that they may believe in falsehood." And the reason behind this is that they did not want to believe in the truth.

76. (Verse 44). *How can you believe*, etc. Here he gives a third rebuke for their quest for vain honor. Because of this quest they were incapable of believing in the truth, as they were seeking after vanity. So the text continues: *How can you believe*, namely, in the truth, *who receive glory from one another*, by clutching onto vanity? For human glory is vanity. Isaiah 40:6 reads: "All flesh is grass, and all its glory is as the flower of grass."[91] An appetite for vanity renders a person incapable of belief in the truth. Thus, Psalm 4:3 laments: "O human beings, how long will you be dull of heart? Why do you love vanity and seek after

---

[90] The Vulgate reads *Ideo mittit illis Deus operationem erroris* ("therefore, God sends to them a work of error") while Bonaventure has *Mittet eos Deus in operationem erroris* ("God will send them into a work of error").

[91] On p. 317 n. 7 QuarEd rightly notice that the Vulgate reads *flos agri* ("flower of the field") while Bonaventure has *flos foeni* ("flower of the grass").

lies?" So you are seeking false glory *and not seeking the glory that is from the only God*, that is, the true glory. This is from God alone. Psalm 83:12 states: "The Lord will give grace and glory." Therefore, 2 Corinthians 10:17-18 reads: "Let the person who glories glory in the Lord. For the person who commends himself is not approved, but the person whom the Lord commends."

77. (Verse 45). *Do not think*. This verse introduces the fourth point, that is, the defect of faith among the Jews, not only in their belief in Christ, but also in Moses. Wherefore, not only has Christ accused them, but also Moses. So the text says: *Do not think that*[92] *I will accuse you to the Father*, for I have not come to accuse, but to pardon. For he himself is a propitiation, not the accuser. 1 John 2:2 states: "He is a propitiation for our sins, not only for ours, but also for those of the whole world." Nevertheless, they do not lack for an accuser. So the text continues: *There is one who accuses you, Moses, in whom you hope*,[93] as his disciples. John 9:28-29 below states: "We are disciples of Moses. We know that God spoke to Moses." He accuses you, since you do not believe in him. Thus the text adds:

78. (Verse 46). *For if you believed Moses, you would believe me also*. The word, *would*, introduces a note of freedom. *In me – for he wrote about me*. Deuteronomy 18:15 reads: "The Lord ... will raise up for you a prophet from your

---

[92] On p. 317 n. 9 QuarEd accurately mention that the Vulgate reads *quia* ("that") while Bonaventure has *quod* ("that").

[93] On p. 317 n. 10 QuarEd correctly indicate that the Vulgate reads *in quo vos speratis* ("in whom you hope") while Bonaventure has *in quo speratis* ("in whom you hope").

people.... You will listen to him as you did to me."[94] And he will accuse you, since you do not believe in him. So the text reads:

79. (Verse 47). *But if you do not believe his writings, how will you believe my words*? As if he were saying: You will not believe. Luke 16:31 states: "If they do not listen to Moses and the prophets, they will not believe even if someone rises from the dead."

Questions

80. Question 1 deals with John 5:41: "I do not receive glory from men and women." – 1. John 21:19 says of Peter: "Signifying by what manner of death he would glorify God." Therefore, human beings do glorify God. – 2. Further, Philippians 1:20 states: "Christ will be glorified in my body whether through death or through life."[95] – I respond. A distinction has to be made between being glorified in humans, by humans, and from humans. "In humans" means to reveal his glory to humans. "By humans" means to be made public by them to others. "From humans" means that one would be enhanced by some glory that humans might give a person. The first two meanings are true whereas the third is false.

81. Question 2 deals with John 5:45: "I will not accuse you to the Father." – Contrary. 1. Christ is just and cannot be unjust. So just as it is his right to praise good people, so too it is his right to accuse evil people. – 2. Furthermore,

---

[94] Deut 18:15 states: "The Lord your God will raise up for you a prophet from your own people and from your brethren like unto me. You will listen to him."

[95] Bonaventure has inverted the order of the Vulgate: "whether through life or through death."

Jeremiah 29:23 states: "I am the judge and the witness." Therefore, it is the right of the true witness to accuse evildoers, etc. – I answer. It has to be maintained that Christ, in as far as he is in himself, offered himself by his death. And since he died for all, therefore, in as far as he is by himself, he accuses no one. Thus the Glossa comments: "The blood of Christ accuses no one, but clamors for forgiveness. The blood of Abel, however, clamors for vengeance," vengeance according to the teaching of Moses.[96] Therefore, it must be understood that by himself he does not accuse, but he does so when we are the cause.[97] – Another interpretation is that Christ is not the primary and principal accuser. Rather it is more the case that the principal accuser is Moses, whom they did not believe when he had foretold the Christ.[98]

82. Question 3 asks about the Lord's argument in John 5:47: "If you do not believe the writings of Moses, how will you believe my words?" – It seems that this is an

---

[96] This is the Glossa Interlinearis on Hebr 12:24: "*A sprinkling of blood that speaks more eloquently than Abel*, since when Christ said: *Father, forgive them*, he was calling for pardon while Abel was calling for vengeance. He was calling for salvation and pardon for his persecutors while Abel was clamoring for damnation."

[97] Behind this tersely worded opinion stands what Bonaventure says in Book I, d. 22. a.1. q. 3 of his *Sentence Commentary*. See Opera Omnia 1.394. See further Bonaventure's source in St. John Damascene, *The Orthodox Faith*, Book II, c. 29 in FC 37, pp. 262-63: "One should also bear in mind that God antecedently wills all to be saved and to attain to His kingdom. For He did not form us to be chastised, but, because He is good, that we might share in His goodness. Yet, because He is just, He does wish to punish sinners. So, the first is called *antecedent will* and *approval*, and it has Him as its cause; the second is called *consequent will* and *permission*, and it has ourselves as its cause."

[98] See Chrysostom's Homily 41 n. 2 in FC 33, p. 419: "Indeed, I am so far from having come in opposition to the Law that he who will be your accuser is none other than he who has given you the Law."

argument from a minor to a major.[99] I negate that
and answer: Even if it seems to be a minor argument
simpliciter, nevertheless the key term, the Jews, is not a
minor, but the major term.[100]

---

[99] If they don't believe the words of Moses, a mere human, how
will they believe the words of Christ the Lord?

[100] The Jews are those who listen to both Moses and Christ. They
are not a minor category.

Chapter Six

John 6: 1-72
Christ as the Conserver

1. *After this Jesus went away*, etc. In the previous chapter the Lord showed himself to be the healer. In this chapter he manifests himself as *the conserver*. And since he is the conserver of bodies and spirits and since people go by means of visible things to invisible things,[1] he first shows himself to be the conserver of *bodies*. Second he shows that he is conserver of *spirits* where verse 22 reads: *The next day the crowd*.

John 6:1-21
Christ the Conserver of Bodies

The Lord showed himself as *conserver of bodies* by miraculously feeding bodily needs. Now this miraculous feeding is described on three planes. First, there are *the antecedents*. Second there are those things that are *concomitant* where verse 10 says: "Jesus then said: Make them," etc. Finally there are *the consequences* where verse 14 states: "But when the people saw," etc.

---

[1] See Rom 1:20: "For since the creation of the world, his invisible attributes are clearly seen – his everlasting power also and divinity – being understood through the things that are made."

John 6:1-9
Antecedents of the Sign

2. (Verse 1) Now *the antecedents* that were the cause or occasion for the performance of the miracle are four: the multitude that was following Christ; the aptness of place and time; the lack of money to buy food; the insufficient amount of food to feed the multitude. So the first occasion for performing the miracle was the multitude that was following Christ beyond his home territory to see his miracles. So the text says: *After this Jesus went away to the other side of the sea of Galilee, which is that of Tiberias.* The sea is called Galilee after the region, and Tiberias after the city.

3. (Verse 2). *And a great crowd was following him.* The Evangelist gives the reason for this: *Because they witnessed the signs that he worked on those who were sick.* Because of these signs that they had seen they were following Christ, for, as 1 Corinthians 1:22 states: "The Jews seek signs." And when they saw the signs, they glorified God. Luke 5:26 says: "They were filled with fear and were ecstatic, saying: We have seen wonderful things today."[2] Through these signs the Jews were drawn to Christ and also strengthened. Exodus 14:13 reads: "Stand and see the great wonders of the Lord, which he will do."

---

[2] Luke 5:26 actually reads: "And astonishment seized upon them all, and they glorified God and were filled with fear, saying: We have seen wonderful things today." Contrast the more prolix interpretation of Hugh of St. Cher, p. 322v,c: "Some followed him to see new miracles. These are the curious. Some to eat of his bread. These are the gluttonous. Some to be restored to health. These are the sick. Some to trap him in his speech. These are the Pharisees. Some to accept his teaching. These are his disciples." See the five reasons that Bonaventure gives in n. 50 below: sickness, signs, food, blasphemy, teaching.

4. (Verse 3) *Jesus, therefore, went away to the mountain.*[3] This verse mentions the second occasion, namely, the aptness of the place and time. The place was fitting for the performance of a miracle, since it was a desert where there was little food. So the text states: *Jesus, therefore, went away to the mountain and sat there with his disciples.* John calls this place "a mountain" because of its height whereas Matthew calls it "a desert" because of its isolation. Matthew 14:13 says: "Jesus withdrew by boat to a desert place apart." And this place was apt for the performance of a miracle, for there was no food there. Thus, Matthew 14:15 notes that the disciples said to the Lord: "This is a desert place.... Send the crowds away, so that they may go into the villages and buy themselves food." – It was also a fitting time, since it was Passover. So the text continues:

5. (Verse 4). *Now the Passover, the feast of the Jews, was near.* On that first Passover the Lord performed miracles, and now he has to renew it by performing a new Passover. It should be noted, as Chrysostom comments, that "from the Passover at the time of the imprisonment of John to this point one year had transpired, although the Evangelist narrates little about it,"[4] since others had narrated these events.

6. (Verse 5). *When, therefore, Jesus had lifted up his eyes,* etc. This is the third occasion, namely, the lack of money to buy food to feed so great a crowd. And to manifest this lack the Lord asks Philip about the cost. So the text continues: *When, therefore, Jesus had lifted up his eyes,* through the

---

[3] On p. 319 n. 1 QuarEd correctly indicate that the Vulgate reads *Subiit* ("went up") whereas Bonaventure has *Abiit* ("went away").

[4] On p. 319 n. 3 QuarEd refer to Chrysostom's Homily 42 n. 1. I have not found the reference.

largess of his mercy, for Psalm 32:18 states: "The eyes of the Lord are upon those who fear him and on those who hope in his mercy." *And seen a great crowd had come to him*, out of loving devotion. For Matthew 14:13 says that "the crowds followed him on foot from the towns." *He said to Philip*, with a view to provident care. 1 Peter 5:7 reads: "God cares for you." *Whence will we buy bread that these may eat?* To feed their bodies, as if he were saying: Do we have sufficient money to make such a purchase? He himself did not need money. Isaiah 55:1 says: "Come, buy without money." He was not asking because he had any doubt, but to test Philip. So the text adds:

7. (Verse 6). *But he said this to try him*, for he had no doubt. *For he himself knew what he would do.* So he said this to try him and through trying him to show that the money was lacking. Thus, Philip's response follows.

8. (Verse 7). *Philip answered him: Two hundred denarii worth of bread is not enough for them that each one may receive a little.* And so a large amount of money would be necessary. And they themselves were poor and didn't have even a little, for they had left everything, according to what Peter said in Matthew 19:27: "Behold, we have left everything and have followed you," etc. And Acts 3:6 states: "Silver and gold I do not have."

9. (Verse 8). *One of his disciples said to him*, etc. This verse introduces the fourth occasion, that is, the insufficiency of food to feed such a large crowd. For although there were five thousand people, they had only five loaves of bread. And Andrew mentions this in his answer. So the text states: *One of his disciples, Andrew, the brother of Simon Peter, said to him*, that is, to the Lord whom Philip was questioning about feeding the crowd.

10. (Verse 9). *There is a boy here who has five barley loaves and two fish.* He is saying that this is the extent of the food they have, but it is not enough. So he continues: *But what are these among so many?* In this, notice the wondrous poverty of the Lord and the disciples that they have just a few coarse loaves. So they frequently experienced hunger with the Lord. Matthew 12:1 reads: "Jesus went through the standing grain, and his disciples, being hungry, began to pluck the ears of grain and to eat."

11. The moral interpretation is this. The five loaves that the boy has are the five things that feed the affections which have their origin in the five considerations of the intellect. From a consideration of one's own sin arises the bread of compunction. About this Psalm 79:6 reads: "You will feed us with the bread of tears," etc. This is the bread, about which Judges 7:13 speaks: "It seemed to me as if a hearth cake of barley bread."[5] – From a consideration of Christ's passion, the bread of affliction. Deuteronomy 16:3 says: "Seven days shall you eat the unleavened bread of affliction, because you came out of Egypt in fear, so that you may remember the day of your coming out of Egypt," etc. Lamentations 3:19 reads: "Remember my poverty and transgression, the wormwood and the gall." – From a consideration of the need of the brothers, the bread of compassion. Qoheleth 11:1 states: "Cast your bread upon the running waters," that is, the waters of tribulation. Without this no one should be placed in command. Isaiah 4 says: "I am no healer, and in my house there is no bread nor clothing. Do not make me ruler of the people."[6] – From

---

[5] Judges 7:13 states: "And when Gedeon had come, a person told his neighbor a dream. And in this manner related what he had seen: I dreamt a dream, and it seemed to me as if a hearth cake of barley bread rolled and came down into the camp of Midian. And when it was come to a tent, it struck it and beat it down flat to the ground."

[6] This citation actually comes from Isa 3:7.

a consideration of eternal punishment, the bread of fear. Tobit 2:5 reads: "He ate bread with mourning and fear," recalling the word that the Lord spoke through Amos the Prophet: "Your feasts will be turned into lamentation and mourning."[7] – From a consideration of the delay of the reward, the bread of loving devotion, which is in the perfect. Psalm 41:4 prays: "My tears have been my bread day and night, while it is said to me daily: Where is your God?"[8]

Questions

12. Question 1 asks about the contradictions within the Gospels. – 1. Now Matthew 14:15 states that "the disciples came to the Lord" and said to him that he should send the crowds away. Likewise, Matthew 14:16 says that the Lord said to them: "they do not have to go away." In John 6:5, however, the Lord seeks counsel from Philip about how to feed them. – 2. Furthermore, John 6:7 states that it was Philip who said: "Two hundred denarii worth of bread is not enough," etc. whereas Mark 6:37 says that the disciples said: "Are we to go and buy two hundred denarii worth of bread and give them to eat?"

---

[7] See Amos 8:10: "And I will turn your feasts into mourning and all your songs into lamentation."

[8] Hugh of St. Cher, p. 323v,a-324d has many interpretations of the five loaves, but very few genuine parallels to Bonaventure's interpretation. See the parallel on p. 324d, for example, "The third bread is recollection of one's past life with sorrow or remembrance of one's sins.... Psalm 41:4 says: My tears have been my bread day and night." See Bonaventure's commentary on Luke 14:15 (n. 34-35) in *Gospel of Luke 9-16*, pp. 1352-54 where he provides seven loaves: sorrow of repentance, work of justice, instruction, Eucharist, internal consolation, supernal contemplation, heavenly kingdom.

In my response I follow Augustine and maintain that the contradictions are solved by what frequently happens among the Evangelists: One notes something that another omits.[9] So it is to be understood that the disciples first went to the Lord, and after the Lord had looked at the crowds, he spoke with Philip. And then Philip gave his answer, and another Evangelist, Mark, attributed Philip's answer to others, through synecdoche. And then the Lord asked how many loaves they had. This part John omits and has Andrew mention that there are five loaves. John alone makes a note of Andrew's role here whereas the others attribute the response to many people, since Andrew was speaking in the name of many individuals.[10]

13. Question 2 deals with the rationale behind John 6:5-7. – Since Philip was not the bursar whereas Judas was, it would seem that the Lord should have asked Judas and not Philip.[11] – Chrysostom answers that the Lord asked Philip to try him and to instruct him, since Philip was in great need of instruction, as is evident from John 14:13 below where he asks: "Show us the Father." So there was good reason for the Lord to ask Philip.[12] – Another interpretation is that Philip haled from this area. So he was known to the crowds and was more solicitous for

---

[9] See Book II, c. 46 n. 96 of *The Harmony of the Gospels*.

[10] See, e.g., Mark 6:38: "They said: Five and two fish."

[11] I have translated *dispensator* by "bursar," for as John 12:6 and 13:29 indicate, Judas kept the purse of Jesus and his disciples. See Chrysostom, Homily 42 n. 3: "Then, too, what took place was a reproach, and not merely a coincidental one, to Judas, since he carried the money box."

[12] See Homily 42 n. 1 in FC 33, p. 426: "Why, then, did He question Philip? He knew those of His disciples who most needed instruction. For he is the one who later said: 'Show us the Father and it is enough for us.' That is why He began to condition him from the start." Hugh of St. Cher, p. 323c quotes a longer section of Chrysostom than Bonaventure, but without attribution.

them. And so one should imagine that he first asked the Lord about the crowds, and afterwards the Lord asked him for his counsel.

14. Question 3 centers on the truth of John 6:6: "But Jesus said this to try him." – Contrary 1. James 1:13 says: "God tempts no one." Wherefore, James 1:13 states: "God is no tempter." – 2. Likewise, temptation leads to sin, but God inclines no one into sin. – If you say that God does not tempt by inclining someone to sin, but by proving that individual, according to what Psalm 25:2 says: "Prove me, Lord, and try me," here is the contrary: One who doesn't know an individual has the responsibility to prove and test him. Therefore, if God knows an individual, God has no need to try or tempt him.

I respond. The point has to be made that there is a temptation that inclines to evil, and this temptation issues from the flesh, the world, and the devil, but not from God.[13] There is also a temptation that proves, and this is threefold. In the first instance it reveals information to the one proving. In the second information comes to others. In the third the person who has been proven gains information about himself. – The first kind of proving does not pertain to God, but to humans. Sirach 13:14 reads: "With many words he will test you."[14] In the second manner God is the one who tempts the perfect man for the sake of example. Genesis 22:1 says: "God

---

[13] See 1 John 2:16: "Because all that is in the world is the lust of the flesh, and the lust of the eyes, and the pride of life, which is not from the Father, but from the world."

[14] On p. 320 n. 9 QuarEd correctly mention that the Vulgate reads *Ex multa enim loquela* ("For with much talk") while Bonaventure has *Ex multis loquelis* ("With many words").

tempted Abraham."[15] The third kind of temptation tests the imperfect person to gain the merit of humility, since a person is humiliated when his weakness is made known to him. Psalm 25:2 states: "Prove me, Lord, and try me."[16]

JOHN 6:10-13
THINGS CONCOMITANT TO THE SIGN

15. *Jesus then says.*[17] After the Evangelist has set down the antecedents to the miraculous feeding, he proceeds to indicate the three *concomitant* things. First is *the seating of those reclining*. Second is *the multiplication of the loaves*. Third is *the gathering of the fragments*.

Verse 10. The first thing noted is the sitting down of those reclining at Christ's command. Thus the text says: *Jesus then says*, namely, to his disciples: *Make the people recline*, that is, to sit down so that they may eat. For to recline or to recline at table is proper for those eating. Thus Luke 14:10 says: "When you are invited to a wedding feast, recline," etc.[18] And the place was fitting for reclining, for the text continues: *Now there was much grass in the place*. And in that appropriate place the disciples made them recline, as the text says: *So the men reclined, in number about five thousand*. The text says *about*, since perhaps there was one more or one less. After all, Scripture is not concerned about minutiae. Other evangelists say that

---

[15] This temptation involves the sacrifice of Abraham's beloved and only son, Isaac.

[16] See Homily 42 n. 2 in FC 33, pp. 426-27 where Chrysostom also deals with the problem of the Lord's testing of Philip and alludes to Gen 22:1.

[17] On p. 320 n. 12 QuarEd accurately indicate that the Vulgate reads *Dixit* ("said") where Bonaventure has *dicit* ("says").

[18] Bonaventure combines words from Luke 14:8 and 14:10.

there were five thousand. Matthew 14:21 has: "Now the number of those who had eaten was five thousand men, without counting the children and women."[19]

16. (Verse 11). *Jesus then took the loaves*, etc. This verse introduces the second point, the multiplication of loaves, which the Lord effected by giving thanks and consummated by *their distribution.* The text states: *Jesus then took the loaves* to multiply them, for his hands had power in them. Thus in Numbers 11:23 the Lord said to Moses: "Is the hand of the Lord impotent? You will presently see whether my word will come to pass." *And when he had given thanks* to make them holy. 1 Timothy 4:4-5 reads: "Nothing is to be rejected that is accepted with thanksgiving.[20] For it is made holy by the word of God and prayer." *He distributed them to those reclining* to eat, through the Apostles, so that they might give to the diverse people whatever they wanted. Esther 1:8 reads: "The king had appointed, who had set one of his nobles over every table, that every person might take what he wanted." *Likewise the fish, as much as they wanted*, that is, until they were full. Exodus 16:12 states: "In the evening you will eat flesh, and in the morning you will have your fill of bread."

17. (Verse 12). *But when they were filled.* Here the third point surfaces, that is, the collecting of the fragments, lest they be wasted. So the text continues: *But when they were filled*, that is, satiated, *he said to his disciples: Collect the fragments, lest they be wasted.* For since bread had been

---

[19] Bonaventure inverts the order of the Vulgate which has *mulieribus et parvulis* ("women and children").

[20] On p. 321 n. 2 QuarEd rightly notice that the Vulgate reads *reiciendum* ("to be rejected") while Bonaventure has *abiiciendum* ("to be rejected"). The Vulgate reads *percipitur* ("is accepted") while Bonaventure has *sumitur* ("is accepted").

made for human consumption, the fragments would be wasted if they were not used for human consumption. Psalm 103:15 states: "May bread strengthen the human heart." And the Lord's disciples followed his command, as the next verse says:

18. (Verse 13) *So they collected them and filled twelve baskets.* Behold, a measure and a full measure. Chrysostom comments: "I not only stand in wonder at the multiplication of the loaves, but also at the exactness of the fragments left over, for the baskets were equal to the number of the Apostles. This indicates that the teaching of the Apostles was to be disseminated to the entire world from the fragments of Christ's teaching."[21] I repeat: *They collected and filled twelve baskets with the fragments of the five barley loaves, left over by those who had eaten.* He made them gather these leftovers, so that the abundance might be manifest. For Psalm 20:13 states: "In your remnants you will prepare their face."

19. The allegorical interpretation.[22] Now one boy had five barley loaves and two fish that were multiplied into twelve baskets of leftovers. This boy is Moses, giver of the Law, who is called a boy, because he was a member of the family. Hebrews 3:2 reads: "Moses was most faithful[23] in all his house," as a family member. – Bread is learning the word. Deuteronomy 8:3 states: "Men and women do not live by bread alone, but by every word that proceeds from the mouth of God." – So the five loaves are the words about which the Apostle speaks in 1 Corinthians 14:19:

---

[21] See Homily 42 n. 3 in PG 59:212. Bonaventure's "quotation" seems a summary of Chrysostom's comment.

[22] As far as I can tell, Hugh of St. Cher has nothing similar. Augustine, Tractate 24 n. 5-6 in FC 79, pp. 234-237 has certain elements, e.g., the five loaves are the five books of Moses.

[23] The Vulgate does not read *fidelissimus* ("most faithful").

"I had rather speak five words with my understanding,"
etc.[24] Jerome teaches: "The five words are the five books
of Moses, about which the Apostle is speaking."[25] – These
loaves are multiplied when the Lord opens up their many
meanings. Luke 24:27 reads: "Beginning with Moses ... he
interpreted to them in all the Scriptures the things that
referred to himself." – From the multiplication of these
loaves twelve baskets of fragments remained, that is,
the teaching of the Twelve Apostles who were dispersed
into the world, according to Psalm 18:5: "Their sound has
gone out into the whole world." And Mark 16:15 states:
"Go into the whole world and preach the gospel to every
creature."

Questions

20. Question 1 deals with the multiplication of loaves. For
if the Lord wanted to display his power and a greater
power is involved in creating bread than in multiplying it,
for the former comes from nothing while the latter comes
from something and it was equally easy for the Lord to
do both, why did he multiply the loaves? – I respond that
it has to be said that both pertain to God's infinite power,
both the multiplication from such puny amounts into
such an enormous quantity, since it issued from infinite
power, and creation. But he multiplied the loaves rather
than create them in order to shut up the mouths of the
heretics who hold that these visible matters pertain to the

---

[24] 1 Cor 14:19 concludes: "... that I may also instruct others than
ten thousand words in a tongue."

[25] See Letter 53 n. 8 in PL 22:545: "Up to this point is the Penta-
teuch. The Apostle was happy that he wanted to speak by means of
these five words in the Church (1 Cor 14:19)."

God of darkness, not to the God of light.[26] So he wanted to multiply things that had already been created, in order to show that he himself was the one who created all visible things.

Next the question occurs whether God multiplied the loaves by affixing new matter to them or by creation or by increasing what was there. It would seem doubtful that God proceeded in these ways. So without prejudicing the matter it should be maintained that the multiplication came about at that time without creation and external affixing of new matter. Nor was there an increase of matter only, as comes about by the power of a natural agent. Rather there was simultaneously an increase in matter and form through God's infinite power. And there is nothing similar in nature or even in creation.[27]

21. Question 2 asks: Why did the Lord in John 2:1-12 above make premium wine, but here distributed coarse barley bread to the crowds? – I answer that an explanation must come from the literal wording of the texts. In John 2 the Lord changed water into wine and gave it the best form.

---

[26] Bonaventure repudiates the teaching of the Manichees in Book II d. 1 p. I dub. 2 and p. II q. 1 d. 34. a. 1. q. 1 of his *Sentence Commentary*. See Chrysostom, Homily 42 n. 2 in FC 33, pp. 428-429: "He did not need the material substance of the bread; however, He made use of the creature itself so that what He made miraculously might not seem to be alien to His wisdom as those afflicted with the disease of Marcion lyingly have asserted."

[27] Some background to Bonaventure's answer may be found in Book I, Part VI, Chapter XXXVII of *Hugh of Saint Victor on the Sacraments of the Christian Faith (De Sacramentis)*, English version by Roy J. Deferrari (Cambridge, MA: The Mediaeval Academy of America, 1951), p. 118: "Indeed, there are six works according to which all things that are done are brought into effect. The first work is to make something from nothing. The second work is out of something to make some things into a greater thing according to substance and quantity." Bonaventure uses this "second work" and adds "form" to "matter."

Here, however, he multiplied and increased the bread. So while the form remained, he gave it perfect quantity, since twelve baskets remained beyond what was necessary.[28] – There is also a spiritual explanation: The five loaves signify the five books of Moses. Now the teaching of Moses was harsh and tough. And therefore, the Lord multiplied barley loaves.[29]

22. Question 3 is raised by Chrysostom: Why does the Lord give thanks in performing this miracle and not when he performed others?[30] – It seems that he showed his powerlessness. – The answer is that he did not give thanks in order to accomplish this miracle. Rather it was his custom, for at the beginning of a meal he gave thanks and blessed the food. In doing this he taught us that we should give thanks and pray when we partake of food.[31]

---

[28] Hugh of St. Cher, p. 323v,c also addresses the issues behind Bo-naventure's questions 1 and 2: "For he did not lack material on which to work, but used the creatures at hand for the matter of the miracles, so that he might show that he himself was their author against Marcion and the Manichees. Likewise as we said above relative to John 2, he did not create new wine, but made it from water. Here in a similar manner he did not create new loaves, but multiplied those which were already made."

[29] See Augustine, Tractate 24 n. 5 in FC 79, pp. 234-235: "... the five loaves are understood as the five books of Moses; rightly they are not wheat but barley because they belong to the Old Testament. For you know that barley was created in such a way that one can scarcely get to its kernel; for this kernel is clothed with a covering of husk, and this husk is tenacious and adhering, so that it is stripped off with effort. Such is the letter of the Old Testament, clothed with the coverings of carnal mysteries; but if one gets to its kernel, it feeds and satisfies."

[30] See Homily 42 n. 2 in PG 59:211-212 and FC 33, pp. 429-430: "But why is it that He did not pray when He was about to cure the paralytic, or to raise the dead, or to calm the sea, while here in the miracle of the loaves He did so?"

[31] See Homily 42 n. 2 in PG 59:212 and FC 33, p. 430: "It was to show that those who are beginning to partake of food ought to give thanks to God. Besides, He did it particularly in the case of a lesser

23. Question 4 introduces the principle that all superfluity is to be avoided. Further, the Lord has made all things according to a certain weight and measure.[32] Therefore, it seems that he should not have multiplied the loaves beyond what was sufficient. – I respond that one has to say that even if the multiplication of loaves went beyond what was necessary, nonetheless it did go beyond what was useful. The usefulness was twofold: nourishment and instruction. Nourishment, since afterwards it provided food for the disciples. Instruction, so that we might know that God is able and prepared to give us what is beyond our mere need. Also that we might know that the miracle was genuine. Further, from the exact number of the fragments left over we might understand the teaching of the Apostles and its great fruit.[33]

JOHN 6:14-21
CONSEQUENCES OF THE SIGN

24. (Verse 14). *Now the people*, etc.[34] The Evangelist has already described those things that came before and accompanied the miraculous feeding. Now he depicts the consequences in a fourfold manner: *the eagerness of the crowds* to honor Christ; *Christ's hiding* to escape the honor; *the descent of the disciples* to the sea to go across it; *Christ's coming* to aid the disciples.

---

miracle that you may learn that it was not out of necessity that He did so."

[32] The allusion is to Wis 11:21.

[33] See Chrysostom's Homily 42 n. 3 in PG 59:212 and FC 33, p. 431: "The fragments, therefore, confirmed the miracle, testifying to it on both counts, namely, that what had happened was not an illusion and that it was with these miraculous loaves that they had been fed."

[34] On p. 322 n. 9 QuarEd accurately indicate that the Vulgate reads *ergo* ("therefore") while Bonaventure has *autem* ("now"). Bonaventure agrees with the Vulgate when he cites this same verse in the next paragraph.

The first consequence of the aforementioned miracle was the eagerness of the crowds to honor Christ. They did this because they recognized him through the sign that he had done. So the text says: *When the people, therefore, had seen the sign that Jesus had worked*, that is, they had considered the magnitude of the sign, *they said: This is indeed the Prophet who is to come into the world*, that is, the Christ, who was expected as Lord of the whole world. They were saying this on account of the sign. John 7:31 below states: "When the Christ comes, will he work more signs that this man performs?"

25. (Verse 15). *So when Jesus*, etc. This verse contains the second point, that is, Christ's hiding to flee from the honor he foresaw that the crowds wanted to confer on him. So the text continues: *So when Jesus perceived*, namely, as God, *that they had come*[35] *to take him by force*, somewhat violently, *and make him king, he fled again to the mountain, alone by himself*, as one in haste and not waiting for his disciples. For they wanted to seize and make him king before the time, as he himself said in John 18:36 below: "My kingdom is not of this world." Augustine remarks: "Christ fled when they wanted to make him king, for the man Christ scorned all earthly goods to show that they were to be contemned. He endured all evil things to show that happiness should not be sought in them and that adversity should not be feared in them."[36]

---

[35] On p. 322 n. 11 QuarEd rightly mention that the Vulgate reads *venturi essent* ("would come") while Bonaventure has *venturi erant* ("had come").

[36] See c.22 n409 *De Catechizandis Rudibus* in *Sancti Avrelii Avgvstini De fide rerum invisibilium*.... Edited by I.B.Bauer. CCSL xlvi (Turnhout: Brepols, 1969), p. 164. Bonaventure's citation is not verbatim, e.g., Augustine reads *homo factus dominus Christus* ("the Lord Christ who was made man") while Bonaventure has *homo Christus* ("the man Christ"); Augustine reads *infelicitas* ("unhappiness") whereas Bonaventure has *adversitas* ("adversity").

26. (Verse 16). *Now when evening had come*, etc. Here is the third point: the descent of the disciples to depart from there. For the Lord wanted to leave the crowds secretly, so that they wouldn't find him. Therefore, he sent his disciples ahead; they were to descend from the mountain and cross the sea. So the text adds: *Now when evening had come*, that is, the hour for returning home, *the disciples went down to the sea*, so that they might cross over.

27. (Verse 17). *And getting in the boat, they went across the sea to Capernaum. They went*, that is, they began to go; the verb is used in anticipation of their arrival there. So *they went* there, because that is where the Lord lived. Matthew 4:13 says: "He went down to Capernaum and lived there."[37] *And it was already dark*, etc. The fourth point occurs here: Christ's coming to help them, since they were in danger from the dark night and the tempestuous sea. So the text reads: *It was already dark*. Note the danger of the night and especially that there were without their captain. So the text continues: *And Jesus had not yet come to them*.[38] So they were in peril. John 12:35 below states: "The person who walks in darkness does not know where he is going." There was also the danger from the storm. So the text says:

28. (Verse 18). *Now the sea was rising, because a strong wind was blowing*. For the sea was being whipped up by the wind. Jonah 1:4 reads: "The Lord sent a strong wind into the sea, and a great tempest arose." And since the Lord was near "to those who are contrite of heart,"[39] the Lord comes to help them. So the text states:

---

[37] The Vulgate reads *venit* ("went") whereas Bonaventure has *descendit* ("went down").

[38] On p. 323 n. 2 QuarEd correctly notice that the Vulgate reads *et non* ("and not") whilst Bonaventure has *nondum* ("not yet").

[39] See Ps 33:19.

29. (Verse 19). *But after they had rowed about twenty-five or thirty stadia.*[40] The text says *about* on account of the difficulty of judging distances on the sea. *They saw*[41] *Jesus walking upon the sea and drawing near to the boat* to help them. But they did not recognize him. So the text continues: *And they were frightened.* Mark 6:49 gives the reason: "They thought it was a ghost." And since the Lord comforts frightened hearts, the text adds:

30. (Verse 20). *But he said to them: I am,*[42] that is, I am the one who protects you. *Do not be afraid.* Since the Lord is present, there is no reason to be afraid, according to Psalm 26:1: "The Lord is my protector.[43] Of whom should I be afraid?" And from this hope flooded their minds.

31. (Verse 21). *So they wanted to take him into the boat,* since they recognized him and were rejoicing that they were safe. *And immediately the boat was at the land, towards which they were going.* That is, at the land, since the Lord almighty was with them and was not being upheld by the boat, but was upholding it. Hebrews 1:3 reads: "Upholding all things by the word of his power." And *immediately,* since Wisdom 12:18 states: "For your power is at hand when you will it." Thus, there was a

---

[40] Augustine, Tractate 25 n. 6 in FC 79, p. 244: "'Twenty-five' would be enough, 'thirty' would be enough, especially since it was a matter of estimation, not affirmation." Then Augustine goes on to do theology by the numbers: "And the fives are multiplied by six, that the Law may be fulfilled by the gospel, that six times five may be thirty."

[41] On p. 323 n. 4 QuarEd correctly maintain that the Vulgate reads *vident* ("they see") while Bonaventure has *viderunt* ("they saw").

[42] On p. 323 n. 5 QuarEd accurately indicate that the Vulgate reads *dicit* ("he says") while Bonaventure has *dixit* ("he said").

[43] The Vulgate reads *Dominus protector vitae meae* ("The Lord is the protector of my life") while Bonaventure has *Dominus protector meus* ("The Lord is my protector").

triple miracle, that is, walking on the sea, stilling the storm, and the fastest docking at port.

32. The spiritual meaning should concern the village to which they were going, their means of travel, and who was their guide. – The village, to which they were going, was Capernaum, which is interpreted most beautiful village.[44] This is the heavenly homeland, where there is the greatest beauty, as Wisdom 5:17 says about the Saints: "They will receive a kingdom of glory and a crown of beauty from the hand of the Lord." – They travel to this village by means of the sea, that is, through bitter tribulations. Acts 14:21 states: "Through many tribulations we must enter into the kingdom of God." – Through this sea the boat of penance, on which men and women are saved, makes its way, according to what Acts 27:31 says: "Unless you remain on the boat,[45] you cannot be saved." In a similar way Sirach 2:22 reads: "If we do not do penance, we will fall into the hands of the Lord." – This boat is buffeted when it is beaten by blasts of temptation. Matthew 7:25 states: "The floods came, and the winds blew."[46] – Those going by boat see the Lord walking as in this passage. Those who are fighting see him standing as in Acts 7:55.[47] Those contemplating see the Lord sitting, according to what Isaiah 6:1 says: "I saw the Lord sitting." – But the

---

[44] See Jerome, CCSL lxxii, p. 139: "Capernaum means field or village of consolation." See Bede's comments on John 2:12 in PL 92:662C: "Capernaum is interpreted most beautiful village, signifying this world, to which our Lord Jesus Christ is said to have descended ... for the salvation of the human race."

[45] The Vulgate reads *Nisi hii in navi manserint* ("Unless these people remain on the boat") whereas Bonaventure has *Nisi in navi manseritis* ("Unless you remain on the boat").

[46] This refrain also occurs in Matt 7:27 and refers to the assault on houses built on rock and on sand respectively.

[47] Acts 7:55 deals with Stephen, who saw "Jesus standing at the right hand of God."

Lord is present and leads them to port, according to what Isaiah 43:2 has: "When you pass through the waters, I will be with you. And the rivers will not cover you." And Psalm 90:15-16 professes: "I am with him in tribulation. I will deliver him and will glorify him. I will fill him with length of days, and I will show him my salvation."[48]

QUESTIONS

33. Question 1 focuses on what the crowds said about Christ in John 6:14: "This is indeed the Prophet." Are they saying something that is true or false? – It seems that their words are true, since Deuteronomy 18:15 states: "The Lord will raise up a prophet for you." And the Glossa maintains that the literal meaning applies to Christ.[49] – Contrary. Prophecy does not pertain to those who possess God,[50] who see clearly whereas others see through a mirror.[51] Therefore, if Christ possessed God, he was not, therefore, a prophet.

---

[48] Hugh of St. Cher, pp. 325-326 has four full columns of interpretation. What he says on p. 325k offers some parallel to Bonaventure: "This boat of penance is necessary for us, if in the evening, that is, in the darkness of this life, we want to cross the sea, that is, the dangers of this world, and arrive at Capernaum, that is, to consolation and the riches of Paradise."

[49] This is the Glossa Ordinaria (from Rabanus Maurus). See PL 113:471BC: "Although historically this can refer to the prophets who from the people of Israel after the time of Moses were filled with the Spirit of God, nonetheless, it is better to take it as referring to the prophets' Lord, about whom the crowds, whose stomachs he had filled, said: *This is indeed the Prophet who is to come into the world* (John 6). Another place has: *A great prophet has arisen among us* (Lk 7)."

[50] Bonaventure uses *comprehensor* whose second meaning, according to Deferrari, p. 191 is "one who comprehends, comprehendor, possessor, especially the possessor of God or of heavenly glory, the opposite of *viator*."

[51] See 1 Cor 13:12: "We see now through a mirror in an obscure manner, but then face to face...."

I answer that one has to distinguish a twofold meaning in the word prophet. A person is called a prophet by reason of interior inspiration and revelation, and this type has ignorance joined to it as a component part. One is also a prophet by reason of infallible and true pronouncements. Christ is not a prophet of the first category, but he is of the second, since he spoke the truth in everything and did so infallibly.

34. Question 2 asks about Christ's flight into the mountain in John 6:15. – 1. For if he was king, therefore he should be received as king and should be willing that his own people receive him as they should. Wherefore, he should not have fled, but rather offered himself to them. – 2. Likewise, when the salvation of the people depends upon an elected individual, that person should not absent himself. So if the salvation of the people depended upon Christ, then, etc. – 3. Furthermore, why did he flee by himself, when earlier he didn't come up by himself, but with his disciples?

I respond that it has to be said that Christ is received as king, when he is received as reigning in the heart through faith. But since the people were not concerned with faith and salvation, but with temporal food, he, therefore, justly absented himself. – 2. And from the previous answer flows the solution to the next objection, for the salvation of the people does not depend upon the carnal reign of Christ, but upon his spiritual reign. – 3. The answer to the query why Christ fled by himself is this. On account of his haste he did not wait for others. On account of his hiding he avoided human association. On account of instruction, so that he might show that one should not seek counsel in receiving honors from family and friends, for in this matter what Micah 7:6 says is verified: "A person's enemies are members of his household."

35. Question 3 focuses on the disciples going down to the sea. – 1. John 6:16 reads: "Now when evening had come, his disciples went down to the sea." Why did they leave their Master all alone? – It would seem that their conduct was reprehensible. – 2. Furthermore, John 6:17 says that the disciples were heading towards Capernaum. But Mark 6:45 says that Jesus commanded them to go to Bethsaida.

I answer that a solution is found in what Matthew 14:22 states: the Lord "made his disciples get into the boat." Therefore, their conduct was not reprehensible, since they had obeyed the Lord. – 2. Relative to the objection about contradictory destinations, the point should be made that Mark mentions the village that was closest whereas John indicates the village that was their ultimate destination.

36. Question 4 is concerned with the Lord's walking upon the sea. – 1. Did this miracle occur because the water was supporting him or because his body kept above the water? – 2. Moreover, why didn't he show this miracle to the crowds? – I respond. Some say that the miracle pertained to the body that for that period of time took on the heavenly gift of agility. This is what Master Hugh maintains.[52] – Others are of the opinion that the miracle

---

[52] On p. 324 n. 5 QuarEd cite Albert the Great's Postilla on John 6:19 where he gives this as the teaching of Hugh of St. Victor: "The Lord took on then, for a time, two heavenly gifts, incorporeality and agility, just as he assumed brightness on the Mount of Transfiguration and impassibility on the day of the Supper when he gave his body to be eaten." The opinion that Bonaventure attributes to Hugh of St. Victor has some basis in Book II, part VIII, c. 3 of his *De Sacramentis*. See PL 176:462-464. See Innocent III, Book IV, chapter 12, *De Sacro Altaris Mysterio* in PL 217:864C: "Subtlety when he was born of the Virgin; brightness when he was transfigured on the mountain; agility when he walked on the water; impassibility when he is eaten at the supper."

pertained to the water that, for the feet of its Creator, made itself capable of being walked on. Gregory holds this viewpoint.[53] – But a more satisfactory opinion preserves both the water and the body in their own natures and with their own properties and states that by divine power the body was carried over the water. – 2. Now he revealed himself to his disciples rather than to the crowds, since, just as his disciples excelled in understanding the words of their Master, so too did they comprehend his miracles. Wherefore, he revealed many things to them in secret.

JOHN 6:22-72
CHRIST AS CONSERVER OF SPIRITS

37. *The next day the crowd*, etc. The Lord has just shown himself as conserver through bodily food. Now in this part he shows that he is conserver through *spiritual food*. And since people are not fed spiritually without their consent and free will does not give its consent unless it is attracted and spurred on, it follows that this part has two sections. The first handles *the rousing up of the crowd* whereas in the second the Lord offers the crowd *spiritual food* where verse 34 reads: "They said to him: Lord, always give us this bread."

JOHN 6:22-33
CHRIST'S ROUSING UP OF THE CROWD

So the Evangelist follows this order in depicting *the rousing up of the crowd*. First, he describes the crowd's *eagerness* in seeking Christ the Lord. Second, the *correction* of those

---

[53] See Homily 10 n. 2 of GGHG in CCSL cxli, pp. 66-67and Hurst, p. 55: "... the sea knew him because it allowed him to walk upon it...."

who were searching for him in an inordinate way. Third, the *instruction* of those who harbor doubts. Finally, the *humiliation* of the haughty.

38. So first the text suggests that the crowds' eagerness to search for Christ stems from the miracle that had been seen. And since they did not know him, there were questing after him. Since they did not know him, they did not know when and how he had left the scene. So the text continues:

Verse 22. *The next day the crowd that had remained on the other side of the sea. Had remained*, I think, out of expectation. Thus, they could say what Peter said in Matthew 17:4: "Lord, it is good that we are here." So they had not immediately departed. *The other side of the sea*, that is, where they had been fed. *They saw*, by means of their reasoning, according to the statement: "I have given you a wise and understanding heart."[54] *They saw that there had been no other boats, but only one at that place*, that is, there was only one boat by which Jesus could have crossed over. *And*, supply: they saw, *that Jesus had not gone into the boat with his disciples, but only the disciples had departed.*[55] And since they did not find him, they believed that he had miraculously crossed over. And they wanted to search for him and could do so, since there were boats there. Thus the text adds:

39. (Verse 23). *But other boats came near from Tiberias*, that is, the city, from which this place derived its name.

---

[54] See 1 Kings 3:12 where this is the Lord's response to King Solomon's prayer.

[55] On p. 325 n. 2 QuarEd accurately mention that the Vulgate reads *sed soli discipuli eius abissent* ("but his disciples had departed alone") whereas Bonaventure has *sed solum discipuli abiissent* ("but only the disciples had departed").

Near the place where they had eaten the bread, when God gave thanks,[56] since food should be eaten with thanksgiving.

40. (Verse 24). *So when the crowd perceived that Jesus was not there nor his disciples.* And they themselves had come on account of Jesus. *They got into the boats and came to Capernaum, seeking Jesus.* Now they were seeking him, because he had fed them in the present, according to what Sirach says: "Those that eat me will still be hungry."[57] By means of wood they were seeking him, who brought about salvation, according to Wisdom 14:5: "Human beings trust their lives to a little wood, and, passing over the sea, are saved."

41. (Verse 25). *And when they had found him,* etc. The second point occurs here, that is, the correction of those seeking Christ inordinately. For the Jews are seeking Jesus, and once they had found him, they question him. So the text adds: *And when they had found him on the other side of the sea* and had not seen him cross over, *they said to him: Rabbi, when did you come here?* In their puzzlement they were inquiring, not knowing how he had arrived there. And in their curiosity they were asking about the time, like the disciples in Matthew 24:3: "Tell us when these things will happen." And the Lord did not answer their query, but responded to the intention behind the question of those asking in an inordinate manner. So the text continues:

---

[56] On p 325 n. 3 QuarEd correctly indicate that the Vulgate reads *Domino* ("the Lord") while Bonaventure has *Deo* ("God").
[57] Sir 24:29.

42. (Verse 26). *Jesus answered*[58] *and said: Amen, amen I say to you. You seek me, not because you have seen the signs* that I have done, so that through these signs you may come to faith and so you are not seeking anything spiritual, but rather carnal matters. *But because you have eaten of the loaves*, that is, that I multiplied, *and have been filled*. And the carnal Jews were seeking after this, that is, bodily satiety, just as their fathers had. Exodus 16:3 reads: "Would that we had died by the hand of the Lord in the land of Egypt, when we sat over the flesh pots and ate bread to the full." And since they were seeking in an inordinate manner, the Lord directs them in an ordinate way.

43. (Verse 27). *Do not labor*, that is, do not search painstakingly, *for the food that perishes*, namely, carnal. For 1 Corinthians 6:13 states: "Food for the belly, and the belly for food. But God will destroy both the one and the other." Matthew 15:17 says: "Everything that enters the mouth passes into the belly," etc. *But for food*[59] *that endures unto eternal life*, that is, spiritual food. This food is the word of God that lasts forever. Thus, Isaiah 40:8 reads: "The word of the Lord endures forever." And so it gives eternal life. John 6:69 below states: "Lord, to whom shall we go? You have the words of eternal life." Christ gives this food. So the text continues: *That the Son of Man will give you*, as the good shepherd. John 10:9 below says: "If anyone enter by me, he will be safe and will go in and out and will find pastures." And that he himself is the one to give this food, he adds: *For upon him God the Father has set his seal. Has set his seal*, by the sign of

---

[58] On p. 325 n. 7 QuarEd rightly notice that the Vulgate reads *eis* ("to them").

[59] On p. 325 n. 10 QuarEd correctly indicate that the Vulgate does not read *cibum* ("food").

his testimony he has shown that he is his Son, who could give life and food. Matthew 3:17 describes Jesus' baptism: "This is my beloved Son."

Another interpretation: *Has set his seal*, that is, he has set someone off from others by his own seal,[60] so that he may be unique "having primacy in all things."[61] For the Father set Christ off from all in a threefold manner. That is, by union with the Word. John 1:14 above says: "The Word became flesh." By fullness of gifts. John 3:34 above reads: "God does not give the Spirit by measure." By immunity from sin. John 1:29 states: "Behold, the Lamb of God. Behold, the one who takes away the sins of the world." This sealing was pre-signified in Haggai 2:24: "I will take you, O Zerubbabel . . . my servant, says the Lord, and will make you as a signet, for I have chosen you, says the Lord of hosts."

44. (Verse 28). *So they said:*[62] *What are we to do*, etc. The Evangelist mentions the third point: instruction for those doubting. For since they did not understand Christ's correction, they began to doubt and ask questions. So the text continues: *So they said to him*, that is, the Jews:

---

[60] See Augustine, Tractate 25 n. 11 in FC 79, pp. 248-249: "What is to set the seal except to put some [mark] exclusively one's own? For to set the seal is this, to apply some [mark] which would not be confounded with others. To set the seal is to put a sign on a thing. You put a sign of something or other; you put the sign precisely so that it may not be confused with other things and can be recognized by you. Therefore, 'upon him the Father has set his seal.' What does 'has set his seal' mean? He has given him something exclusively his own that he might not be compared to other men."

[61] See Col 1:18: "Again, he is the head of his body, the Church. He, who is the beginning, the firstborn among the dead, having primacy in all things."

[62] On p. 326 n. 1 QuarEd rightly notice that the Vulgate reads *ad eum* ("to him"), a reading that Bonaventure also has later in this paragraph.

What are we to do, so that we may perform the good works of God?[63] So they were inquiring about the work, since through it they wanted to get something to eat. For this is the order of things. 2 Thessalonians 3:10 reads: "If any person does not work, let him not eat." Proverbs 12:11 states: "The person who tills his land, will be filled with bread." And the Lord instructs those who are asking. So the text adds:

45. (Verse 29). *In answer Jesus said to them*, that is, to those questioning and doubting: *This is the work of God, that you believe in the one whom he has sent. This is the work* that is good, the beginning of all good works, for Hebrews 11:6 says: "Without faith it is impossible to please God." People who want to do good works must begin with faith. Genesis 15:6 reads: "Abraham believed God, and it was credited to him as justice."[64]

46. (Verse 30). *So they said to him*, etc. Here the Evangelist introduces the fourth point, that is, the humiliation of those who contemn and are arrogant. For they did not want to believe in Christ on account of the signs that they had seen, as if their fathers had seen greater signs. So they said: *What sign, then, do you do that we may see and believe you?* For the Hebrews do not believe unless they see signs. 1 Corinthians 1:22 states: "The Jews seek signs."[65] *What work do you perform?* As if they were

---

[63] On p. 326 n. 1 QuarEd accurately mention that the Vulgate does not read *bona* ("good").

[64] It seems likely that Bonaventure was not quoting Gen 15:6 directly, but through Paul's citation of Gen 15:6 in Rom 4:3. Rom 4:3 reads *Abraham* ("Abraham") whereas the Vulgate of Gen 15:6 does not. Also Rom 4:3 reads *Deo* ("God") while the Vulgate of Gen 15:6 reads *Domino* ("the Lord").

[65] Hugh of St. Cher, p. 327f also cites 1 Cor 1:22.

saying: What great thing have you done? What you did is minor compared to what had been done in the desert.

47. (Verse 31). *Our ancestors ate manna in the desert*, not barley bread, but heavenly bread. So they also add: *As it was written: Bread from heaven he gave them to eat*. It was written in Psalm 77:25: "Humans ate the bread of angels. The Lord sent them provisions in abundance." In this way they were exalting in the miracle shown to their ancestors and contemning Christ's miracle. And the Lord humiliated them by showing that Moses did not fulfill that Scripture passage, but he did. So the text adds:

48. (Verse 32). *Jesus then says:*[66] *Amen, amen I say to you: Moses did not give you the bread from heaven*, as that Scripture passage says. Not truly, I say, but as a type, since, as 1 Corinthians 10:11 states: "All things happened to them as a type." *But my Father gives you the true bread from heaven*. And therefore, we ask him for this in Matthew 6:11: "Give us today our supersubstantial bread."[67] And he provides the reason for this:

49. (Verse 33). *For the true bread*[68] *is that which comes down from heaven and gives life to the world*. And this bread was not the manna, but Christ. John 10:10 below states: "I have come that they may have life and have it more abundantly." *To descend from heaven*, this means to come in the flesh. Thus, Augustine comments: "The Word,

---

[66] On p. 326 n. 6 QuarEd accurately indicate that the Vulgate reads *dixit* ("said") whereas Bonaventure has *dicit* ("says").

[67] See Bonaventure's *Gospel of Luke, Chapters 9-16*, pp. 1024-1025 for a discussion of "supersubstantial."

[68] On p. 326 n. 7 QuarEd correctly mention that the Vulgate reads *Panis enim Dei* ("For the bread of God") while Bonaventure has *Panis enim verus* ("For the true bread").

which was the bread of Angels, when it descended into flesh, was changed into milk for children."[69]

QUESTIONS

50. Question 1 deals with John 6:26: "You seek me, not because you have seen signs." – Contrary. John 6:2 above reads: "A great crowd was following him, because they had seen the signs," etc. – I answer and maintain that this contradiction is resolved in a twofold way. One solution notes that there were *different times*, since the same people first followed him on account of *signs* and, after they had been fed, they followed him on account of *food*. The second solution notes that there were *different people*, and then both statements were true. For some followed him on account of *signs*, and others followed him on account of *food*. – Thus it should be noted that there were five reasons why some followed the Lord. The following jingle contains these reasons: "Sickness, signs,

---

[69] This is a drastic summary of Augustine's commentary on Psalm 119 n. 2. See *Sancti Avrelii Avgvstini Enarrationes in Psalmos CI-CL.* Edited by Eligivs Dekkers and Johannes Fraipont. CCSL xl (Turnhout: Brepols, 1956), p. 1779. See *Expositions of the Psalms (Enarrationes in Psalmos) 99-120*, trans. and notes by Maria Boulding, WSA III/19 (Hyde Park, NY: New City Press, 2003), p. 500: "A mother does this: she eats solid food and processes it through her flesh to pass it on to her baby in the form of milk; similarly the Word, the Lord, the food of angels, was made flesh, and so the apostle could say, *I gave you milk to drink, rather than solid food. You were not capable of it then, nor are you even now* (1 Cor 3:2). He descended to little ones to give them milk, and because he descended, he gave them the one who descended." Hugh of St. Cher, p. 327o has a citation similar to Bonaventureís: "Augustine says that the Word, which is the bread of Angels, was changed into milk for children, when it descended from heaven."

food, blasphemy, teaching were the reasons why the crowd followed the Lord."[70]

51. Question 2 focuses on John 6:27: "Do not work for the food that perishes." Chrysostom asks whether men and women should work for bodily food.[71] It would seem not. – Because of this text. Likewise, because of Matthew 6:31: "Do not be anxious ... what might we eat," etc.[72] – Furthermore, in Luke 10:41 the Lord rebukes Martha who was anxious about bodily food. Therefore, it does not seem that men and women should work for bodily food. – Contrary. 1 Thessalonians 4:11 states: "Work[73] with your own hands, as we charged you." Moreover, 2 Thessalonians 3:10 reads: "If any person does not work, let him not eat."[74] In this passage the Apostle also presents himself as an example.[75]

---

[70] The Latin is: *Morbus, signa, cibus, blasphemia, dogma fuere/Causae, quae Dominum turba secuta fuit.* See Bonaventure's commentary on John 6:2 n. 3 above and note 2 where the five reasons provided by Hugh of St. Cher are listed: miracles, food, sickness, entrapment, teaching.

[71] See Homily 44 n. 1 in PG 59:248 and FC 33, p. 443: "However, since some who wish to live without working misapply this statement by saying that Christ was renouncing manual labor, it is timely to speak also against them."

[72] The Vulgate reads *manducabimus* ("will eat") whereas Bonaventure has *manducetis* ("might eat").

[73] The Vulgate reads *operemini* ("work") while Bonaventure has *operamini* ("work"). 1 Thes 4:11 states: "Strive that you may live peacefully, that you may mind your own business, that you may work with your own hands, as we charged you."

[74] Bonaventure also cited 2 Thes 3:10 in his commentary on John 6:28 n. 44 above.

[75] See 2 Thes 3:8-9: "We worked night and day in labor and toil, so that we might not burden any of you. Not that we did not have the right to do so, but that we might make ourselves an example for you to imitate us."

I answer that it has to be said that it is good to work in order to have bodily food, as it is said: "You will eat the labors of your hands. Blessed are you," etc.[76] But there is a threefold disorder with regard to this work of the hands. There is a disorder of intention with the result that a person wants this food as an end in itself. In this passage the Lord prohibits such desire. There is a disorder of anxiety with the result that a person's mind is preoccupied with earthly matters. The Lord prohibits this in Matthew.[77] There is a disorder in time with the result that when a person should be taken up with hearing the word of God, a person is taken up with work or bodily food. And so Christ rebuked Martha who should have been paying attention to the Lord's preaching.[78]

52. Question 3 asks about the meaning of John 6:29: "The work of God is that you believe in the one whom he has sent." – Contrary. In Romans 3:28 the Apostle states: "We reckon that a person is justified by faith without works of the Law." Wherefore, to believe is not a work. – I respond that work is generally understood as either the work of the performer or the work produced, either a spiritual or a corporeal work, either an interior or an exterior work. But in its proper meaning it refers to the second of the above alternatives: spiritual or corporeal. To believe is a work in the spiritual realm and is hardly one in the corporeal realm.[79]

---

[76] Ps 127:2.

[77] See Matt 6:31 above.

[78] Bonaventure is dependent upon Chrysostom here. See Homily 44 n. 1 in PG 59:248-249 and FC 33, p. 445: "And what was said to Martha did not refer to work and daily labor, but to the necessity of knowing the time for it and of not spending the time, intended for listening to Him, on more material occupations."

[79] See the Glossa Ordinaria in PL 114:382A: "Faith working through love is a work, since if its power is absent, the will seeks in vain. Fittingly, too, is the faith that works through love called a work

53. Question 4 concerns the meaning of John 6:32: "Moses did not give you bread from heaven." For Wisdom 16:20 states: "You gave them bread from heaven already prepared."[80] – Some respond there are a fiery heaven and the heaven of the lower atmosphere. They did not enjoy bread from the first heaven, but from the second.[81] – This solution does not resolve the matter, since Christ was not bread from the fiery heaven. And so Psalm 77:25 states: "Human beings ate the bread of the Angels." But the bread of the Angels was not from the lower atmosphere. – My answer is that the manna has to be taken as material food that is from the material heaven, but effecting a figure of true food, heavenly and spiritual. So authorities that state that this food is heavenly are to be understood according to figure and type which are the opposite of unveiled true reality.

---

which is the beginning and end of every good." See Augustine, Tractate 25 n. 12 in FC 79, pp. 249-50: "Therefore, he did not wish to separate faith from work, but he said that faith itself is a work. For this is the faith which works by love. He did not say, 'This is your work,' but 'This is the work of God, that you believe in him whom he has sent,' so that he who takes glory may take glory in the Lord." Both the Glossa Ordinaria and Augustine refer to Gal 5:6: "Faith that works through charity." See also Hugh of St. Cher, p. 327d.

[80] Wis 16:20 says: "Instead of these things you fed your people with the food of angels and gave them bread from heaven prepared without labor, having in it all that is delicious and the sweetness of every taste."

[81] See Hugh of St. Cher, p. 327m: "Not from the fiery heaven, but from that of the lower atmosphere, according to what Matt 13:4 says: The birds of the heaven eat it up. Also Ps 17:14 reads: The Lord thundered from heaven." See Chrysostom, Homily 45 n. 1 in PG 59: 252 and FC 33, p.451: "Surely, the manna was not from heaven; how is it, then, that He said 'from heaven'? Just as Scripture says: 'The birds of heaven,' and again: 'And the Lord thundered from heaven.' And He calls that bread 'true,' not because the miracle in the case of the manna was false, but because it was figure, not the reality."

John 6:34-72
Christ offers spiritual food

54. *So they said to him*. The Lord has aroused the Jews to seek spiritual food. Now *he provides instruction* for those he has already aroused and who are seeking nourishment. And since Christ is bread that nourishes according to his divine nature and according to his human nature, this part has two sections. In the first he considers the eating of this heavenly bread according to his *divine* nature. In the second according to his *human* nature where verse 52b reads: "And the bread that I will give is my flesh," etc.

John 6:34-52a
Christ is bread that nourishes
according to his divine nature

In its turn this first section has two parts. The first contains *the instruction* Christ gave in answer to the Jews' request. The second deals with *the confirmation of the instruction* on account of the murmuring of the Jews where verse 41 states: "So the Jews murmured," etc.

John 6:34-40
Christ's instruction to the Jews

Christ's instruction of the Jews with regard to eating this heavenly bread proceeds in this order. First he shows *who is* the bread that nourishes and gives life. Second *those* who are nourished by this bread. Third *why* it nourishes these people and not others.

55. (Verse 34). First in response to the Jews' request Christ teaches *who is* the bread that refreshes. For this reason the Evangelist introduces the Jews who make a request: *Lord, give us this bread always*, since he had promised them *living* bread. So they were asking for it that they might not hunger, just as the woman had asked for water.[82] John 4:15 says: "Lord, give me this water that I may not thirst or come here to draw water." So now the Lord presents spiritual bread to those who are asking.

56. (Verse 35). *But Jesus said to them: I am the bread of life*, that is, the bread that *gives life*, for he is Wisdom, about whom Sirach 4:12 says: "Wisdom inspires life in her children." Not only does this bread give life, but it also *satisfied* both affections and intellect. So the text continues: *The person who comes to me*, that is, through love, *will not hunger*. Matthew 11:28 reads: "Come to me, all you who labor and are burdened, and I will refresh you." *And the person who believes in me will never thirst,*[83] since as John 4:13-14 states above: "The person who drinks of the water that I will give him will never thirst. But the water that I will give him will become in him a fountain of water, springing up to eternal life." – It should be noted that love gives nourishment, for among the affections it is the greatest unifier. Faith provides drink, since it deals with the act of the intellect that is the least unifier. And therefore, just as liquids guide the food into the members, so too does faith and the operation of the intellect lead the way for the powers that exist in the affections. This is what it means to have a meal.[84]

---

[82] Hugh of St. Cher, p. 327 also refers to John 4:15.

[83] On p. 327 n. 15 QuarEd rightly notice that the Vulgate reads *unquam* ("never") while Bonaventure has *in aeternum* ("never").

[84] This *notandum* is so condensed that it is obscure. In his Collationes 17-18 of his *Hexaëmeron* Bonaventure provides extensive food imagery.

57. (Verse 36). *But I have told you.* This verse introduces the second point, namely, those who are nourished by this bread: Not non-believers, but believers chosen and called by God. So the text says: I have said that "the person who comes to me will not hunger," but you, because you do not believe, cannot be nourished. Thus he says: *But I have told you that you have seen me and you do not believe.* John 3:11 above said: "We speak of what we know and we bear witness to what we have seen, and you do not accept our testimony." Furthermore, John 5:44 above stated: "How can you believe who receive glory from one another and do not seek the glory that is from the only God?" Moreover, John 6:26 above reads: "You seek me, not because you have seen signs, but because you have eaten of my loaves."[85] And since *you do not believe*, you cannot be nourished. For Bede comments: "You desire bread from heaven? Before you, you have it, and yet you are not eating,"[86] since you do not believe. But those are eating who have been chosen and called by God and believe. So the text continues:

58. (Verse 37). *All that the Father gives to me*, through an eternal election and a temporal calling. *Will come to me*, through faith and love. Psalm 2:8 speaks of this *giving*: "Ask of me, and I will give you the Gentiles as your inheritance." The Lord asked for these gifts in John 17:11 below: "Father, keep in your name those whom you have given me," etc. Isaiah 2:3 speaks of this coming to Christ: "Come ... let us go up to the mountain of the Lord and to the house of the God of Jacob, and he will teach us his ways." Isaiah 55:1 exhorts people to participate in

---

[85] The Vulgate does not read *meis* ("my").

[86] See his commentary on John 6:35 in PL 92:714A. With one exception Bonaventure's citation is verbatim. Instead of *manducatis* ("you eat"), Bonaventure has *comeditis* ("you eat").

this coming: "All you that thirst, come to the waters." He nourishes those who engage in this coming. So the text adds: *And the person who comes to me, I will not cast out. I will not cast out*, but feed and nourish. *I will not cast out*, but *I will lead in*, according to what The Song of Songs 2:4 states: "He led me into the wine cellar," etc. – Another interpretation: *I will not cast him out*, but I will come inside to him. Revelation 3:20 reads: "Behold, I stand at the door and knock. If anyone hears my voice and opens the door for me, I will come inside to him and will dine with him." And in this God shows his justice, since he only nourishes those who come, and his graciousness, since he accepts everyone and rejects no one.

59. (Verse 38). *For I have come down from heaven*, etc. This verse treats the third point, namely, why he feeds only those predestined and called by God. The reason is the conformity of his will to divine will. So the text states: *For I have come down from heaven*, by taking on flesh, *not to do my own will*, at variance with that of the Father, *but the will of the one who sent me*, by being obedient to him in all things. For Philippians 2:8 says: "He became obedient" to the Father "to the point of death, even death on a cross." John 5:30 above reads: "I do not seek my own will, but the will of the one who sent me." But the will of the Father is that those who have been chosen and called may eat of this bread. For which reason the text adds:

60. (Verse 39). *For this is the will of my Father who sent me*[87] *that everything he has given me*, through election. Romans 8:29 states: "Those whom he has foreknown he has

---

[87] On p. 328 n. 7 QuarEd correctly mention that the Vulgate reads *Haec est autem voluntas eius qui misit me Patris* ("Now this is the will of the one who sent me, the Father") while Bonaventure has *Haec est enim voluntas Patris mei, qui misit me* ("For this is the will of my Father, who sent me").

also predestined to become conformed to the image of his Son." *I should lose nothing of that,*[88] through reprobation, according to 1 Corinthians 1:19: "I will destroy the wisdom of the wise, and I will reject the prudence of the prudent." *But that I will raise it up on the last day*, to participation in eternal happiness. Romans 8:11 reads: "If the Spirit of him who raised Jesus from the dead lives in you, then he who raised Jesus Christ from the dead will also bring to life your mortal bodies." For his part he fulfilled that will. John 18:9 below says: "Father, of those you have given me, I have not lost one"[89] And since God chooses us in this manner, so that we may reach happiness through the merits of faith, so that he might show the cooperation of our will, he repeats:

61. (Verse 40). *Now this is the will of my Father, who sent me, that whoever beholds the Son*, according to his humanity, *and believes in him*, through the freedom of his will, since, as Augustine maintains, "no one can believe except willingly,"[90] *will have eternal life* as a reward, *and I will raise him up on the last day*, and thus he will obtain this life through the Son. Ephesians 2:5-6 reads: "When we were dead by reason of sins, he brought us to life together with Christ ... and raised us up together and seated us together in heaven in Christ Jesus." And this occurs *on the last day*, since, as 1 Corinthians 15:26 states: "the last enemy of all,[91] death, will be destroyed."

---

[88] Bonaventure's exposition has necessitated a stilted translation. A more smooth translation of John 6:39b is: "that I should lose nothing of what he has given me."

[89] The Vulgate does not read *Pater* ("Father").

[90] See Tractate 26 n. 2 in FC 79, p. 261; "no one can believe except willingly."

[91] The Vulgate does not read *omnium* ("of all").

QUESTIONS

62. Question 1 concerns John 6:35: "The person who comes to me will not hunger." – Contrary. John 6:67 below states that "many of his disciples turned back." And it follows that these first had come to him. Therefore, he is speaking falsely.[92] – I respond that this text has to be understood of those who came with a perfect, not a false, heart. It is also about those who came with steadfast love. Otherwise, it would be as if they had not come, in that "all their acts of justice are forgotten."[93]

63. Question 2 deals with John 6:36: "You have seen me, and you do not believe." – It seems that this is a nonsense statement, since faith is the substance of those things that are not seen.[94] Wherefore, there can be no basis for his rebuke that they do not believe, since they see. – But if you say, that to see pertains to his humanity, and to believe to his divinity, this is not valid, for the vision of his humanity is more an impediment to faith in his divinity than a help. So he should not have censured them on this point.

I answer that this text should be understood not of looking at pure or weak humanity, but of looking at humanity filled with power and strength manifested in its deeds. And since they were seeing divine power in his deeds, they should have believed. – Relative to the objection

---

[92] It seems that the substance of this question might have been John 6:37: "... the person who comes to me I will not cast out" rather than John 6:35.

[93] See Ez 33:13 where the Vulgate reads *omnes iustitiae eius oblivioni tradentur* ("all his acts of justice will be forgotten") while Bonaventure has *omnes iustitiae in oblivionem dantur* ("all the acts of justice are forgotten").

[94] In the background is Hebr 11:1: "Now faith is the substance of things to be hoped for, the evidence of things that are not obvious."

that seeing is incompatible with faith, the point has to be made that this is true about seeing an essence, but is not true about the seeing that has its origin in a deed done as in a mirror, since it pertains to faith to see "through a mirror and[95] in an obscure manner."[96]

64. Question 3 focuses on John 6:39: "I might lose nothing of all that the Father[97] has given me." – Contrary. John 17:12 below reads: "Not one of those whom you gave me perished except the son of perdition."[98] Therefore, one of those given to him perished. – I respond that one has to put the emphasis on the words "The Father gave," for "to give" can be taken in a twofold manner. If taken according to present justice, he was given Judas, and he perished. If taken according to eternal election, he was given the predestined. None of those perished. Another answer is to put the stress on *I might lose*, for Christ himself guarded them most carefully. So no one perishes because of negligence on the part of the shepherd. However, since he saves no one against his will, some perish out of their own malice. Wherefore, Christ did not lose them. Rather they lost themselves.

---

[95] The Vulgate does not read *et* ("and").

[96] See 1 Cor 13:12. Bonaventure's argument here is a theological version of "where there's smoke, there's fire."

[97] Bonaventure introduces "Father" here from the similarly sounding John 6:37: "All that the Father gives to me will come to me...."

[98] Bonaventure has inverted the parts of John 17:12: "Those whom you gave me I guarded, and not one of those perished except the son of perdition...."

JOHN 6:41-52A
CHRIST OFFERS CONFIRMATION OF HIS INSTRUCTION

65. Christ has just finished giving instruction to the Jews at their behest, now in a second point he offers *confirmation* of his teaching to quell their murmuring. He proceeds in the following order. First there is *the murmuring of the Jews.* Second is Christ's *curbing of the murmuring.* Third is *the removal of error.* Fourth is *confirmation of the true teaching.*

Verse 41. So the first point, the murmuring of the Jews, stems from the Lord's statement that he had come down from heaven. Thus, the text reads: *So the Jews murmured about him.* Murmuring is veiled slander, for Chrysostom says: "They contradicted him, not openly, but in veiled manner, for the sign of his multiplication of the loaves was still recent."[99] They were preserving the custom of their ancestors, about whom Numbers 14:27 says: "For how long does this wicked multitude murmur against me?" And he adds the reason for their murmuring: *Because he had said: I am the living bread that has come down from heaven,*[100] for they were seeking temporal food to eat. Since they were frustrated in getting an answer to their expectation, they were murmuring.

66. (Verse 42). *And they kept saying: Is this not*[101] *the son of Joseph?* Luke 3:23 says: "When he began his work, he

---

[99] Bonaventure's citation contains the gist of Chrysostom's observation. See PG 59:257 and FC 33, p. 462: "On the contrary, they did not listen to Him, but murmured. Of course, they still held Him in awe because of the recent miracle of the loaves. That is why they did not oppose Him openly, but by murmuring they showed that they resented it, because He did not give them the table which they desired."

[100] The Vulgate does not read *vivus* ("living").

[101] On p. 329 n. 10 QuarEd rightly notice that the Vulgate reads *Iesus* ("Jesus").

was about thirty years of age, being, as was supposed, the son of Joseph." *Whose father and mother we know?* From the earth, not from the heavens. Matthew 13:55-56 states: "Is not this the carpenter's son ... and his mother called Mary, and his brothers ... and ... sisters, are they ... not with us?" *How, then, does he say: I have come down from heaven?* For we know that he was born on earth. And in this way what was spoken above in John 4:44 is verified: "A prophet receives no honor in his own country." For since they recognized his temporal generation, they negated his eternal. And since they scorned the humble Christ, they could not see the sublime Christ.

67. (Verse 43). *So in answer Jesus said to them.* This verse introduces the second point, that is, the curbing of their murmuring. For he restrains them in their murmuring. Thus, the text continues: *Do not murmur among yourselves.*[102] The point is well taken, since murmuring profits nothing. Wisdom 1:11 reads: "Keep yourselves from murmuring, which profits nothing." Rather it is an obstacle. 1 Corinthians 10:10 states: "Do not murmur, as some of them murmured." And the reason why they should not murmur is that they do not know Christ. And since they do not know him, they foolishly rebuke him. And truly they do not know him, because they do not believe. And they do not believe, since it has not been given them by the Father. So the text adds:

68. (Verse 44). *No one can come to me,* through faith and love and knowledge, *unless the Father, who sent me, draw him,* through revelation, like Peter, about whom Matthew 16:17 says: "Blessed are you, Simon Bar-Jonah, for flesh

---

[102] On p. 329 n. 12 QuarEd accurately mention that the Vulgate reads *in invicem* ("among yourselves") whereas Bonaventure has *ad invicem* ("among yourselves").

and blood have not revealed this to you, but my Father in heaven." Thus the Father draws people to me through *revelation. And I will raise him up on the last day*, through redemption and freedom from death. 1 Corinthians 15:21-22 says: "Since by a man came death, by a man also comes resurrection of the dead. And as in Adam all die, so[103] in Christ all will be made to live." And in order to impose an even greater silence upon them, he confirms his teaching from Scripture.

69. (Verse 45). *It is written in the Prophets: They[104] all will be taught of God*, that is, all will be taught by God. The text says: *In the Prophets*, for there are many instances. Jeremiah 31:33-34 reads: "I will place my Law in their innards, and I will write it on their hearts.[105] And I will be their God, and they will be my people. And no longer will a man teach[106] his neighbor and man his brother, saying: Know the Lord, for all will know me from the least ... even to the greatest." Likewise, Isaiah 54:12-13 states: "I will make ... all your children to be taught of the Lord." And Joel 2:28 has: "I will pour my Spirit upon all flesh, and your sons and your daughters will prophecy. Your old men will dream dreams."

Everyone who has listened to the Father, etc. The third point is found here, that is, the removal of error. For since he had said that all are taught by God, lest anyone believe that they see God, from whom they are being taught, he

---

[103] The Vulgate reads *ita et* ("so also").

[104] On p. 330 n. 2 QuarEd correctly mention that the Vulgate reads *Et erunt* ("And they will be") while Bonaventure has *Erunt* ("They will be").

[105] The Vulgate reads *corde* ("heart") while Bonaventure has *cordibus* ("hearts").

[106] The Vulgate reads *docebunt* ("they will teach") whereas Bonaventure has *docebit* ("he will teach").

states not that they see, but that *they hear*. So he says: *Everyone who has listened to my Father*[107] *and has learned*, through inspiration, according what Psalm 84:9 says: "I will hear what the Lord God will speak in me." That person *comes to me*, through faith and love, according to what Revelation 22:17 states: "Let the person who hears say, Come."

70. (Verse 46). *And*[108] *not that anyone has seen the Father*, that is, someone who is mortal and capable of suffering, because Exodus 33:20 reads: "Human beings will not see me and live," *except him who is from God, he sees the Father*.[109] This is the only-begotten Son, about whom John 1:18 above says: "No one has at any time seen God, but the only-begotten Son, who is in the bosom of the Father," etc.

71. (Verse 47). *Amen, amen, I say to you*, etc. This verse expresses the confirmation of the previous instruction. So he repeats what he had said and joins an affirmative adverb to it. For this reason he says: *Amen, amen, I say to you*, that is, truly, truly I say: *Whoever believes in me has eternal life*. And he proves this, since he himself is the bread that gives life to believers. So the text continues:

72. (Verse 48). *I am the bread of life*. And I am this for believers, because, as Proverbs 3:18 says: "Wisdom is the tree of life for those who take hold of her," namely, through faith, "and the person who holds onto her is blessed," who

---

[107] On p. 330 n. 4 QuarEd rightly notice that the Vulgate does not read *meo* ("my").

[108] On p. 330 n. 5 QuarEd accurately indicate that the Vulgate does not read *Et* ("And").

[109] On p. 330 n. 5 QuarEd correctly mention that the Vulgate reads *vidit* ("has seen") while Bonaventure has *videt* ("sees").

holds onto her through understanding.[110] And he shows by its effect what the nature of the bread of life is, since it gives the life of grace and the life of glory. The bread that was a type did not give the life of grace. So the text adds:

73. (Verse 49). *Your ancestors ate the manna in the desert*, namely, for forty years, as Deuteronomy 8:3 states: "The Lord gave you manna as your food, with which you were unfamiliar."[111] *And have died*, that is, the death for sin and infidelity. Hebrews 4:2 reads: "The word that was heard did not profit them, since they had no faith...."[112]

74. (Verse 50). *This is the bread that comes down from heaven*, through the incarnation, *so that if anyone eat of it*,[113] through faith and love, that person *will not die*, through prevarication, for, as Habakkuk 2:4 states: "The just person lives by his faith."[114] Just as faith frees from death, so too does love. 1 John 3:14 states: "We know that we have passed from death to life, because we love the brothers and sisters. The person who does not love abides in death." It not only gives the life of grace, but also the life of *glory*. So the text continues:

75. (Verse 51). *I am the living bread*, through his essence, since he has life in himself. John 5:26 above reads: "Just as the Father has life in himself, so he has given to the Son also to have life in himself." *That has come down from heaven*, through an abundance of mercy. Exodus 3:7-8

---

[110] Bonaventure seems to make an explicit identification here between Christ and Wisdom.

[111] Deut 8:2 speaks of the forty years in the desert.

[112] Hebr 4:2 concludes: "... since they had no faith in what they heard."

[113] On p. 330 n. 9 QuarEd rightly notice that the Vulgate reads *ex ipso* ("of it") while Bonaventure has *ex eo* ("of it").

[114] The Vulgate reads *vivet* ("will live") whereas Bonaventure has *vivit* ("lives"). Rom 1:17 and Hebr 10:38 have *vivit* ("lives").

says: "I have seen the affliction of my people in Egypt and ... their sorrow, and I have come down to deliver them."

76. (Verse 52a). *If anyone eat of this bread, he will live forever*, through glory. About this eating The Song of Songs 5:1 states: "Eat, O friends, and drink, and be inebriated, my dearly beloved."[115] This will occur in glory. The sinner in the figure of Adam is prohibited from such a meal. Genesis 3:22 reads: "Now therefore, lest perhaps he ... take from the tree of life and eat and live forever."[116]

QUESTIONS

77. Question 1 deals with John 6:41: "The Jews murmured." – 1. The Lord knew that the Jews would fall from the teaching of the truth into murmuring. Therefore, since he knew that his teaching would not be effective and since he was a physician of salvation, he should not have given them his teaching. – 2. In doing this, he did what Matthew 7:6 writes about: "Do not give to dogs what is holy. Do not cast your pearls before swine." He also did what Proverbs 9:7 warns about: "The person who teaches a scorner, does an injury to himself." Therefore, it seems

---

[115] See c. 11, n. 33 in Bernard of Clairvaux, *On Loving God* with An Analytical Commentary, Emero Stiegman, CFS 13B (Kalamazoo: Cistercian Publications, 1995), p. 34: "Once our bodies come back to life we shall be filled with everlasting life, abounding in a wonderful fullness. This is what is meant by the Bridegroom in the Canticle saying: 'Eat, my friends, and drink; dearest ones, be inebriated.' Eat before death, drink after death, be inebriated after the resurrection. It is right to call them dearest who are drunk with love; they are rightly inebriated who deserve to be admitted to the nuptials of the Lamb, eating and drinking at his table in his kingdom...." See SBOp 3.147.

[116] Bonaventure presupposes what Gen 3:24 says: "And the Lord God cast out Adam and placed before the paradise of delight Cherubim and a flaming sword, turning every way, to guard the way of the tree of life."

that such people should not be given instruction since they use it as a basis for slander.

I answer that as Augustine says in his book *About the Good of Perseverance*, the salvation of one good person is to be preferred to many evils. This opinion is taken from his words.[117] He also says there that when we know that our teaching will be of benefit to good people, even if we know that it will scandalize evil people, we should not keep silent. So since the teaching about the bread of life was opportune and exceedingly useful for the good, both for those present and for us who read about it, and since the timing for this teaching was good, as he had just fed many in a miraculous way, he did well to offer this teaching, not for the sake of evil people, but for the sake of the good. – So this is the solution that even though the Lord was speaking to evil people, he was, nevertheless, teaching good people.

78. Question 2 focuses on John 6:45-46: "Everyone who has listened to the Father ... not that anyone has seen the Father," etc. – Contrary. 1. The point is clear that this passage is speaking of the seeing and the hearing of the intellect itself. But in the intellect there is no difference between seeing and hearing. The person who hears with his intellect also sees with his intellect. Therefore, if the Father is heard interiorly, he is also seen. – 2. Further, if you say that there is another possibility, it is certain that to understand is to see. Therefore, the person who hears either understands or not. If he understands, he sees. If he hears and does not understand and comes to the sound he has heard, he comes not as an intelligent person, but as a brute animal.

---

[117] This is a summary of c. 15 n. 40 of *Liber De Dono Perseverantiae*. See PL 45:1017-1018.

I answer that seeing refers to the individual speaking whereas hearing to the word spoken. Properly speaking, the word spoken by God is God's inspiration, according to the sense of this passage. This inspiration is the effect of God in the soul. The soul can recognize this effect in itself, although it does not fully comprehend from whom it comes. Therefore, it has to be said that a person both sees and hears that inspiration, but it does not follow from this that the person sees God. Thus, the text expresses the matter very well: "Everyone who listens to the Father," that is, the inspiration proceeding from the Father. And I maintain that that person sees as well as hears. But from this it does not follow that that person sees the one who is inspiring, for hearing does not refer to the one inspiring, but to the effect. The same holds with regard to sight.

79. Question 3 concentrates on John 6:44: "No one can come to me, unless the Father ... draw him." – Contrary. 1. Drawing is a violent motion. All merit is voluntary. Therefore, no one is worthy of merit when he does something because he is drawn thereto. – 2. Likewise, if it is impossible unless a person is drawn, then it is not in that person's own power to come to God. And if this is the case, then, since no one is reprehensible if he cannot do the impossible, then no one is reprehensible, if he does not come to God. – 3. Furthermore, although to draw pertains to the whole Trinity, which occurs by revelation, which is proper to the Son or Holy Spirit, how is it attributed to the Father since the attribution is not by characteristic feature, but by appropriation?

I respond that to remain in oneself is what nature has established. To descend or to incline below oneself, that is what corrupt nature has done. But to be elevated above oneself, that is what pertains to nature exalted by grace. Wherefore, to stay put pertains to nature. To go down pertains to sin. To rise up pertains to grace. – So since nature is corrupt and prone to sin, if it is not raised up above itself, there will be not only a raising up, but also on account of the inclination to the contrary, a drawing. So since everyone, who comes to God, is raised up above himself, no one comes, unless that person is drawn. Therefore, he speaks well when he says: "No one comes," etc.[118]

1. With regard to the objection that drawing is a violent motion, the answer is that there is a drawing by means of external compulsion, and one by inducement. The former involves violence while the second has a minuscule amount. – Another answer to the objection is there is the drawing of affection, according to what Augustine says when he quotes the poet: "A person's own pleasure draws him."[119] And this drawing is worthy of merit or demerit. Also there is a drawing that is against one's will. One does not draw by this, and this passage is not speaking about this type of drawing.

2. The answer to the second objection is that it is not in one's complete power to come, but it resides in the power

---

[118] See c. 1, n. 1 in Bonaventure's *Itinerarium Mentis in Deum*. New English translation by Zachary Hayes; Introduction and commentary by Philotheus Boehner, WSB II (St. Bonaventure, NY: Franciscan Institute Publications, 2002), p. 45: "Since happiness is nothing other than the enjoyment of the highest good, and since the highest good is above us, we cannot find happiness without rising above ourselves, not by a bodily ascent, but by an ascent of the heart. But we cannot be elevated above ourselves unless a superior power lift us up."

[119] See Tractate 26 n. 4 in FC 79, p. 262: "Moreover, if it is allowed to a poet to say, 'His own pleasure draws each man,' not need but pleasure, not obligation but delight, how much more forcefully ought we to say that a man is drawn to Christ who delights in truth, delights in happiness, delights in justice, delights in eternal life – and all this is Christ?" The poet is Virgil, and the reference is to his *Eclogue* 2.65.

to prepare oneself for divine help.[120] – 3.With regard to the action that is appropriated to the Father, I am of the opinion that appropriation of a specific characteristic happens in the Trinity by reason of making something comprehensible, removing an error, manifesting humility. So I say that by means of this third way the Son appropriates to the Father actions that pertain to the Trinity, so that he might teach us to be humble. Thus the answer is obvious.[121]

80. Question 4 raises queries about John 6:45: "All will be taught of God.' – 1. Because this is most certainly false in every state of life. – 2. Furthermore, how is what Joel 2:28 says true: "I will pour out my Spirit upon all flesh" and similarly what Isaiah states: "I will make ... all your children to be taught by the Lord"?[122] – I follow Augustine in my answer: he distributes all by the genus to which single individuals belong.[123] – And thus the authorities cited have little bearing on the issue. – For this reason there is an alternate exposition. Those who will be taught

---

[120] See Book II, d. 28 a. 1 and 2 of Bonaventure's *Sentence Commentary* and Part V, c. 2 of his *Breviloquium*.

[121] See Book I, d. 34 q. 3 of Bonaventure's *Sentence Commentary* and Part I, c. 6 of his *Breviloquium*.

[122] See Isa 54:12-13, a text that Bonaventure also cites in his commentary on John 6:45 (n. 69) above.

[123] See c. 27, n. 103 of his *Enchiridion de fide, spe, et charitate* in *Saint Augustine: Christian Instruction, Admonition and Grace, The Christian Combat, Faith, Hope and Charity,* trans. Bernard M. Peebles, FC 4 (New York: CIMA Publishing Co., 1947), pp. 456-57: "Rather, they lead us to understand 'all men' [1 Tim 2:4] as the whole of humankind, in whatever classes it be divided: kings, subjects, nobles ... the sound of body, the weak ... of every tongue, of every fashion ... or according to any other principle of distinction among men. For from which of all these classes does not God wish that men throughout all nations should be saved through His Only-begotten Son our Lord – and therefore does save them, – for the Omnipotent cannot will in vain, whatever it be He wills?"

will be taught by God, and no one will be taught except by God. Therefore, "all are to be taught."And so the authority makes a valid point.[124]

JOHN 6:52B-72
CHRIST OFFERS HEAVENLY BREAD
ACCORDING TO HIS HUMAN NATURE

81. *And the bread that I will give*. Earlier the Lord showed that he was the bread that gave life according to his *divine* nature. Now he makes the same point according to his *human* nature. And since this would seem to be false and harsh or difficult, this section has three parts. The first concentrates on *the teaching* for believers. Second is *confirmation* of this teaching in the face of the quarreling of the Jews where verse 53 states: "The Jews on that account argued," etc. Third is an *explanation* of the teaching because of the scandal of the disciples where verse 60 reads: "These things he said while teaching in the synagogue at Capernaum."

---

[124] In his commentary on John 1 n. 30 Bonaventure comes to a similar conclusion in his discussion of the meaning of John 1:9: "It was the true light, which enlightens every person coming," etc. See Chrysostom, Homily 46 n. 1 in PG 59:258 and FC 33, p. 464: "'But,' you say, 'if he says, "they all shall be taught of God," how is it that not all men are believers?' Because his words were spoken of the majority of men. Besides, even apart from this, the prophecy refers not to all men in general, but to all who will to be taught. For, as a teacher, he is at the disposal of all men, ready to give them His teachings, pouring out His teaching in abundance unto all."

John 6:52b
Christ teaches believers

Verse 52b. This is a brief instruction, in which he says that his flesh is food. Wherefore he says: *And the bread*, etc. Just as I am bread according to my divinity, so too am I bread according to my flesh. So he states: *And the bread that I will give*, namely, as food, according to the petition we make in the Lord's Prayer in Matthew 6:11: "Give us this day our supersubstantial[125] bread." *Is my flesh*, that is, as food. 1 Corinthians 10:16 reads: "The bread that we break, is it not the body of the Lord?" *For the life of the world*, that is, the flesh of Christ was given when it was exposed to punishment, according to what Lamentations 3:30 says: "He will give his cheek to the one who strikes him." For Isaiah 50:6 states: "I have given my body to those who strike and my cheeks to those who pluck." And not only does he give his body over to be beaten, but also to be immolated. Thus, Ephesians 5:2 reads: "He delivered himself up for us as an offering and a sacrifice to God."

John 6:53-59
Christ answers the quarreling of the Jews

82. *The Jews on that account argued.* He has given his teaching. Now for his second point he provides *confirmation* for it in the face of the quarreling of the Jews. First is *the quarreling* of the Jews. Second is *confirmation of the teaching* where verse 54 has: "So Jesus said to them."

Verse 53. So *they were quarreling* that he had said that his flesh was bread, for they had understood his

---

[125] I have transliterated the Latin, *supersubstantialis*, which is frequently translated by "daily."

statement in a carnal manner. So the text says: *The Jews on that account were quarreling*. First, they were murmuring. Now they are quarreling as they contradict a clear and exalted statement. The Jews were engaged in quarreling, something that does not befit the servants of God. For 2 Timothy 2:24 states: "The servant of God must not quarrel, but be gentle towards all." *Saying to one another: How can this man gives us his flesh to eat?* As if they were saying: this is impossible, unless he kills himself. Nicodemus asked a similar question in John 3:4 above: "How can a person be born when he is old? Can he enter a second time into his mother's womb and be born again?" So they were asking a dumb question. Chrysostom comments: "You are asking: How can he give his flesh? Why didn't you ask about the loaves: How did he turn five loaves into so many?"[126]

83. (Verse 54). *So Jesus said to them*. Having set forth the quarreling of the Jews, the Evangelist now presents Christís confirmation of his teaching. He confirms what he had said about his flesh being bread in the following order. First he indicates *the necessity* of eating the flesh of Christ. Second is *the benefit* of such eating. Third is *the reality* of the food. Fourth is *the dignity* of the food.[127]

---

[126] See Homily 46 n. 2 in PG 59:260 where Chrysostom refers to Nicodemus' question right before the comment Bonaventure refers to. Bonaventure's citation is not verbatim. See also FC 33, pp. 467-68: "Nicodemus likewise was disturbed in this way when he said: 'How can a man enter into his mother's womb?' And these men were similarly perturbed when they said: 'How can this man give us his flesh to eat?' Now, if you really are looking for the 'how,' why did you not say this in the case of the loaves: 'How has He multiplied the five into so many?'" Hugh of St. Cher, p. 329v, x also quotes, in his own way, what Chrysostom has to say about Nicodemus and the Jews of John 6:53.

[127] It is impossible in English to capture Bonaventure's rhyming: *necessitas, utilitas, veritas, dignitas*.

So first he shows the necessity of eating, since there is no salvation without it. Thus he says: *Amen, amen I say to you*, that is, truly: *Unless you eat the flesh of the Son of Man*, as true bread, *and drink his blood*, as true drink, *you shall not have life in you*, that is, the life of grace, about which Psalm 118:107 says: "Give me life according to your word." Augustine observes: "The Body of Christ does not live except by the Spirit of Christ. So if you wish to live from the Spirit of Christ, be in the Body of Christ."[128] Now the person who eats the body of Christ is in the Body of Christ. Therefore, the person who does not eat does not live, since John 6:57 below says: "The person who eats my flesh ... abides in me."

84. (Verse 55). *The person who eats*, etc. This verse treats the second point, namely, the benefit of eating, since the person who eats flesh is given life in *soul* and *body*. In *soul*, for the text says: *The person who eats my flesh and drinks my blood has eternal life. Has*, I maintain, in merit. Another interpretation of *has* is this that the person has already begun in some way to have it. Isaiah 55:2-3 states: "Listen diligently to me and eat that which is good, and your soul will be delighted in its richness. Incline your ear and come to me ... and your soul will live, and I will make an everlasting covenant with you, the faithful mercies of David." – It also gives *bodily* life. So the text also says: *And I will raise him up on the last day*, in that hour, about which John 5:28-29 above spoke: "The hour is coming, in which all who are in the tombs, will hear the voice of the Son of God. and those who have done

---

[128] See Tractate 26 n. 13 in CCSL xxxv, p. 266. Bonaventure's citation is not verbatim. See further FC 79, p. 271: "Do you therefore also wish to live from the Spirit of Christ? Be in the body of Christ. For does my body live from your spirit? Mine lives from my spirit, yours from your spirit. The body of Christ can only live from the Spirit of Christ."

good will come forth unto resurrection of life, but those who have done evil unto the resurrection of judgment."

85. (Verse 56). *For my flesh*, etc. The third point occurs here, that is, the realness of the food. For the flesh of Christ really gives life. Since it is true food, it gives life. So the text continues: *For my flesh is food indeed*. So I have truly said that the person who eats it has life. *For my flesh is food indeed*, not imaginary, as bodily food that gives life for the moment and is finished. *And my blood is drink indeed*, since it entirely removes thirst. John 6:35 above states: "The person who comes to me will not hunger, and the person who believes in me will never thirst." And he gives this reason why his flesh is true food that nourishes and gives life: The person who abides in me lives on account of me. Now the person who eats my flesh abides in me. Therefore, the person who eats my flesh lives on account of me. He first provides the minor proposition for his reasoning in what follows:

86. (Verse 57). *The person who eats my flesh*, through spiritual eating, *and drinks my blood abides in me*, through love. 1 John 4:16 reads: "The person who abides in love abides in God, and God in him." *And I in him*, through inhabitation. John 14:23 below states: "If anyone loves me, he will keep my word, and my Father will love him, and we will come to him and make our abode with him." Having stated the minor proposition, he adds the proof for the major proposition, namely, that the person who abides in the Son lives because of him. He manifests this in a simile.

87. (Verse 58). *As the living Father has sent me. Living* is of the Father's essence. *And I live because of the Father*, namely, because I have life from him. John 5:26 above says: "Just as the Father has life in himself, so he has also

given to the Son to have life in himself." And this from the Father who abides in him. John 14:10 below reads: "I am in the Father, and the Father is in me." And from this emerges the major proposition: The person who abides in me, etc. And from this the conclusion is inferred: *So the person who eats me, he also will live because of me*, that is, since he abides in life by eating and truly lives because of me, for, as John 11:25 below states: "I am the resurrection and the life."

88. (Verse 59). *This is the bread*, etc. This verse introduces the fourth point: the dignity of the food, which excels the food of the ancestors that the Jews praised earlier, both because it is more noble and *more permanent*. It is more noble, since it is from heaven. For the text reads: *This is the bread that has come down from heaven*. John 6:32 above states: "Moses did not give you bread from heaven, but my Father gives you bread from heaven." And so it is more noble. It is also more permanent, for the bread from Moses sustained them temporally whereas this bread sustains them *eternally*. For the text continues: *Not as your ancestors ate manna and died*, and thus were sustained temporally, because after forty years they died in the desert, according to Psalm 94:10: "Forty years long was I offended by that generation," etc. Numbers 14:33 states: "Your children will wander in the desert for forty years and will bear your fornication, until the cadavers of their ancestors be consumed in the desert." But Christ's bread sustains eternally. Thus, the text adds: *The person who eats this bread will live forever*. That is, the person who eats it worthily, *will live forever*, because, according to 1 Corinthians 11:29, "The person who eats and drinks

unworthily eats and drinks judgment upon himself...."[129]
The person who eats worthily will live forever. Christ
often promises eternal life,[130] both so that they might
yearn for that food and so that he might draw them away
from the love of earthly life towards eternal life. For as
Matthew 10 reads: "The person who loves his life more
than me is not worthy of me."[131] Deuteronomy 30:19 has:
"Choose life for yourself."

QUESTIONS

89. Question 1 focuses on the quarreling of the Jews in John
6:53. About this verse Chrysostom raises the question:
Why is it that in John 6:41 above they were murmuring
in private,[132] but now they are quarreling in public?[133] – I
answer that there's a twofold reason involved. The first
reason is that evil people and deceivers and the depraved
go from bad to worse the more the truth is explained
to them. The second reason issues from what was said
about his divinity in John 6:27-52 above. Even though
this teaching might seem false, it, nonetheless, was not
inhuman. But now what he had said about eating his flesh

---

[129] Hugh of St. Cher, p. 330m also quotes 1 Cor 11:29.

[130] Hugh of St. Cher, p. 330e-g has some similarities with Bonaventure's exegesis: 1) Christ often said that he has eternal life; 2) citation of John 5:26; 3) Christ is proving his point.

[131] Matt 10:37 reads: "The person who loves father or mother more than me is not worthy of me."

[132] John 6:41 reads: "So the Jews murmured about him because he had said: I am the bread that has come down from heaven."

[133] See Homily 46 n. 1 in PG 59:257 and FC 33, p. 462 for what may be Bonaventure's source: "On the contrary, they did not listen to Him, but murmured. Of course, they still held him in awe because of the recent miracle of the loaves. That is why they did not oppose Him *openly*, but by murmuring they showed that they resented it, because He did not give them the table which they desired" (emphasis mine).

was not only false, but also so inhuman and unclean that the Jews fled from it. Therefore, they were quarreling.

90. Question 2 deals with the eating of the body of Christ and of his flesh. – And it seems that they should not be eaten. – 1. For what is eaten is torn apart and masticated, but the flesh of Christ is impassible and incapable of being torn apart by teeth. Therefore, it is not eaten. – 2. Likewise, what is eaten is transformed into the eater. But the body of Christ is not transformed into us. Rather we into him. Wherefore, we do not eat him, but he us.

I respond that there are three components in eating: mastication, incorporation, and preservation. Mastication is twofold since there is a twofold eating. In sacramental eating there is sacramental mastication, for the species is masticated. There is also spiritual eating, and during this there is spiritual mastication, which is a spiritual scrutinization through faith. There is also incorporation, by which we are incorporated into the body of Christ. Further, there is preservation, by which we are conserved through the spirit of Christ, as bodily members are through the soul. About these three Augustine comments: "O mystery of religion! O sign of unity! O bond of charity! Let the person who wants to live ... come forward, believe, be incorporated ... be given life."[134]

1. The answer to the first objection is obvious, since Christ is not talking about carnal mastication, but spiritual or sacramental. – 2. With regard to the objection that he is not incorporated into us, it has to be said that the ultimate effect of food is to preserve life. And so while it is true that we are incorporated into Christ by eating, it is also true

---

[134] See Tractate 26 n. 13 in CCSL xxxvi, p. 266. Bonaventure's citation is not verbatim.

that we are preserved by him through eating. Thus, he is correctly said to be our food.[135]

91. Question 3 calls into question the meaning of John 6:54: "Unless you eat the flesh of the Son of Man," etc. – From this statement it seems that the Sacrament of the Eucharist is necessary and that no one can be saved without it. – Contra. This is understood either of the life of grace or of the life of glory. It is not of the life of grace, since the person who wants to approach this sacrament worthily must first have the life of grace. Therefore, that person does not obtain it through eating. It is also not of the life of glory, because, if a person could obtain the life of grace without eating, he could do the same with the life of glory.

I answer in the words of Augustine that to believe is to eat, for he says: "Why are you preparing your teeth and your stomach? Believe only, and you have eaten."[136] So according to this one should bear in mind that there is a spiritual eating and also a sacramental eating. Spiritual eating is through faith and love. Sacramental eating is under the form of the sacrament. Without sacramental eating there can be salvation. It is not necessary, in as far as the institution of the Sacrament is concerned. But spiritual eating is necessary.[137]

---

[135] See Bonaventure's commentary on John 4 n. 66 above for a similar discussion of the properties of food.

[136] See Tractate 25 n. 12 in CCSL xxxvi, p. 254. Bonaventure's quotation would be verbatim if he did not have *tantum* ("only").

[137] See Book IV, d. 12. p. II. a. 2. q. 1 of Bonaventure's *Sentence Commentary* in Omnia Opera 4:294-295. Bonaventure's point is that the institution of the Eucharist does not contain the necessity that it be received. Bonaventure writes: "For the word of John or of the Lord in John is to be understood of *spiritual* eating, which is through faith and love. No adult is saved without it. And this is also in a child in some way in as far as incorporation."

92. There are further objections. 1. What about baptized children, who are saved, even though they have never eaten sacramentally or spiritually. – 2. Furthermore, if one adds to the eating of the flesh the drinking of the blood, then without drinking the blood no one is saved. But only the priests consume the blood. Wherefore, only they are saved.

I respond that, as has already been said,[138] eating has a double effect: incorporation and preservation. No one is saved unless that person is a member of Christ and unless he is conserved by Christ. Thus, no one is saved without the effect of eating. So it is said that eating is necessary. – Now since through divine largess there can be in children the effect of eating without eating, they are saved even without any sort of eating. But in adults there can be no incorporation or preservation without spiritual eating, which is through faith and love, but there can be without sacramental eating. Wherefore, spiritual eating is necessary in adults. Now sacramental eating, although it is not necessary, nonetheless provides many benefits, for through the power of the Sacrament every good grows in us.[139] – 2. Concerning the objection about the flesh and the blood, Augustine gives an explanation of spiritual food and drink. He comments: "He wants ... food and drink to be understood as the society of his body and members, which is the holy Church in its saints who are predestined and called ... and believers."[140] Outside of this no one is saved.

---

[138] See question 2 n. 90 above.

[139] See Book I, d. 12. p. II. a. 1 q. 3 and a. 2. q. 2 ad 3 in Bonaventure's *Sentence Commentary* in Omnia Opera 4:297-298.

[140] See Tractate 26 n. 15 in CCSL xxxvi, p. 267 and FC 79, p. 273.

93. Question 4 asks about the benefit behind John 6:55: "The person who eats my flesh ... has eternal life." – 1. For there are many who eat and who, nevertheless, die and are damned such as Judas. – 2. Moreover, as the Son lives on account of the living Father, so too, as John 6:58 states, do we live on account of the Son. But the Son lives without eating. Therefore, by a parallel reasoning the same holds for us. Put another way, if we eat the Son, why doesn't he eat the Father?

I respond to the first objection that two heresies have arisen from this text. The first one maintains that from the fact that a person eats the body of Christ, that person could not be damned, provided that he ate it as a believer. But this is manifest nonsense on account of Judas. – Others have said that if a person has once eaten it worthily, he would never be damned afterwards. And this is obviously wrong, because, as can be proved from Scripture, there were many good people in the Church, who afterwards were damned. – Therefore, the catholic understanding is this: The person who eats, that is, worthily, and does not depart from that worthiness will live forever. – 2. As to the second objection, it must be said that although Christ's point is introduced as a simile, it is not entirely similar. For the Son is said *to live because of the Father*, because he has life from the Father and abides in the Father, and not because he has become better by the participation in the Father. But we live through the Son, since we have life from him and we are better through the Son's abiding in us and his participation. Therefore, since he does not abide in us except by eating, we eat so that we may live and become better.[141]

94. Question 5 raises another question about the worthiness of this eating. For he says that those who eat this bread *will not die,* as those did who ate the manna.[142] – Contrary. This is understood either of spiritual life or of bodily life. If it deals with spiritual life, it says nothing, for the holy ancestors, who ate the manna, were not spiritually dead. If it deals with bodily life, the situation is similar, since those who ate this bread did not live bodily, but died. – If you say, those who eat the manna unworthily are dead by spiritual death and he calls them their ancestors. In a similar way those who unworthily eat the body of Christ died a spiritual death. 1 Corinthians 11:29 reads: "The person who eats and drinks unworthily eats and drinks judgment upon himself...." – So the question arises: What does it mean to eat unworthily? Why does the person who eats unworthily sin?

I respond that Christ's bread is better by reason of its power to give life in two ways. First, because the manna could not give life, except through that which it signified. Therefore, it is said of the just in 1 Corinthians 10:3: "All ate the same spiritual food." But those who had an eye

---

[141] Bonaventure seems to be dependent upon Augustine's Tractate 26 n. 19. See FC 79, p. 275: "He did not say, 'As I eat the Father and I live because of the Father, so he who eats me, also shall live because of me.' For the Son who was begotten equal does not become better by participation in the Father, as by participation in the Son through the unity of his body and blood, the thing which that eating and drinking signify, we are made better. Therefore we, eating him, live because of him, that is, by receiving him as eternal life which we do not have from ourselves...."

[142] John 6:59.

only to see the signifier died spiritually, since they tasted only in a carnal manner. This is Augustine's answer.[143] – Another answer is possible. Manna was ordained to the preservation of bodily life, but Christ's bread of life was ordained for the preservation of spiritual life. And the Lord wanted to say that the manna only continued bodily life for a time, but that this bread continues spiritual life forever for those who worthily receive it. And thus it is more worthy. – But those who receive it unworthily sin, and the bread is turned into poison for them, and these are those who have the remorse of mortal sin on their conscience. The reason why they sin is contempt, since they invite such a great guest into such a vile guest room. – Augustine teaches how one should receive in a worthy manner: "Bring your innocence to the altar. Also your sins. If they are daily, at least let them not be mortal. Before you approach the altar, let these words be said: "Forgive us our debts," etc. Then approach without anxiety. It is bread, not poison."[144]

[143] See Tractate 26 n. 11 in FC 79, pp. 267-268: "Why did they eat and die? Because they believed what they saw, but did not understand what they did not see. For that reason [they are] your fathers because you are like them.... Moses, too, ate manna, Aaron ate manna, Phinees, too, ate manna, many there who pleased the Lord ate it, and they have not died. Why? Because they understood the visible food spiritually, they hungered spiritually, they tasted spiritually, that they might be filled spiritually."
[144] See Tractate 26 n. 11 in CCSL xxxvi, p. 265. Bonaventure's text is not verbatim. See also FC 79, p. 269 for a translation of Augustine's complete text.

John 6:60-72
Christ's explanation because of the scandal of the disciples

95. *These things he said in the synagogue.*, etc. Having provided a confirmation of his teaching on account of the quarreling Jews, he now sets forth *an explanation* of his teaching because of the scandal of the disciples. He proceeds in the following sequence. First is *the murmuring of the disciples*. Second follows Christ's *explanation of his teaching* in the face of this murmuring. Third he gives *the reason for the murmuring*. Fourth he describes *the turning back of those who do not believe*. Fifth is *the confirmation of those who believe*. Sixth is *the separation that occurs within the ranks of those confirmed*.

Verse 60. The murmuring of the disciples arose because he had said that he would give his flesh to eat and that without this there was no salvation. So the text states: *These things he said while teaching in the synagogue of Capernaum*, that is, in public. And so many were furious over his teaching. John 18:20 below says: "I have always taught in the synagogue."

96. (Verse 61). *So many of his disciples, when they heard*, namely, what had just been said about eating his flesh, *said: This is a hard saying*, that is, it is crude and inhuman to eat human flesh. *Who can listen to it?* They did not use the word "believe," but "to listen," on account of the horrible nature of the saying. So they could not listen to it, since their ears had been heavy, according to what Isaiah 6:10 reads: "Blind the heart of this people and make their ears heavy," etc.

97. (Verse 62). *But Jesus knowing in himself*, etc. The second point occurs here, that is, the explanation of the

teaching on account of the murmuring of the disciples. And although the murmuring was in secret, it was not hidden from the Lord. Thus the text continues: *But Jesus, knowing in himself, that his disciples were murmuring at this*. He knew this, not because he was present, but *in himself*. John 16:30 states: "The disciples said: Now we know that you know all things and have no need that anyone should question you." Therefore, knowing that they were murmuring and wanting to nip it in the bud, he explains what he had said: this is not to be understood carnally, but spiritually. So he shows that it is not to be understood in a carnal manner both because it is false and because it is of no benefit. So *he said to them: This scandalizes you*,[145] namely, what I said about eating my flesh, for you believe that it is to be divided in a carnal way, like the Pharisees according to Matthew 15:12: "Do you know that the Pharisees have been scandalized at hearing this saying?"[146] And this is false. So he adds:

98. (Verse 63). *Then if you should see the Son of Man ascending to where he was before* – this construction is defective[147] – then you will know that his flesh is not to be divided to no end, since the total Christ will be whole in heaven. Augustine observes: "He is totally whole in heaven. He abides whole under the form of the Sacrament. He abides whole in your heart."[148] – Not only

---

[145] On p. 336 n. 4 QuarEd state that the Vulgate reads this as a question: "Does this scandalize you?"

[146] In Matt 15:12 Jesus' disciples ask this question of him.

[147] Since Bonaventure does not read John 6:63 as a question, "What then if you should see the Son of Man ascending to where he was before?" the "if" clause has no resolution and is "defective."

[148] On p. 336 n. 6 QuarEd state that they have been unable to find this text in Augustine. Their references to the Glossa Ordinaria on 1 Cor 10:16 (PL 114:536AB) and to "Bede's" commentary on 1 Cor 10:16 in PL 119:335D-336B do not yield a text similar to the one Bonaventure assigns to Augustine. See Tractate 27 n. 3 in FC 79, pp. 278-279:

is their understanding false, it was also of no benefit. So the text continues:

99. (Verse 64). *It is the spirit that gives life*, but *the flesh*, that is, carnal understanding *is of no benefit*. 2 Corinthians 3:6 reads: "The letter kills, but the spirit gives life." And so my words are not to be understood in a carnal manner, since then they are of no benefit. Rather they are to be understood in a spiritual manner, and then they are of benefit. For *the words that I have spoken to you are spirit and life*, since spiritually understood they give life. Thus Hebrews 4:12 states: "The word of God is living and effective." It is living since it gives life. For Deuteronomy 8:3 says: "Not by bread alone do men and women live, but by every word that proceeds from the mouth of God." But these words only give life to the person who understands them spiritually. Augustine comments: "Did you understand them spiritually? *They are spirit and life*. Did you understand them carnally? ... *They are spirit and life*, but not *for you*."[149]

100. (Verse 65). *But there are some*. This verse introduces the third point, that is, the reason for the murmuring, namely, why the disciples were murmuring: They did not have faith. But not all of them, but some, who were not chosen by God. So the text adds: *But there are some among you*. Indeed, my words are to be understood spiritually, but some among you do not understand. For *some do not believe*. And he does not say this from conjecture, but

---

"For they thought that he was going to disburse his body; but he said that he was going to ascend to heaven, whole, of course. 'When you see the Son of man ascending where he was before,' surely then, at least, you will see that he does not disburse his body in the way in which you think; surely then, at least, you will understand that his grace is not consumed in bite-sized pieces."

[149] See Tractate 27 n. 6 in CCSL xxxvi, p. 273 and FC 79, p. 281.

from certain knowledge. Thus the Evangelist says: *For Jesus knew from the beginning who would believe*. John 2:25 above has: "For he himself knew what was in human beings." Sirach 23:28 reads: "The eyes of the Lord are far brighter than the sun, observing all the ways of men and women and the bottom of the abyss, and looking into human hearts, into their most hidden parts." *And who it was who would betray him*. For he was not betrayed unknowingly, as other people are. So the Evangelist says this, lest Christ appear to be deceived, accepting as disciples unbalanced and treacherous people such as his betrayer. Now the reason why they did not believe was that, although they were chosen in an outward manner and according to present justice, they were not chosen according to eternal election. And he had said this above and repeats it here.[150]

101. (Verse 66). *And he said: This is why I said to you: No one[151] can come to me unless it is given to him by my Father*. John 6:44 above says: "No one comes[152] to me unless the Father ... draws him." For to come to the Son "is the good and perfect gift," and therefore, "from above," as James 1:17 states.

102. (Verse 67). *And[153] from this time many of his disciples*. The fourth point surfaces here, namely, *the turning back of those who do not believe*. So the text states: *Ex hoc*, which can be taken as "from this time," but also as "because of this occasion," that is, the occasion of Christ's

---

[150] See John 6:39 (n. 60) and n. 64 above.

[151] On p. 337 n. 1 QuarEd correctly indicate that the Vulgate reads *Quia nemo* ("For no one").

[152] The Vulgate reads *potest venire* ("can come") while Bonaventure has *venit* ("comes").

[153] On p. 337 n. 2 QuarEd accurately mention that the Vulgate does not read *Et* ("And").

rebuke and teaching, *many of his disciples turned back*, not in imitation, as was said to Peter in Matthew 16:23: "Get behind me, Satan," but in indignation. For they not only turned away from him with their hearts, but also with their bodies. So the text continues: *And no longer went about with him.* So many turned back, and a few remained, for according to Matthew 20:16: "Many are called, but few are chosen." And since few were chosen for the kingdom of God, there are few who did not turn away, according to Luke 9:62: "No one who puts his hand to the plow and looks back is fit for the kingdom of God."

103. (Verse 68). *So Jesus said to the Twelve.* The fifth point occurs here, that is, the confirmation of those who believe and are chosen. And indeed, this took place in Peter's confession of faith. So the text describes the Lord's question and Peter's response. The Lord inquires of the twelve whom he had specially chosen: *Do you also wish to go away?* abandoning me like those who have already left me. Jeremiah 2:13 reads: "They have abandoned me, the fountain of living water." But he asks them, not because he has a doubt, but so that he might set forth the faith of Peter as an example of steadfastness.

104. (Verse 69). *Simon Peter answered*[154] *him: Lord, to whom will we go?* As if to say: We don't want to go away, since we cannot find anyone like you. Psalm 85:8 reads: "There is no one like you among the gods, O Lord." The words you have been speaking won't cause us to leave either. So he says: *You have the words of eternal life.* To those others who do not believe they were difficult and death-dealing, but to Peter and those who believe they were life. And he adds the reason:

---

[154] On p. 337 n. 6 QuarEd rightly notice that the Vulgate reads *ergo* ("therefore").

105. (Verse 70). *And we believe*[155] *and have come to know that you are the Christ, the Son of God.* Peter made a similar confession in Matthew 16:16: "You are the Christ, the Son of the living God" "who has come into this world."[156] The text says "we believe," and afterwards "we have come to know," since faith is a journey into knowledge. Isaiah 7:9 states: "For unless you believe, you will not understand."[157]

106. (Verse 71). *Jesus answered them.* This verse treats the sixth point, namely, the separation within the ranks of those who remain. The Lord shows that even though none of the Twelve had turned away, nevertheless not all of them remained faithful. For this reason the text continues: *Jesus responded to*[158] Peter's confession, which he had articulated for all: *Have I not chosen you, the Twelve, and one of you is a devil?* Judas is called *a devil*, because he consented to the devil's suggestions. Psalm 108:6 says of Judas: "Set a sinner over him, and may the devil stand at his right hand." He singles out one for his malice, so that the others might fear. And the Evangelist explains which one Christ had in mind, namely, Judas, as he continues:

---

[155] On p. 337 n. 7 QuarEd correctly mention that the Vulgate reads *credidimus* ("we have come to believe") whereas Bonaventure has *credimus* ("we believe").

[156] Bonaventure has combined Peter's confession of faith with that of Martha in John 11:27 below. The Vulgate does not read *hunc* ("this") before *mundum* ("world") in John 11:27.

[157] On p. 337 n. 7 QuarEd accurately indicate that Bonaventure's text of Isa 7:9 comes from the LXX. I translate the Vulgate: "Unless you believe, you will not remain."

[158] In this instance Bonaventure omits *eis* ("to them"), which he read, along with the Vulgate, at the beginning of #106.

107. (Verse 72). *Now he was speaking about*[159] *Judas Iscariot, the son of Simon. For it was he, although he was one of the Twelve, who would betray him.* This was said, so that they might be fearful and lest they wonder about the others who had gone away, since they had not been so specially chosen. About the choice of the Twelve Matthew 10:1 states: "And having summoned the Twelve ... he gave them power," etc. Luke 6:13 says: "He chose twelve from these," etc. This selection was prefigured in Joshua 4:2: "Choose for yourself twelve men, one," etc.[160]

QUESTIONS

108. Question 1 deals with the meaning of John 6:63: "If you see the Son of Man ascending to where he was before." – This cannot be said of his human nature, since according to his human nature he was not in heaven before. Similarly it cannot be said of his divine nature, because according to his divine nature he was still in heaven, as he said earlier in John 3:13: "No one has ascended into heaven except him who has descended from heaven, the Son of Man, who is in heaven." – I answer that Christ spoke these words to compare the Son of God according to his divine nature after it assumed flesh, in which it was seen to be humiliated, to that same nature before it assumed flesh, since at that time it could not be thought to be physically feeble. So it is the same as if he had said: If you see the Son of Man ascend, that is, only to be glorified, so that you may believe that he is equal to the Father.[161]

---

[159] On p. 337 n. 9 QuarEd rightly notice that the Vulgate does not read *de* ("about").

[160] Josh 4:2 concludes: "... one from each tribe."

[161] Augustine is in the background of Bonaventure's complex thought. See Tractate 27 n. 4 and FC 79, pp. 279-280: "The Son of God

109. Question 2 focuses on John 6:64: "The flesh is of no benefit." – For if it is of no benefit, then it should not be given to be eaten nor is it true food. This is why the heretics maintain that these words are to be understood spiritually, so that the carnal dimension is removed. They also state that it should not be understood that we literally consume the flesh of Christ under the form of the Sacrament. They further hold that his disciples were reprehensible for thinking this. For they say that Christ's flesh is not present in the Sacrament of the altar, except as a sign.[162]

But these people possess a most wretched understanding, since, while they reject the flesh, they flee from the truth. For even if the words of Christ are to be understood spiritually, nevertheless they must be true. For this reason it has to be maintained that the flesh, which he took from the Virgin, is true food. – Now relative to the statement "that the flesh is of no benefit," it is patient of a twofold understanding. First, it is of no benefit without the spirit. For just as coal does not burn unless it's lit, but when it is lit, it burns, so too the flesh of Christ, if it is separated from the Word, does not catch fire, but once joined to the Word, it is like coal that has been lit.[163] – Another answer

---

always, the Son of man in time, nevertheless, one Christ according to the unity of the person. He was in heaven when he was speaking on earth. So the Son of man was in heaven as the Son of God was on earth; the Son of God was on earth in the flesh he had taken, the Son of man was in heaven in the unity of the person."

[162] See Book IV, d. 10. p. I, a. 1, q. 1 in Opera Omnia 4:216-218 for an elaborate refutation of these errors.

[163] See John Damascene, *The Orthodox Faith*, Book IV, c. 13 in FC 37, p. 359: "With eyes, lips, and faces turned toward it let us receive the divine burning coal, so that the fire of the coal may be added to the desire within us to consume our sins and enlighten our hearts, and so that by this communion of the divine fire we may be set afire and deified. Isaias saw a live coal, and this coal was not plain wood but

takes the words "the flesh is of no benefit" to refer to a carnal understanding that states that Christ gives his flesh as one cuts up meat in a meat market and he is materially masticated under the form of flesh. I state that such an understanding is of no benefit, but that true flesh, without being cut up, is eaten in the Sacrament.[164]

110. Question 3 probes Peter's response in John 6:69. – 1. Why was Peter the only one to answer and why did he answer more than the others? – 2. Likewise, why isn't his confession praised as it is in Matthew 16:17?[165] – 3. Further, it seems that he was lying, as least with regard to Judas, since he spoke for everyone. – I answer that it has to be admitted that Peter is the most zealous of all the disciples, as is clear from his words, and spoke audaciously to the Lord. Others were not so courageous, and so he was the mouth of the Apostles both in asking questions and giving answers. And therefore, he answered for all. – 2. To this problem Chrysostom responds: In this instance Peter spoke for all. And since the faith of Judas was not

---

wood joined with fire. Thus also, the bread of communion is not a plain bread, but bread joined with the Godhead."

[164] Again Bonaventure is dependent upon Augustine. See Tractate 27 n. 5 in FC 79, p. 280: "It profits nothing, but as they understood it; for, of course, they so understood flesh as [something that] is torn to pieces or sold in a meat market, not as [something that] is enlivened by a spirit. Accordingly, it was said, 'The flesh profits nothing,' just so as it was said, 'Knowledge puffs up.' Ought we, therefore, to hate knowledge? Far from it. And what does 'knowledge puffs up' mean? Alone, without love. Thus he added, 'but love edifies.' Therefore, add love to knowledge, and knowledge will be useful, not in itself but through love. So too, now, 'flesh profits nothing,' but flesh alone; let spirit be added to flesh, as love is added to knowledge, and it profits very much. For if flesh profited nothing, the Word would not have become flesh to dwell among us."

[165] Matt 16:17 reads: "Blessed are you, Simon Bar-Jonah, for flesh and blood have not revealed this to you, but my Father in heaven."

praiseworthy, he was not praised.[166] – 3. But Peter did not lie, although he spoke falsely, since he was deceived by a pious error in passing a good judgment about his fellow apostles.

111. Question 4 examines the meaning of John 6:71: "One of you is a devil." – Chrysostom asks:[167] Why aren't they sad, as they are in John 13 when Christ said: "One of you will betray me?"[168] – I answer that in John 13 they are not so much saddened by the sin involved as by the injury to the Lord, which was to be inflicted upon him by one of his disciples. But this verse merely refers to the malice of betrayal.[169]

112. Question 5 asks: Why didn't Christ throw out of his band the one who had the devil since he knew that he would always be evil in the future? – I accept Augustine's viewpoint: "God uses evil works in a good way, just as

---

[166] See Homily 47 n. 3 in PG 59:267 and FC 33, p. 481: "What did Christ do then? He did not praise Peter.... Because Peter had said: 'We have come to believe,' Christ excluded Judas from the group.... On this occasion, however, when he said: 'We have come to believe,' Christ with reason did not allow Judas to be included in the group. He did this to check the wickedness of the traitor from the very start, though He knew that He would effect nothing, yet doing what He could."

[167] As far as I can tell, the lack of sadness on the part of the disciples is not Chrysostom's problem. Rather his concern is their lack of fear. See Homily 47 n. 4 in PG 59:267 and FC 33, p. 482: "At this point it is worth while to study why it was that the disciples now said nothing, while later they feared, and doubted, and looked at one another, inquiring: 'Is it I, Lord?'...What, then, is the explanation? Peter had not yet heard: 'Get behind me, Satan;' therefore, he had no fear. But when he had been rebuked ... with reason did he then finally fear."

[168] Christ's statement occurs in John 13:21. John 13 does not mention the disciples' sadness, which occurs in Matt 26:22: "And being very much saddened, they began each to say: Is it I, Lord?"

[169] Hugh of St. Cher, p. 331r-s also quotes Chrysostom and deals with the same issues as Bonaventure, but in a more extensive way.

humans use good things in a bad way."[170] So he chose Judas, a reprobate individual, so that through him the dispensation of divine mercy might be fulfilled for the salvation of the world and so that the wondrous patience of God might be manifested that upheld so evil a person in such a great office, and so that no one might glory in their present call.

---

[170] See Tractate 27 n. 10 in CCSL xxxvi, p. 274 and FC 79, p. 284: "For as the wicked use the good works of God evilly, so, on the other hand, God uses the evil works of wicked men in a good way." Obviously, Bonaventure's quotation is not exact.

Chapter Seven

John 7:1-10:42
Lord as director and enlightener

1. *After these things Jesus went about*, etc. The Lord has just shown himself to be healer and conserver. With this verse the third part commences, during which he manifests himself and shows that he is *director and enlightener*. This part extends to chapter 11. The Lord shows himself to be light and director in three ways. First, by *the word of his teaching*. Second by his *powerful miracle* whose narration begins in John 9:1: "And as Jesus[1] was passing by, he saw a blind man." Third by *the example of a good life* at John 10:1: "Amen, amen, I say to you, the person who does not enter by the door."

John 7:1-8:59
Lord shows he is director by the word of his teaching

So the first part, in which the Lord manifests himself as *director by the word of his teaching*, consists of two chapters, namely, the seventh and eighth and is divided into two sections. The first deals with *the public manifestation of the Teacher*. The second treats *the communication of the*

---

[1] The Vulgate does not read *Iesus* ("Jesus").

teaching where John 7:19 says: "Did not Moses give you the law, etc.?

JOHN 7:1-18
THE TEACHER

Now the manifestation or *public manifestation of the Teacher* is necessary for him to teach. And since his concealment had preceded this, the text first has to deal with *the hiding of the Teacher*. Second comes *the manifestation of the one hidden* where John 7:14 states: "When, however, the feast was already half over," etc.

JOHN 7:1-13
CONCEALMENT OF THE TEACHER

So *the concealment of the supreme Teacher* is described in this order. Since the cause of his hiding was the persecution of the Jews, the first point centers on *the faithlessness of the Jews* in persecuting him. The second point is *the vanity of his relatives* in trying to persuade him to obtain honor. Third is *Christ's humility* in concealing himself. The final point is *the curiosity of the Jews* in seeking after Christ.

2. (Verse 1). This verse hints at the faithlessness of the Jews and their desire to kill Christ. For this reason the Lord had left Judea and remained in Galilee to avoid the furor of the persecutors. So the text states: *After these things*, that is, the things that had been said about the miracle of the loaves and Christ's teaching, *Jesus went about in Galilee*, since there the people were not so zealous concerning the Law and therefore did not persecute him. *For he did not want to go about in Judea.* The text gives

the reason: *Because the Jews were seeking to put him to death*, incited by the devil, a figure of which occurs in Exodus 2:15: "Pharaoh ... sought to kill Moses, who fled from his sight," etc. By avoiding them, he taught how to avoid the furor of persecutors, according to what Matthew 10:23 has: "When they persecute you in one town, flee to another."

3. (Verse 2). *Now it was at hand.* The second point surfaces here: The vanity of his relatives to persuade him to pursue earthly and empty honor. Their reasons for persuading him are: the time is opportune, the edification of one's neighbor, and the trumpeting of his name. – It was an opportune time, as the text states: *Now the Jewish feast of Tabernacles was at hand.* This feast of Tabernacles had to be celebrated in September, according to what Leviticus 23:41-42 reads: "In the seventh month you shall celebrate this feast, and you shall dwell in bowers," etc. They seized the occasion of this feast to persuade him. So the text continues:

4. (Verse 3). *Now his brothers said to him: Leave here and go into Judea. Brothers* are the Lord's kinsmen or relatives of second degree. According to Chrysostom they were James and Jude, who were brothers of the Lord.[2] But it is better to say that these were some kinsmen on

---

[2] See Homily 48 n. 2 in PG 59:270-271 and FC 41, pp. 6-7: "Now, please notice the power of Christ. For, from the ranks of those who were making these remarks, one subsequently became first Bishop of Jerusalem: the blessed James ... and Jude likewise is said to have become famous.... Whence, then, did they conceive such great incredulity? From jealousy and envy, for when some members of a family attain to greater excellence, this can somehow cause envy among those who do not succeed as well." Hugh of St. Cher, p. 332b also cites Chrysostom about the names of James and Jude.

account of what follows in the text.[3] For one has to think that these two Apostles believed in him.[4] – Note that there is a brother by nature. Thus, we are all brothers of Christ. Psalm 21:23 states: "I will declare your name to my brothers." By affection, such are the good. Matthew 12:48-50 reads: "Who ... are my brothers? Everyone who does the will," etc.[5] By blood, like James. Galatians 1:19 says: "James, the brother of the Lord."[6] – And they add yet another reason to persuade him, that is, the edification of one's neighbor. For this reason they say: *So that your disciples may also see the works that you[7] are performing.* I say that these are the disciples, who, having been scandalized, turned back. Now when they saw the great things that he was accustomed to do in Galilee, they would return. About these what was said in John 6:67 applies: "Many of his disciples turned back." – And he adds the third reason, namely, the manifestation of his name.

5. (Verse 4). *For no one does a thing in secret if he wants to be publicly known*, through that deed. These brothers have still not abandoned the viewpoint of the hypocrites, who are criticized in Matthew 23:5: "They perform all their deeds in order to be seen by men and women." That

---

[3] See Augustine, Tractate 28 n. 3 in FC 88, p. 5: "The relatives of the Virgin Mary were called the Lord's brothers. For it was the usual practice in the Scriptures to call any relatives or near relatives brothers; this is outside our usage and not in the manner in which we speak."

[4] See John 7:5: "For not even his brothers believed in him."

[5] Matt 12:48-50 states: "But he answered and said to him who told him: Who is my mother and who are my brothers? And stretching forth his hand towards his disciples, he said: Behold my mother and my brothers. For everyone who does the will of my Father in heaven, that person is my brother and sister and mother."

[6] Gal 1:19 says: "But I saw none of the other apostles, except James, the brother of the Lord."

[7] On p. 340 n. 6 QuarEd rightly notice that the Vulgate does not read *tu* ("you").

is why they were saying: *If you are doing these things, manifest yourself to the world*, that is, if the miracles are true that you are doing as God, manifest yourself. They said this because they were in doubt, and the Evangelist gives the reason:

6. (Verse 5). *For not even his brothers believed in him*. John 4:44 reads: "A prophet is not without honor except in his own country...."[8] John 1:11 states: "He came unto his own, and his own received him not," and this happened because of familiarity. The reason the brothers didn't believe in him was that he was familiar to them.

7. (Verse 6). *So Jesus said*[9] *to them*. This verse introduces the third point, that is, Christ's humility in hiding. So he excuses himself to them. First because of the lack of an opportune time, for it was not an opportune time for him to manifest himself. Thus, the text continues: *My time has not yet come*, that is, the time of my manifestation. And I am the one who judges what is the appropriate time. For Psalm 74:3 reads: "When I select the time, I will surely judge." Qoheleth 3:11 says: "God has made all things good in his time."[10] *But your time is always at hand*, that is, the time of the glory of the world, which you desire. About this time Jeremiah 17:16 states: "I have not desired a human day." Sirach 11:4 has: "Be not exalted on the day of your honor." – So the time is not opportune for me, but

---

[8] The quotation is from Matt 13:57. John 4:44 states: "A prophet receives no honor in his own country."

[9] On p. 340 n. 9 QuarEd accurately mention that the Vulgate reads *Dicit* ("say") while Bonaventure has *Dixit* ("said").

[10] The Vulgate does not read *Deus* ("God"). God, however, is the subject of Qoheleth 3:10.

for you. Further, the exaltation of temporal glory is for you, not for me.[11] Thus:

8. (Verse 7). *The world cannot hate you* and censure you, since you love it and its glory, *but it hates me*, dishonoring me. Galatians 6:14 states: "The world has been crucified to me, and I to the world." *Because I bear witness concerning it that its works are evil*, by proclaiming the truth. Wisdom 2:12 says: "Therefore, let us lie in wait for the just, since he is of no benefit to us and is against our deeds and upbraids us for transgressions of the law and speaks out against us for the sins of our way of life." Amos 5:10 reads: "They hated the person who rebuked at the gate." So someone said: "Truth begets hatred."[12] So since the world does not hate you:

9. (Verse 8). *As for you, go up to this feast*. Now since the world hates and persecutes me, *I am not going up to this feast*,[13] *for my time is not yet fulfilled*, during which I must suffer. About this time John 2:4 above said: "Woman, my hour has not yet come." As he observed the fullness of time in the incarnation, so too in the passion. Galatians 4:4 states: "But when the fullness of time had come, God sent his Son," etc. And in this way he excused himself to

---

[11] See Bede's commentary on John 7:6 in PL 724B: "But the time of Christ's glory had not yet come.... But he wanted humility to precede exaltation, and to arrive at that height through the way of humility. *But your time*, that is, the glory of the world, *is always at hand*: for it will be a time of glory. The one who came in humility will come in exaltation. The one who came to be judged will come to be the judge. The one who came to be killed by the dead will come to judge the living and the dead."

[12] See Terence, *Andria*, act 1, scene 1, v. 41. The full line from LCL is: "Deference begets friends while truth begets hatred." Hugh of St. Cher, p. 332v,q says: "The Philosopher says: Truth begets hatred."

[13] On p. 341 n. 2 QuarEd rightly notice that the Vulgate reads *festum istum* ("this feast") while Bonaventure has *festum illud* ("this feast").

them, so that he could go up secretly. Thus, after they had gone up, he too went up, but by himself and not at the time stipulated by a crowd of relatives.

10. (Verse 9). *After he had said these things*, that is, given his excuse to his brothers, *he*[14] *remained in Galilee*, namely, until his brothers had gone up.

11. (Verse 10). *But as soon as his brothers had gone up to the feast, he, too, went up, not publicly, but as it were privately.* Thus, he went up *privately*, so that he might show the weakness of humanity, and thus invite people to faith.[15] Another interpretation, so that he might teach us to avoid vain praise. Matthew 6:18 states: "Your Father, who sees in secret, will reward you." Gregory comments: "So let our work be in public in such a way that our intention remains hidden."[16]

12. (Verse 11). *So the Jews were looking for him.* This verse states the fourth point, that is, the curiosity of the Jews to look for Christ, although he had secretly gone up. For on previous occasions he had gone up in public. So the text continues: *So the Jews were looking for him at the feast*, since it had been his custom to go up for this feast. They were looking for him out of hatred. Thus the text adds:

---

[14] On p. 341 n. 3 QuarEd correctly indicate that the Vulgate reads ipse ("he himself").

[15] Bonaventure's interpretation here is unclear. Perhaps, Chrysostom's Homily 48 n. 2 in PG 59:272 and FC 41, p. 8 sheds some light on the weakness of humanity: "Further, by adding: 'My time has not yet come,' He seems to be making it clear that it was necessary for miracles to take place, and for groups of people to hear preaching so that more of the crowd might believe, and the disciples become more staunch as a result of witnessing their Master's fearless preaching and His sufferings."

[16] See Homily 11 n. 1 in CCSL cxli, p. 74. Hugh of St. Cher, p. 332v, l also cites Gregory.

And they were saying: Where is he? They did not call him by his proper name either out of hatred or contempt. On the contrary, Wisdom 1:1 exhorts: "Think of the Lord in goodness, and seek him in simplicity of heart." And their searching gave rise to whispering about the absent one. So the text says:

13. (Verse 12). *And there was much murmuring about him in the crowd.* And it arose from a controversy. Thus, the text continues: *For some were saying that he is a good man.* These were the little children. *But others*[17] *No. Rather he seduces the crowds.* And the majority of those saying that he was a *seducer* were the Pharisees. Matthew 27:63 reads: "We have remembered that this seducer said," etc. John 7:47 below states: "Have you also been seduced?" And even though there was a controversy, it was murmured and whispered about and was not in the open. So the text adds:

14. (Verse 13). *Yet for fear of the Jews no one spoke openly about him.* For as John 9:22 below puts it, "The Jews had agreed that, if anyone were to confess him to be the Christ, he should be put out of the synagogue." So they were afraid. For a contrary attitude see Matthew 10:28: "Do not be afraid of those who kill the body, but cannot kill the soul. But rather be afraid of the one who is able to destroy both soul and body in hell."[18]

---

[17] On p. 341 QuarEd rightly notice that the Vulgate repeats *dicebant* ("were saying").

[18] Hugh of St. Cher, p. 332v,h quotes the first part of Matt 10:28.

QUESTIONS

15. Question 1 is this: Since the Lord came not only to teach, but also to suffer, it seems that he should not cease teaching because of his suffering and persecution from the Jews. Therefore, he should not have left Judea where he had the greatest opportunity to teach. – In response it has to be maintained that the Lord, even though he wanted to suffer and was not afraid of suffering, had predetermined the fitting time for his suffering, and before that time did not want to hand himself over into the hands of his persecutors.[19] And so he did not travel about in Judea.

16. Question 2 addresses another angle of the previous question: Since the Jews could not act before the time determined by the Lord, it seems that they could not lay hands on him before that time. Therefore, there was no need for him to absent himself from Judea on this account. – I answer that the point has to be made that the Lord manifested himself to good people in such a way, that he hid himself from evil people. And vice versa he hid himself from evil people in such a way, that he was not hidden to good people. And therefore, he sometimes won out by power and at other times by wisdom, as Job 26:12 states: "His wisdom has struck the proud person." And so, although he could prohibit their opposition with his power, he preferred at that time the wisdom of absenting himself. – Another reason was that he might show his true humanity. So sometimes he showed his power, and at other times his weakness. Thus, another text reads: "For

---

[19] See Chrysostom, Homily 48 n. 2 in PG 59:272 and FC 41, p. 9: "Likewise, He showed that since He foresaw the time when He was to suffer, when at later date this time drew near, then He would especially wish to go up to Jerusalem."

he was unable to go about in Judea."[20] – A third reason is our instruction, so that we might not be amazed when holy men are afraid and steer clear of dangers and not despair for ourselves when we find ourselves in a similar situation.[21]

17. Question 3 focuses on Christ's words in John 7:8: "I do not go up" and what is said later in John 7:10: "Then he also went up." – It seems that he acted contrary to what he had said earlier. – There are multiple answers to this problematic. First, "I do not go up," that is, with you, but "you, go up."[22] – But this exposition raises the further question why he didn't want to go up with them. – So others answer and make their case on these words of John 7:8: "on this day of the feast." The Interlinearis comments:

---

[20] This "text" is an alternate reading of the Greek of John 7:1 found in Chrysostom, Homily 48 n. 1 in PG 59:269 and FC 41, pp. 3-4: "To show this the Evangelist said: 'After these things Jesus went about in Galilee, for he could not go about in Judea because the Jews were seeking to put him to death.' O blessed John, what are you saying? Is it that He who was able to do anything whatsoever He willed 'could not' [go about Judea freely].... It was not in order that he might obtain the reputation of speaking in riddles that John spoke in this way. Perish the thought! On the contrary, he did this to make it clear that at one time Christ's divinity was being attested; at another His humanity." Hugh of St. Cher, p. 331v,g is aware of Chrysostom's reading and cites his solution to the problem raised by this reading.

[21] See Augustine, Tractate 28 n. 2 in FC 88, p. 4: "This is what I meant: he offered an example for our weakness. For he had not himself lost his power, but was comforting our frailness. For it was to be, as I have said, that some believer of his would hide himself that he might not be found by persecutors; and that his hiding place might not be thrown in his face as a crime, that which would be confirmed in the member preceded in the head."

[22] See Chrysostom, Homily 48 n. 2 in FC 41, p. 9: "He did not say with absolute finality: 'I do not go up,' but He meant: 'I do not go up now,' that is, 'with you,' because my time is not yet fulfilled.'"

"That is, on the first day,"[23] which was the most solemn, but on a later day. – But this response likewise leads to the question why didn't he go up on the first day. – The third explanation follows the principle that "discourses are to be interpreted according to their subject matter."[24] And the Lord was responding to his brother's attempts to persuade him that he manifest himself. So he says: "I do not go up" in order to manifest myself. Thus, John 7:10 says: "He went up, not publicly." And so he did not go up with his brothers nor on the first day, lest his going up be in public.

18. Question 4 focuses on the Lord's answer in John 7:6: "My time has not yet come." – Although this statement must not be understood as referring to Fate, it seems, nevertheless, that the Lord's work is dependent upon time. This seems unfitting, since he is omnipotent. – One way of responding is to note that the Lord's work is twofold. This is his work according to his Divinity, and this work does not depend on time. There is also his work according to his humanity, and this requires a precise time. And this was the work of redemption, and relative to this work he said: "My time has not yet come." – Another answer notes that there are two ways by which the time to work is determined. One is determined by need, one by fittingness. According to the first way trees bear fruit at the determined time of autumn. According to the second way God has mercy and judges and saves. Thus, since Passover time was most fitting for our redemption, so the Law might find its goal in the Gospel in the most fitting manner, he, therefore, held off until Passover.

---

[23] On p. 342 n. 4 QuarEd cite the Glossa Interlinearis: *"Not on this day*, when you want to go up, that is, the first or second day. Rather he goes up afterwards during the middle of the feast."

[24] See Book II, c. 2 of Aristotle, *Ethica Nicomachea* in WAE, Volume 9, 1104a

John 7:14-18
Public manifestation of the Teacher

19. (Verse 14). *When the feast was already half over.*[25] After the text had treated the Lord's hiding, now it deals with *the public manifestation of our Teacher*, who had early been hidden. And the order is as follows. First is *the public manifestation of the Teacher in teaching.* Second is the Jews' *marveling in hearing him.* Third, *the commendation of his teaching in their response.*

So the first point is the public manifestation of the Teacher. Thus, the text states: *When, however, the feast was already half over*, and this was "the fourth day of the feast," as the Glossa says, which is the middle of seven days.[26] *Jesus went up into the temple and began to teach*, in a public place, not a hidden one, lest his teaching might be suspect. John 18:20 reads: "I have always taught in the synagogue and in the temple, where all the Jews gather, and I have said nothing in secret."

20. (Verse 15). *And the Jews marveled*, etc. The second point occurs here, that is, the astonishment of the Jews. The reason why they marveled was, as Augustine observes: "They had never seen him learning, but they heard him discussing the Law."[27] For this reason the text states: *And the Jews marveled, saying: How does this man come by learning, since he has not studied?* For the Lord

---

[25] On p. 342 n. 10 QuarEd accurately mention that the Vulgate reads *Iam autem* ("When, however,"). The next time Bonaventure cites the beginning of John 7:14 in this paragraph he will follow the Vulgate.

[26] This is the Glossa Interlinearis: "In the middle of these days, that is, the fourth day of the feast."

[27] See Tractate 29 n. 2 in CCSL xxxvi, p. 285 and FC 88, p. 15. The citation is virtually identical to Augustine's text.

could say what Proverbs 30:3 states: "I have not learned wisdom, and have known[28] the knowledge of the saints." Luke 2:47 reads: "They marveled[29] at his understanding and answers."

21. (Verse 16). *Jesus answered them.* This verse introduces the third point, that is, Christ's answer, by which he provides a satisfactory answer to their marveling, showing that he does not possess knowledge by means of acquisition as other humans do, but from his origin. So the text continues: *My teaching*, that is, what I am teaching, *is not my own*, that is, from me or for my own glory or acquired by me. *But his who sent me*, that is, from the Father, who sent me. For everything that the Son has, he receives from the Father. John 5:30 reads: "By myself I can do nothing," and so he cannot teach anything by himself. And since this answer was only clear to those who hear rightly and these are the ones who hear in order to act upon what is heard, the text adds:

22. (Verse 17). *If anyone desires to do his will*, namely, that of God the Father, *he will know of the teaching whether it is from God or whether I speak on my own authority*, for otherwise a person cannot truly understand my teaching and me. Therefore, 1 John 2:4 states: "The person who says that he knows God[30] and does not keep his commands is a liar." And the one who is commendable by reason of his origin is also commendable by reason of his goal in this

---

[28] On p. 342 n. 13 QuarEd accurately indicate that the Vulgate reads *et non novi* ("and have not known") whereas Bonaventure has *et novi* ("and have known").

[29] On p. 342 n. 13 QuarEd rightly mention that the Vulgate reads *stupebant* ("were amazed") whereas Bonaventure has *mirabantur* ("marveled").

[30] The Vulgate reads *eum* ("him") whereas Bonaventure has *Deum* ("God").

that he does not seek his own glory through his teaching. And he manifests this in this way:

23. (Verse 18). *The person who speaks on his own authority seeks his own glory*, but the person who seeks his own glory is a liar, since he usurps to himself what belongs to another. Isaiah 48:11 reads: "I will not give my glory to another." But in my teaching I do not seek my own glory, but the glory of him who sent me. So my teaching is true. Therefore, he says: *The person who seeks the glory of the one who sent him is truthful, and there is no injustice in him.*[31] Christ did not seek the glory of his Divinity or of his humanity, since all glory was due it. 1 Timothy 1:17 states: "To the King of ages, who is immortal, invisible, the one only God, be honor and glory," etc. He is just and truthful, for contrariwise to usurp to one's self another's honor is falsehood and injustice. The antichrist will usurp in this way. About him 2 Thessalonians 2:4 speaks: "He will be exalted and extolled[32] above all that is called God."

QUESTIONS

24. Question 1 raises the issue: Since the Lord went up to Jerusalem secretly to avoid Jewish furor, why is it that he teaches openly in the temple? – Augustine responds: "That he hid was for the sake of example. That he spoke openly and was not apprehended is an indication of his

---

[31] On p. 343 n. 4 QuarEd correctly notice that the Vulgate reads *in illo* ("in him") whereas Bonaventure has *in eo* ("in him").

[32] The Vulgate reads *qui adversatur et extollitur supra* ("who opposes and is extolled over") while Bonaventure has *Exaltabitur et extolletur super* ("He will be exalted and extolled over").

power."[33] – It can also be said that he deflected the Jewish furor by his own teaching itself, since it changed their fury into admiration.[34]

25. Question 2 deals with John 7:15: "How does this man come by learning, since he has not studied?" – 1. How did they know that the Lord had come by learning? – 2. Likewise, since the Lord had to give us an example not only of humility in his deeds, but also in knowledge, it seems that just as he was baptized and circumcised to give us an example, so too he should have been a disciple before becoming a teacher. – If you say, that he couldn't learn anything, for he knew everything, there arises an objection based on Hebrews 5:8: "He learned obedience from the things that he suffered." If he learned obedience, why not knowledge?

The Glossa answers that the things he said he stated with the authority of Scripture.[35] So they knew that he had learned letters. They also knew that he had not studied, since they knew, according to Augustine, his parents, hometown, and schooling.[36] – 2. With regard to the objection that he had to learn, I say, first of all, that he

---

[33] See Tractate 29 n. 2 in CCSL xxxvi, p. 285 and FC 88, p. 14: "He who was hiding taught and spoke openly, and he was not seized. For that act, his hiding, was for the sake of example; this one [served to show his] power." Bonaventure's quotation is not verbatim.

[34] See Homily 49 n. 1 of Chrysostom in PG 59:274 and FC 41, p. 14: "However, the Evangelist did not state His teachings, but said only that He taught in a wonderful way and that he captivated them and won them over, so great was the power of His words. Even those who had been saying 'He seduces the crowd' were won over and they marveled."

[35] This is the Glossa Interlinearis.

[36] See Tractate 29 n. 2 in FC 88, p. 15: "Because many knew where he was born, and how he had been raised; for they had never seen him learning, but they heard him discussing the Law, putting forward testimonies to the Law, which no one could put forward unless he had

did not need to learn and should have no need to, since he had to assume all of our characteristics except ignorance and sin which were of entirely no benefit to us and our salvation. Further, he did not have to give an example in this matter, for by studying he would show that he was ignorant and that would be a simulation.[37] – So relative to the point about circumcision it has to be said that this was for the purpose of identification, lest he seem to be of a different religion and nation. Therefore, he observed circumcision and baptism, so that he might sanctify the waters and reveal himself.[38] – About the objection that he had to learn, it should be said in a brief compass that one way of learning is to move from ignorance to knowledge by means of teaching. Another way of learning is to experience the known. According to the first way he did not learn, since this modality presupposes ignorance. He did learn according to the second way, since it presupposes the human affections that Christ assumed and experienced.[39]

26. Question 3 focuses on John 7:16: "My teaching is not my own." – 1. This statement seems to be false, for his teaching would be too removed from himself. – 2. Moreover, how would this answer satisfy the Jews? For I could say the same thing: My teaching is not from me,

---

read the Law, and no one could read the Law unless he had learned letters – and so they wondered."

[37] See Book III, d. 15. a. 1. q.1-2 of Bonaventure's *Sentence Commentary*.

[38] See n.35 below for further views about circumcision. See John 1 n. 64 above for Bonaventure's views on baptism: "Now the reason why Christ wanted to be baptized is threefold: so that he might give an example of humility, so that he might confer regenerative powers upon the waters, so that through John's baptism he might reveal himself to all."

[39] See Book III, d. 14. a. 3. q. 2 and d. 15. a. 2. q. 1 ad 2 in Bonaventure's *Sentence Commentary*.

but from God, since "all wisdom is from the Lord God."[40] – Chrysostom answers that he is saying that he did not invent his teaching, but that it came from the Father. So the sense is: my teaching, namely, what I am teaching, is not mine, but is from the Father. – And this covers their question, for it sends them to the Father and cools their furor by humility. Thus, it was his teaching, since he was wisdom itself by his very essence, but he said that it was not his, because he receives it from another.[41]

But why didn't he simply say: I am wisdom personified, and I am humbling myself? – Chrysostom marshals five reasons.[42] First, so that he might show that he was from another and the Son, not unbegotten. Second, so that he might show that he was not against God, as the antichrist will be, who "will be extolled above all that is called God."[43] Third, so that he might show that he is truly human.

---

[40] See Sir 1:1.

[41] See Homily 49 n. 2 in PG 59:275 and FC 41, p. 16: "It was His, on the one hand, because He spoke without having been taught, but it was not His own because it was the teaching of His Father.... Actually the expression 'is not my own' very clearly sets forth the doctrine of His and the Father's Oneness...." Hugh of St. Cher, p. 333k quotes this passage plus much more from Chrysostom.

[42] See Homily 49 n. 2 in PG 59:275 and FC 41, p. 17: "Accordingly, there were many reasons for His speaking in lowly vein of Himself: for example, that He might not be thought unbegotten or in opposition to God; that they might believe that He actually had assumed our flesh; also, because His listeners were so weak; and in order to teach men to act with moderation and not to be boastful with regard to themselves. But only a single reason can be discovered for His making laudatory statements about Himself, namely, the greatness of His nature." Hugh of St. Cher, p. 333s also cites this passage from Chrysostom and does so more faithfully than Bonaventure and also includes the "single reason." Bonaventure's "citation" is both a summary and an expansion, e.g., Bonaventure's introduction of 2 Thes 2:4 in the second reason.

[43] See 2 Thes 2:4. The Vulgate reads *extollitur* ("is extolled") whereas Bonaventure has *extolletur* ("will be extolled"). See John 7:18 n. 23 above where Bonaventure also cites 2 Thes 2:4.

Fourth, on account of the weakness of his listeners. Fifth, to teach humility, according to what Romans 11:20 reads: "Be not high-minded."

Another response is that this contradiction is to be resolved according to the rule of Augustine: Look at the two natures in order to find the sense.[44] My teaching according to my Divinity is not mine according to my humanity. Something is called ours that is acquired by us, and so this is a satisfactory answer to the question. – A third answer accentuates the possible meanings of my, since my refers to the freedom of possessing and the principle of effecting something, as my field and my book, that is, the one I have written. But this can be understood in a twofold manner. Either simply or discretively,[45] as in mine and to me. So speaking simply, this teaching was Christ's, who freely possessed it and from whom it went out to his listeners. But speaking discretively, it did not belong to Christ alone, because this same teaching was the Father's. Further, this same teaching was also from the Father. – Or I may put the answer differently. There is a threefold meaning of my. There is my according to nature or origin. There is my according to divine or human nature. There is my simply or discretively.

---

[44] See Tractate 29 n. 3 in FC 88, pp. 15-16: "What is the doctrine of the Father except the Word of the Father? Christ himself is the doctrine of the Father if he is the Word of the Father. But because the Word cannot be of no one but [must be] of someone, he said both that it was his doctrine, [that is,] himself, and not his, because he is the Word of the Father. For what is so much yours as yourself? And what is so much not yours as you, if what you are is someone else's?"

[45] See Deferrari, p. 304: "after the manner or in the sense of dividing or of discriminating, in a separate or special manner, discretively."

JOHN 7:19-8:59
COMMUNICATION OF CHRIST'S TEACHING

27. *Did not Moses give*, etc. This is the second part which treats the *communication of Christ's teaching*. And since "the task of the wise person is" twofold: "to expose those who are fallacious and not to be fallacious about the things he knows,"[46] so first he confounds *the perversity of the Jews*. Second, he manifests *the nobility of his teaching* in John 8:12 below: "Again Jesus said to them: I am the light of the world."

JOHN 7:19-8:11
CHRIST CONFOUNDS THE PERVERSITY OF THE JEWS

The first part has four sections. In the first he confounds *malignity in heart*. In the second *slander in the mouth* where verse 25 states: "So some of the people of Jerusalem were saying." Third *those rising up in their power* where verse 32 reads: "So[47] the Pharisees heard." Fourth *those lying in wait out of malice* where John 8:1 says: "But Jesus went."

JOHN 7:19-24
CHRIST CONFOUNDS THOSE WHO ARE MALIGNING HIM

So he confounds *those who are maligning him* in this order. First is Christ's *censure*. Second is *the counterattack of*

---

[46] See Aristotle, *De sophisticis elenchis*, c. 1 in WAE, 165a. Bonaventure cites a variant of this teaching in his commentary on Luke 4:1 (n. 1) in *Commentary on Luke, 1-8*, p. 289.

[47] On p. 345 n. 3 QuarEd accurately mention that the Vulgate does not read *ergo* ("So"). When Bonaventure cites John 7:32 below, he does not have *ergo* ("so"), but *autem* ("But").

the Jews. Third is *the explanation for the censure.* Fourth is *the appeal to keep away from evil.*

Verse 19. So the Lord censured them for the hidden malice of their hearts, by which they wanted to kill him against the commandment of the Law. Therefore, the text states: *Did not Moses give you the Law?* which you are obliged to observe as you promised, according to what Exodus 24:7 reads: "All that the Lord has commanded us, we will do." *And none of you observes the Law?* Psalm 13:3 says: "They have all gone aside. Together they have become of no benefit. There is no one who does good, not a single one," since you have already transgressed the law in your hearts. He shows this as he reveals the malice of their hearts.

28. (Verse 20). *Why are you seeking to put me to death,* although the Law commands in the Decalogue of Exodus 20:13 and Deuteronomy 5:17: "You shall not kill."[48] And you are doing this to an innocent person. So he asks: *Why are you seeking to put me to death? Why?* That is, for what reason, as if he were saying: There is no reason. Exodus 23:7 reads: "You shall not put to death the innocent and just person."

The crowd answered. The second point surfaces here, namely, the counterattack of the Jews, since they did not acknowledge their sin, but reviled their accuser. So it is said: *The crowd answered,* not one, but the entire multitude, *and said: You have a demon.* This is the charge they made against him in Matthew 12:24 and John 8:52 below.[49] Behold, their rebuke. Chrysostom

---

[48] Hugh of St. Cher, p. 333t only cites Ex 20:13.

[49] Matt 12:24 reads: "But the Pharisees, hearing this, said: This man does not cast out demons except by Beelzebul, the prince of

comments: "Their rebuke issues from anger and rage and an impudent soul."[50] *Who is seeking to put you to death?* As if they were saying: No one. They are lying, since they themselves have a demon and are children of the devil, who "is a liar and the father of lies."[51]

29. (Verse 21). *Jesus answered and said to them.* This verse introduces the third point, that is, the explanation for Christ's censure, for they wanted to kill him because he had healed on the Sabbath. So the text continues: *I did one work, and you all marvel.* This work was the cure of the paralytic. They were marveling at what he had done and were indignant that he had performed this cure on a Sabbath. John 5:16 above says: "The Jews were persecuting Jesus, because he did this[52] on the Sabbath" as if he were breaking the Law. Therefore, the Lord showed that he had not transgressed against the Law by using a proof from a major premise to a minor premise and argues thus: If circumcision, which is not found in the Law, but comes from the Patriarchs, does not violate the Sabbath, since it is a noble work, therefore, since the healing of an entire human being is a more noble work, how much less does it violate the Sabbath. Wherefore, the text adds:

30. (Verse 22). *For this reason Moses gave you circumcision – not that it was from Moses, but from the Patriarchs*, that is, it was not a commandment first given to him, but to Abraham. Genesis 17:10 states: "Every male among you

---

demons." John 8:52 states: "So the Jews said: Now we know that you have a demon." Hugh of St. Cher, p. 333z also cites Matt 12:24.

[50] See Homily 49 n. 2 in PG 59:276. Bonaventure's citation is not verbatim.

[51] See John 8:44.

[52] The Vulgate reads *haec* ("these things") whereas Bonaventure has *hoc* ("this").

shall be circumcised." *And on a Sabbath you circumcise a man*, because that is what is written in the same place: "An infant of eight days shall be circumcised."[53] Nevertheless, you do not believe that you are breaking the Law, but observing it. From this he argues, using a proof from a major premise to a minor premise, since it seems that circumcision would be a greater violation than restoring a person to complete health.

31. (Verse 23). *If a man receives circumcision on a Sabbath, so that the Law of Moses may not be broken, are you indignant with me because I made a whole man well on a Sabbath?* As if he were saying: Since this action is legitimate and does not break the Sabbath, your indignation is not just, since according to Romans 10:2: "They have zeal for God, but not according to knowledge."

32. (Verse 24). *Do not judge*, etc. The fourth point occurs here, that is, the appeal to keep away from evil. For this reason the text continues: *Do not judge according to appearances*, by accepting the human face. About a good judge Isaiah 11:3 says: "He will not judge according to the sight of the eyes. He will not reprove according to the hearing of the ears." *But give just judgment*, on the merits of the case and not according to the appearances of the persons. Augustine states: "The person who loves equally does not judge according to the person."[54] And since they loved in an unequal way and since they cared more for externals, they were not judging justly. For it is said in Matthew 23:25: You Pharisees "clean the outside." And

---

[53] See Gen 17:12.

[54] See Tractate 30 n. 8 in CCSL xxxvi, p. 293 and FC 88, pp. 28-29: "Who is it who does not judge as to the person? He who loves equally." Bonaventure's citation is not verbatim. Hugh of St. Cher, p. 333v,n also cites Augustine and is closer to Augustine's text than Bonaventure is.

you have justified yourself in the presence of men and women. Luke 16:15 reads: "You are the ones who justify yourselves in the presence of men and women, but God knows your hearts."

QUESTIONS

33. Question 1 asks whether a person should be circumcised on the Sabbath. – What the Lord says in John 7:21-24 seems to give an affirmative answer. And the reason is that it had to be done on the eighth day.[55] – But contrary: The commandment about the Sabbath was the greatest commandment in the Law and was frequently repeated.[56] Therefore, a lesser commandment should yield to a greater one. Therefore, they should desist from circumcising on the Sabbath. – I answer that it has to be admitted that the commandment about the Sabbath is a great one, but did not stand in the way of circumcision, since it did not prohibit a work of salvation, but one of servitude. Thus, the Law is explained on the Sabbath, because teaching is a work of salvation. And therefore, it did not step aside for circumcision. Rather both commandments were observed at the same time.

34. Question 2 addresses the Lord's argument that circumcision does not violate the Sabbath, much less the cure of the paralytic.[57] – It seems that this argument is of no validity. – 1. Since circumcision was of precept and could not be delayed, whereas the cure could be postponed to another day. – 2. Besides, circumcision was a *spiritual*

---

[55] See Gen 17:12 in the commentary on John 7:22 n.30 above.
[56] See, e.g., Ex 20:8 and Deut 5:12.
[57] See John 5:1-18.

work in this regard that it cleansed from original sin,[58] but that healing was a *bodily* work, for the sickness was of the body.

I answer that it has to be noted that the Law of Moses did not command circumcision, but presupposed it as coming from a more worthy source. For it is said in Exodus 12:48: "If any stranger be willing to dwell among you ... he shall be circumcised."[59] But the Sabbath is a commandment in the Law and did not abrogate circumcision that came from the Patriarchs. Therefore, how much less does it not abrogate a healing by God, even though it might not be commanded. – 2. This has to be said relative to the second point. That healing of the paralytic was not only bodily, but also spiritual, for Christ said to him: "Sin no more."[60] And that's why the text says: "I made a whole man well," that is, internally and externally. Even though the work only touched the individual externally through his body, nevertheless it was still a work of compassion and the Law regards works of compassion as spiritual works. Wherefore, on the Sabbath it is licit to give alms. For if it was licit to give water to an ass,[61] how much more to give alms, and even more so to rescue a sick person.

35. Question 3 focuses on circumcision: Why was it given before the Law? For John 7:22 says: "It is not from Moses," etc. – It has to be said that the major reason for the giving of circumcision was to distinguish the people, from whom

---

[58] On p. 346 QuarEd provide no documentation for this opinion.

[59] Ex 12:48 actually reads: "And if any stranger be willing to dwell among you ... all his males shall first be circumcised...."

[60] See John 5:14.

[61] See Luke 13:15: "But the Lord answered him and said: Hypocrites, does not each one of you on the Sabbath loose his ox or ass from the manger and lead it forth to water?"

Christ was to be born, from the nations.[62] And since the first one to be called was Abraham, to whom the promise was made, that is why it began with him. – There are further reasons for the giving of circumcision and what it was given to the people of God rather than another sign. These reasons are contained in these verses: Circumcised flesh signifies and teaches. It is a sign, a good work. It distinguishes or heals.[63] It is the sign of Abraham's faith, the good work of obedience. It distinguishes the people. It heals against original sin. It signifies the eighth day of the resurrection. It teaches chastity.[64]

JOHN 7:25-31
CHRIST CONFOUNDS THOSE WHO SLANDER HIM

36. *So some of the people of Jerusalem said.* He had already confounded those who were maligning him. Now he confounds *those who are slandering him.* And he proceeds in this order. First comes *the slander* itself. Second is *the confounding of the slanderers.* Third *the obstinacy of those who were confounded.* Fourth is *the building up of the little ones* or *lesser ones.*

---

[62] Hugh of St. Cher, p. 333v,g also gives this reason, from the Glossa Ordinaria, and then two others that Bonaventure will shortly mention: Abraham's faith; chastity of mind.

[63] I have been unable to find a source for these lines that read in Latin: *Est signum, meritum, distinguit, sive medetur, Circumcisa caro significatque, docet.*

[64] See the Glossa Ordinaria on Gen 17:10 in PL 113:123B: "There are three reasons why this was commanded Abraham. First, so that he might please by his obedience to the command the one whom Adam displeased by his transgression. Second, so that through this sign the people might be distinguished from all the nations. Third, so that, having been circumcised in that member through which passion is wont to dominate, he might learn that he has to preserve his chastity and stamp out impurity."

Verse 25. So first comes the slander of those who should have known better. And these were the ones who were staying in the kingly city. So the text adds: *So some of the people of Jerusalem were saying*, that is, those who were aware of the schemes of the Pharisees: *Is this not the man that the Jews were seeking to kill?*[65] As someone who is evil. For they were from those, about whom Proverbs 1:16 says: "Their feet run to evil and hasten to shed blood."

37. (Verse 26). *And behold, he is speaking openly, and they say nothing to him*, and they marvel at this and from their admiration that should stir up faith in them, they proceed to falsehood and slander. *Can it be that the rulers have really come to know that*[66] *this is the Christ?* As if they were saying: They could conjecture, but could not know for sure. So the text adds:

38. (Verse 27). *Yet we know where this man is from*, for he is from Nazareth. John 1:45 above says: "We have found Jesus, the son of Joseph from Nazareth." *But when the Christ comes, no one will know where he is from?* And with that they demeaned his origin. They were saying this because of what is written in Isaiah 53:8: "Who will declare his generation?"[67] As if the generation of Christ would be unspeakable and thus impenetrable. Or because he is coming in a hidden manner. Wisdom 18:14 reads: "When all things were held in quiet silence," etc.[68]

---

[65] On p. 346 n. 10 QuarEd rightly notice that the Vulgate does not read *Iudaei* ("the Jews").

[66] On p. 346 n. 11 QuarEd accurately indicate that the Vulgate reads *quia* ("that") whereas Bonaventure has *quoniam* ("that").

[67] Hugh of St. Cher, p. 334f also cites Isa 53:8.

[68] Bonaventure seems to be alluding to Wis 18:14-15: "When all things were held in quiet silence and the night was in the midst of her course, your almighty word leapt down from heaven from your royal throne, as a fierce conqueror into the midst of the land of destruction."

39. (Verse 28). *So he cried out*, etc. The second point surfaces here, that is, the confounding of the slanderers. He confounds those who are slandering the generation of Christ by showing that there is twofold generation: temporal, which they themselves knew about, and eternal which he himself knew about. For the sake of the temporal the text says: *So Jesus, while teaching in the temple, cried out*, so that he might startle those murmuring. Proverbs 1:20 states: "Wisdom preaches abroad. She sounds forth her voice in the streets,"[69] since he teaches openly and freely. Isaiah 58:1 reads: "Cry. Cease not. Lift up your voice like a trumpet." *And said: You both know me and know where I am from*, according to my temporal generation. For Matthew 13:55 states: "His Mother is called Mary." And they knew that he was a human being and was born of Mary. This was said about his temporal generation. But with regard to his eternal generation he said that he was from another, whom they did not know. So the text continues: *Yet I have not come from myself*. Here note his procession from the Father. *But he is true who has sent me*, since he is God. Also God is true, but every human is a liar, according to Psalm 115:11: "Every human is a liar." Numbers 23:19 reads: "God is not a human being that he should lie." *Whom you do not know*. John 5:37 says: "The Father[70] who has sent me has borne witness to me. But you have not[71] heard his voice or seen his face."

40. (Verse 29). *But I know him, and if I said that I do not know him, I would be like you, a liar.*[72] You are lying when

---

[69] Hugh of St. Cher, p. 334h also quotes Prov 1:20.

[70] The Vulgate reads *Pater ipse* ("the Father himself") while Bonaventure has *Pater* ("the Father").

[71] The Vulgate reads *umquam* ("never") while Bonaventure has *non* ("not").

[72] The Vulgate reads *Ego scio eum quia ab ipso sum et ipse me misit* ("I know him, because I am from him, and he has sent me").

you say that you do not know my temporal birth. *But I would be lying if I said that I do not know my eternal birth. For I know him, because I am from him, and he has sent me,* as the Son knows the Father. Matthew 11:27 reads: "No one knows the Father but the Son ... and the person to whom the Son chooses to reveal him." *I know him* with clear knowledge. John 1:18 above states: "No one has seen God," etc.[73] *I am from him,* through generation. John 16:28 below says: "I came forth from the Father and have come into the world." *And he has sent me,* through the incarnation. Isaiah 61:1 has: "The spirit of the Lord is upon me," etc.[74]

41. (Verse 30). *Therefore, they sought to apprehend him.* The third point occurs here, namely, the obstinacy of those who have been confounded. For since he has shown that they were liars and ignorant and therefore confirmed in evil and unable to resist his word, *therefore they sought to apprehend him,* this is, certain of the rulers,[75] as Chrysostom observes.[76] But their malice was ineffectual while divine power was effectual. For they did not apprehend Christ, who is truth. Rather they apprehended falsehood, as Jeremiah 8:5 reads: "They have apprehended falsehood and have refused to return."

Bonaventure's text is almost identical to John 8:55. Hugh of St. Cher, p. 334 has the same text as Bonaventure does for John 7:29.

[73] John 1:18 concludes: "... The only-begotten Son, who is in the bosom of the Father, has revealed him."

[74] Isa 61:1 continues: "... because the Lord has anointed me. He has sent me to preach to the meek...."

[75] I have translated *maiores* as "leaders" here, although I realize that Bonaventure is using the distinction between *maiores* and *minores*. In this instance *minores* ("lesser ones") are the *parvuli* ("little ones").

[76] See Homily 50 n. 2 in PG 59:280 and FC 41, p. 28: "Who? Not the multitude – since it was not desirous of power nor could it be overpowered by envy – but the priests."

Thus, the text continues: *But no one laid hands on him,*[77] that is, by seizing him, *because his hour had not yet come,* the hour during which he deigned to suffer. Wherefore, Augustine comments: "He did not mean an hour in which he would be forced to die, but in which he would deign to die."[78] About this hour John 17:1 below states: "Father, the hour has come. Glorify your Son."

42. (Verse 31). *But many of the crowd believed in him.* This verse introduces the fourth point, that is, the building up of faith in the little ones. Thus, the text continues: *But many of the crowd believed in him,* not the leaders and the mighty or "maiores."[79] Matthew 11:25 states: "You have hidden these things from the wise and the prudent and have revealed them to little ones." 1 Corinthians 1:26 reads: "Consider your own calling, brothers and sisters, that there were not many wise," etc.[80] And the text adds a true confession: *And they kept saying: When the Christ comes,*[81] *will he work more signs than this man works?* So since the signs that they had seen were so many and the greatest, they believed and confessed that another should not be expected. John 15:24 below states: "If I had not done among them works that no one else had done, they would have no sin."

---

[77] On p. 347 n. 7 QuarEd correctly indicate that the Vulgate reads *illum* ("him") while Bonaventure has *eum* ("him").

[78] See Tractate 31 n. 5 in CCSL xxxvi, p. 295 and FC 88, p. 33. Bonaventure also cites this observation of Augustine in his commentary on John 2 n. 17 above.

[79] See n. 75 above.

[80] 1 Cor 1:26 concludes: "... according to the flesh, not many mighty, not many noble."

[81] On p. 347 n. 10 QuarEd accurately mention that the Vulgate reads *venerit* ("comes") whereas Bonaventure has *veniet* ("comes").

Questions

43. Question 1 focuses on John 7:27: "When the Christ comes, no one will know where he is from." – They seem to be speaking falsely, since they knew from Scripture that he is "of the offspring of David and from Bethlehem," as John 7:42 states. – It has to be said that the doctors of the Law were conjecturing according to different scriptures that the Christ would not be born in the same way as others. Thus, they could know that he would be born of a virgin, but did not know how. Thus, Scripture signaled that the manner of Christ's generation would be hidden, but manifested the tribe itself and his place of birth. And they themselves knew where Christ the Lord had come from, since he was from the Virgin Mary, but they did not know how, since they believed that he was born through Joseph. – But there is another explanation according to the twofold generation, namely, temporal and eternal. They had some information about his temporal generation, but were ignorant of other information. However, they were totally ignorant of his eternal generation.[82]

44. Question 2 raises issue with John 7:27: "Yet we know where this man is from," for John 9:29 below states: "We do not know where he is from." Therefore, these statements are contradictory. – Chrysostom responds that it is unremarkable that a disorderly people contradicts itself, because its responses were not consistent.[83] – Another explanation is that the first statement stems from simple knowledge whereas the second statement deals with the

---

[82] This entire question seems a summary of Augustine's Tractate 31 n. 2-3.

[83] See Homily 51 n. 2 in PG 59:285 and FC 41, p. 39: "Their opinion was divided, as it usually is in a disorderly crowd. And certainly they did not pay attention to His words, not even for the sake of acquiring information."

knowledge of affirmation, because they did not know him as approved by God, as Moses was, to whom "God spoke," as John 9:29 says.

45. Question 3 deals with John 7:28: "Jesus cried out," etc., because Isaiah 42:2 states: "He will not cry out ... his voice will not be heard abroad." – I answer that there is a crying out of impatience and of contention, and it is this type of crying out that Isaiah has in mind. And there is also the crying out of affective preaching, and that is the sense here.

46. Question 4 inquires about John 7:28: "You know me." – Contrary is John 8:19: "If you knew me, you would also know my Father." Therefore, they did not know him. – My response is that knowledge of Christ is twofold. One issues from the external senses, to wit, that he was a man and born in such and such a town from such and such a parent. This is what they knew. Another type of knowledge comes from interior revelation, which was of his invisible divinity. And indeed they didn't have this knowledge about him, and it is about this knowledge that John 8:19 is speaking.

JOHN 7:32-51
CHRIST CONFOUNDS, BY HIS POWER, THOSE PERSECUTING HIM

47. *But the Pharisees heard*, etc.[84] The Lord has already confounded those who were maligning in their hearts and those who were lying in their speech. Here he confounds *those who are persecuting him through their deeds* by his power. This section has two parts. In the first *he confronts his persecutors*. The second describes *the overthrowing of*

---

[84] The Vulgate does not read *autem* ("But").

Jewish machination where verse 40 reads: "So some of the crowd," etc.

John 7:32-39
Christ confounds his persecutors

The Evangelist describes Christ's *confounding of his persecutors* in this fashion. First he depicts their *preparation of traps.* Second *their confounding* through teaching. Third *the doubting of those confounded.* Fourth *the invitation to faith for those who do not understand and are doubting.*

Verse 32. So first he mentions the preparation of the snares which the Pharisees and priests had made because of envy, since the crowd seemed to want to believe in him. So the text states: *The Pharisees heard the crowd murmuring these things about him,* since they did not dare to speak openly. *And the rulers and Pharisees sent attendants to seize Jesus.*[85] *The Pharisees heard,* because they were the observers, but they and the rulers *sent,* for they were more powerful. Matthew 22:15-16 says something similar: "The Pharisees went and took counsel how they might trap him in his speech. And they sent to him their disciples with the Herodians." Luke 11:53-54 states: "The Pharisees ... began to press him hard and to make him speak on many things, setting traps for him."

48. (Verse 33). *So Jesus said to them: Yet a little while,* etc.[86] The second point arises here, that is, the confounding of the attendants who are persecuting him and have gone,

---

[85] On p. 348 n. 11 QuarEd rightly notice that the Vulgate reads *eum* ("him").

[86] The Vulgate does not read *eis* ("to them").

armed, to seize him. And he confounds them, displaying their impotence in a twofold manner. First, because now they could not *seize* him, and second, because after a little while they could not *find* him. For this reason the text says: *Yet a little while I am with you*, that is, living a mortal life. Or: *I am with you*, through the daily routines of a mortal life. Luke 24:44 reads: "These are the words I spoke to you, when I was still with you." *And I go to the Father who sent me*,[87] namely, *I go* through my passion, as John 16:5-7 below says. Therefore, you cannot seize me now, because it is not yet the time. John 10:17-18 below states: "I lay down my life, so that I may take it up again. No one takes it from me." And so you cannot now comprehend me nor later find me. So the text adds:

49. (Verse 34). *You will seek me and will not find me.* You will seek my aid during the devastation effected by the Romans under Titus and Vespasian.[88] – Another interpretation is: *You will seek me*, through compunction and sorrow, *and will not find me*, because many have fallen into desperation. But some who repented sought him and did not find him bodily, but did so spiritually. Acts 2:37 reads: "Having heard these things, they were pierced to the heart."[89] – Yet another interpretation: *You will seek*

---

[87] On p. 348 n. 14 QuarEd accurately indicate that the Vulgate reads *ad eum* ("to him") while Bonaventure has *ad Patrem* ("to the Father").

[88] See Chrysostom, Homily 50 n. 2 in FC 41, p. 30: "Yet, where did the Jews seek Him? Luke said that women beat their breast on His account. And it is likely that many others, both immediately after the crucifixion and after the city had been taken, remembered Christ and His wonderful works, and desired that He might be present among them again."

[89] Acts 2:37 continues: "... and said to Peter and the rest of the apostles: Brothers, what shall we do?" See Augustine, Tractate 31 n. 9 in FC 88, pp. 36-37: "Many felt remorse and said, 'What shall we do?'... But they did not need to despair; for the Lord, hanging on the cross,

me and not find me, in judgment. Proverbs 1:28-29 states:
"They will rise in the morning and will not find me, because
they have hated wisdom."[90] – A further interpretation is:
You will seek me, out of a desire to harm me, *and will not
find me*, lacking the power to assault me, since it will be
said to him after his resurrection: "Sit at my right hand
until I make your enemies your footstool."[91] And therefore,
he adds that they could not harm him.[92] *And where I am
you cannot come*. And so you would be unable to find me,
since he would be present in heaven. John 14:2-3 below
states: "I go to prepare a place for you.... And I am coming
again, and I will take you to myself, so that where I am,
you also may be."

50. (Verse 35). *So the Jews said*, etc. The third point
occurs here, that is, the doubting of the Jews that arose
because they did not understand what he had said. So the
text states: *Where is he going that we will not find him?*
And speaking among themselves, they inquired about
his destination: *Will he go to those dispersed among the*

---

deigned to pray for them. For he had said, 'Father, forgive them, for
they know not what they do.'"

[90] The Vulgate reads *disciplinam* ("instruction") while Bonaventure
has *sapientiam* ("wisdom").

[91] Ps 109:1.

[92] Hugh of St. Cher, p. 334v,ab comments: "But where did the
Jews seek him? According to the Glossa and Acts 2:37 when they
felt compunction at the crime of his death. Another interpretation
according to Chrysostom Luke [23:] 27: When the women were wailing
and lamenting. On this score there are many other conjectures.
Moreover, it is believed that when the Romans destroyed the city,
many remembered him and his miracles and wished for his presence,
so that he might tell them what was going to happen and might pray
for them. *And will not find*] him with you in the flesh or merciful in
tribulation or through grace in the future. Prov 1:28 states: They will
rise in the morning and will not find me. Another text (Prov 1:29 in
part) reads: The evil will seek and will not find me, because they have
hated instruction."

Gentiles and teach the Gentiles? Their doubt, as Augustine observed, was a prophecy, for he would go to the Gentiles, not through his bodily presence, but through his apostles.[93] Psalm 17:45 states: "A people that I knew not has served me. When they heard, they obeyed me." And since their doubt was grave, they repeated it.

51. (Verse 36). *What is this[94] statement that he has made: You will seek me and will not find me, and where I am, you cannot come*? Therefore, they did not deserve to understand, since they did not want to humble themselves and believe.

52. (Verse 37). *Now on the last day*, etc. The fourth point surfaces here, namely, *the invitation to faith*, through which wisdom and understanding are fittingly given. So the text reads: *Now on the last day of the great feast*.[95] This was the eighth and last day, which was solemn.[96] *Jesus stood and cried out. Stood*, through unchangeableness.

---

[93] See Tractate 31 n. 10 in FC 88, p. 38: "They did not know what they said; but because he wished it, they prophesied. For the Lord was going to go to the Gentiles, not by the presence of his body but rather by his feet. Who were his feet? Saul wanted to trample upon those feet by persecution when the Head cried out to him, 'Saul, Saul, why do you persecute me?'... Therefore, in no way did they understand this; and yet, as this occasion provided, they foretold our salvation, that the Lord would go to those dispersed among the Gentiles and fulfill what they read but did not understand, 'A people I knew not has served me; at the hearing of the ear, it obeyed me.'" Hugh of St. Cher, p. 334v,g observes: "And although they did not know, they, nevertheless, proclaimed something in their ignorance that was future, namely, that he would teach the Gentiles through the apostles."

[94] On p. 349 n. 5 QuarEd rightly note that the Vulgate reads *hic* ("this") while Bonaventure has *iste* ("this").

[95] On p. 349 n. 6 QuarEd accurately indicate that the Vulgate reads *die magno festivitatis* ("on the great day of the festivity") while Bonaventure has *die magni festi* ("on the day of the great feast").

[96] See Chrysostom, Homily 51 n. 1 in FC 41, p. 34: "Why, then, did he say 'on the last'? Because on that day they were all assembled....

Malachi 3:6 states: "I am the Lord and do not change." *He cried out*, through love. Psalm 68:4 reads: "I have labored, crying out," so that he might spur them on to come. *Let him come and drink*, according to my generosity. *If anyone thirst, let him come and drink*. Isaiah 55:1 says: "All you that thirst, come to the waters.... Come, buy wine and milk without money and without any price." And the manner of coming to Christ is described as that of faith. Thus the text continues:

53. (Verse 38). *The person who believes in me, as the Scripture says, from within him[97] there will flow rivers of living waters.*

54. Chrysostom asks where Scripture says this and says that "it nowhere says this," in a specific passage, but Scripture leads to this understanding.[98] Isaiah 58:11 reads: "You will be like a watered garden and like a fountain of water whose waters never fail." Proverbs 5:16, according to another translation states: "Let your fountains be conveyed abroad, and in the streets divide your waters."[99] And he says rivers, since rivers connote

---

But on the last day, when they were departing for home, He gave them supplies for their journey to salvation."

[97] The Latin is *de ventre eius* ("from his belly"). In Question 1, n. 56, below, Bonaventure will discuss the meaning of "the belly" of the believer.

[98] See Homily 51 n. 1 in PG 59:283 and FC 41, p. 35: "But where does Scripture say: 'From within him there shall flow rivers of living water?' Nowhere. What, then, is the meaning of the words: 'He who believes in me, as the Scripture says'? Here we must place the punctuation so that the words 'From within him there shall flow rivers of living water,' may be part of Christ's words."

[99] The translation that Bonaventure calls "another" is actually the Vulgate text. On p. 349 n. 9 QuarEd mention their unsuccessful efforts to track down "the first translation." Hugh of St. Cher, p. 335d also cites Prov 5:16 and Isa 58:11 as well as Chrysostom's solution of punctuating the sentence differently.

abundance and force and he often spoke of them. For Chrysostom comments: "You will clearly see fulfilled what is said when you consider the wisdom of Stephen, the eloquence of Peter, and the rapid progress of Paul. For nothing withstood them, not the furor of the people, not the insurrection of tyrants, not the snares of the demons, not daily deaths. But like rivers, sweeping all things along with their currents, they moved along."[100] And since this had been spoken in a spiritual, not a carnal sense, the Evangelist gives this explanation:

55. (Verse 39). *Now he said this about the Spirit that they who believed in him were to receive.* About this Acts 2:2 reads: "Suddenly there came a sound from heaven, as of a violent wind blowing." They were to receive this Spirit, but had not yet received it. So the text continues: *For the Spirit had not yet been given, since Jesus had not yet been glorified.* John 16:7 below states: "If I go, I will send him to you."

QUESTIONS

56. Question 1 addresses John 7:38: "Rivers of living water will flow from the belly" of believers. But John 7:39 says that this has to be understood of the Holy Spirit. – 1. But the Holy Spirit proceeds solely from God the Father and the Son. Therefore, it does not flow from the belly of believers. – 2. Furthermore, a holy man, who has the

---

[100] See Homily 51 n. 1 in PG 59:284. Bonaventure's citation is not verbatim. Hugh of St. Cher, p. 335f also cites this passage from Chrysostom. His citation has more in common with Bonaventure's quotation than with the text of Chrysostom. Interestingly enough, Chrysostom mentions *Pauli vim* ("the forcefulness of Paul"), Bonaventure *Pauli cursum* ("the rapid progress of Paul"), and Hugh of St. Cher *Pauli fluxum* ("the flowing tide of Paul").

Spirit, cannot give the Holy Spirit, but God alone gives the Spirit. Wherefore, it does not flow from the belly, etc. – 3. Moreover, how is belly to be understood, since John 7:38 says that the rivers "flow from the belly"?

Chrysostom answers that the rivers of the Holy Spirit are his gifts and graces.[101] Now grace is fittingly called a flowing river, not because it flows from one into another, but because, once it has entered the mind to abide it is greater than any fountain, neither decreasing nor stagnant, but flowing and flowing yet again. It flows from God and makes humans flow back to God, according to the property of water in a tide that moves in only to move out. Thus it is written in John 4:14: "It will become in him a fountain of water, springing up into eternal life." For Qoheleth 1:7 states: "Unto the place whence the rivers come, they return, to flow again." – 3. Relative to the question of what is meant by belly, Chrysostom answers that belly means the heart, according to what Psalm 39:9: "Your law is in the middle of my heart."[102] He also used the word belly for the greater reason that he might signify the abundance of graces. – But the Glossa explains it by the flow of teaching and counsel that issues from the belly of

---

[101] See Homily 51 n. 1 in PG 59:283-284 and FC 41, p. 36: "He is alluding to the wealth and abundance of grace. He spoke in a similar vein elsewhere: 'A fountain of water, springing up unto life everlasting,' that is ['He who drinks of the water that I will give him'] will have much grace. In another context, then, He said 'life everlasting,' while here He speaks of 'living water.' And by 'living' He means 'ever-active.' For, when the grace of the Spirit enters into the soul and takes up its abode there, it gushes forth more abundantly than any fountain and does not cease, nor become exhausted, nor stand still."

[102] See Homily 51 n. 1 in PG 59:283 and FC 41, p. 35: "Here the word *koilias* means 'heart' as Scripture says elsewhere: 'And your law is within my heart.'" See Hugh of St. Cher, p. 335f: "From the belly], that is, from the mind or from the heart. Chrysostom. It calls the heart the belly, as elsewhere in Ps 39:9: Your law is in the middle of my belly, that is, my heart."

a good and pious conscience, according to this: "My belly shall sound like a harp for Moab."[103]

57. Question 2 focuses on John 7:39: "The Holy Spirit had not yet been given." – Contrary. 1. How could the prophets prophesy the truth except through the Holy Spirit? Therefore, they had the Holy Spirit. For David says: "Do not take your holy Spirit away from me."[104] – 2. Likewise, the Apostles performed miracles, but Jerome says that "they could not perform miracles without the grace of the Holy Spirit."[105] – I answer that the gift of the Holy Spirit is threefold: manifest, more manifest, most manifest. It was manifest in those prophesying and performing miracles before the passion. It was more manifest in Christ's breathing upon the disciples after his resurrection, because it was given in a visible sign such as breath.[106] But it was most manifest after the ascension, since it was given in a visible and audible sign.[107] And it was given according to the principle that the most manifest is also the most abundant. Therefore, the meaning of "had not yet been given" refers to a gift that was evident and abundant.[108]

---

[103] See Isa 16:11. See the Glossa Ordinaria in PL 114:388B: "The belly is the conscience of the heart. Once it has drunk of the Spirit, it is purified and becomes a fountain." See Augustine Tractate 32 n. 4 in FC 88, p. 43: "Therefore, when this liquid has been drunk, the cleansed conscience gains life; and drawing [the water] out, it will have a fountain: it will itself even be a fountain."

[104] Ps 51:13. See Chrysostom, Homily 51 n. 1 in FC 41, p. 36: "Then, how did the Prophets prophesy and work countless wonders?"

[105] On p. 350 n. 9 QuarEd quote the Glossa Ordinaria (from Jerome) on John 7:37: "… from the time the Apostles believed in the Lord they had the Holy Spirit. Otherwise they could not have performed signs without the grace of the Holy Spirit…."

[106] See John 20:22.

[107] See Acts 2:1-13.

[108] See Augustine, Tractate 32 n. 6 in FC 88, p. 46: "But of this giving, there was to be a certain mode which had not at all appeared

John 7:40-53
Dispersion of Christ's persecutors

58. *Now*[109] *some of the crowd.* The Evangelist has set forth Christ's confounding of his persecutors through his teaching. Now he presents *the dispersion of Christ's persecutors* and does so in this order. First he points out *dissension within the crowd who are listening.* Second is *the rebuke of the returning attendants.* Third Nicodemus's *upbraiding of the Pharisees who persist in their evil.*

Verse 40. So first he points to the dissension among the multitude about Christ's teaching. For this reason the text continues: *Some of the crowd, when they had heard these words* – some had been enlightened through hearing Christ's teaching – *were saying: This is truly the prophet,* because he was speaking so wisely.

59. (Verse 41). *But*[110] *some were saying: This is the Christ.* And these were the ones who were more enlightened, for they were God-like.[111] Matthew 16:13-16 reads: "Who do people say that the Son of Man is? But they said: Some:

---

before; about this there is a question here. For nowhere before have we read that men, having been gathered together, after the Holy Spirit was received, had spoken in the languages of all nations." See Hugh of St. Cher, p. 335m: "Spirit had not yet been given] as a river. Supply: but rather by dripping or in drops. Another interpretation: not yet under a visible sign such as breath after the resurrection or in fire after the ascension or in strength or in constancy of faith, and revelation of secret matters and knowledge of all languages."

[109] On p. 350 n. 12 QuarEd accurately mention that the Vulgate reads *ergo* ("So") while Bonaventure has *autem* ("Now").

[110] On p. 351 n. 1 QuarEd rightly notice that the Vulgate does not read *autem* ("But").

[111] I have translated *divini* as "God-like." See Hugh of St. Cher, p. 335pq: "This is truly the prophet] These have begun to drink, but not fully. Others were saying: This is the Christ] These agreed with what had been said, but were more perfect."

John the Baptist, but others: Elijah. And others: Jeremiah or one of the prophets. Jesus[112] said to them: But you, who do you say that I am? Simon Peter answered and said: You are the Christ, the Son of the living God."[113] *Some, however, said,* in contradiction, namely, those whose eyes were closed to the light of the Scripture: *Does the Christ come from Galilee?* As if they were saying: No. For even Nathanael said in John 1:46 above: "Can anything good come from Nazareth?" And they were moved by Scripture:

60. (Verse 42). *Does not the Scripture say that he is of the offspring of David?* 2 Samuel 7:12-13 states: "I will raise up your offspring after you, who will proceed from your loins, and I will establish his kingdom ... and I will establish the throne of his kingdom forever." And Psalm 131:11 says: "From the fruit of your loins I will set upon your throne." *And from Bethlehem, the village where David lived, that the Christ is to come?* Micah 5:2 reads: "And you, Bethlehem-Ephrathah, are a little one among the thousands of Judah, for[114] out of you will come forth[115] ... the one who is the ruler in Israel."[116] And in this way they argued back and forth. Thus:

61. (Verse 43). *So there arose a division among the crowd on account of him.* He himself was not the cause. Rather it was their malice. Chrysostom comments: "They were filled with division, not with compunction, for evil does

---

[112] The Vulgate does not read *Iesus* ("Jesus").

[113] See the Glossa Ordinaria on Matt 16:13 in PL 114:141C: "Humans speak about him as the Son of Man. But it is the God-like who understand his deity."

[114] The Vulgate does not read *enim* ("for").

[115] The Vulgate reads *mihi* ("for me") while Bonaventure does not.

[116] Hugh of St. Cher, p. 335v,c also refers to Micah 5:2.

not want to yield to anyone."[117] Because of this division some of them wanted to seize him as an evil person, but some wanted to let him go as a good person. And the Pharisees' plan was frustrated by this contention, since the attendants did not lay hands on him and seize him, although some wanted to. So the text adds:

62. (Verse 44). *But some of them*, namely, the attendants, *wanted to seize him*, that is, according to the command that had been given them. John 7:32 above had said: "The Pharisees and high priests[118] sent attendants to seize Jesus."[119] *But no one laid hands on him*,[120] because God had sent him. Psalm 143:7 reads: "Extend your hand from on high." And so their intention was thwarted. And the reason for this is that "the thoughts of human beings are vain."[121] But "the counsel of the Lord remains forever,"[122] while their plan to apprehend Jesus Christ had not yet waned. Psalm 32:10 proclaims: "The Lord brings to naught the counsels of nations, and he rejects the plans of peoples and casts away the counsels of rulers."

63. (Verse 45). *So the attendants came.* This verse introduces the second point, that is, the rebuke of the returning attendants, for they had done none of the things

---

[117] See Homily 51 n.2-3 in PG 59:285. Bonaventure's citation is not verbatim, but a summary. Hugh of St. Cher, p. 335v,g cites Chrysostom: "... They were filled with division and did not have compunction. For such is the nature of iniquity: it does not want to believe in anyone. It has one goal in sight, to kill the person for whom they lay snares."

[118] The Vulgate reads *principes* ("rulers") while Bonaventure has *pontifices* ("high priests").

[119] The Vulgate reads *eum* ("him") while Bonaventure has *Iesum* ("Jesus").

[120] On p. 351 n. 7 QuarEd correctly mention that the Vulgate reads *super eum* ("upon him") while Bonaventure has *in eum* ("on him").

[121] See Ps 93:11.

[122] See Ps 32:11.

for which they had been sent. So the Pharisees ask them the reason for their behavior in order to censure them. So the text continues: *So the attendants came to the chief priests and Pharisees*; they had not brought him with them. *And these said to them: Why have you not brought him?* because you were sent to accomplish this. Thus you have failed.

64. (Verse 46). *The attendants answered: Never has a human being spoken as this person is speaking.*[123] As if they were saying: This is the reason why we didn't bring him, since we were frightened by the greatness of his teaching, because *never has a human being spoken thus*. Never has anyone spoken so sweetly, for a woman, upon hearing him, said in Luke 11:27: "Blessed is the womb that bore you and the breasts that nursed you." And The Song of Songs 4:11 reads: "Honey and milk are under his tongue."[124] Never has anyone taught so eloquently and so wisely. For Luke 2:47 states: "All were amazed ... at his wisdom and his answers." And Mark 1:22 reads: "They were amazed at his teaching." Never has anyone spoken so powerfully. Matthew 7:29 states: "He was teaching as one having power." And so they were astonished at his teaching. Never has anyone spoken so beneficially. John 6:64 has: "The words that I have spoken to you are spirit and life." And John 6:69 above says: "Lord, you have the words of eternal life."[125]

---

[123] On p. 351 n. 10 QuarEd accurately indicate that the Vulgate does not read *loquitur* ("is speaking").

[124] The Vulgate reads *sub lingua tua* ("under your tongue") while Bonaventure has *sub lingua eius* ("under his tongue").

[125] Bonaventure's five points with their scriptural supports find a very close parallel in Hugh of St. Cher. See Hugh of St. Cher, p. 335v,o: "Never has a human being spoken thus] that is, powerfully. For Mark 1:22 reads: For he was teaching them, as one having power, and not like the scribes. Or [Never thus], that is, with such eloquent teaching. Mark 1:22 reads: All were amazed at his teaching. Matt 5:2: Opening

65. (Verse 47). *So the Pharisees answered them.* Having heard the response of the attendants, the Pharisees rebuke them because they had put faith in his teaching. For they say: *Have you also been led astray?* And through the example of the *"maiores"* or powerful, they try to show that they have been *led astray.*

66. (Verse 48). *Have anyone of the rulers believed in him?* As if they were saying: No one. *Or any of the Pharisees,* namely, those who know the Law. None of those who have knowledge believe him, only the ignorant do.

67. (Verse 49). *But this crowd that is ignorant of the Law,*[126] that is, it believes. And since they are ignorant of what they should know and believe what they shouldn't, *they are accursed.* Deuteronomy 27:26 reads: "Cursed be the person who does not abide in the words of this Law."[127] Chrysostom observes: "Nothing is more clear than the truth, nothing more simple. Nevertheless, nothing is more difficult for those who malign. For behold, the wise, the scribes and Pharisees, who have seen the signs and have read the Scriptures, were wounded by the truth and became blind. But the attendants, who had seen nothing,

---

his mouth, he taught them. The ability to teach is seen in the opening of his mouth. Prov 14:6: The teaching of the wise is simple. Or: [Never thus], that is, so sweetly. For Luke 11:27 says: When he had spoken, a woman, compelled by his sweetness of speech, said: Blessed is the womb that bore you. For the Spouse says to him in The Song of Songs 4:11: Honey and milk are under your tongue. In honey is sweetness; in milk is ability. Thus [Never thus], that is, so beneficially. John 6:69 above states: Lord, to whom will we go? You have the words of eternal life. Or: [Never thus], that is, with such precision and wisdom, since although all were laying traps for him, they never could trap him in his speech."

[126] On p. 351 n. 15 QuarEd rightly notice that the Vulgate reads *non novit* ("does not know") while Bonaventure has *ignorat* ("is ignorant").

[127] Hugh of St. Cher, p. 335v,u also cites Deut 27:26.

were seized by one single speech, and those who had gone to bind him, returned bound themselves."[128] But afterwards the Pharisees tried to turn them from their faith, and so it is said in Matthew 23:13: "Woe to you, scribes and Pharisees ... who shut the kingdom of heaven against men and women. But you yourselves do not enter nor allow those going in to enter." Luke 11:52 reads: "Woe to you, lawyers, because you have taken away the key of knowledge. You yourselves have not entered and have hindered those who were entering."

68. (Verse 50). *Nicodemus said*, etc. The third point surfaces here, that is, the censure of the Pharisees. This was made on the authority of the Law, through which it is shown that they should not have seized him, for he had not yet been judged worthy of death by means of the Law. So *Nicodemus said*, that is, that disciple, *who had come to Jesus at night, who was one of them*,[129] that is, one of the Pharisees. John 3:1 states: "There was a person from the Pharisees, Nicodemus by name."

69. (Verse 51). *Does our Law judge a person unless it first hears from him*[130] *and knows what he is doing?* As if the verse were saying: No. Deuteronomy 17:4 says: "When

---

[128] See Homily 52 n. 1 in PG 59:287. Bonaventure's citation is not verbatim. See Hugh of St. Cher, p. 335v,o where he also cites Chrysostom. Bonaventure's citation of Chrysostom is very similar to the one found in Hugh of St. Cher.

[129] On p. 352 n. 3 QuarEd rightly notice that the Vulgate reads *dixit Nicodemus ad eos* ("Nicodemus said to them") while Bonaventure has *dixit Nicodemus* ("Nicodemus said") and that the Vulgate reads *ad eum* ("to him") whilst Bonaventure has *ad Iesum* ("to Jesus").

[130] On p. 352 n. 4 QuarEd accurately indicate that the Vulgate reads *ab ipso* ("from him") whereas Bonaventure has *ab eo* ("from him").

you have heard it,[131] you will inquire diligently." Job observed this law in Job 29:16: "I searched out diligently for the reason of which I was ignorant." The Romans observed this law. Acts 25:16 reads: "The Romans are not accustomed to condemn[132] any person before the accused has met his accusers face to face and has been given a chance to defend himself against the charges."

70. (Verse 52). *They answered and said,*[133] because they were incorrigible. And although they could not slander him by word, they slandered Nicodemus as being deceived because he believed in Christ. So they say: *Are you also a Galilean?* That is, you believe in a Galilean, just as they are called Christians, since they believe in Christ. For Julian the Apostate called Christians ragged Galileans.[134] And you foolishly believe in him. Thus they say: *Search the Scriptures and see that*[135] *out of Galilee arises no prophet,* that is, the one that we are waiting for. Contrary is what Augustine says: "Not only does a prophet arise from Galilee, but also the Lord of the prophets."[136] He

---

[131] The Vulgate reads *audiensque* ("and upon hearing it") while Bonaventure has *cum audiens* ("When you have heard about it").

[132] The Vulgate reads *donare* ("to give up") whereas Bonaventure has *damnare* ("to condemn").

[133] On p. 352 n. 5 QuarEd correctly indicate that the Vulgate reads *ei* ("to him").

[134] See "Letter 22, to Arsacius," n. 430 in *The Works of the Emperor Julian III*, trans. Wilmer Cave Wright, LCL (London: William Heinemann, 1923), 71: "I order that one-fifth of this (corn and wine) be used for the poor who serve the priests, and the remainder be distributed by us to strangers and beggars. For it is disgraceful that, when no Jew ever has to beg, and the impious Galileans support not only their own poor but ours as well, all men see that our people lack aid from us."

[135] On p. 352 n. 7 QuarEd rightly notice that the Vulgate reads *quia* ("that") while Bonaventure has *quoniam* ("that").

[136] See Tractate 33 n. 2 in CCSL xxxvi, p. 307. Bonaventure's citation is not verbatim. See further FC 88, p. 52: "Search the Scriptures and

was called a *Nazarene*, because he was brought up in Nazareth.[137]

71. (Verse 53). *And they returned,* since they could not avoid a rebuke and were also unable to consummate their evil plan. Thus the text continues: *And they returned, each one to his own home,* so that one did not stay with another. For Sirach 21:10 states: "A gathering of sinners is like twine heaped together, and their end is a flame of fire." Psalm 67:31 reads: "Disperse the nations that desire wars."

QUESTIONS

72. Question 1 inquires about the attendants: If they believed, why didn't they follow Christ?[138] – One must follow Chrysostom's answer: They believed and were his heralds, but they did not follow him, since they had not risen to the status of perfection.[139]

73. Question 2 raises this issue: What great and sublime words did the Lord speak, so that they said in John 7:46: "Never has any person spoken thus"? – Chrysostom

---

see that out of Galilee a prophet arises not.' But the Lord of prophets arose from there."

[137] See Hugh of St. Cher, p. 336m: "For out of Galilee arises no prophet]. It does not read that he has arisen or is; nevertheless the Lord of prophets has arisen from there, who is called a Nazarene."

[138] See John 7:48.

[139] See Homily 52 n. 1 in FC 41, pp. 43-44: "The attendants ... were captivated by a single sermon, and despite the fact that they had gone to seize Him, they returned overwhelmed with admiration. ... Now, it was a much greater thing to come back than to have stayed away. For in the latter case they would have escaped the fault-finding of the Pharisees, while actually they became heralds proclaiming the wisdom of Christ, and so displayed their courage the more."

supplies the answer: "When the mind is uncorrupted, there is no need of long speeches. For such is the nature of truth that when it finds a soul that is well disposed, it wondrously attracts it and adheres to it."[140]

74. Question 3 focuses on the Pharisees: Since the Pharisees have performed all their deeds in the sight of men and women and do not want to be judged wicked,[141] why did they so abandon the rule of law when their sin was obvious? – I answer that three things must come together in the rendering of a just judgment: A just mind, for 2 Chronicles 19:7 reads: "Do all things with diligence, for there is no iniquity with God ... nor respect of persons nor desire for gifts." – The second thing is a just cause. Exodus 23:7 states: "You shall not put to death an innocent or a just person." And Exodus 22:18 says: "You shall not suffer evildoers to live." – The third thing is a just rule or order, which is accomplished through a just investigation. Deuteronomy 16:20 reads: "You shall justly pursue that which is just."

So since an unjust mind dwelt within the hypocrite Pharisees that thirsted after the death of Christ and a just cause was absent, because they could not condemn him according to the law, they were necessarily compelled to subvert the rule of judgment. – Now there are four things that especially pervert the mind, that were in the Pharisees, that are summarized in these verses: These four things – fear, hatred, love, wealth – are wont to

---

[140] See Homily 52 n. 1 in PG 59:287: "For a sincere mind has no need of long speeches. So great is the power of the truth." See Hugh of St. Cher, p. 335v,o: "Chrysostom says: When the mind is uncorrupted, there is no need for long speeches. For such is the nature of the truth."

[141] See Matt 23:5: "In fact, they perform all their deeds to be seen by men and women."

pervert the just sensibilities of people.[142] And all these were in the Pharisees, as is evident by means of induction. Against these Exodus 18:21 states: "Choose for yourself wise men who fear God, in whom there is truth and who hate avarice."[143]

75. Question 4 asks: Since the Lord, in as far as it was in his power, willed that all come to faith, why is it that he hid his origin, so that he would be believed to have been born in Nazareth and because of this Christ would not be believed? – I respond that this was done by divine judgment, divine dispensation, and to fulfill the Scriptures. By divine judgment, because they knew that he was born during the time of Herod and despised him. Indeed, they consented to his death. Therefore, they merited to have his place of birth hidden from them by means of his life in Nazareth. – Second, from divine dispensation, since he wanted to be hidden from evil people, so that when he suffered at the hands of evil people he might redeem good people. – Third, to fulfill the Scriptures, for Scripture not only says that he was born in Bethlehem, but also "he will be called a Nazarene," as it is written in Matthew 2:23. And since the Jews did not search the Scriptures, they were in error.

---

[142] The Latin is: *Quatuor ista: timor, odium, dilectio, census / Saepe solent hominum rectos pervertere sensus.*

[143] The Vulgate reads *Provide autem de omni plebe viros potentes et timentes Deum* ("Now provide out of all the people powerful men who fear God") while Bonaventure has *Elige tibi viros sapientes et timentes Deum* ("Choose for yourself wise men who fear God").

CHAPTER EIGHT

JOHN 8:1-11
CHRIST CONFOUNDS THOSE WHO WERE LYING IN WAIT FOR HIM

1. *But Jesus went*, etc. After describing the refutation of those who were asserting their power, the Evangelist now turns to Christ's *confounding of those who were lying in wait out of malice*. Since they were unable to murder him, they sought to find an opportunity to catch him in his speech. And so they posed a question to trap the Lord. But on the contrary, they themselves were trapped and were confounded. And the text depicts their confounding in this order. First, it mentions *Christ's teaching*. Second, *the malicious questioning* of the Pharisees. Third, Christ's wise response. Fourth, *the confusion of the Pharisees*. Fifth, *the freeing of the woman*.

2. (Verse 1). So the first item to be mentioned is Christ's teaching that was of loving care, public, and truthful. Of loving care, for the text says: "But Jesus went to the Mount of Olives." For in Bethany he received hospitality at the home of Mary and Martha. Luke 21:37 reads: "In the daytime he was teaching in the temple, but as for the nights he would go out and spend them on the mountain called Olivet."[1]

---

[1] Presupposed in Bonaventure's exposition is John 11:1-12:11, esp. 11:5: "Now Jesus loved Martha and her sister Mary, and Lazarus."

3. (Verse 2). *And at daybreak he again came to the temple.*
Loving care is noted in that he went "at daybreak." Wisdom
6:14 states: "She anticipates those[2] who desire her by
showing herself to them[3] first."[4] And Proverbs 8:17 states:
"Those who will watch[5] for me early in the morning will
find me."[6] – What he did was also public. Thus the text
says: *And all the people came to him.* Luke 21:38 reads:
"All the people came early in the morning to the temple
to hear him."[7] – What he did was also truthful. For the
text continues: *And sitting down, he began to teach them.*
"Sitting," because it was characteristic of teachers to sit.
Matthew 23:2 has: "The scribes and the Pharisees have
sat on the chair of Moses." "They sat," that is, to teach, as
Christ is doing here.

4. (Verse 3). *They brought to him,* etc.[8] The second point
surfaces here, namely, the malicious question. The
question concerned a woman who had been caught in
adultery: whether she should be stoned according to the
command of the law. So the text continues: *The scribes and
the Pharisees brought him a woman caught in adultery.*
The text mentions the scribes and the Pharisees, since
they were very shrewd and very envious. The scribes
envied the Lord's wisdom whereas the Pharisees envied
his goodness. Luke 11:53 reads: "The Pharisees and the
lawyers began to press him hard," etc. *And they placed*

---

[2] The Vulgate does not read *eos* ("them").

[3] The Vulgate reads *illis* ("to them") whereas Bonaventure has *eis*
("to them").

[4] Wis 6:14 speaks of wisdom.

[5] The Vulgate reads *vigilant* ("watch") while Bonaventure has
vigilaverint ("will watch").

[6] Prov 8:17 begins with a reference to love: "I love those who love
me and who...."

[7] Hugh of St. Cher, p. 336s also cites Luke 21:38.

[8] On p. 354 n. 3 QuarEd rightly notice that the Vulgate reads
autem ("Now") while Bonaventure has *ei* ("to him").

her right in the middle, because they wanted to question him about her.

5. (Verse 4). *And they said to him: Teacher.* They are speaking out of adulation and deceit, trying to conceal their motives. Chrysostom observes: "They call him teacher, whose disciples they don't want to be."[9] They said something similar in Matthew 22:16: "Teacher, we know that you are truthful and teach the way of God in truth." *This woman has just now been caught in adultery*, either because of the factual evidence or because of witnesses.

6. (Verse 5). *Now in the Law Moses commanded us to stone such a person.* Deuteronomy 22:22 reads: "If a man sleeps with the wife of his neighbor, both shall die,"[10] that is, the adulterer and the adulteress. *What, therefore, do you say?* They were asking this, not as a true question, but as a means of deception. And the Evangelist says this very thing:

7. (Verse 6). *Now they were saying this to test him, so that they could accuse him.* Thus, the Lord answered those questioning him in a similar way in Matthew 22:18: "Why are you testing me, you hypocrites?" *So that they could accuse him*, as in the passion. Matthew 27:12 reads: "And when he was accused by the elders and the leaders, he made no response."[11]

---

[9] See Homily 42 (*Opus Imperfectum*) in PG 56:867: "They call him teacher and truthful: Teacher, as one honored and praised, who opened the secret of his heart to them in a straightforward way, trying to make them his disciples. For this is the primary power of hypocrites: fake praise. For they praise those whom they want to destroy."

[10] Hugh of St. Cher, p. 336v, k also cites Deut 22:22.

[11] The Vulgate reads *principibus sacerdotum et senioribus* ("the chief priests and elders").

But Jesus, bending himself.[12] The third point occurs here, that is, the wise response of Christ. His response is wise, since it is offered with due moderation. For he was duly moderate by not hastening to make a judgment. So the text continues: *Jesus, bending himself, began to write with his finger on the ground,* that is, waiting to see whether they might back off from their painful question. *He began to write with his finger,* in order to suggest that he had written the Law with his finger, as in Deuteronomy 9:10 and Exodus 31:18.[13] – He was also duly moderate in pronouncing judgment, since he did not swerve away from the rigor of the Law that she should be put to death and he did not go against the Law and thereby give them an occasion to accuse him. So the text continues:

8. (Verse 7). *But when they continued to ask him,* and would not desist from their foolishness, *he raised himself and said to them: Let the person among you who is without sin be the first to cast a stone at her.* He had bent down out of mercy. Now *he raised himself,* out of justice. *And he said to them,* in pronouncing judgment. *Who is without sin,* etc., to inflict the punishment? By his duly moderate response he confounded them as hypocrites, according to what Matthew 7:3-5 states: "Why do you see the speck in your brother's eye, and yet do not consider the beam in your own eye? ... First cast out the beam from your own eye, and then you will see clearly to cast the speck from your brother's eye."[14] – His conduct was also duly

---

[12] On p. 354 n. 8 QuarEd correctly indicate that the Vulgate reads *inclinans se deorsum* ("bending himself down").

[13] Deut 9:10 reads: "And the Lord gave me (Moses) two tables of stone written with the finger of God." Ex 31:18 says: "And the Lord ... gave to Moses two stone tables of testimony, written with the finger of God."

[14] Interestingly, Bonaventure does not explicitly cite the words "You hypocrite," that begin Matt 7:5.

moderate after he had pronounced his sentence as the text adds:

9. (Verse 8). *And again stooping down, he began to write on the ground*, so that he might give those who had been confounded a chance to leave without shame. For Bede comments: "In the presence of his tempters he wanted to stoop down and write on the ground, so that, by turning his face to another matter, he might give them freedom to depart. His response had withered them, and now he provides them the opportunity to steal away quickly rather than ask any more questions."[15] Jeremiah 17:13 reads: "All those who forsake you will be confounded. Those who depart from you will be written on the ground." Jeremiah 22:29-30 states: "O ground, ground, hear the word of the Lord ... Write this man sterile."[16]

10. (Verse 9). *But when they had heard this*, etc.[17] This verse introduces the fourth point, that is, the confounding of the Pharisees which is obvious because of their departure. So the text says: *But when they had heard this*, namely, his wise and just answer, *they went away one by one, beginning with the oldest*. Those who had come as a group were dispersed and went away with the eldest the first to depart, because they had been the first in sin and now the first in flight. Daniel 13:5 says: "Iniquity came ... from the eldest judges who seemed to rule the people." And all left, because all had been confounded. Thus the text continues: *And Jesus remained alone with the woman*

---

[15] See Bede's commentary on John 8:8 in PL 92:756B.

[16] I have translated the occurrences of *terra* in Jer 17:13 and 22:29 by "ground" rather than by "earth," so that Bonaventure's reason for citing them is more evident. Hugh of St. Cher, p. 336v, q also cites Jer 17:13 and 22:29-30.

[17] On p. 354 n. 13 QuarEd accurately mention that the Vulgate does not read *haec* ("this").

standing in the middle. He remained alone who required a place of solitude. Hosea 2:14 reads: "I will lead her into a place of solitude and there I will speak to her heart." Another interpretation: He alone had been offended. Psalm 50:6 says: "Against you alone have I sinned, and I have committed evil before you." Augustine observes: "Two remained: misery and mercy."[18] And since mercy had regard for misery, the text adds:

11. (Verse 10). *And Jesus, raising himself.* Here the fifth point occurs, that is, the merciful liberation of the accused woman. And since mercy is a friend of justice and not its enemy, the Lord asks her about the accusation and condemnation lodged against her. So *he says:*[19] *Woman, where are they who accused you?*[20] *Has no one condemned you*? He asks about two matters. And since the answer to his first question is evident in the withdrawal of her accusers, the woman responds to his question about her condemnation.

12. (Verse 11). *She said: No one, Lord,* supply: Has condemned me. It is not the prerogative of human beings to condemn. Matthew 7:1 states: "Do not condemn," etc. And behold, I am left with you. And there follows the merciful liberation of the woman. For the text says: *Then Jesus said: Neither will I condemn you.* Behold, mercy. Romans 8:33-34 states: "It is God who justifies. Who will condemn?" *Go and sin no more.*[21] Behold, justice, that

---

[18] See Tractate 33 n. 5 in CCSL xxxvi, p. 309: "Two were left behind: the miserable woman and mercy." Hugh of St. Cher, p. 337l quotes Augustine exactly.

[19] On p. 355 n. 4 QuarEd correctly indicate that the Vulgate reads *Dixit ei* ("He said to her") while Bonaventure has *dicit* ("he says").

[20] The Vulgate does not read *qui te accusabant* ("who accused you").

[21] On p. 355 n. 6 QuarEd rightly notice that the Vulgate reads *iam* ("from now on").

absolves from sin in such a way that it does not give anyone the freedom to return to sin. Sirach 5:7 reads: "Mercy and wrath quickly come from him, and his wrath looks upon sinners." Thus Augustine comments: "Let those who love gentleness in the Lord be attentive and also fear the truth. For 'The Lord is sweet and just.'[22] Do you love what is sweet? Fear what is just. As a gentle person he says: 'I have kept silent,' but as a just one" he says along with Isaiah 42:14: "I speak like a woman in labor."[23] So he adds: "Sin no more."

QUESTIONS

13. Question 1. This passage raises a doubt. Since this question would easily be determined by the Law and those who are tempting the Lord should ask about doubtful matters, why did the deceitful Pharisees propose such a question to the Lord? – Some respond that this passage is a total human fabrication. For they have said that it was inserted into the Gospel of John just as the story of Susannah was inserted into Daniel.[24] To support their contention they refer to Chrysostom who doesn't mention this story.[25] For he skips over it and comments

---

[22] See Ps 24:8.

[23] See Tractate 33 n. 7 in CCSL xxxvi, p. 309. Bonaventure's citation is virtually verbatim, until the end where he abbreviates Augustine's quotation of Isa 42:14.

[24] See Dan 13. See Book II, c. 33 of Jerome's *Apologia adversus Libros Rufini* in PL 23:476A: "The story against Susannah ... is not found in the Hebrew text."

[25] See Homily 52 n. 2 in PG 59:289 where Chrysostom concludes his commentary on John 7:52 and moves directly into an exposition of John 8:12: "I am the light of the world." Hugh of St. Cher, p. 336v,a makes the same point. Some, however, think that Chrysostom knew of this story from what he says in Homily 60 n. 5 in PG 59:334: The Lord "accepted and cured another prostitute that the Jews had accused."

straightaway on John 8:12: "Again Jesus spoke," etc. –
But Augustine[26] and our commentators give an exegesis
of it in the course of their expositions. – But I don't know
the reason why Chrysostom made no comment about
this story. Some say that this story is not found in the
ancient Greek books, since John added it once his Gospel
was completed.[27] – Therefore, it has to be said that the
Pharisees were envious of the Lord in that he was being
praised for his gentleness and his justice at the same
time, in accordance with Psalm 44:5: "On account of truth
and gentleness and justice." Therefore, they propose the
question in which he would have to resort to the rigors of
justice against gentleness, so that he would be considered
cruel or as one who contradicted the justice of the Law.
And they concocted their position as insoluble, so that,
whatever part Christ took, they would obtain their
objective. But the Lord wisely responds to the person, not
to the question.

14. Question 2 concerns what the Lord was writing on
the ground when he pronounced his sentence. – 1. For
it seemed that this was a puerile action, because it
was not something permanent and no one could read
it. – 2. Likewise, why did he write with his finger? – 3.
Furthermore, what did he write? – I respond that the
moral reason why he wrote on the ground both before and
after his sentence was in order to teach us, as Bede says,
that "before we correct a neighbor who is sinning and
after we have performed the ... ministry of punishment,
let us humbly examine ourselves, lest perhaps we have
fallen into the snare of the same sins that we are rebuking

---

[26] See Tractate 33 n. 4-8.
[27] For a discussion of this matter with translations of relevant
ancient texts, see Brown, pp. 335-36.

or other ... sins."[28] – Another reason is to show that a sentence has to be pronounced with maturity, and first written down and with words that are formed within the confines of the law.[29] – The third reason is to show that a person should condemn unwillingly and that a person should unwillingly and with sorrow render the sentence of punishment.[30] – The fourth reason is that he might distance himself from an evil situation. And this point pertains especially to judges.

3. As to what he wrote, Augustine responds that he wrote what he gave as his sentence.[31] But Ambrose says that he wrote: "O ground, ground, ... write that the men have been disowned,"[32] and thus applied Jeremiah 22:29-30. The Glossa Interlinearis says that he was writing "their sins."[33] Others maintain that he was writing letters through which individuals could make our their own

---

[28] See his commentary on John 8:9 in PL 92:736B.

[29] See the Glossa Ordinaria on John 8:6 in PL 114:389A: "Now he teaches that before judgment is rendered, we must bend, that is, condescend in making our judgment and do so with discretion."

[30] See Bede's commentary on John 8:6 in PL 92:735D: Christ did not immediately pronounce his judgment, but only "after they pressured him with their question."

[31] The closest parallel is not found in Augustine, but in Hugh of St. Cher, p. 337a: "... some say, and I believe, with Augustine, that he was writing what he was about to give as his answer: the one among you who has no sin."

[32] See Epistola XXV, n. 4 in PL 16:1085A: "... the Lord Jesus, bending his head, began to write on the ground. What was he writing except that prophetic word: ' O earth, earth, write that the men have been disowned...." Hugh of St. Cher, p. 337a writes: "Ambrose in a certain letter ... seems to want him to have written: O ground, ground, absorb these men who have been disowned, that is, they are fittingly to be judged. The text is taken from Jer 22:29-30."

[33] See Book II, n. 17 of Jerome, *Dialogus contra Pelagianos* in PL 23:579A: "But Jesus, bending down, was writing on the ground with his finger the sins of those who were accusing her and the sins of all mortals, according to what is written in the prophet: 'Now those who depart from you will be written on the ground' (Jer 17:13)."

sins.[34] – 2. Relative to the question of why he wrote with his finger, I believe that there is a literal reason, because he didn't have another means of writing. There is also a moral and an allegorical reason. The moral reason is that the finger means discernment, and he wanted everyone to examine himself carefully.[35] The allegorical reason is that he might signify that he was the one who had written the Law with his finger. See Exodus 31:18.[36]

15. Question 3 deals with the Lord's response in John 8:7: "Let the person among you who is without sin be the first to cast a stone at her." – From this response it seems that no one could accuse anyone, because "no one is clean from defilement,"[37] and no one is sinless. And if this is the case, then there will be unpunished crimes. – If you say that the Lord meant mortal sin, then it is objected that the commandment is to correct and accuse a brother.[38] Therefore, if no one sins by doing what he was bound to do, and further, if a sinner is bound to accuse, for he is not freed from this obligation because of his sin, then it

---

[34] Hugh of St. Cher, p. 337a comments: "The Glossa says that he was writing their sins. Some say that he was writing a certain figure, which, when they saw it, reminded them of all their sins."

[35] See Bede's commentary on John 8:6 in PL 92:735C: The finger which is flexible for creating things also expresses the subtlety of discernment. See also PL 92:736C: "The judge of another person's crime is commanded to point the finger of discernment at his own heart, lest he, perhaps, may be found guilty of the same crime."

[36] See Ambrose, Epistola XXVI, n. 14 in PL 16:1089B: "Now he was writing on the ground with his finger, by which he had written the Law (Ex xxxi, 18). Sinners are written on the earth (Jer xvii, 13), while the just in heaven...." See also Augustine, Tractate 33, n. 5 in FC 88, p. 55: "What else did he signify to you when he wrote on the ground with his finger? For the Law was written by the finger of God...."

[37] See Job 14:4 in the LXX.

[38] See Matt 18:15-18.

follows that he does not sin when he accuses someone.[39] – If you say, that he does not sin by doing this, but by not doing it worthily, it is objected that this is not a privileged work.[40] – I answer that it has to be maintained that a sinner in mortal sin, who accuses another person, is either a notorious sinner who has committed the same kind of sin and then gives scandal because of what he is and sins in a twofold manner, that is, by giving scandal and acting contemptuously. Now the hidden sinner, whether he has committed the same sin or a different sin, if he knows that he has sinned and considers a brother's sin and judges the brother and neglects himself, he sins by acting contemptuously, not by accusing his brother, but because, although he should have examined himself and cleansed himself of sin, he was negligent and acted contemptuously. So this is how the Lord's response is to be understood. So the answer to this question is obvious.[41]

16. Question 4 revolves about the absolution of the woman's sin. – 1. It seems that the Lord acted directly against the Law, since whom the Law condemned, he himself absolved. And it was still the time of the Law and its observance. – 2. Likewise, it seems that he acted unjustly, for he did not impose a punishment and seemed to have given a license to sin.[42] – I answer that the Lord did not act against the Law, since he was above the Law

[39] Some light is thrown on this discussion by Augustine, Epistola 82 n. 7 in CSEL xxxiiii, p. 357 and FC 12, p. 395: "Surely, when anyone does what he ought to do, he acts uprightly, and therefore that man accuses him falsely who says that he has not rightly done what he knew he ought to do."

[40] See Book II, d. 40 a. 2. q 1 of Bonaventure's *Sentence Commentary*. An example of a privileged work or deed is martyrdom.

[41] See Book IV, d. 19 dub. 4 of Bonaventure's *Sentence Commentary*.

[42] See Augustine, Tractate 33, n. 6 in FC 88, p. 57: "What does it mean, O Lord? Do you, therefore, countenance sins?" Hugh of St. Cher,

and could dispense from a precept of the Law. Further, he did not act against the Law, because the accusers did not persist in their accusations, and the woman remained alone without any accuser, and the Law did not condemn such a person. Thus, he first repulsed his adversaries with the tongue of justice, and afterwards, when she was left by herself, he looked at her with the eyes of mercy.[43] Even if his adversaries had persisted, he would not have condemned her, for as Augustine observes:"Far from it that he, who came to save, would condemn."[44] – 2. With regard to the second issue it has to be said that he was the Lord, and therefore could completely condone. Nevertheless, in condoning, he did not countenance sins, since he forbade her to sin anymore. And he did this, as Augustine says: "God does not condemn the person, but sin."[45]

John 8:12-59
The dignity and nobility of the Lord's teaching

17. *Again, therefore, Jesus said to them*[46] *I am the light of the world.* Now that the perversity of the Jews has been confounded, the Lord manifests the dignity and nobility

---

p. 337v,f raises the same issue that Bonaventure does and phrases it in the words of Augustine just quoted in this note.

[43] See Augustine, Tractate 33, n. 6 in FC 88, p. 56: "But he, who had repulsed his adversaries with the tongue of justice, raising the eyes of gentleness to her...." Hugh of St. Cher, p. 337l writes, without attribution to Augustine:"But he, who had expelled his adversaries with the tongue of justice, looked at her with the eyes of his gentleness."

[44] See Tractate 33, n. 5 in CCSL xxxvi, p. 308 and FC 88, p. 55: "But far be it from him to say, 'Let her be stoned!' For he came not to destroy what he had found but to seek out what had been lost."

[45] See Tractate 33, n. 6 in CCSL xxxvi, p. 309 and FC 88, p. 57: "Therefore, the Lord also condemned, but the sin, not the person."

[46] On p. 357 n. 7 QuarEd rightly notice that the Vulgate has *dicens* ("saying"). But see John 8:12 n. 18 below where Bonaventure does read *dicens* ("saying").

of his teaching in this second part. Now the nobility of his teaching consists in this that it frees from *the blindness of error, the servitude of sin, the condemnation of death*. So it is first shown how it liberates from the blindness of error and infidelity. Second, how it liberates from the servitude of sin where verse 21 states: "So Jesus again said to them," etc. Third, how it liberates from the condemnation of death where verse 51 reads: "Amen, amen I say to you: If anyone keeps my word, he will never taste death."[47]

JOHN 8:12-20
CHRIST'S TEACHING LIBERATES FROM THE DARKNESS OF ERROR

So first he commends his teaching because it liberates from *the darkness of error*, and he does this in the following manner. First, *the commendation of his teaching* is suggested. Second, *the approbation of the commendation* on account of the rebuke of the Jews. Third, *the manifestation of Jewish ignorance*. Fourth, *Christ's evasion from unbelief*.

18. (Verse 12). So first the commendation of the teaching is suggested by this: that the Lord says that those who accompany him and abide by his teaching are freed from darkness. For this reason the text says: *Again, therefore, Jesus said to them*, since after having confounded their perversity, he resumes speaking, so that he might show the nobility of his teaching.

---

[47] On p. 357 n. 8 QuarEd accurately indicate that the Vulgate reads *videbit* ("will see") whilst Bonaventure has *gustabit* ("will taste"). John 8:52 reads: "And you say: if anyone keeps my word, he will never taste death."

So he commends his teaching, *saying: I am the light of the world*, that is, of human beings living in the world. John 1:9 above says: "It enlightens every person," etc.[48] *I am the light of the world*, through instruction. Sirach 24:44 reads: "I make teaching to shine forth to all as the morning light." *The person who follows me*, through the captivity of his intellect, as 2 Corinthians 10:5 states: "bringing every intellect into captivity to the obedience of Christ." Such a person follows Christ. John 12:26 below says: "If anyone serves me, let that person follow me." Such a person *does not walk in the darkness*, through the blindness of error. Ephesians 4:17 has: "You are not to walk, as the Gentiles walk, in the futility of their mind." John 12:35 below reads: "Walk while you have the light, so that darkness may not overtake you." *But* such a person *will have the light of life*, through the vision of divine glory. *But* such a person *will have* this, because in the future it will be the light of life which cannot be extinguished. But it can now. For Psalm 35:10 states: "With you is[49] the fountain of life, and in your light we will see light."[50] Another interpretation. He says *will have*, because now we walk by faith, but then we will have comprehension by sight.[51] But in the present the light is not comprehended, but is obscured by the flesh. Thus Bernard comments: "No one could bear to look at the splendor of that eternal light, unless it were obscured by the thin cloud of his flesh."[52] So he says what

---

[48] John 1:9 says: "It was the true light that enlightens every person who comes into the world."

[49] The Vulgate does not read *est* ("is").

[50] Hugh of St. Cher, p. 338d also cites Ps 35:10 and reads *est* ("is").

[51] Underneath Bonaventure's interpretation is 2 Cor 5:7: "We walk by faith and not by sight."

[52] These words are not found as such in Bernard. See, e.g., Sermon 20 n. 7 on The Song of Songs in SBOp 1.119. See Augustine, Tractate 34 n. 4 in FC 88, p. 64: "Do not despise the cloud of the flesh; he is covered

was said in Luke 1:35: "The power of the Most High will overshadow you."[53]

19. (Verse 13). *So the Pharisees said to him*. This verse introduces the second point, that is, the approbation of the commendation on account of the rebuke by the Jews. For they were rebuking him, because he was commending himself. So they say: *You are bearing witness to yourself. Your witness is not true*, that is, it is not to be accepted as truthful. For it is said in Proverbs 27:2: "Let another praise you, and not your own mouth. A stranger, and not your own lips." The Lord joins his answer to this censure. So he says:

20. (Verse 14). *Jesus responded and said to them* and defended his witness as true, since it was certain, because it was legitimate. Therefore, he states: *Even if I bear witness to myself, my witness is true*, since I am God. Numbers 23:19: "God is not a human being that God should lie." So his witness is true and acceptable, for it is *certain*. For he says: *Because I know where I come from*[54] *and where I go*. Proverbs 12:17 reads: "The person who speaks forth what he knows is a judge of justice,[55] but the person who lies is a deceitful witness." John 13:3 below reads: "Knowing ... that he had come forth from God and was going to God." But you are wrongly rebuking me. Thus he adds: *But you do not know where I came from or where I go*. Psalm 81:5 states: "They have not known or

---

with a cloud not that he may be darkened, but that [his brightness] may be rendered endurable."

[53] Hugh of St. Cher, p. 338h also cites Luke 1:35.

[54] On p. 358 n. 9 QuarEd correctly indicate that the Vulgate reads *veni* ("have come") whereas Bonaventure has *venio* ("come").

[55] The Vulgate reads *index iustitiae* ("index of justice") while Bonaventure has *iudex iustitiae* ("judge of justice").

understood. They walk in darkness." And he shows that they do not know this when he says:

21. (Verse 15). *You judge according to the flesh.* 1 Corinthians 3:3 says: "Since there are jealousy and strife among you, are you not carnal and walking in a human way?" Another interpretation is that in their judgment they believed that he was merely a human being and was seeking his own glory as a human being would. For this reason they rejected his testimony. *But*[56] *I judge no one,* that is, at the present time. John 3:17 above reads: "God did not send his Son into the world to judge the world." *I do not judge,* by condemning someone, as you are now condemning me. And I do this, not because I am unable or do not know. Rather I know and am able. Therefore, he continues:

22. (Verse 16). *Even if I judge, my judgment is true.* It is not carnal, nor uncertain, nor superficial. Isaiah 11:3 reads: "He will not judge according to what he sees nor reprove according to what he hears." And therefore, I cannot err in judgment. *Because I am not alone, but with me is the one who sent me, the Father.* So since I do not separate myself from him in judging, I do not err. John 5:30 above states: "I can do nothing by myself, but[57] as I hear, I judge, and my judgment is just." – Not only is my witness certain, but it is also legitimate, since it was adequate according to the norms of the Law. Thus he says:

23. (Verse 17). *And in your Law it is written that the witness of two persons is true,* that is, acceptable. Deuteronomy

---

[56] On p. 358 n. 12 QuarEd accurately mention that the Vulgate does not read *autem* ("But").

[57] The Vulgate does not read *sed* ("but").

19:15 says: "Through the mouth of two or three witnesses every word stands."[58]

24. (Verse 18). *It is I who bear witness to myself, and the one who sent me, the Father, bears witness to me.* Therefore, my witness is not to be rejected. 1 John 5:7 reads: "There are three who bear witness in heaven: the Father, the Word, and the Holy Spirit."

25. (Verse 19). *So they said to him.* The third point surfaces here, that is, the manifestation of Jewish ignorance. It manifests itself first in their questioning, since they did not understand what he was saying that the Father would give witness to Christ himself. Wherefore, they inquire: *Where is your father?* They do not ask: *Who* he is, but *where* he is. And their question is inordinate, since he is everywhere. Jeremiah 23:24 says: "I fill the heaven and the earth."[59] Therefore, they warrant a rebuke rather than satisfaction. And so the text adds: *Jesus answered them.*[60] Their ignorance is clear in Christ's answer, by which he reproves them and shows that their question about the Father is foolish, since, by ignoring the Son himself, they cannot know the Father. So he says: *You do not know me, and you do not know*[61] *my Father.* And the reason behind this is that I am the way of knowing the Father. So he states: *If you knew me, you would perhaps also know my Father.* Matthew 11:27 provides the reason:

---

[58] The Vulgate reads *stabit* ("will stand") whereas Bonaventure has *stat* ("stands").

[59] Jer 23:24 reads: "Shall a person be hid in a secret place, and I see him not, says the Lord? Do not I fill heaven and earth, says the Lord?"

[60] On p. 359 n. 1 QuarEd rightly notice that the Vulgate does not read *eis* ("them").

[61] On p. 359 n. 2 QuarEd correctly indicate that the Vulgate does not read *scitis* ("you know"). That is, Bonaventure has *scitis* ("you know") twice.

"No one knows the Son except the Father nor does anyone know the Father except the Son, and the person to whom the Son chooses to reveal him." Thus 1 John 2:23 says: "No one who disowns the Son has the Father. But[62] the person who confesses the Son also has the Father."

26. (Verse 20). *Jesus spoke these words.* This verse introduces Christ's wondrous escape from Jewish unbelief, for he was reproving them and was within their grasp, and they did not seize him. So the text states: *Jesus spoke these words in the treasury, while teaching in the temple,* since the treasury was in the right section of the temple.[63] *And no one seized him,* and this by a divine miracle, not by human desire. *Because his hour had not yet come.*[64] The Evangelist frequently repeats these words, in order to show that Christ would be seized and suffer according to his own will, as is said below in John 10.[65]

It should be noted that the place where offerings are made is called a treasury. And there were three places set aside for this purpose. One was called gazophylacium, where offerings for repairs on the temple building were made. Gazophylacium is said to come from gaza, which means riches, and from phylaxe, which means to guard.[66] About

---

[62] The Vulgate does not read *autem* ("But").

[63] See 2 Kings 12:9: "And Jehoiada the high priest took a chest and bore a hole in its top and set it by the altar at the right hand of those who came into the house of the Lord. And the priests who kept the doors put therein all the money that was brought to the temple of the Lord."

[64] On p. 359 n. 3 QuarEd accurately mention that the Vulgate reads *necdum* ("not yet") whereas Bonaventure has *nondum* ("not yet").

[65] See John 10:17-18: "... I lay down my life that I may take it up again. No one takes it from me, but I lay it down of myself."

[66] This etymology is found in Book X of Rabanus Maurus, *Commentariorum in Ezechielem Libri Viginti.* See PL 110:922B: "Since in Greek the word phylaxe means to guard and gazae in Persian

this Luke 21:1 states: "Looking up, Jesus saw those[67] who were putting their gifts into the gazophylacium."–Another place or repository was called corban or corbana and was designated for offerings that pertained to the priests. About this Matthew 27:6 states: "It is not lawful to put them into the corbana, because it is blood money."[68] – The third repository was called musach, where the tribute of kings was placed. 2 Kings 16:18 reads: "Musach of the Sabbath."[69] – Another interpretation: musach pertains to offerings made on solemnities. Corban refers to votive offerings. Gazophylacium refers to freewill offerings.[70]

QUESTIONS

27. Question 1 focuses on what the Lord says in John 8:14: "If I bear witness to myself, my witness is true." – Contrary. Proverbs 27:2 reads: "Let another praise you, and not your own mouth. A stranger, and not your own lips."[71] – Furthermore, no one's witness on his own behalf is accepted, and the Lord said in John 5:31 above:

---

means riches, the place where riches are guarded was customarily called gazophylacium."

[67] The Vulgate specifies these people as *divites* ("rich"). Bonaventure does not read *divites* ("rich").

[68] The "them" refers to the thirty pieces of silver that had been given to Judas.

[69] See Rabanus Maurus' comment on 2 Kings 16:18 in his *Commentaria in Libros IV Regum* in PL 109:247D: "... *musach of the Sabbath* (is) a certain place or a certain structure placed in the vestibule of the temple where the kings, when they come to the temple on the Sabbath to pray, put money for alms. And so *musach of the Sabbath* is the treasury for kings, just as *corbonam* is the one for priests."

[70] Hugh of St. Cher, p. 339h has a similar, but more extended treatment on "the treasury."

[71] In his commentary on John 8:13 (n. 19) above Bonaventure also cited Prov 27:2.

"If I bear witness to myself, my witness is not true."[72] Therefore, he is contradicting himself. – Moreover, there is a question about the Lord's basing his testimony on the Law, "because the witness of two people is true."[73]

1. But this argument does not seem valid, since in the Law, when someone bears witness about himself and another about him, these two witnesses are regarded as one witness only. Wherefore, according to this the Son had nothing but a single witness.[74] – 2. Likewise, his Father was intimately related to him, and such a person, according to the law, is not admitted as a witness.[75] – 3. Further, John 10:30 below states: "The Father and I are one." Therefore, they are one. So they are not two witnesses. Or if they are two witnesses, then the Father and the Son are not one.

My answer is that it has to be said that the Son of God himself is the light, but that every creature is darkness and can, if left to itself, become dark. So since it is characteristic of the light to make itself and other things manifest, light itself can bear witness to itself. But a creature, since it is darkness, needs someone else to make it manifest.[76]

---

[72] See Book XXII, c. 5, n. 10 in *Digest of Justinian* Vol. 1. Translation edited by Alan Watson. (Philadelphia: University of Pennsylvania Press, 1998): "No one is a satisfactory witness in his own cause."

[73] See John 8:17 n. 23 above and its reference to Deut 19:15.

[74] See Chrysostom, Homily 52 n. 3 in PG 59:290-291: "For in the human realm when two people bear witness about a matter outside their pale of interest, then there is a true witness. For their testimony is twofold. However, if someone bears witness about himself, there are no longer two witnesses."

[75] See Book XXII, c. 5, n. 9 in *Digest of Justinian* Vol. 1: "A father is not a satisfactory witness for a son or a son for a father."

[76] See Augustine, Tractate 2 n. 6 in FC 78, p. 66: "Indeed, if he were not enlightened, he was darkness, like all the irreligious people, to whom, once they believed, the Apostle said, 'You were once darkness.'

Furthermore, since he is light, he cannot be darkened or turned aside. Therefore, he can judge and testify at the same time. He can also praise and be praised at the same time. But since a creature can be turned aside, it cannot and should not be both things at the same time.[77] – In addition, Proverbs is addressed to weak people who long for vain praise. – What is said in John 5:30 is understood of Christ according to his human nature. – Relative to the objection from the law that a person cannot testify on his own behalf, a similar response is necessary. If it were the case that someone could bear witness on his own behalf, then one other testimony would be satisfactory. But Christ could bear witness to himself, and presupposing this, his argument is valid. – 2. Similarly about a witness that is intimately related to oneself: Since such a person can deviate and bear false witness, that testimony is not accepted. But the heavenly Father, who is truthful, cannot deviate from the truth.[78] – 3. Now concerning the objection that the Father and Son are one, it should be noted that they are one in essence, but distinct in persons. So since in the case of true witnesses there are a distinction of persons and concord of testimony, and such are found here, therefore, his witness is exceedingly authentic.

28. Question 2 addresses John 8:19: "You do not know me," etc. For John 7:28 above said: "You both know me and know where I come from." – The answer is that John 7:28 was concerned about his humanity, but this statement

---

Now, however, since they had believed, what did he say? 'But now, however, light in the Lord.'"

[77] See Augustine, Tractate 22 n. 10 in FC 79, p. 206: "But your eyes which, when the lamp was not there, were inactive and saw nothing, now they, too, have light, but not in themselves. Accordingly, if they turn themselves away from the lamp, they are darkened; if they turn toward it, they are enlightened."

[78] See John 8:26 below: "but the one who sent me is true."

concerns his divinity. For "the person who sees me also sees the Father."[79]

29. Question 3 focuses on John 8:19: "If you knew me, you would perhaps also know my Father." Since there is no opinion in God, neither is there doubt. So what does this *perhaps* mean? – I answer that it has to be said that by means of this adverb *perhaps* "unbelief is accused here; divinity is not expressing an opinion."[80] It also suggests to us the freedom of the human will.

JOHN 8:21-50
CHRIST FREES FROM THE SERVITUDE OF SIN

30. *So Jesus again said to them*. It has been shown above that the teaching of Christ frees from the blindness of error. Now it is shown and commended as freeing from *the servitude of sin*. The division of this section is as follows. First, it shows that without knowledge of Christ *the servitude is perpetuated*. Second, it makes obvious that through the teaching and words of Christ human beings *are freed from servitude* where verse 31 says: "So Jesus said to those who believed."

---

[79] See John 14:9.

[80] See Augustine, Tractate 37 n. 3 in CCSL xxxvi, p. 333. The quotation is virtually verbatim. See also FC 88, p. 96: "He who knows all things, when he says 'perhaps' does not have doubts, but is chiding. For observe how this 'perhaps' which seems to be a word of doubt is said chidingly. For it is a word of doubt when it is said by a man who doubts precisely because he does not know; but when a word of doubt is said by God, since, of course, nothing is hidden from God, by that doubt unbelief is accused, Divinity is not expressing an opinion."

JOHN 8:21-30
WITHOUT KNOWLEDGE OF CHRIST
SERVITUDE IS PERPETUATED

So the first point proceeds in this order. First, *the threat of perpetual servitude* is set forth. Second, on account of doubt on the part of the Jews there is *an explanation of the threat*. Third is *an explication of things that are believable*. Finally, there is *the increase of those who believe*.

Verse 21. So first he proposes the threat of perpetual servitude. And this occurs when human beings die in sin, and the threat to them is final impenitence. So the text states:

31. *So Jesus again said to them: I go*, namely, to the Father through the passion. *And you will seek me*, that is, to persecute me. *And you will die in your sin*, and I will be rescued from your hands. And the reason follows: *Where I go, you cannot come*, since you could not enter into glory. Thus, he has threatened them with the death of sin and the loss of glory. The Lord said this to the Jews. He said something similar to his disciples in John 13:33 below: "Where I go, you cannot come." But he spoke to the Jews with a threat whereas he made his prediction to his disciples as a means of separation. Thus afterwards he said to Peter: "Where I go, you cannot follow now, but you will follow later."

32. (Verse 22). *So the Jews said.*[81] The Evangelist introduces the second point here, that is, the explanation of the threat on account of doubt on the part of the Jews.

---

[81] On p. 360 n. 13 QuarEd accurately indicate that the Vulgate reads *dicebant* ("kept saying") while Bonaventure has *dixerunt* ("said").

For they were in doubt about what he had said: "Where I am going, you cannot come." So they reply: *Will he kill himself, because he is saying: Where I am going, you cannot come?* Augustine comments: "Stupid words, and completely filled with foolishness. For if he were to kill himself, couldn't they themselves do likewise? If he was speaking about death, are all going to die?"[82] Because of this doubt the Lord explains his threat. And since he had mentioned two things, he gives a twofold explanation. The first item are his words: "Where I am going, you cannot come." Since he had said this about his going to the Father through glory and since sinners cannot ascend to glory, he says:

33. (Verse 23). *And he said to them: You are from below.* John 3:31 above reads: "The person who is from the earth speaks about earthly matters." *But I am from above,*[83] and so I am going above. And therefore, "where I am going, you cannot come," since as it is said in John 3:13: "No one has ascended into heaven except the person who has descended from heaven." Therefore, you descend, but I ascend. Again: *You are of this world,* since you are attached to this world through love. *But I am not of this world.*[84] So I am leaving you in the world, and "where I am going, you cannot come." John 16:28 states: "I have come forth from the Father and have come into the world. Again I leave the world and go to the Father." In this way he explains what he had said: "Where I am going." This

---

[82] See Tractate 38, n. 3 in CCSL xxxvi, p. 3. The first sentence is found in Augustine, but the next two rhetorical questions seem to be Bonaventure's paraphrase of Augustine. Hugh of St. Cher, p. 339y also quotes Augustine's first sentence and then engages in his own paraphrase.

[83] On p. 361 n. 1 QuarEd rightly notice that the Vulgate does not read *autem* ("But").

[84] On p. 361 n. 2 QuarEd accurately indicate that the Vulgate does not read *autem* ("but").

has to be understood as an expression of power, not of weakness. This also explicates what he said: "You will die in your sin."[85] Thus he repeats this, so that he may explain it:

34. (Verse 24). *Therefore, I said to you that you will die in your sins,*[86] and I explain how I understand this. *For if you do not believe that I am, you will die in your sin.* But if you believe, you will not die, which is to be understood as its opposite. Thus, Augustine notes: "Hope has been granted to the despairing, awakening has come to the sleeping."[87] John 3:36 above states: "The person who does not believe in the Son does not have[88] life, but the wrath of God rests upon him. But the person who believes in the Son of God[89] has eternal life."[90] He had promised this.

35. (Verse 25). *So they said*, etc. The third point arises here, that is, the explication of the things that are believable. For since he had explained his threat that without faith in him no one could be freed from death, saying, that they would die in sin unless they believed *that I am* – this indeed was truly implicit in what he had said – the Jews are seeking an explanation and instruction in the meaning of faith. Therefore, *they said to him: Who are you?* that unless we believe in you, we cannot be saved. They asked a similar question of John in John 1:19 above: "Who are you?" And Christ's answer follows, by which he instructed the Jews

---

[85] John 8:21.

[86] On p. 361 n. 4 QuarEd correctly mention that the Vulgate reads *quia* ("that") while Bonaventure has *quod* ("that").

[87] See Tractate 38, n. 7 in CCSL xxxvi, p. 341 and FC 88, p. 109. The citation is verbatim.

[88] The Vulgate reads *non videbit* ("will not see") while Bonaventure has *non habet* ("does not have").

[89] The Vulgate reads *Filium* ("Son") whilst Bonaventure has *Filium Dei* ("Son of God").

[90] Bonaventure inverts John 3:36a and 3:36b.

to believe in him first through those things that point to the creature fashioned by him and second through those things that point to the person of the Father where the text says: *And they did not understand.*[91] – First, for he is the creator. For which reason the text says: *Jesus said to them: Beginning,* that is, I am the creating beginning. For all things have received their existence through him as it is said above in John 1:1: "In the beginning was the Word" and again "All things were made through him."[92] – He is also the teacher, *who is speaking to you.*[93] Hebrews 1:2 states: "In these last days he has spoken to us through a Son, whom he established as heir of all things and through whom he created the world." In a similar way the Lord answered the question of the Samaritan woman: "I am, who is speaking to you."[94] And the blind man in John 9:37 below.[95] – He is also the judge, even though he is not now speaking words of condemnation, but of instruction and invitation. So the text continues:

36. (Verse 26). *I have many things to say concerning you,* that is, against you, *and to judge,* which will not remain unmentioned, not out of malice, but out of justice. *But the one who sent me is true, and the things that I heard from him, these I speak in the world.* And therefore, I judge truly. John 5:30 above states: "As I hear, I judge, and my

---

[91] John 8:27.

[92] John 1:3. Bonaventure cites John 8:25 five times in is commentary on Luke's Gospel: Luke 7:14 n. 25, 8:15 n. 22, 9:35 n. 65, 11:31 n. 66, and 22:44 n. 51.

[93] The Vulgate of John 8:25 is *Principium quia et loquor vobis* which may be translated "What I have said to you from the beginning" or "Why do I speak to you at all?" Bonaventure presupposes *Ego* ("I"), that is, "I am the beginning." For a complete discussion see *Commentary on Luke, Chapters 9-16*, pp. 1091-1092 n. 198.

[94] John 4:26.

[95] John 9:37 reads: "And Jesus said to him: You have both seen him, and he it is who is speaking to you."

judgment is just because I seek not my own will, but the will of the one who sent me." And since he had manifested himself in comparison with a creature, he now manifests himself in comparison to the Father's person, whom the Jews could not understand. So the text says:

37. (Verse 27). *And they did not understand that he was saying that God was his Father.*[96] And since they could not understand the height of his generation, he sent them to contemplate the weakness of his passion, as he says:

38. (Verse 28). *So Jesus said to them: When you have lifted up the Son of Man*, namely, on the cross. John 12:32 below states: "And I, when I am lifted up from the earth, will draw all things to myself." *Then you will know that I am*, that is, a distinct person in the Trinity. Behold, there is a distinction of persons. Exodus 3:14 reads: "I am who I am." *And that I do nothing of myself*, namely, you will know this. *But that I say only what the Father has taught me*, that is, as I have received from the Father, for the Father gives everything to the Son. And in this is manifest the emanation of generation from the Father. John 5:19 above says: "The Son can do nothing of himself, but only what he sees the Father doing." Not only will you know the distinction of persons, but also the indivisibility of essence. So the text continues:

39. (Verse 29). *And the one who sent me is with me*, on account of the unity of essence, in which there is no division. John 14:11 below states: "Do you not believe that I am in the Father and the Father is in me?" *He has not left me alone*, because of a will that disagrees with him. *Because I always do the things that are pleasing to*

---

[96] The Vulgate is different. I translate it: "And they did not understand that he was speaking to them about the Father."

him.[97] Therefore, the Son cannot be separated from the Father, because he can neither disagree with him nor disobey him. Matthew 3:17 reads: "This is my beloved Son, in whom I am well pleased." On the contrary, sinners are separated from the Lord, because they displease him through sins. 2 Chronicles 12:5 states: "You have left me, and I have left you...."

40. (Verse 30). *As he was saying these things*. This verse introduces the fourth point, that is, the increase of those who believe in Christ. This came about through this teaching. So the text continues: *As he was saying these things*, namely, the things that had just been mentioned, *many believed in him*, since his words were efficacious. John 4:41 above says: "Far more believed because of his word."

QUESTIONS

41. Question 1 deals with John 8:24a: "You will die in your sins." – It seems that he would have revealed to them their damnation. Therefore, he was forcing them to despair. Further, according to this it seems that someone could have foreknowledge of his damnation.[98] – But this does not seem to be the case, since knowledge and revelation is a gift for piety. Therefore, he is not forcing them to despair. – There is a threefold answer to this question. The Lord did not say this as a revelation, but as a threat. For he adds this condition in John 8:24b: "unless you believe." – Also it has to be said that the Lord did not

---

[97] On p. 362 n. 2 QuarEd accurately mention that the Vulgate explicitly reads *ego* ("I").

[98] See Book II, d. 4. a. 2. q. 2 of Bonaventure's *Sentence Commentary*.

say this to people who adhered to him out of faith. So he was not forcing them to despair. So he did not say this to believers, but to non-believers. – A third point is this: The Lord was speaking to the multitude. Therefore, his words have to be taken in a general way and not applied to anyone in particular.[99]

42. Question 2 focuses on John 8:25 and the word beginning. Since beginning refers to the cause of emanation, which is fitting first and principally to the Father, how is it that the Son appropriates it to himself? – I answer that it has to be maintained that this word, beginning, sometimes is taken in an essential sense. In this meaning it refers to a relationship to a creature, and thus the entire Trinity is said to be the beginning. At other times this word is taken as a distinguishing characteristic. In this sense the Father and the Son are the single principle of the Holy Spirit. At yet other times it is taken in a personal sense, and thus beginning refers to the very fontal or fundamental emanation that is found in the Father. And so Augustine says: "the Father is the beginning of divinity."[100] – Therefore, it should be said that this word, beginning, in as far as it means in an essential sense is applied to the person of the Son in a twofold manner.

---

[99] See Augustine, Tractate 38 n. 7 in FC 88, p. 109: "I believe, brothers, that in that multitude which heard the Lord there were also those who would believe. But as if that most severe sentence had come forth against all of them, 'In your sin you will die,' and through this even from those who would believe, hope had been taken away, some were furious, some were afraid, nay rather, not afraid, but already in despair. He recalled them to hope; for he added, 'If you do not believe that I am, you will die in your sins.' Therefore, it you do believe that I am, you will not die in your sins. Hope has been granted to the despairing...."

[100] See Book IV, c. 20 n. 29 of *De Trinitate* in *Sancti Avrelii Avgvstini, De Trinitate Libri XV (Libri I-XII)*. Edited by W. J. Mountain. (CCSL 1; Turnhout: Brepols, 1968) 200: "The Father is the beginning of deity." See Bonaventure's commentary on John 1:1 n. 2 above.

The first mode is through the characteristic feature of generation, and thus the Son is said to be beginning from the beginning, that is, begotten. Another mode is through the characteristic feature of the Word, since the Son is the Word, and this is the meaning here: "I am the beginning, who is speaking to you."

43. Question 3 asks about John 8:26.[101] Since truth is appropriated to the Son,[102] how is it that the Son, in speaking of the Father, attributes it to him? – It must be stated that he is said to be true, because he speaks true words. So since the Father speaks the Son, who is the true Word, to whom truth is appropriated, true can rightly be appropriated to the Father because he is its origin.[103]

44. Question 4 inquires about the meaning of John 8:29: "He has not left me alone, because I always do the things that are pleasing to him." – Contrary. In Matthew 27:46 the Son says during his passion: "'My God, my God, why have you abandoned me?"

I respond that it has to be said that there is an abandonment of disposition, probation, permission, eternal damnation. First, through the abandonment of disposition the Father made clear the passion to his Son for the sake of the salvation of the human race. Second,

---

[101] John 8:26 reads: "I have many things to speak and to judge concerning you, but he who sent me in true, and the things that I heard from him, these I speak in the world."

[102] See John 14:6: "I am the way, the truth, and the life."

[103] In the background is Augustine, Tractate 39 n. 7. See FC 88, p. 122: "For the Lord most clearly said, 'I am the way and the truth and the life.' Therefore, if the Son is the truth, what is the Father except what Truth itself said, 'He who sent me is true'? The Son is truth, the Father is true. I seek which is more, but I find equality. For the true Father is not true from that truth, a part of which he took, but which he wholly begot."

the abandonment of probation occurs among the just, just as the Lord left Job in the hand of Satan. The third occurs among sinners at the present time. The fourth occurs among those damned eternally. This is an abandonment without any visitation. So the Lord's word here is to be understood of the abandonment of wrath, not of the disposition of divine wisdom.[104]

John 8:31-50
CHRIST'S TEACHING FREES FROM THE SERVITUDE OF SIN

45. *So Jesus said*, etc. Now that it has been shown that without the teaching of and faith in Christ a person is in perpetual sin, the text now raises a second point: through the teaching of Christ there is *freedom from the servitude of sin*. And this section is divided into three parts. In the first there is *the promise of freedom* from the servitude of sin through Christ's teaching. Second is *the elimination of the glorying of the Jews* where verse 37 says: "I know that you are the children of Abraham." In the third part *the resultant indignation of the Jews* occurs where verse 48 states: "The Jews answered and said to him: "Are we not right in saying?"

---

[104] On p. 363 n. 2 QuarEd indicate how previous editions and some manuscripts tried to solve this obscure sentence. For example, the abandonment of wrath comprehends the third and fourth type of abandonment while the abandonment of divine wisdom encompasses the first and second.

John 8:31-36
The promise of freedom from the servitude of sin through Christ's teaching

So first through Christ's teaching *freedom is promised* and shown to come about in this order. First, *freedom is promised*. Second the promised freedom *is despised by the Jews*. Finally, *its necessity* is shown them.

46. (Verse 31). So freedom is promised to those who remain in the teaching of Christ. Thus the text states: *So Jesus said to those who had come to believe in him.*[105] And since they had come to belief, after being frightened by his threat, he attracts them by his promise, so that they might persevere. For he says: *If you abide in my word.* John 15:4 below reads: "Abide in me, and I in you. As the branch cannot bear fruit of itself, unless it remain on the vine, so neither can you unless you abide in me." Not like those, of whom it is said in Luke 8:13: "They believe for a time, and in time of temptation fall away." These do not bear fruit. But you, if you abide, *you will truly be my disciples.*

47. (Verse 32). *And you*[106] *will know the truth, and the truth will make you free.* He says that three things make a person right. First is the rectitude of affection, and this is noted in being a disciple of Christ. Second is the rectitude of intellect, and this appears in knowledge of the truth. The third is the rectitude of effect through freedom from sin, and this is noted in the freedom of truth. Another interpretation is: You will be disciples on

---

[105] On p. 363 n. 4 QuarEd accurately indicate that the Vulgate reads *ad eos ... Iudaeos* ("to them, the Jews") whereas Bonaventure does not have *Iudaeos* ("the Jews").

[106] On p. 363 n. 5 QuarEd correctly mention that while Bonaventure emphasizes the subject by *vos* ("you"), the Vulgate does not.

the way through imitation. You will know the truth in the beatification of the soul. And you will be freed by the truth from all corruption in the happy union of soul and body. Romans 8:21 states: "Creation itself will be freed from the servitude of corruption into the freedom of the glory of the children of God."[107]

48. (Verse 33). *They answered him*. This verse brings to the fore the second point, namely, how the promised freedom is belittled by the Jews, since they considered themselves to be free. For they were glorying in their *liberty*, and were not taking care of their *liberation*. So they said to him: *We are the children of Abraham, and we have never been slaves to anyone*. And thus we are free by nature. *How do you say: you will be free*, as if somehow we are not free? So they were saying that they were free, since they were born from Abraham through Isaac, who was the son of the free woman, according to what is said in Galatians 4:30: "Cast out the slave woman and her son." This was said of Hagar. "For the son of a slave woman will not be heir with the son of the free woman." This matter is treated in Genesis 21:10.[108]

49. (Verse 34). *Jesus answered them*. The third point surfaces here, as this verse shows the necessity of liberation. He points out that they are *slaves*, and that they have need of *liberation*, and *how they are liberated*. – That they are slaves spiritually, he shows by means of this reason: *The person who commits sin is a slave of sin*. But you commit sin. Therefore, you are slaves of sin. The minor premise of this reason is unspoken, for he will express it below.[109] Likewise the conclusion is left unspoken. But he

---

[107] Hugh of St. Cher, p. 340vi also cites Rom 8:21.
[108] Hugh of St. Cher, p. 341c also cites Gal 4:30 and Gen 21:10.
[109] See John 8:37-41.

does express the major premise, saying: *Amen, amen, I say to you: The person*[110] *who commits sin is a slave of sin.* Blessed Peter proves this in 2 Peter 2:19: "By whatever a person is overcome, of this also he is a slave."[111] This is the worst servitude. Thus Augustine observes: "O miserable servitude…. Sometimes when a human slave is exhausted by the harsh commands of his master, he will find rest in flight. But the slave of sin, where will he flee? With him he drags along his evil conscience wherever he is, because wherever he goes, he does not withdraw from himself."[112] – Thus it is obvious that they are slaves. And from this he proves that they need liberation. The reason is this: The person who does not abide in the house forever needs to be freed by the person who does abide, and through him he can be liberated. But the slave does not abide, but the Son does abide. Therefore, the slave needs to be and can be liberated by the Son. But you are slaves, as has just been said. "So if the Son liberates you, you will truly be free."[113] He states the minor proposition of the first reason in what follows:

50. (Verse 35). *The slave*[114] *does not abide in the house forever. The Son abides there forever.* Augustine explains: The person who is the slave of sin does not abide in the house forever, that is, finally, although he could belong to the number of people in the present Church.[115] Such

---

[110] On p. 363 n. 11 QuarEd rightly notice that the Vulgate reads *omnis qui* ("everyone who").

[111] Hugh of St. Cher, p. 341b also cites 2 Peter 2:19.

[112] This is Bonaventure's adaptation of Tractate 41 n. 4. See CCSL xxxvi, p. 359.

[113] See John 8:36.

[114] The Vulgate reads *servus autem* ("But the slave").

[115] See Tractate 41 n. 8 in FC 88, p. 142: "The house is the Church, the slave is the sinner. Many sinners enter the Church. He did not therefore say, 'The slave' is not in the house, but 'does not remain in the house forever.'"

slaves, even though they are in the house with good people, nevertheless do not have a wedding garment. Therefore, they are cast out, according to what Matthew 22:12-13 says: "Friend, how did you come in here without a wedding garment? ... Cast him forth into the darkness outside."

51. (Verse 36). *So if the Son makes you free, you will be truly free*. The Son alone, I say, is free, since he alone is without sin. For Psalm 87:5-6 states: "I have become like a human being without help, free among the dead." And the reason is given in John 14:30 below: "The prince of this world is coming, and in me he has nothing." This Son is free, so that he might free us, having become like a slave for our sakes. Philippians 2:8 reads: "He humbled himself, taking the form of a slave," etc. So he freed us by redeeming us. Isaiah 52:3 says: "You were sold gratis, and you will be redeemed without money," for, as it is said in 1 Peter 1:18-19: "You were redeemed not by perishable things, with gold and silver ... but by the precious blood of Christ Jesus,[116] as of a lamb without blemish and without spot." Not, I insist, that we might again be slaves, but free. For Galatians 5:13 says: "You have been called to freedom, brothers and sisters. Only do not use freedom as an occasion for the flesh, but be slaves of one another through the love of the Spirit."[117]

QUESTIONS

52. Question 1 examines John 8:33: "We are children of Abraham and have never been slaves." – Contrary. 1. They served the Egyptians. For Deuteronomy 6:13 reads:

---

[116] The Vulgate does not read *Iesu* ("Jesus").
[117] The Vulgate does not have *spiritus* ("Spirit").

"The Lord led you ... out of the house of servitude."[118] – 2. Furthermore, they were slaves of Nabuchadnezzar during the Babylonian captivity of seventy years.[119] – If you say that they were speaking about themselves and not about their ancestors, the objection is raised that even then they were paying tribute to the Romans. For they asked in Matthew 22:17: "Is it lawful to give tribute to Caesar or not?"

One response to this is that they were lying, as they often did, and had become forgetful of God's benefits. For Augustine comments: "Oh, windbag! This is not grandeur, but pomposity! ... How have you spoken truly? Joseph was sold. The ... prophets were led into captivity. The people in Egypt were slaves in mud and brick.... Even you yourselves were paying tribute."[120] – Another answer is that they understood this according to the customary practice that obtained among them by precept of the Law. Leviticus 25:44 reads: "Let your male and female slaves be from the nations that are round about you." – Yet another response makes a distinction among servitudes. There is a servitude that is a condition from origin. Thus, the son of a slave is a slave. And they understand themselves in this way. Such people are called slaves from bodily birth. There is also servitude by oppression through domination. They do not understand themselves as slaves in this manner.[121]

---

[118] Bonaventure has modified Deut 6:13. For example, the Vulgate reads *te* ("you" singular) whereas Bonaventure has *vos* ("you" plural).

[119] See 2 Chron 36.

[120] This is an abbreviation and adaptation of Tractate 41, n. 2. See CCSL xxxvi, p. 358.

[121] Justinian Law seems to lie behind this response. See Book I, title 5, Human Status, n. 5 in *The Digest of Justinian*, Volume 1: "5.Marcian, *Institutes, book 1*: Of slaves, to be sure, there is but a single condition; of free men, on the other hand, some are freeborn (*ingenui*) and some are freedmen. 1. People are brought under our power as

53. Question 2 asks: Since sinners do everything that they want and the just do not, why is it said that sinners are slaves? – It has to be maintained that the sinner is rightly said to be the slave of sin, since it is great servitude to follow an evil will; and on account of the servile conditions that are found in the sinner, on account of which he is rightly called a slave. – For the slave is vile. So too is the sinner. 1 Kings 1:21 states: "I and my son Solomon will be sinners," that is, vile.[122] – Slaves are fed with vile food. So too sinners. Luke 15:16: The prodigal son "longed to fill his belly with the pods of the pigs."[123] – Slaves engage in vile labor. So do sinners. Exodus 1:14 reads: "They overworked them with hard works in clay and brick and all manner of servitude...."[124] – The slave is treated vilely, and so is the sinner. Jeremiah 16:13 states: "You will serve

---

slaves either by the civil law or by the *jus gentium*. This happens by civil law if someone over twenty years of age allows himself to be sold with a view to sharing in the price. By the *jus gentium*, people become slaves on being captured by enemies or by birth to a female slave."

[122] Hugh of St. Cher, p. 341b gives seven reasons why sinners are slaves of sin. His fourth reason reads: "Because, just as slaves are reputed as vile, the opprobrium of men and women, and the abjection of the people. Jer 2:36 says: 'How exceedingly vile have you become, going the same ways over again.' 1 Kings 1:21 states: 'I and my son, Solomon, will be sinners,' that is, we will be reputed to be vile."

[123] Luke 15:16 reads: "He longed to fill his belly with the pods that the pigs were eating." Hugh of St. Cher, p. 341b provides his second reason: "Since sinners like slaves are fed the most vile food. For it is said of the prodigal son in Luke 15:16 that he longed to fill his belly with the pods of the pigs." Hugh of St. Cher goes on to cite Lam 4:5 ('Those who were brought up in scarlet have embraced dung') and Job 30:4 ('The root of junipers was their food'). Hugh of St. Cher then gives a six-line interpretation of the root of junipers.

[124] See Hugh of St. Cher, p. 341b: "The seventh reason is, because they engage in the most vile and most laborious works. For Ps 80:7 says: 'His hands have served with baskets.'" Hugh of St. Cher then goes on to give the various meanings of "basket."

strange gods ... who will give you no rest."[125] – The slave is a stranger to wages. Hosea 8:7 says: "There is no standing stalk in it.[126] The bud will yield no meal. If[127] it should yield, strangers will eat it."[128] – The slave is a stranger to the secrets of his Lord. So too is the sinner. John 15:15 below has: "No longer do I call you slaves ... but friends, because all things that I have heard from my Father I have made known to you." He does not reveal himself to sinners, since they are in darkness.[129] – The slave is a stranger to honorable intimacy. Romans 8:15 reads: "You have not received a spirit of servitude so as to be again in fear."[130] – The slave is a stranger to an inheritance. So too is the sinner. Job 27:19 states: "When the rich person falls asleep, he will take nothing with him."[131] Galatians 4:30 reads: "The son of the slave woman will not be heir with the son of the free woman."

---

[125] See Hugh of St. Cher, p. 341b: "And first, because it is the job of slaves to do much work. For Jeremiah 16:13 says: 'You will serve strange gods day and night who will give you no rest.'"

[126] The Vulgate reads *in eis* ("in them") whilst Bonaventure has *in eo* ("in it").

[127] The Vulgate reads *quodsi et* ("and if") whereas Bonaventure has *quodsi* ("if").

[128] See Hugh of St. Cher, p. 341b: "The third reason: because nothing that the slave earns, is his, but belongs entirely to his master. Thus the sinner does nothing useful to himself for eternal life.... Hos 8:7 reads: 'There is no standing stalk in them. The bud does not yield meal. If it should yield, strangers will eat it....'"

[129] Hugh of St. Cher, p. 341b provides no parallel.

[130] Hugh of St. Cher, p. 341b provides no parallel.

[131] See Hugh of St. Cher, p. 341b: "The sixth reason: because they cannot make a will.... Job 27:19 says: 'When the rich person falls asleep, he takes nothing with him,' since he gives nothing for his soul."

John 8:37-47
Elimination of the glorying of the Jews

54. *I know that you are the children of Abraham.* After it has been shown that freedom derives from the teaching of Christ, here the text presents *the elimination of the glorying of the Jews*, since they were glorying that they were free by nature. And the Lord accomplishes this in the following order. First he suggests that *being a child of a person is of two types*: according to *nature* and *imitation*. Second he shows that *they are not the children of Abraham by imitation*. Third *they are not the children of God*. Fourth, *they are children of the devil*.

Verse 37. So first he suggests that there are two types of being a child of a person: through nature and imitation. *Through natural generation* when he says: *I know that you are the children of Abraham*, that is, begotten according to the flesh. Isaiah 51:2 states: "Look unto Abraham, your father, and to Sarah who bore you." And you have this father through generation, but you have another through imitation. For he says: *But you are seeking to kill me, because my word takes no hold in you.* Sirach 21:17 reads: "The heart of a fool is like a broken vessel. It will hold no wisdom." Proverbs 9.[132] And this indeed is the work of iniquity, and according to this you have another father whom you are imitating. Thus:

55. (Verse 38). *What I have seen with the Father, this*[133] *I speak*, imitating him. Ephesians 5:1 says: "Be imitators of God as dearly beloved sons." *And you do what you have*

---

[132] Bonaventure cites no specific passage. Prov 9:7 is suggested: "The person who teaches a scorner does an injury to himself. And the person who rebukes a wicked person gets a blot for himself."

[133] The Vulgate does not read *hoc* ("this").

seen with your father. Thus they have a father through imitation. Thus they had a twofold father: according to the flesh and imitation. So Abraham had two types of children. Romans 9:7-8 states: "Not all these[134] are children who are descendants of Abraham ... but those who are children of the promise."

56. (Verse 39). *They answered and said to him*. The second point surfaces here, for he shows that they are not children of Abraham by imitation, as they themselves were boasting about. For this reason they said to him: *Abraham is our father*. So they were repeating what he had said: they were doing the works of the father.[135] And the Lord shows that his thought was not fixed on that father. So *Jesus said to them: If you are children of Abraham, do the works of Abraham*, that is, if you want to be children by imitation, as you are according to the flesh. Do the works of Abraham or else you will be glorying in vain. Matthew 3:9 states: "And do not think to say: We have Abraham for our father. For I say to you that God is able out of these stones to raise up children from Abraham." And since you are not doing the works of Abraham, the crippling inference must be drawn that you should not be called his children. So he continues:

57. (Verse 40). *But as it is, you are seeking to kill me, one who has spoken the truth to you which I heard from God*, and so I am righteous and innocent. But *This is not what Abraham did*, since it is wicked and forbidden by the Law. Exodus 23:7 reads: "You shall not kill an innocent and righteous person." Wherefore, you have a different father whom you are imitating. For this reason the text adds:

---

[134] The Vulgate does not have *hi* ("these").
[135] See John 8:33, 37.

58. (Verse 41). *But*[136] *you are doing the works of your father.* Chrysostom observes: "The works of Abraham were faith, obedience, meekness. Yours are non-faith, wickedness, and cruelty."[137] – *So they said to him.* The third point is found in this verse, for it is shown that *they are not children of God.* For since they had already understood that he was speaking about a spiritual father, they commend themselves to him as children of God because they worship God and are not given to idolatry which Scripture calls fornication. Thus the text states: *We have not been born of fornication,* fornicating with idols according to what Jeremiah 2:20 says: "Under every green tree you have committed fornication." And "You have polluted the earth with your fornications."[138] We have not acted in this way, but *we have one Father, God,* whom we worship according to his rule. Exodus 20:3 reads: "You shall not have strange gods before me." Yet they did not have this God. Malachi 1:6 states: "If I am a father, where is my honor? And if I am a Lord, where is my fear?" And since they were vainly glorying, he shows that they are not children of God. Thus the text adds:

59. (Verse 42). *Jesus says to them:*[139] *If God were your father, you would surely love me,* as your brother, since

---

[136] On p. 366 n. 4 QuarEd accurately indicate that the Vulgate does not read *autem* ("But").

[137] See Homily 54 n. 3 in PG 59:300: "But what are his works? Meekness, reverence, obedience. You, on the contrary, are inhuman and cruel." See Hugh of St. Cher, p. 342g: "Chrysostom. What are the works of Abraham? Meekness, humility, obedience, faith. You, on the contrary, are unmerciful, cruel, non-believing."

[138] Jer 3:2. Hugh of St. Cher, p. 342v,a refers to Jer 3:9: "She (Israel) has committed fornication with wood and stone."

[139] On p. 366 n. 7 QuarEd correctly mention that the Vulgate reads *Dixit ergo eis Iesus* ("So Jesus said to them") while Bonaventure has *Dicit eis Iesus* ("Jesus says to them").

the spirit of adoption is the spirit of love.[140] Romans 8:16 says: "You have received the spirit of adoption as children, in whom we cry out: Abba, Father." *For from*[141] *God I came forth*, that is, as the Son through generation. *And have come* into the world through the incarnation,[142] and thus I was begotten by him as well as sent by him.[143] Thus *neither*[144] *have I come of myself, but he has sent me.* I have not come on my own authority. Hebrews 5:5 states: "Christ did not glorify himself that he had become high priest." For a contrary sending see Jeremiah 23:21: "They ran, and I did not send them."[145] Likewise, Exodus 4:13 says: "I beseech you, O Lord. Send whom you are going to send." And nevertheless you do not love me, and he proves this when he asks them:

60. (Verse 43). *Why do you not understand my speech?* by believing in me. The reason for this is hatred, *Because you cannot listen to my word*, on account of hatred and

---

[140] See Augustine, Tractate 42, n. 8 in FC 88, p. 154: "You say that God is your father; recognize me at least as your brother."

[141] On p. 366 n. 8 QuarEd rightly notice that the Vulgate reads *ex Deo* ("from God") while Bonaventure has *a Deo* ("from God").

[142] See Hugh of St. Cher, p. 342v,e: "For I have come forth from God (*ex Deo*)] through eternal generation, having the same essence from him. Likewise, by temporal mission in the flesh."

[143] See Augustine, Tractate 42 n. 8 in FC 88, pp. 154-155: "The sending of Christ, then, is the incarnation. Indeed, that the Word proceeded from God is an eternal procession.... His coming is his humanness; his abiding is his divinity. His divinity is that to which we are going; his humanity is the way by which we are going."

[144] On p. 366 n. 9 QuarEd accurately indicate that the Vulgate reads *neque enim* ("for neither") whilst Bonaventure has *neque* ("neither").

[145] Jer 23:21 reads: "I did not send prophets, yet they ran. I have not spoken to them, yet they prophesied."

envy. Wisdom 2:15 says: "It is burdensome for us ... to see" him.[146]

61. (Verse 44). *The father from whom you are is the devil.* This is the fourth point, for having shown that they are not children of God, he shows that they are children of the devil, so that all their glorying may be eliminated. He sets forth his thesis when he says: *The father from whom you are is the devil.* "From" does not mean generation here, but through imitation of his example. Ezekiel 16:3 reads: "Your father was an Amorite, and your mother a Hittite."[147] And 1 John 3:8 states: "The person who commits sin is from the devil." – He proves his thesis by showing that they are imitating the devil. Thus: *It is your will to do the desires of your father.* These are the desires, of which 1 Timothy 6:9 says: They are "many useless and harmful desires that plunge people into destruction and damnation." He shows this, because they imitate him in two matters, that is, in murder and in lying. In lying the intellect is bent. In murder the affections are bent. So he says: *He was a murderer from the beginning*, that is, after the beginning of the human race, since he led the first human to death by promising life and negating death. Genesis 3:4 reads: "He said: You will never die."[148] And Wisdom 2:23-24 states: "God created human beings incorruptible.... But by the envy of the devil death came into the world," etc. And in this you are imitating him.

---

[146] Hugh of St. Cher, p. 342v,k attributes the Jews' lack of hearing to envy and a malicious and earthly will that does not recognize heavenly words and goes on to cite Wis 2:15.

[147] See Hugh of St. Cher, p. 342v,l: "Since you are from the devil, his children, not through birth, as the Manichees say, but through imitation. For it is said in another place to the Jews: Your father is an Amorite, etc. Ez 16:3."

[148] Gen 3:4 says: "But the serpent said to the woman: You will never die the death."

As was said above, you want to kill me.[149] – They are also imitating him in lying. Thus the text continues: *And he has not stood in the truth*. Rather he has fallen down into falsehood and vanity. Isaiah 14:12 reads: "How have you fallen from heaven, O Lucifer, who did rise in the morning?" *Because there is no truth in him*. For because of the sin of pride he did not recuperate. Ezekiel 28:19 states: "You have become nothing, and you will be never more." *When he tells a lie, he speaks from his own nature*, since it issues from himself and is not suggested by someone else. *For he is a liar and the father thereof*, that is, of the lie. Job 41:25 says: "He is king over all the children of pride." Augustine observes: "The devil is the father of the lie. God is the father of the truth. Depart from the father of the lie and run towards the father of the truth. Embrace the truth, so that you may receive freedom."[150] All liars, who hate the truth, are children of this father. And the Jews are such people. And the Lord proves his point that they hate the truth, as he says:

62. (Verse 45). *But since I speak the truth, you do not believe me*, and therefore you hate the truth. Psalm 4:3 reads: "O human beings, how long will you be dull of heart?" And since they could respond that they do not believe because they hate truth but rather because they hate iniquity, the text adds:

63. (Verse 46). *Who of you will convict me of sin?*[151] As if he were saying: No one can. On this account Job is censured in Job 15:3: "You censure with words the person who is not equal to you." That is, why do you not believe me? *If I*

---

[149] See John 8:37, 40.

[150] This is an adaptation of Tractate 42 n. 13. See CCSL xxxvi, p. 371.

[151] The Vulgate reads *arguit* ("convicts") while Bonaventure has *arguet* ("will convict").

speak the truth, why do you not believe me? Certainly this is not due to my sin, but to your malice. And he proves this:

64. (Verse 47). *The person who is of God hears the words of God.* 1 John 4:6 reads: "The person who knows God listens to us. The person who is not of God does not listen to us." But you do not listen, and why? *The reason you do not hear is that you are not of God*, but rather of the devil. Sirach 3:31 states: "A good ear will listen to wisdom with all desire." The Jews were doing the contrary and not listening. Acts 7:51 says: "Stiff-necked and uncircumcised in heart and ear, you always oppose the Holy Spirit."

JOHN 8:48-50
INDIGNATION OF THE JEWS AT CHRIST'S CENSURE[152]

65. (Verse 48). *So the Jews answered and said.*[153] After he has shown what freedom means and has eliminated the grounds for the boasting of the Jews, the Evangelist treats the *indignation of the Jews* at the Lord's censure. And a sign of their indignation is *the hurling of abuse*. First is *the hurling of abuse*. Second is *a patient response*. Third is *the reason for the patient response*.

First they hurl abuse: *Are we not right in saying that you are Samaritan and have a demon?* Since the Lord had said that they were not children of Abraham, but of the devil, they cast a double aspersion at him. The first one against the Lord's first point: *You are a Samaritan*, not

---

[152] Bonaventure did not indicate this subdivision earlier in n. 54 above.

[153] On p. 367 n. 8 QuarEd correctly maintain that the Vulgate reads *dixerunt ei* ("said to him").

a child of Abraham. The second against the second: *You have a demon* and do not imitate God, but the devil whose teaching you impart and by whose help you perform signs. Thus Matthew 12:24 states: "By Beelzebul, the prince of demons, you cast out demons."

66. (Verse 49). *Jesus answered.* The Evangelist introduces his second point here: the patient answer, for he does not respond to the entire insult, but to a part. So he says: *I do not have a demon*, by whose power I perform works for my own glory. *But I honor my Father*, who is in heaven, since he was doing everything for the glory of the Father, according to what the Apostle says in 1 Corinthians 10:31: "Do everything for the glory of God." *And you dishonor me*, throwing contumely at me, with the consequence that you are dishonoring the Father. John 5:23 above states: "The person who does not honor the Son does not honor the Father who sent him."

67. (Verse 50). *I*[154] *do not seek my own glory.* Here is the third point, that is, the reason for the patient answer. For he was not responding to glorify himself. But he put up with their abuse, not because it was true, but because he didn't care about glory. So he says: *I do not seek my own glory*, and therefore I do not respond to your contumely. Jerome comments: "The person who does not seek glory does not feel contumely."[155] So I am not concerned about the contumely hurled my way, but you may not believe that you are immune from sin and worthy of retribution.

---

[154] On p. 367 n. 12 QuarEd accurately mention that the Vulgate reads *Ego autem* ("But I").

[155] See *Epistola* 108 n. 3 in PL 22:880: "By fleeing from glory, she (Paula) merited glory. She follows virtue like a shadow. Scorning her suitors, she relishes those who contemn her." See Hugh of St. Cher, p. 343v,a where the same citation from Jerome occurs that Bonaventure has.

Thus he says: *There is one who seeks and may judge,*[156] namely, the Father, who seeks the glory of the Son. John 12:28 below says: "I have both glorified it, and I will glorify it again."[157] *And he may judge.* As if he were saying: I reserve these for his judgment. Gregory observes: "The Son reserves judgment to the Father for the contumelies he has received, so that he might truly teach us how patient we must be when the judge himself does not wish to avenge himself."[158]

QUESTIONS

68. Question 1 deals with John 8:38: "You do what you have seen with your father." – But they had never seen the devil. – And besides, weren't they able to sin by themselves? – I answer that it should be noted that even if human beings are aware that they have sinned by themselves, nevertheless, there are few or no instances during which the devil did not play a part by means of suggestion. And they are said to see the works of their father, the devil, when they see his suggestions in their heart and realize them through their actions.

69. Question 2 concerns John 8:44: "The father from whom you are is the devil." – From this verse Manichee argued that the Lord is not the maker and creator of evil people. – To this objection Augustine answers that "father" is not used here as one who generates by origin, but by imitation.[159] In like manner the preposition "from"

---

[156] The Vulgate has *iudicat* ("judges") whilst Bonaventure has *iudicet* ("may judge").

[157] The Father is speaking.

[158] See Homily 18 n. 2 of GGHG in CCSL cxli, p. 138. The citation is almost verbatim.

[159] See all of Tractate 42 n. 10.

does not refer here to an origin in the primordial being, but in a secondary or created being. Thus Augustine says: "Here they are called children not by birth, but through imitation."[160] Adam did not want to imitate God through obedience and imitated the devil through his consent to sin.

70. Question 3 deals with John 8:44: "He was a murderer from the beginning." – From this arose the opposition of Manichee that the wickedness of the devil does not have a beginning. And so it seems that there are two principles: one of good and the other of evil. – My answer is that it has to be maintained that this sentence has a fivefold explanation. – One way of understanding "he was a murderer from the beginning" is this: just as the Word was in the beginning because the Word did not have a beginning. – But this is heretical and is excluded by the words themselves, for the text does not say "in the beginning," but "from the beginning." – Another exposition is that from his very beginning he was made evil, as Psalm 103:26 seems to say: "The dragon that you have formed to play therein." – And this is heretical, because, just as it is impossible that the most intense heat freeze, so too is it impossible that the supreme good make something evil.[161] And the expression in the Psalm and expressions similar to it are to be understood after the fact.[162] – The third explanation of "he was a murderer from the beginning" is this: Immediately after the beginning, since there was a

---

[160] See Tractate 42 n. 10 in CCSL xxxvi, p. 369: "So are the Jews children of the devil? Through imitation, not through birth."

[161] On p. 368 n. 7 QuarEd cite Dionysius, *De divinis nominibus*, c. 4 §19, according to the Vercellens. Version: "Just as it is against the nature of fire that it freeze, so too is it against the nature of the good that it produce something that is not good."

[162] That is, after something has been created good and then fallen through its own free will.

short interval between creation and fall. And this is why the text adds: "He has not stood in the truth," since he did not persevere. – The fourth explanation is this: "he was a murderer from the beginning," not his own beginning, but that of the human race. Thus Augustine: "Human beings could not be murdered unless human beings had been made."[163] – The fifth interpretation of "he was a murderer from the beginning" is that in the very instant he began to be from God he was also evil from himself, just as our soul that is infused in the body. – The first two explanations are heretical while the next two are catholic. The last one is doubtful and leans towards heresy, although it is not heretical. For this reason it is not commonly held.

71. Question 4 raises an objection about John 8:44 where he says that the devil is *the father of lies*. – So since every sin is a lie, it seems that there is a single principle of sin.[164] – I answer that it has to be said that this is not the origin of evil on the level of being, as if it did not have its origin in another. But it is the origin of evil in that there was no other evil that preceded it. And indeed it is the origin of subsequent evils, not always by effecting such evil, but by occasioning and suggesting it. Therefore, the text says: "He is a liar and the father thereof," that is, of the lie.[165]

---

[163] See Tractate 42 n. 11 in CCSL xxxvi, p. 370: "For human beings could not be murdered, unless human beings had first become."

[164] See Book II, d. 5. a. 2 q. 2 of Bonaventure's *Sentence Commentary* in Omnia Opera 2:152.

[165] Bonaventure is giving a philosophical interpretation to Augustine, Tractate 42 n. 13. See FC 88, p. 159: "But the devil is a liar on his own; he himself begot his own lying, he heard it from no one. As God the Father begot his Son, Truth, so the devil after his fall begot a son, so to speak, lying.... But that one, because he did not receive the lie from elsewhere, the lie with which the serpent might kill mankind as if with poison, he is the father of the lie, as God is the Father of the Truth."

72. Question 5 focuses on what John 8:47: "The person who is of God."[166] – Some have based their error on this, maintaining that good spirits are from God materially.[167] I answer these people by saying that it is erroneous to say that there is any matter in God, for God is most simple. – But then the objection arises that if "of" here signifies origin and efficient cause and we are all from God, therefore all hear the word of God.[168] – So they heard him, didn't they? – I answer that as has been already said,[169] "of" refers not to primordial being, but to created being, and this is the being of grace and sin. And this occurs according to conformity and imitation. So "the person who is of God," through conformity of his will, "hears the words of God," by means of the ear of his heart, not his body, but the evil do not hear in this manner.

73. Question 6 seeks an answer to why the Jews raised these two objections against Christ rather than others.[170] – They had some reason why they hurled these slurs at him rather than others. – It must be stated that it seemed to them that Christ had done something or transgressed in some way in observing the Law, such as Sabbath observance and matters like this. And since the Samaritans did similar things and only observed the Law partially,[171] they said that he was a Samaritan.

---

[166] John 8:47 reads: "The person who is of God hears the words of God."

[167] See Book II, d. 17 a. 1. q. of Bonaventure's *Sentence Commentary* where he explains and refutes this opinion of the Manichees.

[168] See the second part of John 8:47: "The reason why you do not hear is that you are not of God."

[169] See question 2 n. 69 above.

[170] See John 8:48: "Are we not right in saying that you are a Samaritan and have a demon?"

[171] See Chrysostom, Homily 31 n. 2 in PG 59:177, who says that the Samaritans "did not accept all the Scriptures, but only the books of Moses. Nor did they care much for the prophets.... Now the Jews

– Furthermore, in his teaching the Lord said some things that seemed to them to be extraordinarily wise and other things that seemed to them to be very improbable because they didn't understand him. So he seemed to them to be speaking like someone who had lost his mind. And since a demon induces loss of mind, they were saying that he has a demon.[172]

74. Question 7 asks why the Lord only addressed the second of the two slurs hurled at him. – Gregory answers: "He denied the second charge, but with his silence consented to the first. For 'Samaritan' means guard, and he was the guard about whom Psalm 126:1 says: 'Unless the Lord guard the city,' etc."[173] – Another response is that it was certain that he was born a Jew. Therefore, there was no need for him to respond to something that was evidently false. – A third answer is that the censure that he was a Samaritan addressed his human nature whereas the censure that he had a demon was an attack on his divine nature and was blasphemy against the Holy Spirit, about which Matthew 12:31-32 speaks,[174] and was derogatory of the Father's glory. Therefore, the Lord taught us to put up with opprobrium directed towards

---

with all others also detested them. Thus they also reproached Christ in these words: 'You are a Samaritan and have a demon.'"

[172] See Chrysostom, Homily 55 n. 1 in PG 59:301: "For when he said anything sublime, the stupid considered it to be madness."

[173] See Homily 18 n.2 in CCSL cxli, p. 137. Bonaventure adapts Gregory's statement. Hugh of St. Cher, p. 343r interprets Samaritan to mean "guard," but supports his position from Ps 120:5 ("The Lord is your guard" and Isa 22[21]:12: "The guard said: The morning comes, and also the night."

[174] Matt 12:31-32 reads: "Every kind of sin and blasphemy will be forgiven human beings, but blasphemy against the Spirit will not be forgiven.... Whoever speaks against the Holy Spirit, it will not be forgiven...."

us, but not when it is directed against God.[175] And this is clear from his response: "I do not have a demon, but I glorify my Father."

JOHN 8:51-59
CHRIST'S TEACHING BRINGS FREEDOM
FROM THE DAMNATION OF DEATH

75. *Amen, amen I say to you.* The Lord has shown that through his teaching there is freedom from the blindness of error and from the servitude of sin. Now in a third point he shows that through it there is *freedom from the damnation of death*. And he shows this in the following way. First he shows the Jews who are reviling him the efficacy of his word. Second he shows his *superiority* to those who are debating him. Third, he shows *his eternity* to those who are wondering. Finally, he manifests *his patient humility* to those who are persecuting him.

Verse 51. So the first point is the commendation of the teaching of Christ, for those who keep it are snatched from death, and this without any doubt. So he says: *Amen, amen I say to you*, namely, I, Jesus, truly assert this: *If anyone keep my word, he will never taste death.*[176] This observation is through keeping the commandments. Qoheleth 8:5 states: "The person who keeps the commandment will find no evil." And Wisdom 6:19-20 reads: "The keeping

---

[175] See Chrysostom, Homily 55 n. 1 in PG 59:301: "When they said that they had God and Abraham as father, he attacked them. But when they said that he had a demon, he gave a meek answer. By this he teaches us that we should avenge attacks against God, but patiently bear up with those against us."

[176] On p. 369 n. 10 QuarEd accurately mention that the Vulgate reads *videbit* ("will see") while Bonaventure has *gustabit* ("will taste").

of the laws is a firm foundation of incorruption. And incorruption brings a person near to God." And such a person does not *taste* death through experience, that is, eternal death, although he might *see* it according to what Isaiah 66:24 says: "They will go out and see the cadavers of the people who have transgressed against me." Matthew 16:28 reads: "There are some standing here, who will not taste death, until they see the Son of Man coming in his kingdom."

76. (Verse 52). *So the Jews said.* In a second point he displays here his superiority over the Jews who are impugning him and his teaching. Thus they say: *Now we know that you have a demon.* They could not recognize the good, but were ready for evil. Jeremiah 4:22 states: "They are wise in doing evil, but they do not know how to do good." And indeed, this is what they want to show by finding fault with the Lord's saying because it is both false and arrogant. They demonstrate that it is false with this reasoning: *Abraham is dead and the prophets.* And they kept God's word. So what you are saying is false: *If anyone keep my word*, etc. They are arguing from the major premise that those who keep God's word are dead and so do not seem to have been immortal. Therefore, etc. So they say: *Abraham is dead*, namely, a person who kept the Lord's word. For it was said to Abraham in Genesis 22:18: "In your descendants will all the nations of the earth be blessed, because you obeyed my voice." *And the prophets are dead*,[177] to whom the Lord spoke. Sirach 46:14 states: "The bones of the prophets spring up out of their place."[178] *And you say: If anyone keep my word,*

---

[177] The Vulgate does not read *mortui sunt* ("are dead").

[178] The Vulgate does not read *prophetarum* ("of the prophets"), for Sir 46:14 is speaking about Israel's judges. Also, the Vulgate reads *pullulent* ("may spring up") while Bonaventure has *pullulant* ("spring up").

he will never taste death. As if they were saying: What you are saying is an obvious falsehood. Not only are you speaking falsely, but arrogantly. Thus they say:

77. (Verse 53). *Are you greater than our father Abraham, who is dead?* As if they were saying: You are not greater, and he is dead. Genesis 25:8 reads: "Declining in age, he died an old man, full of days."[179] *And the prophets are* also *dead.* So neither Abraham nor the prophets could escape death. Much less neither can you. *Whom are you making yourself?* As if to say: Why are you praising and extolling yourself? And thus they deride him in that he was praising himself and speaking falsehood, since he placed himself above Abraham, even though no one escapes death. 2 Samuel 14:14 says: "We all die, and like waters that return no more, we fall down into the earth." – To this attack the Lord answers by showing his superiority over Abraham. But before he mentions his excellence and superiority, he avoids arrogance, lest he seem to be saying this out of pride. Wherefore, he asserts in his response that he is not seeking his own glory. And so the text continues:

78. (Verse 54). *Jesus answered: If I glorify myself, my glory is nothing*, that is, you will consider it vain, just as that glory is deemed vain by which someone praises and commends himself. Thus they said to him in John 8:13 above: "You are bearing witness to yourself. Your witness is not true." That is, *if I* on my own, separating out and highlighting *I.* 2 Corinthians 10:18 reads: "It is not the person who commends himself who is approved, but the person whom the Lord commends." But *I by myself* do not glorify myself. Rather there is another with me. So he says: *It is my Father who glorifies me.* Thus John 1:14

---

[179] This is a paraphrase of Gen 25:8: "And declining, he died at a good old age, and having lived a long time and being full of days."

above states: "We have seen his glory, the glory as of the only-begotten of the Father." 2 Peter 1:16-17 reads: "We had been eye-witnesses of his grandeur, for he received from God the Father honor and glory," etc. *Of whom you say that he is your God*, that is, the one whom you call Father is your God. And therefore, you must believe him. For he is the God of Abraham and Isaac and Jacob, as Exodus 3:6 states.[180] But you do not believe. Thus:

79. (Verse 55). *And you do not know him*. For they belonged to those about whom it is said in Titus 1:16: "They profess that they know God, but they disown him with their works." *But I know him*, and this has to be said not on account of arrogance, but on account of the truth. So: *And if I say that I do not know him, I will be like you, a liar*. And so this has to be said, because I know. Augustine comments: "Arrogance is avoided in such a way that truth is not abandoned."[181] And so he asserts this again: I do not say, because I do not know, *But I know him, and I keep his word*. And this is to truly know God, since it is said in 1 John 2:4: "The person who says that he knows God and does not keep God's commandments is a liar." So having avoided arrogance in this manner, the Lord manifests his superiority and excellence. Since they did not believe that he is greater than Abraham, he shows them that he is greater and so says:

80. (Verse 56). *Abraham, your father, rejoiced that he was to see my day. He saw it and was glad*, as the day

---

[180] Ex 3:6 reads: "I am the God of your father, the God of Abraham, the God of Isaac, and the God of Jacob."

[181] See Tractate 43 n. 15 in CCSL xxxvi, p. 379: "Therefore, may arrogance not be guarded against in such a way that truth is abandoned."

of a greater person.[182] Gregory says that he rejoiced at that time when he saw the three men and worshipped one,[183] according to Genesis 18.[184] Thus Luke 10:23 states: "Blessed are the eyes that see what you see," etc.[185] – Another interpretation is that Abraham *rejoiced that he would see* in the Lord's call to him in Genesis 12.[186] – But *he saw and was glad*, in the firm promise of the Lord. See Genesis 15:1-6 where the Lord promised and "Abraham[187] believed, and it was reputed to him unto righteousness."[188] And again in the confirmation of the covenant when it is said that in the giving of the prescription of circumcision

---

[182] See Augustine, Tractate 43 n. 16 in CCSL xxxvi, p. 380 where he says that the oath of Gen 24:2-4 signifies that from the nation of Abraham was to come in the flesh the God of heaven." Chrysostom, Homily 55 n. 2 in PG 59:304 says: "Now I think that the day here is the day of the cross which he had prefigured by the sacrifice of the ram and Isaac."

[183] See Homily 18 n. 3 in GGHG in CCSL, cxli, p. 139 and Hurst, p. 116: "Abraham saw the day of the Lord when he hospitably received three angels as a prefiguration of the most holy Trinity. After he had received them, he spoke to the three as to one, since although there are three persons in the Trinity, the nature of the divinity is one."

[184] Gen 18:2-3 states: "And when he (Abraham) had lifted up his eyes, there appeared to him three men standing near him. And as soon as he saw them, he ran to meet them from the door of his tent and adored down to the ground. And he said: Lord, if I have found favor in your sight, do not pass away from your servant."

[185] Luke 10:24 follows upon 10:23: "For I say to you that many prophets and kings have desired to see what you see, and they have not seen it...."

[186] See Gen 12:1-3: "Now the Lord said to Abram: Go forth out of your country and from your kin and from your father's house.... And I will make of you a great nation.... In you all the kin of the earth will be blessed."

[187] The Vulgate reads *Abram* ("Abram").

[188] Gen 15:5 reads: "And he (the Lord) brought him (Abram) forth and said to him: Look up to heaven and number the stars, if you can. And he said to him: So shall your descendants be."

that Abraham laughed. Thus he was also glad according to Genesis 17:10-19.[189]

81. (Verse 57). *So the Jews said to him*. In the third point he shows his eternity to the astonished Jews. They were wondering about his statement that Abraham had seen his day. Thus they say: *You are not yet fifty years old, and you have seen Abraham*? As if they were saying: This is totally impossible. And it should be noted that they do not say: Abraham saw you, but you Abraham, as if they were always regarding Abraham as the greater. Chrysostom has "forty years old," because in their estimation the Lord was close to his forty year.[190] So to their bewilderment the Lord gives his answer, in which he manifests his eternity. And so it is no wonder that he might give immortality to others, since he even came before Abraham, as the Creator the creature. So:

82. (Verse 58). *So*[191] *Jesus said to them: Amen, amen, I say to you*, that is, I assert the truth. *Before Abraham came to be*, as a creature is created into being, *I am*. He does not say: *I was made*, because he did not begin to exist. He does not say: *I was*, since his being has no past. Therefore, it is said in Exodus 3:14: "I am who I am,"[192] for his being is uncreated and intransible. Thus Gregory observes: "Divinity does not have a past tense, but always

---

[189] The key verse is Gen 17:17: "Abraham fell on his face and laughed, saying in his heart: Will a son, do you think, be born to him who is a hundred years old? And will Sara who is ninety bring forth?"

[190] See Homily 55 n. 2 in PG 59:304: "'You are not yet forty years old, and you have seen Abraham?' Therefore, Christ has already come close to his fortieth year." Hugh of St. Cher, p. 344n also cites Chrysostom's interpretation.

[191] On p. 371 n. 3 QuarEd accurately indicate that the Vulgate does not read *ergo* ("so").

[192] Hugh of St. Cher, p. 344q also quotes Ex 3:14.

is. Therefore, he rightly says: I am, not I was."[193] Sirach 24:5 states: "I have come from the mouth of the most High, the firstborn before all creatures."

83. (Verse 59). *So they took up stones*, etc. Here in a fourth point the Lord shows his humility to the Jews who are persecuting him. Since they wanted to stone him, the text says: *So the Jews[194] took up stones to cast at him*. Gregory observes: "The minds of the non-believers did not suffer these words of eternity and ran to pick up stones. And they sought to destroy the person they could not understand."[195] Therefore, they wanted to kill him, since he seemed to have blasphemed. For Leviticus 24:16 states: "Let the person who blasphemes the name of the Lord die the death. All the multitude shall stone him." So the Lord humbly flees from this unjust persecution, although he has the power to overcome it. Thus the text states: *But Jesus hid himself and went out from the temple*, according to what Romans 12:19 says: "Do not avenge yourselves … but give place to the wrath." And 1 Peter 2:23 has: "When he was reviled, he did not revile."

Questions

84. Question 1 is this: Since the Jews were scandalized and did not understand the Lord, because their

---

[193] Bonaventure adapts Homily 18 n. 3 of GGHG. See CCSL cxli, p. 139 and Hurst, pp. 116-117: "Because divinity does not have past and future time, but always is, he did not say, 'I was before Abraham,' but *'Before Abraham was, I am.'* Hence it was said to Moses: *I am who I am*, and: *You will say to the children of Israel, 'He who is sent me to you.'*"

[194] On p. 371 n. 5 QuarEd correctly indicate that the Vulgate does not read *Iudaei* ("the Jews").

[195] See Homily 18 n. 3 of GGHG in CCSL cxli, pp. 139-140. The citation is not verbatim.

understanding was only on a carnal level, why didn't the Lord stop preaching? – I answer that it has to be maintained that the Lord was speaking in such a way that they could understand spiritually, but by the just judgment of God they had been blinded. Nonetheless, he did not stop preaching, since, as Gregory says, "When the perversity of evil people increases, preaching should not decrease, but increase."[196]

85. Question 2 deals with John 8:54: "If I glorify myself, my glory is nothing." – Contrary. 1. The person who can bear witness can also give praise. But he said in John 8:14 above that he could bear witness to himself. So he can also glorify himself. – 2. Moreover, heretics formulate this position: The Father glorifies the Son. The Son cannot glorify himself. Therefore he is inferior to the Father.[197] – I respond that there is a twofold solution to this problematic. That which was now said is understood according to his human nature. That "his glory is nothing" is understood not according to the truth, but according to the thinking of the Jews.

86. Question 3 asks about what John 8:55: they do not know the Father, although it is said in the Law: "Your God is one God."[198] And this they believed. – I answer that it

---

[196] See Homily 18 n. 2 of GGHG in CCSL cxli, p. 138: "But when the perversity of evil people increases, not only should preaching not be broken off, but even increased."

[197] See Augustine, Tractate 43 n. 14 in FC 88, p. 171: "Sometimes the Arians misrepresent our faith from this sentence; and they say, See, the Father is greater because, of course, he glorifies the Son. Heretic, have you not read the Son himself also saying that he glorifies his Father? If he glorifies the Son and the Son glorifies the Father, put aside your obstinacy; acknowledge their equality, correct your perversity."

[198] Deut 6:4 says: "Hear, O Israel, the Lord, your God, is one Lord."

has to be said that Father is open to two interpretations. In the first Father is taken essentially, and in this way the Jews knew the Father as God, since this usage is fitting for the whole Trinity in comparison to creation. The second way is taken on the level of persons, that is, the person of the Father in relationship to the person of the Son. And they did not know the Father nor the Son on this level of understanding, as Augustine notes.[199]

87. Question 4 addresses what John 8:59 says about the Lord hiding himself. – It seems that he was afraid and would be imperfect, for it is the trait of the imperfect to be afraid and to flee. – I respond that he hid himself as a sign that "truth, when it does not find a humble mind, flees," as Gregory says.[200] As an example, "so that, even when we can resist, we turn … aside from the wrath of the haughty," as Gregory also teaches.[201] He hides himself to wait for an opportune time, when later on he will offer himself to his persecutors to show that he is truly human. For Augustine observes: "As a human being he flees from stones, but woe to those from whose stony hearts God flees."[202]

88. Question 5 queries the meaning of John 8:50: "There is one who seeks and judges." – Contrary. John 5:22 above states: "The Father does not judge anyone, but has given

---

[199] See Tractate 43 n. 15 in FC 88, p 172: "He, as the Son, was speaking the word of the Father, and he was himself the Father's Word, who was speaking to men."

[200] See Homily 18 n. 5 of GGHG in CCSL cxli, p. 141: "And what does the Lord hiding himself signify but that truth itself is hidden for those who sneer at following his words? Indeed, when truth does not find a humble mind, it flees."

[201] See Homily 18 n. 4 of GGHG in CCSL cxli, p. 140. The citation is almost verbatim.

[202] See Tractate 43 n. 18 in CCSL xxxvi, p. 381. The quotation is verbatim. Hugh of St. Cher, p. 344u also cites Augustine verbatim.

all judgment to the Son." – I answer: There is a judgment of condemnation and of separation. John 5:22 talks of the first while John 8:50 speaks of the second.[203]

---

[203] The Glossa Ordinaria on John 8:50 makes the same distinction. See PL 114:393D.

CHAPTER NINE

JOHN 9:1-41
THE LORD SHOWS HE IS DIRECTOR
BY A POWERFUL MIRACLE

1. *And as he was passing by, Jesus saw a man blind from birth.*[1] In the preceding two chapters the Lord has shown himself to be director through his words of wisdom. Here he likewise manifests himself as director and does so by a *powerful miracle.* For by providing bodily illumination he signifies that he gives spiritual illumination. This is what he does in this chapter. Now the present chapter has three parts. First comes *the wondrous illumination of the blind man.* Second is the *dispute* with or *vilification of the Pharisees* where verse 12 reads: "And they said to him: Where is he?" Third is *the spiritual illumination of the blind man* during the occasion of this dispute where verse 35 states: "But Jesus heard," etc.[2]

JOHN 9:1-11
THE WONDROUS ILLUMINATION OF THE BLIND MAN

So two things are depicted in this part. First is *the wondrous illumination of the blind man.* Second is *the broad-*

---

[1] The Vulgate does not read *Iesus* ("Jesus").
[2] The Vulgate does not read *autem* ("But").

casting of this miracle where verse 8 says: "So the neighbors," etc.

JOHN 9:1-11
THE MIRACLE OF ILLUMINATION AND ITS BROADCASTING

So the description of *the miracle of illumination* follows this order. First is *the compassion of divine goodness*. Second is *the dispensation of divine wisdom*. Third is *the operation of wondrous power*.

Verse 1. The compassion of divine benignity is touched upon here as the Lord looks at the blind man with the eye of mercy. Thus the text says: *As[3] he was passing by, Jesus saw a man blind from birth.[4] He saw*, I say, with the eye of mercy according to what Lamentations 1:20 reads: "Look, Lord, for I am in distress." Another interpretation of *he saw* is that of Chrysostom: "He carefully looked about, so that he might hand on to his disciples a sense of how to examine things."[5] And for this reason the disciples asked him:

2. (Verse 2). *And his disciples asked him.* The second point occurs here, that is, the dispensation of divine wisdom that the disciples want to know and therefore ask him: *Rabbi, who has sinned: this man or his parents, that he*

---

[3] The Vulgate reads *et praeteriens* ("And as he was passing by").

[4] The Vulgate does not read *Iesus* ("Jesus").

[5] Bonaventure adapts Homily 56 n. 1. See PG 59:305 and FC 41, p. 86: "Now, on departing from the Temple, He went expressly to perform this miracle, as is clear from the fact that it was He who saw the blind man, not the latter who came to Him. So intently did He look at him that His disciples also noticed the man. Because of this, at least, they began to question Him." See Hugh of St. Cher, p. 344v,b: "Chrysostom: that is, he carefully looked about, so that he might also hand on to his disciples a sense."

should be born blind? Presupposing that divine wisdom does not inflict punishment unless a sin is involved, they are asking whose sin it was. Indeed, they had learned this from the cure of the paralytic, to whom it had been said in John 5:14 above: "Behold, you are cured. Sin no more, lest something worse befall you." They knew that it was written in Exodus 20:5: "I am … God, mighty, jealous, visiting the iniquity of the fathers upon the children unto the third and fourth generation."[6] And since they had good intentions, but had formulated their question poorly, the Lord did away with their question in his response, when he said:

3. (Verse 3). *Jesus answered: Neither this man sinned nor his parents.* And he goes on to satisfy those questioning him: *But the works of God were to be made manifest in him,* that is, since he was born blind. The works of God are manifest when God is manifest in his works. These are miraculous works. John 2:11 above states: "He manifested his glory." Qoheleth 3:14 reads: "I have learned that all the works that God has done continue forever," etc. Therefore, he was born blind for the manifestation of glory, because the opportunity for this manifestation was present. So he says:

4. (Verse 4). *I must do the works of the one who sent me.* These are the miraculous works that he attributed to the Father, because he appropriated his power. John 14:10 below says: "The Father dwelling in me, it is he who does the works." John 5:36 above states: "The works that the Father has given me to accomplish, these very works that I do bear witness to me that the Father has sent me." The opportunity to perform these works lasts *while it is*

---

[6] See Book II, d. 33 a. 1. q. 1 and d. 36. a. 2 and 3 in Bonaventure's *Sentence Commentary*.

day. Night will come⁷ when no one can work. For then the opportunity ceases. Revelation 14:13 reads: "Yes, says the Spirit, let them rest from their labors, for their works follow them." And Qoheleth 9:10 says: "Whatsoever your hand is able to work, do it earnestly, for neither work nor reason nor wisdom nor knowledge will be in hell, whither you are hastening." But he explains here what this day is. So the text continues:

5. (Verse 5). *As long as I am in the world, I am the light of the world.* So just as the day is nothing other than the presence of light on the earth, so this day is nothing other than the presence of Christ in the world. Malachi 4:2 reads: "The sun of justice will arise for you who fear God."⁸ Wherefore, the Lord says in John 12:35 below: "Walk while you have the light, so that darkness may not overtake you."

6. (Verse 6). *When he had said these things.* This verse introduces the third point, namely, the wondrous working of divine power in this that by his power alone he bestows light through spittle and dark clay. Thus the text states: *When he had said these things,* that is, the aforementioned matters, *he spat on the ground and made clay with the spittle and spread the clay over his eyes.* He made a type of salve to heal the eyes.⁹ Revelation 3:18 says: "Anoint your eyes with salve, so that you may see."

---

⁷ On p. 373 n. 2 QuarEd rightly notice that the Vulgate reads *venit* ("is coming") whereas Bonaventure has *veniet* ("will come").

⁸ The Vulgate reads *timentibus nomen meum* ("who fear my name") while Bonaventure has *timentibus Deum* ("who fear God").

⁹ See Augustine, Tractate 2 n. 16 in FC 78, p. 73: "Indeed, because 'the Word was made flesh, and dwelt among us,' by the nativity itself he made a salve by which the eyes of our heart may be wiped clean and we may be able to see his majesty through his lowliness."

7. (Verse 7). *And he said to him: Go and*[10] *wash in the pool of Siloam.* "Siloam is a fountain at the base of Mount Zion, which flows continuously, but at certain hours water bubbles forth from hollows in the earth."[11] And since this command contains a mystery, the Evangelist added the interpretation of the name: *which is interpreted Sent.* Chrysostom comments: "So that you may learn that the power operating here is that of the sender."[12] And power is revealed by its effect. So the text adds: *And*[13] *he went away and washed and returned seeing.* In this the effect of power and the obedience of the blind man are clear. Thus Chrysostom observes: "Look at the heart of the blind man who obeys everything. For he was not distressed about anything. He was not scandalized, objecting: Why is clay necessary? Why did you anoint my eyes with it? Why did you command me to wash? But he thought nothing of these matters, but obeyed every command."[14]

8. According to the allegorical interpretation, saliva or spittle that comes out of the mouth, that is also salty, signifies God's wisdom, about which Sirach 24:5 says: "I have come out of the mouth of the Most High, the firstborn," etc.[15] – Ground or earth is the flesh of the Virgin.

---

[10] On p. 373 n. 5 QuarEd accurately indicate that the Vulgate does not read *et* ("and").

[11] On p. 373 n. 5 QuarEd state that this citation is from the Glossa Ordinaria apud Lyranum.

[12] See Homily 57 n. 1 in PG 59:311 and FC 41, p. 98: "Further, that is why the Evangelist added the interpretation of the name for us. When he had said: 'to Siloe,' he added; 'That is, "sent," so that you might learn that there also it was Christ who healed the man....'"

[13] The Vulgate does not read *Et* ("And"). Rather it reads *ergo* ("so").

[14] See Homily 57 n. 1 in PG 59:311. Bonaventure's citation is not verbatim.

[15] Sir 24:5 concludes: "... the firstborn, before all creatures."

Psalm 84:13 reads: "Our earth will give its fruit."[16] – Saliva is joined with earth, when the Son of God was born of the Virgin. And it became clay when "the Word was made flesh,"[17] and this for our reformation, according to Augustine.[18] – Our eyes are anointed with this clay when believers in Christ are illumined by the anointing of the Holy Spirit. About this 1 John 2:27 says: "… anointing will teach you concerning all things."[19] – And we wash in the waters of Siloam, that is, Sacred Scripture, which flow silently, since they are not stirred up or agitated by the shrieking words of worldly philosophy, and settle upon

---

[16] See Augustine, Tractate 27 n. 4 in FC 79, p. 279: "For the Son of man is Christ, of the Virgin Mary. Therefore the Son of man began to be here on earth where he took on himself flesh from the earth. For this reason in prophecy it has been said, 'Truth has arisen out of the earth.'" The prophecy is from Ps 84:12. Bonaventure quotes from Ps 84:13.

[17] John 1:14.

[18] See Tractate 44 n. 2 in FC 88, p. 176: "From his saliva he made mud because the Word was made flesh…. And the Evangelist was concerned to explain to us the name of this pool, and he said, 'which is interpreted "Who has been sent."' You already know who has been sent; for unless he had been sent, no one of us would be sent away from wickedness." See the Glossa Ordinaria on John 9:6 in PL 114:395A: "Just as he formed the first human from the slime of the earth, so through the same sort of clay he reformed the human race. From saliva he made clay, since the Word became flesh. Saliva is the wisdom that proceeds from the mouth of the Most High. The earth is the flesh of Christ."

[19] The Vulgate reads *docet* ("teaches") whilst Bonaventure has *docebit* ("will teach").

the humble as they descend from the mountains.[20] Isaiah 8:6 states: "The waters of Siloam that flow silently."[21]

9. According to the moral interpretation, to spit is to announce publicly the filth of sin, lest perchance it putrefies. Psalm 37:6 reads: "My sores have putrefied and are corrupt, because of my foolishness." And Proverbs 28:13 states: "The person who hides his sins will not prosper, but the person who will confess and forsake them, will obtain mercy." – To anoint the eyes with clay is to consider sins with frequency. Jeremiah 31:21 says: "Set up a mirror for yourself. Place bitterness before you." Isaiah 38:15 reads: "I will recount to you all my years in the bitterness of my soul." – To wash with tears. Psalm 6:7 states: "Every night I will wash my bed. I will water my couch with my tears." And Isaiah 1:16 says: "Wash yourselves. Be clean. Take away the evil of your designs from my eyes. Cease to act perversely."[22]

10. *So the neighbors*, etc. After this wonderful illumination has been introduced and described, the next verses depict the *broadcasting of the miracle* in this order. *Doubt* is mentioned first. Second is *certification of the miracle to*

---

[20] Hugh of St. Cher, p. 345v,c comments: "Mystical sense: God spat on the ground when divinity descended into the world. And he made clay from saliva when the Word became flesh and dwelt among us. For saliva is the wisdom of God that proceeds from the mouth of the Most High. Sir 24:5. The earth is the flesh of Christ. Clay from spittle and earth is Christ in both natures, namely, God and man...."

[21] This quotation from Isaiah is interpreted in the same way in Collation 17 n. 27 of Bonaventure's *Hexaëmeron* and in the Glossa Ordinaria apud Lyranum on John 9:7.

[22] See Hugh of St. Cher, p. 345v,c for a relatively long paragraph of moral interpretation that has little in common with Bonaventure's. For example, Hugh of St. Cher writes: "For we must consider our vileness, that is signified by spittle and our fragility that is signified by earth. These two are salve for the eyes, so that a person may see himself and know."

those doubting. Third is *the declaration of the wondrous illumination*.

Verse 8. So first is the doubting of the neighbors, who because of the wonder of his changed sight expressed their doubt that they knew the person who had been illuminated. Therefore, the text reads: *So the neighbors and those who were wont to see him before as a beggar*, since blind people customarily begged. The Lord, gracious and humble, extended his curative power especially towards such miserable and contemptible and poor persons. Thus, Luke 18:35 tells of a similar individual: "A certain blind man was sitting by the wayside, begging." Luke also says that Jesus illumined him while "Jesus was standing."[23] So those who used to see him *began saying: Is not this he who used to sit and beg?* They were saying this in doubt, and since they were doubtful, they disagreed. So the text continues: *Some were saying: It is he*, considering his bodily form.

11. (Verse 9). *But others were saying: By no means. He only resembles him*. Taking into consideration the change in sight, they believed that the person who now saw was another person, although similar. *But*[24] *he said*. The second point surfaces here, namely, the removal of the doubt by the certification that issues from the blind man who certainly knows that he is the one who was cured. So the text states: *But he said: I am he*, that is, the man who was blind and used to beg. Augustine remarks: "A grateful voice, lest he be condemned as ungrateful."[25] The

---

[23] Luke 18:40.

[24] The Vulgate does not read *autem* ("But").

[25] See Homily 44 n. 8 in CCSL xxxvi, p. 385: "A grateful voice, lest an ungrateful one be condemned." Bonaventure reads *ingratus* ("ungrateful person") for *ingrata* ("ungrateful voice"). Hugh of St. Cher, p. 346v, c cites Augustine in the selfsame way as Bonaventure.

blind man was not ashamed to confess to the glory of God that he had been blind. For Sirach 4:25a reads: "There is shame that brings death,"[26] that is, the shame that diminishes God's glory for the sake of our own. "And there is a shame that brings glory and grace,"[27] and which diminishes our glory and manifests our disgrace and thus reveals divine glory.

12. (Verse 10). *So they said to him*. This verse introduces the third point, namely, the declaration of the wondrous illumination, and this at the interrogation by the doubters. So the text continues: *So they said to him: How were your eyes opened?*[28] Through this they would know that he was the person who had been blind. And he pointed out to them *the author and the means* of his illumination.

13. (Verse 11). *He responded: The man, who is called Jesus*, for he did not yet believe him to be God, *made clay and anointed my eyes*.[29] Thus, the action. *And said to me: Go to the pool of Siloam and wash*. Here is his command. *And I went and I washed and I saw*. This is the implementation of the command and through it illumination. For by fulfilling the commandment of Christ, the man is illumined, since as it is said in Proverbs 6:23: "The commandment is a lamp and the law a light." When they have been observed, they illumine. Psalm 18:9 reads: "The precept of the Lord is full of light, illumining the eyes."

---

[26] On p. 374 n. 8 QuarEd accurately indicate that the Vulgate reads *peccatum* ("sin") while Bonaventure has *mortem* ("death").

[27] Sir 4:25b.

[28] On p. 374 n. 9 QuarEd correctly mention that the Vulgate reads *aperti sunt tibi oculi* ("your eyes opened for you").

[29] On p. 374 n. 10 QuarEd rightly notice that the Vulgate reads *unxit* ("anointed") whereas Bonaventure has *linivit* ("anointed").

Questions

14. Question 1. The questions begin with what the disciples ask in John 9:2: "Who has sinned, this man or his parents?" – This seems to imply that children are punished for their parents' sins. – Contrary is what Ezekiel 18:20 says: "The father shall not bear the iniquity of the son nor the son the iniquity of the father." Therefore, the son should not be punished on account of the sin of his parents. – Contrary to this it is said in Exodus 20:5: "I am the Lord your God, mighty, jealous, visiting the iniquity of the fathers upon the children unto the third and fourth generation."

I answer that it has to be maintained that punishment for sin is twofold: temporal and eternal. I state that the son is not punished with eternal punishment on account of the iniquity of the father. Thus, even if unbaptized children are deprived of the eternal vision of God, this occurs not on account of the sin of the father only, but on account of their own sin, since each one has original sin. – But concerning temporal punishment it has to be understood that a son bears the iniquity of the father, because an evil father is often punished in the son. Therefore, the text says: "unto the third and fourth generation," since parents can see their children for that length of time. – Others are of the opinion that this text is understood of children who imitate the crime of their parents, but the first opinion is better.[30]

15. Question 2 deals with John 9:3: "Neither this man has sinned," etc. – Contrary. "No one is clean from defilement,

---

[30] See Book II, d. 33. a. 1. q. 4 of Bonaventure's *Sentence Commentary*.

not even the infant whose life is one day on earth."[31] – Augustine answers that this text has to be supplemented in this way: "He has not sinned by means of a sin, on account of which this punishment might be inflicted upon the blind man."[32] And John Chrysostom maintains that the disciples raised an undifferentiated question, for before he had been born, he could not sin with the result that he be born blind.[33]

But there are *objections*. 1. Since, if every punishment is on account of sin[34] and neither this man nor his parents sinned, it follows that he was unjustly born blind and the punishment was unjustly inflicted. – 2. Likewise, Jerome in commenting on Jeremiah 4:18, "Your ways and your devices have brought these things upon you," says: "Whatever suffering befalls us issues from our sin."[35] – 3. Furthermore, if you say that this occurred on account of the glory of God, could not the glory of God be manifested in some other way than this? And if God does not need our

---

[31] See Job 14:4 in the LXX. See Augustine, Homily 41 n. 9 in FC 88, p. 144: "What does even Job himself say? 'For who is clean? Not even a baby whose life on earth lasts one day.'"

[32] This is a paraphrase of Augustine. See Homily 44 n. 3 in FC 88, p. 177: "If then both his parents had sin and this man had sin, why did the Lord say, 'Neither has this man sinned, nor his parents,' except with regard to what he had been asked about: 'that he should be born blind'? For his parents had sin; but it did not happen that he was born blind because of sin itself. "

[33] See Homily 56 n. 1 in PG 59:305 and FC 41, p. 86: "The question was a blundering one, for how could he have sinned before he was born? And how could he have been punished, if his parents had committed the sin?"

[34] See Book III, c. 18 n. 51 of Augustine's *De Libero Arbitrio* in CCSL xxix, p. 305: "Now every punishment, if it is just, is a punishment for sin and is called a penalty."

[35] See PL 24:737: "Therefore, whatever befalls us, befalls us because of our sin." See also Hugh of St. Cher, p. 344v,g: "And Jerome comments about this (Jer 4:18): Whatever evil befalls us, issues from our sin, not from God."

good things for the sake of his glory,[36] how much less our bad things. – I respond that there are two kinds of causes. One cause is *sine qua non*, and seen from this cause every punishment has sin as its cause, since, if there were no sin, there would be absolutely no punishment. The other cause is meritorious, and seen from this cause not every punishment and suffering has sin in view. The Lord is speaking of this cause in this passage. – Moreover, as Damascene states,[37] sometimes punishments are inflicted on account of the guilt of sin. Sometimes to test and reveal virtue, as in the cases of Tobit[38] and Job. In Job 17:2 Job maintained: "I have not sinned, and my eye abides in bitterness." At other times to preserve virtue, as in the situation of Paul who says in 2 Corinthians 12:7-8: "There was given me a thorn for my flesh, a messenger of Satan, who buffeted me.[39] Concerning this I thrice besought the Lord," etc.[40] Sometimes on account of the dispensation of the divine counsel, as in the case of Christ. At other times to manifest divine power, as in the case of this blind man. – This was not done solely for God's sake, but to give us instruction and to be of benefit to the blind man, since through the occasion of his bodily illumination he was illumined spiritually. Wherefore, it was of great benefit to him.

---

[36] Cf. Ps 15:2: "I have said to the Lord, you are my God, for you have no need of my good things."

[37] Bonaventure has abbreviated and given his own systematization to the more expansive treatment of Book II, c. 29 of St. John Damascene's *De Fide Orthodoxa*.

[38] See Tob 2:12: "So now the Lord permitted this trial (blindness) to happen to him, that an example might be given to posterity of his patience, as also of holy Job."

[39] The Vulgate reads *ut me colaphizet* ("to buffet me") whilst Bonaventure has *qui me colaphizet* ("who buffeted me").

[40] 2 Cor 12:8 concludes: "… that it might leave me."

16. Question 3 concerns John 9:4: "He must work while it is day."[41] – But for God it is always day. Therefore, he never ceases to work. – It should be stated that the text is referring to works that God works for our sakes and in us, according to what Isaiah 26:12 reads: "Lord, you have worked all your works in us."[42] And night descends upon these works when the last day is shut upon us. After that we will be unable to work, nor God in us nor for our sakes when bad things befall us. Thus Matthew 22:13 states: "Bind his hands and feet.[43] Cast him into the darkness outside."[44]

17. Question 4 raises the issue of the manner of the cure. 1. Since the Lord cured others solely by means of his command, why does he perform this cure with clay? – 2. And why does he command him to wash? – I answer that it has to be said that the reason was allegorical and moral, as has been said above,[45] for the guidance and instruction of our mind and conduct. There was also a literal reason. By the just judgment in his coming both the blind were illumined and the Pharisees blinded. He made clay, so

---

[41] John 9:4 actually says: "I must do the works of the one who sent me while it is day."

[42] The Vulgate reads *nobis* ("for us") while Bonaventure has *in nobis* ("in us").

[43] The Vulgate reads *ligatis pedibus eius et manibus* ("Bind his feet and hands") while Bonaventure has *Ligatis manibus et pedibus eius* ("Bind his hands and feet").

[44] See Augustine, Tractate 44 n. 6: "Well then, what shall we say about this night? When will it be, when no one can work? This will be the night of the ungodly, this will be night of those to whom it is said at the end, 'Go into everlasting fire which has been prepared for the devil and his angels.' But night was named, not flame, not fire. Hear that it is also night. About a certain slave he says, 'Bind him hands and feet and cast him into the exterior darkness.' Therefore, let a person work while he is alive that he may not be prevented by that night when no one can work."

[45] See John 9:7 n. 8-9.

that through this action he might seem to break the Sabbath, the filthy might become filthier,[46] and the blind man himself might be illumined and purified.

2. He sent him to the pool, so that the miracle might be public, as Chrysostom says,[47] for all had gathered for so great a spectacle, that by clay which blinds others a blind man might be illumined.

JOHN 9:12-34
CALUMNIATION OF THE JEWS

18. *And they said to him: Where is he?* After the wondrous illumination of the blind man has been made public, the second part follows, in which *the calumniation of the Jews* is described and what arose from this. This part has a threefold division. In the first it is shown how the Pharisees try *to censure Christ*. In the second they try *to deny the miracle* where verse 17 states: "So they again said to the blind man: What do you say," etc. In the third, their first two attempts having failed, they try *to conceal* the miracle where verse 24 reads: "So they called the man a second time."

JOHN 9:12-16
THE PHARISEES TRY TO CENSURE CHRIST

So the first description is how they try *to find fault* with the miracle by their authority. They do so in this way.

---

[46] There is an allusion to Rev 22:11: "He who does wrong, let him do wrong still. And the person who is filthy, let him be filthy still."

[47] See Homily 57 n. 1 in PG 59:311. See Hugh of St. Cher, p. 346c who quotes a number of sentences from Chrysostom whereas Bonaventure merely gives the gist of Chrysostom's comments.

First occurs *the eagerness of those who are finding fault*. Second is *the occasion for the censure*. Third is *the censure itself*.

Verse 12. *The eagerness of those finding fault* is noted in this that they are searching for the person who performed the cure, and not finding him, they hold onto the person cured. So the text reads: *And they said to him: Where is he*? namely, the person who cured you. *He said: I do not know*. And since they could not find the person who had performed the cure, they led the person who had been cured to the Pharisees. So the text continues:

19. (Verse 13). *They took the man who had been blind to the Pharisees*, since they were eager to find fault with Christ. Luke 6:7 says: "The scribes and the Pharisees were watching whether he cured on the Sabbath, so that they might find how to accuse him."

20. (Verse 14). *Now it was a Sabbath*. The second point surfaces here, that is, the occasion for finding fault. The occasion is twofold: when Christ performed the miracle and how. On account of its occurrence on *a festival day* the text reads: *Now it was a Sabbath on which Jesus made the clay and opened his eyes*. John 5:16 above states: "This is why the Jews kept persecuting Jesus, because he did this," namely, works of curing, "on the Sabbath," as if he were contemning the Law. The other occasion arose from the manner of the cure. So they were asking about it, for they could only find out about it from the confession of the blind man. They were asking about the manner, so that even though they could not find fault with the deed, they might find something reprehensible in the manner. So the text continues:

21. (Verse 15). *And*[48] *the Pharisees asked him again how he received his sight.* They were asking about the manner and listening to what he had to say. Thus: *But he said to them: He put clay upon my eyes, and I washed, and now I see.* He repeats his story briefly, since they had already heard it from others, but they wanted to hear from his own mouth for greater certainty. And here the constancy of the blind man is evident, for he was not afraid to confess the truth, preserving what Sirach 4:24 has: "For the sake of your soul be not ashamed to speak the truth."[49]

22. (Verse 16). *So some of the Pharisees said.* This verse introduces the third point, that is, there is dissension among those finding fault. So the text states: *So some of the Pharisees said*, that is, those who are foolishly zealous for the Law. Romans 10:2 says: "They indeed[50] have zeal for God, but not according to knowledge." They were saying: *This man is not from God* by conforming to God's will and doing what is pleasing to God, *who does not keep the Sabbath.* Observance of the Sabbath had been commanded by God in Exodus 20:8 and many other passages. *But others said: How can a man who is a sinner work these signs?* And these were more illumined. So these had some light, but the others were in darkness. So it followed

---

[48] On p. 377 QuarEd correctly indicate that the Vulgate reads *ergo* ("so") while Bonaventure has *et* ("and").

[49] See Chrysostom, Homily 57 n. 2 in PG 59: 313 and FC 41, p. 101: "But please note that the blind man was not perturbed. To be sure, when He (sic) was being questioned in comparative safety and was speaking to the Jews merely, it was not a great thing that he told the truth; but now it was wonderful that, though he was in greater peril, he neither denied nor contradicted his previous statements."

[50] On p. 377 n. 4 QuarEd accurately indicate that the Vulgate does not read *quidem* ("indeed").

that *there was a schism between them*,[51] that is, a division, effected by the just judgment of a God who divides light from darkness and the good from the evil. For which reason he said in Matthew 10:34: "I have not come to bring peace, but the sword."

JOHN 9:17-23
THE PHARISEES TRY TO DENY THE MIRACLE

23. *So they said to the blind man.* In the previous section the Pharisees tried to find fault with Christ. And since they could not agree on how he was at fault, they vigorously attempted *to deny the miracle.* And their attempt is described in this order. First is *the craftiness of the Pharisees in questioning the blind man.* Second is *their hardness in believing.* Third is *their eagerness in questioning.* In last place is *the timidity of the parents of the blind man in responding.*

Verse 17. So the first point to be noted is the craftiness of the Pharisees in questioning the blind man. For they ask the blind man what he thinks of Christ, so that if he answers that he thinks ill of him, they might make him deny Christ's miracle. If he thinks well of Christ, they will not believe what he is saying. So it is said: *So they said again,* namely, the Pharisees: *What do you say of him, who opened your eyes*? Whether he is a good man or an evil man. Their question is malicious, but the blind man's answer is straightforward. *But he said: He is a prophet.* The Glossa comments: "He unswervingly expresses what

---

[51] The Vulgate reads *et schisma erat in eis* ("And there was a schism among them") while Bonaventure has *schisma erat inter eos* ("there was a schism between them").

he perceives."[52] He is like the crowds in Luke 7:16: "A great prophet has risen among us."

24. (Verse 18). *So the Jews did not believe of him that he had been blind*, etc. This verse introduces the second point, that is, the hardness of the Jews to believe. For they did not want to believe for this reason, namely, that he was praising Christ. So they did not trust him. *They did not believe*,[53] that is, *until they called the parents of the one who had gained his sight*. For they were hoping to reject the miracle through them. Thus Chrysostom observes: "They planned to make the miracle abortive through the parents."[54] Thus they were always striving to be rebellious, according to what Job 24:13 says: "They have been rebellious to the light and have not known his ways."[55]

25. (Verse 19). *And questioned them saying*. The third point occurs here, that is, the diligence of the Jews in their interrogation. For they ask the parents about three mat-

---

[52] This is the Glossa Interlinearis. See Augustine, Tractate 44 n. 9 in CCSL xxxvi, p. 386 and FC 88, p. 182: "But he unswervingly expressed what he perceived."

[53] Bonaventure is somewhat elliptical here. The full text is: "The Jews did not believe of him that he had been blind and had regained his sight."

[54] See Homily 58 n. 1 in PG 59:314: "Since they could not scare him and since he boldly proclaimed that he had received a benefit, they hoped that they could reject the miracle through the parents." See Hugh of St. Cher, p. 347a: "Some wanted to make the miracle abortive through the parents." The rare word, *abortivus*, used by both Bonaventure and Hugh of St. Cher, suggests Bonaventure's dependence upon Hugh of St. Cher for this citation.

[55] The Vulgate reads *Ipsi fuerunt rebelles luminis nescierunt vias eius* ("They have been rebellious of the light; they were ignorant of his ways") while Bonaventure has *Ipsi rebelles fuerunt lumini et ignorverunt vias eius* ("They have been rebellious to the light and have not known his ways").

ters: person, condition, and the miraculous change. For this reason it is said: *Is this your son?* They are asking about the person. *Whom you say that he was born blind?* That is, you are saying of him that he was born blind. Their question explores the condition. *How then does he now see?* They are inquiring about the change. They are asking shrewd questions and doing so diligently, since, as it is said in Luke 16:8: "The children of this world in relation to their own generation are more wise than the children of light."

26. (Verse 20). *His parents answered.* The fourth point surfaces here, that is, *the parents' timidity to respond.* And although they had been asked about three matters, they respond to two. They do not dare respond to the third.[56] *His parents,* that is, his father and mother, *responded to* the questions whether he was their son and had been born blind. *And said: We know that this is our son and that he was born blind.* And in this the Pharisees are confounded by the most certain testimony of the parents. Thus Chrysostom comments: "Who would believe that parents would lie about their son in such matters?"[57] And although they had spoken the truth, nonetheless they had not spoken the whole truth. Thus:

---

[56] See Homily 58 n. 2 of Chrysostom in PG 59:316 and FC 41, p. 109: "Well, though there were three questions asked – whether he was their son, whether he was blind, and how it was that he had got his sight – they answered the first two only, but did not grant a reply to the third one. This took place in the interest of the truth, so that no other than the man who had been cured and who was a trustworthy witness should give this answer."

[57] See Homily 58 n. 1 in PG 59:316: "What father would manufacture these things about his son?" Hugh of St. Cher, p. 347b also cites Chrysostom: "...What father would chose to lie about his son in such matters?"

27. (Verse 21). *But how he now sees we do not know or who opened his eyes, we ourselves do not know.* Now since we were not present and know no more than you do, you have no need to interrogate us, but him. So they say: *Ask him*, since he can answer. *He is of age. Let him speak for himself*, because he is more certain than we are. The reason for this response was fear of a Jewish agreement. Therefore, the Evangelist says:

28. (Verse 22). *Now his parents said these things, because they feared the Jews.* Isaiah 51:12 reads: "Who are you that you should be afraid of a mortal human being and of the son of man, who will wither away like grass?" And 1 Maccabees 2:62 states: "Do not be afraid of the words of a sinful man, for his glory is dung and worms." And the reason for their fear is provided: *For already the Jews had agreed that if anyone were to confess him as Christ*[58] *he should be put out of the synagogue.* The agreement is a banding together for evil, as Jeremiah 11:9-10 says: "A conspiracy is found among the men of Judah and among the inhabitants of Jerusalem. They have reverted to the iniquity of their forebears" and conspired to delete the name of Christ. Jeremiah 11:19 reads: "Let us cut him off from the land of the living, and let his name be remembered no more."

29. (Verse 23). *This is why his parents said: He is of age.*[59] *Question him.* For they still belonged to those about whom it is said in John 12:42 below: "Many believed in him, but

---

[58] On p. 378 n. 3 QuarEd rightly notice that the Vulgate reads *esse Christum* ("to be the Christ") whereas Bonaventure has *Christum* ("as Christ").

[59] On p. 378 n. 4 QuarEd correctly indicate that the Vulgate reads *quia aetatem habet* ("Because he is of age") whilst Bonaventure has *aetatem habet* ("he is of age").

because of the Pharisees they did not acknowledge it, lest they should be put out of the synagogue."

JOHN 9:24-34
THE PHARISEES TRY TO CONCEAL THE MIRACLE

30. *So they called the man again.* Already frustrated in their attempts to find fault with Christ and to deny his miracle, the Pharisees try *to conceal the miracle,* so that it would not be attributed to Christ the Lord and his name be kept quiet. So in this section they try to get the blind man to retract his confession in the name of Christ in this way. First by *flattery.*[60] Second by *craftiness.* Third by *insults.* Fourth by *injury.*

Verse 24. So first they try to get him to retract by flattery. With their flattery they admonish the blind man not to believe that Christ performed this miracle as a good person and to confess him as such. So the text reads: *So they again called the man who had been blind and said to him: Give glory to God,* that is, by professing the truth. For *to give glory to God* is to profess the truth about something, as if God were present. Joshua 7:19 states: "Son, confess and give glory to God."[61] And that truth was that he should not attribute this miracle to Christ. For which reason they say: *We ourselves know that this man is a sinner.* So confess that you were not cured by this person, but by God. Chrysostom remarks: "They tried to do this

---

[60] Bonaventure's commentary works with the meaning of flattery as misplaced praise, that is, the Pharisees try to get the blind man to praise God for his cure, not Christ.

[61] Joshua 7:19 reads: "And Joshua said to Achan: My son, give glory to the Lord God of Israel and confess and tell me what you have done. Do not hide it."

under the guise of religion."[62] But they were moving towards evil. Wherefore, Augustine states: "To deny what you have received is not to give glory to God, but rather to blaspheme God."[63] And although they flattered him, they did not prevail, since the blind man rejected their admonition and spoke the truth. So:

31. (Verse 25). *This man says:*[64] *Whether he is a sinner, I do not know. One thing I do know that whereas I was blind, now I see.* As if he were saying: I do not judge the author of my cure, but I acknowledge the benefit I have received. Augustine comments: "Neither does he promote calumny nor does he hide the truth."[65] The blind man responded wisely according to what Sirach 5:14 has: "If you have understanding, answer your neighbor. But if not, let your hand cover your mouth, lest you be surprised in an undisciplined remark and be confounded."

32. (Verse 26). *So they said to him.* Here is the second point, that is, how they try to get him to retract his view by craftiness. So they question him maliciously, so that they might find some objection to the miracle. For this reason the text continues: *What did he do to you? How*

---

[62] See Homily 58 n. 2 in PG 59:317 and FC 41, pp. 109-110: "Now, they did not say to him openly and brazenly: 'Deny that Christ healed you,' but they wished to compass this result by a pretense of piety, 'Give glory to God!' they said.... That is, 'Confess that this man has done nothing.'"

[63] See Tractate 44 n. 11 in CCSL xxxvi, p. 386 and FC 88, p. 182: "What is, 'Give glory to God'? Deny what you have received. Clearly this is not to give glory to God but rather to blaspheme God."

[64] The Vulgate reads *Dixit ergo ille* ("So he said") while Bonaventure has *Dicit homo ille* ("This man says").

[65] On p. 378 n. 9 QuarEd note that this citation is not found in Augustine. See Hugh of St. Cher, p. 347r: "And he said this, so that he might not mouth calumny nor hide the truth."

did he open your eyes?[66] Chrysostom observes: "They scrutinize the manner of the cure like dogs sniffing everywhere."[67] But in their craftiness they are censured by the blind man, who refused to answer, but argued with them. Thus the text adds:

33. (Verse 27). *He answered them: I have told you already, and you have heard. Why do you want to hear again?* As if he were saying: If your questioning is malicious, I will not answer. But if it is serious, I will respond. So the text states: *Would you also become his disciples?* As if he were saying: I believe that you are not willing to do this, but if you were willing, I would tell my story again. He is attentive to what Proverbs 9:7 says: "The person who teaches a scorner does injury to himself."

34. (Verse 28). *So they heaped abuse upon him*, etc. This verse introduces the third point, that, their attempt to get him to retract his opinion through insults. Thus they proceed by heaping insults upon him one at a time: *So they heaped abuse on him, cursed him,*[68] *and said: You are his disciple.* That is, in an abusive and insulting way they said to him that he was Christ's disciple. Augustine observes: "Let this insult and curse come upon me. May

---

[66] On p. 378 n. 11 QuarEd accurately mention that the Vulgate reads *tibi oculos* ("eyes for you") while Bonaventure has *oculos tuos* ("your eyes").

[67] See Homily 58 n. 2 in PG 59:317-318 and FC 41, p. 111: "They were acting like people do who are running about – now here, now there – searching everywhere for a wild beast that is roaming in safety." See PG 59:318 n. 1: "Others read: 'as if dogs were sniffing everywhere for a wild beast hidden in safety.'" Hugh of St. Cher, p. 347t also cites Chrysostom: "like certain hunting dogs mistakenly sniffing everywhere for a hidden wild beast."

[68] I have translated *maledicere* by "to curse" and by "to insult," so that the richness of Bonaventure's interpretation might shine forth.

such a curse be upon us and upon our children."[69] They were contemning the discipleship of Christ and preferring the discipleship of Moses to it. So they say: *We are*[70] *disciples of Moses*, not of that one. And they add the reason:

35. (Verse 29). *We know that God spoke to Moses*, as it is said throughout Exodus and Leviticus. Exodus 33:11 reads: "The Lord spoke to Moses face to face." But as for this man, we do not know where he is from. Therefore, we are disciples of the one whom the Lord approved. But they were speaking falsely, since, as it is said in John 5:46 above: "If you believed Moses, you might also believe in me."[71] And they did not prevail against the blind man through this insult. Rather he attacked the reason behind their insult, for they had said that they did not know Christ. Therefore, the text continues:

36. (Verse 30). *In answer the man said to them: Why, herein is the marvel that*[72] *you do not know where he is from, and he opened my eyes.* He did not say "impiety," lest he provoke them, but "a marvel," because he was astonished at

---

[69] See Tractate 44 n. 12 in CCSL xxxvi, p. 386. Augustine's text does not have the first sentence of the citation, to wit, "Let this insult and curse come upon me." Hugh of St. Cher, p. 347y reads: "Augustine in the original says about this passage: May this curse come upon us and upon our children, Gen 27:13. Let this curse be upon me, my son."

[70] On p. 379 n. 3 QuarEd correctly indicate that the Vulgate reads *Nos autem* ("But we") while Bonaventure has *nos* ("We").

[71] See Chrysostom, Homily 58 n. 3 in PG 59:318 and FC 41, pp. 112-113: "... for you are disciples neither of Moses nor of this Man. For, if you were disciples of Moses, you would also be this Man's. For this reason Christ had said to them previously: 'If you believed Moses, you would believe me, for he wrote of me,' since they were always taking refuge in the words of Moses."

[72] On p. 379 n. 6 QuarEd rightly notice that the Vulgate reads *quia* ("that") while Bonaventure has *quod* ("that").

their hardness. And he provides the reason behind their seeing the most evident sign and not believing, for what Isaiah 6:9 says has been verified: "So that seeing they might not see, and hearing they might not understand."

37. (Verse 31). *We*[73] *know that God does not hear sinners.* For in Isaiah 1:15 the Lord says to sinners: "When you multiply prayer, I will not listen." Job 8:20 reads: "God will not cast away the simple nor reach out his hand to the evildoer." *But if anyone is a worshipper of God and does God's will, he hears him.* John 15:7 below states: "If you abide in me and if my words abide in you, ask whatever you will and it will be done for you." 1 John 3:21-22 says: "We have confidence towards God, so that whatever we ask, we may receive ..."[74] because we keep his commandments and do those things that are pleasing in his sight." And God especially hears this man. And he proves this statement:

38. (Verse 32). *Not from the beginning of the world has it been heard that*[75] *anyone opened the eyes of a man born blind.* But this man opened my eyes. Therefore, he is from God, since this is evident by the taking away of the consequent:[76]

---

[73] On p. 379 n. 8 QuarEd accurately mention that the Vulgate reads *Scimus autem* ("But we know") while Bonaventure has *Scimus* ("We know").

[74] The Vulgate reads *et quodcumque petierimus accipiemus ab eo* ("and whatever we ask, we will receive from him") while Bonaventure has *ut quodcumque petierimus, accipamus* ("so that whatever we ask, we may receive").

[75] On p. 379 n. 10 QuarEd correctly indicate that the Vulgate reads *quia* ("that") while Bonaventure has *quod* ("that").

[76] See Book III, 1198D in *Boethius's De topicis differentiis*. Translated, with notes and essays on the text, by Eleonore Stump. (Ithaca: Cornell University Press, 1978), p. 68: "I take the antecedent: but she has borne a child; I conclude the consequent: therefore, she has lain with a man. From consequents in this way. I take the consequent: but

39. (Verse 33). *If this man were not from God, he could do nothing.*[77] John 15:5 below says: "Without me you can do nothing."

40. (Verse 34). *They answered and said to him.* This verse articulates the fourth point. Since they were not able to get him to retract by means of flattery and guile and insults, they advance to *injury.* Therefore, driven by indignation, *they answered and said to him: You were totally born in sins and do you teach us?* That is, we who have reputation of being just. But these Pharisees were similar to the one who praised himself during his prayer in Luke 18:11.[78] *And they cast him out,* inflicting injury upon him on account of the truth. Chrysostom observes: "You see the herald of truth and how much he suffered. These things have been written, so that we too might imitate him in like manner."[79] Something similar happened

she has not lain with a man; I conclude the antecedent: therefore, she has not borne a child.... The maximal propositions: once the antecedent has been asserted, the consequent follows; once the consequent is taken away, the antecedent is taken away."

[77] On p. 379 n. 11 QuarEd rightly notice that the Vulgate does not read *homo* ("man") and that it reads *poterat* ("could") while Bonaventure has *posset* ("could").

[78] Luke 18:11 reads: "The Pharisee stood and began to pray thus within himself: O God, I thank you that I am not like the rest of human beings, robbers, dishonest, adulterers, or even like this publican."

[79] See Homily 58 n. 3-4 in PG 59:319 and FC 41, p. 115: "Are you taking note of the messenger of Truth, how his lack of learning acted as no deterrent to him? Do you see how much he had to listen to from the start, and how great sufferings he endured, and yet how he bore witness to Christ by word and deed? Now, these things have been recorded in order that we also may imitate him." See Hugh of St. Cher, p. 347v,p: "Do you see the herald of truth, how his lack of learning did not impede him or how he was not hindered by how much he heard and how much he suffered both in words and in actions and how nevertheless he bore witness. But these things were written, so that we might imitate him."

to Stephan in Acts 7:58: "And casting him outside the city, they began to stone him."

QUESTIONS

41. Question 1 concerns what the blind man said in John 9:25: "Whether he is a sinner, I do not know." – He seems to have lied, since in John 9:31 below he acknowledged that he was a sinner.[80] – Let there be a twofold response. First, from Chrysostom that "I do not know" means "I am not declaring this now."[81] Or "I do not know" means that "I am ignorant of his life." Moreover, since I am a blind person, I have never seen him nor followed him.[82]

42. Question 2 focuses on John 9:31: "We know that God does not hear sinners." – Contrary. Didn't God hear the publican?[83] – A twofold answer is found in the Glossa. In the first answer the emphasis should be put on "does not hear *sinners*," since God does not hear those who persist in sin, that is, for their salvation.[84] – The Glossa provides the second answer: The blind man had not yet been besmeared nor interiorly illumined. And therefore he did

---

[80] John 9:31 says: "Now we know that God does not hear sinners...."

[81] See Homily 58 n. 2 in FC 41, p. 111: "'Whether he is a sinner, I do not know,' as if he said: 'I am not now speaking on this Man's behalf, and for the moment I refrain from expressing my opinion.'"

[82] See Chrysostom, Homily 59 n. 1 in FC 41, p. 121: "For, actually, he had not seen Christ before this moment."

[83] See Luke 18:13-14. See Augustine, Tractate 44 n. 13 in FC 88, p. 183: "For God also listens to sinners. For if God would not listen to sinners, in vain would that publican, casting his eyes to the ground and striking his breast, say: 'O Lord, be merciful to me, a sinner.' And that confession won justification as this blind man won enlightenment."

[84] The Glossa Ordinaria apud Lyranum has the same commentary as that of the Glossa Interlinearis, which is dependent upon Augustine. See the previous note and the next note.

speak a falsehood, although he believed he was speaking the truth.[85]

43. Question 3 is about John 9:33: "If this man were not from God, he could do nothing." – Contrary. Many evil people perform multiple miracles, as the Lord himself said in Matthew 7:22: "Lord, did we not cast out demons in your name and work many miracles in your name?" – The response is that the blind man understood that he was performing these miracles by his own authority.[86] Or the response could be given as above.[87]

44. Question 4 raises the further query: Since the Lord cured everyone interiorly whom he cured exteriorly, why wasn't this blind person illumined interiorly?[88] – Two responses are possible. The blind man was a believer, but did not yet possess explicit faith. He was like a catechumen and in John 9:35-38 is given instruction. Second, it was not necessary that he be simultaneously healed interiorly at that time, since his exterior infirmity was not from his own sin, as the Lord testified.[89]

---

[85] This is the Glossa Interlinearis. See Augustine, Tractate 44 n. 2 in FC 88, p. 176: "Ask a man: Are you a Christian? If he is a pagan or a Jew, he has answered you: I am not. But if he said, 'I am,' you still ask him: Are you a catechumen or one of the faithful? If he answered, A catechumen, he was besmeared, not yet washed." In Augustine's interpretation the man born blind was not yet a catechumen and surely did not believe in Jesus as the Son of God (see 9:35-38).

[86] See Chrysostom, Homily 58 n. 3 in FC 41, p. 114: "Well, then, if you acknowledge that God does not hear sinners, and this Man has worked a miracle, yes, such a miracle as no one else has ever worked, it is altogether clear that He has surpassed all the rest in merit and that His power is greater than merely human power."

[87] See the ending of question 2.

[88] See the Glossa Ordinaria on Matt 9:2 in PL 114:115B: "Having taken away the cause of the sickness, he afterwards cured the body."

[89] See John 9:3.

45. Question 5 addresses the Pharisees' statement in John 9:34: "You were totally born in sin." – It could be responded that they were speaking not from reason, but from indignation. Another interpretation is: Since he had not departed from the sins, in which he was born, by religion like the Pharisees. Another viewpoint is: They said that he was born in sins on account of his blindness which was a punishment for sin.[90]

JOHN 9:35-41
THE SPIRITUAL ILLUMINATION OF THE MAN BORN BLIND

46. *Jesus heard.* This verse introduces the third section of the chapter. Having already described the wondrous illumination of the blind man and the dispute of the Jews, the Evangelist turns here to *the spiritual illumination of the blind man* and follows this order. First is *Christ's gracious searching out of the contemptible blind man*. Second is *the internal illumination of the consenting blind man*. Third is the intimation of *the just blinding of the arrogant Jews*.

---

[90] See Chrysostom, Homily 58 n. 3 in FC 41, p. 114: "As long as they continued to expect him to make a denial, they thought him trustworthy, and called on him not once only, but a second time…. Since he spoke the truth, in no way intimidated by them, they condemned him at the moment when they ought most of all to have held him in admiration…. In this way they were harshly reproaching him with his blindness, as if to say: 'From the beginning of your life you have been in sin,' intimating that it was on this account that he had been born blind, which was an unreasonable assumption." See the Glossa Ordinaria on John 9:34 in PL 114:395D: "'You were totally born in sins.' That is, with closed eyes, which they say is on account of his parents' sins, but Christ heals the total person. On the outside he opens the eyes; on the inside he opens the heart."

Verse 35. First is the gracious searching out of the abject blind man. For the Pharisees had cast him out, but the Lord took him in. For this reason the text reads: *Jesus heard that they had cast him out.* He knew of this by himself, but nevertheless it was related to him. *And when he had found him.* His search is not a casual one, but a studious one with the purpose of welcoming him. Luke 15:8 states: "She lights a lamp and searches diligently until she finds it." *He said to him: Do you believe in the Son of God?* By searching after him he enkindles a fire within him and calls the one enkindled, so that he might welcome the rejected according to what Psalm 26:10 states "My father and my mother have left me, but the Lord has lifted me up." Jeremiah 49:11 reads: "Leave your fatherless children, and I will make you[91] live."

47. (Verse 36). *He answered and said.* This is the second point, that is, internal illumination or instruction of a person who is giving his consent. For the blind man consents to faith. For he said: *Who is he, Lord, that I may believe in him?* As if he were saying: I am ready to believe. Thus Chrysostom comments: "He speaks a word of both inquiry and desire."[92] Therefore, he is instructed. So:

48. (Verse 37). *Jesus*[93] *said to him: You have seen him and he it is who is speaking with you. You have seen* through my miraculous deed. *He is speaking with you* through wondrous instruction. John 8:25 above states: "I am the

---

[91] The Vulgate reads *eos* "(them)" whilst Bonaventure has *te* ("you").

[92] See Homily 59 n. 1 in PG 59:322: "A word of longing and strong desire." See Hugh of St. Cher, p. 348a: "Chrysostom: He speaks a word from a longing and very inquisitive soul."

[93] On p. 380 n. 12 QuarEd accurately indicate that the Vulgate reads *Et dixit ei Iesus* ("And Jesus said to him") while Bonaventure has *Dixit ei Iesus* ("Jesus said to him").

beginning who is speaking with you." In a similar way the Lord instructed the Samaritan woman in John 4:26 above: "I am he who is speaking with you." And since "with the heart a person believes unto righteousness and with the mouth profession of faith is made unto salvation,"[94] the true profession of the illuminated blind man follows. And he professed his faith by word, saying:

49. (Verse 38). *I believe, Lord.*[95] And he offers reverent obedience. So the text continues: *And falling down, he worshipped him*, as God, who alone is to be adored with worship. So the Lord answered the devil in Matthew 4:10: "You shall worship the Lord your God and him only shall you serve." Deuteronomy 6:13 states: "You shall fear the Lord your God and him only shall you serve."

50. (Verse 39). *And Jesus said to him.* The third point occurs here, that is, the just blindness of the Jews, which the Lord reveals to the blind man. He had also illumined him bodily to reveal this blindness. Therefore, the text states: *For judgment I have come into the world that those who do not see may see and those who see may become blind. In judgment*, that is, of division, *that those who see*, that is, those who think that they see, like the Jews, *may become blind*. About this judgment it is said in Romans 11:25: "Brothers and sisters, I would not have you ignorant ... lest you should be wise in your own conceits, that a partial blindness has befallen Israel, until the full number of the Gentiles should enter." And again Romans 9:30-31 reads: "Gentiles, who were not pursuing righteousness have secured righteousness.... But Israel,

---

[94] See Rom 10:10.

[95] On p. 381 n. 2 QuarEd correctly mention that the Vulgate reads *At ille ait: Credo, Domine* ("And he said: I believe, Lord") whereas Bonaventure has *Credo, Domine* ("I believe, Lord").

by pursuing a law of righteousness, have not attained to the law of righteousness."[96] And that this judgment is just is obvious from the interrogation of the Pharisees and the response of the Lord, in which the Jews' malice and obstinacy are intimated, since, although they saw, they did not want to believe and to understand. And so by the judgment of God and their own sin they have become blind. So the text continues:

51. (Verse 40). *Some of the Pharisees*[97] *who were with him heard this*, that is, they were present with him. *And said:*[98] *Are we ourselves also blind?* They were indignant at the Lord's word, since they believed that it had been spoken for their sakes and because they regarded themselves as wise. And from this itself the Lord manifests the divine judgment that they have been justly blinded. Therefore:

52. (Verse 41). *Jesus said to them: If you were blind, you would not have sin.* Because then the Lord would illumine you. For 1 Corinthians 3:18 states: "If anyone of you thinks himself wise in this world, let him become a fool that he may be wise." *But now*[99] *that you say that we see*, and consider yourselves wise, *your sin remains*, namely, the sin of unbelief,[100] according to what Romans 1:22

---

[96] Hugh of St. Cher, p. 348m also cites Rom 9:30-31, but does so in a citation from Chrysostom.

[97] The Vulgate reads *Et audierunt ex Pharisaeis* ("And some of the Pharisees heard") while Bonaventure has *Audierunt quidam ex Pharisaeis* ("Some of the Pharisees heard").

[98] On p. 381 n. 6 QuarEd accurately indicate that the Vulgate reads *dixerunt ei* ("they said to him") whereas Bonaventure has *dixerunt* ("they said").

[99] On p. 381 n. 7 QuarEd correctly mention that the Vulgate reads *Nunc vero* ("But now") whereas Bonaventure has *Nunc autem* ("But now").

[100] See Hugh of St. Cher, p. 348m: "They are blinded by their unbelief."

reads: "Professing to be wise, they have become fools." Thus the Lord says in Jeremiah 5:21: "Hear, O foolish people who are without understanding, who have eyes, but do not see, and ears, but do not hear." And since these people who see did not want to believe, they have become blind. Psalm 68:24 states: "Let their eyes be darkened that they do not see," etc.

QUESTIONS

53. Question 1 deals with the Lord's question in John 9:35: "Do you believe in the Son of God?" – 1. It is assured that "Son of God" stands here for the divine nature. But John 9:37 adds: "You have seen him." Now "him" is a relative pronoun that points back to "Son of God." Therefore, the referent is Christ according to his divine nature. So the blind man is seeing the divine nature. – 2. Likewise, if faith concerns things that are not seen,[101] how does the Lord exhort him to believe in someone whom he sees? – I respond that it has to be maintained that it is proper that there is a communication of properties because of the harmony within the one hypostasis.[102] Thus just as the same individual is said to be dead and eternal, so too the same individual, in whom one should believe, because he is equal to the Father, is the same one who speaks and is seen, but in the form of a slave.[103]

54. Question 2 explores the meaning of John 9:39: "For judgment I have come into this world," because in John 3:17 above says: "God did not send his Son to judge the

---

[101] See Hebr 11:1: "Now faith is the substance of things to be hoped for, the evidence of things that are not seen."

[102] See Book III, d. 1. a. q. 3 of Bonaventure's *Sentence Commentary*.

[103] See Phil 2:6-7.

world." – The answer may be that he came for a judgment of division,[104] but not of condemnation.[105] – But there is another possible interpretation. It distinguishes between "to come for judgment" and "to come to judge." "To come to judge" indicates the finality of the intention to judge. Christ did not come in this manner in his first coming. But "to come for judgment" is to effect some judgment among the proud in his first coming, since they were blinded at his coming, although he did not come for this purpose.[106]

55. Question 3 focuses on John 9:38: "That those who do not see may see and those who see may become blind." – Wherefore, it seems that blindness stems from Jesus Christ the Lord. And indeed this seems to have to be said because of this reasoning: if blindness is a punishment, and every punishment is just, and what is just is good, and what is good is from God, it follows that blindness is from God. – But contrary. 1. "God is light,"[107] and is also heat. Therefore, if it is the characteristic of heat not to freeze, it is also the property of light not to darken. Therefore God does not blind. – 2. Moreover, God always desires that reality be conformed to God's image. So if blindness deforms, to blind does not pertain to God.

It may be answered that blindness can be considered according to what it is. And thus it is a privation and does

---

[104] See John 9:39 n. 50.

[105] See John 3:17-21 n. 30-34 and n. 35-37. See also John 5 n. 55-58.

[106] See Chrysostom, Homily 56 n. 1 in FC 41, p. 89: "Furthermore, some maintain that this conclusion (to manifest the glory of God) was stated, not in a causal sense, but because of what resulted, as when He said: 'For judgment have I come into this world, that those who do not see may see, and they who see may become blind.' Now, of course, He did not come with this purpose: that those who saw might become blind."

[107] See 1 John 1:5.

not have an efficient cause, but a deficient cause. But God is the deficient cause of nothing. And so its cause is our malice, for Wisdom 2:21 reads: "Their malice blinded them." However, since blindness and hardness are punishments, they posit an existence according to what it is. And a punishment, according to what it is, is just, and thus, according to what it is, can be from God.[108] – It seems that something further should be said. The statement that some punishment is from God is open to more interpretations. In one sense it is from the one who ordains, and thus sin, which is the punishment of sin, in as far as it is a punishment, is from God, but it is not according to God according to what it is, but only in as far as it is a punishment. – In a second way some punishments are said to be from God according to what they are. And this occurs either from God who inflicts punishment. And in this manner death and other punishments are from God, which are eventually merited. Or by God withdrawing something because of what we have done. And so one lacks nutriment from God. For God has ceased to give to the soul the grace, by which it governed the flesh, because of our fault. Once this grace has been withdrawn, the flesh sinks into the depths. – There is a third manner, namely, from God who does not accompany our deeds. And such is blindness and hardness. For someone is hardened in evil, because that person is not visited by God through a just judgment. Someone is blinded, since that person is not illumined interiorly. This is what Augustine says.[109]

---

[108] See Book XII, c. 7 of Augustine, *City of God* in FC 14, p. 257: "No one, therefore, need seek for an efficient cause of an evil will. Since the 'effect' is, in fact, a deficiency, the cause should be called 'deficient.'" See further Book XII, c. 8 in FC 14, p. 258: "This I know, that the nature of God can never and nowhere be deficient in anything, while things made out of nothing can be deficient."

[109] See Pseudo-Augustine, *De praedestinatione et gratia*, c. 4 in PL 45:1668: "But it should not be understood in this way, as if God creates in a human being that hardness of heart that was not there. For what

is hardness but to go against the commandments of God? ... For God
is said to harden the person whom he does not want to soften. Also
God is said to blind the person whom he does not want to illumine. So
also to reject the person whom he does not want to call. For those he
predestined, he also called, and those whom he called, he also justified
(Rom 8:30). He himself granted that we exist. He also granted that we
could be good."

CHAPTER TEN

JOHN 10:1-41
CHRIST THE GOOD SHEPHERD

1. *Amen, amen I say to you*, etc. Throughout chapters 7-9 the Lord has shown himself to be the director by means of his wise word and powerful miracle. Now he manifests himself to be such by means of *the example of his good life*. In the two ways of his wisdom and power he directed as a *teacher*, but now in a third way he directs as a *shepherd*. Therefore, in this chapter the Lord's intention is to reveal himself as *the true and good shepherd*. This chapter is divided into two sections, since the Lord first shows himself to be the good shepherd *in proverbs and parable*. In the second section *he explains the proverb and applies it to himself*, so that through this he might show that he is the true shepherd where verse 7 reads: "So Jesus said to them again."

JOHN 10:1-6
CHRIST SHOWS THAT HE IS THE GOOD SHEPHERD
THROUGH A PROVERB

So the text describes the good shepherd by means of a proverb in this order. First is *the entrance* of the good and true shepherd. Second is *the proof* that he is the good shepherd. Third is *the office* of the good shepherd. Finally the text says how this proverb *was hidden from the Jews*.

2. (Verse 1). So first Christ distinguishes the entrance of the good and true shepherd by comparing it to its opposite, since when opposites are placed together they become clearer.[1] And the entrance of the shepherd is *through the door*, but the thief comes through another opening. So the text says: *Amen, amen I say to you* – The Lord continues speaking to the Pharisees.[2] – *the person who enters not by the door into the sheepfold*, that is, into the Church of God, in which the Lord's flock is contained, *but climbs up another way*, as an arrogant and ambitious person, *is a thief and a robber. A thief*, because he says that someone else's property is his own. *A robber*, because he destroys and kills the goods of another.[3] Jerome says of this ascent of the evil shepherd: "We rejoice at the ascent. Let us dread the fall. If it was such a great joy to have reached the heights, how much grief there is in falling from them."[4]

---

[1] See Aristotle's *De sophisticis elenchis* in WAE, vol. 1, 174b: "For the placing of their contraries close beside them makes things look big to men, both relatively and absolutely, and worse and better."

[2] On the connection between John 9 and 10 see Glossa Ordinaria on John 10:1 in PL 114:396AB: "Since the Pharisees boasted that they saw, which they could if there were Christ's sheep, the Lord proposes the similitude about his flock and about the door through which one enters the sheepfold against their arrogance and shows that neither wisdom nor observance of the Law nor a good life is of any value unless through him."

[3] See Augustine, Tractate 45 n. 6 in FC 88, p. 191: "'He who does not enter the sheepfold through the gate but climbs in some other way.' Woe to the wretch, because he is going to fall! Let him be humble, let him enter through the gate. Let him come on the level ground and he will not stumble. 'That one,' he says, 'is a thief and a robber.' He wishes to call someone else's sheep his own sheep; *his own*, that is, taken away in theft, for this purpose, not that he may save them but that he may kill them."

[4] This is Bonaventure's adaptation of Book XIII of Jerome's commentary on Ez 44:29-30. See PL 25:444D-445A. Hugh of St. Cher, p.

In this way that leader of thieves and the vainglorious ascended. About him it is said in Isaiah 14:13: "I will ascend into heaven. I will exalt my throne above the stars of heaven." The person who enters in such an inordinate manner is a thief and not the shepherd.

3. (Verse 2). *But the one who enters by the door is the shepherd of the sheep.* The person who enters through the door is the one who enters through the truth.[5] About this entrance 1 Thessalonians 2:1 states: "You yourselves know, brothers and sisters, our entrance among you." And the text continues: "For at no time did we use words of flattery, as you know, nor any pretext for avarice ... nor[6] did we seek glory from people."

4. (Verse 3). *To this one the gatekeeper opens.* This verse introduces the second point, namely, the proof that he is the true shepherd, because he is recognized by the gatekeeper and by the flock. So the text continues: *To this one the gatekeeper opens*, knowing that he is the shepherd. The gatekeeper is Christ, who has the key.[7] For Isaiah 22:22 reads: "I will lay the key of the house of David upon his shoulder, and he will open. And none will shut. And he will shut, and none will open." *And the sheep hear his voice*, because they willingly obey the good shepherd. Hebrews 13:17 says: "Obey your superiors and be subject to

---

348v, e also cites Jerome. His citation does not agree verbatim with that of Jerome or that of Bonaventure.

[5] See Augustine, Tractate 45 n. 5 in FC 88, p. 190: "Let him proclaim the true Christ. Let him not only proclaim the true Christ, but let him seek Christ's glory, not his own."

[6] The Vulgate reads *nec* ("nor") while Bonaventure has *neque* ("nor").

[7] See the Glossa Ordinaria in PL 114:396C: "The gatekeeper, that is, Christ, who opens himself, or Scripture which opens the way to Christ or the Holy Spirit who teaches all truth."

them, for they keep watch as having to render an account for your souls."

And he calls his own sheep by name. This verse points to *the office* of the good shepherd which is threefold: *to call, to lead forth, to direct. He calls* them by name through recognizing them. *He leads them forth* to pasture by teaching them. *He goes before them* by giving them good example. This relationship is fitting for Christ the shepherd by excellence and for others through imitation. Thus, the text first says: *He calls his own sheep by name*, namely, Christ does this. 2 Timothy 2:19 states: "The Lord knows who are his." About imitation of Christ Proverbs 12:10 says: "The just person knows the souls of his beasts." *And he*, that is, Christ, *leads them forth*, to pasture. Ezekiel 34:13 reads: "I will lead them forth from the peoples and will gather them from the countries and will bring them to their own land," that is, which was flowing with milk. So is also the imitator of Christ like Moses and Aaron. Psalm 70:21 states: "You have led your people like sheep by the hand of Moses and Aaron."

5. (Verse 4). *And when he has let out his own sheep, he goes before them*, He goes ahead, giving good example like Christ. Micah 2:13 says: "He will go up to open the way before them."[8] Thus he said in John 13:15 below: "I have given you an example, that as I have done for you, so you also should do." Thus also the imitator of Christ, for 1 Corinthians 11:1 reads: "Be imitators of me, as I am of Christ." And such people are few. Thus Isaiah 24:2 states: "It will be the same for people and priest." – This great and threefold office of the good shepherd has an effect in the sheep, that is, the good shepherd directs the sheep by

---

[8] Hugh of St. Cher, p. 349v,f also cites Micah 2:13.

imitation. For this reason the text says: *The sheep⁹ follow him*, namely, the true shepherd. Sheep are simple and humble. About them Hugh comments: "There is the humility of the sheep that does not desire to be in charge and loves to be obedient. Many, fleeing labor, want to be in charge and despise obedience. These are not *sheep*,"[10] since they do not follow. So the sheep follow, *because they know his voice*, that is, know it to be the voice of consolation, according to what Matthew 11:28: "Come to me, all you who labor and are burdened, and I will give you rest." The good shepherd calls them to refreshment.

6. (Verse 5). *But a stranger they do not follow, but flee from him*,[11] that is, the evil shepherd or wolf, *because they do not know the voice of strangers*, that is, they do not approve. These strangers are the false Christs and false prophets and false apostles, about whom it is said in 2 Corinthians 11:13: They are "deceitful workers, disguising themselves as apostles of Christ." They do not follow such people, for they have been warned by their shepherd. Matthew 7:15 states: "Beware of false prophets, who come to you in sheep's clothing, but inwardly are ravenous wolves."

7. (Verse 6). *Jesus spoke this proverb to them*.[12] The fourth point surfaces here, namely, that the proverb was hidden from them. Thus the text continues: *Jesus spoke this*

---

[9] On p. 384 n. 5 QuarEd rightly notice that the Vulgate reads *Et oves* ("And the sheep") whilst Bonaventure has *Oves* ("The sheep").

[10] This is a paraphrase of Book I, n. 101 of Hugh of Saint Victor, *Miscelanea*. See PL 177:532D: "Humility is twofold. First, you do not desire to be in charge. Second, you love to be obedient. There are many who want to be in charge and flee labor, not honor."

[11] The Vulgate reads *fugient* ("will flee") whereas Bonaventure has *fugiunt* ("flees").

[12] On p. 384 n. 10 QuarEd accurately indicate that the Vulgate reads *eis* ("to them") while Bonaventure has *illis* ("to them").

proverb to them, but they did not understand what he was saying to them. So Matthew 13:13 says: "This is why I speak to them in parables, so that seeing they may not see and hearing they may not hear nor understand."

8. It should be noted that according to Chrysostom "a *proverb* is a useful saying that openly gives practical advice, but also retains much meaning on a hidden level." According to Basil "a proverb is moral instruction, correction of vices, a proven way of life, directing human actions to a higher level." According to common parlance a proverb is a saying that is general and concise that conveys something directly in its articulation, but also conveys something beyond the surface meaning of the words.[13] – It should also be noted in trying to understand what has been said that those who do not enter through the door are deprived of the office of the true shepherd and do so in many ways.

---

[13] On pp. 385-386 nn. 12-14 QuarEd track the possible sources of Bonaventure's citations. It seems that Bonaventure has adapted them from Hugh of St. Cher. See Hugh of St. Cher, p. 350m: "Jesus spoke this proverb to them, etc.] that is, this parable or this obscure saying or common saying about the shepherd. And note: a proverb is a saying that is general and concise that conveys something directly in its articulation, but also conveys something beyond the surface meaning of the words. Basil. A proverb is moral instruction and correction of vices, a proven way of life, directing human actions to a more safe level. And later he says: In ordinary speech the name of proverb is regularly given to human customs, that is, those things that are said with the voice of ancient tradition. But that is the common and unsophisticated meaning, but for us a proverb is a useful saying that openly provides practical advice, but also conveys much meaning on a hidden level."

John 10:7-41
Christ applies the proverb to himself

9. *So Jesus said to them again*. This verse begins the second part of the chapter, in which the Lord *explains the proverb by applying it to himself*, showing that he is the true shepherd relative to the three points made by the proverb. First, with regard to *the entrance of the true shepherd*. Second, with regard to *the love of the true shepherd* where verse 11 states: "I am the good shepherd." Third, with regard to *the proof that he is the good shepherd* where verse 22 reads: "It was the feast of the Dedication."

John 10:7-10
The entrance of the true shepherd

First, he shows that he is the true shepherd with regard to *entrance* in this manner. First, *no one rightly enters except through him*. Second, *whoever enters through him rightly enters*. Third, he is not only *the way of entering*, but he also *enters rightly*.

Verse 7. So he first shows that no one rightly enters the sheepfold except through him. For this reason the text states: *Amen, amen I say to you: I*[14] *am the door of the sheep*. "I" is emphasized and separates Christ from any other, for there is no entrance except through him. Thus the text continues:

10. (Verse 8). *All whoever have come are thieves and robbers*, that is, because they did not enter through me.

---

[14] On p. 385 n. 3 QuarEd correctly indicate that the Vulgate reads *Quia ego* ("That I am") while Bonaventure has *Ego* ("I am").

And the text adds a sign of this: *But the sheep have not heard them.* This door had been closed for a long time, but through the passion it was unlocked, so that "the fullness of the Gentiles might enter."[15] About this door Revelation 4:1 says: "After these things I looked, and behold, a door standing open in heaven." And truly it was open, because, as is said in John 6:37 above: "The person who comes to me I will not cast out."

11. (Verse 9). *I am the door.* The second point surfaces here, namely, that whoever enters through him enters salutarily. So the text states: *I am the door,* that is, through which a person enters salutarily. And the reason is added: *If anyone enter through me he will be safe.* About this entrance Matthew 7:13-14 reads: "Enter by the narrow gate.... How narrow the gate and constricted the way that leads to life," because Christ was poor and little. Through this little door rich people, loaded with riches, do not enter. For this reason it is said in Matthew 19:24: "It is easier for a camel to pass through the eye of a needle than for a rich person to enter the kingdom of the heavens." This entrance is through *faith* and *the sacrament of baptism,* since faith is the door for the virtues while baptism is the door for the sacraments. Persons who enter in this way will be saved. Mark 16:16 states: "Those who believe and have been baptized will be saved." *And will go in and out and will find pasture. He will go in,* through contemplation that calls one back to interior matters. *He will go out,* through action.[16] Numbers 27:16-17 has: "May the Lord God of the spirits of all flesh provide a person ...

[15] See Rom 11:25: "Until the fullness of the Gentiles might enter."
[16] See Hugh of St. Cher, p. 350mn: "will go in] through contemplation: And will go out] through good work."

who can go in and out before them."[17] Another interpretation is that of Augustine: *He will go in*, through contemplation of the Divinity. *He will go out*, to regard humanity. *And he will find pasture*, because he is refreshed in all: the intellect through contemplation of the Divinity and the senses through contemplation of humanity.[18] About these pastures Ezekiel 34:13-14 says: "I will feed them ... on the mountains of Israel.... I will feed them in the most abundant pastures."[19]

12. (Verse 10). *The thief only comes to steal*. Here is the third point, that is, Christ himself enters as the true shepherd, and not as a thief. For this reason the text states: *The thief only comes to steal*, by extorting temporal goods. *And slays*, by temporally tormenting those subject to him. *And destroys*, by casting them into hell through bad example. *I have come that they may have life and have it more abundantly*, that is, to preserve life as a shepherd. *That they may have life*, that is, the life of grace, about which life John 6:33 above stated: "This is the bread that

---

[17] The Vulgate reads *et possit exire et intrare ante eos* ("who can go out and in before them") whilst Bonaventure has *qui possit intrare et exire ante eos* ("who can go in and out before them").

[18] This is Bonaventure's adaptation of *Liber de Spiritu et anima*, c. 9 in PL 40:785: "For since God became man, so that he might beatify in himself the entire human being, and man's entire orientation might be towards him, and man's total love might be directed to him, since God would be seen by the fleshly senses through flesh and be seen by the mental capacities through contemplation of his Divinity. And this was for the total good of human beings, so that whether they go in or go out, they might find pasture in their creator (John 10:9). Pasture outside in the flesh of the Savior and pasture inside in the Divinity of the creator."

[19] The Vulgate reads *eas* ("them," referring to sheep) while Bonaventure has *eos* ("them,") referring to people. See Hugh of St. Cher, p. 350o: "Ez 34:14: I will feed them in the most abundant pastures, and their pasture will be on the high mountains of Israel." Hugh of St. Cher has *eas* ("them").

comes down from heaven and gives life to the world." *That they may have life more abundantly*, namely, the life of glory, about which John 17:3 says: "This is eternal life that they may know you, the only true God and the one whom you have sent, Jesus Christ." The text here says *abundant*, since it is said in Luke 6:38: "They will pour into your lap a measure that is good and[20] pressed down and shaken together and running over."

Questions

13. Question 1 addresses the fact that in John 10:7 the Lord compares himself to a door whereas in John 10:3 above to the gatekeeper. How is the same individual door and gatekeeper and shepherd? – I answer that the point has to be made that is said in John 14:6 below: Christ is the way, the truth, and the life. Since he is the way to the Father, he is the door. Since he is the truth, which teaches the way, he is the gatekeeper. Since he is life, he is the shepherd who provides pasture and preserves life.[21]

14. Question 2 singles out John 9:8 and asks the meaning of "whoever have come are thieves." – Contrary. The prophets and patriarchs and John the Baptist have come. So according to this all these were evil, as the heretics say.[22] – The answer to this is to place emphasis on the

---

[20] The Vulgate does not read *et* ("and").

[21] See Augustine, Tractate 46 n. 4 in FC 88, pp. 205-206: "Let us not, then brothers, be reluctant to take him as the gate and as the gatekeeper, according to certain likenesses. For what is a gate? That by which we enter. Who is the gatekeeper? He who opens. Now who opens himself except he who explains himself? Look, the Lord had said a gate; we had not understood. When we did not understand, it was closed; he who opened it is himself the gatekeeper...."

[22] See Book XVI, c. 12 of Augustine, *Contra Faustum* in NPNF1, Vol. 4, p. 223: "We believe both that Moses wrote of Christ, and that

words "they have come," that is, on their own authority and not on divine authority, like the false prophets, about whom Jeremiah 23:21 says: "I did not send them,[23] yet they ran." Now the good have not come, but were sent. For Augustine comments: "They have not come besides him, but have come with him."[24] For he is the truth, and therefore, whoever preached the truth has come with him.

15. Question 3 asks the meaning of John 10:9: "He will go out and will find pastures." – Contrary. "The person who puts his hand to the plow must not look back."[25] Wherefore, no one who has gone inside will go outside. – I answer that there is a twofold egress. One is contrary to entrance into the faith, and this is egress from the Church through infidelity. There is an objection to this type of egress, about which Augustine says: "To have entered the Church is a good thing, but to have gone forth from it is the worst thing."[26] And about this 1 John 2:19 states: "They have gone forth from us, but they were not of us." The other going out is the movement from contemplation

---

all that came before Christ were thieves and robbers. By their coming He means their not being sent. Those who were sent, as Moses and the holy prophets, came not before Him, but with Him. They did not proudly wish to precede Him, but were the humble bearers of the message which He uttered by them."

[23] The Vulgate reads *prophetas* ("prophets") whereas Bonaventure has *eos* ("them").

[24] See Augustine, Tractate 45 n. 8 in CCSL xxxvi, p. 391: "They have not come besides him, because they have come with him."

[25] See Luke 9:62: "No one, having put his hand to the plow and looking back, is fit for the kingdom of God."

[26] See Tractate 45 n. 15 in CCSL xxxvi, pp. 396-397 and FC 88, p. 201: "To be sure, to go into the Church through the gate, Christ, is exceedingly good; but to go out of the Church, as this John the Evangelist himself says in his epistle, 'They went out from us, but they were not of us,' is surely not good.... To go in through Christ is to work according to faith itself, but to go out through Christ is to work according to faith itself even outside, that is, before men."

to action, and this is not falling away, but moving forward. About this Psalm 103:23 says: "Human beings will go forth to their work and to their labor till evening."[27]

John 10:11-21
Christ is the Good Shepherd because of his Love

16. *I am the good shepherd*. The Lord has shown that he is the good shepherd with respect to the entrance of the good shepherd. Now in a second point he shows that he is the good shepherd relative to *the love of the good shepherd*. He does so in the following manner. First is shown Christ's *friendship* towards his sheep. Second, his *care*. Third, his *providence*. Fourth, his *munificence*. Finally, from this arises *a division among the Jews*.

Verse 11. First Christ's friendship towards the sheep is contrasted with the love of hirelings, which is not true love. So the text says: *I am the good shepherd*, and he demonstrates this: *The good shepherd lays down his life for his sheep*, out of the burning love he has for them. For he himself said in John 15:13 below: "Greater love than this no one has that one lay down his life for his friends." Such a shepherd was Paul who said in 2 Corinthians 12:15: "I will most gladly spend and be spent myself for your souls." This is not how the hireling acts. For this reason the text says:

17. (Verse 12). *But the hireling, who is not a shepherd, whose own the sheep are not*, since he does not love them,

---

[27] Bonaventure continues to be dependent upon Augustine, Tractate 45 n. 15. See FC 88, p. 201: "For this reason it is also read in the psalm, 'A man will go out to his work.' And the Lord himself says, 'Let your works shine before men.'"

but loves lucre for which he serves. About this Gregory observes: "That person is a hireling who indeed holds the place of a shepherd, but does not seek what is profitable for souls. He is eager for earthly advantages, rejoices in being a superior ... enjoys the respect and honor lavished on him by men and women."[28] About this individual one could say what Matthew 6:2 has: "Amen I say to you: They have received their reward." This person *sees the wolf coming and leaves the sheep and flees*, since he is afraid of the wolf and does not love the sheep. "The wolf," as Gregory says, "comes upon the sheep when any unjust person ... oppresses the faithful ... and the humble."[29] About such wolves Paul says in Acts 20:29: "I know that after my departure fierce wolves will get in among you and will not spare the flock." When such a wolf arrives on the scene, the hireling abandons the sheep. Zechariah 11:17 reads: "O shepherd and idol, that abandons the flock." The scattering of the sheep follows upon the flight of this hireling, and so the text continues: *And the wolf snatches and scatters the sheep*. Ezekiel 34:6 states: "My flocks were scattered upon the face of the earth, and there was no one who sought them." And the reason for all these events is provided, namely, the lack of true friendship. For this reason the text says:

18. (Verse 13). *But the hireling flees, because he is a hireling and has no concern for the sheep*, that is, since he loves reward and not the sheep. For Gregory comments: "A person who is in charge of the sheep, not because he loves them but because he is seeking earthly gain, cannot

---

[28] Bonaventure abbreviates Homily 14 n. 2 of GGHG. See CCSL cxli, p. 97.

[29] Bonaventure abbreviates Homily 14 n. 2 of GGHG. See CCSL cxli, p. 98.

make a stand when the sheep are in danger."[30] About such people it is said in Ezekiel 13:5: "You have not gone up to face the enemy nor have you set up a wall for the house of Israel to stand in battle on the day of the Lord." Gregory notes: "He flees, because ... he is silent,"[31] because he was fearful, for fear is flight.[32]

19. (Verse 14). *I am the good shepherd*. The second point is introduced here, that is, Christ's care for the sheep, which consists in singling out and recognizing the sheep. For this reason he calls himself *the good shepherd*. So the text states: *I am the good shepherd, and I know my sheep,*[33] *and mine know me*. And in these things care is highlighted according to what Proverbs 27:23 reads: "Be careful to know the faces of your cattle and to take notice of your flocks." 2 Timothy 2:19 states: "The Lord knows who are his own." – He sheds light on this care by means of a simile. So the text says:

20. (Verse 15). *Even as the Father knows me, and I know the Father*, supply: I know my sheep, and my sheep know me. Chrysostom observes: "*Just as* is a note of similarity,

---

[30] See Homily 14 n. 3 of GGHG in CCSL cxli, p. 99 and Hurst, p. 109. Bonaventure's citation is verbatim.

[31] See Homily 14 n. 2 of GGHG in CCSL cxli, p. 98. See Hurst, p. 108: "He does not flee by changing his place but by withholding his help; he flees because he sees his unrighteousness and is silent; he flees, who conceals himself beneath his silence." Gregory goes on to cite Ez 13:5. See Hugh of St. Cher, p. 351g: "Gregory. He flees, because he fears, because he loved temporal goods more than eternal ones."

[32] See Augustine, Tractate 46 n. 8 in FC 88, pp. 210-211: "Look, the wolf seizes the sheep's throat; the devil has persuaded a believer [to commit] adultery. You are silent, you do not scold. O hired hand, you saw the wolf coming and you fled. Perhaps he answers and says, Look, I am here; I haven't fled. You fled because you kept quiet; you kept quiet because you were afraid. Fear is the flight of the soul."

[33] On p. 387 n. 4 QuarEd accurately indicate that the Vulgate reads *meas* ("mine") whilst Bonaventure has *oves meas* ("my sheep").

not of equality,"[34] as in John 17:11 below the Son, praying to the Father on behalf of his disciples, says: "so that they may be one, as we are." He also manifests his care through its effect, for he says: *And I lay down my life for my sheep*. Likewise, the Apostle says in 1 Corinthians 15:31: "Daily I die for your glory, brothers and sisters." The Lord himself says in Jeremiah 12:7: "I have given my dear soul into the hand of the wicked."[35]

21. (Verse 16). *And I have other sheep*. The third point occurs here, that is, Christ's providence towards the sheep, which consists in the gathering together of his sheep, as a shepherd collects his sheep into a flock, lest they be exposed to an attack. So he says: *And I have other sheep that are not of this fold*, as believers predestined from among the Gentiles. *These also I must bring*, as people going astray. For 1 Peter 2:25 says: "You were like sheep going astray, but now you have returned to the shepherd and guardian of your souls." *And they will hear my voice, and there will be one fold and one shepherd*, on account of the union of the Church from Jews and Gentiles. Thus Ephesians 2:14 reads: "He is our peace, who made the two one," namely, the Gentiles and Jews in one fold.[36] And he is the sole shepherd. Ezekiel 34:23 states: "I will set up

---

[34] Chrysostom doesn't exactly say this. See Homily 60 n. 1 in PG 59:329: "But this knowledge is not equal." In this context Chrysostom cites 2 Tim 2:19.

[35] The Vulgate reads *in manu inimicorum eius* ("into the hand of her enemies") while Bonaventure has *in manu iniquorum* ("into the hand of the wicked").

[36] See Hugh of St. Cher, p. 351v,cd: "And there will be one fold], that is, one Church from Jews and Gentiles. And he gives the source of this unity when he adds: d and one shepherd] ... under one shepherd will be one flock. Which Paul also shows. ... Eph 2:14 says: He is our peace, who made both one."

one shepherd over them, who will feed them, my servant David."[37]

22. (Verse 17). *For this reason the Father loves me.* In this verse the Evangelist makes his fourth point, that is, Christ's munificence towards the sheep, since he, although he owed nothing to death and was not compelled by necessity, laid down his life for the sheep out of sheer liberality. And this commandment he had from the Father, and because of which he merited the Father's love. So the text continues: *Therefore, the Father loves me, because I lay down my life,* namely, in death and the passion, *that I may take it up again,* that is, in the resurrection,[38] and this by the power that is mine to lay down my life and take it up. And he demonstrates this:

23. (Verse 18). *No one takes it from me, but I lay it down of myself,*[39] and so I freely lay it down. Thus the text states: *I have the power to lay it down,* that is, to lay aside, *and the power to take it up again.* So Isaiah 53:7 reads: "He was offered, because it was his own will."[40] And why? He gives the reason, because *I have received this commandment from my Father.* Thus Philippians 2:8 says: "He became obedient" to the Father "to the point of death," etc. So he said to Peter in John 18:11 below: "Do you not wish me to drink the cup that the Father has given me?"[41] As if he were saying: I wish to be obedient.

---

[37] The Vulgate twice reads *ea* ("them," referring to flock) while Bonaventure twice has *eas* ("them," referring to sheep).

[38] See Augustine, Tractate 47 n. 7 in FC 88, p.218: "'The Father loves me for this,' that I die to rise again."

[39] On p. 388 n. 4 QuarEd correctly indicate that the Vulgate reads *a me ipso* ("of myself") whereas Bonaventure has *a me* ("of myself").

[40] Hugh of St. Cher, p. 351v,h also cites Isa 53:7.

[41] John 18:11 reads: "Shall I not drink the cup that the Father has given me?"

24. (Verse 19). *Again there arose a division*. This is the fifth point, that is, the discord among the Jews that arose from the Lord's teaching, because some who did not understand his teaching thought that he was insane. But others thought that he was speaking of sublime matters. So the text states: *Again there arose a division among the Jews*. "Again," since earlier in John 9:16 there was a division over Christ's miracle. *Because of these words*, since they did not understand them. So the text continues:

25. (Verse 20). *Now many of them were saying: He has a demon and is insane*. Thus they were thinking that he was insane. These were from those, about whom 1 Corinthians 2:14 speaks: "The sensual person does not perceive the things of God, for it is foolishness to him, and he cannot understand, because they are examined spiritually." So they were refusing to hear. So they say: *Why do you listen to him*? Thus the Lord said in John 8:43 above: "Because you cannot listen to my word."

26. (Verse 21). *Others were saying: These are not the words of a person who has a demon*. These in some way were beginning to be illumined. For they were having recourse to the miracle of illumination: *Can a demon open the eyes of the blind*? Chrysostom states: "Since they could not stop their mouths with words, they fashioned their proof from the works."[42] So the works provided faith for the words. Wherefore, John 10:38 below notes: "And if you do not … believe me, believe the works."[43]

---

[42] See Homily 60 n. 3 in PG 59:331 and FC 41, p. 141: "Since they were not able to silence His opponents by words, they finally had recourse to His deeds for proof."

[43] John 10:38 reads: "If you are not willing to believe me, believe the works.

Questions

27. Question 1 asks whether the hireling should be cast away and forbidden from caring for the sheep. – It seems that from John 10:12-13 he should be forbidden from caring for the sheep, since he is censured. – But it seems that he should be tolerated, because Philippians 1:18 reads: "Whether in pretense or in truth, Christ is being proclaimed, and in this I rejoice and will rejoice." – Further, he should be praised. Luke 15:17 states: "How many hirelings in my father's house have bread in abundance."[44] Ambrose comments on this passage that they have faith, hope, and charity in abundance.[45] – I answer that one should distinguish between a hireling and a thief, since the hireling speaks the truth and guards the sheep whereas the thief, like a heretic, mouths lies and tears the sheep to pieces. So the thief is entirely to be cast away, but the hireling is to be supported. – But hirelings are of two kinds, since some serve for a temporal reward. Such people are to be tolerated, but nevertheless they are to be censured. Some serve for an eternal reward, and such people are to be supported and given approbation. However, they are not to be completely extolled. Only those serve solely out of love are to be highly extolled.[46]

28. Question 2 concerns John 10:11: "The good shepherd lays down his life for his sheep." – From this it seems: 1.

---

[44] See Hugh of St. Cher, p. 350v,l who cites Luke 15:17 as a reference to good hirelings.

[45] Is this Ambrose? See Bonaventure's commentary on Luke 15:17 n. 29 in his *Commentary on Luke, Chapters 9-16*, p. 1436: "Others are *good* hired men.... And these are the ones who serve for the sake of an eternal reward, and such abound frequently on the bread of faith, hope, and charity."

[46] See Bonaventure's discussion of three types of preachers in his commentary on Luke 9:50 n. 93 in *Commentary on Luke, Chapters 9-16*, pp. 899-900.

The prelate is bound to die for his subjects. – But contrary: To suffer martyrdom is a work of supererogation. But no one is bound to works of supererogation unless they have bound themselves to such by a vow. Wherefore, it seems that a prelate is not obligated to this action. – 2.Likewise, it seems that everyone is bound to this action. 1 John 3:16 states: "We must lay down our lives for our brothers and sisters."

I answer that there can be a threefold meaning to the words "to die for the Lord's flock." There is a dying for the flock by turning something good into something better, and this is a work of supererogation for all prelates. There is also a dying for the flock to free it from imminent danger, and so any prelate is bound, because he has received the care of the Lord's flock, and blood will be required from his hand.[47] There is dying for the flock when it is placed at a point of extreme danger and cannot escape harm unless a person exposes himself to death. And so I say that this is a necessity for everyone, such as the case of selling one's goods and giving to the poor, when they are in extreme necessity. – Here are the basic paths for arriving at reasoned answers to this question.

29. Question 3 concerns John 10:16: "I have other sheep that are not of this fold," because no sheep is a sheep when it is outside the Church. No sheep is innocent when it is outside the Church. – Likewise, why does he say: "I must also bring them"? For Matthew 15:24 reads: "I have not been sent except to the lost sheep of the house of Israel." Therefore, he should not bring these others. – I respond that it has to be maintained that he calls his own those sheep who had not yet been called from the

---

[47] See Ez 3:18: "But I (the Lord) will require his blood at your hand."

Gentiles according to present righteousness, since they had been elect according to eternal predestination. He brought them by merit of his passion and by the word of preaching, not his own preaching, but that of the Apostles, because he himself in his own person had specially and primarily come to preach to the people of Israel, to whom he had been promised and by whom he is to be killed. – And in this way what Matthew 15:24 says is to be understood.[48]

30. Question 4 focuses on John 10:18: "I lay it," that is, my life, "of myself," since it seems that is what anybody can do. For Augustine observes: "Everyone who dies lays down his life."[49] – Now if you say, the other human beings lay down their lives of necessity, an objection arises because of the martyr, who dies voluntarily. – I answer that one has to distinguish between every human being laying down his life, the martyr laying down his life, and Christ laying down his life. Every human being does so of necessity. The martyr does so voluntarily. Christ, however, does so by his will and power simultaneously. For the will of the martyr, even though it is absolutely free to die at a particular time, is, nonetheless, not entirely free from dying. But Christ was totally free.[50]

---

[48] See Augustine, Tractate 47 n. 4 where he also addresses the relationship of Matt 15:24 to John 10:16. See FC 88, pp. 216-217: "To the Gentiles he did not go himself, but he sent; to the people of Israel, in truth, he both sent and came himself so that those who were despising him would receive greater judgment because his presence was also shown to them."

[49] See Tractate 47 n. 11 in CCSL xxxvi, p. 410: "For all men and women, when they die, lay down their lives."

[50] Cf. Ps 87:5-6: "I have become like a person without help, free among the dead."

31. Question 5 also treats John 10:18: "I have the power to lay my life down and ... again to take it up."[51] – 1. Either he is speaking according to his divine nature or according to his body, which separates from the soul. If according to his divine nature, the Divinity has laid aside the soul, which is a sin to say, and those who say it are anathema.[52] – Or he is speaking according to the body, but that doesn't have the power of taking life up again. – 2. Furthermore, it is objected that if the body laid aside the soul and as Damascene says, the soul was the medium of uniting the divine nature to the body,[53] therefore, the divine nature laid aside the body, which is a sinful thing to say.

It has to be said: "the soul" refers here to "life." Thus the sense is: I have the power of laying down my soul, that is, my life, namely, to lay it down through death, and the power to take it up again through the resurrection. – But if it is referring to "the soul" in its proper sense, then Christ is said to lay down his soul, that is, to separate from the flesh, not because the body may do this, but the Son of the God himself does this, who can control both, namely, body and soul.[54] – 2. Now concerning the objection about

---

[51] John 10:18 reads: "I have the power to lay it down, and I have the power to take it up again."

[52] See Book III, d. 21. a. 1. q. 1. fundam. 1 of Bonaventure's *Sentence Commentary* in Omnia Opera 3:437: "Augustine and Damascene: 'Let him be anathema who says that the Word laid aside what it had once assumed': So if he had assumed a soul, he never laid it aside."

[53] See Book III, c. 6 of *De fide orthodoxa* in FC 37, p. 280: "And so, the Word of God is united to the flesh by the intermediary of mind which stands midway between the purity of God and the grossness of the flesh."

[54] See Tractate 47 n. 2 in FC 88, pp. 224-225 where Augustine struggles with the same issues: "Therefore when the soul goes out from the flesh and the flesh remains without the soul, then a man is said to lay down his life. When did Christ lay down his life? When the Word willed it. For in the Word there was sovereignty; therein was the power when the flesh might lay down life and when it might take it up.

the medium or means, it has to be observed that there is a means of distance, connecting, and fittingness. The soul is not a means of distance in that union, because Divinity is immediately united to the body. Nor of connecting, because it does not bind one to another. Rather it is of fittingness, since the body, by that which makes it lovable, is unitable to Divinity in a fitting manner. And therefore, this unity must not be broken.[55]

32. Question 6 inquires about the meaning of John 10:17: "For this reason the Father loves me, because I lay down my life." – Contrary. From the very moment of his conception he was worthy to be loved above all others. – It has to be said that this is spoken according to human nature. And so he is talking here of a meritorious cause, as in the case of Philippians 2:9: "For this reason God also exalted him." The merit involved here exists, not because a debt came about from non-indebtedness[56] nor because from indebtedness there arose greater indebtedness. Rather it came about because what was indebted along one line and one manner, namely, the best interior will, became

---

Therefore, if the flesh laid down its life, how did Christ lay down his life? For is not the flesh Christ? Yes, certainly, the flesh is Christ, and the soul is Christ, and the Word is Christ; and yet these three things are not three Christs, but one Christ."

[55] For greater detail see Book III, d. 2. a. 3. q. 1 and d. 21. a. 1. q. 2. ad 1 in Bonaventure's *Sentence Commentary* in Omnia Opera 3:52-54, 438-439.

[56] A key to what Bonaventure is saying is found in Book III, d. 18. a.1. q.2 ad 4 in his *Sentence Commentary*. See Omnia Opera 3:383-384: "Likewise, whoever merits anything makes from work and obedience something his own from something that is not his own, and from that which is not indebted to him he makes something indebted to him. But Christ could not make a debt from non-debt or make something his own from something not his own, for all things were his through the grace of conception, as he himself bears witness: 'All things that are mine are yours.'"

another kind of indebtedness, that is, through an outward action.

JOHN 10:22-42
CHRIST GIVES PROOF THAT HE IS THE TRUE SHEPHERD

33. *There was*[57] *a feast in Jerusalem.* The Lord has already shown himself to be the true shepherd with regard to the shepherd's entrance and love. Here in a third point he gives a *proof that he is the true shepherd,* one that consists in this that the sheep know him and follow him. There are three elements in this point. First is the Jews' *request for a certain proof.* Second comes *the expression of this certain proof* where verse 25 says: "Jesus answered them: I tell," etc. Third is *the persecution by the Jews* that follows from this where verse 31 reads: "The Jews took up stones."

JOHN 10:22-24
REQUEST FOR A CERTAIN PROOF

The request for a certain proof that he was the shepherd and leader in Israel issues from the questioning Jews. As the Evangelist describes their question, he presents *the time* and *the place* and *the manner of the questioning.*

Verse 22. Relative to time he says: *The feast of the Dedication took place at Jerusalem, and it was winter.* It should be noted that the Latin for Dedication is *encaenia* which comes from *caenon* and means "new." Therefore, *encaeniare* means "to renovate," since at that time the feast was

---

[57] On p. 390 n. 3 QuarEd accurately indicate that the Vulgate reads *autem* ("Now").

being celebrated of the renovation of the Temple which had previously been defiled. And the Latin word *encaenia* is plural to indicate that this solemnity lasted for eight days.[58] 1 Maccabees 4:59 reads: "Judas and his brothers and all the church of Israel decreed that the day of dedication of the temple[59] should be kept ... from year to year for eight days."[60] – With regard to place the text continues:

34. (Verse 23). *And Jesus was walking*[61] *in Solomon's portico*, that is, in the place where Solomon had first made the portico for prayer and which had been destroyed.[62] – With respect to the manner of questioning the text says:

35. (Verse 24). *The Jews gathered around him and said to him: How long will you hold us in suspense?* That is, you are keeping us in suspense.[63] *If you are the Christ, tell us openly*. Give a certain proof about yourself. And so that

---

[58] See Augustine, Tractate 48 n. 2 in FC 88, pp. 228-229: "The Encaenia (feast of the Dedication) was a celebration of the dedication of the temple. For in Greek *kainon* means new. Whenever something new was dedicated, the name *Encaenia* was given. Now, too, common usage employs this term; if anyone is dressed in a new tunic, he is said *encaeniare* – to consecrate it. For the Jews were solemnly celebrating that day on which the temple was dedicated." See Hugh of St. Cher, p. 352n where he cites this passage from Augustine and gives an alternative explanation for *encaenia*.

[59] The Vulgate reads *altaris* ("of the altar") while Bonaventure has *templi* ("of the temple").

[60] See Hugh of St. Cher, p. 352v,a where he also refers to 1 Macc 4:59.

[61] On p. 390 n. 7 QuarEd correctly mention that the Vulgate reads *in templo* ("in the temple").

[62] On p. 390 n. 8 QuarEd cite the Glossa Interlinearis: "*In Solomon's portico*, that is, where Solomon used to stand to pray." See 2 Chron 6:13 and 1 Kings 8:54 for indications of where Solomon was in the temple during his solemn prayer of dedication. See Hugh of St. Cher, p. 352v,c where he cites 2 Chron 6:13 and 1 Kings 8:54.

[63] See the Glossa Interlinearis: "While you leave us uncertain."

they might extract a response from him, they hinted at their power and malice. Power, because they surrounded him. Psalm 21:13 states: "Many calves have surrounded me," that is, so that I could not escape. Psalm 117:12 says: "They surrounded me like bees, and they burned like fire among thorns."[64] Malice, because they pretended to have a desire for learning: *How long will you hold us in suspense?* Psalm 106:26 reads: "They mount up to the heavens." Augustine comments: "They were desiring the truth, but were preparing calumny."[65]

JOHN 10:25-30
CHRIST PROVIDES THE CERTAIN PROOF
THAT HE IS THE TRUE SHEPHERD

36. *Jesus answered them.* After the request has been set forth, *the manifestation of certain proof* is given here. The Evangelist proceeds in this fashion. First the Lord's response contains a *rebuke of the Jews.* Second comes *the expression of the certain proof.* Third is *the reason for this proof.*

Verse 25. First comes the censure of the unbelief of the Jews. For this reason the text states: *I tell you, and you do not believe,* and so you are asking foolishly and maliciously. And I am telling you openly, for I am not only using words, but also works. *The works that I do in my Father's name they themselves[66] bear witness concerning*

---

[64] See Hugh of St. Cher, p. 352v,d where he first cites Ps 117:12 and then Ps 21:13.

[65] See Tractate 48 n. 3 in CCSL xxxvi, p. 413. The citation is verbatim.

[66] On p. 390 n. 13 QuarEd rightly notice that the Vulgate reads *haec* ("these") whereas Bonaventure has *ipsa* ("they themselves").

me. John 7:31 above asks: "When the Christ comes, will he work more signs," through which you should believe?

37. (Verse 26). *But you do not believe because you are not of my sheep.* Wherefore, if you were sheep, you would have proof of your shepherd because of his word and works. Augustine observes: "He said that they were not of his sheep, because he saw that they were ordained for eternal damnation, not to be purchased by the price of his blood for eternal life"[67]

38. (Verse 27). *My sheep,* etc. The second point surfaces here, that is, the manifestation of the certain proof, which consists in this that he is heard by the sheep, and the sheep follow him, and he protects them. So he says: *My sheep hear my voice,* namely, by believing, for "faith comes from hearing," as Romans 10:17 says. *And I know them,* distinguishing them from evil people, not by face, but by their heart. Hebrews 4:12-13 states: "He is a discerner of thoughts and intentions of the heart, and there is no creature hidden from his sight. But all things are naked and open to his eyes."[68] It is said of the evil in Matthew 25:12: "I do not know you." But concerning the good it is said in 2 Timothy 2:19: "The Lord knows who are his." *And they follow me,* through imitation. Matthew 16:24 says: "The person who wants to come after me must deny himself and take up his cross and follow me."

39. (Verse 28). *And I give them eternal life,* by rewarding them as the good shepherd. John 6:40 above has: "That

---

[67] See Tractate 48 n. 4 in CCSL xxxvi, p. 415. Bonaventure's citation is not verbatim. See FC 88, p. 230: "Because he saw that they were predestined for eternal destruction, not purchased at the price of his blood for eternal life."

[68] Bonaventure has adapted Hebr 4:12-13 which describes "the word of God."

whoever beholds the Son and believes in him, may have eternal life."[69] Sirach 4:12 says: "Wisdom has inspired life into her children." *And they will never perish. Nor*[70] *will anyone snatch them out of my hand*, on account of my power. This shepherd was appropriately signified by David, whose name means "mighty hand,"[71] and who freed the prey from the mouth of the lion and the bear, as it is said in 1 Samuel 17:34-36.[72]

40. (Verse 29). *What my Father has given me.* The third point is noted here, that is, the approval of this proof. For this a twofold reason is provided. The first is this: What the Father has given me is greater than all. But what is greater than all does not suffer violence. Therefore, it is impossible that someone snatch something out of his hand. He sets down the means of this reason when he says: *What my Father has given me*, that is, that which my Father has given me, *is greater than all*, since he has given all that he could.[73] John 16:15 below says: "All things that the Father has are mine." The other reason is this. No one can snatch from the hand of the Father. Rather my hand and that of the Father are one.[74] Wherefore, no

---

[69] John 6:40 reads: "For this is the will of the Father who sent me, that whoever beholds the Son and believes in him may have eternal life, and I will raise him up on the last day."

[70] On p. 391 n. 5 QuarEd accurately mention that the Vulgate reads *et non* ("and not") while Bonaventure has *nec* ("nor").

[71] See Jerome in CCSL lxxii, p. 103: "David means mighty hand or desirable."

[72] Shepherd David says in 1 Sam 17:36 how he protected the sheep: "For I your servant have killed both a lion and a bear."

[73] See Augustine, Tractate 48 n. 6 in FC 88, p. 233: "... 'What the Father gave me,' that is, that I be his Word, that I be his only-begotten Son, that I be the splendor of his light, 'is greater than all.'"

[74] See Augustine, Tractate 48 n. 7 in FC 88, pp. 233-234: "If we should understand hand as power, the power of the Father and the Son is one, because their divinity is one; but if we should understand

one can snatch from my hand. So he says: *No one*[75] *can snatch from the hand of my Father*, since he is omnipotent. Psalm 75:8 reads: "You inspire terror, and who will resist you?" Qoheleth 8:4 has: "His word is full of power."

41. (Verse 30). *I and the Father are one*, that is, in unity of essence. We are, in plurality of persons. Wherefore, my hand and that of the Father are one. Chrysostom comments: "When you hear 'hand,' do not think of anything sensible, but understand only strength and power."[76]

John 10:31-41
Persecution by the Jews

42. *The Jews took up stones.* After the declaration of the true shepherd had been made by certain proof, the next point is *the persecution of the evil sheep*, indeed of the wolves, since just as the sheep follow the shepherd, so the wolves persecute him. And the persecution is set forth as follows. First is *the persecution itself*. Second is *the reason for the persecution*. Third is *Christ's wise defense*. Fourth is his *turning away from the furor of the persecutors*. Fifth is *the multiplication of believers*.

Verse 31. First the persecution itself is seen in the fact that they wanted to stone Christ. For this reason the text says: *The Jews took up stones to stone him*, but they didn't succeed. Augustine notes: "Since the time of his passion had not yet arrived, they did not succeed in stoning

---

hand as it was said through the prophet, 'And to whom has the arm of the Lord been revealed?,' the hand of the Father is the Son himself."

[75] On p. 391 n. 7 QuarEd correctly mention that the Vulgate reads *Et nemo* ("And no one").

[76] See Homily 61 n. 2 in PG 59:338: "When you hear 'hand,' do not think of anything sensible, but strength, power."

him."[77] They immediately wanted to kill him like those about whom Proverbs 1:16 speaks: "Their feet run to evil and make haste to shed blood."

43. (Verse 32). *Jesus answered them.* This verse introduces the second point, that is, the reason for the persecution. And first the Lord shows that their motivation is irrational. So he says: *Many good works I have shown you from my Father. For which of these works are you stoning me?* The construction is partitive, that is, for which one of the number of these works are you stoning me? Psalm 34:12 reads: "They have repaid me evil for good." Proverbs 17:13 states: "For the person who renders evil for good, evil will not depart from his house." But the malice that is hidden under the sheep's skin designates the reason. So:

44. (Verse 33). *So[78] the Jews answered him: Not for a good work are we stoning you, but for blasphemy*, since Leviticus 24:16 states: "The person who blasphemes against the name of the Lord, let him die the death." And they point out how he is blaspheming: *And because you, although you are a human being, are making yourself God.* And so a human being, who makes himself God, blasphemes, for he is saying that there are many gods. And this is against the Law of the Jews, which contains the commandment to profess belief in only one God. Matthew 26:65 treats a similar matter: "You have heard the blasphemy. What

---

[77] See Tractate 48 n. 8 in CCSL xxxvi, p. 417 and FC 88, p. 234: "The Lord, because he would not suffer what he did not wish to suffer, and suffered only what he wished to suffer, speaks to them who still desire to stone him." Obviously, Bonaventure's citation is not verbatim.

[78] On p. 392 n. 1 QuarEd rightly notice that the Vulgate does not read *ergo* ("So").

further need do we have for witnesses?"[79] As a human being, he did not make himself God, but although he was God, he became a human being. Philippians 2:6-7 confesses: "He did not consider being equal to God a thing to be clung to. Rather he emptied himself, taking the nature of a slave and having been made like unto human beings, he appeared in the form of a man."

45. (Verse 34). *Jesus answered them.* This verse gives expression to the third point, namely, his wise defense, in which the Lord shows that he has not blasphemed by means of a twofold witness, that is, of the Scriptures and of the works. The testimony of *the Scriptures* is this: Scripture calls "gods" those to whom God has spoken. But how much more is he to be called "God," whom the Father has consecrated and sent. Wherefore, if the Scriptures do not blaspheme, neither do I. *Is it not written in your Law: I have said you are gods?* "Law" here is taken in a comprehensive sense to include the Psalms, in which this citation occurs.[80]

46. (Verse 35). *If he called them gods to whom the word of God was addressed* such as the prophets and other saints. Ezekiel 1:3 reads: "The word of the Lord came to Ezekiel the priest," etc. *And the Scripture cannot be undone*, that is, accused of falsehood[81] or censured for blasphemy. Mat-

---

[79] Matt 26:65 reads: "Then the high priest tore his garments, saying: He has blasphemed. What further need do we have for witnesses? Behold, now you have heard the blasphemy."

[80] See Ps 81:6: "I have said: You are gods and all of you the children of the Most High." See Augustine, Tractate 48 n. 9 in FC 88, p. 235: "And the Lord called all those Scriptures in general the law, although, elsewhere he uses 'the law' in a particular sense.... If God's speech was made to men, that they might be called gods, how is the Word of God himself, who is with God, not God?"

[81] Hugh of St. Cher, p. 353v,s makes the same point.

thew 5:18 states: "Not one jot or one tittle shall be lost from the Law, till all things have been accomplished."

47. (Verse 36). *Whom the Father sanctified*, that is, "he begot him holy."[82] *And sent into the world*. He did not call him from the world and the darkness of the world as he did other saints. *Do you say of him: You blaspheme, because I said: I am the Son of God?* As if he were saying: You are speaking irrationally. "For if those who have been enlightened are gods, is not the light that enlightens them God?"[83] The Lord was not blaspheming. Rather they were since they were saying of God that he was not God. Thus, the Lord said in Matthew 12:31-32: "Every kind of sin and blasphemy will be forgiven men and women. But blasphemy against the Spirit will not be forgiven … either in this world or in the world to come." Thus all were to be stoned. – He also makes the same point that he has not blasphemed by appealing to the witness of the works, which say that he is equal to the Father. So the text continues:

48. (Verse 37). *If I do not perform the works of my Father*, that is, works of omnipotence, *do not believe me*, that is, when I say that I am equal to the Father. In Exodus 4:1 Moses said: "They will not believe me and will not hear

---

[82] See Augustine, Tractate 48 n. 9 in CCSL xxxvi, p. 418 and FC 88, p. 236: "Therefore, 'the Father sanctified his Son and sent him into the world.' Perhaps someone may say, If the Father sanctified him, then was there sometime when he was not holy? As he begot, so he sanctified. For in begetting him, he gave to him that he be holy, because he begot him holy." Whereas Bonaventure reads *sanctum genuit* ("he begot him holy"), Augustine's text has: *sanctum eum genuit* ("he begot him holy"). Hugh of St. Cher, p. 353v,t also has *sanctum genuit* ("he begot him holy") without any reference to Augustine.

[83] See Augustine, Tractate 48 n. 9 in CCSL xxxvi, p. 417 and FC 88, p. 235: "If enlightened lights are gods, is not the Light that enlightens God?" Bonaventure's quotation is not verbatim.

my voice, but they will say," etc.[84] And so the Lord gave him signs.

49. (Verse 38). *But if I do perform them and if you are not willing to believe in me*, that is, in my words, *believe the works*, that is, believe in me through the works, *that you may know and believe that the Father is in me and I in the Father.* And thus what was said above in John 5:30 is true: "I and the Father are one." *That you may believe*, that is, by believing *you may know*, since, according to what Isaiah 7:9 says in the Septuagint: "If you will not believe, you will not understand."[85] In John 14 he says to Philip: "Do you not believe that I am in the Father and the Father in me?"[86] "Otherwise, believe because of the works."[87]

50. (Verse 39). *So they sought to seize him.* Verses 39-40 deal with the fourth point, that is, his turning away from his persecutors, since the time for his suffering had not yet come. So the text states: *So they sought to seize him*, but they were unable. Thus the text says: *And he went forth out of their hands.* Something similar is said in Luke 4:30: "But he, passing through their midst, went his way," when they wanted to throw him off the hill.

51. (Verse 40). *And he went away*[88] *beyond the Jordan, to that place where John was at first baptizing.* About this

---

[84] Ex 4:1 concludes: "…. They will say: The Lord has not appeared to you."

[85] I translate the Vulgate of Isa 7:9: "If you will not believe, you will not continue."

[86] John 14:10.

[87] John 14:12. The "you" in verse 12 is plural whereas the "you" in 14:10 is singular.

[88] On p. 392 n. 12 QuarEd accurately indicate that the Vulgate reads *Et abiit iterum* ("And he again went away") whereas Bonaventure has *Et abiit* ("And he went away").

place it is said in John 3:23: "John was baptizing in Aenon."[89] *And there he stayed*, that is, in solitude. Chrysostom comments: "He urges them to flee noisy crowds and to pray in solitude."[90] *He stayed*, hidden from the Jews, according to what Deuteronomy 32:20 has: "I will hide my face from them."[91]

52. (Verse 41). *And many came*, etc. This verse concentrates on the last point, that is, the multitude of believers after his departure. For this reason the text reads: *And many came to him*, that is, through faith. Isaiah 60:4 states: "Your children will come from afar." *And they were saying: John indeed worked no sign*, through which he would show that he was the Christ, but solely bore witness to Christ.[92]

53. (Verse 42). *All things, however, that John said of this person were true. And*, having been captivated by this twofold witness, *many believed in him*, according to what the Lord himself had said in John 10:38: "And if you do not believe me, at least believe the works."[93] *Many*, according to what Psalm 138:18 says: "I will number them, and they will be multiplied beyond the sand." And Genesis 17:4 has: "You will be the father of many nations."

---

[89] See also John 1:28: "These things took place at Bethany, beyond the Jordan, where John was baptizing."

[90] See Homily 61 n. 3 in PG 59:340 and FC 41, pp. 159-160: "Moreover, He urged us to do this, bidding us to shun market-places and noisy confusion and to pray in our room in secret."

[91] In Deut 32:20 the Lord God is speaking.

[92] See Augustine, Tractate 48 n. 12 in FC 88, p. 237: "John, they say, showed no miracle.... John did none of these things; and yet everything that he said gave testimony to this one. Let us come through the lamp to the day."

[93] John 10:38 reads: "But if I do perform them, and if you are not willing to believe me, believe the works...."

QUESTIONS

54. Question 1 focuses on John 10:28: "No one will snatch them out of my hand." – Are not those who possess present justice in the hand of the Son? Who, however, are scattered according to what is said in John 10:12: "The wolf comes and scatters the sheep"? – The answer to this is that they are snatched, not because of the imbecility of the guard, but because of the weakness of what is being guarded. – Another interpretation is Augustine's: Those who are called sheep here cannot be snatched in a definitive way according to eternal election. Thus Augustine observes: "The wolf does not snatch nor does the thief carry away nor does the robber kill. The one who numbered them is sure of their number."[94]

55. Question 2 deals with John 10:29: "No one can snatch anything out of the hand of my Father." – Therefore, those who are in the hand of God, such as the predestined, cannot be damned. It follows, too, that they do not have the freedom to sin in a definitive manner. In his treatise *On the Gift of Perseverance* Augustine seems to answer this question simply: They cannot lose it. They do not lose their free will, just as free will is not lost in those confirmed in grace.[95] – It must also be said that no one can snatch anything, since the Father does not allow his elect to suffer violence. For "God is faithful and will not permit[96] you to

---

[94] See Tractate 48 n. 6 in CCSL xxxvi, p. 415 and FC 88, p. 232: "… from those sheep neither does the wolf seize nor the robber kill. He who knows what he gave for them is sure about their number."

[95] See c. 14 n. 35 in *De Dono Perseverentiae* in PL 45:1014 and NPNF1, Volume 5, p. 539: "This is the predestination of the saints, – nothing else; to wit, the foreknowledge and the preparation of God's kindnesses, whereby they are most certainly delivered, whoever they are that are delivered."

[96] The Vulgate reads *non patietur* ("will not suffer") whereas Bonaventure has *non permittet* ("will not permit").

be tempted beyond your strength."[97] And the devil cannot inflict violence on God, so that he might tempt his servants beyond what God permits. Wherefore, the freedom of free will to sin remains in them, but there is no power in the devil to violate it or forcibly steal it away.

56. Question 3 deals with the Lord's response in John 10:34. The Lord had said that he is God and the Son of God and shows that he has not blasphemed by means of the Scripture that calls the servants of God gods. – This answer does not seem to carry weight, because Scripture call them gods by adoption. But he was saying that he was God by essence, for he said in John 10:30: "I and the Father are one." – I respond that it has to be said that when the Lord disputed with the Jews, sometimes he answered them concerning the substance of their point. At other times he responded ad hominem. For "it is a general rule to contend with an adversary by using all means of contending."[98] Thus, when they asked him "by what authority" are you doing these things, the Lord answered: "Was the baptism of John of heavenly or human origin?"[99] By means of his question he tied them in knots. Likewise

---

[97] See 1 Cor 10:13.

[98] The general background is Aristotle, *De sophiticis elenchis*, in WAE Vol. 1, 175a: "First then, just as we say that we ought sometimes to choose to prove something in the general estimation rather than in truth, so also we have sometimes to solve arguments rather in the general estimation than according to the truth. For it is a general rule in fighting contentious persons, to treat them not as refuting, but as merely appearing to refute...."

[99] Bonaventure has abbreviated Matt 21:23-24: "And when he had come into the temple, the chief priests and elders of the people came to him as he was teaching and asked: By what authority are you doing these things? And who gave you this authority? Jesus answered and said to them: I also will ask you one question, and if you answer this for me, I in turn will tell you by what authority I do these things. Whence was the baptism of John? From heaven or from human origin?"

in the present passage his answer is ad hominem, so that he might mollify their ire in the same way that he confounded their malice in John 8:7 above: "Let the person among you who is without sin be the first to cast a stone at her."

Be that as it may, it can be said that his response was indeed the best one, since this word "God" has a threefold significance: by nature, participation,[100] and in name only, as in idols. The multiplicity of this name is sound and is rooted in one source. Wherefore, in the most true sense he is called God by nature, in a less true sense by participation, and in the least true sense in name only, because this latter is mere opinion. So since they were calumniating him because he had been attributing to them the name of god, he proved that he can attribute this name to them without blasphemy. The reason is this: if a friend or adopted son is called god and God is truly honored by this without blasphemy involved, how much more when the one concerned is the Son by nature. The argument here is from the minor premise.

57. Question 4 treats John 10:41: "John indeed worked no sign." – 1.Now it is said in Luke 1:17: "He will go before him in the spirit and power of Elijah." Therefore, if Elijah's power consisted in performing miracles, it seems that the Lord had to give him the power of performing miracles. – 2.Furthermore, if no one was "greater than

---

[100] See Augustine's commentary on Ps 94 in CCSL xxxix, p. 1335. See also *Expositions of the Psalms 73-98*. Translation and notes by Maria Boulding. (WSA III/18; Hyde Park, NY: New City Press, 2002) 414: "He calls them *gods* in virtue of participation, not nature; they are gods by the grace through which he willed to deify them. How great must our God be, if he makes us gods?"

John"[101] and the Lord gave his disciples who were bearing witness to him the power to perform miracles,[102] why didn't he do something similar for John?

I respond that it has to be said that John was considered by many to be the Christ, as is obvious from John 1:19-26. Therefore, there had to be a sensible difference between John and Christ that perceptive individuals might discern. But this difference would not lie in sanctity of life,[103] since it was required that a faithful witness be regarded as holy. So it had to consist in the fact that Christ had the power to perform miracles. – 1. With regard to the objection about "spirit and power," it has to be maintained that the word of Elijah was fiery.[104] So too was John's word, as the Lord himself said of him in John 5:35: "He was the lamp, burning and shining." – 2. Relative to the objection about the Lord's disciples it should be said that there was no suspicion about any of the disciples that he was the Christ. And since it was certain to everyone that they had followed Christ, everything that they had in them, be in holiness or power of knowledge, was attributable to their Master. But John never followed the Lord and was not his disciple.

---

[101] See Matt 11:11: "Amen, I say to you: Among those born of women there has not risen a greater than John the Baptist. Yet the least in the kingdom of heaven is greater than he."

[102] See Matt 10:1: "Then having summoned his twelve disciples, he gave them power over unclean spirits, to cast them out, and to cure every kind of disease and infirmity."

[103] See Book XX, c. 7 n. 17 of Gregory, *Moralia in Iob* in CCSL cxliiia, p. 1016: "Indeed, the proof of holiness is not to perform signs, but to love one another...."

[104] See Sir 48:1: "And Elijah the prophet rose up, as a fire, and his word burnt like a torch."

CHAPTER ELEVEN

JOHN 11:1-46
CHRIST AS PERFECT VIVIFIER

1. *Now a certain man was sick*, etc. Earlier the Lord showed himself to be healer and conserver and director. Now he shows that he is *the perfect vivifier*,[1] as he again joins together body and soul in the case of Lazarus who was dead for four days. And this fourth section continues to the end of this chapter where verse 47 reads: "The chief priests gathered together," etc. It is divided into two parts. In the first *the antecedents of the miracle* are set forth. The second deals with *the miracle itself* where verse 43 states: "When he had said this, he cried out with a loud voice."

JOHN 11:1-42
ANTECEDENTS OF THE MIRACLE

The first part has four components according to the four antecedents that set up the miracle. In the first is *the notification of the sickness*. The second concentrates on *the coming of the Physician* where verse 7 says: "Then afterwards he said to his disciples." In the third there is *the plea* or the merit *of faith* where verse 20 has: "So when

---

[1] See John 5 n. 1 above.

Martha heard that Jesus was coming," etc. In the fourth is *the expression of Christ's love* where verse 33 reads: "So when Jesus saw her weeping."

John 11:1-6
Notification of the sickness

So the first point, *the notification of the sickness*, is depicted in this order. First is *the condition of the sick person.* Second is *the notification of who was sick.* Third is *the reason for the sickness.* Fourth is *the delay in the healing.*

2. (Verse 1). So the condition of the sick person is given with a name, as the text says: *Now a certain man was sick, Lazarus.* From *the hometown*, as the text adds, *of Bethany*, to which place the Lord was accustomed to come.[2] The text also mentions Lazarus' family when it says: *the village of Mary and Martha, his sisters.* Luke 10:38 states: "Jesus[3] entered a certain village, and a woman named Martha welcomed him into her home." And the Evangelist gives special attention to Mary:

3. (Verse 2). *Now it was Mary who anointed the Lord with ointment and wiped his feet with her hair.* Through this wondrous description her love is praised. John 12:3 below reads: "So Mary took a pound of ointment, genuine nard of great value." Luke 7:37 states: "Behold, a woman … brought an alabaster jar of ointment." *Whose brother Lazarus was sick* and by whose prayers he was resusci-

---

[2] See Matt 21:17 and 26:6.
[3] The Vulgate reads *ipse* ("he") while Bonaventure has *Iesus* ("Jesus").

tated, as is noted in John 11:33: "So Jesus, when he saw Mary weeping."[4]

4. (Verse 3). *So the sisters sent.* This verse introduces the second point, namely, the notification of Lazarus' sickness that the sisters made to the Lord. For this reason the text says: *So his sisters sent to him, saying: Lord, behold, he whom you love is sick.* They call him Lord and not teacher, for they were requesting a miracle, not teaching. As if they were saying: Lord, you are powerful. Matthew 8:2 states: "Lord, if you will, you can make me clean." And they express the reason for his help: *Behold, he whom you love.* Psalm 9:11 confesses: "Let those who know your name trust in you, because you have not abandoned those who are seeking you, O Lord." And they state the occasion: *He is sick.* Therefore, have mercy. Psalm 6:3 pleads: "Have mercy on me, O Lord, for I am sick."[5]

5. (Verse 4). *But when Jesus heard this, he said to them.* The third point surfaces here, namely, the reason for the illness, which the Lord explains to those who seek healing. For this reason *He said to them: This sickness is not unto death, but for the glory of God.* He says this according to divine dispensation. So he adds: *That through it the Son of God may be glorified,* that is, he may manifest his glory through this work, since in this resuscitation he has revealed his power and through that his glory. Thus John 2:11 has: "Jesus worked this sign and manifested his glory,"[6] before his disciples. Now the Evangelist ad-

---

[4] The Vulgate reads *eam* ("her") while Bonaventure has *Mariam* ("Mary").

[5] The Latin *infirmus* of Ps 6:3 is normally translated as "weak." "Sick" fits the present context better.

[6] John 2:11 reads: "This first of his signs Jesus worked at Cana of Galilee, and he manifested his glory, and his disciples believed in him."

umbrates the reason why his glory was to be manifested in this way: On account of the special love he had towards these persons. For this reason the text continues:

6. (Verse 5). *Now Jesus loved Martha and her sister Mary and Lazarus.* So he loved them, since they loved him, according to what Proverbs 8:17 states: "I love those who love me." One should not wonder at this, since Wisdom 11:25 says: "Lord,[7] you love all things that are and hate none of the things you have made."

7. (Verse 6). *So when he heard.* The fourth point is found here, that is, the delay in the cure, for although he wanted to cure him, nonetheless, he did not want to cure him immediately, but preferred to wait. So the text continues: *So when he heard,* that is, after he heard, *that he was sick, he remained two more days in the same place.* So the Lord, called by his friends, did not come immediately, but waited, so that he might be asked with greater insistence and persistence.[8] Colossians 4:2 reads: "Be insistent in prayer. Be vigilant therein."

8. The sickness or weakness is multiple, namely, the sickness of the grace of integrity is to be embraced. And this is fourfold. There is humility. Proverbs 30:25 states: "The ants, a feeble[9] people, which provide themselves food in the harvest." 1 Corinthians 1:27-28 reads: "God has cho-

---

[7] The Vulgate does not read *Domine* ("O, Lord").

[8] See Book XX, c. 31 n. 61 of Gregory, *Moralia in Iob* in CCSL clxiiia, p. 1047: "God helps the saints to grow in wisdom when they experience a delay in receiving what they asked for. This delay increases desire, and desire helps understanding to grow...."

[9] I have translated the Latin *infirmus* by "feeble." This Latin word is from the same stem as *infirmitas* ("sickness"), which is the word Bonaventure is interpreting.

sen the weak[10] things of the world ... and the despised," etc. Matthew 11:25 says: "For you have hidden these things from the wise and the prudent, and have revealed them to little ones." – There is repentance. Sirach 31:2 reads: "A grievous sickness renders the soul sober." About this Psalm 146:3 states: "Who heals the broken of heart and binds up their bruises" or "sicknesses," according to the other text.[11] – There is patience. 2 Corinthians 12:9 has: "Strength is made perfect in weakness,"[12] that is, in patience, since James 1:4 says: "Patience has its perfect work."[13] Therefore, it is said in 2 Corinthians 12:9: "Gladly will I glory in my infirmities, so that the strength of Christ may dwell in me." – There is suffering with or compassion. 2 Corinthians 11:29 reads: "Who is weak, and I am not weak?"[14] And 1 Corinthians 9:22: "To the weak I became weak that I might gain the weak."[15]

9. Moreover, there is the sickness or weakness of the perversity of sin is to be fled from. This, too, is fourfold. There is avarice. Qoheleth 5:12-13 states: "There is also another grievous sickness that I have seen under the sun: riches accumulated[16] to the hurt of their owner. For they are lost with very great affliction." – There is carnal pleasure. Isaiah 24:7 says: "The vineyard has mourned. The

---

[10] Behind "the weak things" stands the Latin *infirma*. See the previous note.

[11] This "other text" is the Latin of the Hebrew. It actually reads *plagas* ("afflictions").

[12] Behind the words "in weakness" stands the Latin *in infirmitate*. See n. 9 above.

[13] The Vulgate reads *Patientia autem opus perfectum habeat* ("Now let patience have its perfect work").

[14] Behind "is weak" and "I am weak" stand the Latin *infirmatur* and *infirmor* respectively. See n. 9 above.

[15] Behind the three occurrences of "weak" stands the Latin *infirmus*. See n. 9 above.

[16] The Vulgate reads *conservatae* ("kept") whilst Bonaventure has *congregatae* ("accumulated").

vine is sick. All who rejoiced in their hearts have wailed."
– There is arrogance. Isaiah 24:4-5 has: "The arrogance of
the people of the earth is sick,[17] and the earth has been
infected by its inhabitants." – There is obstinacy. Deuteronomy 7:15 reads: "The Lord will take away ... all the
infirmities and all the grievous sicknesses of Egypt that
you knew, he will not bring upon you...." The sicknesses
of Egypt are their obstinacies in evil.

10. Furthermore, the sickness of difficult discipleship is to
be alleviated. And this is fourfold. To resist the evil of sin.
Lamentations 1:14 states: "My strength is weakened. The
Lord has delivered me into a hand from which I am unable to rise." And Isaiah 40:30 has: "Young men will fall in
their infirmity." – To endure the evil of pain. 1 Thessalonians 5:14 reads: "Comfort the fainthearted. Support the
weak." For a contrary exhortation see Ezekiel 34:4: "You
have not strengthened what was weak."[18] – To promote
the good. Sirach 31:27 states: "In all your works be quick,
and no infirmity will come to you." Romans 14:1 has: "But
welcome the person who is weak in faith." – To persevere
in good. 1 Samuel 2:5 reads: "She who has many children
has become weak." All these infirmities are to be alleviated. Romans 8:26 states: "The Spirit himself[19] helps our
weakness."

11. In addition, there is the sickness of the suffering of
pains to be borne. This, too, is fourfold. Endured on account of lies. Psalm 102:3 says: "Who forgives all your

---

[17] Another translation is: "The height of the people of the earth is
weakened."

[18] The Vulgate reads *fuit* ("was") whereas Bonaventure has *erat*
("weak").

[19] The Vulgate of Rom 8:26a does not read *ipse* ("himself"). Rom
8:26c has *ipse Spiritus* ("the Spirit himself"): "The Spirit himself
pleads for us with unutterable groanings."

iniquities, who heals all your sicknesses." Romans 14:2 reads: "Let the person who is weak eat vegetables." – Assumed for our redemption. Isaiah 53:2-3 states: "We have seen him ... the most abject of men, a man of sorrows and acquainted with infirmity." – Inflicted for the sake of purgation. Psalm 15:4 says: "Their infirmities were multiplied.[20] Afterwards they made haste." – Borne for the manifestation of divine glory, as in John 11:4: "This sickness is not unto death, but for the glory of God, so that the Son of God may be glorified through it."[21]

QUESTIONS

12. Question 1 deals with the very first verse where it is said: "Lazarus was from the village of Mary and Martha, his sisters." – Since "the head of the woman should be the man,"[22] the text should rather have put it differently: Martha and Mary were from the village of Lazarus. – It has to be maintained that it is not without reason that Mary and Martha are introduced as principal characters in this verse, since, although they are women by gender, nevertheless they exceeded Lazarus in strength of mind and in virtue. For it was by merit of their faith, as will become clear below,[23] that Lazarus was resuscitated. So pay close attention that the Evangelist says two things. First, from the village of Mary and Martha, so that he gives a preference to the women instead of to Lazarus because of

---

[20] See Hugh of St. Cher, p. 354v,1 where he cites the first part of Ps 15:4.

[21] Hugh of St. Cher has no comparable *distinctio* on sickness.

[22] See 1 Cor 11:3: "But I would have you know that the head of every man is Christ, and the head of the woman is the man, and the head of Christ is God."

[23] See esp. John 11:27.

virtue. Second, his sisters, so that he might mention them last and thus delay mention of the fragility of their sex.

13. Question 2 raises the issue of why the women, when they sent to Jesus, did not request a healing, but just hinted at one. – It seems that either they neglected their brother's health or tempted the Lord with contempt. – I respond that it has to be said that the women, as very good and faithful, knew Christ's power. Therefore, they did not ask that he come as a petty king might ask. They revered his majesty, and therefore did not dare to ask that he issue a command where he was that would be fulfilled where they were, as was the case with the centurion.[24] They hoped in his goodness, and so they hinted and suggested: "Behold, he whom you love is sick." Thus, Master Hugh says that insinuation is one kind of prayer or request and is threefold: With confidence, as the Mother of the Lord in John 2:3 above; with reverence as here, according to what Hugh of Saint Victor himself says; with contempt as an arrogant lord sometimes deals with his servant.[25]

---

[24] See Matt 8:8. See Augustine, Tractate 49 n. 5 in FC 88, pp. 242-243: "They did not say, Come. For to one who loves there is only the need to tell. They did not dare to say, Come and heal. They did not dare to say, Order there and it will happen here. Now why would these women not also say this, if the faith of that centurion is praised for this very thing? ... These women said none of these things, but only, 'Lord, behold, the one you love is sick.' It is enough that you know; for you do not love and abandon." See Hugh of St. Cher, p. 355v,c who cites this passage from Augustine.

[25] See c. 3 of *De modo orandi* in PL 176:981A-D: "*Insinuation* signifies the manifestation of the will by a mere telling without a request. It happens in three ways: in fear or respect, confidence, contempt. It takes place out of respect when either the cause is great that we are engaged in or the person is great whom we are asking, as is the case with: *Lord, if you had been here, my brother would not have died* (John 11:21,32). For she wanted to ask that the Lord resuscitate her dead brother, but since she was afraid on account of the magnitude of the

14. Question 3 singles out John 11:4: "This sickness is not unto death." But Lazarus died. – So Chrysostom queries: How were the sisters not scandalized, when it didn't turn out the way that the Lord had foretold it to them?[26] – I answer that the point must be made that the emphasis lies on it is not unto death, that is, to the final termination of life, so that he no longer lives. For unto death means the dissolution of the soul from the body.[27] – With regard to the issue of the women being scandalized, it has to be said that they still hoped that the Lord would resuscitate him. – Another interpretation is that since things did not turn out literally, they believed that the Lord has spoken in a parable.

15. Question 4 zeroes in on John 11:6 and inquires why the Lord "remained two more days" and waited. – It seems that he should not have done so, since he was a friend,

---

cause and the high standing of the person, she chose to insinuate rather than to ask.... There is also the insinuation of confidence. This occurs when we are confident either on account of the lightness of the matter or the benevolence of the person and we neglect to express our desire openly, for we hope that we can obtain it by mere insinuation. An example is the marriage feast, when the wine ran short, and his Mother said to the Lord: *They have no wine* (John 2:3).... The insinuation of contempt occurs when either the matter is of a vile nature or the person asked is of low estate. This is entirely excluded from divine prayer and request while arrogant and powerful persons most frequently and with great zeal engage in it.... Now insinuation that stems from confidence is fitting for the perfect, that stems from fear for beginners, and that stems from contempt for evildoers."

[26] See Homily 62 n. 1 in PG 59:313 and FC 41, p. 167: "At this point the sisters are worthy of admiration, for the fact that, though they heard 'is not unto death,' yet saw him die, they did not lose confidence because the outcome was just the opposite, but even so came to Him and did not conclude that He had deceived them."

[27] See Augustine, Tractate 49 n. 6 in FC 88, p. 243: "Therefore, he said this: 'It is not unto death,' because even the death itself was not unto death but rather for a miracle, by the performance of which men might believe in Christ and avoid true death."

and it is said in Proverbs 3:28: "Do not say to your friend: Go and come again. Tomorrow[28] I will give to you when you can give straightaway." – I respond that it has to be maintained that he delayed, so that he might do something greater than cure the sick and something more acceptable. For it was greater to raise the dead than to cure the sick.[29] – So he delayed to give greater certitude to the miracle, since, as Chrysostom says, it was then certain that he was not in a trance, but that he was truly dead. To provide a demonstration of his greater power, because it was also greater to reunite the soul to a body that was already putrid than to one that had only recently died. Indeed, he takes into account the appropriate time in all his works.[30]

16. Question 5 is one raised by Chrysostom relative to the description of this Mary, who anointed the Lord with oil.[31] Was she that sinner, about whom it is said in Luke 7:36-50 that she anointed the feet of the Lord in the house of

---

[28] The Vulgate reads *et cras* ("and tomorrow") while Bonaventure has *cras* ("tomorrow").

[29] See Augustine, Tractate 49 n. 5 in FC 88, p. 242: "He put off healing that he might be able to raise up."

[30] This is Bonaventure's summary of Homily 62 n. 1. See PG 59:343 and FC 41, p. 167: "Why did He remain? In order that Lazarus might breathe his last and be buried, that no one might be able to claim that Christ revived a man who was not yet dead; that it was a coma, that it was a faint, that it was a seizure, but not death. And it was for this reason that He remained so long a time, so that corruption of the body might begin and the statement might be made: 'He is already decayed.'" See Hugh of St. Cher, p. 354v,n who cites this passage from Chrysostom.

[31] See John 11:2. See also Chrysostom, Homily 62 n. 1 in PG 59:342 and FC 41, pp. 165-166: "In the first place, they must understand this: that she was not the sinner mentioned in the gospel of Matthew, or the one in the gospel of Luke, for she was a different person. Those others, indeed, were notorious sinners, reeking with many vices, while she was devout and zealous. And I say this for she used to show much concern for the hospitable reception of Christ." See the next note.

Simon the leper?[32] – And he answers that he was not the woman of Luke 7, since the woman of John 11:2 was a good and famous woman whereas the one of Luke 7 was a prostitute.[33] But the Glossa disagrees,[34] and so too does Gregory.[35] – It has to be said that one should agree with the Glossa and Gregory. – But it has to be maintained that Chrysostom holds the contrary opinion. It is not unfitting that interpreters hold contrary opinions, especially with regard to the names of people, for the emphasis of a passage does not reside in a name.

JOHN 11:7-19
COMING OF THE PHYSICIAN

17. *Then afterwards he said to his disciples.* After the announcement of the sickness had been made, *the coming of the Physician* is described in this order. First it is suggested that it is *safe to go.* Second is *the necessity of going.* Third is *the usefulness for the disciples.* Fourth is *Thomas's ardent desire* to die with him. Fifth is *how long*

---

[32] In Luke 7:36-50 a Simon is mentioned, but he is not described as a leper. In this passage the woman is unnamed. In Matt 26:6-7 and Mark 14:3 the woman is also unnamed who anoints Jesus in the house of "Simon the leper." Furthermore, neither Matthew nor Mark describe her as a sinner.

[33] While Luke 7:36-50 says that the woman was a sinner, nowhere does Luke describe the nature of her sin.

[34] The Glossa Interlinearis on John 11:2 observes: "Let us not make a mistake, for it is shown by this most notable action that many bore this name." The Glossa Ordinaria on Matt 26:7, Mark 14:3, and Luke 7:38 expressly states that this woman, who anointed Jesus, was Mary Magdalene, the sister of Lazarus. See, e.g., PL 114:167B on Matt 26:7: "Mary Magdalene, sister of Lazarus."

[35] See Homily 33 n. 1 of GGHG in CCSL cxli, p. 288. I modify Hurst, p. 269: "This woman, whom Luke calls a sinner (7:37), John names Mary (11:2). I believe that she is the same Mary of whom Mark (16:9) says that seven demons had been cast out."

the delay has been. Sixth is *the opportune nature of the place.*

Verse 7. So the first point is Christ's safety. For this reason he exhorts his timid disciples, saying: *Then afterwards he said to his disciples,* that is, Jesus is the speaker. *Let us go again into Judea.* In this way he encourages them, since they are fearful. And this is clear from their answer.

18. (Verse 8). *The disciples said to him: Rabbi, just now the Jews were seeking to stone you,* that is, it was very recent. John 10:31 reads: "They took up stones to stone him." *And you are going there again?* As if they were saying: Do not go. Peter said something similar to the Lord in Matthew 16:22: "Far be it from you, O Lord." He was trying to dissuade Jesus from death and was rebuked, since the Lord had predicted that he was going to die, and he was trying to dissuade him and wanted him to change his mind. But they did not know then that he was willing to die. And so they are instructed and comforted, so that they have no fear. For this reason the text continues:

19. (Verse 9) *Jesus answered: Are there not twelve hours in the day?* That is, during which it is good and safe to walk. Therefore, he says: *If a person walks*[36] *during the day, he does not stumble, because he sees the light of this world.* This light is Christ. John 8:12 above reads: "I am the light of the world." The person who walks with this light does not stumble, because, as it is said in John 8:12 above: "The person who follows me does not walk in the darkness." And therefore, he does not stumble. Thus Wis-

---

[36] On p. 398 n. 5 QuarEd rightly note that the Vulgate reads *ambulaverit* ("would walk") while Bonaventure has *ambulat* ("walks").

dom says in Proverbs 4:11-12: "I will lead[37] you by the paths of justice, which, when you have entered ... and are running, you will not meet a stumbling block." Not only is it safe to walk during the day, but it is also opportune. So he adds:

20. (Verse 10). *But if a person walks during the night, he stumbles, because the light is not in him.* Matthew 15:14 states: "If a blind person guides a blind person, both fall into a pit." For which reason it is said in John 12:35 below: "Walk while you have the light, that darkness may not overtake you."

21. (Verse 11). *These things he spoke, and after this he said to them.*[38] The second point occurs here, that is, the necessity of going for the sake of Lazarus, who was dead unless he could be raised up by him. So the text continues: *Lazarus, our friend, sleeps. But I go that I may wake him from sleep.* His way of speaking is his very own, since to die to God is to fall asleep. Thus Augustine comments: "He was dead to people who were unable to raise him up. But he was asleep to the Lord who roused him from the tomb with such ease as you might rouse a sleeping person from his bed."[39] Wherefore, the Lord said in Matthew 9:24: "The girl is asleep, not dead."[40] But the disciples did not understand this. For this reason the text says:

---

[37] The Vulgate reads *duxi* ("I have led") whereas Bonaventure has *ducam* ("I will lead").

[38] On p. 398 n. 8 QuarEd accurately indicate that the Vulgate reads *eis* ("to them") whilst Bonaventure has *illis* ("to them").

[39] See Tractate 49 n. 9 in CCSL xxxvi, p. 424 and FC 88, p. 246. Bonaventure's citation is almost verbatim.

[40] Hugh of St. Cher, p. 355p also cites Matt 9:24.

22. (Verse 12). *Lord,*[41] *if he is asleep, he will be safe,* for sleep is a good sign in severe sicknesses.[42] They said this because they did not understand. So the Evangelist now says:

23. (Verse 13). *Now Jesus had been speaking of death,*[43] *but they thought that he was speaking of the repose of sleep.* Thus they were mistaken, as the Evangelist hints, through the equivocation of the word "sleep." – From this it is to be understood that there is a fourfold sleep.[44] There is the sleep of sluggishness. Proverbs 6:9 reads: "How long will you sleep, O sluggard?"[45] 1 Thessalonians 5:6 states: "Let us not sleep ... but let us be wakeful and sober."[46] – The sleep of sin. Ephesians 5:14 says: "Awake, sleeper, and arise from the dead, and Christ will enlighten you." 1 Corinthians 11:30 has: "Many among you are sick and weak, and many are asleep." – The sleep of rest. Matthew 26:43 reads: "And he found them sleeping." And the text adds that he said to them in 26:45: "Sleep on now and take your rest." – The sleep of death. 1 Thessalonians 4:13 states: "We would not have you ignorant, brothers and sisters, about those who are asleep, lest you should grieve, even as others who have no hope."[47] Job

---

[41] On p. 398 n. 10 QuarEd correctly indicate that the Vulgate reads *Dixerunt ergo discipuli eius: Domine* ("So his disciples said to him: Lord").

[42] See Augustine, Tractate 49 n. 11 in FC 88, p. 248: "The sleep of the sick is usually a sign of health."

[43] On p. 398 n. 11 QuarEd rightly notice that the Vulgate reads *morte eius* ("his death") while Bonaventure has *morte* ("death").

[44] While I indicate in the following notes the three biblical parallels that Bonaventure's *distinctio* has in common with the exegesis of Hugh of St. Cher, it is largely his own creation.

[45] Hugh of St. Cher, p. 355n also cites Prov 6:9.

[46] Hugh of St. Cher, p. 355n also cites Eph 5:14.

[47] Hugh of St. Cher, p. 355p also cites 1 Thes 4:13.

27:19 says: "The rich person, when he will fall asleep, will take nothing with him."

24. (Verse 14). *Then*[48] *Jesus said to them*. The third point surfaces here, that is, *the benefit for the disciples*. Thus he openly discloses the death of Lazarus, since they did not capture his occult meaning. So *then Jesus said to them plainly: Lazarus is dead*. He does so *plainly*, because, as is said in Matthew 13:11: "To you is given to know the mysteries of the kingdom of the heavens." And he adds the benefit for them and rejoices about it. Thus the text continues:

25. (Verse 15). *But*[49] *I rejoice on your account*, that is, for your benefit, *that I was not there, so that you may believe*. The emphasis here is not on faith, but on rejoicing, that is, *I rejoice that I was not there*, so that afterwards because of our coming your faith may be strengthened. So he says: *But let us go to him*, since it is safe and Lazarus needs us and you need to benefit from this sign. The reason why he went was because he was a friend. John 14:23 below reads: "If anyone loves me, he will keep my word. And my Father will love him, and we will come to him and make our abode with him."

26. (Verse 16). *So Thomas said*. This verse introduces the fourth point, that is, Thomas's ardent desire, even to die with Christ. So the text states: *So Thomas, who is called the Twin, said*,[50] as if he had been in doubt for a long time:

---

[48] On p. 398 n. 16 QuarEd accurately mention that the Vulgate reads *Tunc ergo* ("So then") while Bonaventure has *tunc* ("Then").

[49] On p. 399 n. 1 QuarEd rightly notice that the Vulgate reads *Et* ("And") whilst Bonaventure has *Sed* ("But").

[50] On p. 399 n. 3 QuarEd correctly indicate that the Vulgate reads *ad condiscipulos* ("to his fellow disciples"), a reading that Bonaventure does not have.

Let us also go that we may die with him. – Chrysostom asks why Thomas said this and responds that Thomas spoke out of fear.[51] But a better interpretation is that he spoke out of strength. Inspired by the Lord's exhortation, he spoke both wisely and courageously. Thus 2 Timothy 2:11-12 reads: "If we have died with him, we will also live with him. If we endure, we will also reign with him."

27. (Verse 17). *So*[52] *Jesus came.* Here the fifth point occurs, that is, the delay in time, for this was done according to divine dispensation. So he found him not only dead, but decaying, so that the miracle would be more certain and more wonderful and more glorious. And so the text adds: *And he found him already four days in the tomb,* and thus decayed. John 11:39 below states: "Lord, he is already decayed, for he is dead four days."

28. (Verse 18). *Now Bethany was.* The last point is made here, that is, the opportune nature of the place. For since the place was close to Jerusalem, many Jews had come who would be witnesses of the miracle. Now the reason why they had come was the opportune nature of the place because of its close proximity. Because of its opportune nature the text continues: *Now Bethany was close to Jerusalem, some fifteen stadia distant.* A stadium is one-eighth of a Roman mile, and so the place was close.[53] For which reason the text also says:

---

[51] See Homily 62 n. 2 in PG 59:344: "So all were fearful of the attack of the Jews, most of all Thomas. Therefore, he said: 'Let us go that we may die with him.' Some say that he wanted to die, but this was not the case. Rather he spoke out of fear." Hugh of St. Cher, p. 355v,h cites Chrysostom's opinion.

[52] On p. 399 n. 6 QuarEd accurately mention that the Vulgate reads *itaque* ("So") whilst Bonaventure has *ergo* ("So").

[53] See Chrysostom, Homily 62 n. 2 in PG 59:344: "Now if Bethany was fifteen stadia distant, which is two Roman miles, how was Lazarus dead for four days?"

29. (Verse 19). *And many of the Jews had come to Martha and Mary to console them on account of their brother*, for at that time there was great sadness about the dead. But after the death of Christ there had to be consolation about the good who die, for "blessed are the dead who die in the Lord."[54] So 1 Thessalonians 4:13 states: "... we would not ... have you ignorant concerning those who are asleep, lest you should grieve, even as others, who have no hope."

30. In a spiritual sense three matters are to be noted. The first point is: Why does it mean that Lazarus was loved by the Lord? Second, what does it mean that he was sick, died, and was found dead for four days? Third, what does it mean that the Lord exhorted his disciples to walk during the day? – The name Lazarus means "helped by the Lord."[55] He signifies the man who has helping grace, according to what Isaiah 49:8 says: "In an acceptable time I have heard you, and in the day of salvation I have helped you." This person loves the Lord, and therefore is also loved. Proverbs 8:17 reads: "I love those who love me."

This Lazarus is sick with taking delight in sin. About this sickness Sirach 10:11 states: "A long sickness is troublesome to the physician," since it scarcely happens that morose delight does not fall down into mortal sin. – But he dies through his consent, since then sin is consummated interiorly. James 1:15 says: "When passion has conceived, it brings forth sin. But when sin has been consummated, it begets death." – And he becomes dead for four days and stinks when action follows from consent, habit follows action, and impudence in sinning follows habit. This latter happens when "even though a person has a harlot's fore-

---

[54] Rev 14:13.
[55] See CCSL lxxii, p. 140: "Lazarus means helped."

head, he no longer wants to feel shame."[56] And then he stinks, since his sin has already spread to others. Amos 4:10 has: "I made the stench of your camps to come up into your nostrils," etc.[57]

To raise this sinner from the dead the Lord urged his disciples, whom he had also ordained prelates. Proverbs 6:3 reads: "Run. Hasten. Stir up your friend." – And he exhorts them to walk during the day. "Day" means the time for meriting, since when the sun arises, people go out to their work, and the demons are hidden. Psalm 103:22-23 states: "The sun arises, and they have gathered together.... People go forth to their work," etc. – This day lasts from the coming of Christ till the day of judgment, because John 9:5 above reads: "As long as I am in the world, I am the light of the world." And he is in the world "until the consummation of the world." Matthew 28:20 states: "Behold, I am with you all days, until the consummation of the world." – And this is to be done, so that sinners may be aroused. Galatians 6:10 says: "Let us do good to all, but especially to those who are of the household of faith." – "The twelve hours" of this day can be said to be twelve stages of Christ, which were treated in John 4 above.[58] – Another interpretation is that the

---

[56] Bonaventure adapts Jer 3:3 to his purposes: "You had a harlot's forehead, you would not blush."

[57] See Augustine, Tractate 49 n. 3 for a similar reflection about sin, but one that is based on the three gospel accounts of Jesus' raising the dead: the raising of the synagogue official's daughter while she was lying in the house (interior sin); the raising of the widow's son after he had been carried outside the city gates (external action); Lazarus who had been buried for four days (habitual sin). See Hugh of St. Cher, p. 355v,k: "Another interpretation: the four days are the sin of heart, mouth, deed, and habit."

[58] See John 4 n. 82 above.

twelve can refer to the twelve apostles,[59] who are also signified by the twelve stones, by the twelve fountains in Elim, by the twelve oxen which hold up the golden sea of Solomon, by the twelve precious stones, and now by the twelve hours.[60] – Another interpretation is that they are the twelve virtues that were in Christ, namely the four cardinal, one theological,[61] and the seven gifts. – Still another interpretation is that they are the twelve fruits of the Spirit, about which Revelation 22:2 says: "the tree of life, bearing twelve fruits, yielding its fruit according to each month."

JOHN 11:20-32
FAITH AND LOVE OF THE TWO SISTERS

31. *So when Martha heard*, etc. Previously the two antecedents to the miracle had been determined, that is, the notification of the sickness and the coming of the Physician. Here the Evangelist introduces his third point, that

---

[59] See Hugh of St. Cher, p. 355i: "The twelve hours are the twelve Apostles, whom Christ illumined and through whom he also illumined the world. These are the twelve fountains of Elim. Ex 15:27. About which Isa 12:3 says: You will draw waters with joy from the fountains of the Savior. These are the twelve oxen, 1 Kings 7:25, that hold up the sea, that is, baptism, in which they must wash those who want to enter the Church. These are the twelve gates of the city, made from individual pearls, Rev 21:21. For through the teaching of the apostles and the pellucid example of their lives we enter Paradise."

[60] See Bonaventure's *Commentary on Luke, Chapters 1-8*, pp. 480-481: "This number is also signified in the *twelve sons of Jacob* in Genesis 48:8-27. In the *twelve stones* in Exodus 28:17-21. In the *twelve leaders* of the people of Israel in Numbers 17:2. In the *twelve explorers* sent by Moses in Numbers 13:4-17. In the *twelve fountains* of water in Exodus 15:27. In the *twelve stones* drawn from the River Jordan in Joshua 4:8. In the *twelve oxen* which hold up the golden sea in 1 Kings 7:25. In the *twelve hours* of the day in John 11:9. In the *twelve foundations* of the city in Revelation 21:14, 19-20."

[61] Not faith or hope, but love.

is, *the intercession of faith*, which merited the raising of Lazarus. Now this was the faith and love of the two sisters, namely, Martha and Mary. So first the faith of Martha is noted. Second that of Mary where verse 28 reads: "And when she had said this, she went away," etc.

John 11:20-27
Faith and love of Martha

So the faith and love of *Martha* are noted in this order. First is the *dutiful solicitude* of Martha. Second her *confession of faith*. Third is *the amplification* of her faithful confession.

Verse 20. So Martha's solicitude is suggested in this that she herself met the Lord. She did not wait until he came to the house. So the text continues: *So when Martha heard that Jesus was coming, she went to meet him.*[62] Through this it is evident that Martha was very solicitous, but Mary, on the contrary, was quiet. So the text says: *But Mary remained at home*, that is, quiet. So it is said in Luke 10:41-42: "Martha, Martha, you are solicitous and troubled about many things.... Mary has chosen the best part." The active life is very well signified by Martha meeting. Isaiah 21:14 reads: "Meet the person fleeing with bread." The contemplative life is signified by Mary remaining at home. Thus Lamentations 3:28 says this of the contemplative man: "He will sit solitary and keep quiet, because he had taken it upon himself."[63]

---

[62] On p. 400 n. 11 QuarEd rightly notice that the Vulgate reads *illi* ("him") while Bonaventure has *ei* ("him").

[63] The Glossa Interlinearis comments: "... the active life first meets a person through the works of mercy.... Contemplatives desire quiet."

32. (Verse 21). *So Martha said.*[64] The second point surfaces here, that is, Martha's confession of faith, in which she confesses that the Lord is powerful and gracious, so that he could and would rescue from sickness and now resuscitate. So she says: *Lord, if you had been here, my brother would not have died*, since you would have and could have rescued him, but now you can resuscitate him. So the text continues:

33. (Verse 22). *But even now I know*, that is, I hold by firm faith, *that whatever you will ask of God, God will give it to you*. Augustine observes: "I know that you can. If you wish, you will do it. But whether you will do is your decision, not my presumption."[65] She did not dare to ask for something so great, lest she be rejected. But by expressing her faith, he suggested her desire. God gives not only what Christ asks, but also what is asked in his name. John 16:23 below says: "If you ask the Father anything in my name, he will give it to you."

34. (Verse 23). *Jesus said to her.*[66] The third point arises here, that is, the amplification of the confession of faith. For Martha had confessed that the Lord could petition for her brother's resuscitation. But the Lord wants to lead her to the point that she confess that Christ can resuscitate. For this reason he powerfully states: *Your brother will rise*. And Martha professes her faith in the general resurrection. Thus she says:

---

[64] On p. 400 n. 13 QuarEd correctly indicate that the Vulgate reads *ad Iesum* ("to Jesus").

[65] See Tractate 49 n. 13 in CCSL xxxvi, p. 427. The citation is virtually verbatim.

[66] On p. 401 n. 2 QuarEd accurately mention that the Vulgate reads *illi* ("to her") while Bonaventure has *ei* ("to her").

35. (Verse 24). *I know[67] that he will rise at the resurrection on the last day*. She knew this from *the Law*. Daniel 12:2 states: "Many of those who sleep in the dust of the earth will awake." She knew this through Christ's teaching. John 6:40 above reads: "I will raise him up on the last day." But since she has not yet confessed that he would rise through Christ's power, she is instructed about this. So the text continues:

36. (Verse 25). *Jesus says[68] to her: I am the resurrection and the life*. The predicate is causal, that is, I make some to rise and to live. 1 Corinthians 15:20-21 states: "Christ has risen from the dead, the first fruits of those who have fallen asleep ... since by a man death came, by a man also comes resurrection of the dead." And he reveals this: *The person who believes in me, even if he dies, will live*. And in this way I make him rise. John 5:25 above has: "The hour is coming and now is, when the dead will hear the voice of the Son of God, and those who hear it will live." – I not only make the dead to rise, but also make the living live. So the text continues:

37. (Verse 26). *And who lives and believes in me will never die*. John 6:40 reads: "Whoever sees the Son and believes in him has eternal life." And since "with the heart a person believes unto righteousness and with the mouth profession of faith is made unto salvation,"[69] the Lord asks: *Do you believe this?*

---

[67] On p. 401 n. 3 QuarEd rightly notice that the Vulgate reads *Dicit ei Martha: Scio* ("Martha said to him: I know"). Bonaventure does not have *Dicit ei Martha* ("Martha said to him").

[68] On p. 401 n. 4 QuarEd correctly mention that the Vulgate reads *dixit* ("said") whilst Bonaventure has *dicit* ("says").

[69] See Rom 10:10. Hugh of St. Cher, p. 356a also cites Rom 10:10.

38. (Verse 27). *She said to him: Yes, Lord*. I believe that you will do this. *I believe that you are the Christ, the Son of God, who has come into the world*. And so you can resuscitate and vivify, since, as John 5:26 states: "As the Father has life in himself, so too has he given to the Son to have life in himself." In this one professes both Divinity and humanity: Since as *Son of God*, you can; since *you have come*, you will do it. For you were sent for this purpose.

JOHN 11:28-32
MARY'S CONFESSION OF FAITH

39. *And when she had said this*. After the Evangelist has described Martha's confession of faith, he now presents *Mary's profession of faith* in this order. First is the description of Mary's *haste* after she has been called. Second is *the accompaniment of the Jews*. Third is her *confession of faith and devotedness*.

Verse 28. So the first point is the haste of Mary who has been called. In this *the quiet* and *devotedness* of Mary are signified. *Quiet*, because she did not come until she was called by Martha. So the text says: *And when she had said this, she went away and quietly called Mary her sister*. Lamentations 3:26 states: "It is good to wait with silence for the salvation of God." *She called* her, I say, by the Lord's command. Revelation 22:17 reads: "And let the person who hears say: Come." And this is hinted in that she called, *saying: The Master is here and calls you*. Although this had not been said because of the sake of brevity, nevertheless the facts are to be understood in this manner.[70] Job 14:15 says: "You will call me, and I will answer you." Not only was Mary *quiet*, but she was also *devoted*. So the text continues:

40. (Verse 29). *As soon as she heard this, she rose up*[71] *quickly and came to him.* She did not wait for him to come, but she herself ran out quickly, before he entered the village. So the text states:

41. (Verse 30). *For Jesus had not yet come into the village, but was still at the place where Martha had met him.* In this is signified that a man, called by the Lord, must act quickly, as the good disciples did, about whom Matthew 4:20 says: "At once they left the nets and followed him." Wherefore, that person was rebuked who in Luke 9:59 said: "Let me first go and bury my father." Sirach 31:27 reads: "In all your works be quick." And Proverbs 18:9 states: "The person who is loose and slack in his work is the brother of him that demolishes his own works."[72]

42. (Verse 31). *So*[73] Here the second point surfaces, that is, the accompaniment of the Jews. And the reason for their gathering at the house was their desire to offer consolation. So the text continues: *So when the Jews who were*

---

[70] See Augustine, Tractate 49 n. 16 in FC 88, p. 252: "It should be noticed also that the Evangelist did not say where or when or how the Lord called Mary so that this must be understood from Martha's words instead, thus preserving the brevity of the narrative."

[71] On p. 401 n. 10 QuarEd rightly notice that the Vulgate reads *surgit* ("rises up") whereas Bonaventure has *surrexit* ("rose up").

[72] Contrast the commentary of Hugh of St. Cher, p. 356v,f-g: "When she heard this, she rose up quickly] by turning away from evil. And came to him] by doing good. And the text says 'quickly.' This is expedient, since as Prov 4:12 says: 'When you run, you will not meet a stumbling block.' Sir 5:8 states: 'Do not delay in converting to the Lord.'"

[73] The Vulgate reads *igitur* ("So") while Bonaventure has *ergo* ("So").

with her in the house and were consoling her, for they had come for this purpose, *saw Mary rise up quickly and go away*,[74] as if moved by a grief that she could no longer bear, *they followed her, saying: She is going to the tomb to weep there*. So they were following her, so that they might console her. About this consolation Sirach 38:17-18 says: "Console yourself in your sadness and make mourning for him according to his merit for a day or two, for fear of detraction."

43. (Verse 32). *So when Mary came*, etc. This verse introduces the third point, that is, Mary's confession of faith and devotedness. For this reason the text states: *So when Mary came where Jesus was and saw him, she fell at his feet*. Behold, her *devotedness*, for she is always at the feet of the Lord. Thus Luke 7:38 reads: "Mary, standing behind him at the Lord's feet."[75] And Luke 10:39 has: "She seated herself at the Lord's feet and listened to his word." It is not read about Martha that she fell at his feet, because she was not so devoted and not so warm as Mary was.[76] Deuteronomy 33:3 states: "Those who approach his feet will receive of his teaching." And her confession of faith is added: *And she said to him: Lord, if you had been here, my brother would not have died*.[77] Through her words she

---

[74] On p. 402 n. 1 QuarEd accurately indicate that the Vulgate reads *exiit* ("go out") while Bonaventure has *abiit* ("go away").

[75] Luke 7:38 reads neither "Mary" nor "of the Lord." In commenting on John 11:31, Hugh of St. Cher, p. 356v,l observes: "Now from this it seems that this Mary was not the same one about which Luke 8:37 (=7:37) speaks, since if she were a harlot, not so many would have followed her."

[76] Hugh of St. Cher, p. 356v,o comments: "Her sister had not done this (fallen at the Lord's feet). Chrysostom: This one was warmer than her sister, since she was not ashamed because of the crowd to fall at his feet nor did she abandon him on account of the suspicion that the Jews had about Christ."

[77] On p. 402 n. 5 QuarEd correctly mention that the Vulgate reads *non esset mortuus frater meus* ("my brother would not have died")

insinuates that the Lord has the power, as her sister had done earlier. But this sister speaks more fully because the Lord might still resuscitate Lazarus, if he willed it. And out of respect she kept quiet, and out of love wept, and deeply moved the Lord, as will be clear below.[78] In this it is noted that the Lord more readily hears a groan from the heart than a sound from the mouth. Gregory teaches: "True prayer is to lift up bitter groans of compunction rather than well turned phrases."[79] Thus it is said in 1 Samuel 1:10 that Hannah wept copiously and prayed silently.

Questions

44. Question 1 asks: Why did the Lord so diligently seek Martha's confession of faith in the resurrection, when he knew that she faithfully believed in it?[80] And why was this necessary? – It has to be maintained that the faith of Lazarus' sisters obtained his resuscitation. And since faith is more certain and more firm when it is professed orally, he asked for an oral confession.[81]

45. Question 2 then asks: Whose power is greater to obtain a miracle? – 1. It would seem that the power of faith is greater, since John 11:40 below says: "Have I not told you that if you believe, you will see the glory of God?" – Furthermore, Mark 9:22 reads: "If you can believe, all

whilst Bonaventure has *frater meus non fuisset mortuus* ("my brother would not have died"). Bonaventure's reading corresponds to the text of John 11:21.

[78] See John 11:33-43.

[79] See Book XXXIII, c. 23 n. 43 of *Moralia in Iob* in CCSL cxliiib, p. 1712. The citation is virtually verbatim.

[80] See John 11:25-27.

[81] See John 11:26 n. 37 above and Rom 10:10.

things are possible for the person who believes." And also in Mark 9:27-28 it is said that the Lord told his apostles that they could not cast out the demon on account of their incredulity.[82] – And the Apostle in 1 Corinthians 13:2 says: "If I had faith[83] so as to remove mountains." – 2. But it seems that the power of hope is greater, since in Matthew 9:22 it is said: "Be confident, daughter." Therefore, it seems that it is the power of confidence, and confidence belongs to hope. – 3. But it seems that the power of love is greater, since it joins people to God and makes them friends, and friends are especially worthy of being heard.

I answer that it has to be maintained that since a miracle is not only obtained by good people, but also by evil ones, it is obtained by that power that good and evil people have in common.[84] Now this can be faith and hope. Therefore, the miracle stems from faith as a original principle, but from hope as a consummative principle. And since confidence, properly speaking, embraces both, the obtaining of the miracle issues from confidence. – Note that the operation of the miracle is indebted to faith, because it is common, because it first elevates the intellect, because it has to consider omnipotence.[85]

---

[82] Bonaventure seems to have combined Mark 9:27-28 and Matt 17:18-19. Mark 9:27-28 says: "Why could we not cast it out? And he said to them: This kind can be cast out in no way except by prayer and fasting." Matt 17:18-19 reads: "Why could we not cast it out? He said to them: Because of your incredulity."

[83] The Vulgate reads *omnem fidem* ("all faith").

[84] See Bonaventure's earlier discussion in John 3 n. 6.

[85] See Book III, d. 23. a. 1 q. 1 et dubium 6 in Bonaventure's *Sentence Commentary*.

John 11:33-42
Christ is heard because of his filial love

46. *So when Jesus saw her weeping*. We have now seen three preambles to the miraculous raising of Lazarus. Now the fourth occurs and is Christ's *being heard because of filial love*. For the Lord was moved by compassion to hear and to raise Lazarus. And it is described in this order. First is *the compassion of the one who hears*. Second is *the sign of hearing*. Third is *the power* or authority *of being heard*.

Verse 33. So the compassion of the one hearing is seen in this that Christ wept and was sorrowful at the weeping of Mary and of the Jews. So the text states: *So when Jesus saw her weeping*, namely, Mary, *and the Jews who had come with her weeping. He saw*, that is, with the eyes of compassion. 2 Kings 20:5 says: "I have heard your prayer and have seen your tears." *He groaned in spirit and was troubled,*[86] suffering together with them. And out of this compassion he draws near. Thus:

47. (Verse 34). *He said:*[87] *Where have you laid him? They said to him: Lord, come and see*. And a manifestation of compassion ensues. Thus:

48. (Verse 35). *And Jesus wept*. So from sight arises being troubled. From being troubled arises drawing close. From drawing close arises an expression of sorrow and compassion. Job 30:25 reads: "Up to now I have wept for the person who was afflicted, and my soul had compassion on

---

[86] On p. 403 n. 2 QuarEd rightly notice that the Vulgate reads *turbavit se ipsum* ("was troubled") whereas Bonaventure has *turbavit semetipsum* ("was troubled").

[87] On p. 403 n. 2 QuarEd accurately mention that the Vulgate reads *Et dixit* ("And he said") while Bonaventure has *Dixit* ("He said").

the poor." Luke 19:41 states: "When Jesus saw the city, he wept over it."[88] He wept when he saw Mary weeping. Romans 12:15 says: "Weep with those who weep." And this compassion was a sign of his sorrow, and his sorrow was a sign of his love. So:

49. (Verse 36). *So the Jews said: See how he loved him*, since he was weeping over his death. And they were speaking truthfully according to what is said in Wisdom 11:25-27: "Lord, you have loved all things that are and do not hate any of the things that you have made…. They are yours, O Lord, who loves souls." But from this display of love they fell into doubt, since the person who loves another does not want him to die. It seemed to them that he had died against his will, and they were in amazement. For this reason the text continues:

50. (Verse 37). *But some of them said: Could not the person who opened the eyes of a man born blind*[89] – John 9 above – *have caused that this man should not die?* They are speaking out of doubt. Yet they seem to have a reason for each point. Indeed he could easily do this, for Qoheleth 8:3 states: "He will do everything that pleases him." And Luke 1:37 reads: "Nothing will be impossible with God." But if he had not died, the glory of God would not have been manifested in him. So Lazarus was dead, just as the man of John 9 was born blind. John 9:3 has: "Neither he nor his parents have sinned, but so that the works of God might be manifested in him." Wherefore, he was born blind whereas Lazarus was dead.

---

[88] Hugh of St. Cher, p. 357e cites Luke 19:41 as one of the three places where Jesus is described as weeping. The other two are John 11:35 and Hebr 5:7.

[89] The Vulgate reads *caeci* ("of a blind man") whereas Bonaventure has *caeci nati* ("man born blind").

51. (Verse 38). *So Jesus, again groaning.* The second point is made here, that is, *the sign of Christ's compassionate hearing* that is manifested, because he came to the tomb and had the stone removed. So the text states: *So Jesus, again groaning in himself,* through compassion, *came to the tomb.* And since he had come to raise up Lazarus, he commanded that the tomb be opened, for it was closed. So the text continues: *Now it was a cave, and a stone was laid against it,* that is, to seal off the stench.

52. (Verse 39). *Jesus said: Take away the stone.* And since Martha had been earnest in taking care of the Lord's sensible and bodily needs, the text says: *Martha, the sister of the person who was dead, said to him: Lord, he is already decayed.* Therefore, his tomb should not be opened. *For he is dead for four days.*[90] And since Martha believed that the Lord wanted to see him out of his compassion, not to raise him up out of his power,[91] the text says:

---

[90] See Thomas Aquinas, *Catena Aurea in Quatuor Evangelia.* Vol. II. (Turin: Marietti, 1938) 533: "Theophylactus: Now Martha says this, as if out of doubt, believing it impossible that her brother could be raised up after this length of time. Bede gives another interpretation: These are not the words of desperation, but rather of wonderment." Aquinas then goes on to quote Chrysostom whose observations are found in n. 92. See Hugh of St. Cher, pp. 357-357v,o: "Anselm: She feared that, once the stone had been removed, he would rouse up a stinking cadaver rather than resuscitate her brother."

[91] See Rupert of Deutz, *Commentaria in Evangelium Sancti Iohannis,* p. 558: "She said ... these words: *Lord, he is already decayed, for he is dead for four days,* as if she were saying: Lord, why are you commanding that the stone be taken away? So that you may see your friend who is now dead or to return him alive to his grieving sisters? If you intend the latter, you can do it, for *I know,* as I have already said, *that whatever you ask of God, God will give you.* But if you only want to see him, I say to you: *He is already decayed, for he is dead for four days.* And therefore, it is already past the time when it is fitting to see him."

53. (Verse 40). *Jesus said to her: Have I not told you that if you believe, you will see the glory of God?*[92] That is, the magnitude of divine power. Acts 7:55 reads: "Since Stephen was filled with the Holy Spirit, he looked up to heaven and saw the glory of God."[93] And then they knew that he wanted the tomb opened, not to see a dead person, but to resuscitate a dead person. So obedience follows:

54. (Verse 41). *So they removed the stone.* Through this action it is already made clear that the Lord wanted to raise him up. So they then believed and merited to obtain this.[94] For it is said to Mary in Luke 1:45: "Blessed are you who have believed that the things said to you by the Lord would be accomplished for you."[95]

---

[92] See Chrysostom, Homily 63 n. 2 in PG 59:351 and FC 41, pp. 184-185: "Rightly, then, did I say that the woman failed to understand the words of Christ, namely: 'Even if he dies, he shall live.' At least, see what she said here, as if the thing were impossible because of the length of time.... Further, while He said to His disciples: 'That the Son of God may be glorified,' a statement referring to Himself, He said to the woman, on the other hand, 'Thou shalt behold the glory of God,' referring to his Father. Do you see the weakness of His hearers was the cause of the difference in what He said? Therefore, he was recalling to her mind what He had said to her, all but rebuking her as if she were forgetting it."

[93] The Vulgate does not read *Stephanus* ("Stephen"), even though Stephen is the subject of the sentence.

[94] See Book XXVIII nn. 14, 19 in *Origen, Commentary on the Gospel According to John Books 13-32*. Translated by Ronald E. Heine. FC 89 (Washington: CUA Press, 1993) 294-295: "The delay in the removal of the stone lying upon the cave resulted from the dead man's sister, for she hindered, as it were, those whom Jesus commanded when he said, 'Take away the stone,' by saying, 'He already stinks, for it is the fourth day.... For we must believe that the period of delay concerning the commandment is a time of disobedience for the one who later does what was commanded."

[95] Bonaventure has adapted Luke 1:45: "And blessed is she who has believed that the things said to her by the Lord would be accomplished."

And Jesus, raising his eyes, etc. The third point surfaces here, that is, the power of being heard that is in Christ, which is presented by his words, through which he shows that he has been heard and is always heard and does not ask the Father because he is powerless. For this reason the text states: *And Jesus, raising his eyes to heaven*,[96] *said: Father, I give you thanks that you have heard me.* He gives thanks that the Father hears him, not because the Father might hear him right now and not at other times. Therefore, the text continues:

55. (Verse 42). *Yet I knew that*[97] *you always hear me.* Hebrews 5:7 reads: "With tears and a loud cry he offered prayers and supplications to God ... and was heard because of his reverence."[98] Therefore, not as one who needed to ask did I give thanks, *but because of the people who stand around did I speak, that they may believe that you have sent me.* And I in my works am not against you, but in harmony with you in all things. John 8:28-29 above says: "I say only what the Father has taught me, and the one who sent me is with me and has not left me alone, because I always do the things that are pleasing to him." And thus he gave thanks and prayed, not on account of powerlessness, but to suggest the harmony between him and God. About this harmony John 5:19 above says: "The Son can do nothing of himself, but only what he sees the Father doing. For whatever he does, this the Son also does in like manner."

---

[96] On p. 404 n. 1 QuarEd rightly notice that the Vulgate reads *sursum* ("above") while Bonaventure has *in caelum* ("to heaven").

[97] On p. 404 n. 2 QuarEd accurately indicate that the Vulgate reads *quia* ("that") whereas Bonaventure has *quoniam* ("that").

[98] Bonaventure has adapted Hebr 5:7: "For Jesus, in the days of his earthly life, with a loud cry and tears, offered up prayers and supplications to him who was able to save him from death and was heard because of his reverence."

QUESTIONS

56. Question 1 focuses on John 11:33: "Jesus troubled himself" or "was troubled." – On the contrary it seems: 1. that Isaiah 42:4 reads: "He will not be sad or troubled."[99] – If you say, that he voluntarily troubled himself and not involuntarily as we do, then there is the objection: – 2. Since a disturbance obscures the eye of the mind,[100] therefore, if in Christ the eye of the mind could not be obscured, then he could not be disturbed or troubled. – 3. Furthermore, when a disturbance is voluntary, then it is not only from sensuality, but also from reason and is total. Wherefore, if Christ was voluntarily troubled, it is evident from this that he was completely troubled.

I respond that it has to be said that there are two meanings of disturbance, according to Jerome.[101] One is passion. The other is pre-passion. It is passion as it moves into the realm of reason. It is pre-passion when it remains in the realm of the senses. And this can be twofold. The first deals with a necessity in a sentient being which cannot do otherwise. The second deals with the will. Thus disturbance is threefold, namely, of the reason and this is evil and is found in evildoers. Of sensuality and this is of necessity and concerns the good. Finally, there is the voluntary disturbance that is in Christ.[102]

---

[99] This is from the first of the Servant Songs.

[100] See Book V, c. 45 n. 82 of Gregory, *Moralia in Iob*. Edited by Marcus Adriaen. CCSL cxliii (Turnhout: Brepols, 1979), 279: "About indignation the Psalmist again says: *My eye has been troubled by indignation* (6:8). Indeed, the vice of indignation blinds the eye of the mind...."

[101] See his commentary on Matt 5:28 in PL 26:39C: "Passion is considered sin. Pre-passion, although it contains the beginnings of sin, nevertheless is not considered a sin."

[102] See Book III, d. 15. dubium 4 in Bonaventure's *Sentence Commentary*.

1. So relative to Isaiah 42:4: "He will not be sad or troubled," this verse has to be understood about the disturbance that is of reason or that involuntarily issues from sensuality.[103] – 2. So with regard to the objection that the disturbance that arises from sensuality obscures the mind, at least for a time, it must be said that this is true when it is a case of necessity. But in Christ it increased only in as far as he willed it and directed reason accordingly. – 3. With respect to the objection that voluntary disturbance is complete, this is to be understood when reason troubles and disturbs itself.

57. Question 2 deals with John 11:35: Christ "wept." – For either he wanted Lazarus to die or not. If the answer is yes, then his was a fictitious weeping. If the answer is no, then his will was in discord with the divine will, and he didn't do something that he wanted. – I answer that there was a threefold human will in Christ, namely, of reason, of compassion, and sensuality, as Hugh teaches.[104] And by means of the will of compassion, which is a velleity,[105] he wanted something, but did not want it in an absolute sense. And through this will he suffered along with people and wept, as he wept over Jerusalem.[106] It is to be understood that Christ did not weep on account of the death of Lazarus, but on account of our miserable condition that was signified in the death of Lazarus. – So

---

[103] See Book III d. 15. a. 2. q. 2. ad 1. in Bonaventure's *Sentence Commentary*.

[104] See *Libellus de quatuor voluntatibus in Christo* in PL 176:841B: "So in Christ there was a divine will in as far as Christ was God. And likewise there was a human will in him in as far as he was human. Now the human will is considered in a threefold manner: according to reason, according to compassion, according to the flesh."

[105] See Deferrari, p. 1071: "The conditioned, the imperfect, that does not lead to deeds, that does not attain the aim of the will, velleity." I have corrected Deferrari's "lend to deeds" to "lead to deeds."

[106] See Luke 19:41.

the Lord is read to have wept first at the raising up of Lazarus, and then he wept over human weakness. – Second he wept over Jerusalem in Luke 19:41, and then he wept over our blindness. For Luke 19:42 says: "If you, even you, had known." – Third on the cross. Hebrews 5:7 reads: "When with tears, he offered." And then he wept over our malice.[107] – These are the three origins of sins and the three punishments inflicted upon us on account of sin, which are fittingly mitigated by his tears.

58. Question 3 focuses on how the Lord prayed in John 11:41-42, since he prayed according to his human nature. And according to this he raised him up. Therefore, according to his human nature he raised him up. Wherefore, his manner of resuscitating does not differ from that of Peter.[108] – I respond that as it is evident in John 11:41-42, the Lord neither prayed nor gave thanks, so that he might receive the power of raising Lazarus up, as others. Nor did he pray that he make himself to be believed as inferior to the Father. For, as Chrysostom observes, he did not have to.[109] But he did so in order to show that he

---

[107] See Hugh of St. Cher, p. 357e: "Another interpretation. He wept on the cross on account of our sin. Over the city because of our ignorance. Over Lazarus on account of our miserable condition."

[108] See Acts 9:40: "But Peter, putting them all out, knelt down and prayed. And turning to the body, he said: Tabitha, arise. And she opened her eyes and, seeing Peter, she sat up."

[109] See Homily 64 n. 2 in PG 59:357 and FC 41, pp. 196-197: "However, let us see what the prayer was. 'Father, I give thee thanks that thou hast heard me.' Who, then, has ever prayed in this way? Before saying anything else, He declared, 'I give you thanks,' to point out to us that He did not need the help of prayer. 'Yet I know that thou always hearest me.' He said this, not because He lacked the power necessary for the miracle, but to show that He was of one mind with the Father.... He did not say: 'That they may believe that I am inferior, that I have need of assistance from above, that I can do nothing without prayer.... He declared that the true reason for His prayer was: 'Lest they think that I am an enemy of God....'"

was in conformity with God and that his power was not contrary to the Father. – So with regard to the objection: It is false to say that he raised up in the same manner as he prayed, because he raised up according to his divine nature while he prayed according to his human nature.

John 11:43-46
The Lord raises Lazarus from the dead

59. *When he had said this*, etc. Now that the preliminaries to the miraculous raising up of Lazarus have been set forth, *the matters that accompany and follow upon* the miracle are presented here. The procedure in this section is as follows. First is the powerful *calling forth* of Lazarus himself. Second is his *resuscitation*. Third is his *unbinding*. Fourth follows *the building up of some*, but *the demolition of others*.

Verse 43. Now the powerful calling forth of Lazarus is hinted at by this that *He cried out with a long voice: Lazarus, come forth*. Imperiously did he say: *Come forth. He cried out with a loud voice*, for at his voice the general resurrection will take place according to what had been said above in John 5:28-29: "The hour is coming in which all who are in the tombs will hear the voice of the Son of God. And those who have done good will come forth until resurrection of life, but those who have done evil unto resurrection of judgment."

60. (Verse 44). *And at once he came forth*. The second point occurs here, namely, *the raising up of Lazarus* at the Lord's command. For this reason the text states: *And at once he who had been dead came forth*. In this the obedience of the creature to the Creator is noted. Mark 4:40 reads: "Who, do you think, is this that even the wind

and the sea obey him?"[110] Origen comments: "Although all things obey their Creator, only the rational creature is found to be disobedient."[111] Bonds did not hinder him. Thus the text continues: *Bound hands and feet by bandages.*[112] *Bound* is synecdoche. *By bandages*, that is, strips of cloth, by which his hands and feet were wrapped. *And his*[113] *face was tied up with a cloth*. And therefore, he did not come out of the tomb on his own power, but went forth on account of divine power.[114] Christ used this power at his own death. Matthew 27:52 reads: "The tombs were opened, and many bodies of the saints who had fallen asleep, arose."

Jesus said to them: Unbind him. The third point surfaces here, that is, the unbinding of Lazarus. So the text states that he was unbound by ministers, because the Lord, although he could do everything himself, wanted to communicate his power to others. Bede comments: "The one

---

[110] The Vulgate reads *et ventus et mare* ("both the wind and the sea") while Bonaventure has *ventus et mare* ("the wind and sea").

[111] Origen's Homily 6 is excerpted in Homily 55 of Paul the Deacon's *Homiliarius*. See PL 95:1199D: "He commands the sea, and it does not contemn him.... He commands every creature, and they do not go against his commands. But the one genus, that of human beings, that has been honored by being in the image of God, to which speech and wisdom have been given, only these human beings resist. Only these are disobedient. Only these contemn God."

[112] The Vulgate reads *pedes et manus* ("feet and hands") whilst Bonaventure has *manus et pedes* ("hands and feet").

[113] On p. 405 n. 9 QuarEd correctly mention that the Vulgate reads *illius* ("his") while Bonaventure has *eius* ("his").

[114] See Chrysostom, Homily 64 n. 3 in PG 59:358 and FC 41, p. 200: "At any rate, notice the miracle also testified to His authoritative power. He called, and he who had been dead came forth, still bound. Next, so that the deed might not appear to be an illusion (for it seemed no less wonderful for the man to come forth still bound, than to raise him from the dead), He bade them to unbind him, in order that, by touching him and coming close to him, they might see that it really was Lazarus."

who could raise the dead could also unbind the bonds, but on account of unity and individual charity he said to the ministers: *Unbind him and let him go.*[115] Chrysostom observes: "He did not want to draw to himself the person who had been resuscitated, so that he might teach us to avoid the pomp of the world."[116]

61. (Verse 45). *So many of the Jews.* This verse introduces the fourth point, that is, the building up of some and the demolition of others. For the sake of those who had been built up in faith the text states: *So many of the Jews, who had come to Mary and Martha*[117] *and had seen what he did, believed in him. Who had come*: Proverbs 13:20 reads: "The person who walks with the wise will be wise." John 4:39 above says: "Many believed in him," etc.[118] For the sake of those who became worse, the text has:

62. (Verse 46). *But some of them went away to the Pharisees and told them the things that Jesus had done.* Thus, in the same way that some moved forward, others fell

---

[115] Bonaventure has adapted Bede's commentary on John 11:44. See PL 92:781C: "For the one who resuscitated the dead could unbind the bonds. But on account of the unity of the holy Church of God and individual charity it is said to the ministers, that is, the disciples of Christ: *Unbind him*, since without the unity and faith of the Catholic Church and the charity of ecclesiastical holiness, sins are not unbound."

[116] See Homily 64 n. 3 in PG 59:358 and FC 41, p. 200: "Furthermore, He said: 'Let him go.' Do you perceive His lack of ostentation? He did not draw him to Himself, or bid him follow in His company, so as not to seem to any of them to be showing off – so well did He know to act with moderation."

[117] The Vulgate reads *Mariam* ("Mary") while Bonaventure has *Mariam et Martham* ("Mary and Martha").

[118] John 4:39 says: "Now many of the Samaritans of that town believed in him because of the word of the woman who bore witness: He told me all that I have ever done."

back. 2 Corinthians 2:16 says: "To some we are[119] an odor that leads to death, but for others an odor that leads to life." So Luke 2:34 reads: "Behold, this child is destined for the fall and the resurrection of many in Israel."

63. According to the moral sense there are four things to be noted in the raising up of Lazarus. First the Lord asks where he is. Second he commands that the stone be removed. Third he makes him come forth. Fourth he instructs his disciples to unbind him. – So first the Lord asks where the sinner is, when he shows him the vileness of his sin. Thus the Lord asks of Adam in Genesis 3:9: "Adam, where are you?" And Jeremiah 3:2 reads: "Lift your eyes on high and see where you have not prostrated yourself." – Second, he commanded the stone to be removed, when he makes human beings cease from the habit of sin, which like a heavy stone weighs upon them. Thus, the penitent soul said in Psalm 37:5: "My iniquities have gone over my head, and have weighed me down like a heavy burden." Augustine notes: "How difficult it is to rise for the person whom the weight of an evil habit presses down."[120] Lamentations 3:53 reads: "My life has fallen into the pit," that is, into the death of sin, "and they have laid a stone over me," that is, a tombstone. – So it should be noted that the Lord raised up one dead person in a house in Matthew 9:23-25, that is, he raised up the sinner dead by sin because of consenting to evil. He raised up another outside the house, that is, dead through evil deeds. He raised up another, as is the case here, who was in a tomb through an evil habit.[121] – Third, he commands him to come forth, since he has to confess

---

[119] Bonaventure adapts 2 Cor 2:16 by adding *sumus* ("we are").

[120] See Tractate 49 n. 24 in CCSL xxxvi, p. 431. Bonaventure's citation is verbatim.

[121] Earlier Bonaventure provided a similar explanation in his commentary on John 11:19 n. 30. Also see Augustine, Tractate 49 n. 3.

his own iniquity. To come forth is to come from one's hiding place into the open. Thus Proverbs 28:13 states: "The person who hides his sins will not prosper, but the person who confesses and abandons them will obtain mercy." Augustine comments: "When you despise, you lie dead. If you despise in a mighty way, you lie in the tomb. When you confess, you come forth."[122] – Fourth, he instructs his disciples to unbind him, since at this point the priestly power comes that did not have a place before confession. But the Lord had commanded that they show themselves to the priests to be unbound. In Luke 17:7 it was said to those cleansed from leprosy: "Go, show yourselves to the priests." And the Lord gave them the office in John 20:23 below: "Whose sins you shall forgive, they are forgiven them, and whose sins you shall retain, they are retained." – And it should be noticed that Lazarus, who had been resuscitated and came forth was bound with a triple chain, for a threefold difficulty remains in a person after the remission of sin. Thus the face tied up with a cloth refers to the difficulty in knowing. The bound feet refers to the difficulty in willing the good. The bound hands refers to the difficulty in doing good.[123] About these Matthew 22:13 says: "Bind his hands and feet and cast him forth[124]

---

[122] See Tractate 49 n. 24 in CCSL xxxvi, p. 431 and FC 88, p. 257: "When you despise, you lie dead; and if you despise such things as I have mentioned, you lie buried. When you confess, you come forth." Bonaventure's citation is not verbatim. See Hugh of St. Cher, p. 357v,q: "Augustine. When the sinner despises, he lies as if buried. When he repents, he arises. When he confesses, he comes forth as one coming forth from hiding and showing himself."

[123] See Hugh of St. Cher, p. 357v,r: "Bound feet and hands, that is, with the difficulties of doing good and willing the good…. And his face was tied up with a cloth] By this is understood the obscurity of understanding and of knowing."

[124] The Vulgate has *mittite eum* ("cast him forth") while Bonaventure has *proiicite eum* ("cast him forth").

into the darkness outside."[125] But he is unloosed from this chain when through the satisfaction enjoined upon him he is released from this threefold bondage and restored to a pristine state. Samson pleaded for this status in Judges 16:28: "Remember me, O God, for good and restore to me now my pristine strength."[126]

SECTION II: THE PASSION: JOHN 11:47-19:42[127]

64. *So the chief priests had gathered*, etc. This part of the book, which began with John 1:6, "There was a man sent from God," and which dealt with the Incarnate Word, was divided into two sections. The first considered the incarnation of Christ while the second focused on the manifestation of the incarnate one. The second part of the book describes the passion, and the third concerns the resurrection.

So the second part commences with John 11:47. The goal of this part, which extends to the beginning of John 20, is to treat those things that pertain to the passion. This part is divided into two sections, for certain matters relate to the passion as *preliminaries* while others are *circum-*

---

[125] See Homily 38 n. 13 of GGHG in CCSL cxli, p. 372 and Hurst, p. 350: "A strict judgment will bind the feet and hands of those who are now unwilling to be bound from wicked works by the amendment of their lives. Certainly punishment will bind those whom sin has held bound from good works. The feet of those who neglect to visit the sick are bound; the hands of those who bestow nothing freely now on the needy are bound from good work...."

[126] Bonaventure has adapted Judges 16:28: "But he called upon the Lord, saying: O Lord God, remember me, and restore to me now my pristine strength...."

[127] See Thomas Herbst, "The Passion as paradoxical Exemplarism in Bonaventure's Commentary on the Gospel of John," *Antonianum* 78 (2003): 209-248.

stantial. So the first section describes *antecedent matters* while the second depicts *concomitant matters* were John 18:1 states: "And after saying these things, Jesus went forth," etc.

John 11:47-17:26
Preliminaries to Christ's passion

There are three *preliminaries* to the passion, namely, *the plotting of the Jews, the prediction of Christ's passion, the consolation of the disciples*. So this first part has three sections. The first treats *the conspiracy of the Jews*. The second concerns *the prediction of the passion* where John 12:20 reads: "Now there were certain Gentiles," etc. The third is *the strengthening of the disciples* were John 13:1 states: "Before the feast."

John 11:47-12:19
Plotting of the Jews

The first part, in which is depicted *the plotting of the Jews*, who plotted the death of Christ, has four sections. The first describes *the conspiracy of the Jews*. The second treats *the corroboration of the conspiracy* where John 12:1 reads: "So Jesus six days before." Third is *the deepening of the conspiracy* where John 12:9 states: "So the great crowd knew" Fourth is *obstinacy in the conspiracy* where John 12:12 has: "Now the next day the great crowd."

John 11:47-56
Conspiracy of the Jews

65. (Verse 47). So *the conspiracy of the Jews* is described in this manner. First is *the investigation of human coun-*

cil. Second is *the determination of the council*. Third flows *Christ's hiding* because of this. Fourth is *the search for the hidden Christ*. – The conspiracy of the Jews is set in the context of the manifestation of Christ. For this reason the text states: *So the chief priests and the Pharisees gathered together a council against Jesus*.[128] The ambition of the leaders was united together with the malice of the Pharisees, so that they might fashion by force their wicked counsel. Sirach 21:10 says: "The gathering of sinners is like twisted twine." *They said: What are we doing? For this man is working many signs*. Chrysostom comments: "They are still saying that the one who had provided such a great demonstration of divinity is a mere man."[129]

66. (Verse 48). *If we let him alone as he is, all will believe in him*. And from this follows the undesirable event: *And the Romans will come and take away our place and nation*.[130] So they were saying this, because the Romans ruled over them at that time. And if they were to find for themselves a new emperor or king, they feared that they would incur their indignation. So they were more willing to act against God than human beings. So Proverbs 29:25 reads: "The person who fears human beings will quickly fall." Now the reason behind this is that they loved temporal goods more than eternal ones. Thus Augustine notes: "They did not want to lose temporal goods and gave no

---

[128] On p. 407 n. 5 QuarEd rightly notice that the Vulgate reads *concilium* ("a council") whereas Bonaventure has *consilium* ("a council"). Also the Vulgate does not read *adversus Iesum* ("against Jesus").

[129] See Homily 64 n. 3 in PG 59:358: "They are still saying that the one whose great demonstration of his divinity they had accepted was a mere man." Hugh of St. Cher, p. 358g cites Chrysostom: "They are still saying that the one whose great demonstration of his divinity they had accepted was a mere man."

[130] The Vulgate reads *nostrum et locum et gentem* ("both our place and nation") whereas Bonaventure has *locum nostrum et gentem* ("our place and nation").

thought to eternal life, and so they lost both."[131] And what they feared happened to them. For Chrysostom observes that what Psalm 9:16 says was fulfilled in them: "The Gentiles are stuck fast in the pit that they prepared."[132] Proverbs 10:24 reads: "What the wicked fears will come upon him. What they desire will be given to the just."

67. (Verse 49). *But one of them*, etc. The second point is introduced here, that is, the determination of the council that is made by human authority, divine dispensation, and common agreement. By human authority, because it says: *One of them, Caiphas by name, since he was high priest that year*, and therefore had the authority and would exercise it through this legitimate council, *said:*[133] *You know nothing.*

68. (Verse 50). *Nor do you reflect that it is expedient for us that one man die for the people, instead of the whole nation perishing. One man.* Romans 5:15 states: "For if through the offense of the one man[134] the many died, much more has the grace of God and the gift in the grace of the one man ... abounded unto the many." He did not

---

[131] See Tractate 49 n. 26 in CCSL xxxvi, p. 433. Bonaventure's quotation is not verbatim.

[132] See Homily 65 n. 1 in PG 59:359-361 and FC 41, p. 205: "'The nations are sunk in the pit they have made; in the snare they set, their foot is caught.' This happened in the case of the Jews, for they were saying that Jesus ought to be slain, that the Romans might not come and take away both their nation and their city. But, when they did slay Him, then they suffered this very fate; and when they had taken the measures they deemed necessary to escape it, they did not escape it." The Scripture passage that Chrysostom quotes at the beginning is Ps 9:16.

[133] On p. 407 n. 9 QuarEd accurately mention that the Vulgate reads *dixit eis* ("said to them").

[134] The Vulgate reads *unius delicto* ("by the offense of the one") while Bonaventure has *per unius hominis delictum* ("through the offense of the one man").

give the counsel that he be killed for his own sin, because that counsel would not hold water. Rather he gave counsel for the sake of the salvation of others, so that no one could continue to hold out against him because of Christ's innocence. Jeremiah 18:18 states: "Come and let us fashion plots against Jeremiah.... And let us strike him with the tongue, and let us give no heed to all his words." This counsel that Christ should die proceeded from the priests according to what Daniel 13:5 has: "Iniquity came out ... from the senior[135] judges who seemed to govern the people." The determination of this counsel not only was made by human authority, but also by divine dispensation. So the Evangelist adds:

69. (Verse 51). *This, however, he said not of himself*, that is, by his own invention, but by divine inspiration. Wherefore, the text continues: *But since he was high priest that year, he prophesied*. He attributes the prophetic spirit to the sacerdotal honor.[136] This shows that the Holy Spirit performs many noble deeds even through evil priests. Therefore, they should be held in honor. For this reason after Paul had insulted the high priest and found out that he was the high priest, he said in Acts 23:5: "I did not know ... that he was the high priest." And Saul, after he was anointed, prophesied in 1 Samuel 10:10. The Evangelist explains his prophecy by adding: *He prophesied that Jesus was to die for the nation.*

---

135 The Vulgate reads *senibus* ("old") whilst Bonaventure has *senioribus* ("senior").

136 See Chrysostom, Homily 65 n. 1 in PG 59:361 and FC 41, p. 206: "Do you perceive how powerful the authority of the office of high priest is? For, since he had been at all worthy of the office of high priest – even though undeserving of the honor – he prophesied, but without knowing what he was saying."

70. (Verse 52). *And not only for the nation*, that is, of the Jews, *but that he might gather into one the children of God who were scattered abroad*, that is, that he might collect the predestined into the unity of the Church. That gathering was predicted in Isaiah 11:12: "He will gather the fugitives of Israel and will collect the dispersed of Judah from the four quarters of the earth." Isaiah 60:4 reads: "Your children will come from afar." John 10:16 states: "I have other sheep that are not of this fold. I will also bring them. And they will hear my voice, and there will be one fold and one shepherd."[137] The agreement of the subjects concurs with human authority and divine dispensation. So the text adds:

71. (Verse 53). *So*[138] *from that day forth their plan was to kill him*, and now there was no opposition, because, even if they had questioned earlier, as was said above, "Why are you seeking to kill me,"[139] nevertheless there was no definite plan.[140] About this Proverbs 18 speaks.[141]

72. (Verse 54). *So Jesus no longer went about openly.*[142] The third point surfaces here, that is, Christ's hiding. He hides, that is, he goes out of sight, not out of fear, but for our instruction. He does not hide in order to flee from death, but so that it might come at an opportune time. So

---

[137] Hugh of St. Cher, p. 358z alludes to John 10:16.

[138] On p. 408 n. 5 QuarEd rightly notice that the Vulgate reads *ergo* ("So") while Bonaventure has *igitur* ("So").

[139] See John 7:20 and 8:40.

[140] See Hugh of St. Cher, p. 358a, who quotes the Glossa and Chrysostom and comes to the same conclusion as Bonaventure.

[141] To what verse of Prov 18 was Bonaventure referring? Perhaps, 18:1: "The person who has it in mind to abandon a friend looks for occasions. He will ever be subject to reproach."

[142] On p. 408 n. 7 QuarEd accurately indicate that the Vulgate reads *in palam* ("in the open") whereas Bonaventure has *palam* ("openly").

the text continues: *So Jesus no longer went about openly among the Jews, but withdrew to a district near the desert*, seeking more secluded places in a human way,[143] *to a town called Ephraim. And there he stayed with his disciples*. About this Augustine comments: "It is clear that there is no sin if the faithful, who are members of Christ, should withdraw themselves from the eyes of persecutors and by hiding avoid the wrath of evildoers rather than excite it by offering themselves."[144] He fled from the Jews and remained with his disciples. John 10:4 above has: "The sheep follow him and hear his voice."[145]

73. (Verse 55). *Now the Passover was near*. This verse introduces the fourth point, namely, the search for the hidden Christ, which was conducted by those who had gone up to the feast, since Christ customarily went up on feasts. So the text states: *Now the Passover*, the festival day, *of the Jews was near*. By means of antonomasia Passover is called "the festival day" and occurred during the first month, that is, April. Exodus 12:2-3 reads: "This month shall be to you the beginning of the months. It shall be the first in the months of the year.... On the tenth of this month let every man take a lamb for their families and houses." *And many from the country went up to Jerusalem before the Passover*, that is before the festival day. The text then adds the reason: *in order to purify themselves*, since no unclean person dared to eat the Passover. Numbers 9:10-11 stipulates: "The person,

---

[143] See Hugh of St. Cher, p. 358b: "Furthermore, he hid himself to show that he was truly human. For if he remained with them and by his divine power escaped from them, he would be thought to be God only and not man."

[144] Bonaventure has adapted Tractate 49 n. 28. See CCSL xxxvi, p. 433 and FC 88, p. 259.

[145] John 10:4 actually says: "The sheep follow him because they know his voice."

who has become unclean by occasion of one who is dead or shall be on a journey ... let him celebrate the ritual in the second month." John 18:28 below has: "So that they might not be defiled, but might eat the Passover." These came to cleanse themselves externally, but were defiled internally by willing murder. So the text continues:

74. (Verse 56). *So they were looking for Jesus*, that is, to destroy him. Psalm 39:15 states: "Let those be confounded and ashamed who seek to take my life away." *As they stood in the temple, they were saying to one another*. And the manner of their questioning ensues: *What do you think that he is not coming to the feast*? This questioning took place in the temple, thereby fulfilling what Jeremiah 7:11 has: "This house, in which my name is called upon, has become a den of robbers."[146] Thus Matthew 21:13 reads: "You have made it a den of robbers." Now the Evangelist intimates why they were seeking him in this manner: *Now the chief priests and the Pharisees had given orders that if anyone knew where he was, he should report it, so that they might seize him*. In 1 Samuel 23:23 Saul gave a similar perverse order with regard to David: "Consider and inspect all his lurking holes wherein he is hid.... And if he should ... close himself[147] in the earth, I will search him out in all the thousands of Judah."

Questions

75. Question 1 asks whether the Jews sinned in giving the counsel found in John 11:50. – It seems that they did,

---

[146] Jer 7:11 reads: "Has this house, then, in which my name is called upon, become a den of robbers in your eyes?" Hugh of St. Cher, p. 358v,f also cites Jer 7:11.

[147] The Vulgate reads *se abstruserit* ("should hide himself") whilst Bonaventure has *se obstruxerit* ("should close himself").

since the high priests and the Pharisees are censured because they killed the Lord or had him killed, and the Lord himself censures them in John 7:20 above: "Why do you seek to put me to death?" – It seems that they did not sin: 1. Since it was God's will that Christ be killed, therefore, in willing to kill him they were conforming their will to the divine will. And if this is so, then they did not sin. – 2. Furthermore, the Lord himself wanted his Son to suffer.[148] But he could not suffer unless he was murdered. And the Jews killed him. Wherefore, he willed that the Jews kill him. – 3. Moreover, he had come for the purpose of suffering. So if the Jews had not killed him, his coming would be frustrated. Therefore, since his coming was efficacious because of the counsel of the Jews, it seems that the Jews did not sin.

I respond that it has to be said that the Jews sinned both by reason of action and by reason of intention. By reason of act, because they wanted to kill the person whom they knew was innocent. This action in no way could be good. By reason of intention, since they did not intend to fulfill the divine will, but to satiate their own envy. – 1 and 2. So relative to the objection that the death of Christ pleased God, it has to be maintained that the active killing was permitted, but that the suffering of the passion of death was pleasing, as in the case of the passions of the Saints. For they did the killing from an evil will, and Christ suffered from a good will.[149] – 3. With respect to the objection that Christ's coming would have been in vain, it has to be said that the answer is no, since God had another possible way and has accomplished many good things through

---

[148] See Rom 8:32: "Who has not spared even his own Son, but has delivered him for us all."

[149] See Book III, d. 20 dubia 3 and 4 in Bonaventure's *Sentence Commentary*.

evil ministers, for example, he tests the Saints through the devil. And while the devil only tempts to demerit, God ordains an action to good.

76. Question 2 asks whether Caiphas sinned in giving this counsel. – It seems that he did not. – 1. The text of John 11:51 itself says that "he said this not of himself." And through this it is suggested that he spoke from the Holy Spirit. Therefore, if what he said comes from the Holy Spirit, it is not a sin, etc. – 2. Likewise, John 11:51 reads "being high priest, he prophesied." Wherefore, if the act of prophesying is good, he did not provide evil counsel, but good. So he did not sin. – But contrary. By his words he himself intended to give the counsel that Christ be killed. So in giving this counsel, he was engaged in homicide, etc.

Praepositivus answers that Caiphas sinned out of an evil will, but did not sin in announcing his counsel,[150] since the Holy Spirit used him as an instrument, just as he used Balaam's ass.[151] Thus, Caiphas's words were not the fruit of an evil will, since his will was evil, but his words were good. – Nonetheless, it has to be said that Caiphas not only spoke forth as the ass did, but as a perverse person, intending by his speech to persuade people to evil.

Thus, it has to be maintained that the beginning of this statement was twofold. As it was formed interiorly, namely, by divine inspiration, it was simply good. As it came

---

[150] On p. 409 n. 13 QuarEd refer to the inedited *Summa* of Praepositivus: "... our Masters answer that his (Caiphas's) action was evil and not from God, but that the words that occurred to him, from which the Evangelist could draw the meaning he did, were from the Holy Spirit."

[151] See Num 22:28-24:25. Hugh of St. Cher, p. 358s also refers to Balaam.

from Caiphas's intention, this statement was simply evil. And according to this twofold beginning the intellect responds in a twofold manner to this statement. The first is carnal, and this was evil because it was to avoid offending the Romans. The second is spiritual and good and was for the sake of the salvation of the human race.[152] And thus it has to be conceded that he sinned, for some prophets can sin when they prophesy and perform miracles when they pervert their intentions.[153]

---

[152] See Augustine, Tractate 49 n. 27 in FC 88, p. 258: "Here we are taught that the spirit of prophecy foretells the future even through evil men...."

[153] In Book XXVIII of his *Commentary on John* Origen has a long discussion of Caiphas's prophecy. See FC 89, p. 331 n. 190 for a quasi-conclusion: "... so the Pharisees and the chief priests, because they did not understand correctly the prophecy about our Savior that Caiphas spoke – a prophecy that is true in that it is better for us that one man die for the people and the whole nation not perish – but thought the meaning and intention of his counsel was something else, took counsel together from that day to kill Jesus."

Chapter Twelve

John 12:1-8
Corroboration of the conspiracy of the Jews

1. *So Jesus, six days before the Passover*, etc. After the conspiracy of the Jews has been described, here the second point is depicted, that is, its *corroboration*. The conspiracy itself gained momentum from the indignation of the traitor. Now the indignation of the traitor had its source in avarice, but erupted on the occasion of the anointing of ointment during a banquet. So the description develops in the following way. First is the depiction of *the Lord's banquet*. Second is *the pouring of the ointment*. Third is *Judas's indignation*. Fourth is the *excusing of Mary*.

Verse 1. A banquet was held for Christ the Lord at the place where he had raised Lazarus six days before the festival. So the text states: *So Jesus, six days before the Passover*, that is, on the sixth day before Passover, *came to Bethany where Lazarus whom Jesus had raised to life, had died*. There they held a banquet in the presence of the resuscitated Lazarus. Thus the text continues:

2. (Verse 2). *And they made him a supper there*, for Revelation 3:20 says: "If anyone opens the door for me, I will come in to him and will sup with him and he with me."[1]

---

[1] Hugh of St. Cher, p. 358v,o also cites Rev 3:20.

And although it took place in the presence of Lazarus, Lazarus did not serve the meal, but ate it, so that the truth of the resurrection might be proven. Mark 5:43 says about the girl who had been raised up: "He commanded that she be given something to eat." For this reason the text states: *And Martha served, while Lazarus was one of those reclining at table with him.*[2] Martha was always serving and was solicitous as the prudent woman, for Luke 10:40 reads; "Lord, is it no concern of yours that my sister has left me to serve alone?" So we are right to understand the active life through her, which is anxiously burdened with cares.

3. (Verse 3). *So Mary took a pound.* Here is the second point, that is, the pouring of the ointment, which was made by Mary, who did not recline and was not serving, but she fed the Lord with a special nourishment. For she was burning with an intense love for him, a love that was expressed in the pouring of the ointment. For this reason the text continues: *So Mary took a pound of ointment.* This was an immense quantity of ointment, since her love was immense. It was not any type of ointment whatsoever, but *of nard*, that is, from nard. *Nard* is an aromatic plant, as Isidore says, which has a strong fragrance.[3] Thus it is said in The Song of Songs 1:11: "While the king was in his chamber, my nard gave forth its fragrance." The spikes of nard produced a precious ointment.[4] Thus it is said in Mark 14:3: "Spikenard." *Genuine.* The Glossa ob-

---

[2] On p. 410 n. 5 QuarEd accurately indicate that the Vulgate reads *cum eo* ("with him") while Bonaventure has *cum ipso* ("with him").

[3] See Book XVII c. 9 n. 3-5 of *Isidori Hispalensis Episcopi Etymologiarvm sive originvm* Libri XX. Volume II. Edited by W. M. Lindsay. Oxford: Clarendon Press, 1911.

[4] Nard is also called spikenard.

serves: "That is, the real product" without adulteration.[5] *Precious*, because it was of great price and value. *And anointed the feet of Jesus.*[6] *And the house was filled with the fragrance of the ointment*. The literal sense is that the Jews used ointments that were very aromatic. Therefore, the Lord commanded that the most previous ointment be offered to him in Exodus 30:25-31[7] and forbade others from using it.[8] Thus it was called the holy of holies and was "a most sweet fragrance unto the Lord."[9]

4. (Verse 4). *Then one of his disciples, Judas*. The third point surfaces here, that is, Judas' indignation against the woman who had poured the ointment. For this reason the text states: *Then one of his disciples, Judas Iscariot, the one was about to betray him, said*, that is, out of avarice. And because of avarice he spoke:

5. (Verse 5). *Why was this ointment not sold for three hundred denarii and given to the poor*? Matthew 26:8-9 says: "To what purpose is this waste? For this might have been sold for much and given to the poor." And since this might seem to have been spoken out of compassion, the Evan-

---

[5] See the Glossa Ordinaria in PL 114:401B: "Precious ointment came from nard, especially from spikenard. Now this was said to be genuine because of its place of origin, and was considered the real product, not adulterated with a mixture of something base and inferior."

[6] On p. 411 n. 2 QuarEd rightly notice that the Vulgate reads: *et extersit pedes eius capillis suis* ("and with her hair wiped his feet dry").

[7] See Ex 30:25-26: "And you shall make the holy oil of unction, an ointment compounded after the art of the perfumer, and with it you shall anoint the tabernacle of the testimony and the ark of the testament," etc.

[8] See Ex 30:32: "Human flesh shall not be anointed therewith, and you shall make none other of the same composition, since it is sanctified and shall be holy unto you."

[9] This expression is used of sacrifices, e.g., in Lev 1:13 and 2:2.

gelist shows that he said this out of cupidity. Therefore, he says:

6. (Verse 6). *Now he said this, not because he cared for the poor*, because he did not care for the poor. On the contrary Sirach 4:1 reads: "Son, do not defraud the poor of alms, and do not turn your eyes away from the poor." *But because he was a thief, and holding the purse*, as the bursar, *used to carry what was put in it*, that is, used to carry it off and steal it.[10] And so he was glad when much was given. For it was on account of his avarice that he sold the Lord. Thus it is said in Matthew 26:14-15: "He went to the high priests and said: What are you willing to give me for delivering him to you?" Wherefore, Chrysostom observes: "Avarice subjects the heart to servitude. It turned Judas into a traitor and Gehazi into a leper and handed Ananias over to death."[11]

7. (Verse 7). *So Jesus said to them.*[12] This verse introduces the fourth point, that is, the excusing of Mary, since Judas was insulting her as if she had done something wrong. And the Lord wanted to show that she had done better than if she had given to the poor. So the text states: *Let*[13] *her be*, that is, do not bother her. He does not find fault with them, but excuses Mary. *That she may keep it for the day of my burial*, which indeed is better than to give to the poor.

---

[10] See Augustine, Tractate 50 n. 9 in FC 88, p. 266: "He carried or carried off? He carried by his office, but he carried off by theft."

[11] Bonaventure adapts Homily 65 n. 3. See PG 59:363. On Gehazi see 2 Kings 5:27. On Ananias see Acts 5:5.

[12] The Vulgate does not read *eis* ("to them").

[13] The Vulgate reads *Sine* ("Let") whereas Bonaventure has *Sinite* ("Let").

8. (Verse 8). *For you will always have the poor with you.*[14] Deuteronomy 15:11 reads: "There will be no lack of poor in the land of your habitation."[15] *But you will not always have me*, according to my bodily presence. John 16:10 states: "I go to the Father, and you will see me no more" And therefore, it is most expedient that human kindness be shown me. So you should not bother her. Matthew 26:10 says: "Why are you bothering this woman, since she has done me a good turn?"[16]

9. According to the spiritual sense two matters should be noticed here, namely about the banquet and the ointment. – It should be noted that we read that on three different occasions a banquet was given for the Lord. First, by Matthew, the converted publican in Matthew 9:10: "While he was reclining at table, behold, many publicans and sinners were reclining at table with him." This is the banquet of the penitents. – The second was given by Simon, the Pharisee. Luke 7:36 reads: "A certain Pharisee invited Jesus to eat with him." This is the banquet of the proficient. – Third is the one thrown for Jesus by Mary, Martha, and Lazarus in Bethany, the one described here. Bethany is the house of obedience,[17] and that is a religious institute in which there are people in the state of perfection, according to what Matthew 19:21 has: "If you want to be perfect, go and sell everything that you have

---

[14] On p. 411 n. 9 QuarEd accurately mention that the Vulgate reads *habetis* ("you have") whereas Bonaventure has *habebitis* ("will have") in this half verse and the next one.

[15] Hugh of St. Cher, p. 359v,g also cites Deut 15:11.

[16] Bonaventure has adapted Matt 26:10: "Why are you bothering the woman? She has done me a good turn."

[17] See Book VI n. 206 of *Origen, Commentary on the Gospel according to John Books 1-10*. Translated by Ronald E. Heine. FC 80; Washington: CUA Press, 1989, p. 225: "Bethania, however, means 'house of obedience.'"

and give it to the poor." And this is the banquet of the perfect.

10. In a similar way consider the spiritual sense of the ointment. It, too, is threefold, for Mary is said to have anointed the Lord thrice. There is the ointment of contrition that is signified in Luke 7:38: "She began to bathe his feet with her tears ... and anointed with ointment."[18] – Of devoted love that is signified here and in Matthew 26:6-7: "When Jesus was ... in the house of Simon the leper, a woman came up to him with an alabaster jar of precious ointment and poured it on his head as he reclined at table." – Of compassion, and this is found in Mark 16:1: "Mary Magdalene and Mary the mother of James and Salome bought spices that they might go and anoint Jesus."[19] – During the first anointing his feet were anointed. In the second, his head. In the third, the entire body of the Lord.[20]

---

[18] The woman of Luke 7:36-50 is, however, unnamed.

[19] The Vulgate reads *eum* ("him") whilst Bonaventure has *Iesum* ("Jesus").

[20] See Bernard of Clairvaux, Sermo LXXXVII de diversis n. 6 in SBOp 6.353-353: "So let us say that there are three kinds of ointments. The first arises from recollection of sins since we feel compunction for them and ask forgiveness.... Now it is poured on the Lord's feet.... The second ointment arises from recollection of God's benefits. And this is rightly poured on the head.... The third ointment is composed of precious spices, like those brought by the holy women about whom it is written that *they bought spices, that they might go and anoint Jesus.* But this ointment was not poured out or wasted, since the Lord did not want it poured over his dead body, but kept for his living body, that is, holy Church. So the first ointment is called the ointment of compunction and is consumed by the fire of contrition. The second is of devotion and is consumed by the fire of love. The third is called the ointment of compassion which is not consumed, but kept intact."

QUESTIONS

11. Question 1 deals with John 12:1: "He came, six days before Passover, to Bethany" where he was anointed by Mary. – 1. Since it is said in Matthew 26:2: "You know that after two days Passover will be here" and later in 26:6 that he was anointed by Mary "in the house of Simon." So it seems that it was two days before whereas it is said here that it was six days before. – 2. Likewise there is an objection because this passage says that "she anointed his feet," whereas it is said in Matthew 26:7 that "she poured over his head." If she poured over his head, how did she anoint his feet? – 3. Furthermore, there is another inconsistency, since Matthew 26:8 says: "when the disciples saw this, they were indignant," while in this passage it is said that "one was indignant," namely, the betrayer.

These three inconsistencies are solved by the three rules of Augustine in his *Harmony of the Gospels*:[21] – First, it should be noted that sometimes one Evangelist mentions something according to an historical timeline while another Evangelist mentions something by recapitulation. And this solves the first problematic, since Matthew is dealing with recapitulation as Augustine shows.[22] – The second rule is this: What one omits, another mentions. And both things took place, but both things were not mentioned by both Evangelists. In this way the second question is answered. After anointing the feet, she then poured all the ointment over the head.[23] – The third rule is that it is customary for the Evangelists to use the plu-

---

[21] See Book II, c. 78-79 n. 153-156 of *De consensv evangelistarvm*, pp. 257-263.

[22] See Book II, c. 78 n. 153 of *De consensv evangelistarvm*, p. 257.

[23] See Book II, c. 79 n. 155 of *De consensv evangelistarvm*, p. 263.

ral for the singular through synecdoche. And so some said that the disciples were indignant while John gives the proper name of the person involved.[24]

12. Question 2 raises issues about what the Evangelist says about Judas in John 12:6: "He said this, not that he cared for the poor." – But on the contrary, he was the dispenser of the money in the purse. Therefore, he cared about them. – 2. Moreover, the text says: "He was a thief and held the purse." How is it that the Lord wanted to commit the purse to the care of a thief? – It seems that he would be placing him in an occasion of sin. – 3. Furthermore, Why didn't the Lord correct him since he knew that he was in sin? – 4. Finally, since the Lord lived in extreme poverty and commanded his disciples not to accept money,[25] why is it that he had a purse?

1. I say relative to the first point that "to care for" has two meanings: with respect to affection and with respect of office. In the first meaning he didn't care for them whereas he did according to the second meaning. – 2. My response to the second problem is that there was a twofold reason, namely, the dispensation of divine judgment and our instruction. The dispensation of divine judgment consists in this that the Lord satisfied Judas's evil desire, as he enriches avaricious people in the present, so that even Judas would not have the excuse that he betrayed the Lord because he was hard up for money.[26] Our instruction

---

[24] See Book II, c. 79 n. 156 of *De consensv evangelistarvm*, p. 263.

[25] See, for example, Luke 9:3: "And he said to them: Take nothing for your journey, neither staff nor wallet nor bread nor money. Do not have two tunics."

[26] Bonaventure's question and answer stem from Chrysostom. See Homily 65 n. 2 in FC 41, pp. 210-211: "Now, someone may ask: 'Why in the world did He entrust the purse for the poor to one who was a thief, and why did He give the office of dispensing it to one who was greedy for money? In answer I should reply as follows: God knows the inef-

follows, since the Lord shows that he puts little stock in the riches of the churches, but great stock in the treasure of souls.[27] – 3. The answer has to be that he did not correct him, because he knew that he would not get better, but would become worse. He did not strip him of his office, lest he disclose his sin and incite him to a greater offense.[28] – 4. About this objection one has to follow the opinion of Jerome: The Lord had a moneybag, not for his personal use, but rather for the use of the poor.[29] Thus when he paid the didrachma, he sent Peter to the sea according to Matthew 17:23-26 where he found the money in the mouth of a fish, for he did not wish to turn what had been given to the poor to his personal use. – Another reason is so that he might make it known, against heretics, that it was lawful for his Church to possess riches.

13. Question 3 asks about John 12:7: "Let her be that she may keep it for the day of my burial." For if she had

---

fable explanation; but if we must say something by way of conjecture, it is that He did this in order to deprive Judas of all excuse for the betrayal. For he could not say that he did it for love of money (and I say this for he had enough from the purse to satisfy his desire)."

[27] See Theophylactus, *Commentarius in Joannis Evangelium* in PG 124:118CD: "So some say that the dispensing of money entrusted to Judas was a minor office compared to others. For to dispense money is inferior to dispensing doctrine, as the apostles even say in Acts: 'It is not right for us to give up preaching to serve at table.'"

[28] See Augustine, Tractate 50 n. 11 in FC 88, p. 267: "Let us see what the Lord answers to these words. See, brothers! He does not say to him, You say these things because of your thefts. He knew the thief, but he did not reveal him; rather, he endured him and pointed out to us an example of patience in enduring evil men in the Church."

[29] See his commentary on Matt 17:26 in PL 26:132B: "Such a straightforward interpretation edifies the hearer, for the Lord was in such a state of poverty that when the time came to pay the tribute for himself and the apostle, he didn't have it. Now if someone would object and ask how come Judas carried money in his purse, we will respond that he thought it nefarious to convert money for the poor to his own use and thought to give us the same example."

poured the ointment over his head, how could she keep it for the day of burial? – There is a threefold answer. One interpretation maintains that "to keep it" means that she was to keep part of it.[30] But this exposition is not valid, since Mary did not anoint the body of the Lord on the day of burial. – Another interpretation is that of Victor: "Let her keep it" means her dedication towards it, namely, her dedication to anoint, because she wanted to anoint the body of the Lord, although she would not anoint it.[31] – Yet another interpretation places the emphasis on the word "to keep." "To keep" is used in contrast with "to waste." Ointment that is poured into the ground is wasted, but ointment that is used to embalm the bodies of the dead is not said to be wasted, but to keep. In this interpretation the Lord wanted to say against Judas that this ointment has not been wasted, but kept to prepare for the day of burial. For it is said in Mark 14:8: "She has anointed my body in preparation for burial." And so this passage is to be understood.

JOHN 12:9-11
DEEPENING OF THE CONSPIRACY

14. *So a great crowd learned.* The conspiracy and its corroboration have been determined. Now in a third point *the deepening of the conspiracy* is treated. For first they had planned to kill Jesus, but now not only Jesus, but also resuscitated Lazarus. And the reason was that many had come to believe in Jesus because of him. So two things

---

[30] See Rupert of Deutz in CCCM ix, p. 573.

[31] This is probably Bishop Victor of Capua (d. 554). See also the Glossa Interlinearis: "So that, even if not in reality, nevertheless she would fulfill by her dedication my anointing after my death."

are noted here, that is, *the multitude of believers* and *the deepening of the perversity of the Jews*.

Verse 9. *The multitude of believers* came about on the occasion of the resuscitation of Lazarus. For this reason the text states: *So the great crowd of the Jews learned that he was*[32] *there*, namely, in Bethany, *and came, not only because of Jesus, but that they might see Lazarus, whom he had raised from the dead.* They were still weak, because their eyes not only delighted in seeing the author of the works, but also the works themselves. Wherefore, they were from that group, about whom it is said in John 2:23 above: "Many believed in him, seeing the signs that he was working."[33] So they wanted to see miracles as John 6:2 above reads: "A great crowd followed Jesus, because they saw the signs."[34]

15. (Verse 10). *But the chief priests planned.* The second point surfaces here, that is, the deepening of the conspiracy and perversity against the worker of the sign, because they were not only furious against the Lord, but also against others because of him. So the text states: *But the chief priests planned to put Lazarus to death also*, and not only Jesus. Isaiah 1:15 reads: "Your hands are full of blood." And it adds the reason:

16. (Verse 11). *For on his account many of the Jews began to leave them and to believe in Jesus.* And therefore, they wanted to put him to death. Augustine comments: "O stupid plan! ... The Lord ... who could raise the dead, could

---

[32] On p. 413 n. 12 QuarEd rightly notice that the Vulgate reads *est* ("was") while Bonaventure has *esset* ("was").

[33] John 2:23 reads: "Many believed in his name, seeing his signs that he was working."

[34] John 6:2 says: "A great crowd followed him, because they saw the signs that he worked on those who were sick."

he not raise one who had been killed? When you were bringing death to Lazarus, were you taking power away from the Lord? If a dead man seems one thing to you and a murdered man something else, look: the Lord did both. He raised up both Lazarus who had been dead and himself after he had been killed."[35] They wanted to shut down the road of salvation. Matthew 23:13 says: "You yourselves do not go in, and you have prohibited others from entering."[36]

John 12:12-19
Obstinacy in the conspiracy

17. *Now the next day*, etc. The deepening of the conspiracy has been determined, and now in a fourth and final point the text addresses *the consummation of the evil* through obstinacy. And this obstinacy found a base in the honor shown the Lord. On account of this honor they leapt to an astonishing envy. And things proceeded as follows. First *the honoring of Christ* is determined. Second *the approval of this honoring by means of Scripture*. Third *the reason behind this honoring*. Fourth *the most malevolent obstinacy of the Pharisees*.

Verse 12. Now the honor is depicted in a threefold manner. First with regard to its manner of occurrence, since it occurred with joy. For this reason the text reads: *Now*

---

[35] See Tractate 50 n. 14 in CCSL xxxvi, p. 439 and FC 88, p. 270.

[36] Bonaventure's citation seems to be a mixture of Matt 23:13 ("Because you shut the kingdom of the heavens against people. For you yourselves do not go in, nor do you allow those going in to enter") and Luke 11:52 ("You have not entered yourselves and those who were entering you have prohibited").

the next day the great crowd,[37] *when they heard that Jesus was coming to Jerusalem*, met him with joy. A sign of which is:

18. (Verse 13). *They took branches of palms and went forth to meet him*. They derived this custom from the Law, for it is said in Nehemiah 8:15: "Go forth to the mountain and fetch olive branches and branches of the most beautiful wood … and palm branches." – It is also described according to the manner of praising. For this reason the text says: *And they were crying out: Hosanna*. As the Glossa says: "This cry is that of one pleading, indicating feeling more than anything, as is the case with interjections,"[38] and has the meaning only of "Save, I plead." – *Blessed is he who comes in the name of the Lord, the king of Israel*. By means of this they are confessing that he possesses royal dignity, not by humans, but from God. So they say: *King of Israel in the name of the Lord*, according to what Luke 1:32 reads: "He will be great and will be called the Son of the Most High, and the Lord God will give him the throne of David his father, and he will be king over the house of Jacob forever." – It is also described with respect to the manner of proceeding, because he did not proceed on foot, but was seated on an ass. For this reason the text continues:

19. (Verse 14). *And Jesus found a young ass and sat upon it*. Although he was a true King and might permit regal

---

[37] On p. 414 n. 2 QuarEd accurately indicate that the Vulgate reads *quae venerat ad diem festum* ("that had come to the feast").

[38] On p. 414 n.4 QuarEd state that this is from the Glossa Ordinaria which is dependent upon Augustine. See Augustine's Tractate 51 n. 2 in FC 88, p. 272: "'Hosanna', however, is the word of one supplicating, as some say who know the Hebrew language, more declaring a feeling than signifying anything. Just as in the Latin language there are words which we call interjections…."

honor to be bestowed upon him, nonetheless, he comes not with an array of horses, but seated on an ass. Through this is signified, as Augustine says that "he was a king ..., not to exact taxes, not to equip an army with swords ... but the king of Israel, who rules minds, who counsels ..., who leads those who believe, hope, and love into the kingdom of heaven."[39]

20. *As it is written*. These words introduce the second point, namely, the approbation of Scripture for what he did, and he did this by showing that it had been foretold in Scripture, because this bolsters true faith. Therefore, the text says that he sat on an ass in regal honor. Lest you think that this was a casual gesture, the text states: *As it is written* in Zechariah 9:9:

21. (Verse 15). *Fear not, daughter of Zion*, that is, the Church. The text is abbreviated, and more should be understood, that is, *rejoice*.[40] Zechariah 9:9 states: "Rejoice greatly, O daughter of Zion. Shout for joy, daughter of Jerusalem." And the reason for this rejoicing is given: "Behold, your king is coming to you."[41] Behold, royal dignity. "Seated on the colt of an ass." Behold, meekness and humility.[42] And in such an arrival there should be praise, because it is said in Proverbs 16:15: "In the cheerfulness of

---

[39] See Tractate 51 n. 4 in CCSL xxxvi, p. 441.

[40] A more basic problem is that Zech 9:9 does not read *Noli timere* ("Fear not"). See John 12 n. 27 below.

[41] The Vulgate reads *veniet* ("will come") while Bonaventure has *venit* ("is coming").

[42] See Chrysostom, Homily 66 n. 1 in FC 41, p. 218: "Because all their kings were, for the most part, unjust and covetous and had betrayed them to their enemies, and had perverted the people and made them subject to their enemies, the Prophet said: 'Take courage. This man is not of that kind, but meek and humble,' and he proved this by the ass. For He did not enter with an army in His train, but only with an ass."

the king's countenance is life, and his clemency is like the late rain." And although this honor had been predicted, it, nevertheless, was not recognized by Christ's disciples, so that you might know that this was not done through human device, but through divine dispensation. Therefore, the text adds:

22. (Verse 16). *These things his disciples did not at first understand*, that is, when they conferred this honor. *But when Jesus was glorified*, after his resurrection and ascension, *then they remembered*, that is, adverted to it, *that these things were written about him and that they had done these things to him.* They understood after his glorification, not before, since then for the first time, as it is said in Luke 24:45: "He opened their minds that they might understand the Scriptures."

23. (Verse 17). *So the crowd bore witness to him*, etc. This verse treats the third point, that is, the reason behind the honor shown. And this was Lazarus's wondrous resuscitation which provided bedrock for the crowds. So the text continues: *So the crowd, which had been with him, when he called Lazarus from the tomb*, saying: "Lazarus, come forth," *and raised him from the dead, bore witness to him.*[43] This crowd was bearing witness to his omnipotence, that is, a crowd of simple people, but at the same time a group of wise people. "Wise," because Acts 10:43 states: "To him all the prophets bear witness." "Simple," since Psalm 8:3 reads: "Out of the mouth of infants and those at the breast you have perfected praise." Through this sign and witness such honor was shown to him. Therefore, the text continues:

---

[43] On p. 414 n. 11 QuarEd correctly mention that the Vulgate does not read *illi* ("to him").

24. (Verse 18). *The reason why*[44] *the crowd went to meet him was that they heard that he*[45] *had worked this sign.* The simple crowd, seeing the signs, was moved to faith and dedication. For this reason it is said in Matthew 9:8: "When the crowds saw it, they were struck with fear and glorified God, who had given such power to humans." But the scribes were saying that he was blaspheming.[46]

25. (Verse 19). *So the Pharisees said among themselves.* The fourth point occurs here, that is, the obstinacy of the Pharisees on account of envy. So they were saying among themselves: *See that we are accomplishing nothing,*[47] that is, as long as he lives. 2 Timothy 3:8-9 says: "They resist the truth, people corrupt in mind, reprobate with regard to the faith, but they will make no further progress." The text continues: *Behold, the entire world has gone after him.* In this it is noted that they were moved by an arrow of envy. Therefore, it is said in Matthew 21:15 that when the scribes and the Pharisees saw these things, "they were indignant," since they grieved out of envy, hated him out of arrogance, were furious out of fury itself. And so they were obstinate in evil. Wisdom 2:24 reads: "By the evil of the devil death entered into the world." Sirach 14:10 says: "And evil eye … will be sad at its own table."

---

[44] On p. 415 n. 2 QuarEd rightly note that the Vulgate reads *Propterea et* ("And the reason why") whilst Bonaventure has *Propterea* ("The reason why").

[45] On p. 415 n. 2 QuarEd accurately indicate that the Vulgate reads *eum* ("he") whereas Bonaventure has *ipsum* ("he").

[46] See Matt 9:3: "And behold, some of the scribes said within themselves: This man blasphemes."

[47] On p. 415 n. 3 QuarEd correctly mention that the Vulgate reads *videtis* ("you see") while Bonaventure has *videte* ("see").

QUESTIONS

26. Question 1 deals with this issue: It seems that in performing his works the Lord acted in a contrary manner. – 1. Since it is said in John 11:54 above that the Lord "hid himself" from the face of the Jews who were persecuting him.[48] But here he reveals himself in such an open way. – 2. Likewise, in John 6:15 above the Lord "fled to the mountain," when they wanted to make him king. But here he accepts the honor offered him as to a king and approves of it.

I respond that it has to be maintained that the Lord, as Augustine observes, did not do contrary things, but did diverse things according to the appropriateness of the circumstances, just as first he set forth the Old Testament and later the New Testament.[49] – 1. For this reason it should be said that then the time of the passion had not yet arrived, but now was nigh. So he previously hid himself since he was waiting for the time of the passion. Now, since the time of the passion is nigh and there is opportunity, he manifests himself.[50] – 2. I answer in a similar way to number two: Since he wanted to be unknown before the passion, when it was near and after the passion he was indeed glorified. So he did not accept this royal honor

---

[48] See John 11:54: "So Jesus no longer went about openly among the Jews...." John 8:59 reads: "So they took up stones to cast at him, but Jesus hid himself and went out from the temple."

[49] This seems a global reference to Letter 138 n. 2-8. See, e.g., FC 20, p. 41: "However, it is possible to say in a few words what will probably satisfy a man of keen understanding, that it was fitting for Christ before His coming to be foretold by certain symbolic ceremonies, but after His coming He was to be announced by others, just as, when we speak, the difference of time obliges us to change our expressions, since 'foretell' is not the same as 'announce,' and 'before His coming' is different from 'after His coming.'"

[50] See John 8 n. 87 and John 11 n. 72 above.

beforehand.[51] – Another reason is that these people did not make him king, but recognized him as the one sent from God. But the others wanted to make him king. – A third reason is that since the Lord was to suffer almost immediately after these things, he wanted to be honored, so that the subsequent ignominy of the passion might be heightened by this honor.

27. Question 2 again focuses on contrary matters. – 1. For it is said in Matthew 21:1-11 that first he sent to a village for the ass, and that then the crowd came to meet him. – 2. Furthermore, there it is said: "he sat upon the ass and the colt,"[52] while here, however, it is said that he sat upon "a young ass."[53] – 3. Moreover, this is not written in Zechariah 9:9: "Fear not, daughter of Zion," but "rejoice and shout for joy, daughter," etc.

I answer that it should be said about this last point that the Evangelists were speaking through the Holy Spirit, who set forth all of Scripture and is its author. Wherefore, they did not lay emphasis on the similarity of words, but on the sincerity of understandings. And the very same thing that Zechariah said through the word "rejoice," that the Evangelist says through the word "fear not."[54] – 1 and 2. With regard to the objections about the contrary and preposterous texts, it should be said that the Lord sat upon the ass and also upon its colt. And some say that he did this in the following manner. First he sat upon the

---

[51] See the Glossa Ordinaria on Matt 21:10 in PL 114:152D-153A: "He had frequently entered the city of Jerusalem, but not with this type of praise: He is not called a king, a title he always fled from, but now he accepts it when he goes up to Jerusalem to suffer."

[52] See Matt 21:7: "And they brought the ass and the colt, laid their cloaks on them, and made him sit thereon."

[53] See John 12:14.

[54] See Book II, c. 66 n. 128 of Augustine's *Harmony of the Gospels*.

colt, and since it balked, he afterwards sat on the ass.[55] – But this interpretation is not convincing, since I do not believe that a colt would ever balk when the Lord was sitting upon it. Rather it is to be understood that the Lord, on account of a figure, first said upon the ass, that is, upon the old synagogue, and afterwards upon the colt, that is, the undomesticated gentile populace.[56] – And he first sat upon the ass, which the crowds encountered. So Matthew narrates this first. But later, after the crowds had met him, then he sat upon the young ass. And so John says after the arrival of the crowds: "Jesus found a young ass and sat upon it."[57] John did not care to give all the details which another had mentioned.

---

[55] See Peter Comestor, *Historia scholastica, In evangelia*, c. 117 in PL 198:1599C: "Matthew says that he said upon an ass and a colt. Now even though the journey was short, it could, nonetheless, have happened that he first sat on the colt, and perhaps because it had not yet been broken in and was contrary, he got off it and sat on the ass. Now if he had sat on the colt only, Matthew, nevertheless, put him on both, because both could take place in the mystery." For Peter Comestor, the mystery is that the ass represents the Jews while the colt the Gentiles. See PL 198:1599A.

[56] See Book III of Jerome, *Commentariorum in Evangelium Matthaei Libri Quatuor*, on Matt 21:4-5 in PL 26:153A: "So since the narrative presents either an impossible or a disgraceful situation, its meaning runs on a higher level. Now this ass, which was broken in and domesticated and bore the yoke of the law, may be understood as the synagogue. The colt of the ass, capricious and unbroken, may be understood as the Gentile people...." See also Chrysostom, Homily 66 n. 1 in FC 41, p. 218: "... while in the fact that He was seated upon an ass He was prefiguring the circumstance that in the future He would hold the unclean race of the gentiles under His sway." Hugh of St. Cher, p. 360v, e gives as one interpretation: "The Gentile people are designated by the colt and the Jewish people by the ass."

[57] John 12:14.

John 12:20-50
Second preliminary to the passion:
Prediction of the passion

28. *Now there were certain Gentiles.* Now that the first preliminary to the passion has been determined, that is, the conspiracy of the Pharisees, the Evangelist moves to the second preliminary, namely, *the illumination of the Gentiles*, which is a very beneficial result of Christ's passion. And since at Christ's passion the illumination of the Gentiles and the blinding of the Jews occurred, this section has four parts. In the first part *the prefiguration of the call of the Gentiles* is determined or shown. In the second *the fruitfulness of the passion* is predicted where verse 24 says: "Amen, amen, I say to you," etc. Third is *the explanation of the predicted fruitfulness* where verse 29 reads: "Then the crowd that was standing there and heard the voice." In the fourth *the future blinding of the Jews* is described where verse 36b states: "Jesus spoke these things," etc.

John 12:20-23
Prefiguration of the call of the Gentiles

Thus in the first place *the future call of the Gentiles* is suggested in this that they are seeking for the Lord, and the Lord shows himself benevolent towards them. It is depicted in this order. First is *the eagerness of the Gentiles*. Second is *the request of the disciples*. Third is *the condescension of the Teacher*.

29. (Verse 20). So the text hints at the eagerness of the Gentiles in this that they want to and request to see Jesus. For this reason the text states: *Now there were certain Gentiles among those who had gone up to worship*

on the feast. They were worshipping in the temple, since they, too, had heard. 1 Kings 8:41-43 presents Solomon's prayer: "The stranger, who does not belong to your people … if[58] he shall come and pray in this place, you will hear from heaven," etc.

30. (Verse 21). *So these approached Philip, who was from Bethsaida of Galilee.*[59] John 1:44 above says: "Now Philip was from Bethsaida, the town of Andrew and Peter." They came as to someone who was better acquainted and expressed their wish. Thus the text continues: *And asked him, saying: Sir, we wish to see Jesus.* Do not wonder that they desired to see, because, according to what Psalm 44:3 has: "He was handsome beyond the sons of men and women." "He was totally desirable."[60] Augustine observes: "Look. The Jews wanted to kill him while the Gentiles wanted to see him."[61] For this reason Matthew 21:43 reads: "The kingdom[62] will be taken from you and will be given to a people yielding its fruits."

31. (Verse 22). *Philip came.* Point two surfaces here, that is, the intercession of the disciples with regard to the petition of the Gentiles. And so that Philip might more easily make his petition, he takes along a companion. Therefore, the text continues: *Philip came and said to Andrew,*

---

[58] The Vulgate reads *cum* ("when") whilst Bonaventure has *si* ("if").

[59] See the Glossa Ordinaria on the two disciples Jesus sends in Matt 21:1. PL 114:152A reads: "Some say that these two were Peter and Philip, who were the first to lead the Gentiles to Christ. Relative to Philip, they interpret Samaria as the ass. With regard to Peter, they interpret Cornelius as the colt of Samaria."

[60] See Cant 5:16: "His throat is most sweet. He is totally desirable. Such is my beloved. And he is my friend, O daughters of Jerusalem."

[61] See Tractate 51 n. 8 in CCSL xxxvi, p. 442: "Look. The Jews want to kill him while the Gentiles want to see him."

[62] The Vulgate reads *regnum Dei* ("kingdom of God").

as to his senior. And then Andrew, as the senior, precedes Philip in making the request. Thus the text states: *Again Andrew and Philip spoke to Jesus*. Through this it is suggested that prelates are the mediators between simple folk and the Lord. They offer the desires of the poor to the Lord. Moses said in Deuteronomy 5:5: "I was the mediator and stood between God[63] and you." Hebrews 5:1 reads: "Every high priest taken from among men and women is appointed on behalf of men and women in the things pertaining to God."

32. (Verse 23). *But Jesus answered them*. This verse introduces the third point, namely, the condescension of the Lord, by which he satisfies the desire of the Gentiles, *saying* that now the time had come for him to manifest himself to the Gentiles. So the text says: *The hour has come for the Son of Man to be glorified*, that is, that he might be manifested to the Gentiles, and through this his brightness and glory might be acknowledged. This is the hour of the passion and of our redemption, which, for a long time, had been expected and longed for. In this the Gentiles are called. For this reason the Apostle says in Romans 13:11: "It is now the hour for us to rise from sleep." This is the hour, about which it was said in John 7:30 above: "No one laid hands on him, since his hour had not yet come."

QUESTIONS

33. Question 1 asks: When the Gentiles worship their own idols and have their own gods, why is it that they went up to worship in Jerusalem? – And it should be said that when the Gentiles converted to the rituals of the Jews,

---

[63] The Vulgate reads *Dominum* ("the Lord") while Bonaventure has *Deum* ("God").

they were called proselytes. And about them Chrysostom comments: "Since they were at the point of becoming proselytes, they came, as people beginning to believe, to see the feast and to worship in the temple."[64]

34. Question 2 asks further: Then why didn't Philip repel them? – And it seems that he should have, since he himself had heard what the Lord said in Matthew 10:5: "Do not go in the direction of the Gentiles." And Matthew 15:24: "I was not sent except to the lost sheep of the house of Israel." Therefore, it seems that he acted contrary to the Lord's command when he accepted their petition. – I answer that it has to be maintained that Philip himself had seen that the Lord used to cure not only Jews, but also Gentiles. And it seemed that he wished the salvation of all people. On the other hand, Philip considered the Lord's command and therefore acted cautiously, since neither did he entirely reject it nor completely accept it. And so he consulted Andrew. They, presuming on the Lord's mercy, mentioned the request to Jesus, because he could, as he wanted to and as Lord, manifest himself to everyone.[65]

35. Question 3 pursues the same line of questioning: Why does he manifest himself to the Gentiles now rather than

---

[64] See Homily 66 n. 2 in PG 59:367: "Since they were at the point of becoming proselytes, they had come to the solemnity, and moved by his reputation, they said: *We want to see Jesus*." Hugh of St. Cher, p. 361b says: "Or according to Chrysostom. They were at the point of becoming proselytes and were at the feast."

[65] See Chrysostom, Homily 66 n. 2 in FC 41, p. 220: "Philip stepped aside in favor of Andrew, since the latter was of higher rank than he, and communicated the message to him. However, not even Andrew acted with complete authority in the matter, for he had heard: 'Do not go in the direction of the Gentiles.' For this reason, when he had conferred with the disciple, he brought him to the Master, for they spoke to Him together."

earlier? And the answer has to be that it was because of the nearness of the passion, through which there was salvation for the Gentiles. – Another reason: Since the Jews through the conspiracy of Christ's death had already rejected God's grace, and so after their conspiracy the Lord turned towards the Gentiles.[66]

John 12:24-28
Prediction of the Fruitfulness of the Passion

36. *Amen, amen, I say to you.* After the advance announcement of the call of the Gentiles had been described, the next point is *the prediction of the fruit of the passion.* This description follows this order. First *the fruitfulness of the passion is predicted.* Second, since the passion does not have an effect unless people imitate Christ, *an exhortation to such imitation is given* where verse 25 reads: "The person who loves his life," etc. Third since only those who are called by the Lord imitate him, *it is noted that a prayer is offered for them* where verse 27 states: "Now my soul is troubled." Fourth since he obtains everything he asks for, *it is noted that he is heard* where verse 28 reds: "So a voice came," etc.

Verse 24. So the first point treated is the fruitfulness of the passion through the example of the grain. For this reason the text continues: *Amen, amen, I say to you.* He speaks to assure the Gentiles, who had requested that he confirm them in faith: *Unless the grain of wheat falls into the ground and dies.*

---

[66] See Chrysostom, Homily 66 n. 2 in FC 41, p. 221: "But when they hated Him and hated Him so much as to kill Him, it was useless to adhere to those who were repelling Him."

37. (Verse 25). *It remains alone*. Literally it does not multiply unless it dies. 1 Corinthians 15:36 says: "Senseless person, what you sow is not brought to life unless it dies." *But if it dies, it brings forth much fruit*, since then it produces a harvest. – So it is to be understood of Christ, who is a grain of wheat on account of purity and abundant richness. Wherefore, the best bread is fashioned from him. Thus it is also with the flesh of Christ, who is "the living bread that has come down from heaven," as John 6:51 above states. Psalm 147:14 speaks about this: "He has filled you with the best wheat." This grain, *falling into the ground*, through contempt, *dies* through the bitterness of the passion. Therefore, it is said in Psalm 87:8-9: "You have brought all your waves over me. You have set all my acquaintances far from me. They have set me apart as an abomination to them." This grain *brings forth much fruit*, since it has brought many sons and daughters into glory. Hebrews 2:10 states: "It became him … who brought many sons and daughters into glory, to perfect, through the passion,[67] the author of their salvation." Isaiah 60:5 reads: "When the multitude of the sea will be converted to you, the strength of the Gentiles will come to you."[68] – *The person who loves his life*. The second point occurs here, that is, the exhortation to imitate the passion. And he exhorts by proposing something that is advantageous and an example. Concerning something that is advantageous or injurious he says: *the person who loves his life, loses it*. He calls bodily life "life," as Peter said in John

---

[67] The Vulgate reads *per passiones* ("through sufferings") while Bonaventure has *per passionem* ("through the passion").

[68] See Augustine on Psalm 59 n. 9 in WSA III/17, p. 187: "If a grain did not fall into the earth, it would not be multiplied; it would remain one only. But Christ fell into the earth in his passion, and fruitfulness followed in his resurrection…. He hung on the cross, despised by all; but inwardly he was the grain with power to draw all things after him."

13:37 below: "I will lay down my life for you." *And the person who hates his life in this world*, that is, by giving it for the sake of Christ, *keeps it unto life everlasting.* Matthew 16:25 reads: "The person who would save his life will lose it, but the person who loses his life for my sake will find it." Augustine comments: "If you want to hold onto life with Christ, do not fear to die on account of Christ…. Happy are those who keep their life by losing it, lest by loving it they lose it."[69]

38. (Verse 26). *If anyone serves me, let that person follow me*, as a servant does his Lord. Otherwise, he is not a genuine servant. *Let a person follow*, namely, the footsteps of the passion. 1 Peter 2:21 states: "Christ suffered for us, leaving you an example, so that you might follow his footsteps," so that, as one imitates him in his suffering, so also in his glory. For this reason the text adds: *So that where I am, there also is my servant.*[70] 2 Timothy 2:11-12 reads: "This is a faithful saying: If we have died with him, we will also live with him. If we suffer with him,[71] we will also reign with him." So it is *faithful*, because it has been promised by the Lord. Revelation 3:21 says: "To the one who conquers I will give a place with me on my throne." Lest anyone reject being his servant, he adds the summit of being honored: *If anyone serves me, my Father will honor him*, since that person has honored me. 1 Samuel

---

[69] Bonaventure has adapted Tractate 51 n. 10. See CCSL xxxvi, p. 443.

[70] On p. 418 n. 4 QuarEd rightly notice that the Vulgate reads *et ubi sum ego, illic et minister meus erit* ("and where I am, there also will be my servant") while Bonaventure has *ut ubi ego sum, ibi sit et minister meus* ("so that where I am, there also is my servant").

[71] The Vulgate reads *si sustinemus* ("If we endure") while Bonaventure has *Si compatimur* ("If we suffer with him"). Bonaventure may have been influenced by Rom 8:17c: "If we suffer with him, so that we may also be glorified with him." Bonaventure cites Rom 8:17ab at the end of John 12 n. 38.

2:30 states: "I will honor the person who honors me.[72] But those who despise me will be despised."[73] I say that *he will honor*, because he will make the servant his son. Romans 8:16-17 reads: "The Spirit herself gives testimony to our spirit that we are children of God. But if we are sons, we are heirs also: heirs indeed of God and joint heirs with Christ."

39. (Verse 27). *Now my soul is troubled*, etc. This verse treats the third point, namely, prayer for those to be called. Now the Lord is placed between two concerns. Since his flesh was in flight from death, he had to pray for it. But on the other hand, since he had come for our salvation, he preferred prayer for our conversion to prayer for his own liberation, for which he had first prayed. Thus he says: *Now my soul is troubled*, namely, through fear of death. Matthew 26:37 reads: "He began to be troubled[74] and filled with sorrow." *And what will I say?* As if he were saying: Should I never ask that I escape death? Indeed, I will ask, in order to show my weakness. For this reason he says: *Father, save me from this hour*, that is, the hour of the passion. Matthew 26:39 states: "Father, if it is possible, let this cup pass away from me."[75] But he did not make this petition so that it might be heard, because he adds: *But this is why I have come to this hour*, that is, in

---

[72] Bonaventure has adapted 1 Sam 2:30d which reads: "I will glorify whoever will glorify me."

[73] Hugh of St. Cher, p. 362a also cites 1 Sam 2:30, but does not adapt it as Bonaventure does. See previous note.

[74] The Vulgate reads *contristari* ("to be saddened") whereas Bonaventure has *turbari* ("to be troubled").

[75] Hugh of St. Cher, p. 362e also cites Matt 26:39. See Augustine, Tractate 52 n. 3 in FC 88, p. 282: "Therefore, let him not seem to you to be demoted from his high estate because he wishes you to be promoted from your lowly estate. For he deigned even to be tempted by the devil, by whom assuredly, if he were unwilling, he would not be tempted, just as if he were unwilling, he would not suffer."

order that I might die. Therefore, I do not wish that request to be heard, but this one:[76]

40. (Verse 28). *Father, glorify your name.* And his petition is that the name of God might become known to the Gentiles through his passion. He is praying for us, for whom he also offers himself. Wherefore, in Hebrews 5:7 it is said of Christ: "In the days of his earthly life, with a loud cry and tears, he offered up prayers and supplications to God who could save him from death and was heard because of his reverence."[77] – *So a voice came from heaven.* The last point is made here, that is, the hearing of Christ's petition. As a sign of this the text says: *A voice came from heaven, saying:*[78] *I have both glorified it,* that is, through miraculous deeds, *and I will glorify it again,* through more miraculous deeds, such as our redemption and Christ's lifting up to heaven. The glorification was effected by the Father, for Hebrews 5:5 reads: "Christ did not glorify himself with the high priesthood, but he who spoke to him: You are my son. Today I have begotten you." Wherefore, this voice is attributed to the Father here, as in Matthew 3:17 it is attributed to the Father at Christ's baptism and in Matthew 17:5 it is attributed to the Father at Christ's transfiguration. So the voice bore witness

---

[76] See Chrysostom, Homily 67 n. 2 in FC 41, p. 229: "This was the weakness of His human nature.... It was as if He was saying: 'Even though we are disturbed, even though we are troubled, let us not flee from death.... I do not mean: 'Release Me from this house,' but what? Father, glorify Thy name. Even though My perturbation caused Me to speak as I just did, I mean the opposite: 'Glorify Thy name'; that is, 'lead Me henceforward to the cross.'"

[77] Bonaventure's text differs in four small ways from the Vulgate, e.g., the Vulgate reads *ad eum* ("to him") while Bonaventure has *ad Deum* ("to God").

[78] On p. 418 n. 10 QuarEd correctly indicate that the Vulgate does not read *dicens* ("saying").

to Christ in his coming or incarnation, in his passion, and in his resurrection.

QUESTIONS

41. Question 1 concerns John 12:25: "The person who loves his life loses it." – But all people love their own lives, because it is said in Ephesians 5:29: "No one ever hated his own flesh, but nourishes it," etc. Therefore, how much less does he hate his life. – Let it be understood that the Latin *anima* means "life" and has three different senses. And so in one sense it refers to "carnal" life, according to what is said: "the fleshly person does not perceive the things that are of the Spirit."[79] And this life is not to be loved, because it conveys sin, as Sirach 18:31 states: "If you yield your life to its concupiscences, it will make you a joy to your enemies."[80] – In another sense *anima* is said to be "natural life," according to what John 13:37 below says: "I will lay down my life for you." – In a third sense it is "spiritual life," according to what Psalm 10:6 states: "Those who love iniquity hate their lives." – In the text at hand it is said of life, as it signifies sin. – But this interpretation does not resolve the question of why the Lord exhorts unto death. So does he wish that people give themselves to death and thereby hate their natural life? But if that is the case, those who kill themselves in order to obey Christ would be engaged in a meritorious act. – But this is obviously false, because it is not licit for anyone to kill himself, as is proved in the first book of *The City of God*.[81]

---

[79] See 1 Cor 2:14.

[80] Hugh of St. Cher, p. 361v, f also cites Sir 18:31.

[81] See Book I, c. 20-27 in *Sancti Avrelii Avgvstini De civitate Dei Libri I-IX*. Edited by Bernard Dombart and Alphonsus Kalb. CCSL xlvii (Turnhout: Brepols, 1955), pp. 22-28. See also Augustine, Tractate

I answer that it has to be maintained that this text be understood of the life "of nature." But it should be noted that "to love" and "to hate" must not be taken in an absolute sense, but in relationship to something else. So that person is said "to love," who loves life more than fulfilling the divine command. While another person is said "to hate," who fulfills the command rather than preserving his life. Wherefore, people are not bound to die or to kill themselves and should not cast themselves headlong to their deaths. For Augustine maintains: "If a person is forced to make a choice, with his persecutor threatening death, then let him choose to die loving God than to live having offended God."[82]

42. Question 2 focuses on Christ's petition in John 12:27 that he be saved from the hour of death. – 1. He himself knew that God would not hear his petition. Therefore, he was petitioning without any purpose. – 2. Likewise, he asked for this and was not heard. So it follows that he was not heard in all things. Contrary to this is what John 11:42 says above: "I knew that you always hear me." – 3. If you say that this petition issued from his sensual nature, here is the counter argument: The sensual nature does not turn itself towards God the Father. Therefore, if there was a petition, it issued from his reason.

I answer that it has to be held that in Christ there was a twofold will, namely, of reason and of sensuality. The

---

51 n. 10 in FC 88, pp. 276-277: "But watch out that a wish to destroy yourself not creep upon you unawares, by so understanding that you ought to hate your life in this world. For, from this, certain evil and wicked men, in themselves crueler and more criminal murderers, give themselves to flames, suffocate in water, smash themselves by leaping from a height, and perish. Christ did not teach this...."

[82] This is Bonaventure's adaptation of Tractate 51 n. 10. See CCSL xxxvi, p. 443.

will of reason is always in conformity with God in what is willed, and therefore is always heard. But the will of sensuality is not in harmony with the will of God in what is willed, but not in the way a thing is to be willed. And so the will of sensuality in Christ did not always obtain what it willed, because what happened is only what God willed. – Therefore, the petition under discussion did not proceed from the will of reason, but from that of sensuality. And so it was not heard. – 1. Relative to the objection: What was the object of his prayer? it has to be maintained that just as the Lord commands something not for it to be fulfilled, but to instruct us, so also he instructed us through this petition that it is legitimate for us with the will of sensuality to will something for ourselves. Also the petition itself must be subordinated to the divine will. Further, that we should not think we lack faith if we fear death. – 3. With regard to the objection that this petition stemmed from reason, it should be said that the words themselves were formulated at the direction of reason and that reason proposed the petition. And just as an attorney sometimes does not make a request for himself, not because he wants it himself, but wants it for another and because the other person wants it, so too reason made the petition for sensuality. Christ didn't want this petition granted, but rather to die for our salvation.[83]

JOHN 12:29-36A
EXPLANATION OF THE PREDICTED FRUITFULNESS

43. *So the crowd that was standing.* After the fruitfulness of the upcoming passion has been determined, a third

---

[83] For more detail on the discussion in n. 42, see Book III d. 17. a. 1. q. 2 and 3 and d. 17. a.2. q. 2 and 3 of Bonaventure's *Sentence Commentary* in Omnia Opera 3:365-370, 373-375.

point is joined here, that is, *its explanation*. The Evangelist proceeds in this order. First he indicates *the astonishment of the crowd*. Second is *Christ's explanation*. Third is *doubt on the part of the crowd*. Fourth is *the removal of the doubt*.

Verse 29. So first is the astonishment of the crowd when they heard that voice, since they did not know whence it came. For this reason the text states: *So the crowd, that was standing round and heard,*[84] that is, that voice. *Said that it had thundered*, noting its loudness and effect on their senses. And these belonged to the Sadducees, about whom Matthew 22:23 and Acts 23:8 say: "They say that there are no angels or spirits."[85] But *others said:An angel has spoken to him*, noting how articulate the voice was, although they did not understand what it meant.[86] These were from the party of the Pharisees, who hold that there are angels, for in Acts 23:9 they say: "What if a spirit has spoken to him or an angel?"

44. (Verse 30). *Jesus answered and said*. This verse covers the second point, that is, the explanation of this voice, since they did not know why it had sounded and what it meant. So he says relative to why it sounded: *Not for me did this voice come, but for you*, since it was not for my instruction, but for yours. So he gives the meaning of the voice:

---

[84] On p. 419 n. 10 QuarEd correctly mention that the Vulgate reads *audierat* ("had heard") while Bonaventure has *audiebat* ("heard").

[85] The citation is from Acts 23:8. Matt 22:23 reads: "On that same day some of the Sadducees, who say there is no resurrection, came to him and questioned him."

[86] See Chrysostom, Homily 67 n. 2 in FC 41, p. 230: "Was the voice not clear and distinct? Yes, but it quickly sped past them, since they were somewhat unspiritual and carnal and immortified. Moreover, some merely detected the sound, while others knew that the voice was articulate, but they did not yet comprehend what it meant."

45. (Verse 31). *Now is the judgment of the world*, that is, in the passion. *Now will the prince of this world be cast out*, namely, the one who believes he is the prince, since he was worshipped by many Gentiles. Rather he is accounted the worst demon. Luke 11:21-22 reads: "When the strong man, fully armed, guards his courtyard.... If a stronger than he attacks and overcomes him, he will take away all his weapons that he relied upon and will divide his spoils." And Christ conquers the world and its prince, for John 16:33 below says: "Take courage. I have conquered the world." And the text says that the way of casting out the prince is through the passion. For this reason the text continues:

46. (Verse 32). *And I, if I be lifted up from the earth*, through the passion of the cross, *will draw all things to myself*, through faith and love. The Song of Songs 1:3 reads: "Draw me after you." John 21:11 below says: "Simon Peter ... drew the net onto the land full of large fish," etc. John 3:14 above states: "Just as Moses lifted up the serpent in the desert, so must the Son of Man be lifted up." And the Evangelist gives an explanation of this:

47. (Verse 33). *Now he said this signifying by what death he was to die*, since it was death on the cross, which was the most vile. Wisdom 2:20 says: "Let us condemn him to the most shameful death."

48. (Verse 34). *The crowd answered him*. The third point is introduced here, that is, the doubt among the people in the crowd who had been instructed in the Law, since they had heard that the Christ was immortal, and here he was saying that he was the Christ and that he was mortal and was going to die. For this reason the text continues: *We have heard from the Law that the Christ abides forever.* – But where had they heard this in the Law? It should be

understood that the Law also encompasses the Prophets, and it is said in Micah 5:2: "His going forth is … from the days of eternity." Daniel 7:14 reads: "His power is an everlasting power … and his kingdom, one that will not be destroyed."[87] 2 Samuel 7:12-13 states: "I will raise up your descendants after you…. And I will establish the throne of his kingdom forever." – *And why are you saying: The Son of Man must be lifted up? Who is this Son of Man?* In this passage Christ did not use the form he employed in John 8:28 above: "When you have lifted up the Son of Man, then you will know."[88] But now he uses this formulation: "And I, if I be lifted upon from the earth."[89] They were not asking about what they had just heard, but about what they had previously understood.

49. (Verse 35). *So Jesus said to them.* This verse gives voice to the fourth point, namely, the removal of their doubt. And the Lord indicates that their doubt does not issue from an evil intellect, but from a lack of understanding, since Scripture says both things of the Christ: both that he is eternal and that he is mortal. So the text states: *Yet a little light is among you.*[90] *The light* is that you believe that the Christ is eternal, but *a little*, since you do not believe that he is going to die.[91] Therefore, he exhorts them

---

[87] Hugh of St. Cher, p. 363c also cites Micah 5:2 and Dan 7:14. In addition, he quotes Isa 9:7 twice.

[88] John 8:28a reads: "So Jesus said to them: When you have lifted up the Son of Man, then you will know that I am he."

[89] See John 12:32.

[90] See Chrysostom, Homily 68 n. 1 in FC 41, p. 236 where he follows the Greek text: "… 'Yet a little while the light is among you,' making it clear to them that His death was a change of state. And this is so for the sunlight is not extinguished, but disappears for a little while, and appears again."

[91] See Augustine, Tractate 52 n. 13 in FC 88, pp. 288-289: "'Therefore, Jesus said to them: Yet a little light is among you.' From this you can understand that the Christ remains forever…. Walk, approach, understand wholly that the Christ will die and he will live forever….'"

to make progress in faith while they have time. So he says: *Walk while you have the light*. That "walking" consists of drawing near to Christ through faith. Psalm 33:6 reads: "Draw near to him and be enlightened." And the reason is added: *That the darkness may not overtake you*, that is, the blindness of non-belief, about which John 3:19 above speaks: "The light has come into the world, and men and women have loved the darkness rather than the light." And it is dangerous to be overtaken by the darkness, since *the person who*[92] *walks in darkness does not know where he is going*. Proverbs 4:19 says: "The way of the wicked is dark. They do not know where they may fall." And he explains what he means by "walk." It means "believe." So the text continues:

50. (Verse 36). *While you have the light, believe in the light, so that you may become children of the light*. "Children of the light" are children of God, since he is "the true light."[93] And this takes place by faith. John 1:12 above reads: "To those who believe in his name he gave the power of becoming children of God." The Lord gives the best answer to their doubt, because they could only be freed from their doubt by approaching him through faith." For Augustine comments: "Approach, understand completely that the Christ will die and the Christ will live forever and will pour out his blood, by which he may redeem, and will ascend on high where he may lead the way."[94] This is what "to walk" means.

---

[92] On p. 420 n. 9 QuarEd rightly notice that the Vulgate reads *et qui* ("and the person who") while Bonaventure has *qui* ("the person who").

[93] See John 1:9.

[94] See Tractate 52 n. 13 in CCSL xxxvi, p. 451 and FC 88, p. 289. Bonaventure's citation is almost verbatim.

Questions

51. Question 1 focuses on John 12:31: "Now is the judgment of the world," since it had been said that he judges no one and did not come to judge.[95] – I answer that there is a judgment of condemnation and of separation. Through the judgment of separation the world is judged in the passion, by which the sheep are separated from the wolves, not at the primal judgment.

52. Question 2 probes John 12:31: "The prince of this world will be cast out" and asks: Who is this prince? – If the answer is the devil, then it seems that this sensible world is under the control of the devil. And then the wicked impiety of the Manichees would be true. – I respond that it has to be maintained that "the world" here refers to those who have fallen in love with the world. Their prince is the devil, but not with regard to nature, but with regard to his pre-excellence in sinning, since as Job 41:25 says: "He is king over all the children of arrogance."[96]

53. Question 3 focuses on "he will be cast out" of John 12:31, because this does not seem to be the case. For he still rules in those who have surrendered to the world, and his rule becomes stronger, since they are sinning more grievously. – I answer that it should be said that the devil is said "to be cast out of the world," not in the sense that he no longer tempts, but in the sense that he does not rule intrinsically. He is not said "to be cast out," in that he has no complete sway over anyone intrinsically, but that he doesn't hold sway over everyone. He does not rule

---

[95] See John 3:17: "For God did not send his Son into the world to judge the world." Note also John 12:47: "I do not judge him, for I have not come to judge the world, but to save it."

[96] See Book II, d. 1. p. I. n. 2. q. 1 ad 1-3 in Bonaventure's *Sentence Commentary*.

with such great power, since his hand that drags us has been cut off, since "the handwritten bond that was hostile to us"[97] has been destroyed in the passion and nailed to the cross. His hand that urges us on has been debilitated while our hand to resist him has been strengthened through faith. 1 Peter 5:9 reads: "Resist him (the devil as a roaring lion), strengthened in faith."[98]

54. Question 4 deals with John 12:31 that he will draw all things to himself, for not all, not even a majority have been converted to faith. Moreover, there are more evil people than good people. – I respond that it has to be maintained, as Augustine says, that those whose tendency is towards non-existence should not be numbered.[99] And evil people

---

[97] See Col 2:14: "canceling the handwritten bond that was hostile to us. Indeed he has taken it completely away, nailing it to the cross."

[98] For the imagery and theology behind this third question see Book III, d. 19. a. 1. q. 3 of Bonaventure's *Sentence Commentary* in Omnia Opera 3:406: "For the devil, before Christ's passion, had a two-fold hand, that is, one that dragged us and one that urged us. The hand that dragged us was the power of dragging down to limbo even the just and the saints. The hand that urged us was the power of pushing us into evil either through falsehood or through violence, because he tempts like a dragon and like a lion. And the first hand, namely, that of dragging us, was of such great power that no one could resist it. And this one was entirely amputated through the passion, for now he can drag down to limbo no just person, because through Christ's passion the handwritten bond of the sin of Adam has been destroyed. But he has such great strength with his hand that urges us that with great difficulty can anyone resist it. And so he rules in many, indeed almost in everyone, for he overcomes all either through fraudulence or by violence. And this power had been weakened through the passion, by which the light of truth has been opened against diabolic fraudulence and the assistance of virtue is given against diabolical violence."

[99] See Tractate 1 n. 13 in FC 78, p. 52: "Certainly sin was not made through him, and it is clear that sin is nothing and that men become nothing when they sin." See also Tractate 52 n.11 in FC 88, p. 287: "He did not, however, say all men but 'all things', for not all men have the faith. And so he did not refer this to the totality of mankind, but to the wholeness of the creature.... Or if men themselves are to be under-

are such. Therefore, "all" only applies to the elect, who are children of God by election. And he drew all these to himself and "gathered them into one."[100] – Another interpretation: "I will draw all," that is, from every people and kingdom, not only the Jews, but also the Gentiles, without a distinction between nations.

John 12:36b-50
Future blindness of the Jews

55. *Jesus spoke these things.* After describing the future call of the Gentiles and giving the prediction and exposition of the upcoming passion, the Evangelist moves to the fourth point here: *the future blindness of the Jews.* And he proceeds to declare this reality in this order. First he signals *the blindness itself.* Second *the election of others.* Third *the strengthening of the elect who are weak.* Fourth *condemnation is pronounced on the blind.*

Verse 36b. The blindness of the Jews is signaled by the fact that the Lord hid himself from the very Jews who had begun to contradict him. For this reason the text states: *Jesus spoke these things, and he went away and hid himself from them.* Augustine observes: "Not from those who had come to meet him with palm branches... but from those who saw and became envious upon seeing."[101] Deuteronomy 32:20 reads: "I will hide my face from them and will consider what their last end will be, for it is a perverse generation and unfaithful children."

---

stood as 'all things', we can say all things predestined for salvation.... Or certainly all kinds of men, whether in all languages, or in all ages, or in all degrees of honor...."

[100] See John 11:52.

[101] See Tractate 52 n. 14 in CCSL xxxvi, p. 451.

And this physical hiding was a sign of spiritual hiding.[102] And the following verse intimates this:

56. (Verse 37). *Now although he had worked so many signs in their presence, they did not believe in him.* Such a sign was the sign of raising Lazarus. Nevertheless, *they did not believe*, because their malice would not allow it. Wisdom 2:21 states: "Their malice blinded them. Nor did this happen per chance, but was foreseen by the Lord and predicted by Isaiah the prophet. For this reason the text continues:

57. (Verse 38). *That the word that Isaiah the prophet spoke might be fulfilled: Lord, who has believed,* as if he were saying: nary a one or no one. *Our report?* That is, what we have heard from the Lord. Or what we have heard from those prophesying to us, since "faith is from hearing," as Romans 10:17 states.[103] *And to whom has the arm of the Lord been revealed?* The arm of the Lord, as Augustine says, is the Son of the Father: "For just as it is your arm through which you work, so too God's arm is called the Word, through which he formed the world.... This arm is neither stretched forth and extended nor drawn in and pulled back."[104] Not only was it foreseen, but also it occurred according to the just judgment of God. For this reason the text adds:

---

[102] On p. 422 n. 1 QuarEd cite the Glossa Interlinearis: "*He hid himself from them*, both physically and spiritually." In CCCM ix, p. 592 Rupert of Deutz notes that John diverts from the other evangelists who present Jesus teaching daily in the temple and comments: "So what does this intimate mystically except their blindness?"

[103] Hugh of St. Cher, p. 364e also cites Rom 10:17.

[104] See Tractate 53 n2-3 in CCSL xxxvi, p. 452 and FC 88, pp. 290-291. Bonaventure's citation is almost verbatim.

58. (Verse 39). *This is why they could not believe* in him, that is, because they were blind, and Isaiah said this. Therefore, the text adds: *Because Isaiah said again:*

59. (Verse 40). *He has blinded their eyes and hardened their hearts.* Isaiah 6:10 reads: "Blind the heart of this people, and make their ears heavy and shut their eyes," etc. And Romans 1:28 says: "God has given them up to a reprobate sense." *Lest they see with their eyes and understand with their heart and,* through their understanding, *be converted, and,* through their conversion, *I heal them.* Jeremiah 3:22 states: "Be converted to me[105] ... and I will heal your rebellions." And lest you believe that this authority has been usurped, he adds:

60. (Verse 41). *Isaiah said these things, when he saw his glory and spoke of him.* See Isaiah 6:1-3 where it is said that he saw the Lord sitting upon a throne high and elevated ... and "all the earth was full of his majesty."[106]

61. (Verse 42). *Yet[107] among the rulers.* The second point surfaces here, that is, the election of certain ones. So this statement is to be taken adversatively:[108] Although it had been said that they did not believe, *yet among the rulers many believed in him.* Romans 11:5 reads: "At the present time there is a remnant left, saved according to an election of grace."[109] But nonetheless, they were not perfect in faith. For this reason the text adds: *But because of the*

---

[105] The Vulgate does not read *ad me* ("to me").

[106] The Vulgate reads *gloria* ("glory") while Bonaventure has *maiestate* ("majesty").

[107] On p. 422 n. 8 QuarEd accurately indicate that the Vulgate reads *Verumtamen et* ("And yet") whereas Bonaventure has *Verumtamen* ("Yet").

[108] That is, in contrast to John 12:39.

[109] The Vulgate does not read *salvae* ("saved").

Pharisees they did not acknowledge it, lest they might be cast out of the synagogue. John 9:22 above says: "For the Jews had already agreed that if anyone confess him to be the Christ, he should be put out of the synagogue." And indeed, they feared this as imperfect believers. For this reason the text adds the reason for their fear:

62. (Verse 43). *For they loved human glory more than the glory of God.* And they acted foolishly according to what is said in 1 Maccabees 2:62-63: "Fear not the words of a sinful man, because his glory is dung and worms. Today he is lifted up, and tomorrow he will not be found." Psalm 52:6 reads: "God has scattered the bones of those who please men and women." Galatians 1:10 states: "Am I seeking to please human beings? If I were still trying to please them, I would not be a slave of Christ."

63. (Verse 44). *But Jesus cried out and said.* The third point is found here, that is, the strengthening of those who are weak in faith. This strengthening is brought about by Christ's loving exhortation by which he lifts up the minds of the believers to the divine dignity. For this reason he says: *The person who believes in me does not believe in me,* according to my visible nature, *but in the one who sent me.*[110] Another interpretation is: By believing you not only honor me, but the one who sent me. Through this he shows that to believe in him is not to believe in a human being, but in God. And he shows this:

---

[110] See Augustine, Tractate 54 n. 2 in FC 88, p. 302: "Now, however, how are we to understand his words, 'He who believes in me believes not in me but in him who sent me,' except that the man appeared to men while the God was hidden?" See also Chrysostom, Homily 69 n. 1 in FC 41, p. 243: "It was as if He said: 'Why are you afraid to believe in me? Faith in God comes through Me, as also, accordingly, does unbelief.' Notice how by every means He showed the complete identity of Their substance."

64. (Verse 45). *And the person who sees me sees the one who sent me*. Therefore, they are one in essence, the one sending and the one sent, since the person who sees one also sees the other. For John 14:9 below states: "Philip, the person who sees me also sees my Father." And the reason is unity of essence, since "I am in the Father and the Father in me."[111] And the Son himself is the cause of seeing the Father, as the word comes from the speaker and as the brightness comes from the light.[112] For this reason the text continues:

65. (Verse 46). *I have come a light into the world, so that whoever believes in me may not remain in darkness*, but may see and also become light. Ephesians 5:8 reads: "You were once darkness, but now you are light in the Lord."[113] And this occurs because you believe in him about whom it is said in Hebrews 1:3: "Since he is the brightness of the glory and the image of his substance," etc.[114]

66. (Verse 47). *And if anyone hears my words*. The fourth point occurs here, that is, the threat against those who do not believe. And at the same time he shows his benignity in threatening and the severity of the judgment. So he says: *If[115] anyone hears my words and does not keep them*,

---

[111] See John 14:10: "Do you not believe that I am in the Father and the Father in me?"

[112] See the examples in Chrysostom, Homily 69 n. 1 in FC 41, p. 244: "As one might say: 'He who bears water from the river takes not the water of the river, but really that of its source.... 'I have come a light unto the world.' Since the Father is called by this name in the Old as well as the New Testament, He also used this name for Himself. That is why Paul likewise called Him 'brightness,' since he learned from Scripture to do so."

[113] Hugh of St. Cher, p. 364c also refers to Eph 5:8.

[114] Hugh of St. Cher, p. 363v,b also refers to Hebr 1:3.

[115] On p. 423 n. 2 QuarEd rightly notice that the Vulgate reads *Et si* ("And if") while Bonaventure has *Si* ("If").

it is not I who judge him, that is, I do not condemn him, and this on account of my benignity. *For I have not come to judge the world, but to save the world.* John 3:17 above says: "God did not send his Son into the world in order to judge the world, but that the world might be saved through him." Luke 9:56 reads: "The Son of Man did not come to destroy people's lives, but to save them." But nevertheless they will not escape the severity of the judgment. For this reason the text continues:

67. (Verse 48). *The person who rejects me and does not accept my words has one to judge him*, And he shows what does the judging: *The word that I have spoken will judge him on the last day*. Matthew 24:35 states: "Heaven and earth will pass away, but my words will not pass away." Rather, as Chrysostom says: "They will be as an accusation, convicting them and depriving them of all excuse."[116] What Matthew 5:25 says is understood of Christ: "Come to terms with your adversary quickly while you are with him on the way," etc.[117] And he shows that his word has the power of judging us in that it is not a human word, but divine and true. Therefore, the text states:

68. (Verse 49). *For I have not spoken on my*[118] *authority*, as those who glory in their vanity, about whom John 7:18 above says: "The person who speaks on his own authority seeks his own glory." *But the one who has sent me, the*

---

[116] See Homily 69 n. 2 in PG 59:379. Bonaventure's citation is not verbatim.

[117] See Augustine Sermon 9 n. 3 in WSA III/1, p. 261: "So who is the adversary? The word of God. The word of God is your adversary. Why is it your adversary? Because it commands things against the grain which you don't do...."

[118] On p. 423 n. 5 QuarEd accurately indicate that the Vulgate reads *ex me* ("on my") while Bonaventure has *a me* ("on my").

Father, he[119] *has commanded me what I should say and what I should declare.* And so I speak in accord with his command.

69. (Verse 50). *And I know that his commandment is everlasting life.* For Matthew 19:17 states: "If you want to enter into life, keep the commandments." Deuteronomy 30:19-20 reads: "So choose life that both you and your descendants may live. And you should love the Lord your God and obey his voice." And so I do not waver from his commandment. For this reason the text continues: *So the things that I speak, I speak as the Father has bidden me,* so that what he says as a human being is always in accord with the divine commandment and will. John 8:26 states: "The things I have heard from the Father[120] I speak to the world." And this is why he wants his word to be accepted as divine and not to be rejected. As it is said about the good in 1 Thessalonians 2:13: "When you heard and received the word of God ... you welcomed it not as a human word, but, as it truly is, the word of God, who works in you who have believed."

QUESTIONS

70. Question 1 deals with John 12:39-40: "This is why they could not believe, because Isaiah said: He has blinded," etc. – First of all, it seems that this is badly said, because, if they could not believe, then sin should not be imputed to them. – To this Chrysostom answers: "They

---

[119] On p. 423 n. 5 QuarEd correctly mention that the Vulgate reads *ipse* ("he himself") while Bonaventure has *ille* ("he").

[120] The Vulgate reads *ab eo* ("from him") whilst Bonaventure has *a Patre* ("from the Father").

could not, that is, they would not."[121] But this does not solve the problem, 1. because then it would be easy to solve all issues. Why didn't the Evangelist say: They did not want, since such an expression was right at his fingertips? – 2.Furthermore, let the proposed sense stand: They did not want to believe, for Isaiah said: "He has blinded their eyes." Then it would seem that God is the cause of their evil will.

I respond that it has to be maintained that there are two types of possibility. In one case something cannot exist in any way whatever. In the second instance something can exist with great difficulty. Thus it is said that a man accustomed to evil cannot do good. Jeremiah 13:23 states: "If the Ethiopian can change his skin and the leopard his spots, you also can do good, although you have learned evil." – According to this way of viewing the matter it is said that a blind man cannot believe. And the Evangelist wishes to say that they could not believe, because they had been blinded, as Isaiah had foretold, not that the prediction of Isaiah was the cause, but the cause of their blindness was their own evil and the divine judgment, that is, the judgment of abandonment. Augustine comments: "God blinds and hardens by abandoning, and not assisting. This can take place by a hidden judgment, which, nonetheless, is not unjust."[122]

71. Question 2 focuses on John 12:44: "The person who believes in me believes not in me," etc. – It seems that

---

[121] See Homily 68 n. 2 in FC 41, p. 239: "Further, if the words 'they could not' occur instead of 'they did not wish,' do not be surprised. I say this for elsewhere Scripture says: 'Let him accept it who can.' Thus, it is apt frequently to say 'can' for 'will.'" Hugh of St. Cher, p. 363v,h also cites Chrysostom's opinion.

[122] See Tractate 53 n. 6 in CCSL xxxvi, p. 454. The citation is not verbatim.

there is a contradiction here. – Now if you say that "only" should be understood here, so that the sense is: The person who believes in me does not believe in me only, but also in the one who sent me. According to this way of taking the sentence one must say in like manner: The person who sees me does not see me only, but the one who sent me. – I answer that it has to be held that the faith has different articles, and when a person is thinking of one article, she is not thinking of another. Further, some believe in one article while others are believing in another. But in the matter of seeing, since essence is singular, those who see one person see all persons. Therefore, there is unity in sight: "Who sees me also sees the Father,"[123] for it is impossible to see one without the other. But while there is a distinction in the articles of faith, this distinction does not mean solitariness: The person who believes in me does not believe in me only, but in me and in the one who sent me. – Matters can be put in another way. To believe relates to authority, but to see and to understand pertain to reason.[124] So since authority and power pertain to the Father by appropriation and belief is the appropriate response, the Son appropriates belief to the Father. And so it was said "the Father draws people to the Son."[125] But through sight and revelation the Son leads people to the Father by his being word and light. And therefore, he does not appropriate seeing to the Father. Rather he

---

[123] See John 12:45: "The person who sees me sees the one who sent me."

[124] There is some parallel in Augustine, *De utilitate credendi* c. 11 n. 25. See *The Advantage of Believing*. Translated by Luanne Meagher in *Writings of Saint Augustine*, Volume 2. FC 4 (New York: CIMA Publishing Co, 1947), p. 425: "What we understand, accordingly, we owe to reason; what we believe, to authority; and what we have an opinion on, to error."

[125] See John 6:44: "No one can come to me unless the Father who sent me draws him...."

appropriates believing to the Father when he says: "The person who believes in me," etc.

CHAPTER THIRTEEN

JOHN 13:1-17:26
STRENGTHENING OF THE DISCIPLES

1. *Before the feast of the Passover*. Now that the two preliminaries to the passion have been presented, namely, the conspiracy of the Jews and the prediction of the passion, this third part deals with *the strengthening of the disciples*. Now the Lord confirms and strengthens the disciples against the imminent tribulation first by *his example of humility*. Second, by *his word of instruction and consolation* at the beginning of chapter 14: "Let not your hearts be troubled." Third by *the assistance of prayer* at the beginning of chapter 17: "Jesus spoke these things and raising his eyes," etc.

JOHN 13:1-38
THE LORD ENCOURAGES HIS DISCIPLES BY HIS EXAMPLE

So this present chapter, in which the Lord encourages his disciples by means of his *example*, presents four sections. First the Lord proposes *an example*. Second *he exhorts to imitation* where verse 12 says: "Now after he had washed," etc. Third he *shows* or discloses *the perversity of Judas* who turned aside where verse 21 reads: "When he had said these things, he was troubled in spirit." In the fourth *he shows the weakness of the disciples* in following him to his passion where verse 33 states: "Little children, I am with you just a little while."[1]

John 13:1-11
The Lord gives an example

So *the example*, which he proposes for imitation, is described in this order. First he shows *the fittingness of the hour*. Second, *Christ's humility*. Third, *Peter's fearful reverence*. Fourth, *his obedience*.

2. (Verse 1). The fittingness of the time is shown since the time of his death was imminent when he had to show special signs of his love. So the text states: *Before the feast of the Passover*, that is, before the first day of unleavened bread which occurs in the evening of the fourteenth day and is the time when the lamb is slaughtered.[2] *Jesus, knowing that his hour had come for him to pass over from this world to the Father*. Passover means "to pass over," and so the Lord wanted to die at Passover, because his dying was a passing over. This passing over was signified in the passing over of the Red Sea, about which 1 Corinthians 10:1 says: "All our forebears passed over through the sea."[3] *Since he had loved his own, who were in the world, he loved them to the end*, that is, he then showed extraordinary signs of his love. Augustine observes: "Far be it that he who did not end with death ended his lov-

---

[1] It seems that Bonaventure actually commences this section with John 13:31. See below.

[2] See Ex 12:1-18.

[3] 1 Cor 10:1 reads: "For I would not have you ignorant, brothers and sisters, that our forebears were all under the cloud and all passed over through the sea."

ing with death."⁴ And "this is not an end that consumes, but consummates."⁵ The Lord loved *his own*. Isaiah 49:15 says: "Can a woman forget her infant, so as not to have pity on the child of her womb?" Having considered the time frame, the Evangelist now mentions the hour.

3. (Verse 2). *And during the supper, the devil having already put it into the heart*, that is, had suggested, *of Judas Iscariot, the son of Simon, to betray him*, since from this time he had determined to betray him. By means of this betrayal Christ was not humiliated, but exalted. Thus the text adds:

4. (Verse 3) *knowing that the Father had given all things into his hands*, according to what Matthew 28:18 states: "All power has been given to me in heaven and on earth." *And* knowing *that he had come forth from God and was going to God*, according to what John 16:28 below says: "I have come forth from the Father and have come into the world. Again I leave the world and go to the Father." *Knowing* this, that is, recognizing in advance that his death was imminent.

---

⁴ See Tractate 55 n. 2 in CCSL xxxvi, p. 464. The citation is verbatim. The translation is from *St. Augustine Tractates on the Gospel of John 55-111*. Translated by John W. Rettig. FC 90 (Washington: CUA Press, 1994), p. 5.

⁵ See Augustine, Tractate 10 n. 5 on 1 John in PL 35:2057. The quotation is not verbatim. See *St. Augustine Tractates on the Gospel of John 112-24 and Tractates on the First Epistle of John*. Translated by John W. Rettig. FC 90 (Washington: CUA Press, 1995), p. 268: "Do not think of consumption but of consummation. For one says, 'I have put an end to this bread,' in one way, but 'I have put an end to this tunic,' in another way. I have put an end to the bread by eating it; I have put an end to the tunic by weaving it." Thus Augustine interprets Ps 118:96: "I have seen an end of all consummation."

5. (Verse 4). *He rose from the supper*, to give an example, since the opportune time was already present, as it was said to the minister of the Church in Acts 12:7: "Rise up quickly."[6] – *And laid aside his clothes*. The second point is found here, that is, *Christ's humility*, since he took off his clothes, so that he might easily minister. Therefore, the text says: *He laid aside his clothes*, so that he might also be prepared to minister. So the text continues: *And taking a towel, he girded himself*. Luke 12:37 reads: "Amen I say to you: He will gird himself," etc.[7] The office of a minister follows. So the text continues:

6. (Verse 5). *Then he poured*[8] *water into the basin and began to wash the feet of the disciples and to dry them with the towel with which he was girded*. This is the office of the minister. Such an office the Lord of majesty assumed. Luke 22:27 says: "I am in your midst as one who ministers." "The Son of Man has not come to be ministered to, but to minister and to give his life as a ransom for many."[9] And this washing of feet is the most humble ministry.

7. (Verse 6). *So he came to Simon Peter*, etc. The third point occurs here, that is, Peter's fearful reverence, by which he refused obedience to the Lord. For which reason the text reads: *He came to Simon Peter*, that is, to wash his feet. *And Peter said to him: Lord, are you going to wash my feet*? Peter was speaking as one terrified: *You are doing this for me*? You, as Lord, are doing this for me,

---

[6] Bonaventure refers to the words of the Lord's angel to Peter as he breaks out of prison. See Matt 20:26: "Whoever wishes to become great among you will be your minister."

[7] Luke 12:37 concludes: "... and will make them recline at table and will come and minister to them."

[8] On p. 425 n. 9 QuarEd rightly notice that the Vulgate reads *mittit* ("pours") while Bonaventure has *misit* ("poured").

[9] Matt 20:28.

a servant? You, the Master, are doing this for me, the disciple? You, the Almighty, are doing this for miserable me? Chrysostom notes: "Are you washing my feet with the hands, by which you opened eyes, cleansed lepers, raised the dead?"[10] As if he were saying: I don't dare let this happen, and since he was overcome by fearful reverence, the Lord warned him that he should desist on account of the mystery. So it follows:

8. (Verse 7). *Jesus said to him:*[11] *What I do you know not now, but you will know afterwards*. So you have to wait until later. But Peter is not deflected by this admonition. So:

9. (Verse 8). *Peter said to him: You will never wash my feet*. And since he had decreed that he would remain steadfast in his stance, he is deterred by a threat. So the text continues: *Jesus answered him: If I do not wash you, you will have no part with me*. "Part" means eternal union with God. About this it is said in Psalm 15:5: "The Lord is the part of my inheritance and of my cup." And Psalm 141:6 reads: "My portion in the land of the living."[12]

10. (Verse 9). *Simon Peter said to him*. The fourth point surfaces here, that is, *Peter's obedience*, after being faced with a threat. For in John 13:8 the text read "Peter": "Peter said to him," but in this response it is said: "*Simon Peter said to him*," that is, the obedient,[13] fervent one who

---

[10] See Homily 70 n. 2 in PG 59:383. Hugh of St. Cher, p. 366b also cites Chrysostom.

[11] On p. 426 n. 2 QuarEd accurately indicate that the Vulgate reads *Respondit Iesus et dixit ei* ("Jesus answered and said to him") whereas Bonaventure has *Dixit ei Iesus* ("Jesus said to him").

[12] Ps 141:6 reads: "I cried to you, O Lord: I said: You are my hope, my portion in the land of the living."

[13] See CCSL lxxii, p. 148.

offers more than what the Lord commanded. Thus the text states: *Lord, wash not only my feet*, as you command, *but also my hands and head*. Thereby, Simon Peter, truly obedient, could say with Psalm 56:8: "My heart is ready, O God, my heart is ready." But since he had previously erred in his fearful reverence and now was excessive in his obedience, he was earlier called Peter the terrified, but now is called Peter the instructed. For this reason the text adds:

11. (Verse 10). *Jesus said to him: The person who has bathed*, that is, with this bath. About this bath it is said in Isaiah 1:16: "Wash yourselves, be clean" and in Zechariah 13:1: "There will be a fountain open to the house of David and to the inhabitants of Jerusalem for the washing of the sinner" and Jeremiah 4:14: "Wash your heart from iniquity, Jerusalem, that you may be saved." That person, I say, *does not need to wash except his feet*,[14] that is, the affections, about which The Song of Songs 5:3 says: "I have washed my feet. How will I defile them?"[15] These feet are in greater need of washing than other members, since they more frequently come in contact with filth. Lamentations 1:9 reads: "Her filthiness is on her feet, and she has not remembered her end." *And*, when these feet are washed, then *he is clean all over*. Ezekiel 36:25 says: "I will pour upon you clean water, and you will be cleansed from all your filthiness." *And you are clean*. Therefore, you need only to have your feet washed. John 15:3 below states:

---

[14] The Vulgate reads *non indiget ut lavet* ("does not need to wash").

[15] See Augustine, Tractate 56 n. 4 in FC 90, p. 11: "Nevertheless, when life goes on afterwards (after baptism) amid human affairs, naturally the ground is stepped on. Therefore the human affections themselves, without which one does not live in their mortal state, are, as it were, the feet whereby we are affected in consequence of our human condition; and we are so affected that, if we say that we do not have sin, we deceive ourselves and the truth is not in us."

"You are clean because of the word that I have spoken to you." But lest he seem to be ignorant of the crime of a disciple, he adds: *But not all*. And the Evangelist gives the reason why he had said this:

12. (Verse 11). *For he knew who it was who would betray him. This is why he said: You are not all clean.* So the Evangelist, where he speaks of the traitor, shows that the Lord knew, lest anyone think that Christ as a human being could be deceived. John 6:65 says: "Jesus knew from the beginning who would not believe and who would betray him."

QUESTIONS

13. Question 1 deals with the meal "before the feast of Passover" in John 13:1. – And from this it seems that the Lord confected the sacrament from leavened bread. – But the other Evangelists hold a contrary time frame and say that the Lord ate the Passover according to the common custom.[16] – To this problem the Greeks respond, as it is said in the Glossa, that the Lord anticipated the day of Passover, as it is said here, and confected the sacrament from leavened bread and that John is correcting the other Evangelists.[17] – But their opinion is foolishness, since

---

[16] See Matt 26:17, Mark 14:12, and Luke 22:7.

[17] On p. 426 n. 11 QuarEd quote the Glossa Ordinaria apud Lyranum: "*Before the feast*, calling the solemn day Passover. But the Greeks maintain that only the day on which the lamb is slaughtered is called Passover, and on that day they say that Christ was crucified at midday. And they say that he anticipated one day before so that he might eat the lamb with his disciples. And the words that follow in the Gospel lead to this firm conclusion: *They did not want to enter the praetorium*, that is, Pilate's house, *lest they be defiled and not eat the Passover* (John 18:28). They understood that Passover referred solely to the eating of the lamb. They are not ashamed to say that the other

there is no instance in which the other Evangelists lie since they were speaking by means of the same Spirit.[18] Thus it is not said here that the day of Passover is the day of slaughtering the lambs, but that it is the first day of unleavened bread. In the late evening of the preceding day the lambs are slaughtered.

14. Question 2 focuses on John 13:2: "The devil having already put it into the heart of Judas to betray him." – 1.So it seems that the devil is the one who puts forth evil thoughts. 2. And it seems that this is so, since he is "the god of this world,"[19] and rules over unbelievers, according to Ephesians 2:2.[20] Therefore, just as God puts good thoughts into the hearts of the elect, over whom he rules, so too does the devil put evil thoughts, etc. – But contrary is this: Since, if the devil sends evil thoughts, then it follows that human beings will sin whether they want to or not. Wherefore, according to this the devil would be superior to the mind itself, a position that is contrary to reason and to Augustine.[21]

Evangelists lie when they say that the Lord ate the flesh of the lamb with others at the common time. They say that John corrected the others on this matter."

[18] On p. 426 n. 12 QuarEd refer to the Glossa Ordinaria apud Lyranum: "But they (the Greeks) are in error, for since it is true that all (Evangelists) have spoken through the same Spirit, if in one matter they lie, then they may not be believed in others."

[19] See 2 Cor 4:4: "In their case, the god of this world has blinded their unbelieving minds that they should not see the light of the gospel of the glory of Christ, who is the image of God."

[20] Eph 2:2 says: "wherein once you walked according to the fashion of this world, according to the prince of the power of the air about us, the prince of the spirit which now works on unbelievers."

[21] See Book XI, c. 5 n. 8 of *De Trinitate* in CCSL 1, p. 344. I adapt the translation of WSA I/5, p. 310: "This trinity therefore is not the image of God. For it is produced in the soul through the senses of the body out of the lowest level of creation, which is the bodily one, and the soul itself is superior to this."

I answer that it has to be held that "to send into the heart" or "to put into the heart" admits of two meanings: propri_etary or common. "To send in a proprietary manner" is virtually to form the interior thought, and this is charac_teristic of God alone. "To send in a common manner" is to offer suggestions on a given occasion. The first manner is not fitting for the devil while the second is.[22] – 2.With re_gard to the objection that the devil rules, it has to be said that he does not rule because of power proper to himself, but through the consent of a perverse will that desires to give its consent to the devil, according to what Gregory says: "The enemy is weak against those who resist, but strong against those who consent."[23] So "to put into" is used in the sense of "to suggest" or "to enkindle."

15. Question 3 asks why only Peter resisted the Lord when he wanted to wash his feet and why all the rest said nothing. And if all the others remained silent, why did he want to be unique? – If you say, that the Lord came to him first, and he, as the first, resisted and that afterwards the others were rebuked, the text is against this opinion, for John 13:5 says: "He began to wash ... and to dry"[24] and afterwards John 13:6 reads: "So he came to Simon Pe_ter."[25] – Chrysostom answers that he believes that he first

---

[22] See Book II, d. 8. p. II. q. 4 and 5 of Bonaventure's *Sentence Commentary*. See Augustine, Tractate 55 n. 4: "This putting is a spiri_tual suggestion."

[23] See Book V, c. 22 n. 43 of *Moralia in Iob* in CCSL 143, p. 248: "... just as the ancient enemy is strong against those who consent, so too is it weak against those who resist."

[24] The Vulgate reads *extergere* ("to dry") whereas Bonaventure has *tergere* ("to dry").

[25] See Augustine, Tractate 56 n. 1 in FC 90, p. 9: "For these words of the Gospel are rather easily so understood because when it was said, 'He began to wash the feet of his disciples and to dry them with the towel he had tied around himself,' then it was conjoined, 'He comes to Simon Peter,' as if he had already washed some and after them had come to the first. For who would not know that the first of the Apostles

washed the feet of Judas, because he, as a presumptuous individual, had anticipated Jesus' action. And afterwards he came to Peter, and he resisted.[26] – But what the Glossa states is to be considered better: He first came to Peter, and what was said was by means of anticipation.[27]

John 13:12-20
Christ exhorts his disciples to imitate him

16. *So after he had washed their feet*, etc. After he had given them an example, *he exhorts them to imitate him* and does so in the following fashion. First out of consideration of *the dignity of the Master*. Second out of consideration of *the greatness of the reward*. Third out of consideration of *the excellence of the merit*.

Verse 12. So he exhorts them through a consideration of the dignity of the Master: Since he as Master and Lord has done this, they too must do it. And so once he had risen up as their minister, he then began to instruct them as their teacher. And so he puts his clothes back on and asks for their attention. For this reason the text states: *So after he had washed their feet, he put on*[28] *his clothes*,

---

was the most blessed Peter? But one must not so understand that after some he came to him, but that he began from him.... And then Peter trembled in fear at what each of them would also have trembled at...."

[26] See Homily 70 n. 2 in PG 59:383 and FC 41, p. 255: "It seems to me that He first washed the traitor's feet, and came next to Peter, and that the rest were instructed by his example.... Even if Peter was first in rank, it is likely that the traitor was forward and took his place at table ahead of the leader."

[27] On p. 427 n. 7 QuarEd cites the Glossa Interlinearis: "Not after the others, but first he came to the prince of the Apostles. Therefore, he was terrified that God would wash a human's feet...."

[28] On p. 427 n. 8 QuarEd correctly indicate that the Vulgate reads *et accepit* ("and put on") while Bonaventure has *accepit* ("put on").

that is, those he has taken off so that he might minister to them, *and when he had reclined again, he said to them: Do you know what I have done for you*? He prompts them to be eager and attentive, since he has to teach them as their Teacher. And it is his teaching that they should imitate. So the text continues:

17. (Verse 13). *You call me Master and Lord, and you say well, for so I am*. For he is Master. Matthew 23:8 says: "One is your Master, the Christ." He is also Lord, for David called him his Lord in Psalm 109:1: "The Lord said to my Lord: Sit at my right hand."

18. (Verse 14). *Therefore, if I, the Lord and Master, have washed your feet, you also ought to wash the feet of one another*, Philippians 2:3-5 reads: "In humility let each one regard the others as his superiors.... Have this mind in you which was also in Christ Jesus," etc. And the reason for this is added: Because he did this, so that he might be imitated. For he performed miracles which is something we cannot imitate, because he did not perform them as an example, but as an indication of his power. He also performed works of humility to be imitated such as here. Thus:

19. (Verse 15). *I have given you an example,*[29] *that as I have done for you, so you also should do.*[30] Matthew 11:29 reads: "Learn from me, for I am meek and humble of heart." And

---

[29] On p. 427 n. 11 QuarEd rightly notice that the Vulgate reads *Exemplum enim dedi* ("For I have given an example") whilst Bonaventure has *Exemplum dedi* ("I have given an example").

[30] See Chrysostom, Homily 71 n. 1in FC 41, p. 260: "Therefore what is the meaning of 'so'? He meant: 'with the same zeal.' That is why He selected His examples from matters of greater importance: namely, that we might at least accomplish the lesser ones. I say this for teachers write the letters for children very beautifully, so that they may attain to at least an imperfect imitation."

he gives the following reason why he is to be imitated in works of humility: The servant is not greater than his Lord. Therefore, if the lord does not refuse humiliation, much less his servant. And this is what he says:

20. (Verse 16). *Amen, amen, I say to you*, as something true and certain: *No servant is greater than his lord, nor is the one sent greater than the one who sent him.* Matthew 10:24 reads: "No disciple is above his teacher."[31] And John 15:20 states: "No servant is greater than his lord." And therefore, all Christ's servants must serve their fellow servants. Therefore, it is customary for the Pope to write that he is "the servant of the servants of God."[32] For Chrysostom observes: "Where are those who despise their fellow servants? Where are those who seek honors? The Lord washed the feet of the traitor, who was engaged in sacrilege and theft at the time of his betrayal, and you yearn for great things and to be lifted on high?"[33]

21. (Verse 17.) *If you know these things*, etc. Here in a second point he exhorts them to imitate him by a consideration of the greatness of the reward, since those who do this will be blessed. For this reason the text continues: *If you know these things, you will be blessed if you do them.* Not if you know them only, but rather if you do them. James 1:25 reads: "The one who is a doer of the work is the one who will be blessed in his work." Matthew 5:19 has: "The person who does away with one of these least commandments and so teaches men and women, will be called least in the kingdom of heavens. But the person

---

[31] Hugh of St. Cher, p. 366v,u also cites Matt 10:24.

[32] On p. 428 n. 1 QuarEd state that Gregory the Great was the first Pope to use this title of himself.

[33] See Homily 71 n. 1 in PG 59:386. Bonaventure's citation is not verbatim. Hugh of St. Cher, p. 366v, s has the selfsame quotation from Chrysostom.

who does them and teaches them, this one will be called great in the kingdom of the heavens." And he had promised them beatitude, but lest you think that he promised it to his traitor, he adds:

22. (Verse 18). *But I do not speak of all,*[34] that is, that you are blessed, but of the elect. For he says: *I know whom I have chosen.* Matthew 20:16 states: "Many are called, but few are chosen." 2 Timothy 2:19 reads: "The Lord knows who are his own." So what I said, "Blessed are you," is to be understood of some of you and of many. *But that the Scripture might be fulfilled, the person who eats bread with me,*[35] that is, a table companion, *has lifted up his heel against me*, as Psalm 40:10 says. According to the other translation: "A person who was at peace with me, in whom I trusted, who ate my food, plotted treachery against me." Now *to lift up the heel*, as Chrysostom says, is to mount kicks, deceit and fraud and hidden snares.[36] And he is speaking by means of similitude: Just as a person, when he wants to tread upon a thing, lifts his heel against it, so too has Judas lifted up his heel against Christ. And he said this of Judas, not to accuse him, but to instruct his disciples, lest they might believe that he was handed over as a mere human being. So the text adds:

23. (Verse 19). *I tell you now before it comes to pass that when it has come to pass, you may believe that I am*, that is, God, who knows all things, before they come to pass.

---

[34] On p. 428 n. 4 QuarEd correctly indicate that the Vulgate reads *omnibus vobis* ("all of you") while Bonaventure has *omnibus* ("all").

[35] On p. 428 n. 5 QuarEd accurately mention that the Vulgate reads *adimpleatur* ("might be fulfilled") whilst Bonaventure has *impleatur* ("might be fulfilled").

[36] See Homily 71 n. 2 in PG 59:387: "He did not say: He betrays me, but *He has lifted his heel against me* to declare his deceit and hidden snares." Hugh of St. Cher, p. 367i cites Chrysostom in much the same way as Bonaventure does.

Sirach 23:29 has: "All things were known to the Lord God, before they were created," etc.

24. (Verse 20). *Amen, amen, I say to you.* Here he touches his third point as he exhorts them to imitate him in the honor granted his servants by a consideration of the greatness of the merit. For persons receive great merit who honor the Lord, and the Lord himself considers honor rendered his servant honor rendered him. And the person who honors Christ's servant has such great merit. Therefore, the text says: *The person who receives the person I send, receives me,* that is, the person who honors the one sent honors me the one who sends. Matthew 25:40 reads: "As long as you did it to one of my least, you did it to me." *And the person who receives me receives the one who sent me,* that is, the person who honors the Son honors the Father, who sent him. In Matthew 10:40 something similar is said: "The person who receives you receives me, and the person who receives me receives the one who sent me." And from this it is made clear that just as it is a grave transgression to despise God, so too it is a great merit to honor God. So also to show honor to the servants of God.

Questions

25. Question 1 is: Why did the Lord give his disciples an example of humility rather than of some other virtue, since there are other excellent virtues. – It has to be maintained that the Lord recommended unity to his disciples above everything else. And since pride truly fractures unity, because "there are always contentions among the proud,"[37] and the disciples were contending "who of

---

[37] See Prov 13:10.

them was reputed to the greatest,"[38] he gave them an example of humility so that each one might be subject to the other, lest through their contention the unity of the Church be rent asunder.[39] – Another reason is that since damnation had its origin in pride, salvation might thus have its origin in humility.

26. Question 2 focuses on John 13:18: "I do not speak of all. I know whom I have chosen." – Contrary to this is what is said in John 6:71 above: "Have I not chosen you, the Twelve?" If he chose twelve, Judas was chosen. And now he is speaking contrary to what he said earlier. – I answer that it has to be held that he was chosen to a present dignity. And in this manner Judas was chosen, just as evil bishops and prelates are chosen, not through error, but through wondrous dispensation. There is also a choosing to a eternal solemnity. And in this manner Judas was not chosen, since this state pertains to those who are good to the end.[40]

27. Question 3 addresses John 13:20: "The person who receives the one I send receives me." – 1. According to this the person who honors the messenger honors the one who sent him. Therefore, just as "the honor paid to the image redounds to the original,"[41] so too the honor given the

---

[38] See Luke 22:24.

[39] See Chrysostom, Homily 70 n. 1-2 in FC 41, pp. 261-262: "They were presently going to enjoy honor: some of them more, some less. Therefore, in order that they might not magnify themselves at the expense of one another, and say again what they said before this: 'Who is greater?' and that they might not wax indignant toward one another, He took down the pride of all of them by declaring: 'Even if you are very great, you ought not to lord it over your brother.'"

[40] See John 6 n. 100 above.

[41] See *De fide orthodoxa*, c. 89 in *Saint John Damascene, De fide orthodoxa*. Versions of Burgundio and Cerbanus. Edited by Eligius M. Buytaert, Franciscan Institute Publications, Text Series No. 8 (St. Bo-

messenger redounds to the Lord. Wherefore, if we must adore the image of Christ with the adoration of service to God, so too must we adore the messengers of Christ with the same adoration. – 2. The same thing seems to be found in John 5:23 where one finds a similar expression: "The person who honors him honors the Father who sent him."[42] And both are to be honored with the same honor.

I answer that it has to be maintained that the honor to be paid anyone is twofold: either as an object or as a goal. So I say that the honor paid to an image refers to the original as to an object, since stone is not honored, but God. And the honor paid to the one sent redounds to the sender with regard to motive and goal. And since people do not honor the one sent except on account of the sender, and consequently do not honor the one sent as an object, since from their action God regards himself as honored or dishonored, so the image is to be adored with the adoration of service to God while the messenger is to be adored with the adoration of service.[43] – 2. With regard to the objection based on a similar expression, it has to be said that the expressions are not completely similar, for in John 5:23 the issue is conformity of nature, but John 13:20 deals with conformity brought about by grace.

---

naventure, NY: Franciscan Institute, 1955), p. 331. See also Book IV, c. 16 in FC 37, pp. 370-371: "As the inspired Basil, who is deeply learned in theology says: 'the honor paid to the image redounds to the original,' and the original is the thing imaged from which the copy is made."

[42] John 5:23 says: "The person who does not honor the Son does not honor the Father who sent him."

[43] Bonaventure makes a distinction between *adoratio latriae* ("adoration of service to God") and *adoratio duliae* ("adoration of service"). See Deferrari, p. 36. See Book III, d. 9 a. 1 q. 2-5 of Bonaventure's *Sentence Commentary*.

JOHN 13:21-30
PERVERSITY OF JUDAS

28. *When Jesus had said these things, he was troubled.*
After an example has been given and the disciples have
been exhorted to imitate it, these verses present the third
part of the chapter, in which the Lord shows *the perversity of Judas* to turn aside. And he accomplishes this in
the following order. First there is *a general hint of a traitor*. Second follows *the hesitant questioning of the disciples*. Third is *the secret response of the Lord*. Fourth is *the
haste of the traitor*.

Verse 21. So the first point is a general hint of a traitor,
and although it is in general, there is no doubt, but certainty. And the fact that Christ was troubled manifests
this. For this reason the text continues: *When Jesus had
said these things*, namely, those that pertain to the instruction of the disciples, *he was troubled in spirit*, that
is, in his will.[44] *And he solemnly said*, because he asserted
this most certainly: *Amen, amen, I say to you that one of
you will betray me*. That is, that one would betray him.
About this one John 6:71 says: "One of you is a devil."

29. (Verse 22). *So the disciples looked at one another.* This
verse introduces the second point, that is, the questioning by the disciples. And first they began to doubt. For
this reason the text states: *So the disciples looked at one
another, uncertain of whom he was speaking*. Therefore,
they were looking at one another, since one disciple had
doubts about another. Augustine comments: "While there
was devoted love in them toward their Teacher, nonetheless, human weakness spurred between them, one about

---

[44] See Bonaventure's lengthy discussion about the similar phrase
of John 11:33 in John 11 n. 56 above.

the other."⁴⁵ And since doubt leads to questioning, and questioning demands intimate friendship, the friendship of John is shown, so that the questioning might be done through him. So the text says:

30. (Verse 23). *Now one of his disciples was reclining at Jesus' bosom*, as the best friend among the others, and this was the result of the privilege of love. *Whom Jesus loved*. This disciple was John, for Chrysostom observes: "Look at the ingloriousness of John, for he did not give his name, but says *whom Jesus loved*, as the Apostle in 2 Corinthians 12:2 says: *I know a man*."⁴⁶ He did not say: "I know Paul." So this disciple who was such a friend was the most fitting person to question Jesus. For this reason the text states:

31. (Verse 24). *So Simon Peter beckoned to him and said to him: Who is it, of whom he is speaking?* As if he were saying: Ask him. Peter was always eager to ask questions by himself or through others. At Peter's request that disciple asks:

32. (Verse 25). *So as he was leaning back upon the bosom of Jesus*, as beloved and familiar and close friend, which is a sign of love. The Song of Songs 8:5 reads: "Who is this, who comes up from the desert, flowing with delights, leaning upon her beloved?" *He said to him: Lord, who is it?* Supply: the one who will betray you. He leans upon Jesus' breast, so that he might hear the secret, because in him were "hidden all the treasures of wisdom and knowl-

---

⁴⁵ See Tractate 61 n. 3 in CCSL xxxvi, p. 481 and FC 90, p. 34. Bonaventure's citation is almost verbatim.

⁴⁶ See Homily 72 n. 1 in PG 59:390. Bonaventure's quotation is not verbatim.

edge."[47] For Augustine says of John: "He drank the rivers of the Gospel from the very foundation of the Lord's breast."[48]

33. (Verse 26). *Jesus answered* him. The third point occurs here, namely, the secret response of the Lord, by which he satisfies the request of his closest disciple. For this reason he did not say who it was in words, but revealed who it was by the sign itself. So the text continues: *It is he for whom I*[49] *will dip the bread and give it to him.* The dipping of the bread signifies the dissimulation of Judas.[50] *And when he had dipped the bread, he gave it to Judas Iscariot, the son of Simon,* and by this John knew who it was who would betray him. Augustine notes: "The bread offered to the traitor is a demonstration of grace, for which the traitor was ungrateful."[51] For in Psalm 54:13-15 there is complaint of the ingratitude of Judas: "If my enemy had reviled me, I would truly have borne it.... But you, a person of one mind with me, my guide, and my intimate friend, who did partake of the best of foods with me," etc.

---

[47] See Col 2:3: "in whom are hidden all the treasures of wisdom and knowledge."

[48] See the Prooemium n. 4 where Bonaventure cites the same passage from "Augustine." This citation is not so much from Augustine as it is from the responsory to the second and eighth readings at Matins in the Roman Liturgy for the Feast of St. John the Evangelist on December 27.

[49] On p. 430 n. 5 QuarEd rightly notice that the Vulgate reads *ego* ("I") while Bonaventure does not.

[50] See Hugh of St. Cher, p. 367v,p: "The dipping of the bread signifies the dissimulation of Judas, who came to the meal under the guise of a friend." See Augustine, Tractate 62 n. 3 in FC 90, p. 39: "... the Lord most openly exposes his traitor through the morsel dipped and proffered, perhaps signifying through the dipping of the bread that man's pretence."

[51] See Tractate 62 n. 1 in CCSL xxxvi, p. 483. The citation is not verbatim.

34. (Verse 27). *And after the morsel.* The fourth point arises here, namely, the haste of the traitor, which was effected by the vehement infestation of the devil, which he had in Judas after he had turned against Jesus. For this reason the text states: *And after the morsel Satan entered into him,* so that he might more efficaciously possess him and might more quickly consummate the iniquity that had been planned. For Psalm 108:6 reads: "Set the sinner over him, and may the devil stand at his right hand." *And,* since he did not hide this from the Lord, *Jesus said to him: What you do, do quickly.* He was speaking in a predictive mood, not in an imperative one.[52] But lest it might seem that his iniquity had been uncovered, the Evangelist shows that this word escaped all. So he says:

35. (Verse 28). *But none of those reclining at table understood what*[53] *he said to him,* not even John himself, who already knew of his iniquity. For Chrysostom comments: "It was not characteristic of a gracious and meek mind to suspect evil of another."[54] Rather, on the contrary, they interpreted others' actions as good. So the text continues:

36. (Verse 29). *For some thought that since Judas held the purse,* as its dispenser, *that Jesus had said to him:*

---

[52] See Augustine, Tractate 62 n. 4 in FC 90, p. 39: "He did not foreordain a crime, but foretold an evil for Judas, a good for us." See Chrysostom, Homily 72 n. 2 in FC 41, p. 272: "However, the words, 'Do quickly,' were not spoken as a command or as advice, but in reproof, and to show that Christ Himself wished him to mend his ways."

[53] On p. 430 n. 9 QuarEd accurately mention that the Vulgate reads *ad quid* ("why") whereas Bonaventure has *quid* ("what").

[54] See Homily 72 n. 2 in PG 59:391 and FC 41, p. 273: "Not even he (John), for he could not have supposed that a disciple would come to such a pitch of wickedness. Indeed, since they themselves were far removed from such evil-doing they could not even suspect such things of others."

Buy the things that are necessary[55] *for the feast* or that he should give something to the poor, for it was especially for these purposes that he had the purse.[56] In this is signified that it is legitimate for prelates to buy from the purse of the Church "what is needed," that is, the things that are necessary and to give the rest to the poor. And to these a special commandment is given to support the poor, for Sirach 29:12 states: "Because of the commandment help the poor person, and do not send him away empty handed because of his penury." And as the devil had suggested and Christ had predicted, Judas hastened off. So the text states:

37. (Verse 30). *So when he*[57] *had received the morsel, he went out quickly*, so that he might rapidly fulfill his deed. And the time fit the deed. *Now it was night.* Job 24:15 reads: "The eye of the adulterer looks for darkness." And John 3:20 above says: "Those who do evil hate the light."

QUESTIONS

38. Question 1 inquires about the Lord's being troubled, since John 13:21 reads: "He was disturbed in spirit." If all things were at peace in Christ, since he is signified through Noah's ark, in which all things were at peace,

---

[55] On p. 430 n. 10 QuarEd accurately mention that the Vulgate has *nobis* ("for us"). Bonaventure does not.

[56] See Chrysostom, Homily 72 n.2 in FC 41, pp. 273-274: "But how is it that He who bade them to carry neither wallet, nor money, nor staff, provided a purse for the service of the poor? He did so that you might learn that, though He was very poor and destined to be crucified besides, He had to concern Himself a great deal about this matter. Indeed, He did many things to provide for our instruction."

[57] On p. 431 n. 1 QuarEd correctly indicate that the Vulgate reads *ille* ("he"). Bonaventure does not.

how was he troubled in spirit?[58] – And it has to be said that this disturbance created no inordinate movement in Christ, since his sensuality was subjected to his will and he was voluntarily troubled. In witness of this the text reads: "He was troubled in his spirit."

39. Question 2 pursues the issue further: About what was his sensuality disturbed? – If the answer is given that he was troubled about his future death, then this is nothing, for that did not proceed into his senses, because it was future. Since it was future, it did not proceed into his sensuality. Therefore, his sensuality was not sorrowful about this. – It has to be maintained that death was being imagined in the interior sense, not proceeding from the senses, but issuing from the knowledge of reason. For when we have prior knowledge of something, we can imagine it, and through this imagination that we consider certain we can be troubled. – And if you object that this order is irregular, there are some who hold that there was no impediment to this order in Christ, in whom the inferior powers were subject to the superior. – But one doesn't have to say this, since the order would only be irregular, if the intelligible species would issue into the senses and would become sensible. But when the species are in the imagination and the reason considers and does something, then the same thing that has become sensitive in the imagination can frighten a person. In this instance there is no irregular order.[59]

---

[58] See Book III, d. 17. a. 1 q. 3 of Bonaventure's *Sentence Commentary* in Omnia Opera 3:369: "In whom (Christ) all rational movements were righteous and all movements of sensuality at peace, according to what Augustine says: This was signified by the animals in Noah's ark which were quietly at peace." On p. 369 n. 1 QuarEd indicate that they have not found this interpretation in Augustine.

[59] See Book III, d. 15. dub. 4 of Bonaventure's *Sentence Commentary*.

40. Question 3 continues the questioning: Since Christ from the beginning knew of his death as he does now, why wasn't he always troubled about it as he is now? – The answer has to be that knowledge of death was not the total reason for his being troubled. Rather it was knowledge of his imminent death. Thus, nature is more frightened by an imminent danger than by one that is distant. But still this is not the total reason, but knowledge of imminent death with his willingness to be disturbed. And he willed this at the present time, in order to show that he was truly human.[60]

41. Question 4 asks about the disciples' questioning. – 1. So why is it that the disciples dared to ask about a hidden sin? – This seems to stem from curiosity. – 2. And it is also asked: Since Peter was the most audacious of all the disciples, why didn't he ask by himself, but asked "through an intermediary,"[61] namely, John? For almost always it is Peter who answers for all the disciples.[62]

It has to be said that the disciples were not asking out of curiosity about knowing the sin of their neighbor, but because each one of them, as Chrysostom observes, was fearful of himself and was being tormented by that fear. They wanted to be certain. And since they knew that the Lord was not speaking openly, they themselves did not want to disturb him openly. Rather they asked in a roundabout way, and the response was given to them in a

---

[60] See Augustine, Tractate 60 n. 2 in FC 90, p. 29: "Such immense power is troubled, the strength of the Rock is troubled. Or is it rather that our weakness is troubled in him?… The very same one who died for us was troubled for us."

[61] The same Latin expression, *per interpositam personam*, occurs in c. 4 of the 1223 Rule of St. Francis.

[62] See John 6 n. 110 where Bonaventure interprets John 6:69 and Peter as the disciples' spokesperson.

roundabout way.[63] – 2. And so Peter did not speak up, but pointed to him who was near the Lord and could secretly ask, for he was reclining upon Jesus' breast and could also ask secretly whereas Peter could not do so.[64]

42. Question 5 asks about the Lord's response in John 13:26: "It is he for whom I will dip the bread and give it to him." – It seems that the Lord betrayed Judas. – To this Chrysostom comments that the Lord gave dipped bread to everyone.[65] But then it is first asked: What sign would it have been to John that he would be the one "for whom I will dip the bread and give it to him"? – Second, it is said in Matthew 26:22-25: "Each began to say: Is it I, Lord.... And Judas, who betrayed him, answered: Is it I, Rabbi?" And it is said in Matthew 26:25 that the Lord's response was: "You have said it." Wherefore, it seems that the Lord openly revealed him and that not only by sign, but also by word.

---

[63] See Homily 72 n. 1 in PG 59:389-390 and FC 41, p. 269: "Once again He struck them all with terror by not mentioning the traitor by name. Moreover, some were in doubt, even though they were conscious of no wrongdoing, for they considered Christ's statement more to be trusted than their own reason. And that is why they looked at one another. Therefore, by limiting their entire matter of His betrayal to one man He reduced their fear, but by adding 'One of you" he disturbed them all."

[64] See Chrysostom, Homily 72 n. 2 in FC 41, p. 272: "I say this for John leaned back on His bosom for the purpose and asked the question practically in His ear, so that the traitor was not revealed. Furthermore, Christ replied in the same way, and so, not even then did He made him known."

[65] On p. 431 n. 10 QuarEd indicate that they have not found this opinion in Chrysostom. See Hugh of St. Cher, p. 367v,p: "But it is asked that it seems according to this that the Lord betrayed the identity of Judas.... But this is solved according to certain authors in this that in offering bread to him, he did not betray him, since he acted similarly with the others."

I answer that it has to be said that the Lord revealed who his traitor was, but not to all, but to some disciples and did so secretly. Now he revealed to John who the traitor was for a twofold reason, for he was suffering with him in his desolation[66] and he would be the witness that Christ had certain foreknowledge and was not speculating who the disciple was who would betray him. – As to the point that the name of the sinner should be betrayed, it has to be understood that the name is not to be broadcast about. But nonetheless, it can be mentioned to those who can benefit from the information and would be at a disadvantage without it.[67] – 2. With regard to what Matthew 26:22-25 says, it has to be said that this particular word of the Lord, as Augustine states in his *Harmony of the Gospels*, provides no certain and definite meaning.[68] When the Lord said: "You have said it," it's as if he had said: Not I, but you have said it. – Another interpretation can be that the Lord spoke to him in such a way that nobody else understood it. – So what Matthew narrates was spoken first, and since Peter and John were not certain of its meaning, John secretly asked about it.

43. Question 6 focuses on John 13:27: "After the morsel Satan entered into him." – 1. It seems that the Lord

---

[66] See Chrysostom, Homily 72 n. 1 in FC 41, p. 271: "But why did he lean on His bosom? They did not yet have any suspicion of His great dignity; besides, He was in this way soothing their troubled spirits.... If they were troubled in their souls, much more would their faces reveal this. Well, then, to put them at their ease, He prepared the way both for His own statement, and for the disciple's question, by permitting him to rest on His bosom."

[67] There is a slight parallel in what Bonaventure says about Luke 22:23 (n. 33) in *Gospel of Luke, Chapters 17-24*, p. 2059: "But the Lord preferred that all might be troubled rather than that Judas's name might be revealed. He did this to give a model that hidden sins are not to be blithely publicized.... For that, which is revealed out of charity to safeguard a prelate and to avoid danger, is not considered public."

[68] See Book III, c. 1, n.2-3.

did not do well in giving the morsel to Judas, because through it there was a wretched effect. – 2. Furthermore, what is the reason for saying "after the morsel"? – 3. It also seems to be speaking a falsehood, since, as Augustine states, only God enter into the soul.[69] And therefore, Satan does not. – 4. Moreover, earlier the text stated that the devil had put it into the heart of Judas.[70] So why now "after the morsel"?

I answer. There are diverse opinions about these matters. Some were of the opinion that the bread that had been dipped was the body of Christ. And this is what the Master maintains in his *Histories*.[71] That is why we do not receive communion by intinction. And it seems that Augustine says this in his original text: "Why do you wonder," he says, "if there was given to Judas the bread of Christ, by which he is subjected to the devil, since you see on the opposite side there was given to the Apostle an angel of the devil by whom he makes progress in Christ?"[72] And therefore, they say that it is then that Satan entered him,

---

[69] See *De ecclesiasticis dogmatibus*, Liber Gennadio tributus, c. 50 in PL 42:1221: "Now to enter the soul is the sole prerogative of the one who created it...."

[70] See John 13:2: "And during the supper, the devil having already put it into the heart of Judas Iscariot, the son of Simon, to betray him...."

[71] See Peter Comestor, *Historia scholastica, In Evangelia*, c. 151 in PL 198:1617C: "He gave the intincted morsel to Judas. From this it follows that the Eucharist is not given by intinction."

[72] See Homily 62 n. 1 in CCSL xxxvi, p. 483 where the text reads *Paulo* ("to Paul") whereas Bonaventure has *Apostolo* ("to the Apostle"). It also reads *perficeretur* ("was perfected") while Bonaventure has *proficeret* ("makes progress"). and FC 90, p. 38. Augustine is referring to 2 Cor 12:7.

since he unworthily received the body of Christ and ate and drank judgment upon himself.[73]

Some have a different viewpoint, and I believe that it is better. It is the opinion of the Glossa: The bread that was intincted or dipped was not the body of Christ.[74] Rather, as Augustine says in his *Harmony of the Gospels*, the body of Christ had already been distributed to the disciples, and Judas, along with the others, had consumed it.[75] Rather it was a different bread, and after Judas had consumed it, Satan entered him, since, having been spurred to repent in so many ways, he did not repent. Thus the devil took more full possession of him.[76] – 3. With respect to the objection that God alone enters the soul. That is true, and God does so by penetration, but the devil by suggestion.[77] – 4. With regard to the objection that the devil had earlier suggested betrayal, it has to be maintained that this is true. But from that time he assaulted him on all sides and more vehemently impelled him to fully get the evil deed done.

---

[73] See 1 Cor 11:29: "For the person who eats and drinks unworthily, without distinguishing the body, eats and drinks judgment upon himself."

[74] See the Glossa Ordinaria in PL 114:406B.

[75] See Book III, c. 1 n. 4.

[76] See Augustine, Tractate 62 n. 3 in FC 90, p. 38: "After this bread, then Satan entered into the Lord's betrayer in order that, after he was delivered over to him, he might possess more fully him into whom he had already entered in order to deceive."

[77] See Book II, d. 8 p. II q. 2, 4, and 5 in Bonaventure's *Sentence Commentary*.

John 13:31-38
Weakness of the disciples

44. *So when he had gone out*, etc. After the perversity of Judas has been shown in his turning away from the Lord, *the weakness of the disciples* in following the Lord is demonstrated. And this is the fourth part of the chapter, and the Evangelist fashions it in this order. First, the future *passion of Christ* is foretold. Second, *the imperfection of the disciples*. Third, *the instruction for those who are imperfect*. Fourth *the presumption of Peter is censured*.

Verse 31. So first the future passion of Christ is foretold, and through his passion his *glorification*, which was moving forward once his betrayer had hastened to do his deed. For this reason the text states: *So when he had gone out*, namely, Judas, to bring to fruition what he had conceived, *Jesus said:*[78] *Now is the Son of Man glorified*. He says "now" because his passion is at hand, through which he was to be raised on high. Philippians 2:8-9 reads: "He humbled himself.... Therefore, God also exalted him." *And God is glorified in him,*[79] since through Christ God became known to all. John 17:6 says: "Father, I have manifested your name to the men and women you have given me out of the world."[80]

---

[78] The Vulgate reads *dicit* ("says") whilst Bonaventure has *dixit* ("said").

[79] On p. 433 n. 4 QuarEd rightly notice that the Vulgate reads *in eo* ("in him") while Bonaventure has *in illo* ("in him").

[80] *Pater* ("Father") does not occur in John 17:6. Bonaventure carries this address over from John 17:5.

45. (Verse 32). *And*[81] *if God is glorified in him,*[82] in his passion through a great manifestation of power, since his death and passion were extraordinary manifestations for God's glory, as it is said of Peter in John 21:19 below: "Signifying by what manner of death he would glorify God." *God will also glorify him in himself*, through the glory of the resurrection, *and will glorify him at once*, because he could not delay his resurrection. For Psalm 15:10 says: "You will not give your Holy One to see corruption." And he wants to say that Christ was to be immediately glorified by his Father through resurrection, because he had to endure the passion in order to manifest the glorification of the Father. So the weakness of Christ as human glorified God. And therefore, the power of God raised up and glorified Christ who had died.[83]

46. (Verse 33). *Little children, yet a little while*, etc. This verse introduces the second point, namely, the imperfection of the disciples in following Christ. Therefore, he calls them "little children," that is, weak in faith, since strong faith makes people "children" whereas weak faith makes them "little children."[84] – Another interpretation is that "little children" is used out of tender love, for Priscianus maintains that the diminutive sometimes bespeaks famil-

---

[81] On p. 433 n. 5 QuarEd accurately indicate that the Vulgate does not read *Et* ("And").

[82] On p. 433 n. 5 QuarEd correctly mention that the Vulgate reads *in eo* ("in him") whereas Bonaventure has *in illo* ("in him").

[83] See Augustine, Tractate 63 n. 3 in FC 90, p. 45: "That is, 'if God is glorified in him,' because he did not come to do his own will but the will of him who sent him, 'God also will glorify him in himself,' so that the human nature in which he is the Son of Man, which had been taken on by the eternal Word, may also be endowed with immortal eternity."

[84] See Book 32 n. 368 of Origen, *Commentary on the Gospel according to John* in FC 89, p. 411: "The diminutive is significant, I think, and teaches the smallness of the apostles' soul even at that time."

iarity and love,[85] as in the expression "Sergiolus" or "little Sergius."[86] So he reveals their imperfection when he adds: *Yet a little while I am with you*, through my bodily presence, *and as I said to the Jews* – in John 7 and 8 above[87] *– you will seek me. Where I go you cannot come. To you I say now*.[88] The reason is that you cannot endure the arduousness of the passion. Indeed they could not, for they had not received power from on high. Thus it is said to them in Luke 24:49: "Wait in the city until you are clothed with power from on high," since without the strength of this power it is impossible to stand in battle.[89]

47. (Verse 34). *I give you a new commandment.* Here is the third part, that is, instruction for the imperfect disciples. And since they were imperfect, the Lord gives them the remedy of love, so that they might love one another and be sustained by one another. For this reason the text states: *I give you a new commandment that you love one another*. So it is "new," because it must always be fresh in one's heart and because love must always be owed and

---

[85] On p. 433 n. 7 QuarEd quote from Book III, c. 5 of Priscianus' *Institutiones grammaticae*: "But diminutives are customarily used either for the sake of necessary signification ... or affability ... or adulation and especially with regard to little boys. Examples are Catulaster, Antoniaster, Patritiolus, Sergiolus."

[86] In Latin "little child" is *filiolus*. In Latin "little Sergius" is *Sergiolus*.

[87] See John 7:34: "You will seek me and will not find me, and where I am you cannot come" and John 8:21: "So again Jesus said to them: I go, and you will seek me, and in your sin you will die. Where I go you cannot come."

[88] On p. 433 n. 8 QuarEd rightly notice that Bonaventure has changed the word order of the Vulgate. I translate: "You will seek me, and, as I said to the Jews: Where I go you cannot come. And I say to you now." See Augustine, Tractate 64 n. 4 in FC 90, p. 48: "But when he said this to the Jews, he did not add 'now.' And so these men could not then come where he was going, but they could later on; for a little later he says this quite openly to the Apostle Peter."

[89] Hugh of St. Cher, p. 369d also cites Luke 24:49.

never grow old. For Romans 13:8 reads: "Owe no one any-thing except to love one another." And he gives expression to the manner of love: *That as I have loved you, you also love one another.* Now he loved in such a way that he loved our salvation more than his own life. So too each person should love the life of his neighbor more than his own body. 1 John 3:16 says: "In this we have come to know the love of God,[90] that he laid down his life for us, and we should lay down our life for our brothers and sisters." And he adds the reason that moves one to love:

48. (Verse 35). *By this will all people know that you are my disciples if you have love for one another*, since, as Augustine says: "Love is the proper and special virtue of the merciful and of the saints.[91] It is the means by which one distinguishes the children of the kingdom from the children of perdition."[92] Ephesians 4:30 reads: "Do not grieve the Holy Spirit of God, in whom you were sealed for the day of redemption." Now this sealing of the Spirit is love. Romans 5:5 states: "The love of God has been poured out into our hearts through the Holy Spirit who has been given to us."

49. (Verse 36). *Simon Peter said to him.* The fourth point surfaces here, namely, the stifling of the presumption of Peter through which he offered to imitate the Lord. So Peter asks the Lord, so that he might offer himself: *Lord,*

---

[90] The Vulgate does not read *Dei* ("of God").

[91] This citation is based on Book I, n. 7 of Prosper of Aquitane, *Sententiae ex Augustino delibatae*. See PL 45:1859: "Love of God and neighbor is the proper and special virtue of the merciful and of the saints, since all the other virtues can be common to both good and evil people."

[92] This citation is based on Book XV, c. 18 n. 32 of *De Trinitate*. See CCSL la, p. 507: "Nothing is more excellent than this gift of God. It alone is what separates the children of the eternal kingdom from the children of eternal perdition."

where are you going? And since he wanted to offer himself, the Lord shows him his impotence, lest he rush ahead and say more: *Jesus said to him:*[93] *Where I am going, you cannot follow me now*, on account of your weakness, *but you will follow me later*, once you have been confirmed in strength. But Peter was not deterred by his admonition. So the text continues:

50. (Verse 37). *Peter answered him: Why can I not follow you?*[94] *I will lay down my life for you*. And this is perfect following. John 15:13 below states: "Greater love than this no one has that one lay down his life for his friends." Therefore, if I can do this, I can truly follow you. And since the Lord's admonition concerning Peter's weakness did not deter Peter from his presumption, now he is censured through the prediction of his future prevarication. For this reason the Lord resumes speaking to Peter, so that he might rebuke him:

51. (Verse 38). *Jesus answered him: Will you lay down your life for me*? Augustine comments: "Can you who are unable to follow go on ahead? ... What do you believe that you are? Listen to what you are."[95] *Amen, amen I say to you: The cock will not crow before you deny me three times*. Augustine observes: "You who promise me your death will thrice deny your Life. For as great a life as it is to confess

---

[93] On p. 434 n. 5 QuarEd accurately indicate that the Vulgate reads *Respondit Iesus* ("Jesus answered") while Bonaventure has *Dicit ei Iesus* ("Jesus said to him").

[94] On p. 434 n. 6 QuarEd correctly mention that the Vulgate reads *Dicit ei Petrus: Quare non possum te sequi modo?* ("Peter said to him: Why can I not follow you now?" while Bonaventure has *Respondit ei Petrus: Quare non possum sequi?* ("Peter answered him: Why can I not follow?").

[95] See Tractate 66 n. 1 in CCSL xxxvi, p. 493 and FC 90, p. 55.

Christ, so great a death it is to deny Christ. By fearing the death of your flesh, you will give death to your soul."[96]

QUESTIONS

52. Question 1 asks about the meaning of what was said first in this part in John 13:31: "Now is the Son of Man glorified." In his passion and Judas's betrayal he is more humiliated than glorified. – Augustine answers that this is said in a "sign," because in the going out of Judas only good people remained. And then his future glorification was signified in which God will be only with the good.[97] – It can also be said that he says this according to "merit," since in his passion he merited to be glorified and to the extent he was glorified he glorified the Lord.

53. Question 2 deals with John 13:33: "Where I am going, you cannot come." – Contra. 1. In John 12:26 above it was said: "If anyone serves me, let him follow me." Therefore, he was exhorting them to do the impossible. – 2. Likewise, Peter says in 1 Peter 2:21: "Christ suffered for us,[98] leaving you an example that you may follow in his steps." Therefore, he was giving an example to all. So why does he say: "You cannot come"?

---

[96] See Tractate 66 n. 1 in CCSL xxxvi, p. 493 and FC 90, p. 55. Bonaventure does not quote exactly.

[97] See Tractate 63 n. 2 in FC 90, pp. 44-45: "Therefore, just as Scripture is accustomed to speak, calling the things doing the signifying as if [they were] the things that are signified, so the Lord spoke, saying, 'Now the Son of Man is glorified.' When the most wicked one has been separated from them and his holy ones remain with him, his glorification has been signified when, after the separation of the wicked, he will remain forever with the saints."

[98] The Vulgate reads *pro vobis* ("for you") whilst Bonaventure has *pro nobis* ("for us").

To this the response has to be that just as "the possibility of believing" is taken in a twofold sense – in one way as one talks about its "possibility" and that pertains to nature, and the second way as one speaks of "an active power" and that pertains to grace – so too is "the possibility of imitating the passion" taken in a double meaning. The "imperfect possibility" is found in us whereas "the complete activation" comes through the power of the Holy Spirit. But the Apostles had not yet been clothed with that power.[99]

But contrary to this: Since with a minimum of love a person can resist whatever temptation there is, it, therefore, follows that if the Apostles had a minimum of love, they could have resisted temptation. – The response to this stems from a twofold opinion. Some say "from a minimum of love," not however "from a love that remains minimal," because love increases. And according to this opinion the problem is solved as before, that is, they could not resist with what they had. – I answer on the basis of the other opinion: They could from a minimum of love, but not easily. As a matter of fact, it would be exceedingly difficult. And therefore, few resist.[100]

54. Question 3 focuses on John 13:34: "I give you a new commandment," etc. – 1. Why didn't he command them to love God, which "is the first and highest commandment"?[101] 2. Furthermore, why does he say "new," because it was given from the very beginning? For 1 John 2:7, speaking of this commandment, says: "I am not writing

---

[99] The reference is to Luke 24:49.

[100] See Book III, d. 30. q. 1 in Bonaventure's *Sentence Commentary*.

[101] This is an allusion to Matt 22:38: "the greatest and the first commandment."

you a new commandment, but an old commandment…."[102]
– I answer that it has to be maintained relative to the
first objection that love of God is understood in love of
neighbor.[103] – Relative to the second objection it should be
said that even though this commandment was given in
the Old Testament, it was, nevertheless, renewed in the
New Testament with respect to its manner, since in the
OT one was commanded to love one's friends. In the NT
one is commanded to love one's enemies. In the OT one is
commanded to do good to one's friends whereas in the NT
one is commanded to do good to one's enemies. And this is
the import of what he adds: "As I have loved you."[104]

55. Question 4 addresses what the Lord said to Peter in
John 13:38: "You will deny me three times."[105] – From
this it seems that he revealed to Peter his sin and that
he forced Peter to despair. – I answer that it should be
said that there is a difference between "to predict" and
"to reveal." God does not make a revelation to anybody,
but, nonetheless, truly predicts, since what is revealed is
known with certitude, but what is predicted is not known
with certitude, for sometimes what has been said is believed because of a threat, but at other times it is believed
because of a condition. In this instance Peter understood

---

[102] Hugh of St. Cher, p. 368v, *g also cites 1 John 2:7.

[103] See Augustine, Tractate 65 n. 2 in FC 90, p. 52: "But to those
who understand well, both (commandments) are found in each. For
he who loves God cannot despise him when he teaches him to love his
neighbor; and he who loves his neighbor in a holy and spiritual way,
what does he love in him except God?"

[104] See Chrysostom, Homily 72 n. 3 in FC 41, p. 278: "He Himself
made it new by the way they were to love and to this end He added: 'as
I have loved you. For in loving you I have not been discharging a debt
to you for things already carried out by you, but it is I Myself who have
initiated the process,' He meant."

[105] This is actually Matt 26:34. John 13:38 reads: "Before you deny
me three times."

the Lord's words as a condition: If you do not watch yourself. And so he did not despair.[106]

---

[106] See Book II d. 4. a. 2. q. 2 ad 1 in Bonaventure's *Sentence Commentary*.

CHAPTER FOURTEEN

JOHN 14:1-16:33
THE LORD ENCOURAGES HIS DISCIPLES
BY THE WORD OF HIS INSTRUCTION

1. *And he said to his disciples.*[1] *Let not your heart be troubled*. Earlier the Lord encouraged his disciples by his example.[2] In this part he encourages them by *the word of his instruction*. This part comprises three chapters and is divided in a threefold manner. In the first section the Lord instructs them to be constant *in faith*. In the second to be constant *in love*, and this commences at the beginning of chapter 15: "I am the true vine." In the third to be constant *in the waiting of hope*, a little past the beginning of chapter 16: "But I did not tell you these things from the beginning."[3]

The first section, which consists of the present chapter, has three parts. In the first the Lord *exhorts the disciples to constant faith*. In the second, however, since "faith without works is dead,"[4] *he exhorts them to good works* where verse 15 reads: "If you love me, keep my commandments." While in the third *he foretells the imminence of*

---

[1] On p. 435 n. 8 QuarEd correctly indicate that "And he said to his disciples" is not found in the Vulgate.

[2] See John 13:1-38.

[3] Bonaventure is referring to John 16:5.

[4] See James 2:25: "For just as the body without the spirit is dead, so also faith without works is dead."

his departure where verse 25 states: "These things I have spoken to you while yet dwelling with you."

John 14:1-14
The Lord exhorts his disciples to constant faith

So first he exhorts his disciples that they not vacillate in faith because of his departure, as he shows them first *the manner* of his departure. Second, its *way*. Third, its *end* and fourth, its *fruit* or result.

Verse 1. So first he exhorts them that in considering the manner of his departure they be not troubled by his departure nor have weak faith, bur rather that they have strong faith. Therefore, he says: *Let not your heart be troubled*, but believe. Thus he continues: *You believe in God. Also believe in me.* Let your heart not be disturbed by my absence, but believe in me who will be absent, just as you believe in God, whom you do not see. And the reason why they must not be troubled, but believe is this: The Lord does not entirely depart from them, but precedes them, so that he may again assume them into the glory in which there are many mansions that have already been prepared according to eternal election, but still need preparation according to merit. Wherefore, the verb "to prepare," according to Augustine's exposition of this passage, is patient of these two meanings. So this passage should be read in this manner:[5]

---

[5] See Augustine, Tractate 68 n. 1 in FC 90, p. 63: "He who made things that are going to be does not prepare other dwelling-places, but those which he has prepared; those which he has prepared by predestining he prepares by working. Therefore they already are, with respect to predestination; if they were not, he would have said, 'I shall go and shall prepare,' that is, I shall predestine. But because they are not

2. (Verse 2). *In my Father's house there are many mansions*, namely, already prepared according to eternal election, for Ephesians 1:4 reads: "He chose us before the foundation of the world." Jerome comments: "Different mansions have been prepared in heaven for different virtues. Persons do not accept these mansions, but works do."[6] Thus, they have been prepared. *Were it not so*, that is, if it were not so. But Chrysostom reads a different phrase. Where it says "Were it not so," he reads: "If it were not so," that is, if they had not been prepared through predestination, *I would have told you, because I go to prepare a place for you*.[7] But it is impossible that I now prepare them, since it is impossible that I should again predestine someone, as Augustine says.[8] Therefore, I have said that "there are many mansions in my Father's house," already prepared by predestination, but they are still to be prepared by the merit of faith that has its greatest merit in my absence. So the text adds:

3. (Verse 3). *And if I go and prepare a place for you*, namely, through your faith while I am absent. For Augustine maintains: "Let the Lord Jesus go and prepare a place. Let him go that he may not be seen. Let him be concealed that he may be believed in. For then a place is being prepared, if a person lives by faith. Believed in, let him be de-

---

yet, with respect to working, 'And if I shall go,' he says, 'and prepare a place for you, I am coming again, and I shall take you to myself.'"

[6] Bonaventure slightly adjusts Book II, c. 28 of *Adversus Jovinianum*. See PL 23:339B.

[7] See Homily 73 n. 2 in PG 59:396.

[8] Bonaventure seems to be referring to Tractate 68 n. 1. See FC 90, p. 63: "He chose by predestining before the foundation of the world; he chose by calling before the consummation of the world. So also he has prepared and prepares dwelling-places. He who made things that are going to be does not prepare other dwelling-places, but those which he has prepared; those which he has prepared by predestining he prepares by working."

sired, so that, desired, he may be possessed. The desire of love is the preparing of the mansion."[9] After I have thus prepared a place for you while I am absent, *I am coming again and will take you to myself*, namely, through glory, *so that where I am, you also may be there*. John 12:26 above says: "If anyone serves me, let him follow me. And where I am, there, too, is my servant."[10] Therefore, he exhorts them to faith while he is absent, since he absents himself for this purpose that they may have the merit of faith. This is the way that Augustine[11] and the Glossa[12] interpret this text.

4. But this entire verse can be explained by another meaning of the verb "to prepare."[13] Thus the sense is: "Let not your heart be troubled," but believe in me, for "in my Father's house there are many mansions," in one of which you will rest with me. I prepare the way to them. Therefore, you should not be sad. But then you would have been

---

[9] See Tractate 68 n. 3 in CCSL xxxvi, p. 499 and FC 90, p. 65. Bonaventure's citation is virtually verbatim.

[10] The Vulgate reads *illic et minister meus erit* ("there, too, will my servant be") whilst Bonaventure has *ibi sit et minister meus* ("there, too, is my servant").

[11] See Augustine, Tractate 68.

[12] See the Glossa Ordinaria on John 14:3 in PL 114:407C: "Augustine. Faith that does not see believes, for if it would see…. The desire of love is the preparing of the mansion."

[13] See Hugh of St. Cher, p. 369v,k: "The mansions have already been prepared, as he had said, through predestination. But nonetheless, the doors have to be prepared by opening them and through meritorious works. Now Jerome against Jovinian the heretic reads the entire text above with one distinction. If there were not many mansions with my Father, I would have told you that I am going to prepare a place for you. That is, if each one would not have to prepare a mansion for himself from his own works, I would have told you that I am going to prepare a place for you. But it is not my task to prepare a place, but yours. And this is said in accordance with what Matthew 20:23 has: 'To sit at my right hand or at my left is not mine to give to you.'" For Jerome's opinion, see PL 23:339A.

sad. "Were it not so, I would have told you," that is, if I had not told you: "Because I go to prepare a place for you, I will again take you," etc.[14] But I have said this and continue to say it. Therefore, "If I go and prepare a place for you, I am coming again and I will welcome you," etc. Nevertheless, in whatever manner the text is read, it is an exhortation to faith.

5. (Verse 4). *And where I am going, you know.* The second point surfaces here, namely, the way of departure. And lest it would seem that he was saying something new to them about his departure, he says that they themselves knew both the way and the final destination. Therefore, he says: *And where I am going, you know, and you know the way.* But some of them did not fully understand. So they ask, namely, Thomas and Philip. Thus:

6. (Verse 5). *Thomas said to him: Lord, we do not know where you are going, and how can we know the way?* Doubting Thomas was late in understanding, and this was for our progress in faith, for, just as Peter's denial is instrumental in eliminating presumption, so too is Thomas's ignorance instrumental in sorting out the elements of faith and strengthening faith. So the Lord gives him sure knowledge about the way and the destination. Thus:

7. (Verse 6). *Jesus said to him: I am the way, truth,*[15] *and life.* Truth and life with regard to destination, since truth pertains to the intellect and life pertains to the affections. *I am the way* for those who are seeking, *the truth* for those finding, *life* without death for those who endure

---

[14] On p. 436 n. 9 QuarEd indicate that some texts omit "I will again take you."

[15] On p. 437 n. 3 QuarEd accurately mention that the Vulgate reads *et veritas* ("and truth").

and abide.[16] – *I am the way* that does not lead astray.[17] Psalm 106:40 says: "They went astray along impassible roads and were not on the way."[18] *I am the truth* that does not deceive. Psalm 144:13 states: "The Lord is faithful in all his words." *Life* unfailing. Luke 10:42 says: "Mary has chosen the best part which will not be taken away from her."[19] – *I am the way* that leads. Proverbs 4:11-12 reads: "I will lead you by the paths of equity. When you have entered them, your steps will not be impeded. When you run

---

[16] On p. 437 n. 5 QuarEd helpfully cite the Glossa Interlinearis: "*The way* without error for those seeking, *the truth* without falsehood for those finding, *life* without death for those who endure and abide." Hugh of St. Cher, p. 370g quotes these same words and attributes them to Augustine. See Augustine, Tractate 22 n. 8 in FC 79, p. 204: "Do you wish to walk? 'I am the way.' Do you wish not to be deceived? 'I am the truth.' Do you wish not to die? 'I am the life.'"

[17] Bonaventure's primary source for this distinctio seems to be Cardinal Hugh. See Hugh of St. Cher, p. 370g: "The way that does not lead astray. Ps 10b [= Ps 106:40] says: They went astray along impassable roads and were not on the way…. The truth that does not deceive. Prov 25:19 states: To trust in an unfaithful person in the time of trouble is like a rotten truth [Hugh's text mistakenly reads: *Deus putridus*] and weary feet. Life unfailing. Matt 25:46: These will go into eternal life. The part, which Mary chose, that will not be taken away from her. Luke 10:42. Likewise, the way that leads. Prov 4:11: I will lead you by the paths of equity. Truth that enlightens. Mal 4:2: The sun of justice will arise for those who fear God. The life that provides pasture. Ps 36:4, 3: Delight in the Lord, etc. Dwell in the land, and you will be pastured with its riches. Furthermore, he is the way by example. John 13:15 above states: I have given you an example, etc. Truth in what has been promised. Ps 88:35 reads: The words that proceed from my mouth I will not make void. Life in reward. Rom 6:23 states: The wages of sin is death, but the grace of God is eternal life…."

[18] Bonaventure adjusts Ps 106:40: "God caused them to wander where there was no passage and out of the way."

[19] See Book VII, n. 33 in *Saint Hilary of Poitiers The Trinity*. Translated by Stephen McKenna. FC 25 (New York: Fathers of the Church, Inc., 1954), p. 262: "He who is the way does not guide us to the wrong roads or to those that are impassable, nor does He who is the truth deceive us by falsehoods, nor does He who is the life leave us in the error of death."

along them, you will not meet an obstacle." *I am the truth*
that enlightens. Malachi 4:2 states: "The sun of justice
will arise for you who fear God."[20] *The life* that provides a
pasture. John 10:9 says: "If anyone enters by me, he will
be safe and will go in and out and will find pastures."[21] – *I
am the way* by example. John 13:15 reads: "I have given
you an example that just as I have done to you, so too you
should do." *I am the truth* through what has been promised. Psalm 88:35 states: "The words that proceed from
my mouth I will not make void." *I am the life* in reward.
Romans 6:23 has: "The wages of sin is death, but the gift
of God is eternal life...."[22] And he shows what the way is:
No one comes to the Father but through me, and through
me he certainly comes.

8. (Verse 7). *If you had known me, you would also have
known my Father*, since, as it is said in John 10:30 above:
"The Father and I are one." Matthew 11:27 reads: "No
one knows the Son except the Father, nor does anyone
know the Father except the Son, and the person to whom
the Son chooses to reveal the Father." *And henceforth you
will know him*,[23] *and you have seen him. You will know
him*, namely, in the coming of the Holy Spirit. John 16:13
below states: "When he, the Spirit of Truth, has come, he

---

[20] The Vulgate reads *vobis timentibus nomen meum* ("you who fear
my name") whereas Bonaventure has *vobis timentibus Deum* ("you
who fear God").

[21] See Chrysostom, Homily 73 n. 2 in FC 41, p. 287: "Besides, if I
am the Way, you will not be in want of a guide; and if I am the Truth,
there is nothing false in what I have said; and if I am the Life, even
though you die you will receive the fulfillment of My words."

[22] See Bernard of Clairvaux, Sermon 2 on the Lord's Ascension n.
6 in SBOp 5.130-131: "But let us, who are your people and the sheep of
your pasture, follow you, through you, to you, because you are the way,
the truth, and the life: the way in example, the truth in what has been
promised, the life in reward."

[23] The Vulgate reads *cognoscitis* ("you know") while Bonaventure
has *cognoscetis* ("you will know").

will teach you all the truth." In you will be verified what Jeremiah 31:33 says: "I will give my law into your inner depths, and I will write it in their hearts."

9. (Verse 8). *Philip said to him*. This verse introduces the third point, namely, the destination of Christ's departure, which Philip wanted to see. For this reason *Philip said to him: Lord, show us the Father, and it is enough for us*, as if he were saying: We would seek nothing beyond this from you. For he is "all in all," as 1 Corinthians 15:28 says. Not only he himself, but also his grace, as 2 Corinthians 12:9 states: "My grace is sufficient for you." And since Philip was asking about something that he should not have asked about, the Lord instructs Philip that he is asking about something that he should know. Thus:

10. (Verse 9). *Jesus said to him: Have I been so long a time with you, and you have not known me?*[24] As if he were saying: Since you are asking about the Father, you are asking about me, whom you should know. So he says: *Philip, the person who sees me also sees my Father. How can you say: Show us the Father? The person sees* with the eye of faith, according to what is said of Abraham in Genesis 18:2-3: "He saw three and worshiped one."[25] And that he should believe in this way he shows because they are one. For this reason the text continues:

11. (Verse 10). *Do you not believe that I am in the Father and the Father is in me?* As one. As if he were saying: You

---

[24] On p. 487 n. 11 QuarEd correctly indicate that the Vulgate reads *cognovistis me* ("you [plural] have known me") while Bonaventure has *cognovisti me* ("you [sing.] have known me").

[25] This is not exactly what Gen 18:2-3 says. See Bonaventure's commentary on John 8:56 n. 80 above where he cites Gregory the Great: "Gregory says that he rejoiced at that time when he saw the three men and worshipped one...."

should believe this. And he demonstrates this by works: *The words that I speak to you I speak not on my own authority, but the Father dwelling in me, it is he who does the works.* And so if the operation is one, so too is the substance.[26] John 5:19 above says: "Whatever the Father[27] does, this the Son also does in like manner." And John 8:28 above states: "Of myself I do nothing."

12. (Verse 11). *Do you not believe that I am in the Father and the Father in me?*[28] He says this simply, without persuasive argument, just as right faith believes.

13. (Verse 12). *Otherwise believe because of the works themselves.* John 10:37 reads: "If I do not perform the works of my Father, do not believe me." Therefore, Augustine observes: "If we had been separated, we could never work inseparably."[29] And thus it is explained in what sense he had said that he would be going away, since he was not going to the Father as to someone *extra se*, but he wanted to make them believe that he was equal to the Father. And, truly, the disciples already knew this, because they believed that he was true God and thus equal to the Father in all things. Otherwise, he would not be true God. – *Amen, amen I say to you.* The fourth point occurs here,

---

[26] See Book I, d. 19. p. I. q. 4 of Bonaventure's *Sentence Commentary*. See also Book III, c. 14 of John Damascene, *De fide orthodoxa* in FC 37, p. 296: "For the will and operation of things having the same substance is the same, and the will and operation of things having different substances is different. Conversely, the substance of things having the same will and operation is the same, whereas that of things having a different will and substance is different."

[27] The Vulgate reads *ille* ("he") while Bonaventure has *Pater* ("the Father").

[28] On p. 438 n. 4 QuarEd rightly notice that the Vulgate reads *Pater in me est* ("the Father is in me").

[29] Bonaventure adapts Augustine. See his Tractate 71 n. 2 in CCSL xxxvi, p. 506 and FC 90, p. 78.

namely, the fruit of Christ's departure or its usefulness and benefit for those who believe. For this reason he says: *The person who believes in me, the works that I do he will also do and greater than these he will do.* Matthew 17:19 states: "If you have faith like a mustard seed, you will say to this mountain: Remove yourself from here to there,[30] and it will remove itself. And nothing will be impossible for you." And the reason for this is Christ's departure from us. Therefore, the text adds: *Because I am going to the Father*, namely, so that I may appear before the face of God "to make intercession for you."[31] Thus 1 John 2:1 reads: "We have an advocate with the Father, Jesus Christ...."[32] And so the text continues:

14. (Verse 13). *Whatever[33] you ask the Father[34] in my name, I will do it.* Wherefore, he says that we have to ask of the Father in the name of the Son, namely, *so that the Father may be honored in the Son*,[35] because the Son does not seek his own glory, but that of the Father. Therefore, it had been said in John 7:18 above: "The person who seeks the glory of the one who sent him is truthful." And for even greater certitude, since a promise becomes more secure through a twofold affirmation, the text adds:

---

[30] The Vulgate reads *transi hinc* ("remove yourself from here") while Bonaventure has *transi hinc illuc* ("remove yourself from here to there").

[31] See Hebr 7:25: "Therefore, he is able at all times to save those who come to God through him, since he lives always to make intercession for them."

[32] 1 John 2:1 says: "We have an advocate with the Father, Jesus Christ the just."

[33] The Vulgate reads *Et quodcumque* ("And whatever").

[34] The Vulgate does not read *Patrem* ("the Father").

[35] On p. 438 n. 9 QuarEd accurately indicate that the Vulgate reads *glorificetur* ("may be glorified") whereas Bonaventure has *honorificetur* ("may be honored").

15. (Verse 14). *If you ask anything*[36] *in my name, I will do it*. And he does not repeat the Father's name, in order to show that even if they ask something of him, they will obtain it, since he is equal to the Father. 1 John 3:21-22: "If our heart does not condemn us, we have confidence towards God, and whatever we ask, we will receive from him."

QUESTIONS

16. Question 1 deals with what the Lord said to his disciples in John 14:4: "Where I am going you know, and you know the way." – 1. Since Thomas in John 14:5 immediately asks about this as one who does not know about it and even says that he does not know. – 2. Furthermore, Philip in 14:8 asks about the Lord's destination, namely, about the Father, and by doing this, shows that he does not know. Wherefore, either the Lord has spoken falsely or they were asking about something that they knew.

Let there be a triple response to this. First, the Lord was not speaking about all of them, but about some of them. – But this solution is not apt, since the Lord in the preceding verses had made an exception of Judas. John 13:18 reads: "I do not speak of you all." – There is another response: that they knew both the way and the destination, but did not know them from the perspective the Lord was using. As in this example: I know Coriscus, but not insofar as he is coming. And therefore, even though I know Coriscus, I can ask and be in doubt about the perspective of the com-

---

[36] On p. 438 n. 10 QuarEd correctly mention that the Vulgate reads *quid petieritis me* ("you ask me anything") whilst Bonaventure has *quid petieritis* ("you ask anything").

ing of Coriscus.[37] – Another response is that they knew, but did not advert or actually consider the matter, and so Philip was chastised for his inconsideration.[38]

17. Question 2 focuses on the Lord's response to Thomas in John 14:6: "I am the way, the truth, and the life." – How is he himself, who is going, the way? How also is he himself both life and destination? This seems to be extraordinarily inapt. – It has to be maintained that he himself is the one, who is going, and through whom the journey is made, and to whom one arrives. And thus he is the truth that is going. He is the way, through which one journeys. He is the life, to which one arrives. And this happens because of the plurality of natures, for, as a human being, he goes and as God he arrives at his destination. Since he is "the mediator between God and human beings,"[39] he creates the way.[40]

18. Question 3 addresses the Lord's response to Philip in John 14:9: "Have I been with you so long a time, and you

[37] Bonaventure is dependent upon Aristotle's discussion in c. 24 of his *De sophisticis elenchis*. See WAE, vol. 1, 179b: "… they say that it is possible to know and not to know the same thing, only not in the same respect: accordingly, when they don't know the man who is coming towards them, but do know Coriscus, they assert that they do know and don't know the same object, but not in the same respect." On p. 439 n. 2 QuarEd cite Herm. Bonitz: Coriscus "is the name used to signify any person whosoever."

[38] See Augustine, Tractate 69 n. 1 in FC 90, pp. 67-68: "The Lord had said that they knew both; he (Thomas) says that they did not know either, either the place to go or the way to go. But he knew not how to lie. Therefore, they knew and did not know that they knew."

[39] See 1 Tim 2:5.

[40] See the commentary on John 14:6 above with its notes. See Augustine, Tractate 69 n. 2 in FC 90, p. 68: "Therefore, he himself was going to himself by way of himself. And where do we go except to him? And by what way do we go except through him? He himself, therefore, to himself through himself; we to him through him, and indeed also to the Father, both he and we."

have not known me?" – From this it seems that Philip had not yet believed in Christ. – But then how was it said to him in John 13:10 above that he was clean, for no one is clean except through faith? – If you say that he did believe, how, then, since he would say in faith that the Father and the Son are of one essence, did he raise the question about seeing the Father?[41] It seems that he would have believed in a way contrary to faith. – To this it has to be said that Philip believed in him and believed that he was equal to and one in substance with the Father. But since at that time he heard the Son speaking distinctly about the Father, he wanted and asked to see him distinctly. He would not have asked for this, if he had considered the unity of their essence. Therefore, through this error of judgment he sinned venially, and therefore was censured by the Lord.

19. Question 4 asks about the meaning of John 14:9: "The person who sees me also see the Father." – Since the Son has become visible, but the Father remained invisible. – If you say: that he is speaking according to Divinity, that means nothing, since "no one has even seen God,"[42] neither the Father nor the Son, because, if the person has seen the Son, he has also seen the Father. – I answer that one must maintain that he is speaking of the vision of Divinity, not of humanity. But this is twofold, namely, by faith, as "we see now through a mirror in an obscure manner,"[43] and by sight.[44] And he is speaking here of the vision of faith, since no one has perfect belief in the Son without also believing in the Father.

---

[41] See John 14:9: "Philip, the person who sees me also sees the Father. How can you say: Show us the Father?"

[42] See John 1:18.

[43] See 1 Cor 13:12.

[44] See 2 Cor 5:7: "For we walk by faith and not by sight."

20. Question 5 concerns John 14:11: "I am in the Father, and the Father in me." – Contrary. Therefore, one can argue from this: Therefore, the Father is in the Father. – Also it can be asked: Why is this formulation not made: the Father is in the Father? – I respond that it should be said that this preposition "in," since it is a preposition, expresses a distinction. But since it is this preposition, it expresses unity of essence. Therefore, it is granted that the Father is in the Son and the Son in the Father. But it does not follow that the Father is in the Father. Rather he is there accidentally, as in this example: I am similar to you, and you are to me; therefore, I am similar to myself. Accidentally, since a similitude expresses correspondence and distinction at the same time.[45]

21. Question 6 asks about John 14:12: "The person who believes in me, the works that I do that person will also do." – 1. This is false, for those works were of infinite power. Therefore, no one performs them except God. – 2. Moreover, what is the meaning of "he will do works that are greater"?[46] For the greatest work is to raise up a dead person who is decayed.[47] How can there be a greater miracle? – 3. Furthermore, if the servant is not greater than his master,[48] it is not appropriate that God perform greater works through Christ's servants than through his very Son.

I answer that it must be said that the Lord performed more miracles at the request of the Apostles than he had done by himself. – 1.But it is said that a believer will do.

---

[45] See Aristotle, *Metaphysics* in WAE, vol. 8, 1021a: "Those things are the same whose substance is one; those are like whose quality is one; those are equal whose quantity is one."

[46] See John 14:12.

[47] See John 11:39.

[48] See John 13:16.

This means that the works will happen at the request of the believer or because people think that he did them. – 2. Again when it is said that the works will be greater, it should be maintained that greater does not refer to number, but to kind or manner. For it is read in Acts 5:15 that the sick were cured through Peter's shadow.[49] Likewise, it is said of the Apostles that through touching their clothing the ill were healed and the dead resuscitated.[50] – 3. The servant is not greater than the master, since the Apostles did not perform their works for their own glory, but for Christ's glory.

22. Question 7 yet again considers John 14:12: "The person who believes in me, the works that I do he also will do." – It is asked whether this should be understood of faith unformed by charity or of faith formed by charity. – There are two considerations why it seems to refer to faith unformed by charity. 1. For it is said in 1 Corinthians 13:2: "If I have faith[51] so as to remove mountains, but do not have charity," etc.[52] Therefore, the works were performed by faith unformed by charity. – 2. Likewise this seems to be the case, because many evil persons worked miracles, as is said in Matthew 7:22. – But against this is: the sinner is unworthy of the bread by which he is nour-

---

[49] Acts 5:15 reads: "... they carried the sick into the streets and laid them on beds and pallets that, when Peter passed, his shadow at least might fall on some of them." See Augustine, Tractate 71 n. 3 in FC 90, p. 78: "For it is a greater thing for a shadow to heal than a hem. The one by him, the other by them, but nevertheless he himself did both." Relative to "hem," see Matt 9:20-22; Mark 5:2529; Luke 8:43-44. Hugh of St. Cher, p. 370v,t writes: "And greater than these will he do], for if the Lord cured by means of his hem in Matt 9:20-22, Peter healed by means of his shadow. Acts 5:15."

[50] See Acts 19:12: "so that even handkerchiefs and aprons were carried from his (Paul's) body to the sick, and the diseases left them and the evil spirits went out."

[51] The Vulgate reads *omnem fidem* ("all faith").

[52] 1 Cor 13:2 concludes: "... it profits me nothing."

ished.[53] Wherefore, if the person who has faith unformed by charity is in sin, in no way does he merit to be heard.

I answer that a distinction has to be maintained between hearing that is by largess and a hearing that is by justice. The person who has faith unformed by charity is heard frequently and merits to be heard solely by largess relative to those matters about which he has faith that the Lord might hear him.[54]

23. Question 8 deals with John 14:12 from another angle and queries: If those who have faith perform miracles and if today few people or no one perform miracles, then few people or no one has faith. – To bolster this viewpoint what is said in Matthew 21:21 is brought forth: "If you have faith ... and say to this mountain: ... hurl yourself into the sea, it will be done." But who is there who could do this? – I answer that it has to be said according to Gregory[55] and Augustine[56] that miraculous works are of two kinds: sensible and spiritual. Sensible miracles such

---

[53] This saying is attributed to Augustine. I have been unable to locate its exact source.

[54] See Book III, d. 23. a. 2. q. 2 and Book I. d. 41. a. 1. q. 1in Bonaventure's *Sentence Commentary*.

[55] See Homily 29 n. 4 of GGHG in CCSL cxli, pp. 247-249. See Hurst, p. 229: "These things were necessary at the Church's beginning.... Holy Church does daily in a spiritual way what it did then materially through the apostles.... Surely these miracles are all the greater to the extent that they are spiritual; they are all the greater to the extent that it is not bodies but souls which are being raised up."

[56] See Sermon 88 n. 3 in *Sermons III (51-94) on the New Testament*. Translation and notes by Edmund Hill. WSA III/III; Brooklyn: New City Press, 1991, p. 420: "So the Lord did all these things (miracles), in order to invite people to faith. This faith is now glowing white-hot in the Church, which is spread throughout the whole world. And now he is achieving greater healings, for the sake of which he was then prepared to perform those lesser ones. Just as the spirit, you see, is better than the body, so too the health of the spirit is worth more than the health of the body. Nowadays, while indeed blind flesh does not

as raising the dead and things of this kind are necessary to build up the faith of simple people. On the other hand, spiritual miracles are raising people from spiritual death by means of the sacraments. The first kind of miracle has ceased, since the faith has been spread abroad. The second kind will always remain for our salvation. So it is to be understood that the Lord was speaking to them either about spiritual miracles or was speaking about the time of the primitive Church when Gentiles and uneducated people were nurtured in the faith. But nonetheless, miracles occur now, but the Lord does not extend his hand so generously in performing them, since there is not such a great need.

JOHN 14:15-24
THE LORD EXHORTS HIS DISCIPLES TO OBSERVANCE OF HIS COMMANDMENTS

24. *If you love me*, etc. The Lord had just exhorted his disciples to constant faith, now in this second section, since "faith without works is dead,"[57] he exhorts them *to keep the commandments*. And he does this in the following order. First he exhorts them by promising them *assistance*. Second by promising them *consolation*. Third by promising them a *reward*. Fourth he states what *the merit* is of these things.

Verse 15. So first he exhorts them to keep his commandments. And since it happens that commandments are observed out of fear, as with regard to the Law – and this he does not ask for – and it also happens that they are

---

open its eye at a miracle of the Lord's, blind hearts do open their eyes to the world of the Lord...."

[57] See James 2:25 and John 14:1 above.

observed out of love – and this he does ask for – the text reads: *If you love me, keep my commandments*, namely, out of love for me.[58] 2 John 6 states: "This is love that we walk according to his commandments." To such people he promises assistance. For which reason the text continues:

25. (Verse 16). *I[59] will ask the Father and he will give you another Paraclete. Paraclete* means consoler or advocate.[60] He says "another," and in doing so intimates that he himself was a consoler and advocate. 1 John 2:1 says: "We have an advocate with the Father, Jesus Christ the righteous." He promises them that the other advocate will be with them forever, since he was their consoler in his bodily presence but for a time. *To dwell with you forever*, not as in Saul, about whom 1 Samuel 16:14 states: "The Spirit of the Lord departed from Saul," etc. And he adds who this advocate is:

26. (Verse 17). *The Spirit of truth*, who proceeds from the Father, the Father will give, that is, the other Paraclete is the Spirit of truth. He describes this Spirit with the perspective of his effect. Therefore, he calls him "the Spirit of truth," since he teaches the truth, just as the spirit of

---

[58] Augustine, *Contra Adimantum*, c. 17 n. 2 in PL 42:159: "The most obvious difference between the two Testaments, to put the matter most concisely, is fear and love. Fear pertains to the old man while love pertains to the new man. Nevertheless, both Testaments have been set forth and are joined together by the most merciful dispensation of the one God."

[59] The Vulgate reads *Et ego* ("And I").

[60] See Homily 30 n. 3 of GGHG in CCSL cxli, p. 258: "Many of you know, my brothers and sisters, that the Greek word 'paraclete' means 'advocate' or 'consoler' in Latin."

error teaches falsehood.[61] John 16:13 below reads: "When he ... has come, he will teach you all the truth." He also describes him from the perspective of his lodging, because he does not abide in non-believers, but in believers, not in human beings who are dominated by animal instincts, but in spiritual people. For which reason the text adds: *Whom the world cannot receive.* And the reason is that it is blind because of non-belief: *Since it does not see him,* by means of clear recognition, *and does not know him,* by means of any type of understanding. Wisdom 1:5 says: "The Holy Spirit of discipline will flee from the deceitful and will withdraw himself from thoughts that are without understanding."[62] And 1 Corinthians 2:14 reads: "The sensual person does not perceive the things that are of God."[63] *But you will know him, because he will dwell with you and be in you.* Revelation 2:17 states: "To the person who overcomes, I will give the hidden manna, and I will give him a white pebble, and upon the pebble a new name written, which no one knows except the one who receives it." About this knowledge Wisdom 15:3 says: "To know you is perfect justice, and to know your justice and power is the root of immortality." And it should be noted that the text says "he will dwell with you and will be in you," signifying the twofold grace of the Holy Spirit: grace that comes before and grace that follows.[64] Psalm 58:11 reads: "God's mercy will come before me." And Psalm 22:6 has: "And your mercy will follow me all the days of my life."

---

[61] See Theophylactus' commentary in PG 124:179D: "'The Spirit of truth,' he says, that is, the Spirit, not of the Old Testament (for that is figure and shadow), but of the New, which is what is true."

[62] Hugh of St. Cher, p. 371n also cites Wis 1:5.

[63] The Vulgate reads *Spiritus Dei* ("of the Spirit of God").

[64] Technically: *gratia praeveniens* ("prevenient grace") and *gratia subsequens* ("subsequent grace").

27. (Verse 18). *I will not leave you orphans*. Here in his second point he promises consolation through his visitation to disciples who keep his commandments. For this reason he says: *I will not leave you orphans*, that is, desolate. *I will come to you*, namely, by visiting you. In Mark 16:7 the angel said: "He goes before you into Galilee. There you will see him, as he told you." And just as the Holy Spirit is sent only to good people, so too the visitation of Christ comes only to good people. So the text continues:

28. (Verse 19). *Yet a little while and the world no longer sees me*, because after his passion he did not appear to earthly people, but to his Apostles. Acts 10:40-41 reads: "God caused him to be plainly seen, not by all the people, but by witnesses designated beforehand by God." *But you will see me*,[65] *for I live*, through the life of glory, *and you will live*, through the life of grace, which commences in faith.[66] About faith Habakkuk 2:4 states: "But my just one lives by faith." And that they may have this life of perfect faith, he shows in what follows:

29. (Verse 20). *In that day you will know that I am in my Father*. In this sentence the distinction of persons and the unity of essence is noted, and this pertains to faith in the Trinity. *And you in me, and I in you*, through grace, and this looks forward with faith in redemption. *You in me*, like branches on the vine. John 15 below says: "I am the vine. You are the branches."[67] "Abide in me."[68] *And I*

---

[65] On p. 441 n. 9 QuarEd rightly notice that the Vulgate reads *videtis* ("you see") while Bonaventure has *videbitis* ("you will see").

[66] See Augustine, Tractate 75 n. 3 in FC 90, p. 94: "Therefore, elegantly and briefly, by two verbs of the present and future tense, he promised two resurrections, namely, his own, soon to be, and ours, to come at the end of [this] age."

[67] See John 15:5.

[68] See John 15:4.

in you, like one who dwells in a dwelling. 1 Corinthians 3:17 reads: "Holy is the temple of God, and this temple you are."

30. (Verse 21). *The person who has my commandments.* The third point surfaces here, namely, a reward is promised to those who keep the commandments. And the reason for this is that the person who keeps the commandments is loved by the Lord, and therefore receives benefits and is glorified. For this reason the text reads: *The person who has my commandments and keeps them is the one who loves me*, since, as Gregory comments, "the proof of love is its manifestation in deeds."[69] For Psalm 102:17-18 states: "The Lord's justice is unto children's children, to those who keep his covenant and are mindful of his commandments to do them." The person who serves in this manner is one who indeed loves in a true sense, not in word only, like those, about whom it is said in 1 John 3:18: "Let us not love in word, neither with the tongue, but in deed and in truth." *Now the person who loves me will be loved by my Father*, and also by me, *and I will love him*. Proverbs 8:17: "I love those who love me." And I will show my love by means of a reward. Thus: *And I will manifest myself to him*, and this is the reward. Psalm 90:16 states: "I will show him my salvation." The Glossa comments: "The vision of Christ is the total reward."[70] John 17:3 below says: "This is eternal life that they may know you, the only true God, and the one whom you have sent, Jesus Christ."

---

[69] See Homily 30 n. 1 of GGHG and CCSL cxli, p. 256 and Hurst, p. 236. Homily 30 is on John 14:23-31. This citation is virtually verbatim.

[70] On p. 442 n. 1 QuarEd cite the Glossa Interlinearis: "This vision will be the reward of faith." See Augustine, Tractate 75 n. 5 in FC 90, p. 96: "For now he has loved for this purpose, that we may believe and hold fast to the commandment of faith; then he will love for this purpose, that we may see and may obtain this very vision as the reward of faith."

31. (Verse 22). *Judas said to him*, etc. This verse expresses the fourth point: there is merit in keeping the commandments. For since he had said that he must manifest
himself to the Apostles and not to the world, a disciple
began to have doubts about what he was saying. So this
text follows: *Judas, not the Iscariot, said to him: Lord,
how is it*, that is, what is the reason *that you are about
to manifest yourself to us and not to the world?*[71] And the
Lord answered him that the reason was their merit, because those in the world did not keep his commandments
and therefore did not merit to see him.[72] For this reason
the text continues:

32. (Verse 23). *Jesus answered and said to him: If anyone
loves me, that person will keep my word.* Luke 6:46 reads:
"Why do you call me Lord, Lord, and do not do the things
that I command you?" "God's love is never idle, for where
it exists, it does great things. But if it refuses to work, it
is not love."[73] And from this observance one merits the
manifestation of the Lord. Thus *and my Father will love
him.* And the manifestation follows from this love. Therefore, the text continues: *And we will come to him.* And if
the Lord comes, nothing that is good is absent. Wisdom
7:11 states: "All good things came to me together with

---

[71] See Augustine, Tractate 76 n. 2 in FC 90, p. 97: "Look, the reason why he is going to manifest himself to his own, but not to those
who belong to another, whom he designates by the name of 'the world,'
has been set forth. And this is the cause, because these love, but those
do not love."

[72] See Augustine Tractate 75 n. 5 in FC 90, p. 96: "For now he has
loved for this purpose, that we may believe and hold fast to the commandment of faith; then he will love for this purpose, that we may see
and may obtain this very vision as the reward of faith."

[73] Bonaventure has modified Homily 30 n. 2 of GGHG. See CCSL
cxli, p. 257 and Hurst, p. 237.

her." *And we will make our abode with him,*[74] and this by merit of the keeping of his commandments. For Gregory observes: "The Lord makes his abode in that person who truly loves God and perfectly keeps his commandments, for the love of Divinity so penetrates that person, that he does not depart from this love during the time of temptation."[75] – And therefore, supply: I will manifest myself to you, who keep my commandments, and in so doing love me and thereby merit.

33. (Verse 24). *The person who does not love me does not keep my word.* And therefore, such a person does not merit to see me. Such are the world and worldly people. John 15:18 below states: "If the world hates you, know that it has hated me before you." And therefore, it does not keep his commandments. And so he does not manifest himself to the world. And lest you think that he referred to his own words and not those of the Father, he adds: *And the word that you have heard is not mine,* that is, my word. This is an instance of "antiptosis," in which one case is substituted for another.[76] John 12:49 above says: "I have not spoken on my own authority, but the one who sent me, the Father, has commanded me what I should say and what I should declare."

---

[74] The Vulgate reads *mansiones* ("abode") while Bonaventure has *mansionem* ("abode").

[75] Bonaventure has modified Homily 30 n. 2 of GGHG. See CCSL cxli, p. 257.

[76] In brief, in the sentence, "and the word that you heard is not mine," "the word" is in the accusative case while "mine" is in the nominative case. Bonaventure uses the figure of antiptosis to explain this infelicity.

Questions

34. Question 1 deals with John 14:15-16: "If you love me, keep my commandments. And I will ask the Father, and he will give you another Paraclete." – So it seems that they could love and keep the commandments before the Holy Spirit would be given to them. Or if they have the Spirit, why will he give it and how? – I answer that it has to be maintained that they have the Holy Spirit so that they may love and keep the commandments, but the Spirit was promised them by the Lord, so that they might have the Spirit more fully and with greater effects. For Augustine comments: "It remains for us to understand that the person who loves has the Holy Spirit, and by having deserves to have more, and by having more to love more."[77]

35. Question 2 focuses on John 14:16: "I will ask the Father." – Augustine says in *About Nature and Grace* that "no one prays for that which he can do by himself."[78] Therefore, if the Son prays for the gift of the Holy Spirit, the Son cannot give the Holy Spirit. – The response to this has to be that he asks in such a way that he may merit the gift of the Holy Spirit. And he does this according to his human nature, through which he suffered and was exalted by his passion and merited by his prayer the gift of the Holy Spirit for us. And according to that nature he could not give, but asked for the gift of the Holy Spirit.[79]

---

[77] See Tractate 74 n. 2 in CCSL xxxvi, p. 513 and FC 90, p. 90.

[78] See c. 18 n. 20 of *De natura et gratia* in PL 44:256: "For what is more foolish than to pray that you accomplish something that lies within your own power?"

[79] See Book III d. 17 a. 2 q. 1 of Bonaventure's *Sentence Commentary*.

36. Question 3 concerns John 14:16: "The Father will give you another Paraclete." – Now if the Paraclete is an advocate, and an advocate is a mediator, the Holy Spirit cannot be a mediator. Therefore, the Holy Spirit is neither the Paraclete nor an advocate. – I respond that it must be insisted upon that the Holy Spirit is said to be the Paraclete in a twofold meaning, because the Holy Spirit is the consoler through the hope of forgiveness, for he has been given us "as a pledge of our eternal inheritance."[80] The Holy Spirit is also an advocate. Now there is a double meaning to advocate: either with regard to the person or with regard to the effect. The Son is the advocate with regard to the person of the advocate, because he is the mediator. But the Holy Spirit is the advocate with regard to his office. – Now the office of the advocate is threefold. The first function of the advocate is to plead. And this the Holy Spirit does, for Romans 8:26 reads: "The Spirit himself pleads for us with unutterable groanings."[81] The second function is to speak. Matthew 10:19-20 states: "Do not be anxious how or what you are to speak, for what you are to speak will be given to you in that hour. For it is not you who are speaking, but the Spirit of your Father who speaks through you." The third function is to convict the opposing party. And this the Holy Spirit does as John 16:8 below says: "And when he comes, he will convict the world of sin," etc.

---

[80] See Eph 1:14. See Homily 30 n. 3 of GGHG in Hurst, p. 238: "The same Spirit is called a consoler because when he prepares a hope of pardon for those grieving over their sins he is lifting up their hearts from sorrow and affliction."

[81] See Homily 30 n. 3 of GGHG in Hurst, p. 238: "He is called an advocate because he intervenes before the Father's justice on behalf of the wrongdoings of sinners; he who is of one substance with the Father and the Son is said to plead earnestly on behalf of sinners because he causes those whom he fills to do so. Hence Paul says: *For the Spirit himself pleads for us with unutterable groanings.*" Hugh of St. Cher, p. 373v,c also cites Gregory.

37. Question 4 is taken up with John 14:17: "The world does not know the Holy Spirit, but you will know him, because he will be in you."[82] – But it is objected that the Holy Spirit is in all, both in the good and in the evil, since he is God. Therefore, all know him. – But if you say that the text is not speaking about his existence because of his presence, but because of his grace, that is false, since "no one knows whether he is worthy of love or of hatred."[83] Therefore, no one knows whether he has the Holy Spirit with respect to the effect of grace. – I respond that it has to be said that the text is speaking here of knowledge of the Holy Spirit in his manifest effect, for it speaks of his existence in us, not by his essence, but by his effect. And this is a sufficient response to objection one. – But it should be noted that the effect of the Holy Spirit is two-fold. Certain effects that are in us and involve us directly, such as loving, believing, and fearing, are ones that, when we have them, we are certain of having them. But others that involve something outside ourselves, such as being graced by God and made pleasing to God, are not known to us in their effect except through a special revelation. Nonetheless, we can know these effects in a probable way, but not in a certain way.[84]

38. Question 5 zeroes in on John 14:23 where it is said that "The Father will come," for the text actually reads: "We will come to him." – 1. Why does Christ speak about himself and the Father rather than about the Holy Spirit? – 2. And it seems that he should not have spoken about the Father, since the Father is the one who sends the Son.

---

[82] John 14:17 reads: "The Spirit of truth whom the world cannot receive, because it neither sees him nor knows him. But you know him, because he will dwell with you and be in you."

[83] Qoh 9:1.

[84] See Book I d. 17. p. I. q. 3 of Bonaventure's *Sentence Commentary*.

Even if the Father would come together with the Son, by reason of his sending the Son, by the same reason he is sending himself. – Furthermore, how does the Father come who is everywhere and did not assume a creature?

I answer that it has to be maintained that the coming of God to us, as Augustine observes, is understood according to its effect and not through its essence. For Augustine comments: "They come to us while we come to them. They come to our help; we come by obeying. They come by enlightening; we come by seeing. They come by filling; we come by receiving."[85] So since the works of the Trinity are undivided, when the Holy Spirit comes, the Father and the Son actually come, but this coming is attributed to the Father, another of the three persons, by appropriation. – But to send, beyond what is to be said of its effect, involves a distinction of persons by means of authority and sub-authority. And therefore, even though the Father comes with the Son, nonetheless, he does not send himself with the Son. – There is no mention of the Holy Spirit in this passage, since about him John 14:16-17 above had spoken.[86]

JOHN 14:25-31
THE LORD PREDICTS THE IMMINENCE OF HIS DEPARTURE

39. *I have spoken these things to you*, etc. This is the third section of this chapter. Having given his exhortation, *he foretells the imminence of his departure*, so that when it

---

[85] See Tractate 76 n. 4 in CCSL xxxvi, p. 519 and FC 90, p. 99.

[86] See Augustine, Tractate 76 n. 4 in FC 90, p. 99: "... so that no one may think that only the Father and the Son, without the Holy Spirit, make a dwelling place among those who love them, let him recollect what was said a little earlier about the Holy Spirit." Augustine then cites John 14:17.

does take place, they may believe. And lest they be downcast about this, he does not propose it right away, but first provides consolation and then mentions his imminent departure when verse 29 says: "Now I have told you," etc.

And he offers them much consolation. First by means of the expectation of the Holy Spirit. Second by the gift of peace. Third through the promise of his visitation. Fourth from rejoicing with him about his exaltation.

Verse 25. So first he formulates consolation on the basis of the expectation of the Holy Spirit. For which reason the text says: *I have spoken these things to you, while yet dwelling with you.* Luke 24:44 states: "These are the words that I spoke to you while I was still among you." You need not be troubled if you do not understand, for you will understand when the Holy Spirit arrives. Thus:

40. (Verse 26). *But the Paraclete, the Spirit,*[87] *whom the Father will send in my name*, that is, through faith in my name, because he was given only to those who believe in Christ, as John 7:38 says: "The person who believes in me, as the Scripture says, from within him there will flow rivers of living water" and as Acts 4:12 states: "For there is no other name under heaven given to men and women by which we must be saved." *He*, I supply "the Spirit," *will teach you all things and bring to your mind whatever I have said to you.* Wisdom 7:21-22 reads: "Wisdom, the worker of all things, taught me, for in her is the spirit of understanding, holy."[88]

---

[87] On p. 444 n. 2 QuarEd accurately indicate that the Vulgate reads *Spiritus sanctus* ("Holy Spirit").

[88] Wis 7:22-23 goes on to give twenty-three other adjectives that characterize wisdom.

41. (Verse 27). *Peace I leave you.* The second consolation stems from the gift or benefaction of peace, in which there is great consolation. For this reason the text continues: *Peace I leave you, my peace I give to you.* He repeats the word "peace" to suggest that there is a peace of grace and a peace of glory. For Augustine comments: "He leaves his peace for us, abiding in which we conquer our enemies. He gives us his peace when we will reign without an enemy."[89] Isaiah 27:5 says: "The Lord will make peace with me. He will make peace with me."[90] He gives this to those who keep his commandments. Isaiah 48:18 reads: "Would that you had hearkened to my commandments. Your peace would have been like a river." By using "my," he distinguishes his peace from that of the world. And so he adds: *Not as the world gives do I give to you,* since the world gives in a carnal way, but I give in a spiritual way. The world gives in a temporal manner, but I give in an eternal manner. The world gives in an external way, but I give in an internal way. Wherefore, it is written in Philippians 4:7: "May the peace of God that surpasses all understanding guard your hearts and minds in Christ Jesus." The peace of the world guards human bodies and possessions. About this peace Matthew 10:34 states: "I have not come to bring peace, but the sword." – *Do not let your heart be troubled.* The third consolation, namely, that of the promise of his visitation, occurs here. He had also promised this above. For this reason he says: *Do not let your heart be troubled or be afraid.* And this is the reason:

---

[89] Bonaventure has adapted Tractate 77 n. 3. See CCSL xxxvi, p. 521.
[90] Bonaventure has modified Isa 27:5, so that "the Lord" is the subject. Hugh of St. Cher, p. 373v,n also cites Isa 27:5.

42. (Verse 28). *You have heard me say to you: I go away, and I am coming to you.* See John 14:3 above: "If I go," etc. John 16:22 below states: "I will see you again, and your heart will rejoice, and no one will take your joy away from you." – *If you loved me.* Here the fourth basis for consolation occurs, namely, that from rejoicing with him about his exaltation. For they must rejoice at his exaltation, if they love him. For this reason the text continues: *If you loved me, you would indeed rejoice that I am going to the Father*, since my exaltation consists in this journey. Thus he adds: *For the Father is greater than I*, and thus, when I sit at the right hand of the Father, I am exalted. About this exaltation Hebrews 1:3-4 states: "He has taken his seat at the right hand of the Majesty on high, having become so much superior to the angels," etc. And the disciple who loves Christ rejoices with him at his exaltation, for Romans 12:15 says: "Rejoice with those who rejoice," etc.

43. (Verse 29). *And now I have told you.* After consolation has been extended, the imminence of his departure is added here. And first the reason for saying this beforehand is noted. Second is the reason for the imminent departure. Third is an indication of said imminence. So first the reason for him saying this beforehand is noted, namely, to strengthen their faith. For this reason the text continues: *Now*[91] *I have told you before it comes to pass, so that, when it has come to pass, you may believe.* Through this he has strengthened their faith, since they will see things take place in just the way he had predicted. For if he had not foretold these things, they would have doubted whether he had willingly endured them. Thus after the resurrection he recalled these things to their memory. Luke 24:44-46 reads: "These are the words that I spoke

---

[91] On p. 444 n. 11 QuarEd correctly notice that the Vulgate reads *Et nunc* ("And now").

to you when I was still with you that all things must be fulfilled that are written about me…. Since it is written that the Christ should suffer," etc.

44. (Verse 30). *I will no longer*, etc. The second point surfaces here, that is, the reason for his imminent departure, and this on account of the attack of the devil and the divine will. On account of the attack of the devil, who has armed his servants to seize Christ. Therefore, the text says: *I will no longer speak much with you, for the prince of this world is coming*, that is, the devil is speedily drawing near. The devil was drawing near in his servants, but he does not compel what is going to happen, because *in me he has nothing*. The devil did not have any basis by which he might command Christ or censure him, for he had no sin, and the devil rules over sinners.[92] Thus Job 41:25 states: "He is king over all the children of pride." So he is the prince of darkness. Ephesians 6:12 says: "Against the world rulers of this darkness." And in Christ there is no darkness, since he is "the true light that enlightens everyone coming into this world."[93] – But another reason, the divine will, is far more compelling. So the text says:

45. (Verse 31). *But he comes, so that the world may know that I love the Father*. So I die at his command. Thus: *As*[94] *the Father has commanded me, so I act*. About this command John 10:18 above says: "I have received this commandment from my Father." God the Father gave him this commandment, not because he himself deserved to

---

[92] See Augustine, Tractate 79 n. 2 in FC 90, p. 113: "… 'and in me he has not anything' – no sin at all, obviously. For thus he shows the devil to be the prince, not of created things, but of sinners, whom he now calls by the term 'this world.'"

[93] See John 1:9.

[94] On p. 445 n. 2 QuarEd accurately mention that the Vulgate reads *Et sicut* ("And as").

die, but for our salvation. Thus 2 Corinthians 5:21 reads: "For our sakes he," God the Father, "made him to be sin who knew nothing of sin, so that in him we might become the righteousness of God." Now he did this out of love for us. John 3:16 above states: "God so loved the world that he gave his only begotten Son." – *Arise, let us go.* The third point occurs here, namely, an indication of his imminent departure, which consists of this that he warns his disciples to depart from here. For which reason the text says: *Arise, let us go from here.* Through this he demonstrates that he suffers willingly.[95] Something similar is said in Matthew 26:46: "Arise, let us go. Behold, the one who betrays me is at hand."

Questions

46. Question 1 asks first about John 14:26: "The Holy Spirit will bring to your minds all things" that the Son had said. Now "to bring to mind" is an inferior action. Gregory responds to this: "The Holy Spirit is said to 'bring to mind,' not because he provides knowledge as an inferior, but as one who knows what is hidden."[96]

47. Question 2 addresses John 14:28: "You would indeed rejoice that I am going to the Father, for the Father is greater than I." – 1. From this verse Arius argued that the Son is inferior to the Father. – But if you say that this was said according to his human nature, then one would have to say by the same reasoning that I am greater than I myself. – 2. Furthermore, Hilary says that the Father

---

[95] See Augustine, Tractate 79 n. 2 in FC 90, p. 114: "But 'let us go,' he said. Where, except to that place from which he was to be handed over to death, he who had nothing deserving of death?"

[96] See Homily 30 n. 3 of GGHG in CCSL cxli, p. 259, and Hurst, p. 239.

is greater than the Son according to divine nature.[97] And then it is argued from the being of the relationship each has with the other[98] that the Son is lesser than the Father, and therefore is no equal.

The answer to this problem is found in Augustine's rule in Book I of *On the Trinity* that all things that are said of the Son that indicate equality refer to the divine nature and that all things that are said of the Son that indicate inequality refer to the human nature. And this verse should be understood accordingly.[99] Thus Augustine observes: "Congratulations should be extended to human nature precisely because it has been so taken up by the only-begotten Word that it was established immortal in heaven, and earth was made so sublime that dust incorruptible sat at the right hand of the Father."[100] Therefore, according to the determination granted, the Son, insofar as he is God, is greater than himself, insofar as he is a human being. – 2. Relative to the objection taken from Hilary, it has to be said that Hilary accepts that the Father is greater, not according to what he calls the abundant magnitude of power or strength, but according to what he calls authority. And since the Father has authority with respect to the Son as the beginning, he says that he is greater than the Son. Nevertheless, the Son is not called

---

[97] See Book IX, n. 54 of *De Trinitate* in FC 25, p. 377: "Hence, the Father is greater than the Son, and surely greater, since He allows Him to be as great as He Himself is...."

[98] See Book III, 1198A in *Boethius's De topicis differentiis*, p. 67: "The maximal proposition: contraries cannot agree with each other when they are adverse, privative, or negative; and when they are relative, they cannot occur without each other."

[99] See Book I, c. 7 n. 14 in CCSL l, pp. 44-46.

[100] See Tractate 78 n. 3 in CCSL xxxvi, p. 525 and FC 90, pp. 109-110.

lesser, as if he bears a name that conveys the notion of imperfection.[101]

48. Question 3 draws attention to John 14:29: "Now I have told you before it comes to pass, so that, when it has come to pass, you may believe." – 1. So it still seems that the Apostles did not have faith, because he told them beforehand, so that they might believe. – 2. Moreover, "There is no merit in faith, when human reason provides a proof."[102] Therefore, if he foretold these things to them and they saw the things take place that he had foretold, they experienced them as true. Wherefore, they didn't have the merit of faith. – I respond that it has to be said that the Apostles had faith, but that their faith was not fully articulated nor was it perfectly firm, as it obvious, because they in no way wanted to believe the resurrection.[103] – So it has to be maintained that the Lord foretold his passion to them, so that they might already believe in it. About it they had no prior knowledge. He was also speaking in a way to strengthen their faith, so that, seeing his passion and vacillating, they might recall that he suffered willingly and as God. So they saw one thing and believed another thing, because they saw that he had suffered as a human being, but they believed that he voluntarily suffered and as God handed over his own life. His prediction was a sign of this, but it was not a compelling cause that might take away their merit.

49. Question 4 deals with John 14:30 and what it says that the devil did not have any jurisdiction over Christ. – 1. So it seems that the Lord acted unjustly when he al-

---

[101] See Book IX, n. 51-57 of *De Trinitate*.

[102] See Homily 26 n. 1 of GGHG in CCSL cxli, p. 218, and Hurst, p. 201.

[103] See John 20:9, 25 below.

lowed him to be oppressed by the devil. – 2. Furthermore, he says that he did this on account of the commandment of the Father. Wherefore, if he had to be obedient, then he died out of a sense of duty, not out of sheer generosity.

I answer that it has to be said that any person who does not want to be punished for his own sin acts out of anger and severity.[104] Anyone who is willingly punished for his own sin acts of our justice and truth. Anyone who is willing to suffer for the sin of another acts out of a wondrous and gracious disposition. – So since Christ underwent punishment and did so freely for our salvation, God was pleased "to lay upon him the iniquities of us all"[105] and to punish him for our crimes. "He was offered because it was his own will."[106] And therefore, no injustice was done on God's part, but on the part of the devil. And so, since the devil unjustly usurped dominion over Christ, by this very fact he lost the just dominion he had over the members of Christ.[107] – 2. With regard to the objection that he had to die, it has to be maintained that there is the necessity that is deserved and the necessity that stems from a commandment. The sinner must die, since he deserves death, but Christ dies because the Father has commanded him. Now this necessity does not contravene graciousness and liberality when it transpires out of love. And this is how Christ acted, and therefore he says: "So that the world may know that I love the Father."[108]

---

[104] On p. 446 n. 5 QuarEd give evidence for the reading "perversity."

[105] See Isa 53:6.

[106] See Isa 53:7.

[107] See Book III d. 19. a. 1. q. 2. ad 5 and dub. 3-4 in Bonaventure's *Sentence Commentary*.

[108] See John 14:31.

Chapter Fifteen

John 15:1-27
The Lord exhorts his disciples to constant love

1. *I am the true vine*, etc. In the previous chapter the Lord exhorted his disciples to constant faith. In this chapter he exhorts them to *proven and true love*. And since true love first loves God, and then the friend in God, and finally loves and bears up with the enemy for God's sake, the Lord first exhorts his disciples to the love of God, then to love of friends where verse 12 reads: "This is my commandment that you love one another," etc., and finally to love and bear up with enemies where verse 18 states: "If the world hates you, know," etc.

John 15:1-11
The Lord exhorts his disciples to love of God

He exhorts them first to *love of God*. And since "the person who abides in love abides in God,"[1] he exhorts them to abide in him and does so in the following manner. First, he describes *the place where one abides*. Second, *the fruit*. Third, *the manner*. Fourth, *the effect*.

2. (Verse 1) So first the place where one abides is said to be Christ himself, on whom believers must abide like

---

[1] 1 John 4:16.

branches abide on the vine. So the text states: *I am the true vine*. He says "true," because he produces the true wine, about which Genesis 49:11: "He will wash his robe in wine[2] and his garment in the blood of the grape, tying his foal to the vineyard and his ass ... to the vine."[3] This vine is not uncultivated, for the text says: *And my Father is the vinedresser*, who not only tends to the exterior, but also increases the interior.[4] 1 Corinthians 3:6,9 reads: "I have planted. Apollos watered, but God has given the growth.... You are God's tillage; you are God's building." Therefore, the Father is the true vinedresser, because he performs his tasks. Thus, the text continues:

3. (Verse 2). *Every branch in me that bears no fruit, he will take away*. Matthew 3:10 states: "The axe is laid at the root of the tree.[5] Every tree that is not bringing forth good fruit, will be cut down and thrown into the fire."[6] *And every branch that bears fruit he will cleanse, so that it may bear more fruit*. "He will cleanse" through repentance. Thus 1 John 1:9 reads: "If we acknowledge our sins, he is faithful and just to forgive us all our[7] sins and cleanse us from all iniquity." He also cleanses through patience. Thus Psalm 65:10-11 says: "Because you, O God, have proved us. You

---

[2] The Vulgate reads *vino* ("in wine") whilst Bonaventure has *in vino* ("in wine").

[3] On p. 446 n. 12 QuarEd correctly indicate that Bonaventure has inverted the two clauses of this verse.

[4] See Augustine, Sermon 87 c. 1 n. 1 in *Sermons III*, p. 407: "... we cultivate God, in the sense of worshiping him, and God cultivates us.... He, however, cultivates us as a farmer does his fields. So his tending or cultivating us means he makes improvements in us, because a farmer improves his fields by tending them...."

[5] The Vulgate reads *arborum* ("trees") while Bonaventure has *arboris* ("tree").

[6] The Vulgate reads *exciditur* ("is cut down") whilst Bonaventure has *excidetur* ("will be cut down"). Also the Vulgate reads *mittitur* ("is thrown") whereas Bonaventure has *mittetur* ("will be thrown").

[7] The Vulgate does not read *omnia nostra* ("all our").

have tried us by fire, as silver is tried. You have brought us into the net," etc.[8] So on this vine cleansed branches are optimally located. Therefore, he exhorts the apostles, who are already cleansed, that they abide in him. For this reason the text states:

4. (Verse 3). *You are already clean because of the word that I have spoken to you.* This was the word of faith that purifies those who believe. Acts 15:9 says: "... cleansed their hearts by faith."[9] So since you are clean:

5. (Verse 4). *Abide in me*, as on a vine, *and I in you*, as in a temple. About this 1 John 4:16 has: "The person who abides in love abides in God and God in him." Therefore, there is a mutual abiding, because there is a mutual love. John 14:21-23 above reads: "The person who loves me will be loved by my Father, and I will love him and manifest myself to him.... And we will come to him and will make our abode with him." – *As the branch*, etc. He had treated the place of the abiding. Now here in a second point he addresses the fruit of the abiding. The branch bears this fruit, not without the vine, but on the vine. So he shows that fruit has its origin from the branch on the vine, first by showing its opposite, namely, separation, and secondly, by showing the situation at hand, namely, abiding.[10] For which reason the text says: *As the branch cannot bear*

---

[8] See Book IX, Letter 102 of *S. Gregorii Magni Registrvm epistvlarvm Libri VIII-XIV, Appendix*. Edited by Dag Norberg. CCSL cxla (Turnhout: Brepols, 1982), p. 614: "For he takes away the unfruitful branch, because the sinner is pulled out at the roots. But the fruitful branch is said to be cleansed, since it is cut back through discipline so that it may be led to more abundant grace."

[9] This verse occurs in Peter's speech to justify God's call of the Gentiles at the Council at Antioch.

[10] See Book IV, c. 4 of Aristotle, *Topica* in WAE, Volume I, 124a.

fruit of itself unless it remains on the vine, so you, too,[11] *bear fruit only if you abide in me.* And wherefore, if they want to be fruitful, it is necessary that they remain in him from whom the fruit issues. Ephesians 1:22-23 reads: "Him he gave as head over all the Church which is his body and the fullness of him who has filled all with all."[12] John 1:16 above states: "Of his fullness we have all received, grace for grace." So you cannot bear fruit, unless you remain in me. But you can bear fruit in me, because:

6. (Verse 5). *I am the vine, and*[13] *you are the branches.* And therefore, remain in me as in the source of the fruit. *For without me you can do nothing* Isaiah 26:12 says: "Lord, you have performed all our works in us." And that they can do nothing without him, he shows through a similitude:

7. (Verse 6). *If anyone does not abide in me, he will be cast outside like the branch,* namely, separated from the vine. Outside the vine one is cast aside through separation from the unity of the Church. Revelation 22:15 reads: "Outside are the dogs and the sorcerers and the lewd," etc.[14] And they will not produce fruit. Therefore, *and he will wither,* through the loss of the moisture of grace. *And they will gather him up and cast him into the fire, and he*

---

[11] On p. 447 n. 7 QuarEd accurately indicate that the Vulgate reads *sic nec* ("so neither") while Bonaventure has *sic et* ("so, you, too").

[12] I translate the Vulgate: "Him he gave as head above everything of the Church, which is his body, the fullness of him who fills all with all."

[13] On p. 447 n. 8 QuarEd correctly mention that the Vulgate does not read *et* ("and").

[14] Hugh of St. Cher, p. 375v,d comments: "be cast outside] from the saints in the future society. For they will be with the goats, not with the sheep in the judgment, Matt 25:32. Likewise, Rev 22:15 says: "Outside are the dogs.""

will burn,[15] since he will burn through the affliction of punishment. – Thus four evils follow. First, that it is cast out. Matthew 15:13 states: "Every plant that my heavenly Father has not planted will be rooted out." – Second, it withers. In Matthew 21:19 the Lord said to the fig tree on which he found nothing but leaves: "May no fruit ever come from you forever. And it immediately withered up."[16] Psalm 21:16 says: "My strength is dried up like a potsherd." – Third, it is gathered up through the ministry of the angels. Thus, Matthew 13:41 reads: "They will gather up from his kingdom all scandals."[17] – Fourth, it is burnt with fire. Ezekiel 15:2-4 states: "Son of man, what will happen with the wood of the vine? ... Behold, it has been cast into the fire for fuel."[18]

8. (Verse 7). *If you abide in me.* In verses 4-6 above he showed that he was the source of the fruit by showing what was opposite to abiding. Here he makes his point by the abiding itself, which produces fruit with regard to itself and with regard to one's neighbor. With respect to self the text reads: *If you abide in me and if my words abide in you*, not like those about whom Luke 8:13 speaks: "They believe for a while, and during temptation fall away," but like those about whom Psalm 102:18 speaks: "Who keep his covenant and are mindful of his commandments to do them." *Ask whatever you will, and it will be done for you.* John 9:31 above has: "If anyone does the will of God, God hears him." Not only is there fruit with regard to self, but also with regard to converting the neighbor to the glory of God. So the text adds:

---

[15] The Vulgate employs the plural: "They will gather *them* up... and *they* will burn."

[16] The Vulgate reads *arefacta* ("became parched") while Bonaventure has *exaruit* ("withered up").

[17] Matt 13:41 concludes: "... and those who work iniquity."

[18] Hugh of St. Cher, p. 375v,h also cites Ez 15:2-4.

9. (Verse 8). *In this is my Father glorified that you may bear much fruit*, namely, that men and women be converted by your word and example. Matthew 5:16 reads: "So let your light shine before men and women that they may see your good deeds and give glory to your Father, who is in heaven." *And* by this *you become my disciples*, that is, imitators of me, who bore much fruit through my death, as John 12:25 above says: "If a grain of wheat dies, it brings forth much fruit." It is the same with the apostles. Thus the Church sings of them: "they planted the Church with their blood."[19] Colossians 1:24 states: "I fill up those things that are lacking of the sufferings of Christ."

10. (Verse 9). *As the Father has loved me*. Here the third point surfaces, that is, the manner of abiding, which is through love, to which he must invite us through his prior love. Therefore, the text says: *As the Father has loved me, I also have loved you*. And so *Abide in my love*. 1 John 4:19 reads: "Let us, therefore, love God, because God first loved us." And since true love is shown by deeds, the text continues:

11. (Verse 10). *If you keep my commandments, you will abide in my love, as I also have kept my Father's commandments and abide in his love.* John 14:31 above states: "That the world may know that I love the Father and that I do as the Father has commanded me." We too must do likewise. 1 John 2:6 reads: "The person who says that he abides in him must also walk just as he walked." Deuteronomy 10:12-13 says: "And now, Israel, what does the Lord your God require of you, but that you fear the Lord your God and walk in his ways and love him and serve the Lord your God with all your heart and with

---

[19] See the responsory to the first reading for the third nocturn of the Common of Apostles in the Roman Breviary.

all your soul and keep the commandments of the Lord
and his ceremonies which I command you today, so that
it may be well with you?"

12. (Verse 11). *These things I have spoken to you.* Here
he touches upon the fourth point, namely, the effect of
abiding. And the effect is joy in the present and joy in the
future. About the joy in the present the text says: *that
my joy may be in you,* that is the pure joy which a person
enjoys in the Lord, not in the world.[20] About it Philippians
4:4 says: "Rejoice in the Lord always. Again I say: rejoice."
– Concerning future joy the text states: *And that your joy
may be made full.* About this John 16:24 below says: "Ask,
and you will receive, so that your joy may be full." Our joy
is filled by the joy of the Lord. About this Matthew 25:21
has: "Enter into the joy of your Lord."[21]

QUESTIONS

13. Question 1 deals with John 15:1: "I am the true vine."
Augustine objects: If Christ is said to be a vine, as he is
said to be a lion and a rock, and these are not said of him
in a proper sense, but in the sense of a similitude, and
yet they are said of him as true and therefore as proper,
it does not seem that he should say that he is the true
vine, but that he is like a vine.[22] – And Augustine answers

---

[20] See Augustine, Tractate 83 n. 1 in FC 90, p. 130: "But this joy of
ours grows and progresses, and by persevering it persists in reaching
for its perfection. Therefore, it is initiated in the faith of those who are
born again; it will be fulfilled in the reward of those who rise again."

[21] See Letter 114 n. 1 of Bernard of Clairvaux in SBOp 7.292: "And
verily that joy is true and singular that is not born of creatures, but
from the Creator and that, when you possess it, no one can take it
from you. Compared to it, every other felicity is sadness...."

[22] See Tractate 80 n. 1 in FC 90, p. 115: "For he is called the vine
through metaphor, not through proper designation, in the same way

that by adding true, "he distinguishes himself from that [vine] to which it was said: 'How have you turned into bitterness, O strange vine?'"[23] Jeremiah 2:21 states: "How have you turned into something that is good for nothing, O strange vineyard?"[24] So "true" is not used by way of similitude, but in the sense of "not strange."

Now it can be said that just as wine is true that works like wine, so too is a vine true that works like a vine. So in a literal sense a vine is true when it produces wine. It is not true when it bears no fruit. Thus by similitude a vine is said to be true which acts as a vine should, and not true when it does not act like a vine.[25] So also Christ, who performs the action of a vine, is the true vine. The Synagogue, however, is not. About it Isaiah 5:2 reads: "He expected that it should bring forth grapes, but it brought forth thorns."[26]

14. Question 2 addresses the same question from a different angle: Why does the Lord compare himself to a grain

---

as he is called a sheep, a lamb, a lion, a rock, a cornerstone, and other things of this sort, which are rather themselves true things from which are drawn these metaphors, not proper designations." Hugh of St. Cher, p. 373v, c also cites this passage from Augustine.

[23] See Tractate 80 n. 1 in CCSL xxxvi, p. 528 and FC 90, p. 11. Bonaventure's quotation is virtually verbatim. Augustine has modified Jer 2:21 by changing "vineyard" into "vine" and by taking the word "bitterness" from the LXX. Jer 2:21a talks about the "true vineyard."

[24] Hugh of St. Cher, p. 374v,d also cites Jer 2:21.

[25] See Book IV, c. 12 of Aristotle, *Meteorologica* in WAE, Volume 3, 390a: "What a thing is is always determined by its function: a thing really is itself when it can perform its function; an eye, for instance, when it can see."

[26] On p. 448 n. 11 QuarEd rightly notice that the Vulgate reads *labruscas* ("wild grapes") while Bonaventure has *spinas* ("thorns"). Was Bonaventure thinking of Matt 7:16: "By their fruits you will know them. Do people gather grapes from thorns, or figs from thistles?"

of wheat rather than to some other grain[27] and why does he compare himself to the wood of the vine rather than to some other wood? – I respond. This is said on account of the true body and the mystical body. The true body of Christ is true food, and his true blood is true drink.[28] So since from the grain of wheat the best bread comes and from the vine the best wine comes, therefore he compared himself to a vine and to a grain. And so too it is from these two species that the Sacrament of the altar is confected. – Another reason is due to the mystical body, since, as from the most pure grains of wheat and the fruit of the grape bread and wine are made, so too from the pure faithful is the mystical body of Christ fashioned.[29]

15. Question three inquires about the nature by which Christ is the vine, whether his divine or his human nature. – And for the case that it was according to his human nature Augustine observes: "The vine and the branches are of one nature. And for this reason, since he was God – of whose nature we are not – he became human in order that in him human nature might be the vine, of which we too could be the branches."[30] – But contrary to this is: 1. Since the vine causes moisture to flow through the branches and if the flow of the moisture of grace issues solely from God and as God,[31] therefore, it follows that

---

[27] See John 12:24-25: "Amen, amen I say to you, unless the grain of wheat falls into the ground and dies, it remains alone. But if it dies, it brings forth much fruit."

[28] See John 6:56 above.

[29] See Augustine, Tractate 26 n. 17 in FC 79, p. 274: "For this reason ... Our Lord, Jesus Christ, manifested his body and blood in those things which are reduced from many to some one thing. For the one is made into one thing from many grains, the other flows together into one thing from many grapes."

[30] See Tractate 80 n. 1 in CCSL xxxvi, p. 527. Cf. FC 90, p. 115. Bonaventure's quotation is virtually verbatim.

[31] See Ps 83:12: "The Lord will give grace and glory."

Christ is the vine according to his divine nature.[32] – 2. Furthermore, on this vine all the saints from Abel to the last just person have remained and grown, but Christ according to his human nature followed after Abel.[33] Therefore, the branches were not in him according to his human nature.

I answer that it should be maintained that certain things are said of Christ according to his divine nature solely, so that these are said, abstracting from his human nature, such as his eternity and impassibility. Other things are said of his human nature solely, such as his mortality and possibility. Certain other things are said according to his human nature as it is united to the divine nature, and vice versa, as in the case of his mediatorship. For if he were only God, he is not straightaway a mediator. If he were only human, he would not immediately be a mediator. If he were God and human, then he is a mediator.[34] And according to this viewpoint he is the vine and the head of the Church in as far as he is the mediator. So when the text says "vine," this is not according to his human nature solely, but according to it as joined to the divine nature in the unity of hypostasis. And because of the unity of the hypostasis Christ is the object of faith according to both natures. And therefore, we believe Christ to be God and

---

[32] See Augustine, Tractate 81 n. 3 in FC 90, pp. 121-122: "Moreover, although Christ would not be the vine if he were not a man, nonetheless he would not offer this grace to the branches if he were not also God."

[33] See the Glossa Ordinaria on Col 1:18 in PL 114:610C: "And since the Church began with Abel, how can he be its head? It is true because he is the beginning of the Church, that is, its founder…. Of the church, according to his divinity, that is, the founder of the Church, because he has illumined by the gift of his mercy all the just who are begotten by the power of his divinity from Abel to the last just person."

[34] See Book III. D. 19 a. 2. q. 2 of Bonaventure's *Sentence Commentary*.

man. And since without this faith, implicit or explicit, no one is saved, the moisture of the grace from this vine overflowed into all the saints. – 2. And so it is clear how he was the vine with regard to those who went before and those who came after. For "and those who went before him and those who followed kept crying out: Hosanna to the son of David."[35] So Christ is very well signified by "the cluster of grapes,"[36] which was taken from the promised land, according to Numbers 13:24, and which they carried on their shoulders.[37] And those who went ahead were carrying it and did not see, but those who followed carried and saw.[38]

16. Question 4 stems from Augustine who asks about John 15:3: "You are clean because of the word that I have spoken to you."[39] Since a word is external and cleanliness is internal, how can an external word clean internally?[40] – I respond that it has to be said that this is either on account of faith or account of the sacrament of faith. On account of faith, since "faith depends upon hearing," that

---

[35] Bonaventure conflates Matt 21:9 and Mark 11:9. See Bede's commentary on Mark 11:9 in CCSL cxx, p. 573: "Those that went ahead are the Jewish people. Those who followed are the Gentile people. And since all elect ... believed and believe in the mediator of God and human beings, those who go before and those who follow cried out Hosanna."

[36] Bonaventure stops short of saying what the signification was. See the commentary of Bede on Num 13:24 in PL 91:564D: The Jews are represented by the first man carrying the pole while the Gentiles are signified by the second man who sees the cluster of grapes.

[37] As the two men carried the cluster of grapes on the pole, one went ahead and did not see the cluster while his carrying partner did.

[38] This detail is not found in Num 13:24. Cf. Deut 1:24-25.

[39] The Vulgate reads *Iam vos mundi estis* ("You are already clean").

[40] See Tractate 80 n. 3 in FC 90, p. 117-19.

cleanses the heart.[41] On account of the sacrament of faith which is baptism. Thus Augustine observes: "… in the water the word cleansed. Take away the word, and what is the water except water? The word is added to the element, and it becomes a sacrament."[42] Now this word of faith and of sacrament, although external, nonetheless cleanses, as Augustine says "not because it is spoken, but because it is believed. Romans 10:16 states: *If you confess with your mouth*, that the Lord has ascended into heaven, and *you believe in your heart*, that *God raised him from the dead, you will be saved.*"[43]

17. Question 5 focuses on John 15:2: "The Father takes away every branch that bears no fruit." – Either he takes it away from the vine or from life. Not from the vine, since the Father separates no one from his Son. Or if he takes it away, how does he take it away from the vine? For the person who does not do good, by that very fact has been separated from the vine, Christ. And since he does not have grace, he by all means perishes. – If the Father takes it away from life, that is false, because there are more evil people than good who are alive, as we see. – Moreover, he would also take good as well as the evil away from bodily life. – I answer that it has to be maintained that the branches draw from Christ not the life of nature, but the life of grace and the life of glory. The text says the branches "are taken away" or separated from this vine, not by death of nature, but by the death of sin or final damnation. Wherefore, unfruitful branches and those who receive the grace of God in vain are separated from

---

[41] Bonaventure refers to Rom 10:17 ("faith depends upon hearing") and Acts 15:9: ("faith cleansed their hearts").

[42] See Tractate 80 n. 3 in CCSL xxxvi, p. 529. Cf. FC 90, p. 117. Hugh of St. Cher, p. 375f also cites this passage from Augustine.

[43] Bonaventure adapts Tractate 80 n. 3. See CCSL xxxvi, p. 529 and FC 90, pp. 117-118.

the vine by merit of their own sin through the judgment of divine justice. Thus Revelation 3:16 states: "Since you are lukewarm, I will begin to vomit you forth," since by his just judgment God does not apportion grace to them. By the judgment of final damnation they are taken away and cast into the fire, when the time for meriting is over.[44] Therefore, the text says "he will take away," not because he immediately takes them away, since he provides a time for repentance.

18. Question 6 concerns John 15:9: "As the Father has loved me, I also have loved you." – Against this statement is this that the love of the Father is natural, but the love of Son towards us is purely gratuitous. Wherefore, there does not seem to be a likeness. So the question is: How much love is behind the statement: 'As the Father has loved me," etc.? – I respond that one must say, as Richard of St. Victor maintains, that in the divine persons there is love that is purely gratuitous, that is due, and that is a mixture of the two. The love of the Father towards the Son is purely gratuitous, because the Father gives to the Son and receives nothing. Now the love of the Holy Spirit to the Father and the Son is purely due, because he is solely a receiver. And the love of the Son towards the Father is due, for he receives. The love of the Son towards the Holy Spirit is gratuitous, since he gives. So since the Son has loved us with purely gratuitous love, he, therefore, compares the love by which he loves us to the love of the Father towards him.[45]

---

[44] See Augustine, Tractate 81 n. 3 in FC 90, p. 122: "One of two things is suitable for the branch, either the vine or the fire; if it is not in the vine, it will be in the fire. Therefore, that it may not be in the fire, let it be in the vine."

[45] See Book V, c. 16-20 of *De Trinitate* in PL 196:961B-964B. In his *Explicatio aliquorum passuum difficilium Apostoli* Richard of St. Victor gives a clear articulation of these three types of love. See PL

John 15:12-17
The Lord exhorts his disciples to love
of their brothers and friends

19. *This is my commandment.* After the Lord has exhorted them to love of God, here in a second place he exhorts them to *love of their brothers and friends*, and he does this in the following manner. First, he binds them to fraternal love from the perspective of *obedience*. Second from the perspective of *divine friendship*. Third from the perspective of *eternal remuneration*.

Verse 12. First he binds them by the commandment of obedience, indicating that this is entirely in accordance with his will and is the principal commandment. For this reason the text says: *This is my commandment that you love one another.* Thus John 13:34 above states: "I give you a new commandment that you love one another." And he adds the manner: *As I have loved you,* "not in word or tongue, but in deed and in truth,"[46] as I have loved you. And that he loved them in deed, he shows:

20. (Verse 13). *Greater love than this no one has than*[47] *that one lay down one's life for his friends.* As if to say: There is nothing more to do than to give one's life which is dearest to all people. Ephesians 5:2 reads: "Christ loved us and delivered himself up for us as an offering and a sacrifice to God in a sweet fragrance." And this was the most burn-

---

198:682D. See also Augustine, Tractate 82 n. 2 in FC 90, pp. 125-126: "... he does not show an equality of our nature and his, as there is of the Father's and his, but grace whereby the mediator of God and men is the man Christ Jesus."

[46] The quotation is from 1 John 3:18, but is not verbatim. See Hugh of St. Cher, p. 376v, d who cites 1 John 3:18, but not verbatim.

[47] On p. 450 n. 7 QuarEd accurately indicate that the Vulgate does not read *quam* ("than").

ing love, not only in Christ who handed over himself and his life, but also in the Father. For Romans 8:32 states: "Who did not spare his own Son, but has delivered him up for us all. How can he fail to grant us also all things with him?" – Thus it is to be noted that the love by which a mother loves her child is great. But Christ's love for us went beyond this love. Isaiah 49:15 states: "Can a woman forget her infant, so as not to have pity on the child of her womb? And if she should forget, yet I will not forget you." – The love of a wife for her husband is greater. But Christ's love for us went beyond this love. Jeremiah 3:1 reads: "It is commonly said: If a man puts away his wife and she goes forth from him and marries another man, will he return to her any more? ... But you have prostituted yourself with many lovers. Nevertheless, return to me ... and I will welcome you."[48] – The greatest love is that of the soul for the body. But Christ's love for us exceeded that love. Jeremiah 12:7 says: "I have forsaken my home. I have left my inheritance. I have given my beloved soul into the hands of her enemies." And therefore, what The Song of Songs 8:6 states is true: "Love is strong as death," etc.

21. (Verse 14). *You are my friends.* Here in a second point he exhorts them to mutual love from the perspective of divine friendship. Thus he offers his friendship to those who observe his commandments, so that they may love one another according to the Lord's command. For this reason the text states: *You are my friends if you do the things that I command you.*[49] He promises something great when he promises friendship. Augustine comments:

---

[48] See Vulgate, p. 1169 where *et ego suscipiam te* ("and I will welcome you") is a variant reading and in a footnote.

[49] On p. 451 n. 1 QuarEd accurately mention that the Vulgate makes "I" explicit by reading *ego*.

"The Lord's esteem is great when he has esteemed us by calling us friends"[50] because "friend" is a word of equality. "For friendship … is an accord in things divine and human conjoined by means of a mutual will."[51] For if wisdom makes people friends of God as Wisdom 7:27 says: "She conveyed herself into holy souls and made them friends of God," then how much more love? This love is proven in deeds. Wherefore, the text continues: *You are my friends, if you do the things I command you*,[52] out of love as friends, not out of fear as slaves, because you have not been called into servitude. For this reason the text adds:

22. (Verse 15). *No longer do I call you servants*, although you were such before. Romans 8:15 reads: "You have not received a spirit of servitude so as to be again in fear, but … a spirit of adoption as children." And he shows this by means of a sign: *because the servant does not know what his master is doing*. But it is not so with you. Therefore, he says: *But I have called you friends, since all things that I have heard from my Father I have made known to you.* This is a sign of great friendship: the revelation of secrets. Ephesians 1:9 has: "He has made known to us the mystery of his will."[53] Matthew 13:11 states: "To you have been given to know the mysteries of the kingdom of God," etc.

---

[50] This is a paraphrase of Tractate 85 n. 1. See CCSL xxxvi, p. 539.

[51] Bonaventure adapts Cicero's definition of friendship found in c. 6 n. 20 of his *De amicitia*. See *Cicero, De senectute, de amicitia, de divinatione*. Translated by William A. Falconer. LCL (Cambridge: Harvard University Press, 1964), p. 131: "For friendship is nothing else than an accord in all things, human and divine, conjoined with mutual goodwill and affection…."

[52] In this citation of John 15:14 Bonaventure reads *ego* ("I"). See note 49 above.

[53] Eph 1:9 reads: "so that he might make known to us the mystery of his will…."

23. (Verse 16). *You have not chosen me.* Here in a third point he exhorts them to love from the perspective of eternal reward to which they have been called through eternal predestination. They had not made their way there on their own. Wherefore, the text reads: *You have not chosen me, but I have chosen you.* Ephesians 1:4-5 says: "He chose us ... before the foundation of the world that we might be holy and without blemish in his sight in love. He predestined us to be adopted through Jesus Christ as his children, according to the purpose of his will." He adds why he had chosen them: *And I have appointed you that you should go and bear fruit* by converting others.[54] This happens through the preaching of the word of God that, like a seed, bears fruit when it is received into good soil. Thus Luke 8:15 states: "But that upon good soil, these are they who, with a right and good heart, hear the word and ... bear fruit in patience."[55] 1 Peter 1:23 reads: "You have been reborn, not from corruptible seed but from incorruptible, through the word of God who lives and abides forever." *And that your fruit should remain*, for your salvation and consolation through divine reward.[56] And the reward is added: *that whatever you ask the Father in my name*, that is, that which is for your salvation, *he may give you*. Now what is to be asked for is our salvation. Thus Matthew 6:33 says: "Seek first the kingdom of God and his righteousness, and all these things will be given you besides." In this way the holy soul asked for these things in Psalm 26:4: "One thing I have asked of the Lord,

---

[54] Hugh of St. Cher, p. 377v,b comments: "And that you bear fruit] through the conversion of men and women."

[55] I translate the Vulgate of Luke 8:15: "Now that upon good soil, these are they who, with a right and good heart, having heard the word, hold it fast, and bear fruit in patience."

[56] See Homily 27 n. 5 of GGHG in Hurst, p. 216: "I have appointed you for grace. I have planted you to go willingly and bring forth fruit by your works.... What we do for eternal life remains even after death...."

this will I seek after, that I may dwell in the house of the Lord all the days of my life." And from the perspective of this reward they should observe the commandment of Christ. Therefore, he repeats it:

24. (Verse 17). *These things I command you, that you may love one another*. The commandment of love is said to be like something given by hand, for he gave it by means of his example. Thus John 13:34 says: "I give you a new commandment that you love one another."[57] And 1 Thessalonians 4:9 reads: "We have no necessity to write to you about fraternal love, for you yourselves have been taught by God that you love one another."

QUESTIONS

25. Question 1 comes from Gregory and focuses on John 15:12: "This is my commandment that you love one another." Gregory asks: "Since all the divine sayings are full of the Lord's commandments, why does he single out love by saying 'This is my commandment'?"[58] And he answers: "The divine commandments are many and yet one: many on account of the diversity of deeds, but one in their root in love." And he states that love is a root, because "the little branch of a good work does not flower unless it remains rooted in love."[59] So since the commands are related to the commandment of love, in which all were united and fulfilled, he says plain and simple: "This is my commandment."

---

[57] Jesus said this after he had washed his disciples' feet by hand.

[58] See Homily 27 n. 1 of GGHG in CCSL cxli, p. 229.

[59] Bonaventure has adapted Homily 27 n. 1 of GGHG. See CCSL cxli, pp. 229-230.

26. Question 2 concerns John 15:13: "Greater love than this no one has that he lay down his life for his friends." – Contrary. 1. Out of a little love one person does something while another can die for a friend out of greater love. So what does he mean when he says "greater love"? 2. Moreover, in the heavenly homeland there will be much greater love than there is on the journey thereto. So what does he mean by "greater love? – I answer that the text is not speaking about the habit of love or about its principal act. Rather it is speaking about its sign or effect, since this is the principal sign of love.[60]

27. Question 3 continues the previous question and objects: Since it is greater to die for an enemy than for a friend, it is still not the greatest sign of love to die for a friend. In this manner the Apostle argues in Romans 5:10 *a minori*: "If, when we were enemies we were reconciled to God through the death of his Son, much more, having been reconciled, will we be saved by his life." – Gregory responds that the word "friends" stands not only for those who loved the Lord, but also for enemies, because they became the friends of the Lord when the Lord loved them by "laying down his life for them."[61] – Another interpretation is that the Lord was speaking about the love of friends, and relative to that type of love there is no greater sign than to die for one's friend. In a similar way this holds relative to the true love of enemies, because there is

---

[60] On p. 452 n. 1 QuarEd cite the Glossa Interlinearis: "To lay down one's life for friends is not love, but the effect of love."

[61] See Homily 27 n. 2 of GGHG in Hurst, p. 213: "The Lord had come to die even for his enemies, and yet he said he would lay down his life for his friends to show us that when we are able to win over our enemies by loving them even our persecutors are our friends."

no greater sign than to die for the enemy. Thus this excellence is not to be taken *simpliciter*, but *in genere*.[62]

28. Question 4 addresses John 15:15: "I no longer call your servants." – Contrary. 1. Matthew 25:21 says: "Well done, good and faithful servant." And if he calls these servants blessed, what does he mean by: "I do not call you servants"? 2. Furthermore, in John 13:13-15 above he said that he was their master. Therefore, on the basis of relative contraries he said that they were servants.[63] – I answer that it has to be maintained that "servant" is taken in a twofold sense. In the first sense it refers to obedience and subjection, and in this sense a servant is not to be distinguished from a friend, because all friends of God are God's servants. In the other sense servant means someone who fears in a servile manner. And such a person, who serves solely out of fear, is not a friend. And about such a person he is speaking in this verse, because he did not want people to fulfill his commandments in a servile way, but rather in a lovely manner.[64]

---

[62] Bonaventure seems to be employing a distinction found in Book IV, n. 16 of Aristotle's *Metaphysica*. See WAE, Volume 8, n. 1021b: "Things, then, that are called complete in virtue of their *own* nature are so called in all these senses, some because in respect to goodness they lack nothing and cannot be excelled and no part proper to them can be found outside them, others in general because they cannot be exceeded in their several classes and no part proper to them is outside them."

[63] See Book III n. 1198A in Boethius, *De topicis differentiis*, p. 67: "The maximal proposition: contraries cannot agree with each other when they are adverse, privative, or negative; and when they are relative, they cannot occur without each other."

[64] It seems that Bonaventure is adapting Augustine, Tractate 85 n. 3. See FC 90, pp. 138-139: "For as there are two fears that make two kinds of those who fear, so there are two servitudes, which make two kinds of servants. There is a fear that perfect love casts out, and there is another pure fear, enduring for ever and ever.... In the fear that love casts out, there is also a servitude that must be cast out at the same time together with this same fear; for the Apostle has joined the two

29. Question 5 queries the meaning of John 15:15: "All things that I have heard from my Father I have made known to you." Contrary: The Son heard infinite matters from the Father. Therefore, he has made known infinite matters. – They respond that he is not speaking of those things concerning which he heard in his divine nature, but in his human nature.[65] If this is the case, then the following objection results: Although Christ as a human being knew the day of judgment, nonetheless, he did not want to reveal it to his disciples.[66] – For this reason they give the further explanation that he made known to them everything pertaining to salvation. – Contrary to this is John 16:12 below: "I still have many things to say to you, but you cannot bear them now." And it is certain that these things pertain to their salvation. Therefore, etc.

Augustine answers: "He has made everything known," that is, he was disposed to make them known. For the Scripture often speaks in this manner, using the past tense for the future as a sign of certitude.[67] Another interpretation is that he has made known all things necessary for salvation, in as far as they were able to comprehend them.[68] – And so all things are clear.

---

together, that is, servitude and fear, by saying, 'You have not received the spirit of servitude again in fear'...."

[65] On p. 451 n. 8 QuarEd indicate that the Glossa Interlinearis suggests this answer and the one that follows: "Whatever I have heard, I, as a human being, with regard to work of human beings."

[66] See Matt 24:36: "But of that day and hour no one knows, not even the angels of heaven, but the Father only."

[67] Bonaventure is paraphrasing Tractate 86 n. 1. See FC 90, p. 140: "For just as he says through a prophet, 'They have dug my hands and my feet,' and does not say, 'are going to dig,' as though speaking of past events and yet foretelling those as still future, so also in this passage he says that he has made known to the disciples all things that he knows he is going to make known...."

[68] See John Chrysostom, Homily 77 n. 1 in PG 59:415: "Now when he says *all things*, you may understand those things that they had

30. Question 6 asks about the meaning of John 15:16: "You have not chosen me." Contrary. 1. Deuteronomy 26:17 states: "You have chosen the Lord ... to be your God." 2. Likewise, if the merit of free will consists in making a choice,[69] how were they to merit if they had not chosen him? – I respond that the matter is to be understood in this way. First, we have not first chosen the Lord. Second, he has chosen us beforehand through predestination and afterwards has chosen us by calling us from among others, and after that we have chosen God by consenting to God's call.[70]

John 15:18-16:4
The Lord exhorts his disciples to endure the persecution of their enemies

31. *If the world hates you*, etc. This is the third part of the chapter,[71] in which the Lord exhorts his disciples *to endure the persecution of their enemies*. And he does this in the following order. First, *he predicts the hatred of the world*. Second, he predicts *the harm that results from this persecution*. Third, he manifests *the malice of those per-*

---

need to hear." See also Theophylactus's commentary on John 15:14-16 in PG 124:199CD: "For a servant does not know the secrets of the master, but you, since you are now my friends, have been made worthy of the secrets. 'For I have made known to you all the things that I have heard from my Father.' But why does he say in another place: 'I have many things to say to you, but you cannot bear them now'? He has made known to them everything that they could hear and of which they were capable."

[69] See Book II, c. 22 of John Damascene, *De fide orthodoxa* in FC 37, p. 249: "Choice is the choosing and picking out of this one rather than the other of two things proposed."

[70] Bonaventure seems to be summarizing Augustine's lengthy treatment of "election" in Tractate 86 n. 2.

[71] Bonaventure's division actually goes to verse 4 of the next chapter, John 16.

secuting or hating the disciples. Fourth, he tells of his innocence. Finally, he *arms his disciples with patience.*

Verse 18. So first he predicts the world's hatred, which was to fall upon the members after the example of the head. For there had been the world's hatred against the head which is Christ. For this reason the text says: *If the world hates you, know,* that is, consider, *that it has hated me before you.* The Lord gave the reason for this hatred in John 3:20 above: "Everyone who does evil hates the light." And John 7:7 above states: "The world hates me, because I bear witness against it that its works are evil."[72] Because of this very same reason the world hates the members. Thus he provides the reason for this hatred: because they did not agree with the world. So the text continues:

32. (Verse 19). *If you were of the world,* that is, if you had remained in the world by means of an evil way of life, *the world would love what is its own.* Thus it is said in John 7:6-7 above: "But your time is always at hand. The world cannot hate you." *But because you are not of the world,* that is, involved in a worldly way of life,[73] *but I have chosen you out of the world, therefore the world hates you.* This hatred was signified in Genesis 27:41 in the hatred of Esau where it is said: "Esau hated Jacob for the blessing wherewith his father had blessed him." "Esau" signifies the worldly and rejected whereas "Jacob" signifies the chosen.

33. (Verse 20). *Remember the word.* So the second point surfaces here, that is, the harm that hatred inflicts

---

[72] John 7:7 reads: "The world cannot hate you, but it hates me, because I bear witness against it that its works are evil."

[73] See Hugh of St. Cher, p. 378h: "But you are not of the world] that is, you are not worldly cohorts in malice."

against the members in the same way as against the head. It harms the members for the sake of the head and follows the example of what it did to the head. For this reason the text states: *Remember the word that I have spoken to you:*[74] *No servant is greater than his master.* John 13:16 above reads: "Amen, amen I say to you: No servant is above his master nor is the one sent greater than his master."[75] And therefore, he argues: *If they have persecuted me, they will also persecute you.* And so it follows that, if they hate and persecute the head, they will do the same to the members. Thus Augustine comments: "The person who does not want to endure the hatred of the world with the head refuses to be in the body."[76] About the persecution of the head Psalm 108:17 says: "They persecuted the poor person and the beggar and the broken in heart."[77] They persecute not only in deed, but they contemn in their heart: *If they have kept my word, they will keep yours also*, that is, as they have contemned my word, they will scorn yours also. Luke 10:16 states: "The person who hears you hears me, and the person who scorns you scorns me." – Another interpretation: *They have kept my word*, that is, they have observed what I was saying so that they might calumniate me. Matthew 22:15 reads: "The Pharisees went and took counsel how they might trap him in his speech." And Psalm 36:12 says: "The sinner will watch the just person." – And the worldly people persecute head and members. They do not persecute the

---

[74] On p. 453 n. 9 QuarEd correctly indicate that the Vulgate reads *sermonis mei* ("my word").

[75] John 13:16 reads: "Amen, amen I say to you: No servant is greater than his master, nor is one who is sent greater than the one who sent him."

[76] See Tractate 87 n. 2 in CCSL xxxvi, p. 544. Bonaventure changes the second person singular into third person singular. Hugh of St. Cher, p. 378e cites this passage from Augustine verbatim.

[77] Ps 108:17 concludes with: "... to put him to death."

head for the sake of the members, but vice versa. Therefore, the text continues:

34. (Verse 21). *But all these things they will do to you for my name's sake,* namely, to erase it. For this reason you are blessed. Matthew 5:11 states: "Blessed are you, when men and women persecute you and, speaking falsely, utter all manner of evil against you, for my sake."[78] The reason for this is the blindness of unbelief. Thus the text says: *Because they do not know him who sent me.* John 8:19 above says: "You know neither me nor my Father." And John 17:25 states: "Righteous Father, the world has not known you."

35. (Verse 22). *If I had not come.* Now in a third point the malice of those who hate and persecute is shown. So he shows that their malice is inexcusable both through the things they have heard and from the things they have seen. Through the things that they have heard when he says: *If I had not come and had not*[79] *spoken to them,* namely, through the words of faith and teaching, *they would have no sin.* Supply: a sin so grave and inexcusable since as Luke 12:47-48 states: "The servant, who knew his master's will ... and did not do it, will be beaten with many stripes, but the one who did not know it ... will be beaten with few stripes."[80] And wherefore, if they had not heard, they would be excusable in some manner on account of ignorance.[81] *But now they have no excuse for their sin,* because they do not believe out of ignorance, but out

---

[78] Hugh of St. Cher, p. 378v,b alludes to Matt 5:11.

[79] On p. 454 n. 1 QuarEd rightly notice that the Vulgate does not have this second *non* ("not").

[80] Hugh of St. Cher, p. 378v,g alludes to Luke 12:47-48.

[81] See Book II. d. 22 a. 2. q. 3 of Bonaventure's *Sentence Commentary* where he shows that ignorance excuses from sin either in total or to a great extent.

of hatred. This hatred overflows towards the Father. So the text adds:

36. (Verse 23). *The person who hates me also hates my Father.* These people have been raised on high by their pride, according to what Psalm 73:23 says: "The pride of those who hate you rises up continually." So since they refused to hear out of malice, they were inexcusable. Matthew 12:42 reads: "The Queen of the South will rise in judgment with this generation and will condemn it, since she came from the ends of the earth to hear the wisdom of Solomon." Romans 2:1 states: "You are inexcusable, O human being whoever you are, who judges, for wherein you judge another, you condemn yourself." The Jews are also inexcusable on account of the things they have seen. So the text continues:

37. (Verse 24). *If I had not done among them works such as no one has done, they would have no sin*, namely, by not believing in something so great, since as John 5:36 above states: "The works that I do bear witness to me." *But now they have seen and have hated both me and my Father.* And therefore, they knowingly and out of malice refuse to believe and engage in persecution. So they are inexcusable. Matthew 11:21-22 states: "Woe to you, Chorazin. Woe to you, Bethsaida. For if the mighty deeds, that had been done among you, had been done in Tyre and Sidon, they would have repented long ago in sackcloth and ashes. But I tell you: It will be more tolerable for Tyre and Sidon on the day of judgment than for you." And this malignity of the Jews was expressed in Scripture. Therefore, he says:

38. (Verse 25). *But that the word written in their Law may be fulfilled* – "Law" is taken in the broad sense and thus

includes the Psalms[82] – *they have hated me without cause.* In Psalm 34:19 it is written: "Who are my enemies wrongfully, who have hated me without cause, and give consent with their eyes." And Psalm 119:7 reads: "When I spoke with them, they fought against me without cause." This hatred was prefigured in Genesis 37:4 where it is said: "The brothers of Joseph hated him and could not say anything peaceably to him."

39. (Verse 26). *But when the Paraclete has come.* Here in a fourth point he suggests the innocence to be expressed in the witness of the Holy Spirit and the Apostles. For this reason the text states: *But when he has come.* They have persecuted me as they would a wicked man and one deserving death. *But when the Paraclete has come, whom I will send you from the Father, the Spirit of truth who proceeds from the Father, he will bear witness concerning me.* Acts 5:32 says: "The Spirit is a witness, whom God has given to all who obey him." And by giving witness to my innocence, he convicts the world of malice. John 16:8 reads: "When he has come, he will convict the world of sin," because it did not believe. – Not only will he give witness to me, but also you who have been strengthened by him will give witness to me.[83] Thus:

40. (Verse 27). *And you will bear witness, because you are with me from the beginning.* Acts 1:21–22 states: "So of these men who have been in our company all the time that the Lord Jesus moved among us.... Of these one must become a witness with us of his resurrection." The Apostles did not bear witness before the coming of the

---

[82] See Hugh of St. Cher, p. 379g: "That the word written in their Law might be fulfilled] that is, given to them in the Law, or, that is, in the Psalms."
[83] See Hugh of St. Cher, p. 379q: "And you] the Apostles who are illumined and strengthened by him."

Holy Spirit, but afterwards. Therefore, Peter, who denied Christ at the word of a maid,[84] answered with great authority after the sending of the Holy Spirit the leader of the priests in Acts 5:29: "We must obey God rather than human beings."

---

[84] See John 18:17 below.

CHAPTER SIXTEEN

JOHN 15:18-16:4
THE LORD EXHORTS HIS DISCIPLES TO ENDURE
THE PERSECUTION OF THEIR ENEMIES (CONTINUED)

1. (Verse 1). *These things I have spoken to you*, etc. He now brings forth the fifth point as he arms his disciples with patience, namely, that they may not grow weak because of tribulation, but endure. Therefore, the text states: *These things I have spoken to you that you may not be scandalized*. For, as Gregory observes, "blows that we see coming strike us less forcefully, and we accept the evils of the world more patiently, if we are fortified against them by the shield of providential knowledge."[1] In this way he fortifies them in advance of future tribulation.

2. (Verse 2). *They will expel you from the synagogues*. Acts 8:1 reads: "A great persecution broke out against the church in Jerusalem, and all were scattered abroad throughout the land of Judea and Samaria." And the reason for this bitter persecution is added: *Indeed, the hour is coming for everyone who kills you to think that he is offering worship to God*. This hour was the time of the persecution of the Apostles. At that time they thought that by killing them they were doing good. Thus there is the example of Paul, about whom it is said in Acts 9:2: "he

---

[1] See Homily 35 n. 1 of GGHG in CCSL cxli, p. 321 and Hurst, p. 301. The citation is virtually verbatim.

sought letters from the high priest for Damascus that if he found any," etc.[2] Now such a plan has its basis in non-belief. And so the text continues:

3. (Verse 3). *And they will do these things, because they have not known the Father nor me*, that is, on account of ignorance and unbelief. An example is found in Paul. 1 Timothy 1:13 says: "I was formerly a blasphemer and a persecutor and a bitter adversary, but ... I acted ignorantly, in unbelief."[3] Therefore, he arms his disciples against these things by warning them beforehand. Therefore, he says:

4. (Verse 4). *But I have spoken these things to you that when the time for them has come*, namely, the time of persecution,[4] *you may remember that I told you.*[5] Remembering and recalling God's words are of great help in bearing up with all evils. On the contrary, forgetting is harmful. So Deuteronomy 8:11 states: "Beware lest at any time you forget the Lord your God and neglect his commandments." Recollection of God's words lifts up and directs a person. Therefore, it is said in Matthew 26:75: "Peter remembered the word of Jesus ... and he went out and wept bitterly."[6] Psalm 21:28 states: "All the ends of the earth will remember and will be converted to the Lord."

---

[2] Acts 9:1-2 reads: "But Saul ... went to the high priest and asked him for letters to the synagogues at Damascus, that if he found anyone belonging to the Way, he might bring them in bonds to Jerusalem."

[3] 1 Tim 1:13 states: "For I was formerly a blasphemer, and a persecutor, and a bitter adversary, but I obtained the mercy of God because I acted ignorantly, in unbelief."

[4] See Augustine, Tractate 93 n. 4 in FC 90, p. 179: "Their hour, an hour of darkness, an hour of night."

[5] The Vulgate concludes John 16:4 with this sentence.

[6] Matt 26:75 says: "And Peter remembered the word that Jesus had said, 'Before a cock crows, you will deny me three times.' And he went out and wept bitterly."

QUESTIONS

5. Question 1 focuses on John 16:3: "They did not know me"[7] and asks whether the Pharisees themselves knew Christ. – It seems that they did know him. 1. For it is said in Matthew 21:38 in the parable of the vineyard: "These vinedressers … said: This is the heir. Come, let us kill him." 2. Furthermore, in John 15:24 it is said: "But now they have seen and have hated both me and my Father." Wherefore, they knowingly hated him." – But contrary to this are: 1. Acts 3:17 reads: "And now, brothers and sisters, I know that you acted out of ignorance, as did your rulers too." So the rulers killed Christ in ignorance. Therefore, they did not know him. 2. Moreover 1 Corinthians 2:8 states: "If they had known, they would not have crucified the Lord of glory." Thus, they did not know the Christ. – I respond that it has to be said that he was Christ and God and the Messiah or the ruler promised in the Law. So it should be said that the Jews were evil in knowing that he was the Christ promised them and true and innocent. However, they did not know that he was the Son of God.[8] But since they assailed the truth known to them, willing to show that he was neither good nor holy, they became blinded and did not recognize the divinity in him because they hated his humanity. – So it is said that either they knew or they did not. Now knowledge is relative to the different things known. Now some refer to the different times when they knew.[9] They knew in the beginning, but

---

[7] John 16:3 says: "And these things they will do because they have not known the Father nor me."

[8] See Augustine, Tractate 93 n. 3 in FC 90, p. 176: "That is, they have not known God or his Son to whom they think they are offering service in slaying you."

[9] See Bonaventure's commentary in John 6 n. 50 where he also employs this distinction.

afterwards when they maliciously assailed him, they became blind.[10]

6. Question 2 deals with John 15:22: "If I had not come and spoken to them, they would have no sin." – 1. So according to this reasoning those who did not hear and did not believe are not damned because of unbelief. This is manifestly false, since no one is saved without faith. – 2. Likewise, according to this the people of Tyre and Sidon, who did not believe, will not be damned. This is obviously false on the basis of the witness of the gospel.[11] – I answer that it has to be maintained that there is an order in sins and that different types of sins are generally understood by the word "sin." But the gravest sin among others is that against the Holy Spirit. It is sin pure and simple with no excuses. So by the word "sin" is understood here the sin against the Holy Spirit that has been augmented by the sin of unbelief. And the Jews would not have had this, but

---

[10] See Peter Lombard's exposition of 1 Cor 2:8 in PL 191:1549AB: "Or it can be interpreted of the Jews, some of whom knew he was the Christ, but others did not. About those who did not know Peter said: *I know, brothers and sisters, that you acted out of ignorance* (Acts 3). These did not know that he was the one who had been promised them in the law. But the leaders such as the high priests, Scribes and Pharisees knew that he was the one who had been promised in the law. But they did not know that he was God or the Son of God. And so this verse can be interpreted of both of these: If they had known, either the ordinary people that he was the Messiah promised in the law or the leaders that he was God or the Son of God, they would never have crucified the Lord of glory. For they would not have done this if they knew that he was God. For if the demons did not understand that he was God made human, how much less could human beings? So the demons did not know anything more than the rulers. For if they knew that he was the one promised in the law, they, nevertheless, did not know his mystery that he was the Son of God and that from eternity. Neither did they know the sacrament of the incarnation, passion, and redemption."

[11] See Matt 11:21-22 and Luke 10:13-14. Cf. Bonaventure's commentary on John 15:24 n. 37 above.

would have remained only in unbelief, if the Lord had not manifested himself to them by clear signs.

7. Question 3 then asks about John 15:24: "If I had not done among them works that no one else has done," etc. – 1. This statement seems to be false, since we read about greater and more wondrous signs in the Old Testament. For we read about the dividing of the Red Sea and the Jordan, men and women being fed from heaven for forty years, the raising of the dead, and many such miracles.[12] – 2. Furthermore, the Lord himself said: "The person who believes in me will do greater things than these."[13] Therefore, the sign of miracles was not a certain nor unique sign that he was the Christ. – To this the Glossa responds that the text is not talking about miraculous works, but about wonderful works such as "a woman has encompassed a man,"[14] he was born of a virgin, and similar wonders.[15] – But this does not resolve the issue, since these things were not known to them.[16] – Therefore, a different answer must be given. One explanation is that this passage is talking about the number and diversity of his works, because no one had ever performed so many, so various

---

[12] See Ex 14:21-31 (Red Sea), Joshua 3:13-17 (Jordan River), Ex 16:35 (manna for 40 years), 1 Kings 17:21-24 (Elijah raises up a child), and 2 Kings 4:33-37 (Elisha raises up a child). Augustine, Tractate 91 n. 2 lists many of these same miracles.

[13] See John 14:12: "... Amen, amen I say to you: he who believes in me, the works that I do he also will do, and greater than these he will do, because I am going to the Father."

[14] See Jer 31:22: "... for the Lord has created a new thing upon the earth: A woman will encompass a man."

[15] On p. 456 n. 6 QuarEd cite the Glossa Ordinaria: "He is not talking about such things here (that he satiated a multitude with a few loaves, that he walked upon the water). Christ also surpassed the miracles of all of them in that he was born of a Virgin, that he rose from the dead."

[16] On p. 456 n. 7 QuarEd again cite the Glossa Ordinaria: "But these things were not done among them and in their presence."

and diverse miracles as Christ had. – Another explanation is to put stress on these words "had done works that no one else had done," because that person was not God, but performed such works by petitioning God. But Christ did them as one who was omnipotent.[17]

8. Question 4 concerns John 15:24: "Now they have seen and have hated me and my Father." – Against this is: 1. As Augustine says: "No one's conscience can hate God."[18] Therefore, how could they hate the Father? 2. Further, no one hates what one does not know, but he himself said "They have not known the Father," both now in 16:3 and in many earlier verses.[19] Wherefore, they did not regard God with hatred.

There is a twofold answer to this. First, one must distinguish between two types of hatred. There is genuine hatred that is an affect of aversion towards someone.[20] And in this sense no one hates God. There is also interpreta-

---

[17] On p. 456 n. 8 QuarEd continue their quotation of the Glossa Ordinaria: "So he was speaking of cures. There were so many and so great that no one else had performed among them. And since he did them by himself and no one without him."

[18] See Book II, c. 14 n. 48, *Sancti Avrelii Avgvstini, De sermone Domini in monte libros duos*. Edited by Almut Mutzenbecher. CCSL xxxv (Turnhout: Brepols, 1967), p. 139: "For almost no one's conscience can hate God."

[19] See, e.g., John 5:37-39; 8:19, 55. Augustine, Tractate 90 n. 1 sees the problem Bonaventure is addressing. See his answer in FC 90, p. 160: "But if they perceive this about him, namely what he is, how are they said not to know him? And indeed with regard to men it is possible for us oftentimes to love those whom we have never seen; and on this account neither is the contrary impossible, for us to hate those whom we have never seen."

[20] See Book II, d. V c. 1 in Peter Lombard, *Sententiae in IV libros distinctae*. Volume I, Part II, Books 1 and II. Third Edition. Spicilegium Bonaventurianum IV (Grottaferrata: Collegium S. Bonaventurae, 1971), p. 351: "To be turned towards God was to join oneself to God out of love; to turn away from God was to regard God with hatred or envy,

tive hatred when some person disposes himself after the manner of one who hates. Thus, it is said that someone hates his soul when he does something contrary to his own salvation.[21] So it is also said that a person hates God when that person is opposed to God's will. – The second answer is to consider God as the supreme good from whom all good comes and to consider God as just in his actions. No one can hate God or does hate God in himself. Rather an individual hates God in as far as God is just.[22] – Relative to the first objection raised by Augustine, it should be noted that Augustine retracted that statement.[23] Nevertheless what he says about hatred has some truth in it as it has been interpreted.[24] – With respect to the second objection that they did not know, it has to be said that there is knowledge that is certain and clear and of the essence. And the only ones who know God with this type of knowledge are those in heaven. And there is a knowledge that

---

for pride, by which they wanted to be equal with God, is the parent of envy."

[21] See Ps 10:6: "The person who loves iniquity hates his soul."

[22] A biblical parallel to Bonaventure's point is Wis 2-5 where people attack the just person who trusts in God. On p. 456 n. 14 QuarEd cite Cicero, *De amicitia*, c. 24. See LCL, p. 197: "A troublesome thing is truth, if it is indeed the source of hate, which poisons friendship."

[23] See Book I, c. 19 n. 8 of *Sancti Avrelii Avgvstini, Retractionvm Libri II*. Edited by Almut Mutzenbecher. CCSL lvii (Turnhout: Brepols, 1984), p. 60: "Likewise what I said: 'For almost no one's conscience can hate God,' I see should not have been said. For there are many about whom it is written: The pride of those who hated you.'" Augustine cites Ps 73:23 which reads: "Forget not the voices of your enemies; the pride of them who hate you ascends continually."

[24] Bonaventure is referring to what he wrote about it in Book II, d. 5. dubium 1 of his *Sentence Commentary*. See Omnia Opera 2:158: "It should be noted that Augustine retracted that statement. Nevertheless, his statement has some manner of truth to it if it is understood of God, in as far as God is the supreme good, in which rational creatures have been made to participate. Therefore, since this creature always wants to be beatified it never hates the one who beatifies it...."

is certain, but obscure.[25] Now only believers know God by this type of knowledge. And there is the knowledge of opinion, and by this type of knowledge unbelievers and many evil people know God. And so they knew the Father and consequently could hate him.

9. Question 5 focuses on John 16:2: "The hour is coming for everyone who kills you to think that he is offering worship to God." Therefore, according to this statement those who killed the Apostles did so with a good intention. Wherefore, they were worthy of merit. If you say that this could not happen with a good intention, your statement is false, because evils *in genere*, which are not evils *secundum se*,[26] can become good. And such an evil is killing. – I answer that it has to be maintained that there are certain deeds that could never become good such as lying, as Augustine says,[27] because "the minute they are even mentioned they are linked with evil," as the Philosopher says.[28] There are other deeds that can immediately become good when a good intention is present such as

---

[25] See 1 Cor 13:12: "We see now through a mirror in an obscure manner, but then face to face...."

[26] See Deferrari, p. 950: "*Secundum se,* according to itself, in itself...."

[27] See c. 14 n. 25 of *De mendacio* in *Sancti Avreli Avgvstini De fide et symbolo ... De mendacio ... De patientia.* Edited by Joseph Zycha. CSEL xli (Prague: F. Tempsky, 1900), p. 444: "For first to be avoided and to be fled faraway from is that capital lie that is done in the teaching of religion. To such a lie no one should be induced under any circumstances."

[28] See Book II, c. 6 of Aristotle's *Ethica Nicomachea* in WAE, volume 9, 1107a: "But not every action nor every passion admits of a mean; for some have names that already imply badness, e.g. spite, shamelessness, envy, and in the case of actions adultery, theft, murder; for all of these and suchlike things imply by their names that they are themselves bad, and not the excesses or deficiencies of them."

good deeds *in genere*.[29] There are other deeds, that cannot become good solely by someone's intention, but need a reason and governing order, and such deeds are killing and actions similar to it. Therefore, whenever a person kills another for God's sake, unless there are present a governing order that judges and a reason, this action is in no way good. Such was the case with the Apostles, since there were no just reason and judicial interrogation.

John 16:5-33
The Lord strengthens his disciples
in the waiting of hope

10. *But I did not tell you these things from the beginning*, etc. Earlier the Lord through his word of teaching strengthened his disciples in faith and in love. In this part he intends to strengthen them *in the waiting of hope*, comforting them in many ways against the distress and desolation that will occur at his departure. And this third part is divided according to the threefold genus of consolation. The first consolation comes from *the sending of the Holy Spirit*. The second comes from *the visitation of the Son* and is indicated in verse 16: "A little while, and you will not see me." The third issues from *the Father's listening to the disciples' prayer*, as verse 23b states: "Amen, amen, I say to you: If you ask the Father," etc. And so the entire Trinity offers consolation to the soul. The first consolation gives understanding; the second, joy; the third, peace and confidence. The first deals with the rational part of the soul; the second, the concupiscible; the third, the irascible.

---

[29] See Book II d. 36 dub. 5 in Omnia Opera 2:858. The gist is that a good deed *in genere* has the potency to become a specific good deed when a good intention is added.

John 16:5-15
The Lord consoles his disciples by the sending of the Holy Spirit

So first he consoles them by *the sending of the Holy Spirit*. This consolation is depicted in this way. First is set forth *the desolation of the disciples*. Second, *the promise of the Holy Spirit*. Third, *the office of the one sent*. Fourth, *the commencement of the sending*.

Verse 5. *I did not tell you these things from the beginning*,[30] namely, the things that I have predicted about the sending of the Holy Spirit and your persecution. *Because I was with you*, consoling you by my presence, and so I was not telling you any sad news. Thus Matthew 9:15 states: "Can the wedding guests mourn as long as the bridegroom is with them." *And now I am going to the one who sent me*, namely, to the Father. So I am telling you beforehand. And at this departure his disciples have not become loving, but sad. So he says: *And no one of you asks me: Where are you going?* They were listening and not understanding and neglected to ask him. And this was the result of sorrow.

12. (Verse 6). *But since I have spoken these things to you, sorrow has filled your heart*. These words signify the depth of their sorrow, because they were only considering

---

[30] On p. 457 n. 10 QuarEd rightly notice that the Vulgate reads *autem* ("But") and has a slightly different word order. Augustine, Tractate 94 n. 1-2 addresses the apparent inconsistency between John and the Synoptics about when Jesus told his disciples about their future suffering. See FC 90, p. 181: "What, then, does what he said here mean: 'But these things I did not say to you from the beginning because I was with you,' except that the things that he says here about the Holy Spirit, that he will come to them and bear testimony when they will suffer those evils, these [are the] things he did not say to them from the beginning when he was with them?"

his absence and not the fruit of his absence. Against this attitude it is said in 1 Thessalonians 4:13: "Do not be sorrowful like the rest who have no hope." Such people are filled with sorrow. 2 Corinthians 2:7 reads: "Console him, lest perchance he might be overwhelmed by too much sorrow."[31] Lamentations 3:15 states: "He has filled me with bitterness. He has made me drunk with wormwood."

13. (Verse 7). *But I speak the truth to you*, etc. Here he touches upon the second point, namely, the promise of the Holy Spirit. This is fulfilled when he departs, and they should be consoled by this fact. So he continues: *But I speak the truth*, etc., as if to say: Now you are sorrowful, but when I depart, then you must be comforted. *It is expedient for you that I depart.* And he gives the reason: *For if I do not go, the Paraclete will not come to you.* And the reason for this is: unless you were desolate, you would not be consoled. Matthew 5:5 reads: "Blessed are those who mourn for they will be consoled." Bernard observes: "Exceedingly delightful is divine consolation, and it is not given to those who have another consolation."[32] *But if I go, I will send him to you*, because once your visible consolation has been removed, an invisible consoler will be given you. Isaiah 28:9 says: "Whom will he teach knowledge? And whom will he make to understand? Those who are weaned from milk, withdrawn from the breasts?" And the reason for this is given in Hebrews 5:13: "Everyone who is fed on milk is unskilled in the word of justice, for he is a child."[33]

---

[31] Hugh of St. Cher, p. 380b also cites 2 Cor 2:7.

[32] See c. 55 n. 66 of Abbot Geoffrey, *Declamationes de Colloquio Simonis cum Jesu, Ex S. Bernardi sermonibus collectae* in PL 184:472A. Bonaventure's citation is a paraphrase.

[33] Hugh of St. Cher, p. 380v,h also cites Hebr 5:13.

14. (Verse 8). *And when he has come.* The third point surfaces here, namely, the office of the Holy Spirit. This office is twofold. In comparison to earthly people the Spirit's task is to convict while in comparison to good people the Spirit's task is to teach. So the text expresses this office in comparison to the evil people when it states: *And when he has come, he will convict the world of sin and of justice and of judgment.* And the Savior himself explains:

15. (Verse 9). *Now of sin, because they have not believed in me.*[34] And this is the sin of unbelief, about which John 8:24 above says: "You will die in your sins, for if you do not believe that I am he, you will die in your sin."[35]

16. (Verse 10). *Of justice, because I go to the Father, and you will see me no more.* The Glossa comments: "Not of the justice that they have done, but of the justice they refuse to imitate." And this is the justice of faith, which believes what it does not see.[36] So the text reads: *Because I go to the Father*, etc. And then you believe, since "faith is the substance of things hoped for," etc. as Hebrews 11:1

---

[34] The Vulgate reads *non credunt* ("do not believe"). Bonaventure has *non crediderunt* ("have not believed").

[35] See Augustine, Tractate 95 n. 2 in FC 90, pp. 187-188: "He put this sin before the others as if it were the only one because, while this one remains, the others are retained, and when this one departs, the others are remitted."

[36] It seems that Bonaventure has combined the Glossa Interlinearis and the Glossa Ordinaria. On p. 458 n. 5 QuarEd cite the Glossa Interlinearis: "*Of sin*, which the world has, *and of justice* which it does not imitate, *and of judgment* which it does not fear." For the Glossa Ordinaria see PL 114:413B: "*And of justice*, not its own, but the world is convicted of the justice of believers, in comparison with which it is condemned. Thus the text does not read: The world will not see me, but *you will not see me*, you apostles. Against the unbelievers who say: How will we believe what we do not see?, it is true justice to believe what is not seen, so that those who have seen this person believed that he was God."

states. And this is the justice, namely, of faith, by which the just person is saved.[37] Romans 3:28 says: "We reckon that a person is justified by faith without works of the Law."[38]

17. (Verse 11). *And of judgment,*[39] *because the prince of this world has already been judged.* John 12:31 above reads: "Now is the judgment of the world. Now will the prince of this world be cast out."

18. Now these verses can be explained in another way. For "to convict the world" means to make manifest to the world, according to what Ephesians 5:13 has: "The things that are convicted are made manifest by the light." Through the coming of the Holy Spirit three things have been manifested to the world: sin, justice, and judgment: the sin of the world, the justice of Christ, and the judgment of the devil. And the reason for these three is that Christ was the redeemer of the world, the devil its deceiver, and the world has been detained by the devil on account of the sin of unbelief. Ephesians 6:12 states: We are "against the world rulers of this darkness." – And of this sin the Holy Spirit convicts the world. When the Spirit shows the world its unbelief, it convicts it of sin. And this agrees with John 16:9: "Of sin, because they have not believed." – But Christ redeemed the world by his justice, for since he was just and did not merit to suffer, he saved the world by suffering for the sake of the world. As a proof of his justice, he was exalted to the right hand

---

[37] Hugh of St. Cher, p. 381a explains "justice" as the justice of faith and cites Rom 3:28.

[38] In his Sermon 144 Augustine explains John 16:10 by means of Phil 2:3-11: Christ came out of mercy, but returns to the Father out of God's justice. See *Sermons* III/4, pp. 431-432.

[39] On p. 458 n. 7 QuarEd accurately indicate that the Vulgate reads *autem* ("and") whereas Bonaventure has *vero* ("and").

of the Father. And this interpretation accords with verse 10: *Of justice*, namely, my own, *because I go to the Father*, through exaltation, and this by merit of justice. Philippians 2:8-9 reads: "He humbled himself, being obedient until death, death on a cross. Because of this God has exalted him and given him the name which is above every name." – But the devil has been unjustly detaining the world and has unjustly fought against Christ. Therefore, he has been judged, because he has lost dominion over the human race. And the present verse accords with this interpretation: *And of judgment, because the prince of this world has already been judged*, that is, he was found guilty in the cause against the Savior. – Thus verses 8-11 are to be read in this wise: "He will convict the world of sin," namely, its own, "because they have not believed in him." "Of justice," namely, my justice, "because I go to the Father," bearing witness to my justice. "Of judgment," namely, of the devil, "because the prince of this world has already been judged."[40] – In this way he has set out the office of the Spirit with regard to worldly people. Now he adds a description of his office with respect to the disciples, and this office is to teach, since they could not be fully taught while Christ was present. So he says:

19. (Verse 12). *I still have many things to say to you, but you cannot bear them now.* And the reason for this was that they were still carnal. Thus 1 Corinthians 3:1-2 says: "I could not speak to you as to spiritual men and women, but as carnal.... For you were not yet ready for it ... and still are not ready."[41] But their carnal viewpoints would

---

[40] Hugh of St. Cher, p. 380v,efg reads: "Of sin] its own. And of justice] my justice. And of judgment] of the devil."

[41] Bonaventure adapts 1 Cor 3:1-2: "And I, brothers and sisters, could not speak to you as to spiritual men and women, but as to carnal, as to little ones in Christ. I fed you with milk, not with solid food,

be removed by the coming of the Holy Spirit. So the text adds:

20. (Verse 13). *But when he, the Spirit of Truth, comes, he will teach you all the truth*. Thus 1 John 2:27 reads: "The anointing will teach you about all things."[42] And that he is teaching the truth, he shows because he does not teach by his own authority, but by the authority of another. Therefore, the text says: *For he does not speak*[43] *on his own authority*, as the devil does who "is a liar and the father of lies" as John 8:44 above states: "When he tells a lie, he speaks from his very nature." *But whatever he will hear he will speak*. Wherefore, he will speak the truth. John 8:26 above reads: "The one who sent me is true, and the things that I heard from him, these are the things I speak." Not only will he teach the truth about past events, but also about future ones. Thus: *And the things that are to come he will declare to you*. So 1 Timothy 4:1 states: "The Spirit expressly says that in the last days some will depart from the faith."

21. (Verse 14). *He will glorify me*. The fourth point occurs here, namely, the principle of the Holy Spirit. This not only involves the Father, but also the Son. And so just as the Son, since he proceeds from the Father, glorifies by his works the Father from whom he is, so too the Holy Spirit glorifies the Son. So the text states: *He will glorify me*. And the reason for this is given: *because he will receive of what is mine and declare it to you*. Since the Holy Spirit

---

for you were not yet ready for it. Nor are you now ready for it, for you are still carnal."

[42] Hugh of St. Cher, p. 382g* also cites 1 John 2:27.

[43] On p. 459 n. 5 QuarEd correctly mention that the Vulgate reads *loquetur* ("will speak") while Bonaventure has *loquitur* ("speaks").

is supremely simple, he is whatever he has.[44] Therefore, if he accepts anything from the Son, he accepts it totally and so it follows that he proceeds from the Son. But lest you believe from this that he proceeds solely from the Son or primarily from him, he shows that he proceeds from him at the same time that he proceeds from the Father. Therefore, he adds:

22. (Verse 15). *All things that*[45] *the Father has are mine.* John 17:10 says: "All things that are mine are yours, and yours are mine." *That is why I have said that he will receive of what is mine and will declare it to you.* "Of what is mine" refers to what I have received from the Father. Thus the Holy Spirit declares the Son, from whom he proceeds, just as the Son declares the Father. John 1:18 above states: "The only begotten Son, who is the bosom of the Father, he has revealed him."

QUESTIONS

23. Question 1 focuses on John 16:5: "No one of you asks me: Where are you going?" – Contrary to this is what John 13:36 above says: "Peter said to him: Lord, where are you going?"[46] – I answer that it has to be said that the Lord was going to the ignominy of the passion; he was going to the glory of the resurrection. And when he had spoken earlier that he was going to his passion, Peter asked him:

---

[44] See Augustine, Tractate 99 n. 4 in FC 90, p. 222: "When, therefore, it is said of the Holy Spirit, 'For he will not speak of himself; but what things soever he will hear, he will speak,' much more a simple nature must be understood or believed there wherein it is most truly simple, one that far and profoundly exceeds the nature of our mind."

[45] On p. 459 n. 9 QuarEd accurately indicate that the Vulgate reads *quaecumque* ("whatever") while Bonaventure has *quae* ("that").

[46] See also John 14:5: "Thomas said to him: Lord, we do not know where you are going, and how can we know the way."

"Where are you going?" But now he wanted to tell them that he was going to the glory of his resurrection. Thus: "I am going to the one who sent me."[47] And they were troubled only by the journey to his passion and thought nothing of glory. So they were not questioning him about this, but the Lord wanted to console them when they did ask this question.[48]

24. Question 2 deals with John 16:7: "If I do not go away, the Paraclete will not come to you." – It seems from this that Christ was not omnipotent, since he could not give the Spirit unless he personally went away. – If you say that this was not on account of Christ's impotence, but on account of the incapability of the disciples,[49] the response against this is that Christ's presence disposed people to grace rather than hindered them from receiving it. This is clear, since before the coming of Christ was not the time of grace, but afterwards. – It might be responded that they were impeded because they were loving him in a carnal way.[50] But this is nothing, for in that love they were not sinning. Therefore, it was not opposed to grace, for grace remained with love. – If you say that Christ's remaining with the disciples was not something impossible, but rather a hindrance, this is nothing, because,

---

[47] John 16:5a.

[48] See Hugh of St. Cher, p. 380a: "For when they saw him ascending in the cloud, they were certain of his glory. Earlier in John 13:36 they had asked him about the suffering he was predicting for himself: Lord, where are you going?"

[49] See the Glossa Ordinaria on John 16:7 in PL 114:413A: "It is not that while he was placed on earth he could not give the Spirit, but that they were incapable of receiving the Spirit, until they ceased knowing him according to the flesh."

[50] See Augustine, Tractate 94 n. 4 in FC 90, p. 183: "I do indeed dwell among you, the Word made flesh, but I do not want you to love me still according to the flesh and, satisfied with this milk, to desire to be infants always.... If you stick fast to flesh according to flesh, you will not have the full capacity for receiving the Spirit."

when someone loves another person sensually and spiritually, he loves that person more fervently, for natural love tends toward spiritual love. – I answer that it has to be said that there was a threefold reason why the Holy Spirit was not given before the ascension of Christ. One reason comes from the side of those receiving the Spirit, since, having been consoled in their senses by the bodily presence of Christ, they were not desirous of another type of consolation. But God does not want his gifts to be scorned and so only gives them to those who merit them. So it was necessary that Christ be separated from them. – Another reason comes from the side of the one sending, since it was not fitting that the one giving to his servants be wretched. Rather he has to appear in a glorious state. Therefore, it is said in John 7:39 above: "The Spirit had not yet been given, because Jesus had not yet been glorified." – The third reason comes from the side of both, since enmity between God and us still existed. And so first there had to be reconciliation through the gift of the Holy Spirit.[51] So first Christ had to suffer before the Holy Spirit would be sent.

25. Question 3 explores the meaning of John 16:13: "When the Spirit comes, he will teach you all the truth." – 1. First of all, it seems that when he says "the Spirit will teach," his words are poorly chosen, since "to teach" is an act of wisdom, and wisdom is appropriated to the Son, not to the Holy Spirit. – 2. Further, how "will he teach all the truth"? According to this statement it would seem that the Apostles would know geometry and all the arts. And that is false, since they barely knew the elements of grammar. For the Apostle used to say in 2 Corinthians 11:6: "Even if I am unskilled in speech, yet I am not in

---

[51] See Rom 5:10: "For if when we were enemies we were reconciled to God by the death of his Son...."

knowledge."[52] – I respond that it has to be maintained that "to teach" is characteristic of the entire Trinity, but sometimes it is attributed to the Son and sometimes to the Holy Spirit. For knowledge is twofold, namely, the knowledge of contemplation, and this is attributed to the Son. There is also the knowledge of experience and devotion, and they are attributed to the anointing of the Holy Spirit. It is about this latter that this text is speaking. – 2. And because of what was just said, the solution is at hand to objection two, for this verse is not to be understood of "all truth" plain and simple, but the truth that is "in accord with piety."[53] And this is the truth that is necessary for salvation, which the Apostles fully knew.

Or another interpretation of this verse is: it should not to be understood as if "all" is to distributed by means of the genus to which single individuals belong, bur rather of the individuals to whom the genera belong.[54] For there is the truth of doctrine, life and justice. And he has taught these. Matthew 22:16 says: "Master, we know that you are truthful and teach the way of God in truth." – Concerning the truth of life, Isaiah 38:3 reads: "Remember, Lord, how I walked before you in truth." – About the truth of justice, Proverbs 18:5 states: "It is not good to be an accepter of a person[55] during a trial and thereby render a judgment that goes against the truth."[56]

---

[52] 2 Cor 11:6 reads: "Even if unskilled in speech, but not in knowledge."

[53] See Titus 1:1: "Paul, a servant of God and apostle of Jesus Christ, in accordance with the faith of God's elect and the full knowledge of the truth that is according to piety."

[54] For more detail see John 6 n. 80 above.

[55] On p. 460 n. 10 QuarEd rightly notice that the Vulgate reads *personam impii* ("of a wicked person").

[56] See Bonaventure's commentary on Luke 17: 1 n. 3 in *Bonaventure on Luke Chapters 17-24*, pp. 1623-1624 for a similar listing of the

26. Question 4 queries about the meaning of John 16:15: "The Spirit will receive of what is mine." – 1. This seems to be false, because if the Holy Spirit is God and God can have nothing new, therefore, he can receive nothing further. So what does "he will receive of what is mine" mean? – 2. Likewise a question is raised about the reason the Lord provides: "That is why I have said that he will receive of what is mine, because all things that the Father has are mine."[57] – Either he distributes all things by reason of essentials or by reason of characteristic feature. If by reason of a characteristic feature, the statement is false, for the Son does not possess the ability not to be born. If by reason of essentials – but from this it does not follow, even if the Holy Spirit proceeds from the Father, that on account of this he proceeds from the Son, for "to proceed" is personal. By dint of the same reason the Holy Spirit could say of the Son: "he will receive of what is mine," since everything that the Father has, the Holy Spirit has.

To these matters the Greeks respond that there is a two-fold procession of the Holy Spirit, namely, eternal and temporal. With regard to the eternal procession, he proceeds from the Father alone, and thus he receives from the Father and not from the Son. With respect to the temporal procession, he proceeds from the Son. They give as proof of this the verb "he will receive," for he proceeds in a temporal manner. And they find the reason for their error in this word of the Lord, since the Lord sometimes says that "he will send" the Holy Spirit, but never says that he proceeds from him, but always from the Father. – But nevertheless, preserving peace with them, they are

truth of doctrine, life, and justice and Alexander of Hales' explication of this threefold truth.
[57] Bonaventure inverts the normal reading of John 16:15.

saying nothing, because, as is clear from this text, the Holy Spirit receives from the Son. What does he receive? Whatever he receives is nothing other than himself since he is supremely simple. Wherefore, if he receives himself, how can he receive in time and not be temporal? Therefore, it is to be said that the Holy Spirit proceeds from the Son eternally and is sent in a temporal manner into creatures.

1. So the answer to the meaning of "he will receive" is found in the Glossa: "Just as eternity encompasses every time on account of its diverse characteristic features, it follows that it is said 'he will receive' in the future, not because he receives anything new, but because he is not lacking."[58] – Now it must be said that the expression "he will receive" is the same as if he were saying: He will show that he has received. – 2. It should be said concerning the second point that the reason given is not a cogent reason why the Holy Spirit proceeds from the Son. Rather it is the reason for the statement, namely, why he had said "He will receive of what is mine," not because it is proper to me and excludes the Father, but because he is together with the Father. Therefore, this is the reason behind the statement: "All things that the Father has are mine."[59]

---

[58] On p. 461 n. 4 QuarEd state that this is the Glossa Ordinaria. See Augustine, Tractate 99 n. 5 in FC 90, p. 224: "... nevertheless, on account of the changeableness of the times in which our mortality and our changeableness are involved, we do not falsely say *was* and *will be* and *is*.... Was, because he was never lacking; will be, because he will never be lacking; is, because he always is.... Accordingly, when, following the revolution of times, human expression varies, because through no times was he able or is he able or will he be able to be lacking, true verbs of any time whatever are said about him."

[59] See Sermon 76 n. 5 of St. Leo the Great in *St. Leo the Great, Sermons*. Translated by Jane P. Freeland and Agnes J. Conway. FC 93 (Washington: CUA Press, 1996), p. 338: "For this reason it was said, 'He will receive from what is mine,' seeing that, with the Father giving, the Son gives what the Spirit receives." See also Book II, n. 31 of

John 16:16-23a
The Lord consoles his disciples by the promise of his visitation

27. *A little while, and you will see me no longer.* This is the second part of this chapter. In it he consoles them through *the promise of his visitation* and proceeds in the following manner. First *the promise* of Christ's visitation. Second, *the doubt* of the disciples. Third *the explanation* for their doubting. Fourth *an exemplification.* Fifth *an application* of the example.

Verse 16. So first he promises his visitation after his departure. So the text states: *A little while, and you will see me no longer*, namely, because I am leaving you. *And again a little while and you will see me*, since immediately after his passion he would visit them. Therefore, "a little while" was just until the passion, during which he ought not be seen. And "a little while" from his passion up until his resurrection, in which he ought to appear. Isaiah 54:7 reads: "For a small moment I have forsaken you, but with great mercies I will gather you." And he provides the reason why they would not see him: *Because I go to the Father.*[60] – Another interpretation focuses on the glorious vision. In this reading the little time would be up until

---

St. Hilary of Poitiers, *De Trinitate* in FC 25, p. 59: "In regard to what we read in the Gospels: 'Because God is Spirit,' (John 4:24) we must carefully examine in what manner and for what reason they were uttered. There is a motive for every statement that is made and we shall grasp its meaning when we understand the purpose for which the words were spoken, in order that, because the Lord replied 'God is Spirit,' there may not be a denial of the use and the gift together with the name of the Holy Spirit."

[60] See Chrysostom, Homily 79 n. 1 in FC 41, p. 352: "Moreover, on closer scrutiny, there is consolation in the very fact that He said: 'I go to the Father.' For these words made it clear that He would not perish but that His death would simply be a kind of metamorphosis."

Christ's departure and ascension to the Father, and again a little while until his coming to them to assume them into glory. For John 14:3 above states: "And if I go and prepare a place for you, I am going again, and I will take you to myself, that where I am, there you too may be."[61]

28. (Verse 17). *So some of his disciples said*, etc. Here the second point is introduced, namely, the doubt of the disciples is based on what he had said: in a little one he is not to be seen, and in a little while he is to be seen. For this reason the text states: *So some of his disciples said to one another: What is this he is saying to us: A little while and you will not see me, and again a little while and you will see me?* Their first doubt about his words is that he seems to be saying two contradictory things. Their second doubt concerns his destination: *I go to the Father*, for they did not know how he understood this. They were in doubt about the meaning of his words.

29. (Verse 18). *So they kept saying: What is this 'little while' of which he speaks? We do not know what he is saying*. They did not know what he meant by these words. The disciples still had little understanding, for the Lord rebuked them in Matthew 15:16: "Are you too still without understanding?"[62]

30. (Verse 19). *But Jesus knew*. The third point occurs here, namely, the removal of doubt, which was done by the Master before the disciples questioned him. For this

---

[61] See Augustine, Tractate 101 n. 6 for this interpretation.

[62] See Chrysostom, Homily 79 n. 1 in FC 41, p. 353: "How is it, then, that they did not understand? Either because of their sadness, as I for my part think – for it drove His words from their minds – or else because of the obscurity of what was said. And therefore it seemed to them that He was setting forth two contradictory things, though actually they were not contradictory."

reason the text continues: *Jesus knew that they wanted to ask him*, etc. Sirach 23:28 states: "The eyes of the Lord are far brighter than the sun, beholding round about all the ways of men and women and the bottom of the deep and looking into human hearts, into the most hidden parts." And Sirach 16:20-21 reads: "Every heart is understood by him.[63] And who understands his ways?" And he anticipates their doubt or questioning: *And he said to them: You are asking among yourselves, because I said to you.*[64] *A little while, and you will not see me, and again a little while, and you will see me.* He resolves their doubt by showing that there is a twofold time involved, namely, one of sorrow and one of consolation. And on account of one it was said: "And you will not see," and for the sake of the other: "and you will see." And therefore, there is no contradiction, for he was not referring to the same time, but because of different times he twice said "a little while." Therefore, the text continues:

31. (Verse 20). *Amen, amen, I say to you that you will weep and lament.* "You will weep" externally. "You will lament" internally, during the time when you will not see me. And then you will be blessed. Luke 6:21 says: "Blessed are you, who weep now, for you will laugh." *But the world will rejoice, and*[65] *you will be sorrowful.* The world rejoices. Job 21:12 states: "They rejoice at the sound of the tympani."[66] But the good are sorrowful. 1 Peter 1:6 has: "Now for a little while, if need be, you are made sorrowful by vari-

---

[63] I translate the Vulgate: "And every heart will be understood."

[64] On p. 462 n. 5 QuarEd accurately mention that the Vulgate does not read *vobis* ("to you").

[65] On p. 462 n. 6 QuarEd correctly indicate that the Vulgate reads *autem* ("and") while Bonaventure has *vero* ("and").

[66] On p. 462 n. 6 QuarEd rightly notice that the Vulgate reads *organi* ("of the organ") whilst Bonaventure has *tympani* ("of the tympani").

ous trials."[67] *But your sorrow will be turned into joy*, and therefore, it was said: "And a little while, and you will see me." Tobit 3:22 says: "After tears and weeping you pour in rejoicing." Thus it is said in Qoheleth 7:5: "The heart of fools is where there is rejoicing. The heart of the wise is where there is sorrow."

32. (Verse 21). *A woman about to give birth*. This is the fourth point, namely, an exemplification. And the exemplification deals with something that quickly and in a short time changes from sorrow into joy. And it is the example of a woman giving birth, who, when she is giving birth, is sorrowful, although she is accomplishing a good. But once she has given birth, she is immediately happy. So the text says: *A woman, about to give birth, has sorrow, because her hour has come*, namely, to give birth, which she would still like to delay because of the sorrow and pain, because there is great sorrow in giving birth. Isaiah 13:8 reads: "They will be in painful sorrow as a woman giving birth." And 1 Thessalonians 5:3 states: "And like birth pangs upon her who is with child, and they will not escape."[68] *But when she has brings forth a child*,[69] *she no longer remembers the anguish for her joy that a human being is born into the world*. Concerning the joy a woman has in her child, see Genesis 21:6: Sarah said: "The Lord has made me laugh. Whoever hears of this will laugh with me."

---

[67] Hugh of St. Cher, p. 382v,a and e and p. 383g also cites 1 Peter 1:6.

[68] 1 Thes 5:3 has: "For when they will say, 'Peace and security,' even then sudden destruction will come upon them, as birth pangs upon her who is with child, and they will not escape."

[69] On p. 462 n. 9 QuarEd accurately mentions that the Vulgate reads *pepererit* ("has brought forth") whereas Bonaventure has *peperit* ("brings forth").

33. (Verse 22). *And so you.* Here is the application of the example to their situation. In a similar way they will be sorrowful during Christ's passion, but they will rejoice at his glorification or resurrection. For this reason he says: *And so you indeed have sorrow now*, and this at the departure of the bridegroom. Matthew 9:15 reads: "The days will come when the bridegroom will be taken away from them. And then they will be sorrowful."[70] But this sorrow will last just a little while. Therefore, he says: *I*[71] *will see you again, and your heart will rejoice.* John 20:20 states: "The disciples rejoiced at the sight of the Lord." And this not for time, but for eternity. So the text states: *And no one will take your joy away from you*, because Christ, who was their joy, "having risen from the dead, dies now no more."[72] Revelation 7:17 reads: "God will wipe away every tear from the eyes of the saints," etc. And then your questioning has been ended; they will not disturb you as they do now. So the text adds:

34. (Verse 23a). *And in that day you will ask me nothing*, that is, you will not interrogate me. If this refers to the day of glory, it is true, since then they will clearly see all things. Isaiah 54:13 says: "I will determine that all your children are taught by God."[73] But if it is understood to refer to the time after the glorification of Christ, it is still true, because then they had an interior teacher, according to what had been said in John 16:13: "When he, the Spirit

---

[70] On p. 462 n. 10 QuarEd accurately indicates that the Vulgate reads *ieiunabunt* ("they will fast"). Matt 9:15a states: "And Jesus said...: Can the wedding guests mourn as long as the bridegroom is with them?"

[71] On p. 462 n. 11 QuarEd correctly mention that the Vulgate reads *autem* ("But").

[72] See Rom 6:9: "For we know that Christ, having risen from the dead, dies now no more. Death will no longer have dominion over him."

[73] The Vulgate does not read *ponam* ("I will determine").

of truth, comes, he will teach you all the truth." And "his anointing will teach you about all things."[74] – Another interpretation is: "You will not ask," since you need nothing, but will be blessed. All things you asked for have come true.

QUESTIONS

35. Question 1 addresses John 16:15: "A little while and you will not see me, because I go to the Father." The reasons for this question are: 1. It is said in Matthew 28:20: "Behold, I am with you … unto the consummation of the world." 2. Furthermore, what is the meaning of "A little while, and you will see me," since those words are said in the same verse. How does he depart and remain, be seen and not seen? – I answer that it has to be understood that in Christ there is divine existence and human existence, visible and invisible, wretched and glorious. So with regard to his divine existence he never departs from the elect. With regard to his human and invisible existence under the Sacrament he does not depart "until the consummation of the world." With respect to his human, visible and impassible existence he does not depart until the ascension. With regard to his human and visible existence that was capable of suffering, he departs at his passion, since when he was seen he was not capable of suffering nor did he afterwards associate with them as someone who was capable of suffering.[75]

36. Question 2 deals with John 16:20: "You will weep and lament," etc. – The question is: Did the Apostles merit

---

[74] See 1 John 2:27
[75] Cf. Bar 3:28: "Afterwards he was seen upon earth and associated with human beings."

in this sorrow or did they not merit? It seems that they did merit: 1. For it is said in 2 Timothy 2:12: "If we suffer with him, we will also reign with him."[76] Therefore, to suffer with him was meritorious for them. 2. Furthermore, unhealthy sorrow is changed into worse sorrow whereas this sorrow is changed into joy. This sorrow, I maintain, is healthy sorrow, for the sorrow of the Apostles has been changed into joy, as it is said in this very verse: "Your sorrow will be turned into joy." Wherefore, their sorrow was healthy, good, and meritorious.

Against this are the following: 1. Either they wanted that Christ would die or they did not. If not, then they were sinning, for Peter was rebuked about this matter.[77] But if they wanted him to die, they would have no sorrow. 2. Moreover, it seems from the Gospel itself that the Lord was exhorting them not to be troubled.[78] But the Lord does not give admonitions about what is good. So to be troubled was not something good. 3. Likewise, it is said in John 14:28: "If you loved me, you would indeed rejoice."[79] Wherefore, there should have been rejoicing about his passion. But the person who is sorrowful, when he should be rejoicing, is inordinately sorrowful. So the Apostles were troubled inordinately and culpably.

I answer that it has to be said that sorrow admits of a twofold evaluation: one from its origin and one from its

---

[76] On p. 462 n. 6 QuarEd correctly indicate that Bonaventure is conflating 2 Tim 2:12 and Rom 8:17. 2 Tim 2:12 reads: "If we endure, we will also reign with him." Rom 8:17 says: "… provided, however, that we suffer with him that we may also be glorified with him."

[77] See Matt 16:23: "He turned and said to Peter: Get behind me, satan, …"

[78] See John 14:1: "Let not your heart be troubled" and 14:27: "Do not let your heart be troubled or afraid."

[79] John 14:28 reads: "… If you loved me, you would indeed rejoice that I am going to the Father…."

manner of expression. – Relative to its origin sorrow stems from love.[80] Therefore, there is a certain sorrow that springs from voluptuous and carnal love as in the case of a glutton weeping over the loss of a tasty morsel. Another sorrow springs from natural love as the soul in its separation from its body or a mother at the death of a child. Another sorrow issues from social love as the sorrow of a friend when he is bodily separated from a friend whose companionship he treasures. Yet another sorrow stems from spiritual love as the case of a person loving out of charity and suffering with someone who is in pain. – The first sorrow is culpable. The second and third are supportive. The fourth is laudable.

So it is to be understood that the Apostles had a two-fold love for the Lord, namely, a social love, by which a person loves a companion, because they did not want to be separated from him. They also had a spiritual love towards him. Therefore, the sorrow in them was something laudable, for they were suffering with Christ. And their sorrow was also supportive, since they did not want to be separated from Christ.[81] – From the perspective of the manner of being sorrowful it is to be understood that there is a prescribed manner of being sorrowful, for the Apostle says: "May you not grieve as the others who have no hope."[82] Therefore, sorrow must be tempered by joy. And in this regard the Apostles were excessive and engaged in reprehensible conduct, since they had no measure of joy. Rather they were sorrowing like those who

[80] See Book XIV, c. 7 n. 2 of Augustine's *City of God* in FC 14, p. 360: "Thus, love yearning to possess the object loved is desire and love delighting in the object possessed is joy; its avoidance of what is abhorrent is fear and its sufferance of a present evil is sadness."

[81] As far as I can tell, Hugh of St. Cher, p. 383 has no parallel to Bonaventure's fourfold origin of sorrow.

[82] See 1 Thes 4:13.

lack hope. And the Lord exhorted them to remove this manner or immoderation and not to be sorrowful. He was exhorting them to rejoice. Thus Chrysostom comments: "The tyranny of sadness is great, and we must use all our strength to resist this passion. And purifying from it what is useful, let us reject what is superfluous in it."[83] So they were laudable in their sorrow, but their manner of being sorrowful was to be censured.

John 16:23B-33
The Lord consoles his disciples:
The Father hears their prayers

37. *Amen, amen, I say to you.* This is the third part of the chapter, in which the Lord consoles his disciples through the fact that their prayers will be heard. And he proceeds here in this manner. First *the gracious promise* of the Lord is noted. Second is *the consolation of the disciples* in verse 29: "His disciples said to him." The first section is described in this way. First *the Lord's graciousness* in making this promise is singled out. Second *the opportune time* to make a petition. Third *the prompt willingness* to hear.

Verse 23. So the first item to occur or to be noted is the Lord's graciousness in making a promise to them with certitude. For this reason he says: *Amen, amen, I say to you*, this is a sign of certitude. *If you ask the Father some thing in my name, he will give it to you.* "If you ask some thing," that is, if you ask anything. That "anything" is

---

[83] Bonaventure paraphrases Homily 78 n. 1. See PG 59:419-420: Useful sorrow concerns sins committed. Hugh of St. Cher, p. 380b also cites Homily 79 n. 1 in paraphrase.

eternal life.[84] For Augustine comments: "If anything else is asked for, no matter what, nothing is asked for, not because it is altogether not a thing, but because in comparison with so great a thing, whatever else is desired is nothing."[85] Thus James 1:5 has: "If any one of you lacks wisdom, let him ask God who gives abundantly to all, and it will be given to him."

38. (Verse 24). *Hitherto you have not asked.* The second point occurs here, namely, the right time to petition. Until this time it was not the right time, but from now on it will be. So the text continues: *Hitherto you have not asked anything in my name,* since it was not the opportune time, for the Lord himself was with them who was giving them everything. Thus John 17:12 below states: "While I was with them, I kept them in your name." But now the time has come. So he says: *Ask, and you will receive that your joy may be full,* for every one of your petitions must refer to that joy. This fullness of joy consists in the gifts of soul and body. About this Isaiah 66:14 says: "You will see, and your heart will rejoice, and your bones will flourish like a herb." And it will be clear when the time for petitioning arrives, because until now they did not know nor understand whom they should ask. But now they do know. So the text adds:

39. (Verse 25). *I have spoken these things to you in proverbs.* Thus I have spoken in similitudes, since as 1 Corinthians 3:1 says: "I could not speak with you as spiritual people, but as carnal." But *the hour is coming, when I no*

---

[84] See Augustine, Tractate 102 n. 2 in FC 90, p. 242: "Therefore, whatever is asked for of such a sort as pertains to attaining their joy, this is to be asked for in the name of Christ, if we understand divine grace, if we request the truly blessed life."

[85] See Tractate 102 n. 2 in CCSL xxxvi, p. 595 and FC 90, p. 242. Bonaventure's citation is virtually verbatim.

longer speak to you in proverbs, namely, in an obscure way, *but will plainly proclaim to you about my Father.*[86] That hour was the time of the sending of the Holy Spirit.

40. (Verse 26). *On that day,* it is the time, *you will ask in my name,* for then you will know the Father and me. For Jeremiah 31:34 states: "A man will not say to his brother: Know the Lord, for all will know me, from the least to the greatest." And this happened in the period after the reception of the Holy Spirit, who not only taught them, but also compelled them to petition. Romans 8:26 reads: "The Spirit petitions for us with unutterable groans," that is, he makes us petition. – *And I do not say to you.* Here the third point is noted, namely, promptness in hearing, because the Father is ready to hear the petitions of the Apostles without any intermediary intercessor. So he says: *And I do not say to you that I will ask the Father for you,* since that is not necessary.[87]

41. (Verse 27). *For the Father himself loves you,* and therefore, he willingly listens to you. And the reason for this is: *Because you have loved me.* John 14:21 above states: "The person who loves will be loved by my Father." Not only was love involved in the reason, but also faith. *And have believed that I came forth from God.* And by the merit of faith they are worthy to be heard, since Matthew 21:22 reads: "All things that[88] you ask for in prayer with belief,

---

[86] On p. 464 n. 8 QuarEd rightly notice that the Vulgate does not read *meo* ("my").

[87] See Chrysostom, Homily 79 n. 2 in FC 41, p. 356: "And I will not ask the Father – your love for Me will be sufficient to win His favor, because you have loved Me and have believed that I came forth from God." See Theophlactus in PG 124:222B: "I will keep the Father friendly towards you, so that afterwards you have no need for me as an intercessor."

[88] The Vulgate reads *quaecumque* ("whatever") while Bonaventure has *quae* ("that").

you will receive." So since you have believed, you merit to be heard. But up to that point it had been sufficient to believe that he had come from God. From now on they had to believe that he was returning to God. So in order to deepen and complete their faith he adds:

42. (Verse 28). *I have come forth from the Father and have come into the world*, through the incarnation, and you believed this. Thus John 11:27 reads: "You are the Christ, the Son of the living God, the one who has come into this world."[89] *Again I leave the world*, through the passion, *and go to the Father*, through a glorious resurrection. Thus after he had been raised up, he sent through Mary to say to his disciples in John 20:17 below: "Say to my brothers and sisters: I ascend to my Father and your Father, to my God and your God." About these two it is said in Psalm 18:7: "From highest heaven is his going forth, and his circuit even to height of heaven."

43. (Verse 29). *His disciples said to him*. After Christ's promise had been set forth, next comes the consolation of the disciples which is described in this order. First he makes note of the consolation. Then since they were befuddled, he gives them instruction. Third since they were vacillating, he strengthened them. So first the disciples' consolation is suggested by the Lord's words which they now understood and believed that the promised time of consolation was present. For this reason *his disciples said to him: Behold, now you are speaking plainly and are uttering no proverb*. And thus the time had arrived, about which you said: "The hour is coming when I will no

---

[89] The Vulgate does not read *hunc* ("this"). This confession of faith is that of Martha. Did Bonaventure maintain that she was among the other disciples during Jesus' last hours?

longer speak to you in proverbs, but I will proclaim things plainly."[90]

44. (Verse 30). *Now we know that you know all things and do not need that anyone should question you.* And so the hour had come, about which you had spoken earlier: "On that day you will ask me nothing."[91] *For this reason we believe that you have come forth from God*, namely, because you knew all things. John 6:70 above reads: "We have come to believe and to know that you are the Christ, the Son of God," etc. For it is only God's prerogative to know hidden things. Jeremiah 17:9-10 states: "The human heart is perverse ... and inscrutable, and who can know it? I am the Lord who searches hearts[92] and probes the affections."

45. (Verse 31). *Jesus answered them.* The second point surfaces here, namely, the instruction of the disciples. Since they had been comforted by the Lord's word, they believed that they had been consoled and made perfect in faith. So the Lord teaches them to be humble as he had done for Peter above. Thus he picks up their words to correct them. So the text states: *Jesus answered them: You now believe.*[93] That is, you are proud of yourselves that you believe.

46. (Verse 32). *Behold, the hour is coming and has already come*, that is, it is drawing near, *for you to be scattered, each one to his own house*, that is, "for you to be scattered," in such a way that each one goes "to his own house," since

---

[90] See John 16:25.

[91] See John 16:23.

[92] The Vulgate reads *cor* ("the heart") while Bonaventure has *corda* ("hearts").

[93] On p. 465 n. 6 QuarEd state that the Vulgate reads Jesus' words as a question: "Do you now believe?"

one person will not remain with another in a bodily manner or through faith. Zechariah 13:7 reads: "Strike the shepherd, and the sheep of the flock will be scattered." *And you will leave me by myself.* Isaiah 63:3 states: "I have trodden the winepress alone, and of the Gentiles there is not a man with me." But this anxiety was not due to a lack of divine assistance, but of human. So he says: *But I am not alone,*[94] *because the Father is with me.* John 8:29 above says: "The one who sent me is with me and has not left me alone." This is not against what is said in Psalm 21:2: "Why have you forsaken me?" for that verse is understood to be about exposure to punishment.

47. (Verse 33). *I have spoken these things to you.* The third point is introduced, namely, the strengthening of the disciples. Since he had just predicted their future scattering, he adds a word to strengthen them, since he had not said this that they might despair, but that they might have peace through confidence. Therefore, the text continues: *I have spoken these things to you that in me you may have peace.* About this peace Isaiah 66:12 reads: "I will bring upon her a river of peace, as it were." One does not arrive at such peace except through affliction. So he says: *In the world you will have affliction.* Acts 14:21 has: "Through many tribulations we must enter the kingdom of God." They should not despair amidst these afflictions. Thus he adds: *But take courage. I have conquered the world.* 1 Corinthians 15:57 states: "Thanks be to God who has given us victory through our Lord Jesus Christ." Those who believe in Christ gain this victory. 1 John 5:4 says: "This is the victory that conquers the world, our faith."

---

[94] On p. 465 n. 8 QuarEd rightly notice that the Vulgate reads *Et non sum solus* ("And I am not alone") whereas Bonaventure has *Sed non sum solus* ("But I am not alone").

Questions

48. Question 1 deals with John 16:23: "If you ask the Father something in my name, he will give it to you." – The first question is this: Since he had said the same thing above in John 14:13-14[95] and 15:16,[96] why does he now repeat himself in John 16:23? – It seems to be superfluous. Therefore, if there was nothing superfluous in the words of Christ,[97] why does he say it so often? – The second question proposes that this statement seems to be false, for although Paul asked that the thorn be removed from his flesh, he did not obtain his request in 2 Corinthians 12:9. – Furthermore, every single day we see that the saints make a petition, but are not heard. What does he mean when he says: "If you ask...."?

I respond that it has to be maintained that for any prayer to be worthy of being heard it is required that the one praying be worthy, persistent, petition for what pertains to salvation, and petition for his own good.[98] The promise of Christ is to be understood in such a way that these

---

[95] John 14:13-14 says: "And whatever you ask in my name, that I will do, in order that the Father may be glorified in the Son. If you ask me anything in my name, I will do it."

[96] John 15:16c reads: "that whatever you ask the Father in my name he may give you."

[97] The reasoning behind this question seems based on Book I, c. 4 of Aristotle's *De caelo*. See WAE, Volume 2, 271a: "But God and nature create nothing that has not its use."

[98] Contrast Hugh of St. Cher, p. 383v,k: "Four things are to be considered here: What things should be petitioned, why, by whom, and how." See Book III, Tractatus 27, c. 3, q. 1 of Guillelmus Altissiodorus, *Summa aurea*. Edited by Jean Ribaillier; Spicilegium Bonaventurianum XVIIA (Paris: Editions du Centre National de la Recherche Scientifique/Grottaferrata: Collegium S. Bonaventurae, 1986), p. 517: "It is said that four things are required (for prayer to be efficacious), namely, that the person who prays petitions with piety, perseverance, for salvation, and for himself."

conditions are running concurrently. And then a person's prayer will be heard. – Now that a person be worthy it is necessary that the person have faith, hope, and charity. That is why the promise was made three times. First by merit of faith, second by charity, and here now in the third instance by hope. – With regard to the perseverance of the one praying it is necessary that the person pray frequently. That is why he often repeated this injunction, "If you ask anything," to show that the same thing had to be asked for many times. – It is also required that one's request be salutary. So he often said: "If you ask in my name." Augustine comments: This is in the reality behind his name, since Jesus means "salvation."[99] "Ask in the name of Jesus, that is, ask what pertains to salvation. And for this reason Paul was not heard.[100] – Fourth, ask for yourself, for the text says: "He will give you." The text does not say: He will give to others, but to you.[101]

40. Question 2 focuses on John 16:25: "I have spoken these things to you in proverbs." – 1. But it is said in Matthew 13:11: "To you it has been given to know the mystery of

---

[99] See Tractate 73 n.3 in FC 90, p. 86: "Christ signifies king. Jesus signifies Savior. Not any king whatsoever, surely, will save us, but the King Savior; and because of this whatsoever we ask that is opposed to what is advantageous for salvation, we do not ask in the name of the Savior." See also Tractate 102 n. 1 in FC 90, p. 241: "… that whatever is asked for contrary to the essential character of the faith is not asked for in the name of the Savior."

[100] See Homily 27 n. 6 of GGHG in Hurst, p. 217: "He means, 'You who do not know how to seek eternal salvation have not asked in the Savior's name.' That is the reason too why Paul was not heard. If he had been freed from temptation it would not been of help to his salvation."

[101] See Augustine, Tractate 102 n. 1 in FC 90, pp. 241-242: "For indeed, the saints are favorably heard for [themselves, but are not favorably heard for] all, either of their friends or enemies or of anyone else; but it was not said unqualifiedly 'will give' but 'will give to you.'"

the kingdom of God, but to others in parables."[102] There-fore, he should not be speaking to his disciples in prov-erbs. – 2. Furthermore, why does he speak in proverbs, because the text immediately goes on in 16:29: "Behold, you are speaking plainly, and are uttering no proverb"? Wherefore, either the disciples were speaking falsely or the Lord was. – 3. Finally, since they had little under-standing, why was he speaking to them in proverbs and in an obscure manner? – It seems that he wanted to waste time.

I respond that it has to be said "a proverb" is sometimes called "parabolic speech," and sometimes it is called "an obscure sentence." The Lord used to speak to the crowds in parabolic language, but he would speak to his disciples in obscure sentences. Indeed he spoke to the crowds in parables, so that seeing that might not see. He spoke to the disciples in obscure sentences, so that afterwards his teaching might be more understandable and pleasing, as Augustine says in his book on Christian Instruction.[103] –Relative to question two, when the disciples said that he was speaking plainly, they said that as people who did not understand, because they believed that they understood him when they did not.[104] – Relative to the third objec-tion, why he spoke to his disciples in such a way that they did not understand, I answer that then they understood in some manner, but afterwards through the coming of

---

[102] Bonaventure is actually quoting Luke 8:10.

[103] See Book II, c. 6 n. 8 in *Sancti Avrelii Avgvstini De doctrina christiana, De vera religione*. Edited by Joseph Martin and K.-D. Daur; CCSL xxxii (Turnhout: Brepols, 1967), p.36. See also FC 4, p. 66: "... no one is uncertain now that everything is learned more willingly through the use of figures, and that we discover it with much more delight when we have experienced some trouble in searching for it."

[104] See Augustine, Tractate 103 n. 1 in FC 90, p. 248: "... those men still do not understand to such an extent that they do not even at all understand that they do not understand."

the Holy Spirit, who interpreted the words of Christ, they saw clearly, just as someone has greater delight in something obscure when he comes to understand it than if it had been entirely clear to him.[105]

50. Question 3 asks about the meaning of John 16:30: "Now we know that you know all things." – 1. By what means did the disciples arrive at the knowledge that the Lord knew all things? – 2. Likewise, what is the meaning of the words that follow, "You do not need that anyone should question you"? Rather this is totally contrary, since, if he knows all things, then he is the good teacher and anyone whosoever should ask him about individual matters. – I respond that it has to be maintained that they knew that he knew all things, because he had no need that anyone question him, thereby expressing a doubt about this. For he knew about the things human beings would doubt, and he would not have had this knowledge unless he was searching hearts as God does.[106] And therefore, he knew all things.[107] – And it would not be necessary that anyone open his doubt to him, for he knew that they had previously doubted the words that he had spoken: "A little while."[108] And he did not wait for their question: "They wanted to ask him,"[109] but anticipated it and gave them

---

[105] See Book II, c. 6 n. 8 of Augustine's *On Christian Instruction* in FC 4, p. 66: "Those who do not find what they are seeking are afflicted with hunger, but those who do not seek, because they have it in their possession, often waste away in their pride."

[106] See 1 Chron 28:9: "The Lord searches all hearts and understands all the thoughts of minds."

[107] Augustine also deals with this question. See Tractate 103 n. 2 in FC 90, p. 249: "But he who knows all things did not even have this need; nor did he have need to come to know, through his askings, what anyone might wish to become aware of from him, because before he was asked, he knew the will of the one who was going to ask."

[108] See John 16:18.

[109] See John 16:19.

a satisfactory answer. Wherefore, they now say: "Now we know," etc.

CHAPTER SEVENTEEN

JOHN 17:1-26
THE LORD STRENGTHENS HIS DISCIPLES
BY THE AID OF PRAYER

1. *Jesus spoke these things*, etc. Earlier the Lord had strengthened his disciples by his example and the word of his instruction. Now he strengthens them by *the aid of prayer*. And he does this in the present chapter by setting forth Christ's prayer. And the present chapter has four parts. In the first *the Lord petitions for a manifestation of glorification for himself*. In the second *he petitions for the preservation of holiness for the Apostles* where verse 6 reads: "Father, I have manifested your name," etc.[1] In the third *he petitions for the strengthening of grace upon those who are to believe through the Apostles* where verse 20 states: "Yet not only for these do I pray, but also for those," etc. In the fourth *he asks for the perpetuity of glory for both the Apostles and these others* where verse 24 says: "Father, I will that those you have given me," etc.

---

[1] On p. 467 n. 5 QuarEd accurately indicate that the Vulgate does not read *Pater* ("Father").

John 17:1-5
The Lord asks for the manifestation
of glorification for himself

2. (Verse 1). So first the Lord asks for the manifestation of glorification for himself in this order. First comes *the manner of petitioning* or praying. Second comes *the fruit of the petition*. Third comes *the reason for being heard*. Fourth is *the petition itself*. – Thus the manner of petitioning is suggested in this that Christ made his petition devoutly and intently. A sign of this occurs in his raising his eyes to heaven. Therefore, the text says: *Jesus spoke these things*, which had been mentioned earlier, *and raising his eyes to heaven* out of devotion. John 11:41 reads: "Jesus, raising his eyes, said: Father, I give you thanks because you have heard me." Psalm 122:1 has: "I have raised my eyes to you, who dwell in the heavens." Lamentations 3:41 states: "Let us raise our hearts with our hands to the Lord."[2] – Not only does the Lord pray devoutly, but also humbly. Thus *he said: Father*. He calls God "Father," because he honors him as Father. John 8:49 above states: "I honor my Father, and you dishonor me." – He also prays in a specific manner. So he says: *The hour has come. Glorify your Son*. He petitioned in a specific way, because he prayed to be glorified when the opportune time had arrived. About this hour frequent mention has been made. John 2:4 and 7:30 say: "My hour has not yet come." Therefore, he did not want to be glorified by miracles, but when this hour had come, he asked to be glorified. – Therefore, through this manner of prayer we learn that we should pray devoutly, humbly, and specifically.[3]

---

[2] Hugh of St. Cher, p. 385i also cites Lam 3:41.

[3] See Bernard of Clairvaux, Sermon 4 n. 4 *In Quadragesima* in SBOp 4.371: "Prayer that is faithful and humble and fervent will without doubt penetrate heaven...."

3. *That your Son*, etc. These words introduce the fruit of petition, and this is twofold, namely, the manifestation of the divine name and our beatification. Relative to the manifestation of the divine name the text states: *That your Son*, etc. Father, glorify your Son in such a way *that your Son may* also *glorify you*, since he was going to die for this reason. Thus John 12:28 above reads: "Father, glorify your name." – Another fruit is our glorification. For this reason the text continues:

4. (Verse 2). *Even as you have given him power over all flesh*, that is, show that you have given him power over all flesh, that is, to save all flesh. Matthew 28:18 says: "All power has been given me in heaven and on earth," and this for the sake of salvation. *In order that to all you have given him*, namely, through predestination, *he may give eternal life*, through glorification. The neuter "to all" (*omne*) stands for the personal "to all" (*omni*). John 6:39 above reads: "This is the will of the one who sent me, the Father, that of all[4] that he has given me, I should lose nothing, but that I should raise it up on the last day." And he explains what this eternal life is:

5. (Verse 3). *This is*,[5] he says, *eternal life, that they may know you, the one true God, and him who have sent, Jesus Christ*. 1 Kings 10:8 states: "Blessed are your men and blessed are your servants, who stand before you always and hear your wisdom." Wisdom 15:3 reads: "To know you is perfect justice." And glory is nothing other than perfect

---

[4] The Latin here is the neuter *omne* ("all").

[5] On p. 468 n. 2 QuarEd correctly indicate that the Vulgate reads *Haec est autem* ("Now this is") while Bonaventure has *Haec est* ("This is").

justice, since "to know your justice and power is the root of immortality,"[6] and therefore of eternal life.

6. (Verse 4). *I have glorified you.* The third point surfaces here, namely, the reason for being heard. And this was the Christ's merit, by which he merited to be glorified or exalted. So the text continues: *I have glorified you on earth.* Therefore, I merit to be glorified by you. *I have accomplished the work that you have given to me to do.*[7] Therefore, he has accomplished it because he was obedient till death. Luke 12:50 reads: "I have a baptism to be baptized with, and how distressed I am until it is perfected." About this perfection and accomplishment Hebrews 2:10 states: "It was fitting for him, for whom are all things and through whom are all things, who had brought many children into glory, to perfect through sufferings the author of their salvation." And since he had done everything, it was fitting that he be heard.

7. (Verse 5). *And now you, Father, glorify me.* This verse contains the fourth point, namely, the petition itself, by which he prays for the manifestation of his glorification. For this reason he says: *And now you, Father, glorify me with yourself with the glory that I had with you before the world came to be.*[8] That is, manifest that glorification, so that, just as I was equal to you from eternity before the world came to be, that might also be manifested to others. For this reason it is said in John 17:10 below: "I

---

[6] This seems to be a paraphrase of Bernard of Clairvaux, *Liber de gratia et libero arbitrio*, c. 6 n. 19. See SBOp 3.180: "Now the fullness of glory should be joined to such perfect justice, because these two are so linked that neither can there be perfect justice except in full glory nor the fullness of glory without perfect justice."

[7] On p. 468 n. 3 QuarEd accurately mention that the Vulgate reads *faciam* ("to do") while Bonaventure has *facerem* ("to do").

[8] On p. 468 n. 4 QuarEd rightly notice that the Vulgate reads *esset* ("existed") whilst Bonaventure has *fieret* ("came to be").

have been glorified in them," that is, in the Apostles, since they believed that he is equal to the Father. John 16:30 above reads: "Now we believe that you have come forth from God. John 1:1 above says: "The Word was with God," namely, equal to God, "and the Word was God."

QUESTIONS

8. Question 1 asks why the Son is praying, for, if to pray is a sign of need and impotence and the Son can do all things, therefore, he should not be praying. – If you say that he was praying in as far as he was human, that is nothing, because whatever he merited in as far as he was human, he merited from the first moment of his conception. – I answer that it should be maintained that Christ prayed in as far as he was human, for according to his human nature he could not do all things. Even if he were worthy through grace, there was nothing to hinder him from meriting through his good deeds. Therefore, by suffering and praying he merited to be glorified. But he was not acquiring merit that he did not previously have, but he was increasing in some way his due merit for many others.[9]

9. Question 2 has two aspects. 1. About the petition in John 17:1, "Father, glorify" or "exalt your Son."[10] – Contrary is that John 8:50 says: "I do not seek my own glory." Therefore, he should not be asking for his own glory or

---

[9] See Book III d. 18. a. 2 q. 1 of Bonaventure's *Sentence Commentary*.

[10] I have translated *glorifica* with "glorify" and *clarifica* with "exalt." Both verbs, however, have the same meaning. See Augustine, Tractate 104 n. 3 in FC 90, p. 255: "... *dozason* which the Latin translator renders as *clarifica*, although he could also have said *glorifica*, which is an exact equivalent."

his own glorification. – 2. Moreover, according to which nature is he making this petition? – Not according to his divine nature, since according to this he has everything. Not according to his human nature, because he says a little later in John 17:5: "Glorify me with the glory I had before the world came to be." This could not be according to his human nature.

I answer relative to the first point that it has to be maintained that he was asking for glorification, so that God might be glorified through it. For he added: "So that your Son may glorify you." And this is not to seek one's own glory, since the person who seeks his own glory is the one who seeks his own praise without any reference to God. – Another interpretation is to say that he was not seeking glory from human beings, for that is vain, but from God.[11] – 2. With respect to the question of the nature by which he is praying, the heretic began his reasoning from this that the Son existed before the world and was praying according to that human nature, because he was inferior to the Father. This is what Arius was maintaining.[12] – But Augustine says that this is understood according to his human nature and gives this exposition: "With the glory which he had with you," namely by predestination, for Romans 1:4 reads: "He was predestined Son of God in power."[13]

---

[11] Bonaventure has similar discussions above in John 5 n. 75-76, John 7 n. 23, and John 8 n. 66-67.

[12] See John 8 n. 85 above and Augustine, Tractate 43 n. 14 in FC 88, p. 171: "Sometimes the Arians misrepresent our faith from this sentence; and they say, See, the Father is greater because, of course, he glorifies the Son. Heretic, have you not read the Son himself also saying that he glorifies his Father? If he glorifies the Son and the Son glorifies the Father, put aside your obstinacy; acknowledge their equality, correct your perversity."

[13] See Tractate 105 n. 7 in FC 90, pp. 262-263: "... when the Son says, 'And do you now glorify me, Father, with yourself, with the glory

Another response stems from distinguishing between "who is petitioning" and "to whom" or "for what" one is petitioning, for the person who is petitioning or praying does so in as far as he is inferior or powerless. But relative to why he is praying, there is a twofold meaning. Either the person is praying for himself in himself, so that his needs may be supplied as in the case of me praying for myself as a sinner. Or the person is praying to himself for others, so that his glory may be manifested. And thus I could petition God for something: God, manifest yourself; honor yourself. – So I say that when you ask "according to what nature was he praying?" if you are asking about the person who is asking, according to what is he asking, I say according to his human nature. If you ask: To whom was he praying? I say according to his divine nature. Thus he shows here that behind "glorify me" is the divine hypostasis equal to the Father from eternity. He was asking that this equality be manifested.[14]

10. Question 3 focuses on John 17:2: "Even as you have given him power over all flesh." – Contrary. 1. It is said in Matthew 28:18 that after his resurrection all power was given him. 2. Furthermore, "if he gave him power over all flesh" and he "gives eternal life to all whom the Father has given him,"[15] it follows that all are saved. – Augustine

---

which I had before the world was, with you,' we should understand the predestination of the human nature that is in him, as in the future to be, from mortal, immortal with the Father, and that this was already done by predestining before the world was, which would also come to be in the world at its own time."

[14] On p. 469 n. 4 QuarEd cite Book IV of Basil, *Adversus Eunomium* where he explains "Father, glorify me" in this way: "So he is not petitioning for additional glory, but that there might be a manifestation of the dispensation.... So the matter is clear that he was saying such things according to the dispensation of humanity, not according to a defect in deity."

[15] See John 17:2.

answers that "you have given" is understood according to his foreknowledge and means "you have foreseen that it be given."[16] – But Chrysostom maintains that this is understood according to the divine nature: "you have given" from eternity. In Matthew it is written "has been given," not at that time shown for the first time, but manifested.[17] – 2. With respect to this objection about "all flesh," the distribution is according to the individuals to whom the genera belong, that is, the text is dealing with all flesh. Another interpretation: if the distribution is by means of the genus to which single individuals belong, then stress has to be put on the word "you have given," because the text does not say "he has given him all flesh," but "he gave him power over all flesh." But he gave him those who had been predestined that he might save them. Also he gave him power over the evil to judge them.

11. Question 4 takes up John 17:3: "This is eternal life that they may know you, the only true God." – 1. There is not only knowledge, but also love. Or if you say that there is love in knowledge, why didn't he set forth love here? 2. Likewise, God is either taken in an essential manner or in a personal manner. If in a personal manner, then the Holy Spirit is excluded. If in an essential manner, then it is useless to add: "him whom you have sent, Jesus Christ,"

---

[16] Bonaventure seems to be summarizing Tractate 111 n. 1. See FC 90, p. 300: "And here he shows that he indeed has received power over every man, so that he who will judge the living and the dead may set free whom he would, may damn whom he would, but that these were given to him that he may give eternal life to all of them."

[17] Bonaventure seems to have summarized Homily 80 n. 1. See, e.g., FC 41, p. 369 for Chrysostom's rhetorical questions: "Did He not have power before over His own works? Notwithstanding the fact that He had created them, did He not have power over them after He had made them?"

because knowledge of the Christ as man does not pertain to substantial reward,[18] but of Christ as God.

It has to be said to the first objection that in knowledge, which is face to face, love is necessarily understood. For when it is said "vision is the total reward,"[19] love is not excluded. But greater emphasis should be placed on vision than on love, since vision distinguishes what pertains to the heavenly homeland from what is on the journey whereas love does not. For now we do not see, but love. – 2. Relative to the question of how one should view God, it should be said that if the meaning of the text here is to be construed essentially, then what is added, "And him you have sent," is understood according to human nature, according to which, even if the essence of the reward is not in view, nonetheless there will be the most penetrating delight in Christ as man. And so this is added: "And him whom you have sent, Jesus Christ." – Or if God is taken in a personal manner, then Jesus Christ stands for the Son according to his divine nature, and the Holy Spirit is not excluded, since there is a union of Father and Son. Wherefore, the word "only" is not supplied to exclude persons, because the person who sees one person sees another, but to exclude false gods.[20]

---

[18] On p. 469 n. 10 QuarEd indicate that editions with Gorranus read: "the substantial reward of beatitude."

[19] See Augustine, Sermon 2 n. 13, "Enarratio in Psalmum 90" in CCSL xxxix, p. 1277: "Our total reward is vision." See 1 Cor 13:12: "We see now through a mirror in an obscure manner, but then face to face." Hugh of St. Cher, p. 386H ends a long discussion of this point: "The solution is that vision is the reward and our beatitude, similarly love and enjoyment, but once a person enjoys the vision, love and enjoyment necessarily follow. Therefore, it is said that the vision is the total reward."

[20] See Chrysostom, Homily 80 n. 2 in FC 40, p. 371: "He said 'the only true God' to differentiate Him from the gods that do not exist."

John 17:6-19
Petition for the preservation of sanctification
for the Apostles

12. *I have manifested your name to the men and women.* This is the second part of this chapter. In it he prays for *the preservation of holiness* for the Apostles. And first he asks that they be steadfast in good. Second he asks that they be freed from evil where verse 12 reads: "While I was with them," etc.

So the first petition is that the Apostles be preserved in good. And since petitions to be heard must be rational, many reasons are set forth. So he proceeds in this order. First is shown *the loving guarding of the words of Christ by the Apostles.* Second, *divine election.* Third, *the desolation of the disciples.* Fourth, *the petition itself* is set forth.

John 17:6-11
The Lord prays that the disciples
be steadfast in good

13. (Verse 6). So first is set forth or intimated the loving preservation of the words of Christ. They lovingly preserved the teaching of Christ that had been manifested to them. Therefore, the text states: *I have manifested my name to the men and women whom you have given me out of this world,* that is, those out of the world you have called to me through the present justice. John 6:44 above says: "No one comes to me, unless the Father draws him." And the reason why he has drawn them from the world is added: *They were yours,* through eternal election, *and you have given them to me,* to be instructed in my teaching. Isaiah 8:18 states: "Behold, I and my children, whom the Lord has given me." The Apostle interprets this pas-

sage as pertaining to Christ.[21] And they fittingly accepted his teaching. Thus the text says: *They have kept my word*. About this keeping of his word John 14:21 above has: "The person who has my commandments and keeps them, he it is who loves me." And he shows how they have kept the word or message of the Father. For since they had neither heard nor seen the Father, someone might doubt that they could keep his word. Therefore, the text says that they have kept the Father's word by believing in the Son.

14. (Verse 7). *And*[22] *now they have learned that all that you have given me is from you*, and therefore, they have known you by knowing me. For John 5:19 above says: "The Son can do nothing of himself." John 14:10 above reads: "The Father, dwelling in me, it is he who does the works." And therefore, "the person who sees me also sees the Father."[23] And they have also heard the word of the Father. Therefore, the text continues:

15. (Verse 8). *Because the words that you have given me I have given to them*. John 15:15 above states: "Whatever[24] I have heard from my Father, I have made known to you." And these have kept my words, which I have given to them, and consequently your word. Therefore, the text reads: *And they have received them*, by understanding them, *and have truly known that I have come forth from you*, according to divine nature, *and have believed that you have sent me*, namely, into flesh. And so they have believed and have known the divinity in Christ and his

---

[21] Bonaventure refers to Hebr 2:13 which quotes Isa 8:18.

[22] On p. 470 n. 8 QuarEd correctly mention that the Vulgate does not read *Et* ("And").

[23] See John 14:9.

[24] The Vulgate reads *omnia quaecumque* ("all things whatever") while Bonaventure has *quaecumque* ("whatever").

humanity. And it should be noted that the text says: "And they have believed that you have sent me" and afterwards "And they have known that I have come forth from you." They had said in John 16:30 above: "For this reason we have known[25] that you have come forth from God," because through faith in his assumed humanity a person arrives at an understanding of his eternal generation. Thus Augustine observes that those who contemned the humble Christ did not merit to acknowledge the sublime Christ.[26] So this is the first reason why they should be heard, namely, their keeping of Christ's words. Thus John 15:7 says: "If you abide in me and my words abide in you, you will ask for whatever you will and it will be done for you."

16. (Verse 9). *And I pray for them*. Here the second reason for hearing the Apostles surfaces, namely, the divine election itself, since our Lord himself was praying for the elect, not for the reprobates. Therefore, he says: *I pray for them*, namely, because they are elect, and goes on to say: *Not for the world do I pray*, "that is, those given over to the world,"[27] whom you have blinded. *But for the ones[28] you have given me*, that is, you have saved through me. In Acts 27:24 it was significantly said to Paul: "Behold, God

---

[25] The Vulgate reads *credimus* ("we believe") whilst Bonaventure has *cognovimus* ("we have known").

[26] This quotation is not found verbatim in Augustine. See Augustine, Exposition of Psalm 93 n. 8 in *Expositions of the Psalms 73-98*. Translated by Maria Boulding. WSA III/18 (Hyde Park, NY: New City Press, 2002), p. 384: "Do you think that because they laid hands on a humble man, they will lay their hands on him in his high glory?"

[27] This citation comes from the Glossa Interlinearis. See Augustine, Tractate 107 n. 1 in FC 90, p. 273: "He now wishes the world to be understood as those who live according to the lust of the world and who are not in that allotted portion of grace so that they may be chosen by him out of the world."

[28] On p. 470 n. 13 QuarEd rightly notice that the Vulgate reads *pro his* ("for those") whereas Bonaventure has *pro eis* ("for the ones").

has given you the souls of all who are sailing with you." Nor have you taken away for yourself any that you have given me: *Because they are yours.*

17. (Verse 10). *And all things that are mine are yours, and yours mine.*[29] John 16:15 above reads: "All things that the Father has are mine," and vice versa. Therefore, he said earlier in John 7:16: "My teaching is not mine." Wherefore, my servants and my elect are your elect. And this is the second reason for hearing the Apostles, namely, their election. For John 15:16 above states: "You have not chosen me, but I have chosen you and have appointed you that you should go and bear fruit, and that your fruit should remain, that whatever you ask the Father in my name he may give you."

18. *And I[30] am glorified.* The third reason occurs here, namely, the desolation of the disciples at Christ's departure which was at hand. On account of its nearness he says that he has been glorified and departed, since what was future was near at hand. So he says: *And I am glorified in them*, because they have known him and should acknowledge him in the immediate future.[31]

19. (Verse 11). *And I am no longer in the world*, for as John 14:30 states: "I will no longer say much to you." *But these are in the world, and I am coming to you*, and thereby leaving them desolate. John 16:5-6 reads: "I am going

---

[29] On p. 471 n. 1 QuarEd accurately indicate that the Vulgate reads *sunt* ("are"): and mine *are* yours.

[30] On p. 471 n. 2 QuarEd correctly mention that the Vulgate does not read *ego* ("I").

[31] See Chrysostom, Homily 81 n. 1 in FC 41, p. 380: "Next He set forth the reason and the proof by saying: 'And I am glorified in them,' that is, either 'because I have power over them' or 'because they will glorify Me, since they believe in You and in Me, and they will glorify Us alike.'"

to the one who sent me.... But since I have spoken these things to you, sorrow has filled your heart." This was the third reason for their being heard. Therefore, John 14:12-13 states: "I am going to the Father, and whatever you ask the Father[32] in my name, that I will do."

20. *Holy Father*. After the multiple reasons for petitioning have been set forth, here, in a fourth point, is the petition itself, in which he prays that they be preserved in good. For this reason the text says: *Holy Father, keep in your name those whom you have given me*, that is, through the power of your name. John 10:29 above reads: "No one can snatch anything from the hand of my Father." *Keep*, it says, in good. Thus he says: *so that they may be one even as we are one*, namely, in the unity of concord and peace. God preserves this unity in the elect, but, nonetheless, needs their care. For Ephesians 4:3 states: "Be careful to preserve the unity of the Spirit in the bond of peace."

Questions

21. Question 1 asks why the Lord is praying for the Apostles at this point. 1. For it is said in John 16:26-27 above: "I do not say to you that I will ask the Father for you, for the Father himself loves you." So what he is doing here is contrary to what he had said. – 2. Furthermore, the Lord himself did not pray for any except those who were predestined. He knew that God willed to save them at the end. So they would be saved without his prayer. Therefore, he was praying in vain. – 3. Moreover, why was he praying out loud? What was the necessity of doing so?

---

[32] The Vulgate does not read *Patrem* ("the Father").

I answer that it has to be said that there was a threefold reason behind the Lord's prayer for the Apostles, namely, the accomplishment of salvation, the consolation of salvation, and teaching about salvation since he was meriting for them, since they were being consoled as they heard these words, since they, and we too, were being taught to pray from this. Therefore, he prayed out loud. – With respect to the first objection that the Lord had earlier said, "I do not say to you that I will ask the Father, etc." the Lord did not want to deny that he would pray for them since it is said in Hebrews 9 that "he was appearing before the face of God to make intercession for us."[33] So he would pray to the Father who was not ill disposed, but was rather well disposed towards the Apostles. – 2. With respect to objection two: Why is he praying? Augustine says in his *De praedestinatione sanctorum* that our prayers are only heard for the predestined and for them we are not praying in vain, because "they have perhaps been predestined, that they may be granted this by our prayers."[34] Thus in Christ.

22. Question 2 deals with John 17:9: "I pray for them, not for the world." Contrary. 1. John 17:21 below states: "That the world may believe that you have sent me." Therefore, he was praying that the world believe. – 2. Moreover, he had to pray for those, on whose behalf he had been sent and was to die. Indeed he died for the sake of the world.

---

[33] Hebr 9:24 says: "… to appear now before the face of God on our behalf." Hebr 7:25 reads: "… since he lives always to make intercession for them."

[34] The text actually comes from Augustine, *De dono perseverantiae*, c. 22 n. 60. See PL 45:1029: "For why is it not rather phrased in this way: And if they have not yet been called, let us pray for them that they may be called? For they have perhaps been predestined in such a way that they may be granted this by our prayers and may receive the same grace by which they would want to be and would become elect." See also Augustine, Book XXI, c. 24 n. 1, *De civitate Dei*.

John 3:16 above reads: "God so loved the world that he sent his only begotten Son." – 3. In addition, sinners are meant by "the world," but "it is not the healthy who need a physician, but those who are sick."[35] Wherefore, for such people especially should prayers be said.

I answer that it has to be maintained that "world" in his prayer is patient of a threefold meaning, and this generates ambiguity. Besides there is a fourth meaning. For "world" is said to be this orb that is visible to us. And in this sense it is used in John 1:10 above: "The world was made by him." Sometimes "world" refers to the status of our existence in as far as it had suffering with it. And in this sense John 17:11 says: "These are in the world, and I am coming to you." At other times "world" refers to the status of our present existence as a sinful one. And in this sense John 17:14 reads: "The world has hated them." At yet other times "world" carries the meaning of eternal reprobation, and that is the meaning here: "I pray for them, but not for the world do I pray." – The first way of speaking refers to nature; the second to nature and suffering; the third to nature and suffering and sin; the fourth to nature and suffering and sin and divine reprobation.

John 17:12-19
The Lord prays for liberation from evil

23. *While I was with them*, etc. After he has asked for their preservation in good, he now petitions for their liberation or rescue from evil. And he gives voice to this petition or prayer in this wise. First he notes *the necessity of praying*. Second is *the form of the prayer*. Third is *the reason for be-*

---

[35] See Luke 5:31.

ing heard. – So the necessity of praying for steadfastness stems from two causes: from the absence of the one who preserves and from immersion in tribulation.

24. (Verse 12). Christ, who had been guarding them, is absent from them. So the text states: *While I was with them, I kept them in your name.* He had kept the disciples in the name of the Father, since he did so through the power of the Father and for the glory of the Father. And afterwards the Father kept them in the name of the Son. For John 16:23 above says: "If you ask the Father anything in my name, he will give it to you." And he has kept them well. So the text continues: *Those whom you have given me I have guarded,*[36] as the good leader to whom it is said in 1 Kings 20:39: "Guard this man. If he escapes, it will be your life in exchange for his." About this guarding Psalm 120:4 has: "Behold, the one who guards Israel will not slumber or sleep." And again Psalm 126:1 reads: "Unless the Lord guard the city, he watches in vain who guards it."[37] Thus Psalm 16:8 states: "Guard us, Lord, as the apple of your eye." Deuteronomy 32:10 says: "The Lord led him about, and taught him, and guarded him as the apple of his eye." And he did this well. For the text continues: *And not one of them perished except the son of perdition*, that is, Judas, who is said to be "of perdition," because his death had been known beforehand. For he ruined himself in a temporal way. Matthew 27:5 reads: "He went away and hanged himself with a halter." He ruined himself in an eternal manner. Matthew 26:24 states: "Woe to that person through whom the Son of Man is betrayed. It were better for that person if he had not been born." For the same reason it is said of the Antichrist in

---

[36] On p. 472 n. 5 QuarEd rightly notice that the Vulgate does not read *ego* ("I").

[37] Hugh of St. Cher, p. 386v,y quotes Ps 126:1 and 120:4.

2 Thessalonians 2:3: "Then the sinful person will be revealed, the person destined for ruination."[38] This one did not perish accidentally or because of Christ's negligence, but because of his own malice, which was foreseen from eternity and foretold in Scripture. So the text states: *in order that the Scripture might be fulfilled*, namely, Psalm 108 which bears the title "God, my praise."[39] So I have kept them in a good state, and thus they had no need that I should pray for them.

25. (Verse 13). *But now I am coming to you*, and am leaving them, and therefore I am praying that they may experience a deepening of faith through my prayer. So he says: *These things*[40] *I am speaking in the world*, that is, I am making this prayer, with them listening, *in order that they may have my joy made full in themselves*, so that they not be disturbed by lack of faith, but that they may rejoice in themselves because of the hope instilled in them by listening, according to what John 16:24 says: "Ask, and you will receive, so that your joy may be full." So he was praying that they experience full joy. – So this is the first reason for the necessity of prayer, namely, the absence of the one guarding them. Now the other reason is their immersion in the tribulation that would rush upon them because they were guarding the divine word. For this reason the world hated them. So the text continues:

26. (Verse 14). *I have given them your word.* John 14:24 says: "The word that you have heard is not mine, but that of the Father who sent me." And because of this they have

---

[38] Hugh of St. Cher, p. 387f also cites 2 Thes 2:3.

[39] See esp. Ps 108:7: "When he is judged, may he go out condemned, and may his prayer be turned to sin." Hugh of St. Cher, p. 387g also refers to Ps 108, "God, my praise."

[40] On p. 472 n. 10 QuarEd correctly indicate that the Vulgate reads *Et haec* ("And these things").

experienced the world's hatred. Therefore, he says: *And the world has hated them*. And the reason is that they have left the world. So he continues: *Because they are not of the world, just as I*[41] *am not of the world*, that is, they are segregated from worldly conduct just as I am. John 15:19 says: "If you were of the world, the world would love what is its own.... But since I have chosen you out of the world, therefore the world hates you." The Apostles had been set aside from the world, for Romans 1:1 says: "Paul, Apostle of Jesus Christ, set apart," indeed segregated, for he says in Galatians 6:14: "The world has been crucified to me, and I to the world."

27. (Verse 15). *I do not pray that you take*. The second point occurs here, namely, the form of the prayer, in which he asks that they be removed from a twin evil, namely, perverse affection and error. – So he asks that they be kept from perverse affection to which the world draws them and entices them that they should live that way. Therefore, he says: *I do not pray that you take them out of the world*, namely, through the death of their flesh, as it is said of Enoch in Genesis 5:24: "Enoch[42] walked with God and was seen no more, because God had taken him." He took him for this reason that he preserve him from evil. Wisdom 4:11 reads: "He was taken away, lest wickedness should alter his understanding." But he did not ask that they be preserved in this way, but in the world. So he adds: *But that you keep them from evil*.[43] And the reason given why they should be preserved from evil:

---

[41] On p. 472 n. 12 QuarEd accurately mention that the Vulgate reads *sicut et ego* ("just as I, too").

[42] Gen 5:24 does not explicitly mention Enoch, but the context indicates that he is the subject.

[43] The Glossa Interlinearis comments: "*I do not ask that you take them out of the world*, where they are still necessary, even if they are not of the world."

28. (Verse 16). *They are not of the world, even as I*[44] *am not of the world,* namely, through my conduct. So he was asking that they be saved and preserved, lest they be turned to love of the world. About this keeping Revelation 3:10 states: "Since you have kept the word of my patience, I too will keep you from the hour of trial that is about to come upon the whole world to try those who dwell upon the earth." So he prays that they be kept from the evil of prevarication. He prays also that they be kept from the evil or error. For this reason he says:

29. (Verse 17). *Sanctify them in the truth.* "Holy," that is, outside the earth.[45] "To sanctify," that is, to cleanse and purge. Now "truth" is found in the word of God. So the text reads: *Your word is truth.* And by means of this word of God the disciples are sanctified, that is, purged from error. Chrysostom comments: "*Sanctify them in truth,* that is, instruct them, teach them the truth, for correct teachings sanctify the soul."[46] For he knew that the word of God cleanses, for it was said in John 15:3 above: "You are clean because of the word I have spoken to you." And Ephesians 5:26 reads: "Christ sanctified the Church,

---

[44] On p. 473 n. 2 QuarEd accurately note that the Vulgate reads *sicut et ego* ("even as I too"). See n. 41 above.

[45] See Origen, Homily 11 n. 1 on Leviticus 19:2 in *Origen, Homilies on Leviticus 1-16.* Translated by Gary W. Barkley. FC 83; Washington: CUA Press, 1990, pp. 210-211: "Moreover, we say to be set apart, not from places but from deeds, not from regions but from ways of life. Finally, this same word which is called *hagios* in the Greek language signifies that it is something outside the earth. For whoever consecrates himself to God will deservedly appear to be outside the earth and outside the world...."

[46] See Homily 82 n. 1 in PG 59:442-443. Bonaventure summarizes Chrysostom's observations. Hugh of St. Cher, p. 387v,d also cites Chrysostom: "... make them holy through the gift of the Spirit and correct teachings, that is, instruct them and teach them the truth...."

cleansing her in the bath of water by the word of life."[47] About sanctification of this kind 2 Timothy 2:21 states: "If anyone has cleansed himself from these, he will be a vessel ... sanctified, useful to the Lord, ready for every good work."

30. (Verse 18). *Just as you have sent me.* The third point is found here, namely, the reason for hearing his prayer which is twofold: the office to which they have been appointed and the sacrifice offered for their sakes. By reason of the office appointed them they should be kept and sanctified, because they have been sent among evil people. So he says: *Just as you have sent me into the world,* to the passion, *so*[48] *I also send them into the world,* namely, to suffer. For Matthew 10:16 reads: "Behold, I am sending you like sheep in the midst of wolves." So by reason of their office it was fitting that they be preserved. Also by reason of the sacrifice offered. So he adds:

31. (Verse 19). *I sanctify myself for them.* Chrysostom observes: "That is, I offer a holy sacrifice. All sacrifices were said to be holy."[49] Romans 12:1 states: "Present your bodies as a sacrifice, living, holy, and pleasing to God." And as Chrysostom says: "For in ancient times sanctification occurred in a sheep as a type, but now it occurs not in a type, but in truth itself, for the text says: *so that they may*

---

[47] Eph 5:25-26 has: "Husbands, love your wives, just as Christ also loved the Church, and delivered himself up for her, that he might sanctify her, cleansing her in the bath of water by the word." Hugh of St. Cher, p. 387v,g observes: "This truth or this word sanctifies, that is, cleanses. For John 5:3 (=15:3) reads: "You are clean, because of the word I have spoken to you. And it is said in Eph 5:26 about the Church that he sanctified it by the word."

[48] On p. 473 n. 6 QuarEd correctly indicate that the Vulgate does not read *sic* ("so").

[49] Bonaventure paraphrases Homily 82 n. 1. See PG 59:443.

be sanctified in the truth."[50] Hebrews 9:13-14 reads: "For if the sprinkled ashes of a heifer and the blood of goats sanctify the unclean to cleanse the flesh, how much more will the blood of Christ ... cleanse our conscience from dead works to serve the living God?"[51]

QUESTIONS

32. Question 1 deals with John 17:12: "While I was with them, I kept them." – 1. This seems to imply a certain powerlessness on his part, since in his absence he could not preserve them. – 2. It also seems from this that works of the Trinity are divided and it alternately happens that first the Son keeps them and now he asks the Father to keep them. – I respond that one has to hold that "to keep" has a twofold significance, namely, to keep in an effective manner and to keep by means of preparation. The first way of keeping pertains to the one who gives existence whereas the second way pertains to someone who can enhance existence. In the first way God keeps a human being in good. In the second a person keeps another through sound teaching and example, as a leader for his subjects. – So I say that Christ is speaking here of a keeping that is on the level of preparation, namely, by example and exhortation and teaching. And this will be removed when his bodily presence is removed. On the other level he was keeping them interiorly with the Father in as far as he was God. But he is not speaking here of this and he does

---

[50] Bonaventure paraphrases Homily 82 n. 1. See PG 59:443.

[51] Hebr 9:13-14 says: "For if the blood of goats and bulls and the sprinkled ashes of a heifer sanctify the unclean to cleanse the flesh, how much more will the blood of Christ, who through the Holy Spirit offered himself unblemished unto God, cleanse your consciences from dead works to serve the living God?"

not remove it, but he continues to manifest it together with the Father.[52]

33. Question 2 continues to ask about John 17:12: "I guarded those you have given me, and not one of them perished except the son of perdition." – Contrary are John 6:37: "All that the Father gives to me will come to me" and John 10:29: "No one will snatch my sheep from my hands."[53] Wherefore, none of the sheep should perish. – I answer that it has to be said that the Father gives the Son individuals in a twofold sense, namely, those whom he has predestined by eternal foreknowledge and knew beforehand that they would be conformed to the image of his Son.[54] He gives other individuals according to present justice. – So when it is said that none of those given to him perished, he is speaking according to predestination. When he excepts Judas, he is speaking of present justice.

34. Question 3 focuses on the Lord's petition that his disciples be kept from evil.[55] – It seems that this is an inordinate request. 1. For they were in the state of love and grace, but from whatever little grace or charity one has, a person can resist whatever large temptation arises. Therefore, etc. 2. Moreover, from that grace a person cannot fall except by mortal sin and a person can only sin willingly. Therefore, it is through the freedom of our will that any of us is kept from evil. So his petition is superfluous. – The response to this should be that of Augustine:

---

[52] For more detail see Book II d. 37. a. 1. q. 2 ad 3 in Bonaventure's *Sentence Commentary*.

[53] John 10:29 says: "What my Father has given me is greater than all, and no one can snatch anything from the hand of my Father."

[54] See Rom 8:29. See also Bonaventure's commentary above on John 6 n. 60, 64, and 100.

[55] See John 17:15.

To remain in the good that has been received stems from divine beneficence and our effort, for grace is kept in us by means of its continuous influence. And therefore it is asked of the Lord that he continuously help. For if we can fall away by our will alone, unless divine aid intervenes, we cannot remain.[56]

John 17:20-23
The Lord prays for those who would believe through the Apostles

35. *Not only*[57] *for them*[58] *do I pray*. This verse commences the third part of the chapter, in which the Lord prays for conformity to grace on the part of those who are to believe because of the Apostles. And he proceeds in this fashion. First he sets forth *the petition*. Second is *the reason for hearing the prayer* where verse 22 reads: "And I have given them the glory you have given me." Further, in the petition he asks *a twofold unity* for those who are to believe, namely, of love and of faith.

Verse 20. For the sake of the unity of love, which he asks for those who are to believe because of the Apostles, he says: *Not only for them*, that is, for the Apostles, *do I pray, but also for those who through their word are to believe in me*. For these, he says, I pray:

---

[56] This seems a summary of *De correptione et gratia*, c. 6 n. 10. See PL 44:921-923.

[57] On p. 474 n. 7 QuarEd accurately mention that the Vulgate reads *autem* ("Now").

[58] The Vulgate reads *his* ("these") whereas Bonaventure has *eis* ("them").

36. (Verse 21). *That they*[59] *may be one*, through the conformity of love, *even as you Father in me, and I in you*, that is, as we are one, *that they also be one in us*. Galatians 3:18 says: "You are all one in Christ Jesus." This unity comes about through the cleaving of love. 1 Corinthians 6:17 states: "The person who cleaves to God[60] is one spirit." So when they are united with one another in God, then they are one in God. For 1 Corinthians 12:13 reads: "In one Spirit we have been baptized into one body."

37. Thus his prayer for them is for the unity of love. He also prays for the unity of faith. So he says: *That the world may believe that you have sent me*. "The world," that is, the universality of the children of God dispersed through the world, whom he must gather into the unity of faith. In John 11:52 above it was said that he was about to die "so that he might gather into one the children of God who were scattered abroad." And he does this by uniting them in faith in his name, because as John 1:12 above says: "To those who believe in his name he gave power to become children of God." And Acts 4:12 states: "There is no other name under heaven given to men and women, by which we must be saved."

38. (Verse 22). *The glory I*. The second point surfaces here, namely, the reason for being heard, since he had communicated his glory to the Apostles that the world might be converted to faith. Now he had communicated a triple glory to them, namely, that of power, wisdom, and goodness: power in performing miracles, through which

---

[59] On p. 474 n. 9 QuarEd correctly indicate that the Vulgate reads *Ut omnes* ("That all").

[60] The Vulgate reads *Domino* ("the Lord") while Bonaventure has *Deo* ("to God").

the Jews, who "seek signs,"[61] were converted to faith; wisdom in proclaiming teachings, through which the Greeks, who "seek wisdom," were converted. On account of this twofold glorification he says: *And the glory that you have given me, I have given to them.* Chrysostom comments: "The glory that came through signs; the glory that came through teachings."[62] About the giving of glory through signs Luke 9:1 reads: "Having gathered together the Twelve, he gave them power and authority over all demons and to cure diseases." – About the bestowal of the glory of teachings Luke 21:15 states: "I will give you utterance and wisdom that all your adversaries will not be able to resist or gainsay." – He also gave them the glory of goodness. For this reason the text adds: *that they may be one, just as we are one,* according to their capacity. And this is their capacity:

39. (Verse 23). *I in them, and you in me, that they may be perfected in unity,* that is, perfect in the unity of love, and that through this they may become glorified. For Chrysostom observes: "This is great glory that they may be one, and this glory is greater than signs. For just as they stand in awe of God that there is no contention and discord in God's nature and this is the greatest glory, so through the lack of discord they may become glorified."[63] For John 13:35 above says: "In this will all people know that you are my disciples if you have love for one another." And he has given this glorification to his Apostles. – *And that the*

---

[61] See 1 Cor 1:22: "For the Jews seek signs and the Greeks seek wisdom."

[62] See Homily 82 n. 2 in PG 59:444: "That is, through signs, through teaching, and that they may be in accord with one another." Hugh of St. Cher, p. 388e also cites this passage.

[63] See Homily 82 n. 2 in PG 59:444. Bonaventure's citation is a paraphrase. Hugh of St. Cher, p. 388f also quotes Chrysostom and does so in a paraphrase that is different than Bonaventure's.

world may know that you have sent me, namely, through the glorification you have given them in my name. *And that you have loved them just as you have loved me*. And the world will know this through the unity and concord that it will see in them. Chrysostom states: "Showing by this that peace attracts more people than miracles, for just as contention drives people away, so does harmony draw them together."[64] Acts 2:42-43 reads: "They continued steadfastly in the teaching of the Apostles and in the communion of the breaking of the bread and in the prayers. And fear came upon every soul."

QUESTIONS

40. Question 1 focuses on John 17:20 and asks: If only those for whom Christ prayed for were saved through him and he prayed only for the Apostles and those who were to believe through them, so it follows that those who had believed through Christ, such as Nicodemus,[65] lacked the benefit of his prayer and therefore of salvation. – I answer that it should be maintained that "those who were to believe through the Apostles" refers not solely to those converted at their preaching, but also to those who followed in their footsteps. – Alternately it can be said that the Lord was praying for those who had already believed in him in a general way, not only for the Apostles.[66]

---

[64] Bonaventure paraphrases Homily 82 n. 2. See PG 59:444.

[65] See John 3:1-21 and 7:50-52.

[66] Augustine devotes his entire Tractate 109 to this problematic. While mentioning Jesus' Mother, women disciples, and Joseph of Arimathea, Augustine does not mention Nicodemus. See Tractate 109 n. 2 in FC 90, p. 285: "Therefore, the Savior did not pray for them then because he prayed for those who were with him then and for others who through their word had not already believed in him but would believe. These, however, neither were with him then and yet had already believed in him before."

41. Question 2 deals with John 17:21: The Lord prayed for those who were to believe through the Apostles that "they may be one." – Contrary: Many have believed who later became deviant and fell away. Therefore, his prayer for all was not heard. – I respond that certain people are members of the faithful by name only, such as evil Christians. Certain people by merit of present justice. Certain by knowledge of eternal foreknowledge, about which 2 Timothy 2:19 says: "The Lord knows who are his own." And for such the Lord prays, but not for the others, since 1 John 2:19 states: "They have gone out from among us, but they were not of us."

42. Question 3 addresses John 17:22: "That they may be one, just as we are one." – 1. What is he saying, for they are one in essence while human beings cannot be one in essence? 2. Moroever, John 17:23 reads: "Just as you in me and I in them." There seems to be no likeness whatsoever. Arius maintained that there was a likeness. And when it is said, just as we are one, it does not follow from this that we are one in essence. Just as it is not the case when the Son says in John 10:30: "The Father and I are one."

And he is speaking in an evil manner, since, when it is said that some individuals are one, as Augustine maintains, one must of necessity add a determinative or of necessity speak of conformity in nature, not only in will. For when it is said of two or more people that they love one another, it is rightly said that they are one, but this is never said of the love of a human being and God.[67] For it

---

[67] See Book VI, c. 4 of *De Trinitate* in *The Trinity*, WSA I/5, p. 208: "So when 'one' is predicated without it being stated 'one what,' and several things are just called one, it signifies sameness of nature and being without any variance or disagreement. But when a specification is added to state 'one what,' then it can signify one made out of

is necessary, if the Son is truly saying to the Father: "You and I are one," that they have the same nature. But if the divine nature is indivisible, then they are one *simpliciter*. – Relative to the question about the likeness between God and humans, it has to be said that the likeness or similitude is extraordinarily distant, as in Luke 6:36: "Be merciful as your Father is merciful." Just as divine mercy infinitely exceeds my mercy, so too does divine unity exceed human unity.

But why does the church of evildoers not form a unity like the Church of Christ? The response is: Since, if evil people gather externally for some evil deed, nonetheless, they differ internally in their will and in their goal, for each one seeks his own advantage.[68] But good people gather together unified in will and goal.

JOHN 17:24-26
THE LORD PRAYS FOR LASTING GLORY

43. *Father, I will.* This is the fourth part of the chapter, in which he petitions *lasting glory* for those for whom he had asked to be conformed to grace. The order is twofold:

---

several things, even though they differ in nature. Thus soul and body are certainly not one (could two things be more different?), unless you add or understand one what, namely one man or one animal.... Nor do I think it is without significance, seeing how much and how often the Lord spoke in the gospel according to John about unity, whether his with the Father or ours with each other, that he nowhere said 'That we and they may be one,' but *That they may be one as we are one* (Jn 17:22). Father and Son are of course one with the unity of substance...."

[68] See Phil 2:21: "For they all seek their own interests, not those of Jesus Christ." See Book I, d. 31. a. 2 q. 2 ad 2 of Bonaventure's *Sentence Commentary*.

the petition is set forth. Second is *the reason for hearing the petition.*

Verse 24. The petition is for glory. And since glory consists in the vision of the Divinity that we will see in the heavenly homeland, the text reads: *Father, whom you have given me*, through predestination, *I will that where I am, they also may be*,[69] through dwelling together in glory. John 12:26 above has: "If anyone serves me, let him follow me. And where I am, there also will my servant be." *Where I am*, that is, where I will presently be according to my humanity.[70] – Another interpretation: "Where I am" according to my Divinity, that is, that they may be with me who am everywhere. Augustine observes: "To be with him is a great good, for even the wretched can be where he is who is everywhere. But the blessed are with him, since they are always enjoying blessedness by adhering to him."[71] And how this is to be understood is clear from what follows: *That they may behold my glory which you have given me*. This is the magnificence of the Divinity. Therefore, the text continues: *Because you have loved me before the creation of the world*. John 5:20 above reads: "The Father loves the Son and shows him all." Only the good will see this glory. Isaiah 26:10 states: "May the wicked be taken away, lest he see the glory of God."[72] To this glory we are now being conformed through grace. 2 Corinthians 3:18 says: "We all, with faces unveiled, re-

---

[69] On p. 476 n. 4 QuarEd rightly notice that the Vulgate has *mecum* ("with me").

[70] See Augustine, Tractate 111 n. 2 in FC 90, p. 301: "... but he could have said, 'where I am,' in such a way that we might understand that he was soon going to ascend into heaven, so that he said that he now was where he was going to be in the near future."

[71] Bonaventure adapts Tractate, 111 n. 2. See CCSL xxxvi, p. 630.

[72] Isa 26:10 reads: "Let us have mercy on the wicked, but he will not learn justice. In the land of the saints he has done wicked deeds, and he will not see the glory of the Lord."

flecting as in a mirror the glory of God,[73] are being transformed into his very image from glory to glory, as through the Spirit of the Lord."[74]

44. (Verse 25). *Righteous Father, the world*, etc. The second point occurs here, namely, the reason for being heard: Why these must see through glory since they now know through grace. But the evildoers do not know now nor will they know then. So he says: *Righteous Father*, because "you render to each one according to his works."[75] *The world has not known you*. John 1:9 above reads: "He was the true light that enlightens," etc.[76] Therefore, I am not praying for the world. *But I have known you, and these have known that you have sent me*, and this is what I am revealing. So he continues:

45. (Verse 26). *And I have made known to them your name*. Psalm 21:23 says: "I will proclaim your name to my brothers and sisters." Matthew 11:27 has: "No one knows the Son except the Father, and no one knows the Father except the Son, and to whom the Son wishes him to be revealed." He made him known not only through himself, but he will make him more fully known through the Holy Spirit, who is the love of the Father and the Son. Therefore, he says: *In order that the love with which you have loved me, may be in them*, through the gift of the Holy Spirit. Romans 5:5 reads: "The love of God has been poured forth into our hearts through the Holy Spirit who

---

[73] The Vulgate reads *Domini* ("of the Lord") whereas Bonaventure has *Dei* ("of God").

[74] Hugh of St. Cher, p. 388v,c also cites 2 Cor 3:18.

[75] See Matt 16:27 where the Vulgate reads *reddet* ("he will render") whereas Bonaventure has *reddes* ("you will render") and *secundum opus eius* ("according to his work") while Bonaventure has *secundum opera sua* ("according to his works").

[76] See John 1:10: "He was in the world, and the world was made through him, and the world did not know him."

has been given to us."[77] *And I in them*, since 1 John 4:16 states: "The person who remains in love remains in God, and God in him."[78] And so it is said in 1 John 4:13: "In this we know that we remain in him and he in us, because he has given us of his Spirit." And the person who has this Spirit also has the Son and is secure that he has the Father. For Augustine comments: "The Father gave his Son as the price of redemption, the Holy Spirit as a pledge of adoption, himself as the inheritance for those adopted."[79]

QUESTIONS

46. Question 1 rivets our attention on John 17:24: "That where I am, they also may be with me." – Contrary. John 14:2 above says: "In the house of my Father there are many mansions." – I answer: "There is equal joy in the disparate glorifications," by reason of different glorifications within the multitude, by reason of communal joy where the head and members are.[80]

---

[77] See Theophylactus's commentary on John 17:26 in PG 124:142B: "Now how does he make him known? By sending them the Holy Spirit, who 'will lead them into all the truth.'"

[78] See Augustine, Tractate 111 n. 6 in FC 90, pp. 306-307: "I have made known by faith, and I shall make known by direct vision; I have made known to those sojourning with an end, I shall make known to those reigning without end."

[79] See c. 54 Pseudo-Augustine, *De spiritu et anima*, c. 54 in PL 40:820: "He gave the Son as the price of redemption, the Holy Spirit as the special right of love. Finally he keeps himself as the inheritance for those adopted."

[80] See Prosper Aquitane, *Liber Sententiarum ex operibus S. Augustini delibatarum*, 364 in PL 51:486C: "So many mansions refer to the various dignities of merits in one life. But since God will be all in all, there is also equal joy in the disparate glorifications, so that what each one has individually may be common to all, for through the connection of love no part of the body will be without the glory of the head." This "sentence" is taken from Tractate, 67 n. 2. See FC 90, p. 59: "But the many dwelling-places signify the varied values of merits

47. Question 2 raises an objection based on 1 Timothy 6:16: "The Lord lives in inaccessible light."[81] – I respond that the light is inaccessible either because there is no entry or because it is difficult to enter or because one does not enter by human power or because one has access solely by divine glory.

48. Question 3 focuses on the magnificence of the Divinity. Now something that is excessive destroys, but the glory of God is most excessive.[82] – I answer that if what is comprehended is bodily, then the thing comprehended can be harmful.

49. Question 4 deals with John 17:25 and asks why the world, that is, earthly people, have not known. – Contrary. Romans 1:21 says: "Although they had known God, they did not glorify him as God," etc. – I respond that there is simple knowledge and knowledge of acknowledgment. They knew with simple knowledge, but not with that of acknowledgment. And so their knowing merited them nothing.

---

in the one eternal life.... because God is love, it may come to pass through love that what each has may be common to all. For in this way each one himself also has, when he loves in another what he does not have himself. And so there will not be any envy of unequal brightness, because the unity of love will reign in all."

[81] And so who is going to gain access to the inaccessible?

[82] It seems that Bonaventure is dependent upon Book III n 2 of Aristotle, *De anima*. See WAE, Volume 3, 426a-b: "That is why the excess of either the sharp or the flat destroys the hearing. (So also in the case of savours excess destroys the sense of taste, and in the case of colours excessive brightness or darkness destroys the sight, and in the case of smell excess of strength whether in the direction of sweetness or bitterness is destructive)."

CHAPTER EIGHTEEN

JOHN 18:1-19:42
EVENTS THAT OCCUR ALONGSIDE THE PASSION

1. *After saying these things*, etc. Earlier he treated the antecedents of the passion, namely from John 11:47 to 17:26. Now he considers those things by which *the passion is consummated*. And since he was seized and judged, killed and buried in his passion, this section is divided into four parts. The first part focuses on Christ's *arrest*. His *condemnation* is the subject of the second part where verse 13 says: "And they brought him to Annas." The third considers his *passion* where John 19:16 reads: "So they took Jesus," etc. The fourth deals with the nature of his *burial* where John 19:38 states: "Now after these things Joseph," etc.

JOHN 18:1-12
THE ARREST OF CHRIST

So in the first part, in which is shown the details of Christ's arrest, three points stand out. First that *a betrayal* led to his arrest. Second that it was *voluntary* where verse four has: "Now Jesus, knowing all that was to come upon him." Third that it was *ignominious* where verse 12 reads: "So the cohort and the tribune," etc.

John 18:1-3
Betrayal led to Christ's arrest

2. (Verse 1). So the first part proceeds in this fashion. First he shows Christ coming into a place known to his betrayer. Second is the arrival of the betrayer into that place where verse 3 reads: "Judas, then," etc. – So the evangelist continues what has to be said: *After he had said these things.* Supply: Which had preceded. *Jesus went forth with his disciples beyond the torrent of Cedron.* This journey had been prefigured in 2 Samuel 15:23: "The king also went over the torrent of Cedron." "Cedron" is genitive plural, that is, beyond the torrent of cedars, since there were many cedar trees there. *He went forth*, from the city, for he was arrested and suffered outside the city. Hebrews 13:12 states: "Christ suffered outside the gate." *Where there was a garden into which he and his disciples entered*, not as if they were fleeing or hiding themselves, but because they were seeking quiet. The Song of Songs 6:10 reads: "I went down into my garden ... to see." Psalm 75:3 says: "His place is in peace." Thus he adds:

3. (Verse 2). *Now Judas, who betrayed him, also knew the place.* And the reason is added: *Since Jesus used to meet*[1] *there frequently with his disciples.* Victor comments: "Judas had known about this place, because the Lord was accustomed to go there frequently."[2] This place was at the foot of the Mount of Olives. Jesus went there often. Luke 21:37 states: "In the daytime he was teaching in the

---

[1] On p. 478 n. 4 QuarEd accurately indicate that the Vulgate reads *convenerat* ("had met") while Bonaventure has *conveniebat* ("used to meet").

[2] This citation is probably from Bishop Victor of Capua (d. 554) whose works are not extant. See John 1:1 n. 3 above.

temple, but during the nights he would go out and stay on Mount Olivet."[3]

4. (Verse 3). *Judas, then, taking the cohort*. This verse notes the arrival of the betrayer with such people as could seize and hold and lead him away. So, *taking the cohort*, namely, from the Gentiles, *and attendants from the leaders*[4] *and Pharisees, for he was handing him over to them*. It is said in Matthew 26:14-15: "He ... went to the chief priests and said to them: What are you willing to give me for delivering him to you?" *Came there*, as if he were the leader of the others, *with lanterns and torches and weapons*, lest he might remain hidden at night. For since they were walking in darkness, they were begging light from torches. Job 24:17 states: "If daylight suddenly arises, they think it is the shadow of death. And so they walk in darkness as if it were in light." Another interpretation is that they wanted to defend themselves. And they were doing this, because they believed that there was nothing divine in him, but only human power.

QUESTIONS

5. Question 1 deals first with John 18:1: after his prayer "Jesus went forth beyond the torrent of Cedron, since, as Augustine observes in his *Harmony of the Gospels*, once Jesus' words were completed, "a contention arose as to which of them would be the greatest."[5] – But it should

---

[3] Luke 21:37 says: "Now during the days he was teaching in the temple, but during the nights he would go out and stay on the mountain called Olivet."

[4] On p. 478 n. 6 QuarEd correctly mention that the Vulgate reads *pontificibus* ("high priests") whereas Bonaventure has *principibus* ("leaders").

[5] See Book III, c. 3 n. 9 with reference to Luke 22:24.

be said that the word of Blessed John should not be construed in such a precise way that this took place immediately after the prayer. Rather the meaning is that it was after the prayer and not before.[6]

6. Question 2 still deals with the place. Matthew 26:36 says: "Jesus came to a country place, which is called Gethsemani." But Luke 22:39 says: "He came out and went, according to his custom, to the Mount of Olives." John says: "beyond the torrent of Cedron." – It seems that there are contraries here. – Augustine answers in Book III of his *Harmony of the Gospels*: "This place is the Mount of Olives, whose name Matthew and Mark gave as Gethsemani. And we understand that there was a garden there, which John recalls."[7] And Victor says: "The country place was situated at the foot of the Mount of Olives."[8]

7. Question 3 asks why the Lord left the city at night? – It seems that he wanted to remain hidden. – Chrysostom responds that he not only did this at this time, but that he was accustomed to slipping away often, so that he might extricate himself from the tumult of human congress and might discourse about important matters.[9]

---

[6] See Augustine, Tractate 112 n. 1 in FC 92, p. 4: "Let us then not take what he says ... in such a way as though he had entered into that garden immediately after those words. But let the statement, 'When Jesus had said these things,' have this effect, that we do not suppose that he entered before he finished those words."

[7] Bonaventure summarizes Book III, c. 4 n. 10 of *De consensu Evangelistarum*. See CSEL xliii, p. 281.

[8] See n. 2 above on Bishop Victor of Capua.

[9] Bonaventure summarizes Homily 83 n. 1. See PG 59:447 and FC 41, p. 400: "He did this for He frequently held meetings with them in private to talk with them of important matters and those which it was not right for others to hear. These conferences took place, for the most part, on hilltops and in gardens, as He always sought out a place free from distractions so that the minds of His listeners might be bet-

8. Question 4 queries Judas's actions: Since Judas left him at the house, why didn't he lead the cohort there rather than to the garden? – Chrysostom answers that he would have more easily gone to the house to find him asleep there, but he knew that his custom was to frequently spend the night outdoors.[10]

9. Question 5 asks: Since that cohort was made up of Gentile soldiers, why were they following Judas? – I respond that they had been corrupted by money given or promised them. For Chrysostom observes: "They were genuine soldiers, conniving to do anything for the sake of money."[11]

10. Question 6 asks: "Why didn't they come to arrest him during the day since they had such a large cohort? – And Chrysostom answers that they feared the crowds that followed him during the day.[12]

---

ter able to concentrate." Hugh of St. Cher, p. 389i cites Chrysostom verbatim.

[10] See Homily 83 n. 1 in PG 59:447 and FC 41, p. 400: "From his (Judas') coming there it is clear that Christ had spent the night many times out of doors. For, if He ordinarily passed the night in a dwelling, Judas would not have gone to seek Him out in that lonely spot, but to His lodgings, expecting to find Him sleeping there." Hugh of St. Cher, p. 389h summarizes Chrysostom's thought in his own way.

[11] See Homily 83 n. 1 in PG 59:447: "They were soldiers who were prepared to do anything for money's sake." Hugh of St. Cher, p. 389k cites Chrysostom in almost the selfsame manner as Bonaventure.

[12] See Homily 83 n. 1 in PG 59:448 and FC 41, p. 401: "They feared His followers, and it was for this reason, also, that they approached at an untimely hour of the night." See Hugh of St. Cher, p. 389q: "Because they were in dread of those who were following Christ. Therefore, they also initiated the arrest at an untimely hour of the night."

John 18:4-12
Christ's arrest was voluntary and ignominious

11. *But[13] Jesus, knowing.* Here it is shown in a fourfold manner that the arrest of Christ was *voluntary* on his part. First although he could have hidden, *he offered himself.* Second by offering himself, *he caused his enemies to fall on the ground.* Third by offering himself *he freed his disciples* solely by his command. Fourth *he did not permit them to resist.*

Verse 4. So first it is noted that he was voluntarily arrested, because he could have hidden himself. For the text says: *But Jesus, knowing all that was to come upon him,* and therefore, he could have escaped from them before they arrived. Sirach 23:28 says: "The eyes of the Lord are far brighter than the sun," etc. And nevertheless, he handed himself over. For it is said: *He went forth and said to them: Whom do you seek?* "He went forth," that is, he freely offered himself. Isaiah 53:7 reads: "He was offered, because he willed it," etc.[14] Psalm 34:4 states: "Let those who seek my life be confounded and ashamed." Augustine comments: "In their raging they were seeking to kill him, but he was seeking us by dying."[15]

12. (Verse 5). *They answered:[16] Jesus of Nazareth.* It is clear from this that they did not know him. Chrysostom observes: "Standing in their midst, he blinded them and

---

[13] On p. 479 n. 4 QuarEd rightly notice that the Vulgate reads *itaque* ("therefore") while Bonaventure has *autem* ("but").

[14] Hugh of St. Cher, p. 389s also cites Isa 53:7.

[15] See Tractate 112 n. 3 in CCSL xxxvi, p. 635. Bonaventure's citation is almost verbatim.

[16] On p. 479 n. 7 QuarEd accurately indicate that the Vulgate reads *responderunt ei* ("They answered him").

therefore could have hidden himself."[17] *Jesus said to them: I am.* Here it is noted that he was voluntarily arrested, since by offering himself he caused them to fall prostrate. For the text continues: *Now Judas, who betrayed him, was also standing with them*, namely, with the others who were standing. But having heard his word, they did not remain standing, but fell down. For this reason the text states:

13. (Verse 6). *So when he said to them: I am, they drew back*, turning their face from him according to Psalm 34:4: "Let those who devise evil against me be turned back and confounded." *And fell to the ground.* Augustine notes: "With one word and without any weapon he smote, repulsed, struck down so great a crowd, fierce in its hatreds and frightful in its weapons by the power of his hidden Divinity.... What will he do when he comes to judge, when he has done this when he was about to be judged? What will he be able to do when he comes to reign, who was able to do this when he was about to die?"[18] Job 26:14 says: "And since we have heard scarcely a ... moment of his word, who will be able to behold the thunder of his greatness?"

14. (Verse 7). *So he asked them again.* This verse indicates the third reason why he was freely arrested, namely, by showing himself to them he freed his disciples. So he showed himself to them when he asked them again:

---

[17] See Homily 83 n. 1 in PG 59:448 and FC 41, p. 401: "Do you perceive His insuperable power and how he stood in their midst and blinded them? For the Evangelist has made it clear that darkness was not responsible for the question, since he mentioned that they also had lanterns." Hugh of St. Cher, p. 389r also cites this passage from Chrysostom. Neither in Chrysostom nor in Hugh of St. Cher is there a parallel to Bonaventure's "and therefore could have hidden himself."

[18] Bonaventure has modified Tractate 112 n. 3. See CCSL xxxvi, p. 634 and FC 92, pp. 5-6.

Whom are you seeking? And they said, as before, *Jesus of Nazareth*. And just as he asked them again, so too does he offer and reveal himself to them for the second time.

15. (Verse 8). *Jesus answered them:*[19] *I have told you that I am*. And since you did not know me then, I repeat myself, so that you may know. They had been blinded, lest they recognize him, as Luke 24:16 says: "Their eyes were held that they should not recognize him." After he had handed himself over, he freed his disciples solely by his word. For the text adds: *If*[20] *you seek me, let these go their way*. Augustine observes: "He commands his enemies to do what he commands. They let those go whom he does not want to lose."[21] And the Evangelist shows that he did this through his own power, for he says:

16. (Verse 9). *That the word that he said might be fulfilled*, in John 17:12 above, *Of those whom you have given me, O Father, I have not lost one*,[22] because he wanted to suffer alone. Isaiah 63:3 reads: "I have trodden the winepress alone, and there is not a man from the Gentiles with me."

17. But why is he saying this: "I have not lost one of them"? Is it not said in Matthew 16:25: "The person who loses his life for my sake will find it"? Therefore, Augustine explains eternal perdition: "Because they were not yet believing in him, as all those who do not perish be-

---

[19] On p. 479 n. 10 QuarEd correctly mention that the Vulgate does not read *eis* ("them").

[20] On p. 479 n. 11 QuarEd rightly notice that the Vulgate reads *Si ergo* ("Therefore, if").

[21] See Tractate 112 n. 4 in CCSL xxxvi, p. 635. Bonaventure has *Inimicis iubet* ("He commands his enemies") while the critical text reads *Inimicos videt* ("He sees his enemies").

[22] John 17:12 has: "Those whom you have given me I have guarded, and not one of them perished...."

lieve."[23] Now this was said to those who were believing in a perfect manner.

18. (Verse 10). *But*[24] *Simon Peter*. The fourth sign that Christ was freely arrested is now found: he restrains Peter who resists. So Peter's fervor to protect the Lord is suggested by this that *having a sword, he drew it*, as if he is unable to contain himself, *and struck the servant of the high priest*, as if he were not distinguishing who was who, *and amputated*[25] *his right ear*. Chrysostom comments: "He hints at Peter's fury, for he attacked the head itself."[26] *Now the servant's name was Malchus*. The Evangelist said this, as Chrysostom maintains, to have the greatest certitude.[27] Peter, burning with zeal for the Lord, struck those malefactors. 1 Maccabees 2:24 states: "Mathathias saw and was grieved ... and his zeal was kindled according to judgment of the Law, and he ran upon him and slew him."[28] – According to the spiritual sense: Peter, the understanding one, amputated the right ear, that is, obe-

---

[23] See Tractate 112 n. 4 in CCSL xxxvi, p. 635 and FC 92, p. 6. Bonaventure's citation is virtually verbatim.

[24] On p. 480 n. 4 QuarEd correctly mention that the Vulgate reads *ergo* ("therefore") whilst Bonaventrue has *autem* ("but").

[25] On p. 480 n. 5 QuarEd accurately indicate that the Vulgate reads *abscidit* ("cut off") while Bonaventure has *amputavit* ("amputated").

[26] Bonaventure summarizes Homily 83 n. 2. See PG 59:449 and FC 41, pp. 403-404: "Moreover, it was not undesignedly that he mentioned the right ear, but it seems to me that he wished to say that the Apostle just missed beheading the man when he attacked him." See Hugh of St. Cher, 389v,m who cites Chrysostom in full.

[27] See Homily 83 n. 2 in PG 59:449 and FC 41, p. 403: "And it was also for the following reason that the Evangelist gave the name: that it might be possible for those who read it at that time to make inquiry and ascertain whether the miracle actually had taken place."

[28] 1 Macc 2:24 reads: "And Mathathias saw and was grieved, and his reins trembled, and his zeal was kindled according to the judgment of the Law, and running upon him, he slew him before the altar."

dience.[29] – So in this manner he restrained Peter who was resisting, for the text continues:

19. (Verse 11). *So Jesus said to Peter: Put your sword back into its scabbard.* Victor comments: "Let revenge cease, and let patience reign,"[30] according to what Matthew 5:39 states: "I say to you: Do not resist the evildoer. On the contrary, if someone strikes you on the right check, turn to him ... the other." And he gives the reason: *Do you not want[31] me to drink the cup that the Father has given me?* As if he were saying: If you rightly understood, you would need to will what the Father wills. About this cup Matthew 26:39 says: "Father, if it is possible, let this cup pass away from me." The Son drank from this cup, for Matthew 20:22 states: "Can you drink of the cup from which I am going to drink?" And about the will of the Father Romans 8:32 reads: "He did not spare his own Son, but handed him over for us all."[32]

20. (Verse 12). *So the cohort and the tribune,* etc. Here in a third point it is shown that the arrest of Christ was ignominious since a cohort arrested him and bound him as a robber. So the text states: *So the cohort,* that is, a multitude of soldiers gathered together into one company, *and*

---

[29] See Bonaventure's commentary on Luke 6:14 n. 36 in *Bonaventure on Luke, Chapters 1-8,* p. 486: "*Simon,* to whom he gave an additional name, means *one who submits. Whom he named Peter,* which means *understanding.* By this is designated the virtue of *prudence,* from the combination of Peter as *understanding* and Simon as *one who submits.*" Hugh of St. Cher, p. 389v,k: "... zealous prelates ... using the sword of excommunication ... amputate the right ear of their subjects, that is, the slight obedience which they had previously displayed."

[30] This citation is from Bishop Victor of Capua. See n. 2 above. See the Glossa Interlinearis on Matt 26:52: "Let revenge cease, let patience reign, so that we might learn patience, not revenge."

[31] Bonaventure reads *vis* ("you want") which the Vulgate does not.

[32] Hugh of St. Cher, p. 389v,q also cites Rom 8:32.

the tribune, who was over them, *and the attendants of the Jews arrested Jesus and bound him*. Victor says: "It was customary for the Jews that they would hand over to the ruler, in bonds, the person whom they judged worthy of death,"[33] and as a malefactor. So in Matthew 26:55 the Lord said to them: "As against a robber you have come out, with swords and clubs, to seize me." And they bound him, lest he flee, since Judas had said in Mark 14:44: "Whomever I kiss that is he. Lay hold of him and lead him safely away."

QUESTIONS

21. Question 1 asks first of all why the Lord handed himself over to the Jews. – It seems that he presented them with the occasion of doing evil. – Chrysostom answers: "The Lord offered them every opportunity to change their minds," namely, by blocking their vision lest they recognize him and by casting them to the ground solely by his word. "But since they were persisting in their malice and had no justification for their action, then he handed himself into their hands."[34]

22. Question 2 queries: Since Peter alone was the one who provoked them to anger, why didn't they arrest him? Chryrostom responds: "No one else prevented them, but

---

[33] This citation is from Bishop Victor of Capua. See also the Glossa Ordinaria in PL 114:418C: "It was customary for the Jews that they would hand over to the ruler, in bonds, the person whom they judged worthy of death." Hugh of St. Cher, p. 389v,r attributes to the Glossa the citation that Bonaventure attributes to Victor.

[34] See Homily 83 n. 1 in PG 59:448. Bonaventure's quotation is a paraphrase.

it was through that power by which he had previously cast them to the ground."[35]

23. Question 3 asks: Since Peter had been prohibited from possessing a bag, how is it that he now possessed a sword? – Victor responds to this question. The Lord gave that commandment to them when he sent them to preach, but during the time of persecution, he enjoined that they carry along the necessary food and that they buy swords. And he took this from Luke 22:36: "Let the person who has a purse take it and a bag, and let him who has no sword, sell his tunic and buy a sword."[36] – Another possible answer is that the Lord did not command this, because he wanted them to defend themselves, but to show those arresting him his patience, since, although he had arms, he didn't want to use them.[37]

24. Question 4 raises this issue: Since it was said to the Apostles in Matthew 5:39, "If someone strike you on the right cheek, turn to him the other also," it seems that Peter did an evil deed because he struck. – Chrysostom answers: "He was not avenging himself, but his Master. For they were not in any way perfect or without defect,"[38] as they were afterwards when the Holy Spirit came. And then they experienced the perfection enjoined on them earlier.

---

[35] See Homily 83 n. 1 in PG 59:448. Bonaventure's citation is not verbatim.

[36] Luke 22:36 says: "Let the person who has a purse take it, and likewise a bag. And let the person who has no sword sell his tunic and buy one."

[37] See the Glossa Ordinaria on Luke 22:36 in PL 114:340A: "... that the readers might know that the disciples did not lack the power to resist...."

[38] See Homily 83 n. 2 in PG 59:449. Bonaventure's quotation is paraphrastic. Hugh of St. Cher, p. 389v,l has wording similar to that of Bonaventure, but does not say it stems from Chrysostom.

25. Question 5 queries whether Peter's successor can bear a material sword and strike with it. – And it seems that the answer is yes because of Peter's example. – Bernard's "To Eugene" speaks of the material sword in these words: "Your sword, perhaps with your approval, even though not with your hand, is to be taken from its scabbard. Otherwise, if it in no way pertained to you, when the Apostles said, 'Behold, there are two swords here,' the Lord would not have responded, 'It's enough,' but rather 'It's too much.' So both swords pertain to the Church, but the material sword is to exerted on behalf of the Church while the spiritual sword is to be exerted by the Church."[39]

JOHN 18:13-19:15
CHRIST'S CONDEMNATION

26. *And they brought him first to Annas.* With this verse the second principal section of this part commences. It deals with *Christ's condemnation.* And since many interrogations preceded his condemnation, this section is divided into three. The first one deals with *the interrogation conducted by Annas.* The second with *that of Caiaphas* where verse 24 reads: "And Annas sent him bound to Caiaphas." The third with *that of Pilate* where verse 28 states: "So they led Jesus to Caiaphas."[40]

---

[39] See Book IV, c. 3 n. 7 of *Tractatus de Consideratione ad Eugenium Papam* in SBOp 3.454. Bonaventure's quotation is almost verbatim.

[40] The Vulgate reads *a Caiapha* ("from Caiaphas") while Bonaventure has *ad Caipham* ("to Caiaphas").

John 18:13-23
Interrogation by Annas

In the first section three matters are noted: *a defect in judgment, a defect in testimony, the oblation of the one reviled*. They are noted in this order. First *Christ is presented to an evil judge*. Second *he is denied by Peter* where verse 15 says: "Now Simon Peter was following Jesus." Third *he is examined* where verse 19 reads: "So the high priest questioned Jesus."

27. (Verse 13). So relative to Christ's presentation, it is said: *And they brought him*, namely, Jesus, *first to Annas*, since he was the senior and the elder and more seasoned in malice. Daniel 13:5 states: "Iniquity came out ... from the old judges who seemed to govern the people."[41] And he gives the reason, when he says: *Now he was the father-in-law of Caiaphas, who was the high priest that year*. So it seemed, in a certain way, that judgment pertained to him. Christ suffered under these high priests. Under them John had preached. Luke 3:2 states: "Under the high priests, Annas and Caiaphas, the word of the Lord came to John, son of Zechariah, in the desert." And the text points him out with the suspicion that he would not judge justly, since he was the father-in-law of the one who had conspired in the death of Christ. For the text continues:

28. (Verse 14). *Now it was Caiaphas who had given the counsel to the Jews* in John 11:49-50 above that it was expedient that one person die for the sake of the people. Chrysostom observes: "So the evangelist recalls that

---

[41] Dan 13:5 says: "And there were two of the elders of the people appointed judges that year, of whom the Lord said: Iniquity came forth from Babylon from the old judges who seemed to govern the people."

prophecy, because his death was the salvation of the world, and therefore, the person who heard about Christ's chains should not be disturbed."[42]

29. (Verse 15). *Now he was following Jesus.* This verse begins the treatment of Peter's denial, which is depicted in this order. First is the occasion for the denial. Second is the denial itself. Third is love's growing cold because of the denial. – The occasion for the denial was set up when, although he was weak, Peter wanted to follow the Lord. So the text states: *Now Simon Peter was following Jesus,* but not perfectly. For Matthew 26:58 says: "Now Peter was following from afar," with another leading the way. For he was not alone, but *there was another disciple,* and this one was the leader. Thus: *Now that disciple was known to the high priest.* And so he moved with confidence, for the text adds: *And he entered with Jesus into the courtyard of the high priest.* Who he was, the Glossa gave no definite answer.[43] But it seems that he was John, as Victor says, who spoke about himself as the other disciple, and was not afraid to do so.[44]

30. (Verse 16). *Now Peter was standing outside the gate,* either because he didn't dare enter or because he was not allowed. Therefore, what had been spoken to him in John 13:36 was true: "Where I am going, you cannot follow me

---

[42] Bonaventure paraphrases Homily 83 n. 2. See PG 59:449. Hugh of St. Cher, p, 390c also cites Chrysostom in a paraphrase different from that of Bonaventure.

[43] See the Glossa Ordinaria in PL 114:418D: "Let one not rashly specify who this disciple was, since the text is silent on the matter. But John was accustomed to signify himself in this way."

[44] This is the opinion of Bishop Victor of Capua. On p. 482 n. 4 QuarEd provide additional interpretations of who "the other disciple" was.

now." *So that*[45] *other disciple, who was known to the high priest, went out,* and by reason of familiarity *spoke to the portress and brought Peter in.* And so it is manifested that the person whose love is tenuous was brought in by another. In this action it is signified that disciples must help one another. For Galatians 6:2 reads: "Bear one another's burdens, and so you will fulfill the law of Christ."

31. (Verse 17). *The portress said to Peter.*[46] The second point surfaces here, namely, a denial that proceeded from weakness. And this is clear from the fact that Peter denied the Lord because of a maid's voice. So the question of the maid is introduced: *Are you also one of this man's disciples?* She did not say "of this deceiver," but "of this man," as if speaking with compassion. But Peter, overcome with timidity, denied it. For the text continues: "He said: I am not." Chrysostom comments: "What is this, Peter, did you say: I will lay down my life for you? – See John 13:37 above. – So why did it happen that you did not bear up under the questioning of a maid?"[47]

32. (Verse 18) *Now the servants were standing.* The third point occurs here, namely, from denial love turns cold.

---

[45] On p. 482 n. 5 QuarEd rightly note that the Vulgate does not read *ille* ("that").

[46] On p. 482 n. 7 QuarEd correctly indicate that the Vulgate reads *ancilla ostiaria* "(the maid, who was portress")."

[47] See Homily 83 n. 2 in PG 59:450. Bonaventure's citation is a paraphrase. See Hugh of St. Cher, p. 390n; his quotation is similar to that of Bonaventure's. See FC 41, pp. 405-406: "What are you saying, Peter? Did you not declare, just a little while ago, 'Should it be necessary even to lay down my life for You, I will do so'? Well, then, why does it happen that you cannot even bear up under questioning of the portress? It is not a soldier who is asking the question, is it? ... It is merely a portress asking a casual question, and her manner of asking is not even impertinent. For she did not say: 'Are you a disciple of that deceiver and scoundrel? but "of this man"' and this was the question of a sympathizer, rather than of a fault-finder."

This is suggested by Peter, already having forgotten the Lord, standing at a coal fire with the servants, and again, his interior warmth having become tepid, he was seeking refuge in exterior warmth. Therefore, the text says: *Now the servants and attendants*, namely, those who had taken the Lord, *were standing at a coal fire and warming themselves, for it was cold.* Augustine notes: "It was not winter, and nonetheless, it was cold, as is apt to happen sometimes at the vernal equinox."[48] *Now Peter was also with them, standing and warming himself,* for he had lost that light, about which Luke 12:49 says: "I have come to cast fire on the earth," because he had become lukewarm. Bede comments: "The prince of the Apostles grew so cold with the frost of infidelity that he trembled to confess Christ at the voice of one maid."[49]

33. (Verse 19). *Now*[50] *the high priest.* Etc. Having presented Peter's denial, the evangelist adds the examination of Christ here. In this examination four points are made, namely, the questioning of the high priest, Christ's response, afflicting of injury, the support of patience. – So the questioning of the high priest occurs when the text states: *Now the high priest,* namely, Annas, *was question-*

[48] See Tractate 113 n. 3 in CCSL xxxvi, p. 637 and FC 92, p. 11. Bonaventure's quotation is virtually verbatim. Hugh of St. Cher, p. 390o cites Augustine verbatim.

[49] See Book IV, commentary on Mark 14:54 in CCSL cxx, p. 621: "Numb from the cold at that time, the Apostle Peter wished to warm himself at the coal fire of the attendants of Caiaphas because he was seeking the refuge of temporal comfort in the company of those treacherous people." The citation carries the gist.

[50] On p. 483 n. 2 QuarEd correctly mention that the Vulgate reads *ergo* ("Therefore") while Bonaventure has *autem* ("Now").

ing[51] *Jesus about his disciples and his teaching,*[52] so that, since he could not accuse him of a crime, he at least might catch him in his speech. He did this, not to learn from him, but to trap him, as Matthew 22 says.[53]

34. (Verse 20). *Jesus answered him.* This is the second point, namely, Christ's answer, in which the Lord confounds the intention of the high priest. For he considered Christ's teaching to be suspect, and so wanted to examine him about it. Therefore, the Lord shows that his teaching is not suspect, because it was not hidden, but public. So he says: *I have spoken openly to the world.* And he proves this: *I have always taught in the synagogue and in the temple, where all the Jews gather.* And since the high priest could say: In public you taught what is true, but in secret you taught what is false, he says the following for greater certitude: *And in hiding*[54] *I have said nothing.* Isaiah 45:18-19 states: "I am the Lord, and there is no other. I have not spoken in hiding, in a dark place of the earth."[55] In this way he removed suspicion of his teaching by reason of its hiddenness. Then he removes suspicion by reason of its falsity. Thus he sends him to others, not wishing to respond himself. So the text continues:

35. (Verse 21). *Why do you question me,* since you do not believe me and can learn from others? *Question those who*

---

[51] On p. 483 n. 3 QuarEd rightly note that the Vulgate reads *interrogavit* ("questioned") whilst Bonaventure has *interrogabat* ("was questioning").

[52] On p. 483 n. 3 QuarEd accurately indicate that the Vulgate reads *de doctrina eius* ("about his teaching").

[53] See Matt 22:15: "Then the Pharisees went and took counsel how they might trap him in his speech."

[54] On p. 483 n. 4 QuarEd correctly mention that the Vulgate reads *occulto* ("secret") while Bonaventure has *abscondito* ("hiding").

[55] Hugh of St. Cher, p. 390v,c cites Isa 45:19.

have heard what I spoke to them,[56] so that you may believe them. For *behold, these know what I have said.* Chrysostom remarks: "These are not the words of a defiant individual, but of one who has confidence in the truth of what he had spoken."[57] Proverbs 8:8 reads: "All my words are just. There is nothing wicked nor perverse in them."

36. (Verse 22). *When*[58] *he had said these things.* This is the third point, namely, the affliction of injury both in deed and in word. With regard to the deed: *One of the attendants who was standing by struck Jesus a blow.* Lamentations 3:30 states: "He will give his cheek to the person who strikes him." And Micah 5:1 says: "They will strike the cheek of the judge of Israel."[59] He was injured by word: *Saying: Is that the way you answer the high priest?* As if he were saying: Your answers are stupid, because the high priest should be answered in a humble way. Thus they said to Paul in Acts 23:4: "Are you insulting the high priest of God?"

37. (Verse 23). *Jesus answered him.* Here is the fourth point, namely, the support of patience, which is suggested in the Lord's answer, because he endured the wicked servant. For the text adds: *If I have spoken evilly, bear witness to the evil,* as if to say: I am ready to endure the pun-

---

[56] On p. 483 n. 5 QuarEd correctly mention that the Vulgate reads *ipsis* ("to them") while Bonaventure has *eis* ("to them").

[57] See Homily 83 n. 3 in PG 59:450: "These are not the words of an arrogant person, but of one confident in the truth of what had been said." Hugh of St. Cher, p. 390vi also cites Chrysostom: "These words are not those of a presumptuous person, but of one confident in the truth of the things that were spoken."

[58] On p. 483 n. 6 QuarEd correctly mention that the Vulgate reads *autem* ("Now").

[59] Hugh of St. Cher, p. 390v,k also cites Lam 3:30 and Micah 5:1.

ishment. And he teaches, for he says: *But if well, why*[60] *are you striking me?* As if he were saying: You will realize that you have acted wrongly. In this the wondrous benignity of Christ is noticed, for he not only sustained an injury, but he also taught by its means, according to what Leviticus 19:17 has: "You shall not hate your brother ... but reprove him openly, lest you incur sin through him."

Questions

38. Question 1 points to what is said in Matthew 26:57: "Those who had taken Jesus led him away to Caiaphas the high priest" and asks: Why does John 18:13 say that they led him to Annas? – 2. Furthermore, since Annas was not the high priest, why was he led to him? – Augustine answers that he was led to both. Matthew, wishing to give an abbreviated account, says that he was led to Caiaphas, since he was examined more extensively in his house.[61] – 2. There are four reasons why he was led to Annas. By reason of dignity, since, as Victor says, he was the priest the previous year, for at that time he bought the high priesthood.[62] – The second reason is one of blood relationship, because he had attained the high priesthood as father-in-law. – The third reason is that of convenience, for his house was on the way.[63] – The fourth rea-

---

[60] On p. 483 n. 8 QuarEd rightly notice that the Vulgate reads *cur* ("why") while Bonaventure has *quid* ("why").

[61] See Tractate 113 n. 1 in FC 92, p. 9: "And Matthew, since he wanted to relate it more briefly, properly recounts that he was led to Caiaphas; for he was also taken first to Annas precisely because he was his father-in-law, and here one must understand that Caiaphas himself wanted this to be done."

[62] This opinion stems from Bishop Victor of Capua.

[63] See Augustine, Tractate 113 n. 5 in FC 92, pp. 14-15: "Therefore, according to Matthew, when he was arrested, he was led to him; but according to John they first came with him to Annas, not because he

son stems from maliciousness, as Victor states: "so that Caiaphas would seem to have the lesser sin, if Christ was condemned by the sentence of the other priest."[64]

39. Question 2 asks with Chrysostom: Who was that other disciple, about whom it is said in John 18:15 that he was following Jesus? – And he answers that it was John, who did not mention his name out of humility.[65]

40. Question 3 continues this line of questioning: Why then didn't he eliminate mention of himself entirely? – The response is that he mentioned himself to bolster our faith, but didn't mention his name to teach us how to avoid pride.[66]

41. Question 4 raises these issues. 1. With regard to John 18:20 where the Lord says, "I have said nothing in secret," it is remarked that the Lord himself had spoken many things to his disciples in secret.[67] – 2. Moreover, there is a question about John 18:20, "I have always taught in

---

was his colleague but because he was his father-in-law. And one must believe that this was done in accordance with the will of Caiaphas, or even that their houses had been so situated that Annas ought not to have been passed up by those passing by."

[64] This quotation stems from Bishop Victor of Capua. The Glossa Interlinearis on John 18:13 reads: "He wanted him to be led to him first, so that he might have the lesser sin...."

[65] See Homily 83 n. 2 in FC 41, pp. 404-405: "Who was the other disciple? The author of this Gospel himself.... Yet, notice how he deprecated what redounded to his praise."

[66] See Chrysostom, Homily 83 n. 2 in FC 41, pp. 404-405: "... but he was forced to mention himself, as well as Peter, that you might learn that he was giving a more accurate account than the others did, of the events in the courtyard, since he was actually inside. Yet, notice how he deprecated what redounded to his praise."

[67] See, e.g., Matt 17:18: "Then his disciples came to him privately and said: Why could we not cast it out?" and Mark 7:17: "And when he had entered the house away from the crowd, his disciples began to ask him about the parable."

the synagogue and in the temple," since it is said in Matthew 5:1 that he was teaching on a mountain. Likewise, it is said in Luke 6:17 that he was teaching on the plain. – 3. Finally, John 18:20 reads, "I have spoken openly to the world." But the Lord would speak in parables and in obscure sentences, as it is said in Matthew 13:3.[68] – With respect to the first issue Augustine answers: "Since, even if he said some things only to his disciples, he was not speaking in secret, ... for he wanted these things to become known to many through them. For Matthew 10:27 states:[69] 'What I tell you in darkness, speak it in the light, and what you hear whispered, preach it from the housetops.'"[70] – Chrysostom responds: "I have spoken nothing in secret," since "he was not speaking out of fear or deceit, as these were thinking. He was teaching his disciples by themselves, but concerning those things that others could not grasp."[71] – 2. With regard to the second issue it has to be said that "always" is to be taken to apply to the three solemnities: Passover, Pentecost, Tabernacles when the people generally came together.[72] – 3. Relative to the third issue it has to be maintained that "he spoke openly," not that he was clearly understood, but that many heard what he was saying. Augustine comments: "In a certain way he spoke 'openly,' since many heard him. In a certain

---

[68] Matt 13:3 says: "And he spoke to them many things in parables...."

[69] Hugh of St. Cher, p. 390v,g also cites Matt 10:27.

[70] Bonaventure abbreviates Tractate 113 n. 3. See CCSL xxxvi, p. 638.

[71] See Homily 83 n. 3 in PG 59:450: "But not, as those were thinking, because he was afraid and moved by thoughts of sedition. Rather since he was speaking about those things that were beyond the grasp of the multitude."

[72] See Deut 16:16: "Three times a year shall all your men appear before the Lord your God in the place which he shall choose: in the feast of unleavened bread, in the feast of weeks, and in the feast of tabernacles."

way he did not speak 'openly,' because they did not understand."[73]

42. Question 5 asks: Since the Lord says in Matthew 5:39, "If someone strikes you on the right cheek, also turn to him the other," why didn't the Lord do this, but rebuked those persecuting him? – Augustine responds: "He answered truthfully, gently, and justly.[74] He not only prepared his other cheek for the person who would strike it again, but also his entire body to be fixed on the cross. And from this he shows that the commandments of patience are not to be fulfilled by an ostentatious bodily show, but by preparation of the heart."[75]

JOHN 18:24-27
INTERROGATION BY CAIAPHAS

43. (Verse 24). *And Annas sent him*, etc. This section deals with the examination made under Caiaphas and has two components. The first is *the leading of Christ to the judge*. The second is *his denial by a disciple* where verse 25 states: "Now Simon Peter was," etc. – With regard to the first the Evangelist is brief and says that Christ was sent to Caiaphas, saying nothing about the examination conducted by Annas, since the other Evangelists had spoken about this sufficiently. So he says: *And Annas sent him bound to Caiaphas the high priest*, by whom he was

---

[73] Bonaventure paraphrases Tractate 113 n. 3. See CCSL xxxvi, p. 638. See Hugh of St. Cher, p. 390v,g: "Augustine: ... For he was speaking openly in one way, but in another way he was not speaking openly. It was openly because many heard it, and again it was not openly, since they did not understand."

[74] Hugh of St. Cher, p. 390v,m quotes this first sentence from Augustine.

[75] Bonaventure adapts Tractate 113 n. 4. See CCSL xxxvi, p. 638.

dishonored and reviled in many ways, as it is said in Matthew 26:67: "They spat in his face and buffeted him, while others struck his face with their palms," etc.

44. (Verse 25). *But Simon Peter.* The denial of Peter is set here, and the occasion for his denial comes about because he was intermingled with the attendants. For the text states: *Now Simon Peter was standing and warming himself,* namely, with the attendants, as above.[76] And from the fact that he was among them, it happened that they were asking about him. *So they said to him: Are you also one of his disciples?* And this presented the occasion for the denial. So the repetition of his denial follows: *Now*[77] *he denied it and said: I am not.* Peter was afraid of the multitude standing about. Sirach 7:7 says: "Do not offend against the multitude of a city. Do not cast yourself in among the people."

45. (Verse 26). *One of the servants of the high priest said to him.* Here is the completion of his denial. First comes the question of the servant, then follows Peter's denial and its sign which is the cock's crowing. *One of the servants of the high priest, a relative of the person whose right ear he had cut off, said to him.* The reason why he was accusing him more vehemently was to avenge his relative: *Did I not see you in the garden with him?* as if he were saying: You cannot hide from me.

46. (Verse 27). *So Peter again denied it.* Now Peter's denial is complete, since it is threefold. And as a sign of its completeness the text adds: *And at that very moment a*

---

[76] See John 18:18 says: "... And Peter was with them, standing and warming himself."

[77] On p. 485 QuarEd correctly indicate that the Vulgate does not read *autem* ("now").

cock crowed. Augustine observes: "Look, the prediction of the Physician has been proven out; the presumption of the sick man has been proven wrong. For, what this fellow had said, 'I shall lay down my life for you,' did not happen; but what he [i.e., Christ] had predicted, 'you will deny me thrice,' did happen."[78]

QUESTIONS

47. Question 1 stems from Chrysostom who notes that the Evangelists' accounts of Peter's denial agree with one another when it seems that they should have covered up the sin of an associate. Why did they do this? – He answers that they did this "not to blame a disciple, but in an effort to teach us how wicked it is not to put everything in God's hands, but to trust in ourselves."[79]

48. Question 2 is a query about the manner of Peter's denial. – For the Lord had said to him beforehand in John 13:38: "You will deny me three times." But here Blessed John says that he denied one single time that he was his "disciple." – Augustine answers: "We should truly notice … in this denial of … Peter, not only that Christ is denied by the person who says that he is not the Christ, but also

---

[78] See CCSL xxxvi, p. 640 and FC 92, p. 15. Bonaventure's quotation is verbatim. Hugh of St. Cher, p. 391b quotes the first sentence of Augustine: "Augustine. Look, the prediction of Christ has proven out; the presumption of Peter is proven wrong."

[79] See Homily 83 n. 3 in PG 59:451: "Now why are the Evangelists in agreement in writing about this? Not so that they might blame a disciple, but to instruct us how wicked it is not to commit ourselves totally to God, but to trust in ourselves." Without attribution to Chrysostom, Hugh of St. Cher, p. 391b states: "But it is asked: Why did all the Evangelists write with such agreement about Peter's denial. We answer: Not to blame a disciple, but in a effort to teach us how wicked it is not to put all things in God's hands, but to trust in ourselves."

by the one who, although he is a Christian, denies that he is a Christian.... For Peter denied Christ, when he denied that he was Christ's disciple."[80]

49. Question 3 asks about the location of Peter's denial. – Some Evangelists seem to say that it took place in the house of Caiaphas, as it is said in Matthew 26.[81] John seems to say that it took place in the house of Annas. – I answer that there are contrary opinions among the expositors,[82] for Bede[83] and Jerome[84] say that the denial began in the house of Annas, but was completed in the house of Caiaphas. While the other Evangelists address the final denial, John is concerned about the beginning of Peter's denial. – But Augustine maintains that the denial was total and completed in the house of Annas, as the Evangelist seems to say. And when the others say that it took place in the house of Caiaphas, they are saying

---

[80] Bonaventure abbreviates Tractate 113 n. 2. See CCSL xxxvi, p. 637.

[81] See Matt 26:57-58, 74.

[82] It seems that Bonaventure's interpretation is dependent upon Cardinal Hugh. See Hugh of St. Cher, p. 391b: "It is customary to ask: In what location did Peter's denial take place? And to this it can be said that according to the order of this text it seems that Peter's threefold denial began in the courtyard of Annas and was completed in the courtyard of Caiaphas. According to other Evangelists, who do not mention Annas, it seems that everything took place in Caiaphas' courtyard. Augustine, in his book *De concordia evangelistarum* and even in what he says about this passage, maintains that everything took place in Annas's courtyard and that everything that was said there was recapitulated after Jesus had been sent to Caiaphas. Jerome *On Matthew* and Bede *On Luke* seem to be of the opinion that Peter's denial took place in the courtyard of Caiaphas."

[83] See Bede on Luke 22:54-62 in CCSL cxx, pp. 390-392. As far as I can ascertain, in his commentary on these verses Bede does not hold the opinion Bonaventure ascribes to him.

[84] See Jerome on Matt 26:75 in PL 26:211C. In his commentary on this verse Jerome does not hold the opinion ascribed to him by Bonaventure.

this since Caiaphas was the high priest and that what had happened at Annas's house also took place at Caiaphas's.[85]

50. Question 4 asks about the time of the denial. – For John says here that the cock crowed after the third denial, but in Mark 14:68 it is said that he crowed after the first denial. – I answer that things literally took place as Mark says they did. The cock crowed before the third denial and immediately after the third, but Peter did not pay attention to the first crowing of the cock. At the second he paid attention and returned to his heart.[86] And so the other Evangelists did not mention the first crowing, but all mention the final cockcrow.[87]

JOHN 18:28-19:15
INTERROGATION BY PILATE

51. *So they led Jesus*, etc. This section deals with Christ's third interrogation which is done under Pilate. And it shows the malice of the Jews first in that they persuaded a reluctant Pilate *to render judgment*. Second in that they persuaded him *to condemn* Christ whom he was willing

---

[85] See Book III, c. 6 n. 21-26 of *De consensu evangelistarum* in CSEL xliii, pp. 292-301. In these passages I have been unable to locate Bonaventure's summary of Augustine's viewpoint. See Augustine, Tractate 113 n. 6 in FC 92, p. 15: "But when the Evangelist had said that Annas sent him bound to Caiaphas, he returned to the place in the story where he had left Peter in order to give an account of what happened in the house of Annas in regard to his threefold denial. 'And Peter,' he said, 'was standing and warming himself.' With this he recapitulates what he has already said before...."

[86] See Isa 46:8: "Remember this, and be ashamed: return, you transgressors, to the heart."

[87] See Book III, c 3, n. 7 of Augustine, *Harmony of the Gospels* for a detailed resolution of this question.

to set free where verse 38 says: "And when he had said this, he went outside again," etc.

JOHN 18:28-37
JEWS PERSUADE PILATE TO RENDER JUDGMENT

The first section has two parts, for first comes *the offering of Christ*. Second is *the examination of what has been offered* where verse 33 reads: "So Pilate entered again,"

JOHN 18:28-32
CHRIST'S OFFERING

52. (Verse 28). In this offering first is noted *the perversity of the Jews*. Second, *their lies*. Third, *their unsound character*. Fourth, *how the divine will is fulfilled in this*. – Perversity, since on a festival day they are leading an innocent person to the place of condemnation. Thus the text says: *So they led Jesus*, namely, the attendants, *to*[88] *Caiaphas into the praetorium*, since they had come there to hand Christ over to Pilate. *Now it was early morning*. The time increased their malice, since it was morning. They were thirsting only for the death of Christ which they could not expect to be far away. It was also a festival time. So the text continues: *And they themselves did not enter the praetorium, lest they might be defiled, but might eat the Passover*, since they could not be defiled. Numbers 9:6 states: "Those who were unclean because of a person's death could not celebrate Passover." Augustine comments: "O impious blindness.... They feared

---

[88] On p. 486 n. 8 QuarEd correctly indicate that the Vulgate reads *a* ("from") while Bonaventure has *ad* ("to"). Augustine, Tractate 114 n. 1 tries to explain the meaning of the reading "to Caiaphas into the praetorium."

to be defiled at the praetorium of a foreign judge, and did not fear to be defiled by the blood of an innocent brother."[89]

53. (Verse 29). *So Pilate went outside to them and said.* The falsity of the Jews occurs here, since they are accusing Christ of a false crime and bringing him to be interrogated by Pilate. Thus the text says: *What accusation do you bring against this man?* As if he were saying: Without a cause I will not take his case. Acts 25:16 reads: "Romans are not accustomed to condemn[90] a person before the accused has met his accusers face to face and has been given a chance to defend himself against the charges." The Jews responded that the cause was evildoing. Thus the text adds:

54. (Verse 30). *They said to him in answer: If he were not a criminal, we would not have handed him over to you,* wishing to observe the law in Exodus 23:7: "You shall not kill the innocent and the righteous." As if they were saying: He is a malefactor. They do not prove their charge, but falsely impose it on him. Augustine notes: "Let those freed from unclean spirits, the sick who were healed … answer whether Jesus is an evildoer. But they were saying these things that had … been predicted by the prophet: They repaid me evil for good."[91] Job 36:17 reads: "Your cause has been judged as that of the wicked."

---

[89] See Tractate 114 n. 2 in CCSL xxxvi, p. 641.

[90] The Vulgate reads *donare* ("to give up") while Bonaventure has *condemnare* ("to condemn").

[91] Bonaventure abbreviates Tractate 114 n. 3. See CCSL xxxvi, p. 641. Augustine quotes Ps 34:12.

55. (Verse 31). *So Pilate said to them.* The third point surfaces here, namely, the deceit[92] of the Jews, since they wanted to pass the blame off to another, but Pilate refused to judge him, for he did not see that they had a fitting cause. Thus the text says: *So Pilate said to them: Take him yourselves and judge him according to your law,* which says in Exodus 22:18: "You shall not suffer evildoers to live." On the contrary, the Jews showed that it was necessary for him to judge, because the case involved the death penalty, and it was not lawful for them to put anyone to death. So the text continues: *So the Jews said to him: It is not lawful for us to put anyone to death.* But this pertains to you, and this one "is liable to death."[93] So it is necessary for you to look into this case. They want to put him to death deceitfully, through another person, and not be accused. So it is said to them in Acts 7:52: "Whose betrayers and murderers you have been."[94]

56. (Verse 32). *This was in fulfillment of what Jesus had said.* Here is the fourth point, namely, that the will of Christ is being fulfilled. For he wished to die through death on a cross which was the Gentile way of putting people to death. So the text says: *This was in fulfillment,* that is, it was done in this way to fulfill his word. *Of what he had said* in John 3:14 above: "Just as Moses lifted up the serpent in the desert, so too must the Son of Man be exalted." And John 12:33 above states: "signifying,

---

[92] In John 18 n. 51 above Bonaventure had *improbitas* ("unsound character") as the third point. Here the third point is *dolositas* ("deceit").

[93] See Matt 26:66.

[94] Acts 7:52 says: "Which of the prophets have not your fathers persecuted? And they killed those who foretold the coming of the Righteous One, of whom you have now been the betrayers and murderers."

by what death he was to die," on the cross.[95] Matthew
20:19 says: "He will be handed over to the Gentiles to be
mocked and scourged and crucified." And the Lord chose
this death as the most wretched.

QUESTIONS

57. Question 1 asks about the meaning of John 18:28,
"They led him to Caiaphas in the praetorium," since the
text immediately goes on to say: "They did not enter the
praetorium." – And Augustine answers that it is called the
praetorium, first of all, because it was the place "where
the praeses or governor lived."[96] Secondly it is said to be
the place where he renders judgment. If they entered into
this place, they would consider themselves defiled.

58. Question 2 inquires about John 18:28, "it was early
morning," since in John 18:24 it is said that before the
cockcrow "Annas sent him bound to Caiaphas." – I respond that Chrysostom and Augustine do not agree about
an answer to this question. For Augustine states that
they led him from Annas to Caiaphas into the praetorium
and says that this verse can be understood in two ways.
Pilate had his administration in the house of Caiaphas
or Caiaphas came to the house of Pilate.[97] Chrysostom,
however, states that they did not immediately lead him
from Annas, but at cockcrow they led him to the house
of Caiaphas, and afterwards, in the early morning, from

---

[95] John 12:32-33 reads: "And I, if I be lifted up from the earth, will
draw all things to myself. Now he said this signifying by what death
he was to die."

[96] See Tractate 114 n. 1 in CCSL xxxvi, p. 640.

[97] See Tractate 114 n. 1 in FC 92, p. 16: "… Caiaphas had proceeded
from the house of Annas … to the governor's praetorium … or Pilate
had had his praetorium given to him in the house of Caiaphas…."

his place to him who had come to the place of the praetorium.[98]

59. Question 3 focuses on John 18:28: "That they might not be defiled, but might eat the Passover." – Therefore, they had not yet eaten the Passover. Therefore, since Christ had eaten it on the preceding day, he had not eaten it at the proper time. – To these matters the Greeks answer that it is true that Christ anticipated the Passover because of his death. Thus they say that he ate leavened bread and that he confected the Eucharist with this bread and they do likewise. But their interpretation of this verse is the reason for their error. – But we interpret that the Passover was the same, that the food was that of a Passover meal. Among these foods was unleavened bread, which they ate for seven days.

60. Question 4 deals with John 18:31: "It is not lawful for us to put anyone to death." – But it is said in Exodus 22:18: "You shall not suffer an evildoer to live." And the Law states the same on several occasions.[99] – Augustine answers: "It should be understood that they said ... this on account of the holiness of the festival day that they had just begun to celebrate."[100] – Another interpretation is that they were saying this because of the imperial rule of the Romans who took away from them the power to put

---

[98] See Homily 83 n. 2 in FC 41, p. 409: "Before cockcrow He was led to Caiphas, and in the early morning to Pilate."

[99] See, e.g., Deut 18:20: "But the prophet, who being corrupted with pride, shall speak in my name things that I did not command him to say, or in the name of strange gods, shall be put to death."

[100] Bonaventure abbreviates Tractate 114 n. 4. See CCSL xxxvi, p. 641. Hugh of St. Cher, p. 391o also cites Ex 22:18 and Augustine, Tractate 114 n. 4 in his own abbreviation.

a person to death.[101] They also had to purchase the high priesthood from them.

JOHN 18:33-38A
EXAMINATION BY PILATE OF WHAT HAD BEEN OFFERED

61. *So Pilate again entered*, etc. Having described how Christ was handed over, that is, how the Jews handed him over to Pilate, here he sets forth Pilate's examination. Four things are suggested. First is *the interrogation*. Second is *the origin of the interrogation*. Third is *the answer to the interrogation*. Fourth is *the discussion of the answer*.

Verse 33. So first is the interrogation itself. So the text states: *So Pilate again entered the praetorium*, for he had gone outside to ask the Jews about their case against Jesus and had found none. So he went inside to ask the accused about the case against him: *And he summoned Jesus and said to him: Are you the king of the Jews?* Surely he was a king, since it was about him that Jeremiah 23:5 speaks: "I will raise up to David a just branch, and a king will reign." So he was especially interested in this, since by saying yes, he would seem to be against Caesar, who ruled over the Jews at that time.

62. (Verse 34). *Jesus answered*, etc. The second point surfaces here, namely, the source of Pilate's question. And so that he might learn its source, the Lord asks Pilate: *Do you say this of yourself or have others told you about*

---

[101] See the commentary on John 18:31 by Rupert of Deutz in CCCM ix, p. 727: "However, it was not lawful for them to put to death anyone that they had judged worthy of death, unless the Roman governor confirmed their judgment."

me? He did not ask because he had a doubt, but so that through his answer he might uncover the malice of the Jews. And this indeed occurred in Pilate's answer. Thus:

63. (Verse 35). *Pilate answered: Am I a Jew?* As if he were saying: I am not laying this upon you. *Your own people and your*[102] *chief priests have delivered you to me.* As if he were saying: I have accepted your case from them. *So what have you done?*[103] Why are they accusing you in this manner?

64. (Verse 36). *Jesus answered.* This is the third point, namely, the Lord's answer in which the Lord himself confounds the evil intention of the Jews, for the Jews intended to persuade Pilate and Caesar to act against him, because they won't want to share their rule with him. Thus the Lord excludes this possibility by saying: *My kingdom is not of this world.* Augustine observes: "Listen to this, Jews and Gentiles.... 'My kingdom is not of this world.' I will not impede your rule in this world.... What more do you want?"[104] – He gives the reason why his kingdom is not of this world, and his reason is this: For an earthly king attendants fight lest he be handed over to death. But for me my attendants do not fight. Therefore, I am not an earthly king. And he sets forth the major premise of this reasoning: *If my kingdom were of this world, my attendants would have fought that I might not be delivered to the Jews, but now.* Supply: But now it appears. This is the conclusion. *My kingdom is not from here,* since no one is defending me. And wherefore, his kingdom is not of this world, because as is said in 1 John 5:19: "The entire world

---

[102] On p. 488 n. 7 QuarEd rightly notice that the Vulgate does not read *tui* ("your").

[103] The Vulgate does not read *ergo* ("So").

[104] Bonaventure has abbreviated and adapted Tractate 115 n. 2. See CCSL xxxvi, p. 644.

is in hands of the evil one." And so we pray: "Your kingdom come."[105] Rather my kingdom is in the heavens, for Matthew 5:19 reads: "Whoever carries these commandments out and teaches them, will be called great in the kingdom of the heavens."

65. (Verse 37). *So Pilate said to him*. Here is the fourth point, namely, the discussion of Jesus' answer. And since the Lord had said that he has a kingdom, Pilate, almost in admiration, follows up on his answer: *So*, he says, *Are you a king?* As if he were saying: From your admission that you are a king, it seems from your words that you want to rule. And the Lord answers, conceding Pilate's conclusion and giving a satisfactory answer to what he intends. He concedes Pilate's conclusion when he says: *You say that I am a king.* As if he were saying: I am not denying what you are saying, but nonetheless I have not come as a temporal ruler as you think. Thus he adds: *This is why I was born and why I have come into the world, to bear witness to the truth. Have been born*, namely, through a temporal birth, not to rule, but to teach the truth. Isaiah 55:4 reads: "Behold, I have given him as a witness to the people, for a leader and a teacher for the Gentiles." And he adds a sign of this: *Everyone who is of the truth hears my voice.* John 8:47 states: "The person who is from God hears the words of God." And since Pilate still did not fully understand, he continues his questioning. So the text continues:

66. (Verse 38). *And Pilate said to him: What is truth?* He did not hear the answer to his question, since he did not wait for it. In John 14:6 above Jesus answered this question: "I am the way, the truth, and the life."[106]

---

[105] See Matt 6:10.
[106] Hugh of St. Cher, p. 391v,q also quotes John 14:6.

Questions

67. Question 1 focuses on John 18:36: "My kingdom is not of this world." – From this the heretics argue that this world does not pertain to the God of light, but to the god of darkness. – Contrary to John 18:36 is John 1:11: "He came to his own." Now if you say that the world is not to be equated with nature, but refers to human beings living in a worldly manner, contrary to this is what is said in Matthew 13:41: "The angels will gather out of his kingdom all scandals."[107] But it is obvious that scandals take place only in this world. – I answer. Chrysostom says briefly that it is the same as if he were saying: My kingdom is not earthly or corporal.[108] – Another interpretation is possible. The kingdom of Christ are those in whom he rules – and they obey him – not by power, but by obedience. Now such people are only the Saints, and these are not of the world. John 17:14 above says: "They are not of the world, even as I, too, am not of the world." But they are in the world, for John 17:15-16 states: "I do not pray that you take them out of the world, but that you guard them from evil."

68. Question 2 treats John 18:37: "Everyone who is of the truth hears my voice." Either he is saying this of truth as

---

[107] Matt 13:41 says: "The Son of Man will send forth his angels, and they will gather out of his kingdom all scandals and those who work iniquity."

[108] See Homily 83 n. 4 in FC 41, p. 413: "The heretics, basing their claims on this passage, allege that He is independent of the Creator. What, then, of the words, 'He came unto his own?' And what of the words, 'they are not of the world, even as I am not of this world?' Thus, He says that His kingdom is not from here, not to deprive the world of His providence and overlordship, but to show, as I have said, that His kingdom is not a human one, nor is it transient." Hugh of St, Cher, p. 391v,h quotes Chrysostom at length and says briefly: "my kingdom is not human, not corruptible."

a material cause, and then no one is of the truth. Or he is saying this of an efficient cause and then all are of the truth.[109] But not all hear the truth.

Augustine answers that in this verse: "He has commended the grace by which the Saints are predestined and called according to his purpose.... For if we think of the nature in which we were created, since Truth created all, who is not of the truth? But it is not granted to all by truth that they hear the truth. But those hear to whom it has been granted," as John 6:66 states.[110]

69. Question 3 asks why Pilate didn't wait for the Lord's answer to his question in John 18:38a. – Augustine observes: "The custom of the Jews suddenly came to mind, by which he was accustomed to release a person to them during the Passover."[111] So since he wanted to release him, he went out immediately. – Chrysostom gives another interpretation: "He knew that that question needed time, and he hastened to release Christ. Therefore, he went out immediately."[112] – This is another possible interpretation:

---

[109] See Book II d. 1 p. 1. a. 1. q. 1. ad 6 of Bonaventure's *Sentence Commentary* where he gives the example: iron is the material cause of a small knife, and the father is the efficient cause of the son.

[110] Bonaventure has abbreviated and adapted Tractate 115 n. 4, in which Rom 8:28, "according to his purpose," occurs. See CCSL xxxvi, pp. 645-646 and FC 92, p. 25.

[111] See Tractate 115 n. 5 in CCSL xxxvi, p. 646. Bonaventure's citation is virtually verbatim. See FC 92, pp. 25-26: "... there had immediately come into his mind the custom of the Jews whereby one man was usually released to them at the Pasch, and therefore he did not wait for Jesus to answer him as to what the truth is, so that there might not be a delay once he had recalled the practice by which he could be released to them by reason of the Pasch. And it is clear that he very much wanted this."

[112] Bonaventure adapts Homily 84 n. 1. See PG 59:455: "For he saw that such a question needed time, but he wanted to free him from the fury of the Jews."

Pilate began his judgment on the basis of the truth, but he did not remain in the truth. Therefore, he was worthy to begin his interrogation on the basis of the truth, but not worthy to hear the answer to his question.[113]

John 18:38b-19:16a
Pilate unwillingly condemns Christ

70. *And when he had said this*, etc. Earlier the malice of the Jews had been shown, because they compelled Pilate to interrogate Christ. In this section it is shown in that that they make him condemn a person he was willing to release. This section is divided into two. In the first the Jews *resist the judgment of truth*, lest he be released. In the second they plead for and *extort a false judgment* that he be condemned where John 19:13 states: "So Pilate, when he had heard these words."

John 18:38b-19:13
Pilate's attempts to release Christ

Now there is a threefold mode of judging: according to benignity, severity, and equity. Pilate strives to free Christ through this threefold manner of rendering judgment, and on their part the Jews resist such judgment. Wherefore, there are three components to this section. In the first *they resist the judgment of benignity*. In the second *they resist the judgment of severity* where John 19:1 reads: "Then Pilate took him." In the third *they resist the judgment of equity* where John 19:6 states: "Pilate said

---

[113] On p. 489 n. 10 QuarEd cite Alcuin's commentary on this passage: "He did not wait to hear Jesus' answer to his question, for perhaps he was not worthy to hear it."

to them," etc. – With regard to the first judgment three things are signaled: *the allegation of innocence in Christ, the remembrance of clemency on the part of the judge, obdurate iniquity on the part of the Jews.*

71. (Verse 38b). So the innocence of Christ is alleged, and so he should be released, for the Evangelist states: *And when he had said this*, namely, the aforesaid question, in an attempt to liberate Christ, *he went outside again to the Jews*, who were outside the praetorium, so that he might make a case for Christ's innocence. Thus *he said*[114] *to them: I find no case against him*, namely, worthy of death. And he spoke truly, for Psalm 58:5 states: "Neither is it my iniquity nor my sin, O Lord."

72. (Verse 39). And since it was not enough to make a case for his innocence, in a second point he recalls a custom of clemency: *But you have a custom that I should release someone to you at Passover*. Victor comments: "Since they were freed from slavery at Passover, this custom of releasing someone to them at Passover arose."[115] *Do you wish*[116] *that I release to you the king of the Jews*? Augustine observes: "It could not be wrested from his heart that Christ was the king of the Jews, as though Truth Itself, about which he had asked what it was, fixed this notion there, as on the title."[117]

---

[114] On p. 489 n. 14 QuarEd accurately indicate that the Vulgate reads *Et dicit* ("And he said") while Bonaventure has *Et dixit* ("And he said").

[115] This is Bishop Victor of Capua. See the Glossa Ordinaria on John 18:39 in PL 114:420B for virtually the same words.

[116] On p. 490 n. 2 QuarEd correctly mention that the Vulgate reads *Vultis ergo* ("So do you wish").

[117] See Tractate 115 n. 5 in CCSL xxxvi, p. 646 and FC 92, p. 26. Bonaventure's citation is virtually verbatim. Hugh of St. Cher, p. 391v,z quotes in adapted form this same passage from Augustine.

73. (Verse 40). Next is added the obdurate malice among the Jews who were not bent by Christ's innocence or by the clemency of the judge, but persisted in their point. So the text continues: *They cried out again and said:*[118] *Not this man, but Barabbas*, namely, not this innocent person, but the one that we know as an evildoer, for the Evangelist adds: *Now Barabbas was a robber*. In this action the astonishing malice of the Jews is expressed, for they preferred a robber and his release to Christ the Lord. Thus Chrysostom comments: "O you of a defiled decision. You seek the release of a criminal, and command that the innocent be crucified."[119] Acts 3:14-15 states: "You disowned the Righteous and Holy One[120] and asked that a murderer should be granted to you. But you killed the author of life."

---

[118] On p. 490 n. 3 QuarEd rightly notice that the Vulgate reads differently: "They all cried out again, saying."

[119] See Homily 84 n. 1 in PG 59:455 and FC 41, p. 418: "Oh what an accursed decision! They lay claim to those who are like themselves and they set free the guilty, while they decree punishment for the innocent One...."

[120] The Vulgate has the reverse order: "Holy and Righteous One."

CHAPTER NINETEEN

JOHN 18:38B-19:16A
PILATE'S ATTEMPTS TO RELEASE CHRIST (CONTINUED)

1. *Then*[1] *Pilate took him*, etc. Now Pilate intends to release him by means of the *judgment of severity* by which he scourges the innocent one to mitigate the anger of the Jews. There are three sections. In the first *the ignominious flagellation of C*hrist is described. In the second *the one flagellated is displayed* where verse 4 says: "So Pilate went outside again." In the third *the stubbornness of the Jews* is depicted where verse 6 reads: "So when the chief priests saw him."

Verse 1. The ignominious scourging of Christ is suggested first in the affliction itself and then in the derision. – The punishment is stated in the words: *Then Pilate took Jesus and had him scourged.* Chrysostom comments: "Pilate had him scourged, perhaps wishing to exhaust and mitigate Jewish anger."[2] Thus in Luke 23:16 Pilate said: "I will release the one who has been chastised," that is, the one afflicted through scourging for the sake of miti-

---

[1] On p. 490 n. 5 QuarEd accurately indicate that the Vulgate reads *Tunc ergo* ("So then").

[2] See Homily 84 n. 1 in PG 59:455: "*Pilate had him scourged*, perhaps, so that, having quieted the fury of the Jews, he might free him." See also FC 41, p. 418. Hugh of St. Cher, p. 392b quotes Chrysostom in the same words that Bonaventure has.

gating the anger of the Jews. – Derision is added to the affliction:

2. (Verse 2). *And the soldiers, plaiting*, etc. And since kings were customarily honored by a sign, clothing, and a word of salutation and a token of respect, he is derided in a fourfold manner. First in the sign of a crown, which was a kingly symbol. Thus the text says: *Plaiting*, that is, twisting together, *a crown of thorns*, that is, made of marine bulrushes that were sharply pointed like thorns.[3] *They put it upon his head*. About this crown The Song of Songs 3:11 says: "Go forth, you daughters of Zion, and see King Solomon with his diadem, with which his mother crowned him," that is, the synagogue.[4] – Then they mock him by means of clothing or a garment. Thus it is said: *And arrayed him in a purple cloak*, as if he were a king. Through this is signified that his flesh was made purple by his blood. That had been signified in Genesis 37:31: "They took Joseph's[5] coat and dipped it in the blood of a kid that they had killed." And Isaiah 63:2 has: "Why is your apparel red and your garments like those who tread in the winepress?" – What follows is derision by means of salutation. So the text continues:

3. (Verse 3). *And they kept coming to him and saying: Hail, King of the Jews*, and they did this to reproach him. Lamentations 3:30 reads: "He will be filled with re-

---

[3] Bonaventure apparently gets this information from Peter Comestor, *Historia scholastica in Evangelia*, c. 168. See PL 198:1628D: "They say that those who have considered this matter assiduously assert that these thorns were marine bulrushes whose point pierces no less than a thorn since it is hard and able to puncture." Hugh of St. Cher, p. 392e has the same interpretation of the thorns as Bonaventure.

[4] Hugh of St. Cher, p. 392h also cites Cant 3:11 and interprets the passage as pertaining to the synagogue.

[5] The Vulgate reads *eius* ("his").

proaches."[6] – Not only in word do they reproach him, but also by a token of reverence that consists of blows. Thus the text says: *And they were striking him.* Lamentations 3:30 reads: "He will give his cheek to the one who strikes him."[7] And Isaiah 50:6 states: "I have given my body to those who were striking me and my cheeks to those who were plucking them."

4. (Verse 4). *Pilate again went outside.* Next is the display of Christ scourged and mocked, so that they might be moved to pity. And first he repeats his verdict of innocence, for the text says: *He said: Behold, I bring him out to you.* He adds the reason: *That you may know that I find no guilt in him,* that is, nothing guilty "of death"[8] or of scourging. And nevertheless I have had him scourged.

5. (Verse 5). *So Jesus came forth.* Augustine states: "Not with the bright renown from power but with the full burden of shame."[9] So the text continues: *Wearing the crown of thorns and the purple cloak,* in which they have mocked him, according to what Matthew 20:19 says: "They will deliver him to the Gentiles to be mocked and scourged." *And he said to them: Behold, the man.* "Behold," as he displays the one scourged and mocked as if he had made himself a king. Augustine comments: "He has been crowned with thorns, clothed in a mocking robe, scoffed at with bitter taunts, smitten with blows. [His] disgrace seethes and cooks, let [your] dislike slacken and cool."[10]

---

[6] Hugh of St. Cher, p. 392o also quotes Lam 3:30.

[7] Hugh of St. Cher, p. 392k also quotes this portion of Lam 3:30.

[8] This is the interpretation of the Glossa Interlinearis.

[9] See Tractate 116 n. 2 in CCSL xxxvi, p. 647 and FC 92, p. 28. Bonaventure's citation is verbatim. Hugh of St. Cher, p. 392o also cites Augustine verbatim.

[10] See Tractate 116 n. 2 in CCSL xxxvi, p. 647 and FC 92, p. 28. Bonaventure's quotation is verbatim. Hugh of St. Cher, p. 392q cites these selfsame words of Augustine.

6. (Verse 6). *So when they had seen him.* After Pilate's display of Christ the third point follows, namely, the pertinacious obduracy of the Jews, especially of the chief priests. Thus the text states: *So when the chief priests and the attendants saw him, they cried out, saying: Crucify, crucify him.* Isaiah 5:7 reads: "I waited for him to render judgment, and behold a cry." Twice they say "Crucify," to show forth their pertinacity. Jeremiah 12:8 says: "My inheritance has become like a lion in the forest. It has cried out against me." And Psalm 21:14 reads: "They have opened their mouths against me, as a ravening and roaring lion," because of their crying forth against him.

7. *Pilate said to them.* Earlier Pilate had tried to free Christ through judgments of benignity and severity. Now he attempts the judgment of equity, returning to his innocence, for it is just to release an innocent person and never to put a person to death without a just reason. And the Jews resist this twice. First, by accusing and afterwards by threatening. Thus in this section many matters are treated. First, the justification of Christ's innocence. Second, his accusation where verse 7 states: "The Jews answered." Third, questions about the accusation where verse 8 says: "So when Pilate heard these words." Fourth is added the threats by the Jews where verse 12 reads: "But the Jews cried out." – So in first place is the justification of Christ's innocence. Because of his innocence Pilate did not want to condemn him, but offered him to the Jews. So the text says: *Pilate said to them,* who were petitioning that Christ be crucified: *Take him yourselves and crucify him, for I find no guilt in him.* And wherefore, I do not want to crucify him if he is not guilty. Indeed, he found no guilt in him, because 1 Peter 2:22 states: "He committed no sin; nor was deceit found in his mouth."

8. (Verse 7). *The Jews answered him.* The accusation of
the Jews occurs here, as they say: *We have a Law,* namely,
that we observe with the permission of the Roman authorities. They present the Law in their favor, although
it is against them. John 7:19 above says: "Didn't Moses
give you the Law, and none of you observes the Law?"
*And according to the Law he must die, because he has
made himself Son of God,* and therefore has blasphemed.
Leviticus 24:16 reads: "Let the person who blasphemes ...
shall die the death." For John 10:33 above states: "Not for
a good work are we stoning you, but for blasphemy, and
because you, although you are a human being, are making yourself God."

9. (Verse 8). *So when Pilate heard.* The third point occurs here, namely, questions about the accusation. So
moved by the accusation of the Jews, he needed further
questioning, for the text says: *Pilate, when he had heard
this statement, feared the more,* lest, if he released him,
he would be acting against the Law and, if he did not release him, he would be crucifying the Son of God. A good
judge should not fear, for Sirach 7:6 says: "Do not seek
to become a judge, unless you have sufficient strength to
extirpate iniquities." So the text adds:

10. (Verse 9). *Having again gone back into the praetorium,
he said to Jesus:*[11] *Where are you from?* He questioned him
about his origin, since they were accusing him of this. He
was asking a question that was momentous and beyond
his grasp, for Isaiah 53:8 states: "Who will tell of his generation?" And therefore, he did not hear the answer. Sirach 3:22 reads: "Do not ask about the things that are too

---

[11] On p. 491 n. 11 QuarEd correctly indicate that the Vulgate reads
Et ingressus est praetorium iterum et dixit ad Iesum ("And he again
entered the praetorium and said to Jesus").

high for you, and do not search into things that are beyond your ability." Thus the text continues: *But Jesus gave him no answer*, so that what Isaiah 53:7 says might be verified: "He will be dumb as a lamb before his shearer, and he will not open his mouth."[12] Augustine observes: "The comparison with the lamb was given for this purpose: that in his silence he be held not guilty, but innocent."[13] Lamentations 3:38 reads: "Shall not both good and evil proceed from the mouth of the Most High?"[14] So he tried to get such a taciturn individual to respond. Thus:

11. (Verse 10). *Pilate said to him:*[15] *Do you not speak to me?* As if he were saying: You're making a mistake in scorning my question since you should be currying my favor as one subject to my power. And he says this straightaway: *Do you not know that I have the power to crucify you and that I have the power to release you?* And therefore, I am someone to be both feared and begged. Thus he was marveling in that Christ, who was in such dire straits, was not seeking his favor. Matthew 27:14 reads: "And he did not answer him a single word, so that the procurator wondered." And since Pilate was exalting himself, Christ gave a prudent answer that leveled his pride as he taught him "not to be high-minded."[16]

---

[12] Hugh of St. Cher, p. 392v,e also cites Isa 53:7.

[13] See Tractate 116 n. 4 in CCSL xxxvi, p. 648 and FC 92, p. 29. Earlier Augustine has referred to Isa 53:7. Bonaventure's citation is verbatim.

[14] In the Vulgate *mala* ("evil") comes before *bona* ("good.").

[15] On p. 491 n. 13 QuarEd rightly notice that the Vulgate reads *Dicit ergo ei Pilatus* ("So Pilate said to him").

[16] See Rom 11:20: "Be not high-minded, but fear."

12. (Verse 11). *Jesus answered: You would have no power over me,*[17] *were it not given to you from above.* Augustine notes: "From above," that is, from God, according to what Romans 13:1 says: "There is no power except from God."[18] – But according to this exposition there does not seem to be the consequence that follows in the text: *Therefore, the person who handed me over,* etc. Thus Victor gives this explanation: "From above," that is, from Caesar. And since you are exercising your authority out of fear, *the person who handed me over to you has the greater sin,* since that person sins more grievously out of malice than the person who sins out of weakness or impotence.[19] And since he had answered wisely, Pilate intended to release him. Thus he says:

13. (Verse 12). *And from then on Pilate was looking for a way to release him.* He realized that his power was constituted under another power and did not want to condemn an innocent person. Wherefore, he wanted to release him. – *But the Jews cried out.* Here the fourth point surfaces,

---

[17] On p. 492 n. 2 QuarEd accurately indicate that the Vulgate reads *potestatem adversum me ullam* ("any power at all against me") while Bonaventure has *in me potestatem* ("power over me").

[18] See Tractate 116 n. 5 in FC 92, p. 29: "Let us learn, therefore, what he said, that which he also taught through the Apostle, that 'there is no power except from God....'" Hugh of St. Cher, p. 392v,k also cites Rom 13:1.

[19] This opinion is that of Bishop Victor of Capua. Victor's opinion seems much the same as the interpretation that Augustine gives in Tractate 116 n.5 after he had voiced the exposition given in n. 18. See FC 92, pp. 29-30: "For indeed God had given to Pilate a power of such a kind that he was also under Caesar's power.... For indeed, that man delivered me up to your power, feeling ill-will; but you are going to exercise the same power against me, feeling fear. Nor from being afraid indeed ought a man slay a man, especially an innocent man; nevertheless, it is much more evil to do it from being jealous than from being afraid." Hugh of St. Cher, p. 392v,I quotes parts of this same passage from Augustine.

namely, the threat by the Jews. And since they could not condemn Christ by means of their accusation, they turned to clamorous threats. Thus they were accusing Pilate of disloyalty towards Caesar if he released him. So the text continues: *But the Jews cried out*, namely, against Pilate because he wanted to release Christ, *saying: If you release this man, you are not a friend of Caesar*, but rather a traitor, since he is releasing Caesar's enemy. And they prove their case: *For everyone who makes himself a king, sets himself against Caesar*, because at that time Caesar was a monarch. Thus he had it in his power to bestow the title of king. So the person who set himself up as a king, set himself against Caesar. And this threat caused Pilate to retreat from the truth of his judgment to release Christ, since he was afraid of being accused to Caesar. Proverbs 29:25 states: "The person who fears human beings will quickly fall." For this reason the Lord said to his disciples in Matthew 10:28: "Do not fear those who kill the body."

14. *So Pilate, when he heard*. The perversity of the Jews has been shown in their malignity in resisting the judgment of the truth. Here their perversity is shown in extorting the false judgment that results in the condemnation of Christ. The judgment of the condemnation of Christ is described here and follows this order. First are noted the circumstances of place and time. Second comes the reason for the condemnation. In third place is the sentence itself.

Verse 13. The place is noted when the text says: *So Pilate, when he heard these words*. In this verse it is noted that he had already fallen from his just resolve because he feared Caesar, as if the verse were saying: He was frozen with fear. *Brought Jesus outside*, that is, to a public place. So he was "outside," so that he might be condemned in the sight of all. *And he sat down on the judgment seat, at a place called Lithostratos*.[20] This place is given special detail. "Judgment seat," that is, for pronouncing a sentence, for "judgment seat" is for judges. It is also the throne of kings and the chair of professors. "Lithos," as Victor says, is interpreted to mean "judgment" while "stratos" refers to a pavement laid out with various stones.[21] In this place was the consistory where judgments were rendered. And this place was *In Hebrew, Gabbatha*, that is, sublimity, since judges were accustomed to sit on an elevated or sublime level.[22] – Another interpretation is that "Gabbatha" means painted and polished and signifies the same thing as Lithostratos, that is, a place of judgment that was adorned and polished.[23]

15. (Verse 14). *Now it was the preparation day*. Behold, the circumstance of time is added, since it was Friday, which is called the parasceve for Passover, that is, the preparation day for Passover, since preparation took place on Friday for Sabbath, as it said in Exodus 16:5 that they are to gather enough on that day for two days.[24] *About the sixth hour*. Here special note is taken of the time, and it says "about," for it is difficult to determine the exact hour. – *And he said to the Jews*. Here mention is made of the

---

[20] On p. 492 n. 6 QuarEd accurately mention that the Vulgate reads *Lithostrotos*.

[21] This interpretation stems from Bishop Victor of Capua.

[22] On pp. 492-493 n. 6-7 QuarEd assemble various other interpretations of Lithostrotos and Gabbatha.

[23] On p. 493 n. 1 QuarEd cite Blessed Albert's commentary on this passage: "But Victor says that Gabbatha is interpreted as painted and polished, and thereby signifies the same thing as Lithostratos. And on such high seats ambition delighted to take a seat."

[24] See Ex 16:5: "But on the sixth day let them provide ... let it be double the amount they were wont to gather each day."

reason for Christ's condemnation, and this was not due to his sin, but to the hardened perversity in the Jews and the negation of the truth. The former because they were asking that he be condemned to the cruelest death. Thus the text states: *Behold, your king*, as if Pilate were saying: You do not have any other cause against him.

16. (Verse 15). *But they cried out: Away with him, away with him, crucify him.* Their twofold cry signifies the intensity of their emotion at the death of Christ. Jeremiah 26:11 reads: "The priests and the prophets spoke to the leaders and to all the people, saying: The judgment of death is upon this man." And since hardened perversity was not sufficient unless the negation of the truth were added to it, Pilate's question follows: *Shall I crucify your king?*[25] As if underlining to them in these words their perverse will in seeking their own ignominy, for the defamation of the king redounds upon the people. But in order that they might seem to escape this defamation, they deny the truth. So the text continues: *The chief priests answered, saying:*[26] *We have no king but Caesar.* And so this man here is not our king, and so we don't have any ignominy. And Pilate condemned him for this cause. So the text states:

17. (Verse 16a). *Then*[27] *he handed him over to them to be crucified.* Here the third point occurs, namely, the sentence itself, through which he was condemned to the punishment of the cross. And the text well says: *He handed*

---

[25] On p. 493 n. 5 QuarEd correctly indicate that the Vulgate reads: *Dicit eis Pilatus: regem vestram crucifigam?* ("Pilate said to them: Shall I crucify your king?").

[26] On p. 493 n. 6 QuarEd rightly notice that the Vulgate does not read *dicentes* ("saying").

[27] On p. 493 n. 7 QuarEd accurately indicate that the Vulgate reads *Tunc ergo* ("So then").

over to them, because he did this because of their petition. Acts 3:13 reads: "God … glorified his Son Jesus, whom you indeed handed over and disowned in the presence of Pilate, when he had decided that he should be released." And Luke 23:24 states: "Pilate pronounced sentence that what they had petitioned for should be done," namely, the petition of the Jews. Pilate acted against the Law. Exodus 23:2 says: "You shall not follow the crowd to do evil. Neither shall you yield in judgment to the opinion of the majority to stray from the truth."

QUESTIONS

18. Question 1 asks whether the custom of releasing a prisoner was praiseworthy.[28] – It seems that it was, because the Lord welcomes mercy rather than judgment, as is clear from the adulterous woman in John 8:1-11.[29] – But then there is the objection that the Law prescribed that malefactors should be put to death.[30] Wherefore, to release wrongdoers was against the Law and an evil custom. – It should be said that it was a good custom, when the release of the prisoner was congruous with Passover, since, even though the time of justice was in existence then, they should have been mindful of the mercy done for them and to be done for them on Passover. And therefore, this was lawful for them as a quasi sign. – Relative to the objection about the Law, it has to be said that the great solemnity of the festival outweighed the harshness of the Law.[31]

---

[28] See John 18:39.

[29] See John 8:11: "Neither will I condemn you." See also Matt 9:13: "'I desire mercy, not sacrifice.'"

[30] See Ex 22:18: "You shall not suffer malefactors to live."

[31] On p. 493 n. 13 QuarEd refer to Book I, tit. 7 (3) of Justinian's Code: "Where the first day of Passover is celebrated, let no one be kept

19. Question 2 asks whether they sinned in asking for Barabbas.[32] – It would seem so, since Acts 3:14-15 reproaches them: "You ... asked that a murderer should be granted to you, but you killed the author of life." – But it seems that they did not sin, because it was lawful for them to ask for whom they wanted without distinction. – I respond that they did not sin in this that they released a person who was worthy of death, but in this that they preferred him to an innocent person. Therefore, it was a case of favoritism. Thus Augustine comments: "We do not censure you, O Jews, because you freed an evildoer during Passover, but that you put to death an innocent person."[33]

20. Question 3 deals with the soldiers' mockery of Christ when they are not said to have a mandate from Pilate to do this. Why did this happen? – Chrysostom answers that they were doing this for money, since they had been corrupted by the chief priests.[34]

21. Question 4 focuses on the discrepancy that in this section John says that Christ was mocked by the soldiers before the sentence of condemnation whereas it is said in Matthew 27:27-31 that the soldiers mocked him after

---

in jail, let the chains of all be released, etc." But see Book II, Tit. 12 n. 9 of *The Digest of Justinian*, Vol. 1: "The deified Trajan issued a rescript to Minicius Natalis to the effect that holidays gave a vacation from legal business only; but business pertaining to military discipline was to be transacted even on holidays. Included here is examination of prisoners."

[32] See John 18:40.

[33] This is a verbatim quotation from Tractate 115 n. 5. See CCSL xxxvi, p. 646.

[34] See Homily 84 n. 1 in FC 41, p. 419: "To curry favor with the Jews, because even from the start it was not by his (Pilate's) orders that they set out against Him during the night, but rather to please the Jews, since they would dare anything for the sake of money."

his condemnation which is recorded in Matthew 27:26: "He handed Jesus over to them to be crucified."[35] – It can be said that this mockery occurred twice, once before the condemnation and once after. – Another interpretation is that Matthew says this by way of recapitulation, for it had taken place beforehand.[36]

22. Question 5 highlights John 19:9: Why did the Lord not answer Pilate when he asked: "Where are you from?" – It would seem that this silence stemmed from arrogance. – I respond that he did not answer that question, because he could not comprehend the answer. For the Lord had told his disciples in John 16:12 above: "I still have many things to say to you, but you cannot bear them now." What was true then is also true now.

23. Question 6 asks about John 19:11: "You would have no power over me were it not given you from above." – So it seems that Pilate did not sin when he crucified Christ, because this was given him by God. – It has to be maintained that two factors must be considered in this power, namely, the power of presiding and the power of passing sentence. The first is from God, as the Apostle says,[37] but the actual passing of a sentence is not always from God. Therefore, the Lord wanted to say to Pilate that he did not have this power from himself. So he should not glory

---

[35] The Vulgate reads *eis* ("to them") whilst Bonaventure has *illis* ("to them").

[36] See Book III c. 9 n. 36 of Augustine's *Harmony of the Gospels* in NPNF1, Volume 6, p. 197: "This makes it evident that Matthew and Mark have reported this incident in the way of a recapitulation, and that it did not actually take place after Pilate had delivered Him up to be crucified. For John informs us distinctly enough that these things took place when He yet was with Pilate."

[37] See Rom 13:1: "There exists no power except from God."

in that power by itself. However, the sentence he passed was only with God's permission, as Chrysostom says.[38]

24. Question 7 deals with John 19:11: "The person who betrayed me to you has the greater sin." – This seems false, since the Jews sinned out of ignorance. For they believed that he was a blasphemer and worthy of death, but Pilate knowingly put an innocent person to death. – I respond that both sinned, but the Jews had a greater sin, because it rose from malice, whereas Pilate's sin stemmed from weakness and fear of Caesar. – With regard to the objection that they sinned out of ignorance, it has to be maintained that they did not know that he was God, but they were not ignorant about his innocence. Or if they did not know about both of these, their sin issued from malice, for Wisdom 2:21 reads: "Their malice blinded them."

25. Question 8 treats John 19:14 and its statement that Christ was condemned "about the sixth hour." Now it is said in Mark 15:25: "Now it was about the third hour of the day, and they crucified him."[39] Furthermore, it is said in Matthew 27:45: "Now from the sixth hour to the ninth hour there was darkness...." Therefore, he was sentenced before the sixth hour. – Augustine answers: "At the third hour the Lord was crucified by the tongues of the Jews, at the sixth hour by the hands of the soldiers, so that we may understand that the fifth hour was already past and something of the sixth hour begun when Pilate sat down in the judgment seat ... and when he was led ... and those things were done ... that are related as having been done,

---

[38] See Homily 84 n. 2 in FC 41, p. 422: "'Yet, if it was actually given [from above] neither he nor they would be blameworthy.' In vain do you say this, for the word 'given' here means 'permitted,' as if He said: 'These things have been allowed to take place, but you are not on that account free from guilt.'"

[39] The Vulgate does not read *quasi* ("about") or *diei* ("of the day").

the ... sixth hour would be completed, and from this hour to the ninth the sun was obscured...."[40] – Victor gives a different answer. The Lord was crucified during an hour between the third and the sixth. And since the extremes are mentioned by name and the middle often bears the name of the extremes, Mark says the third hour while John says the sixth hour, but not *simpliciter*, but with the specification "about the sixth hour."[41]

26. Question 9 looks at John 19:15 and the Jews' petition that the Lord be crucified. Why did they want the Lord to be put to death by this means rather than by some other? – Chrysostom answers: "This death was the most reproachable. So afraid that some memory of him might persist afterwards, they were striving to bring him to an accursed punishment, not realizing that the truth is exalted by prohibitions."[42] – On God's part the reason was multiple. It was a mystery, since we have sinned by means of a tree.[43] It was an example, lest anyone fear a shameful death.[44] It was judgment, since "it pleased God,

---

[40] Bonaventure abbreviates Tractate 117 n. 1. See CCSL xxxvi, p. 651 and FC 92, p. 33. Hugh of St. Cher, p. 393b also cites this passage from Augustine, but commences with his equivalent of "so that we may understand."

[41] Hugh of St. Cher, p. 393b gives a third solution to this problem: "Between the third and sixth hour the Lord was crucified, but more towards the third hour. And so Mark says that it was the third hour, but John says about the sixth hour. He does not say the sixth hour *simpliciter*. So in the Church Mass is celebrated between the third and the sixth hours."

[42] Bonaventure adapts Homily 84 n. 2. See PG 59:457 and FC 41, p. 423. Hugh of St. Cher, p. 393g quotes Chrysostom in the selfsame words as Bonaventure, but does not have "not realizing that the truth is exalted by prohibitions."

[43] See Ambrose's commentary on Luke 4:1 in Book IV, n. 7 of CCSL xiv, p. 108: "... death by means of a tree, life by means of the cross...."

[44] See Augustine's Exposition of Psalm 140 n. 20 in *Expositions of the Psalms ... 121-150*. Translation and notes by Maria Boulding. WSA III/20 (Hyde Park, NY: New City Press, 2004), p. 321: "It was not

by the foolishness of our preaching, to save those who believe."[45]

John 19:16b-37
Christ's passion and its consummation

27. *Now they took Jesus.* Having treated the arrest and
condemnation of Christ above, the Evangelist now depicts his *passion*. This part is divided into two sections.
The first section *describes his passion* whilst the second
treats *the consummation of the passion* where verse 28
reads: "After this Jesus, knowing," etc.

John 19:16b-27
Christ's passion

In this first section his passion is depicted from the four
angles that are suggested there. For first is described the
vileness of the passion. Second is *the dignity of the one suffering* where verse 19 states: "Now Pilate also wrote an
inscription." Third is *the cruelty* or cupidity *of those crucifying him* where verse 23 says: "So the soldiers, when
they had crucified him." Fourth is *the paucity of those suffering with him* where verse 25 states: "Now there were
standing by the cross."

28. (Verse 16b). Now the vileness of the passion is depicted in its procession, its place, the type of suffering, and in
the company of those suffering. So first with regard to the

---

just death that they faced without fear but the cross as well, a death
more horrible than any other that could be imagined. The Lord accepted it so that his disciples might not only be unafraid of death itself
but would shrink from no manner of death."
    [45] See 1 Cor 1:21.

vileness of the passion in its procession, it is to be noted that he was led away like a robber and he was bearing his own cross. So the text states: *Now they took Jesus.* Psalm 16:12 says: "They have taken me, as a lion prepared for the prey," namely, the soldiers took Jesus. *They led him away,*[46] as a malefactor, namely, outside the camp. For this reason Hebrews 13:13 states: "Let us go forth to him outside the camp, bearing his reproach" of the cross.

29. (Verse 17). *And bearing the cross for himself*, namely, in the way a robber would be punished. Then was fulfilled what had been said in Isaiah 22:22: "I will lay the key of ... David upon his shoulder." And Isaiah 9:6: "The government is upon his shoulder,"[47] because he has triumphed there. About this Augustine comments: "A grand spectacle. But if ungodliness should watch, a grand ridiculous absurdity. If godliness should watch, a grand mystery."[48] – *He went forth to the place which is called the place of the Skull.*[49] In this verse the vileness of the place is suggested, for he suffered in this place where robbers and evildoers were punished. For that place was called "Calvary," because it was there that the heads of the condemned were

---

[46] On p. 495 n. 8 QuarEd rightly notice that the Vulgate reads *et eduxerunt* ("and they led him away") while Bonaventure has *duxerunt* ("they led him away").

[47] Hugh of St. Cher, p. 393n also cites Isa 22:22 and 9:6 back to back.

[48] See Tractate 117 n. 3 in CCSL xxxvi, p. 652 and FC 92, p. 35. Bonaventure's citation is verbatim. Hugh of St. Cher, p. 393r gives a more extensive citation from Tractate 117 n. 3.

[49] On p. 495 n. 10 QuarEd accurately mention that the Vulgate reads *Calvariae locum* ("place of the Skull") while Bonaventure has *Calvariae locus* ("place of the Skull").

shaven. For "Calvary" means the head without flesh.[50] *In Hebrew, Golgotha, that is, "the place of beheading."*[51]

30. (Verse 18). *Where they crucified him.* In this verse is noted the vileness of the passion from the type of death, for this type of death was the vilest. Wisdom 2:20 reads: "Let us condemn him to the most shameful death." – *And with him two others, one on each side, with Jesus in the middle.* Here is noted vileness by companionship, since these two were robbers. Thus Mark 15:27 states: "They crucified with him two robbers." Then was fulfilled what was said in Isaiah 53:12: "He was reckoned with the wicked." But he was in the middle to signify that he was the mediator, for in his birth he was in the middle of animals, as Habakkuk 3:2 says, while in his passion he was in the middle of robbers, because he was true peace, as Ephesians 2:14 states.[52]

31. (Verse 19). *Now Pilate also wrote an inscription.* The second principal section of this part occurs here, namely, the dignity of the one suffering. And this is intimated in the title, for it is the inscription of a king. And this inscription is described in the following order. First, the inscription itself. Second is the publication of the inscription. Third is the opposition to the inscription. Finally comes the approbation of the inscription. – So the text touches upon the inscription when it reads: *Now Pilate also wrote an inscription and placed it on the cross.* Isa-

---

[50] See Bonaventure's commentary on Luke 23:33 (n. 39) in *Bonaventure on Luke, 17-24*, pp. 2148-2149: "So it is called *the place of the Skull* because it contained the skulls of the condemned whose heads were cut off there and hung on a pole."

[51] This is the interpretation of the Glossa Interlinearis.

[52] Hab 3:2 in the LXX reads: "You will be known in the midst of two animals." Eph 2:14 states: "For he himself is our peace. He it is who has made both one...."

iah 19:19 states: "In the midst of the land of Egypt there will be an altar of the Lord and an inscription of the Lord at its borders." – And notice that there is a memorial inscription to commemorate the deceased. There is an inscription of commendation on houses.[53] Finally there is an inscription to commemorate a victory. And this inscription was that of a victory and triumph.[54] Thus it was in praise of Christ and to the shame of the Jews, because, even though he had been condemned as a robber, he was indeed no robber, but a king. And this is what the inscription said: *Now there was written: Jesus of Nazareth, The King of the Jews.* Scripture approved of this inscription, for Psalm 2:6 says: "I have been constituted by him king over Zion, his holy mountain," etc. In this inscription Pilate described him by his name, since he wrote "Jesus." Luke 1:31 reads: "You will call his name Jesus." By his hometown, "Nazareth." Luke 2:51 states: "He went down with them and came to Nazareth." By his royal dignity, since he says "king." Jeremiah 23:5 says: "I will raise up for David a just branch, and a king will reign." – According to Matthew the inscription noted the charge against him. Matthew 27:37 states: "They put above his head the written charge against him," because in that inscription is intimated why he died, namely, to save, because he was Jesus,[55] and "to make us a kingdom for our God." Revela-

---

[53] See Hugh of St. Cher, p. 393v,c who lists these three types of inscriptions and gives an example of this second one: "As a rose is the flower of flowers, so is this house the house of houses."

[54] See Bonaventure's commentary on Luke 23:38 (n. 47) in *Bonaventure on Luke, 17-24*, p. 2160: "Now titles are threefold. There is a *memorial* title such as those written on the tombstones of the dead. *A public commendation* such as those written on the gates of cities. *A celebration of a triumph* that contains the reason for and course of the victory and is customarily written on arches. And such was this title, concerning which Isaiah 19:19 says...."

[55] See Matt 1:21: "... and you will call his name Jesus, for he will save his people from their sins."

tion 5:9-10 reads: "Worthy are you, O Lord God,[56] to take the scroll… for you were slain and have redeemed us for God with your blood … and have made us[57] a kingdom for our God.…'"

32. (Verse 20). This verse treats the public notice of the inscription. Thus the text continues: *So many of the Jews read this inscription, because the place where Jesus was crucified was near the city.* Thus many read it, since many passed by that place, not only Jews, but also others. Isaiah 34:16 says: "Search diligently in the book of the words of the Lord[58] and read. Not one of them was wanting." *And it was written in Hebrew, Greek, and Latin,* so that everyone could read the inscription, since he was future king for all, as is said in Revelation 19:16: "He is king of kings and lord of lords." It was written in three languages, since Deuteronomy 19:15 says: "Let every word be confirmed by the mouth of two or three witnesses."

33. (Verse 21). *So the chief priests of the Jews said to Pilate.* Here the opposition of the Jews is noted, for they wanted to destroy the inscription, as it promoted their ignominy. So they say: *Do not write: King of the Jews, but that he[59] said: I am the King of the Jews,* namely, so that no dignity might be shown him, but rather that the presumption with which he said that he was king might be demonstrated. On the contrary, it is said in Hebrews 5:5:

---

[56] The Vulgate does not read *Domine Deus* ("Lord God").

[57] The Vulgate reads *eos* ("them") while Bonaventure has *nos* ("us").

[58] The Vulgate reads *in libro Domini* ("in the book of the Lord") while Bonaventure has *in libro sermonum Domini* ("in the book of the words of the Lord").

[59] On p. 497 n. 1 QuarEd correctly indicate that the Vulgate makes "he" explicit and reads *ipse*.

"Christ did not glorify himself that he might become high priest," etc.

34. (Verse 22). *Pilate answered*. This verse introduces the affirmation of the inscription or its approval against the malice of the Jews, for Pilate does not destroy it, but approves it: *What I have written, I have written. What I have written* is true. *I have written*, as something indelible and irrevocably true. Augustine observes: "If what Pilate wrote cannot be destroyed, can what Truth said be destroyed?"[60]

35. (Verse 23a). *So the soldiers, when they had crucified him*. Here the third principal point surfaces, namely, the cruelty or cupidity of those crucifying him, for they stripped Christ and then divided his garments. And three things are noted here, namely, the division of the garments by parts, then by lots, and third the confirmation of both through an authoritative voice, lest it seem that something in the death of Christ happened by chance. – So they divided his garments by parts. Thus the text says: *They took his garments and made of them four parts, to each soldier a part*. From this action it seems that, as Augustine observes, there were four soldiers who crucified the Lord. *And the tunic*. Understood is "They took."

36. (Verse 23b-24). This verse indicates that the distribution of the tunic was done by lots. And the reason is given: *Now the tunic was without seam, woven in one piece from the top*, that is, one integrated piece. And since it could not be divided in a fitting way, the soldiers *said to one an-*

---

[60] This is a verbatim citation. See CCSL xxxvi, p. 653 and FC 92, p. 37.

other:[61] *Let us not tear it, but let us cast lots for it,* for as is said in Proverbs 18:18: "Casting lots suppresses contentions and determines who wins among the powerful."[62] – And lest anyone think that this took place by chance, it is shown that this had been predicted by the Prophet, for the text reads: *That the Scripture might be fulfilled which says.* Psalm 21:19, which has the heading, "God, my God, look upon me," says: "They parted my garments," with regard to the soldiers' first action, "and upon my vesture they cast lots," relative to the division of the tunic. And this Scripture was not understood by the Jews, but by the soldiers. Therefore, the text continues: *And the soldiers indeed did these things.*

According to the spiritual meaning Christ's tunic, which is undivided, signifies love, which is a garment, because it covers turpitude. 1 Peter 4:8 reads: "Because love covers a multitude of sins." And it is a garment that is adorned. So it is said to be the wedding garment, without which no one enters into the joy of the wedding feast of the Lamb. So Matthew 22:12 says: "Friend, how did you come in here without a wedding garment?" This tunic is seamless, since it is not tied to something else, but is the bond that holds others together. Colossians 3:14 states: "But above all these things have love, which is the bond of perfection." – This tunic is not to be divided by being torn asunder. So 1 Corinthians 1:10 reads: "I beseech you, brothers and sisters, ... that you all say the same thing."[63]

---

[61] On p. 497 n. 4 QuarEd rightly notice that the Vulgate reads *dixerunt ergo* ("So they said").

[62] The Vulgate reads *inter potentes quoque diiudicat* ("also determines among the powerful") while Bonaventure has *inter potentes quosque diiudicat* ("determines who wins among the powerful").

[63] 1 Cor 1:10 continues: "... and that there be no dissensions among you, but that you be perfectly united in one mind and in one judgment."

And Ephesians 4:3 says: "Careful to preserve the unity of the Spirit in the bond of peace."[64] – Those who sever this tunic are worse than the soldiers who crucified him and didn't want to divide the seamless garment of the Lord.

37. (Verse 25). *Now there were standing by the cross*, etc. This verse indicates the few people who were suffering with him. Of all those dear to him three women were present, among whom was also the Mother of the Lord, with whom the Lord was also suffering. Four things are noted here: the compassion of the women towards the Lord; the Lord's care towards his Mother; from this care arises a commendation, and finally from this commendation arises an acceptance. – So the compassion of the women is noted here: *There were standing near the cross of Jesus.* So they were near the body, because the affection of compassion drew them. But others were far removed through non-compassion, for it is said in Psalm 37:12: "Those who were close to me stood far off." But these women stood close by, for they loved him more, namely, his Mother, who was suffering with him beyond everyone else, for Luke 2:35 states: "A sword will pierce your own soul." *And his Mother's sister, Mary of Cleophas.* This woman was the mother of James. – It should be noted that Anna is said to have had three husbands: Joachim, Cleophas, and

---

[64] See Hugh of St. Cher, p. 393v,p: "The mystery of this tunic is clear in the Glossa." See PL 114:421D: "The tunic, for which they cast lots, signifies the unity of all parts (which had been signified by the four garments). This unity is held together by the bond of love." See Augustine, Tractate 118 n. 4 in FC 92, p. 42: "But the tunic for which lots were cast signifies the unity of all the parts which is held together by the bond of love. Now the Apostle, just before he speaks about love, says, 'I show you an outstanding way.' And in another place he says, 'To know also the love of Christ which stands out above knowledge.' And likewise elsewhere, 'But above all these things love which is the bond of perfection.'" It is clear that Bonaventure, while dependent upon tradition, elaborates the spiritual sense of the tunic in his own way.

Salome, and from these three husbands she had three Mary's, namely, the Lord's Mother, who was the daughter of Joachim; James's mother, who was the daughter of Cleophas; Simon's and Jude's mother, who was the daughter of Salome.[65] – *And Mary Magdalene*, who was named after Magdala, a fort.[66] These three women as those who suffered most closely with him were standing by the Lord's cross.

38. (Verse 26). *So when Jesus saw*. Here the second point occurs, namely, the Lord's care for his Mother, and it is shown in this that he looked at her and the one to whom he could commend her. So the text continues: *So when Jesus saw his Mother*. "When he saw" with a regard of care. 1 Timothy 5:8 reads: "If anyone does not take care of his own and especially those of his own household," etc.[67] And Chrysostom observes: "Here the Lord shows his great love for his Mother and commends her to the disciple, teaching us to have every care, to the last breath, for those who have given us birth."[68] Exodus 20:12 states:

---

[65] See Peter Lombard's commentary on Gal 1:19 in PL 192:101D: Mary, the mother of the Lord, was the daughter of Joachim and Anne. "Now when Joachim passed away, Cleophas, the brother of Joseph, married the same Anne and begat from her a daughter whom he called Mary, who married Alphaeus, who begat from her four sons, namely, James, Joseph, Simon, Jude. Now when Cleophas died, a certain Salome married the same Anne and begat from her a daughter, by the name of Mary, who married Zebedaeus, and he had from her sons, namely, James, who was called the Greater, and John the evangelist."

[66] See CCSL lxxii, p. 137: "Magdalene tower."

[67] 1 Tim 5:8 concludes: "... he has denied the faith and is worse than an unbeliever." Hugh of St. Cher, p. 394q cites 1 Tim 5:8 in its entirety.

[68] See Homily 85 n. 2 in PG 59:461. Bonaventure's citation has more in common with Hugh of St. Cher than with Chrysostom. See Hugh of St. Cher, p. 394o: Chrysostom: "Through this he teaches us to have every care, to the last breath, for those who have given us birth."

"Honor your father and your mother," etc. What this text commanded, he fulfilled. *And the disciple standing by whom he loved.* And so he could commend her to him as a member of the family. John "was standing by." He had not moved far away, for he was one of those to whom it was said in Luke 22:28: "You are the ones who have remained with me in my trials." – *He said to his Mother.* Here is the third point, namely, the loving commendation, for he says: *Woman, behold, your son,* as if he were saying: So you may trust and confide in him as your son.

39. (Verse 27). *Then he said to the disciple: Behold, your mother,* as if he were saying: Protect her as your mother. *And from that hour the disciple took her as his own mother.*[69] Here is the acceptance of the commendation. "As his own," that is, as his mother. "He took," so that, as a son, he might honor, protect, and serve her as a mother. But Augustine reads this verse in this way. "Into his own" is an accusative plural and then asks: How could he take her into his own when he did not have anything of his own? He answers his own question: "Into his own," namely, his official duties, services, and benefits, not into his possessions which he did not have.[70]

QUESTIONS

40. Question 1 focuses on John 19:17: "Jesus, bearing the cross for himself, went forth." But it is said in Matthew

---

[69] On p. 498 n. 6 QuarEd rightly notice that the Vulgate reads *in sua* ("into his home") while Bonaventure has *in suam* ("as his mother").

[70] Bonaventure seems to expand upon Tractate 119 n. 3. See FC 92, p. 47: "Therefore he took her to his own, not properties – none of which he possessed on his own – but official duties which by special dispensation it was his care to carry out."

27:32 that they forced a certain Simon to take up his cross. – In Book III of his *Harmony of the Gospels* Augustine answers: "Jesus was carrying the cross when he went forth to Calvary. But Simon was forced to carry it along the way.... Afterwards the cross was given him to carry to the place. So we read that both were done: first, what John says, then what Matthew has."[71]

41. Question 2 asks about the inscription that John 19:19 mentions: Did Pilate write this in truth or in derision? – It seems that he wrote it in truth, since, despite the request of the Jews, he refused to destroy it, but answered them in John 19:22: "What I have written, I have written." – It seems, though, that it was a derisory inscription, because he permitted him to be mocked by the soldiers not as a true king, but as a foolish one, for as John 19:2-3 says the soldiers "plaited a crown of thorns" and "struck him." – To this question it has to be said that Pilate had some inkling, by which he knew that he was innocent, for as Matthew 27:18 says, "He knew that they had handed him over out of jealousy." By this inkling he also knew that he was the king promised to the Jews. Therefore, he always called him king. Thus Augustine comments: "It could not be wrested from Pilate's heart that Christ was the king of the Jews, as if Truth itself had fixed it in his heart."[72] – With regard to whether he ordered or permitted the soldiers' mocking of Christ, I say that he permitted them to mock the king and to scourge the innocent, so that he might placate the Jews by means of these shameful punishments and incline them to mercy.

---

[71] Bonaventure has adapted Book III, c. 10 n. 37 of *De consensu evangelistarum*. See CSEL xliii, p. 322.

[72] Bonaventure paraphrases Tractate 115 n. 5. See CCSL xxxvi, p. 646.

42. Question 3 raises the question of why Pilate dared to hand him over to death. – The answer to this must be that he was petrified by the fear that he be accused before Caesar and that he was deceived by the error of thinking that the entire blame was the Jews', basing his thought on the fact that they had put his petition into his hands. For it is said in Matthew 27:24: "He took water and washed his hands and said: I am innocent." And the Jews took full blame upon themselves, for they said in Matthew 27:25: "His blood be upon us and upon our children." But he was mistaken, since he could not consent in the death of an innocent person without sin.

43. Question 4 notes that in Matthew 27:35 it is said: "They divided his garments, casting lots." It seems that they cast lots not only for his tunic, but also for all his garments. But John says that they cast lots solely for his tunic. – The same is said in Mark 15:24: "They divided his garments, casting lots over them to see what each should take." – To this question Augustine answers and says: "What Matthew says is understood of the entire dividing up of the garments. When they were dividing up the garments and came to the tunic, they cast lots for it."[73] – With regard to what Mark says, it has to be maintained that this is its sense: "They divided his garments first. Then they cast lots over the tunic, which had remained over or was left over, who should take it."[74]

44. Question 5 asks about John 19:26-27: Why did the Lord commend his Mother in this way when in John 2:4 above he responded so harshly to her: "What is this to me

---

[73] Bonaventure abbreviates Tractate 118 n. 3. See CCSL xxxvi, p. 655 and FC 92, p. 40.

[74] Bonaventure paraphrases Tractate 118 n. 3. See CCSL xxxvi, p. 656 and FC 92, p. 41.

and you, woman?" – Augustine responds, and his answer is found in the Glossa: "For at that time he was about to perform divine works and rebuffed his Mother as ignorant... Now he shows that the hour has come which he had foretold then and during which he would die. He acknowledges her from whom he was mortally born, and in his suffering he commends her with human affection and also instructs by his human example that care should be given to parents by devoted children."[75] – Now relative to the reason why he commended her to John, the answer on the part of the Lord is found in the text: Because he had a special love for him. But the evangelist is silent on his part. And the Saints say that this occurred, so that a virgin should guard the Virgin.[76]

John 19:28-37
Consummation of Christ's passion

45. *Afterwards Jesus, knowing*, etc. Earlier the Evangelist treated Christ's passion. Now he considers *the consummation of the passion* in three parts. First he deals with its consummation relative to *the testimony of Scripture*. Second he considers it with respect to *its occurrence* where verse 30 says: "And bowing his head." Third he treats it with regard to *its effect* where verse 31 states: "So the Jews, since it was the Preparation Day."

---

[75] Bonaventure greatly adapts Tractate 119 n. 1-2. See CCSL xxxvi, p. 658 and FC 92, p. 45. Hugh of St. Cher, p. 394q cites the last clause of Augustine: "He also instructs by his human example that care should be given to parents by devoted children."

[76] See Theophylactus's commentary on John 19:27 in PG 124:279B: "So the disciple took Mary to his own home, for the pure lady had been entrusted to the pure man."

46. (Verse 28). So the consummation of Christ's passion relative to the testimony of Scripture is seen in this that all things concerning him that had been foretold by the prophets were accomplished. This consummation is intimated in the following sequence, namely, the intention of the one consummating, the consummation itself, the assertion of the consummation. – Thus the intention of the one consummating is suggested here: *Afterwards Jesus, knowing that all things had now been consummated.* Supply: that have been written about the Son of Man. But not fully, for he says *Now, that the Scripture might be fulfilled*, that is, he is willing to accomplish in a perfect way the Scripture that says in Psalm 68:22: "In my thirst they gave me vinegar to drink," *he said: I thirst.* And this was a sign of weakness assumed and of the truth of nature against those heretics who were saying that he had not truly suffered. And indeed he said this not only on account of need, but also to fulfill the Scripture.

47. (Verse 29). *Now there was a vessel.* The consummation itself occurs here. During it they gave him vinegar[77] to drink, something that they had at hand. Thus the text states: *Now there was standing there a vessel full of vinegar, and having put a sponge soaked with the vinegar on a stalk of hyssop*, that is, putting the sponge which was bound to the hyssop, *they put it to his mouth*, by means of a reed, as it is said in Matthew 27:48: "One of them ran and, taking a sponge, soaked it in vinegar, and put it on a reed, and offered it to him to drink."

48. (Verse 30). *So when Jesus had taken the vinegar.* The assertion of the consummated is found here. Thus the text continues: *So when Jesus had taken the vinegar, he said: It is consummated*, namely, what had been writ-

---

[77] Another possible translation of *acetum* is "common wine."

ten about me before the sending of the Spirit. About his consummation Luke 18:31 says: "All things will be consummated which have been written ... about the Son of Man." Hebrews 5:9 reads: "Having been consummately perfected,[78] he became to all who obey him the cause of eternal salvation."

And bowing his head, etc. Having detailed the consummation in Scripture, the Evangelist now sets down the occurrence of the consummation. And this consummation took place in death, since the end of present sufferings is death. Thus the text states: *Bowing his head, he handed over the spirit.* Augustine observes: "'He handed over the spirit,' as the one who 'has the power of laying down his life and taking it up again.' And the words, 'bowing his head': Who so goes to sleep when he wants to, as Jesus died when he wanted to?"[79] Thus he offered his spirit, as it is said in Hebrews 5:7: "With tears and a loud cry he offered" his spirit.[80] And this was the consummation of what had been foretold as it is said in Hebrews 10:14: "By one offering he has consummately perfected forever those who have been sanctified." And Hebrews 2:10 reads: "It became him ... who had brought many children into glory, to consummately perfect him through his passion."

49. *But*[81] *the Jews, since it was the Preparation Day.* The consummation is described here with regard to the effect

---

[78] I have tried to preserve the translation "consummated" for *consummatus* which can also bear the translation of "accomplished" and "perfected."

[79] Bonaventure rearranges Tractate 119 n. 6. See CCSL xxxvi, p. 660 and FC 92, p. 49.

[80] Bonaventure inverts the word order of Hebr 5:7: "... with a loud cry and tears he offered."

[81] On p. 500 n. 5 QuarEd accurately indicate that the Vulgate reads *ergo* ("So") whilst Bonaventure has *vero* ("But"). But note that in his commentary on John 19:31 Bonaventure uses *ergo* ("So").

of the passion that was seen in the opening of Christ's side, from which flowed "blood and water." Thus the Sacraments have their efficacy, as the Glossa says.[82] And four things are noted here, namely, the petition to take down the bodies of the crucified; the breaking of the bones of the robbers; the opening of Christ's side; and the confirmation by witness.

Verse 31. The petition that the bodies of the crucified be taken down was made by the Jews. And the reason proffered was that the following day was the great day of the Sabbath. For this reason the text says: *So the Jews, since it was the Preparation Day*, that is, the day before the Sabbath, *in order that the bodies might not remain upon the cross on the Sabbath*, namely, because of its solemnity, *for that Sabbath was a solemn day*, because it occurred during the solemnity of unleavened bread, *besought Pilate that their legs might be broken and that they might be taken down*. Augustine comments: "... So their legs were broken, so that they might die and be removed from the wooden cross, lest they might, by hanging on crosses, pollute the great festival day by the horror of their crucifixion occurring on that day."[83] Deuteronomy 21:22-23 reads: "When a person has committed a crime for which he is to be punished with death, and having been condemned to death has been hanged on a gibbet, his body shall not remain upon the tree, but shall be buried the same day."[84]

50. (Verse 32). *So the soldiers came.* This verse covers the breaking of the legs of the robbers: *So the soldiers came*, at the bequest of the Jews, *and broke the legs of the first*,

---

[82] This is the Glossa Ordinaria apud Lyranum on John 19:34.

[83] See Tractate 120 n. 1 in CCSL xxxvi, p. 661 and FC 92, p. 50. Bonaventure's citation is virtually verbatim.

[84] Hugh of St. Cher, p. 394vi, also cites Deut 21:22-23.

namely, the one to whom they came first, because he was still alive. *And of the other, who had been*[85] *crucified with him.* Supply: They broke their legs, and so they died, so that they might be so distinguished from the Lamb whose bones were fittingly preserved intact, since he alone was untouched by sin. They could say what Psalm 6:3 has: "Heal me, Lord, for my bones are troubled."

51. (Verse 33). *But when they came to Jesus.* Here the opening of Christ's side is noted. And first the text says why they did not break his legs, namely, because he was dead. And this is what the text says: *And saw that he was dead,*[86] *they did not break his legs,* since they were doing this to hasten death. And the opening of Christ's side is added. Thus the text continues:

52. (Verse 34). *But one of the soldiers opened his side with a lance.* Augustine comments: "He does not say 'he wounded,' but 'he opened,' so that there, in a manner of speaking, the door ... was thrown open, from which the Sacraments of the Church have flowed."[87] And therefore, the text adds: *And immediately there came out blood and water.* Augustine remarks: "That blood was shed for the remission of sins. That water provides the proper mix for the salutary cup and offers both bath and drink."[88] Revelation 1:5 reads: "He has washed us from our sins in his

---

[85] On p. 500 n. 9 QuarEd accurately mention that the Vulgate reads *est* ("was") whereas Bonaventure has *erat* ("had been").

[86] On p. 500 n. 10 QuarEd correctly indicate that the Vulgate reads *iam mortuum* ("already dead").

[87] Bonaventure adjusts Tractate 120 n. 2. See CCSL xxxvi, p. 661 and FC 92, p. 50.

[88] See Tractate 120 n. 2 in CCSL xxxvi, p. 661 and FC 92, 50. Bonaventure's citation is virtually verbatim.

own blood." And Ephesians 5:25-26 states: "Christ loved the Church ... cleansing her in the bath," etc.[89]

53. (Verse 35). *And he who saw it*, etc. Here is the fourth point, namely, the confirmation by testimony. And he confirms this by his own testimony and by the testimony of Scripture. "His own," because he saw and was present, for the text states: *And he who saw it has borne witness*. And he approves the testimony as true, for the text continues: *And his witness is true*, and approves it as certain, because the text adds: *And he knows that he tells the truth*. And so he says: *that you also may believe*, for faith more quickly inclines to the person who has seen than to the person who knows something through another's account of it. Proverbs 12:17 reads: "The person who speaks what he knows is the just judge,[90] but the person who lies is a deceitful witness." And 1 John 1:1 has: "What was from the beginning, what we have heard, what we have seen with our eyes, what we have looked upon and our hands have handled: of the Word of life," etc. – Not only does he confirm this by his own testimony, but also by that of Scripture. Thus he continues:

54. (Verse 36). *These things*[91] *came to pass that the Scripture might be fulfilled: Not a bone of him shall you break*, from Exodus 12:46.[92] And therefore, they did not break his legs.

---

[89] Eph 5:26 concludes: "... in the bath of water by means of the word."

[90] The Vulgate reads *index iustitiae* ("pointer to justice") while Bonaventure has *iudex iustitiae* ("judge of justice").

[91] On p. 501 n. 4 QuarEd rightly notice that the Vulgate reads *facta sunt enim* ("For these things").

[92] Ex 12:46 deals with the paschal lamb: "In one house shall it be eaten. Neither shall you take its flesh forth from the house, nor shall you break a bone thereof."

55. (Verse 37). *And again another Scripture says: They will look upon him whom they have pierced.* Zechariah 12:10 reads: "They will look upon me, whom they have pierced." And therefore, it is true, because a soldier opened his side. This Scripture is not yet completely fulfilled, but will be on the day of judgment. Revelation 1:7 reads: "Every eye will see him, and they also who pierced him." Chrysostom comments: "Let no one be incredulous or look upon this with shame, for those things that seem to be the most ignominious are those that are the foundations of the goods we have."[93]

Questions

56. Question 1 focuses on John 19:28 where it says that Jesus asked for a drink "that the Scripture might be fulfilled." – The order involved here seems preposterous, since the Lord is not for the sake of the Law, but the Law and Scripture are for the sake of Christ, for "Christ is the end of the Law."[94] – It has to be maintained that the Latin *ut* ("that") is not to be interpreted to state the cause of an action, but to state its consequence. So it is not the sense that the Lord did this to fulfill the Scripture, but that this was a consequence of what the Lord did, namely, the fulfillment of the Scripture that had foretold this.

---

[93] Bonaventure paraphrases Homily 85 n. 3. See PG 59:463 and FC 41, p. 436: "Let no one, therefore, be incredulous; let no one cast aspersion on our words through shame. For the details which seem to be most ignominious of all are the ones that preach most eloquently of our blessings." Hugh of St. Cher, p. 394v,t quotes Chrysostom in words similar to those of Bonaventure: "So let no one be incredulous or look upon the things that are ours with shame, for those things that seem to be the most ignominious are those that are the foundations of the goods we have."

[94] See Rom 10:4.

57. Question 2 builds upon the first question and asks: Why it is said that the Lord consummated Scripture in taking a drink of vinegar rather than in doing something else? – And the answer is that the Lord had been suffering in all his members. He needed to suffer also in his mouth and tongue so that his suffering might be total. Therefore, when all his members were totally in pain, then it is said that his passion was consummated in a certain manner, and as a consequence Scripture too was consummated.

58. Question 3 continues the questioning about Jesus' drink: How is it that they immediately had the drink of vinegar ready? Did they know that he would ask for a drink? – In answer to this certain people say that they had taken wine along to drink, but that because of the heat it had turned to vinegar. – Others say that they had purposely taken vinegar along, so that he might die more quickly by drinking it.[95] – Others maintain that it was wine mixed with myrrh which was most bitter[96] and sharp as vinegar, to increase the torment of one already crucified, for they say that then too the Scripture was fulfilled: "They gave me gall for my food, and in my thirst they gave me vinegar to drink."[97]

---

[95] See Peter Comestor, *Historia scholastica* in Evangelia c. 177 in PL 198:1632D: "There were some who would say that those crucified would die more quickly if they drank vinegar mixed with gall, and that is why the soldiers took vinegar with them, so that they could more quickly be freed from guarding those they had crucified if they died sooner. It could also be that they took a cheap wine with them to drink, and that it had turned to vinegar because of the heat." Hugh of St. Cher, p. 394b cites this passage from Peter Comestor almost verbatim.

[96] See Book III, c. 11 n. 38 of Augustine, *Harmony of the Gospels* in NPNF1, Volume 6, p. 197: "And wine mingled with myrrh is remarkable for its bitterness. The fact may also be that gall and myrrh together made the wine exceedingly bitter."

[97] See Ps 68:22.

59. Question 4 asks about John 19:30: "He said: It is consummated, and bowing his head, he handed over his spirit." But Luke 23:46 says that he cried out: "Father, into your hands I commend my spirit." Matthew and Mark, however, state that he cried out with a loud voice: "Eli, Eli," etc.[98] – Now it is to be understood that he said all these words. First he said: "I thirst." Then, while they were preparing the vinegar, he cried out: "Eli." And at this cry the one who was preparing the drink hastened to bring the vinegar and present it. When the vinegar had been taken, he said: "It is consummated." And then bowing his head, he died with a loud cry, saying: "Into your hands," etc.[99]

60. Question 5 centers on John 19:34 and asks: Why was his side opened or wounded after his death and not before? – And it should be understood that nothing happened in his regard that God did not permit for a fitting reason. Now there is an allegorical and a literal reason for this. The allegorical reason is this: Just as Eve was formed from the side of Adam when he was asleep, so too the Church was formed from the side of Christ sleeping on the cross. For Augustine maintains: "Because of this the second Adam ... slept on the cross, so that from there his wife might be formed, that flowed from his side."[100] – The literal reason is this: The Lord Christ, even though he would manifest his humanity, wanted at the same time to show the truth of his Divinity. Therefore, he showed the former before his passion in his arrest and during the passion in the darkness. But he manifested his Divinity after his death through the flow of water and blood. Thus

---

[98] See Matt 27:46 and Mark 15:34.

[99] For this answer see Book III, c. 17-18, n. 54-55 of Augustine, *De consensu evangelistarum* in CSEL xliii, pp. 341-343.

[100] Bonaventure adapts Tractate 120 n. 2. See CCSL xxxvi, p. 661.

Ambrose comments: "Although the nature of the body of Christ was mortal, it was, nonetheless, ... dissimilar by grace. For the blood in our bodies congeals after death, but from this incorrupt ... body the life of all flowed forth. Water and blood came out. The former to cleanse, the latter to redeem. We drink our ransom, so that by drinking we may be redeemed."[101]

JOHN 19:38-42
BURIAL OF THE LORD

61. *Now after these things Joseph requested*, etc. Earlier passages dealt with the Lord's arrest, condemnation, and passion. Here in a fourth section the subject is *his embalming and burial* and is presented in the following sequence. First is *the taking down of the body from the cross*. Second is *the embalming of the one taken down* where verse 39 reads: "And Nicodemus also came." Third is *the placing of the embalmed one in the tomb* where verse 41 states: "Now in that place," etc. The first was done by Joseph. The second was done by Nicodemus. The third was done by both.

Verse 38. So Joseph took down the body of Jesus. And since he could not do this without permission, *he made his petition* and *obtained what he had petitioned* and *took down what he had obtained*. – He petitioned, because he was a disciple of Christ, although a secret one. Therefore, the text states: *After these things*, that is, after the consummation of the passion, *Joseph of Arimathea asked Pilate*. Arimathea is the same as Ramathaim, the village of Elkanah, Samuel, and Hannah. At its beginning

---

[101] Bonaventure adapts Book IV, c. 135 of Ambrose's Commentary on Mark. See CCSL xiv, p. 384.

1 Samuel speaks about it.[102] Now Joseph petitioned, *because he was a disciple of Jesus, but a secret one for fear of the Jews*, because, as it was said in John 9:22 above: "The Jews had already agreed that if anyone were to confess him to be the Christ, he should be put out of the synagogue." Even though he was a secret disciple, he was a true one, because he loved him not only when he was alive, but also when he was dead. Proverbs 17:17 reads: "The person who is a friend loves all the time." *He petitioned*, the text says, *that he might take away the body of Jesus*, that is, that he might take it down from the cross. And he obtained what he asked for, for the text continues: *And Pilate gave permission*, namely, so that he might be buried. *So he came and took away the body of Jesus*, namely, he came from the place where Pilate was to the cross and took him down.

62. (Verse 39). *Now Nicodemus also came*. This verse deals with the embalming with spices performed by Nicodemus and with Nicodemus' loving devotion in the preparation of many spices and in embalming the body. *Now Nicodemus also came*, namely, *who at first had come to Jesus at night*, as John 3:2 states. The text narrates this coming, in which the reason for coming is intimated, since he too was a disciple, although a secret one. *Bringing a mixture of myrrh and aloes*, that is, an ointment made from these, which would preserve the body from putrefaction. For he was not yet a believer in the resurrection, nor were the other disciples. Nevertheless, he loved much, for the text reads: *In weight about a hundred pounds*, for he still did

---

[102] The Glossa Interlinearis on Matt 27:57 says: "*From Arimathea*, which is Ramathaim, the city of Elchia (sic) and Samuel." Hugh of St. Cher, p. 395c says: "From Arimathea] which is Ramathaim, city of Elkanah, the father of Samuel. 1 Sam 1:1-3."

not understand what is said in Psalm 15:10: "Nor will you give your Holy One to see corruption."

63. (Verse 40). *So they took*. This verse addresses the devoted love of Nicodemus in embalming the body. *So they took*, namely, Nicodemus and Joseph, *the body of Jesus and wrapped it in linen clothes and spices*.[103] Supply: They had anointed. *After the Jewish custom of preparing for burial*, namely, in an honorable way. Genesis 50:2 states: "Joseph commanded his servants, the physicians, to embalm his father with spices." Chrysostom comments: "They buried him, not as one who had been condemned, but, as is the custom of the Jews, namely, with great honor, as someone great and admirable."[104]

64. (Verse 41). *Now in the place*. The third point surfaces here, namely, the placing of the body in the tomb. And the reason why it was put into this place is suggested as twofold, namely, the convenience of the place and the shortness of the time. Relative to the fittingness of the place, it was nearby and new. Thus the text states: *Now in this place where he was crucified there was a garden, and in the garden a new tomb*. And since it was new, *in which no one had yet been laid*.[105] And this tomb was fitting for the Lord, lest, once the resurrection took place, it be thought to be the resurrection of another person who had been placed with the Lord. Augustine observes: "As in the womb of the Virgin Mary no one had been conceived

---

[103] On p. 503 n. 2 QuarEd correctly mention that the Vulgate reads *cum aromatibus* ("with spices").

[104] See Homily 85 n. 3 in PG 59:464: "And he buried him, not as one who had been condemned, but, as was the custom of the Jews, to bury a great and admirable man." See Hugh of St. Cher, p. 395r who quotes Chrysostom in wording similar to that of Bonaventure.

[105] On p. 503 n. 4 QuarEd accurately say that the Vulgate has *positus erat* ("was laid") while Bonaventure has *positus fuerat* ("had been laid").

before him, no one after him, so in the tomb no one was buried before him, no one after him."[106]

65. (Verse 42). *So there because of the Preparation Day of the Jews*, and thus the festival day was imminent. Because of this day it was not permitted to carry the body far. *For the tomb was close at hand*, that is nearby, *they laid him*,[107] that is, Jesus. Augustine comments: "He wants it understood that the burial was hurried, that the evening might not come when because of the parasceve (which the Jews among us more commonly in Latin call 'the pure supper') it was no longer allowed to do any such thing."[108]

Questions

66. Question 1 asks why none of the Lord's disciples stepped forward to bury him. – If you say that they didn't dare for fear of the Jews, the objection is that Joseph had much more to fear. So he should have been more eager to abandon him. – I respond that the answer is both human and divine.[109] The human reason lies in this that although the disciples and Joseph feared the Jews, Joseph was a

---

[106] See Tractate 120 n. in CCSL xxxvi, p. 662 and FC 92, p. 53. With the exception of one word Bonaventure's citation is verbatim.

[107] On p. 503 n. 5 QuarEd rightly notice that the Vulgate reads *Iesum* ("Jesus").

[108] See Tractate 120 n. 5 in CCSL xxxvi, p. 663 and FC 92, p. 53. Bonaventure's quotation is verbatim.

[109] See Chrysostom, Homily 85 n. 3 in FC 41, p. 437: "If, indeed, someone should claim that it was because they feared the Jews, these men were just as likely to be hindered by that same fear.... It seems to me that Joseph was one of the most prominent Jews (and this is clear from the lavishness of the funeral). He was well known to Pilate and for this reason obtained the permission."

person of noble rank, as it is said in Mark 15:43.[110] And therefore, he was confident when he made his petition, because he was known to Pilate.[111] The divine reason is this: If the disciples had buried the body, the Jews would have had the probable argument that his body had been stolen afterwards.[112]

67. Question 2 asks whether Joseph's fear was good. – It seems that it was not, since preservation of his own life was more beloved than worldly scorn. So if he did not dare to confess the name of Christ because of fear, his fear was evil.[113] – But on the contrary, it is said in Luke 23:50: "He was a good and righteous man." – I answer that this fear was not evil, but stemmed from a certain natural weakness, by which a person fears shame. Nor was it sinful, since he was not afraid that he would deny Christ, as Peter did, but he was afraid to preach him publicly. And this obligation was not then one of necessity, but one of perfection. Ambrose observes: "Was it amazing that a righteous person was in hiding, when the Apostles, the teachers of the righteous, were also in hiding?"[114]

[110] Mark 15:43 reads: "Joseph of Arimathea, a councilor of high rank, came."

[111] Hugh of St. Cher, p. 395y has a long section on this question and concludes that both Joseph and Nicodemus "were rich and of high rank, as is obvious from the funeral, and known to and in the favor of Pilate – at least Joseph was."

[112] See Matt 27:64: "Give orders, therefore, that the tomb be guarded till the third day, or else his disciples may come and steal him away...."

[113] See Matt 10:32-33: "So everyone who acknowledges me before men and women, I too will acknowledge that person before my heavenly Father. But whoever disowns me before men and women, I, in turn, will disown that person before my heavenly Father."

[114] See Ambrose's commentary in Book X n. 138 on Luke 23:50 in CCSL xiv, p. 385. Bonaventure's citation is verbatim.

68. Question 3 makes inquiry about the loving devotion of Nicodemus. – For it seems that he sinned, for just as there is sin in hoarding, so is there sin in superfluous prodigality. But the piling up of ointments was superfluous, since there was no necessary benefit derived from it. Therefore, there was no need for so great an outlay. – I respond that the loving devotion of Nicodemus is to be praised. There was no squandering of goods here, but loving devotion, as it is said in John 12:3-6 above.[115] And since a person cannot serve the Divinity too much, so too no one can offer too much respect for the body of Christ, crucified for us. Therefore, even though this action would be superfluous relative to another individual, it was not with respect to this most holy body. – With respect to the objection that this ointment was not needed, it has to be maintained that he believed that it was needed.[116] And seen from this perspective, his action was not to be praised, for it was done out of ignorance. But seen from the perspective that he believed that the body was worthy of great honor and gave it such honor, his loving devotion is to be commended.

69. Question 4 focuses on the Lord. Since the Lord himself had to provide us with every form of perfection and he himself taught us in Matthew 8:22 to spurn burial,[117] it seems that by his being placed in a vile location he also

---

[115] Bonaventure alludes to Mary's anointing of Jesus' feet with ointment worth three hundred days of wages and Judas' objection to Mary's act of loving devotion.

[116] On p. 504 n. 1 QuarEd cite Blessed Albert's postill on John 19:39: "It should be said that this objection is impious, since the body is considered in a threefold way. That is, as equal to the sanctity of the soul and therefore honor is due it; and as ordained to the resurrection of glory, and therefore veneration is due it; and as divine, united to the Divinity, and therefore it is also due divine worship...."

[117] Matt 8:22 reads: "Follow me, and let the dead bury their own dead."

forced himself to be buried contemptuously just as he was forced to suffer in a vile manner. – I respond that it has to be maintained that burial is commended to us on account of faith in the resurrection, since we believe that although ashes have been scattered everywhere, they will be gathered into one by the Lord and will not escape the vastness of divine knowledge and power. But the burial of Christ occurred to strengthen the faith of our resurrection, for from our belief that our head was raised up, we also believe that we will be raised up. And so, in order for his resurrection to be certain, he had to be buried honorably in a public place and also guarded by soldiers to remove any suspicion. – So with respect to the objection that he had to give us an example that we should not be concerned about the vileness of burial, it has to be said that he had to give us an example of good behavior in such a way that he would not hinder our faith, so that humility and truth might be concurrent.[118] Nevertheless, he gave us a sufficient example that we should not be concerned about burial. For if, when he was alive, he was not concerned about punishments to and ignominious treatment of the body, he showed us after death that even less care should be taken of the vileness of a soul-less body.[119]

---

[118] Bonaventure's thought here is not clear. There are no interpretive parallels in Augustine, Rupert of Deutz or Hugh of St. Cher.

[119] Might Bonaventure be inveighing against expensive funerals? See Chrysostom, Homily 85 n. 5 in FC 41, p. 444: "What excuse shall we have if we richly adorn the body which is destined to be consumed by decay and worms, while we ignore Christ who is thirsty as he goes about, naked and friendless? Let us cease, then, from this senseless, exaggerated care of the dead…. Let us make payment in their behalf of generous alms; let us send with them the best traveling expenses."

Chapter Twenty

1. *Now on the first day of the week*, etc. Earlier the Evangelist dealt with the matters that pertained to the Lord's incarnation and passion. From this place to the end of the gospel he considers matters that concern his *resurrection*. So in this part he treats the manifestation of the resurrection of Christ. And since the solicitude of the disciples preceded this manifestation and our instruction or certitude in faith followed, there are three sections in this part. The first describes *the eagerness of the disciples and the women*, to whom he manifested himself. The second depicts *the manifestation itself* where John 20:10 reads: "So the disciples went away." The third describes *the confirmation of our faith* where John 21:24 states: "This is the disciple," etc.

John 20:1-9
Anxious care of the disciples and the women

The first section is further divided, for since the Lord had redeemed both sexes and wanted to manifest himself to both, the text not only addresses the eagerness of the men, but also of the women. So first comes the eagerness of *Mary*, then of *the disciples* where verse 3 says: "So Peter went out," etc.

2. (Verse 1). Mary's loving care is emphasized both by her *vigilant searching* and *diligent proclamation*. – Thus she was vigilant in *searching*, since she came at the very first light. Thus the text says: *Now on the first day of the week*, that is, Sunday, which is the first day, that is, the beginning of the week, which has seven days, according to what Luke 18:12 reads: "I fast twice a week." *The Sabbath* is even called the seventh day. Exodus 20:8 states: "Remember that you keep holy the Sabbath." *Mary Magdalene came early*, as one eager to see the Lord's body. And so she did not wait for broad daylight. And so the text adds: *While it was still dark, she came to the tomb*. Chrysostom comments: "Mary, who had the greatest affection towards the Master, since the Sabbath had passed, did not remain at rest. But she came at the crack of dawn to the tomb, wishing to find some consolation from the place."[1] And since she came *in the morning*, she found him. Proverbs 8:17 reads: "Those who vigilantly watch for me in the morning will find me." – *And she saw the stone*. Here is noted her diligence in *proclaiming*, because, having seen that the tomb was open, she related this to the disciples. Thus the text continues: *And she saw the stone rolled away*[2] *from the tomb*. This removal of the stone had been signified in Judges 16:3 where it is said that "Samson ... took both the doors of the gate with their posts and the

---

[1] See Sermon 85 n. 4 in PG 59:464. Bonaventure follows Chrysostom's gist, but uses different words. Hugh of St. Cher, p. 395c also cites Chrysostom and uses a text that is similar to Bonaventure's.

[2] On p. 505 n. 2 QuarEd rightly notice that the Vulgate reads *sublatum* ("taken away") while Bonaventure has *revolutum* ("rolled away").

bolt,[3] and laying them on his shoulders[4] carried them up to the top of the hill."

3. (Verse 2). *So she ran and came to Simon Peter*, who especially loved Christ among the others, *and to the other disciple, whom Jesus loved*,[5] that is, to John, who does not give his name out of humility. *And said to them: They have taken the Lord from the tomb.* The Greek texts add "my" to "Lord" to express affection.[6] *They have taken*, namely, some indefinite "they," either the Jews or the guards. *And I do not know[7] where they have laid him.* This was a cause of great sorrow for her, for since she still knew and loved him in a fleshly way, once his flesh had been removed, she had no consolation left.

4. (Verse 3). *So Simon Peter went out.* Notice is made here of the anxiety of *the disciples* both in haste with which they ran and in their curiosity in looking inside where verse 5 reads: "And stooping down." So they were anxious, since, once they heard that he had been taken away, they went running. Thus the text says: *So Simon Peter went out and the other disciple and they went to the tomb.* This has been said via anticipation, that is, they embarked on

---

[3] The Vulgate reads *sera* ("bolt") while Bonaventure has *seris* ("bolt").

[4] The Vulgate reads *humeris* ("shoulders") while Bonaventure has *humeris suis* ("his shoulders").

[5] On p. 505 n. 3 QuarEd accurately indicate that the Vulgate reads *amabat* ("loved") while Bonaventure has *diligebat* ("loved").

[6] It is the Greek of John 20:13, not 20:2 that has "my Lord." See Augustine Tractate 120 n. 6 in FC 92, pp. 53-54: "Some Greek codices also have 'They have taken my Lord' – that which can be seen to have been said from a quite well-disposed feeling of love or devoted service – but we have not found this in the several codices which we have at our disposal."

[7] On p. 505 n. 4 QuarEd correctly mention that the Vulgate reads *nescimus* ("we do not know") whilst Bonaventure has *nescio* ("I do not know").

a journey that brought them to the tomb.[8] And they went on the run. Thus the text continues:

5. (Verse 4). *The two were running together*, that is, rapidly. But they were not running at the same speed. Thus the text states: *And the other disciple ran on before, faster than Peter, and came ahead of him*[9] *to the tomb.* So they were running *quickly*, since they wanted to obtain the prize. 1 Corinthians 9:24 has: "Those who run in a race, all indeed run, but one receives the prize. So run so that you may obtain the prize." – Another interpretation is that since he was younger, he could run faster. Yet another interpretation is that he was more fervent in seeing while Peter was more diligent in considering. Therefore, there was a disparity on the level of diligence in considering. For:

6. (Verse 5). *And stooping down, he saw the linen clothes lying there, but he did not enter.* And so he was quicker in finding, but slower in considering. But Peter was the exact opposite. So the text continues:

7. (Verse 6). *But*[10] *Simon Peter came following him and went into the tomb*, not being content only to look in from the outside like John. And so Matthew 19:30 was verified: "The first will be last, and the last first." *And he saw the linen clothes lying there*, separately.

8. (Verse 7). *And the handkerchief, which had been about his face, not lying with the linen clothes*, as if this would

---

[8] See Augustine, Tractate 120 n. 7 about this narrative anticipation.

[9] On p. 505 n. 8 QuarEd rightly notice that the Vulgate reads *primus* ("first") whereas Bonaventure has *prior* ("ahead of him").

[10] On p. 505 n. 11 QuarEd accurately mention that the Vulgate reads *ergo* ("So") while Bonaventure has *autem* ("But").

have been done in a hurry, *but folded in a place by itself. Linen clothes* to cover the body. John 19:40 above reads: "They took the body of Jesus and wrapped it in linen clothes." *A handkerchief* to cover the face. John 11:44 above states: "And his face was tied up with a handkerchief." And so he had diligently inspected everything before John, who had arrived ahead of him, but came after him in diligence of consideration. So the text adds:

9. (Verse 8). *So then that other[11] disciple also entered, who came[12] to the tomb first*, that is, following Peter's example, *and saw* what had been foretold,[13] *and believed.* – But Chrysostom gives another interpretation and so does Augustine, for Chrysostom maintains that he believed that he had risen. And he argues from this that if anyone had taken the body away, he would not have left everything behind in such an orderly manner when these items were more useful than a body.[14] But Augustine gives another interpretation: He believed, namely, that the body had been taken away as the woman had said.[15] And he supports his exegesis from the following verse:

---

[11] The Vulgate does not read *alius* ("other").

[12] The Vulgate reads *venerat* ("had come") while Bonaventure has *venit* ("came").

[13] See Augustine, Tractate 120 n. 9 where he brings in Jesus' predictions of his passion and resurrection from the Synoptics to support his interpretation. See n. 15 below.

[14] See Homily 85 n. 4 in PG 59:465 and FC 41, p. 440: "But why in the world were the linen clothes lying there in one spot and the handkerchief folded up in another? That you might realize that it was not the work of men in haste or agitation to put the cloths in one place and the handkerchief in another, and to fold the latter. Because of this fact the Apostles believed in the Resurrection. That is why it was after this that Christ appeared to them, since they were now disposed to believe because of what they had seen."

[15] See Tractate 120 n. 9 in FC 92, pp. 54-55: "Here some, paying little attention, suppose that John believed this, that Jesus arose;

10. (Verse 9). *For as yet he did not understand*[16] *the scripture that he must rise from the dead.* Therefore, he did not believe that he had risen, but that he had been taken away. – Nevertheless, if we want to hold the position of Chrysostom that stresses verse 8, "he saw and believed," the meaning is this: At that time he first believed through what he had seen, since earlier he had not believed, "for as yet he did not understand the scripture."

QUESTIONS

11. Question 1 straightaway raises the issue: Since other women had come with the Magdalene to the tomb, why does John speak only of her? – Augustine responds in the third book of his *Harmony of the Gospels*: "Mary Magdalene was more ardent than the other women who had ministered to the Lord. For this reason John not unfittingly mentioned her by herself and kept quiet about the others who were with her, as others bear witness."[17]

12. Question 2 asks about John 20:1: "She came early to the tomb." – Contrary. It is said in Matthew 28:1: "In the evening they came to see the tomb."[18] – Augustine answers: "In the evening of the Sabbath means the same

---

but what follows does not indicate this.... And he believed what the woman had said, that he was taken from the sepulcher."

[16] On p. 506 n. 4 QuarEd correctly indicate that the Vulgate reads *nondum enim sciebant* ("For as yet they did not understand") while Bonaventure has *nondum enim sciebat* ("For as yet he did not understand").

[17] Bonaventure has adapted Book III, c. 24 n. 69 of *De consensus evangelistarum*. See CSEL xliii, p. 362. Hugh of St. Cher, p. 395a comments: "Mary Magdalen] who was more ardent than the others."

[18] Matt 28:1 says: "Now in the evening of the Sabbath as the first day of the week began to dawn, Mary Magdalen and the other Mary came to see the tomb."

as on the night of the Sabbath."[19] And it is proven by the next phrase that this is the way the text must be understood: "as the first day of the week began to dawn." Now this could not happen if we understand that it was only the beginning of the night. But "evening" is understood by synecdoche to mean "night," when light begins to dim.[20] – Others answer that this wording was used, since they prepared the evening before by purchasing spices, but came early in the morning, as John says.[21]

13. Question 3 is still concerned with John 20:1: Why is it said, "While it was still dark," when it is said in Mark 16:2: "When the sun has just risen"? – I answer by repeating what Augustine says in his book about *Harmony of the Gospels*. Mary came twice: First, before she called the disciples, and second when she returned again. And the first time she went it was still dark, but when she returned, the sun was shining.[22]

14. Question 4 continues to focus on John 20:1: "She saw the stone rolled away," etc. – Would not it have taken greater power to come out of a tomb that was shut by a stone? It seems that the answer is yes. – And it is to be said that the Lord rose, with the tomb shut tight, and that the tomb was opened afterwards by an angel. Chrysostom observes: "Indeed, Jesus rose, and the stone and the

---

[19] See Book III, c. 24 n. 65 in CSEL xliii, p. 355.

[20] Bonaventure adapts Augustine. See Book III, c. 24 n. 65 in CSEL xliii, pp. 355-356.

[21] See Bede's comment on Matt 28:1 in PL 92:127D-128A: "Indeed on the evening of the Sabbath they began to come, but when light dawned on the first day of the week they came to the tomb. That is, in the evening they prepared the spices, but brought what they had prepared to the tomb early in the day. These things Matthew, for the sake of brevity, expressed in an obscure way. However, the other evangelists more clearly showed the order in which things happened."

[22] See Book III, c. 24 n. 69.

seals[23] were lying aside.[24] Now since it was necessary for others to be informed, the tomb was opened after the resurrection, and so what had taken place was believed."[25]

15. Question 5 deals with John 20:3: Why did just this two run and not the others? – It has to be said that the answer is either because it was related to them only[26] or because, as Gregory states: "They ran ahead of the rest because they loved more than the rest."[27]

16. Question 6 has two parts. First, since Luke says in 24:12 of his gospel that Peter went to the tomb, he only mentions Peter. What is it that John says here that there were two who ran? Second, what need was there for John to mention himself here? It would seem better for him to have made no mention whatever. – Augustine answers in Book III of his *Harmony of the Gospels* that Luke singles out Peter, since the Magdalen gave him the news first.[28] Nonetheless, he also mentions both, since Cleophas said: "Some of our company went to the tomb," etc.[29] – Relative to the second question of why he mentions himself,

---

[23] See Matt 27:66: "So they went and made the tomb secure, sealing the stone, and setting the guard."

[24] On p. 506 n. 12 QuarEd indicate that Hugh of St. Cher and Thomas Aquinas read *iniacentibus*, that is, the stone and the seals were intact. Bonaventure's *iacentibus* ("were lying on the side") does not agree with the rest of his citation from Chrysostom.

[25] See Homily 85 n. 4 in PG 59:464: "For he rose, while both the stone and the seals were intact. Now since it was necessary that others be also informed, the tomb was opened after the resurrection, and so there was confirmation of what had happened."

[26] See Chrysostom, Homily 85 n. 4 in PG 59:465: "When she had come and said these things, they, having heard it, immediately ran to the tomb."

[27] See Homily 22 n. 2 of GGHG in CCSL cxli, p. 181. Bonaventure's citation is verbatim.

[28] See Book III, c. 25 n. 70.

[29] See Luke 24:24.

there is a twofold reason. The first reason stems from the literal sense, that is, for he wanted to elevate Peter above him, so that he might praise Peter and humble himself, because, even though he was the first to arrive, the one who came later entered the tomb.[30] – The second reason is allegorical, since the Jewish people are designated by John whereas the Gentile people are designated by the older Peter. John ran ahead, but did not enter, since the Jewish people received the Law first, but did not believe whereas the Gentile people, coming later, believed.[31]

JOHN 20:10-23
MANIFESTATION OF THE RESURRECTION

17. *So the disciples went away*[32] *to their home*. Earlier the text considered their anxious care. Here consideration is given to *the manifestation*. And since the manifestation was made to both sexes, this section is divided into two parts. So the first describes the manifestation made to a woman whereas the second depicts a manifestation made to the disciples where verse 19 reads: "So when it was late," etc.

---

[30] See Chrysostom, Homily 85 n. 4 in FC 41, p. 440: "Notice here, also, the humility of the Evangelist as he testified to the carefulness of Peter's examination of the tomb. For, though John had arrived there first and had seen the linen cloths lying there, he did not investigate any further, but stood aside."

[31] See Homily 22 n. 2-3 of GGHG in CCSL cxli, pp. 181-182.

[32] On p. 507 n. 6 QuarEd rightly notice that the Vulgate reads *iterum* ("again").

John 20:10-18
Manifestation made to a woman

The manifestation made to a *woman* is described in this order. First is the suggestion of Mary's *desolation*. Second is the depiction of the *consolation* offered to the desolate one where verse 11 reads: "So as she wept," etc. Third, *the manifestation of Christ* is offered to the one who doesn't want to be consoled where verse 14 states: "When she had said this, she turned around," etc. Fourth is the *command* given her to make the revelation public where verse 17 says: "Jesus said to her: Do not touch me." Fifth is the *relating* of the manifestation or apparition where verse 18 reads: "Mary Magdalene came."

18. (Verse 10). So the intense *desolation* of Mary did not permit her in her discomfort to leave the tomb, even though the other disciples had gone away. So the text states: *So the disciples went away to themselves,*[33] "that is, where they lived,"[34] before returning to the tomb to find some consolation.

19. (Verse 11). *Now Mary was standing outside the tomb,* "that is, before the stone tomb,"[35] and remained there with perseverance. Therefore, she found what she was looking for. Luke 11:8 says: "But if he perseveres in his knocking,[36] I tell you that, even if he would not get up to give to

---

[33] I have translated *semetipsos* by "to themselves," so that I can make Bonaventure's next point. The normal translation of *semetipsos* in this context is "to their home."

[34] See Augustine, Tractate 121 n. 1 in CCSL xxxvi, p. 664: "*id est, uti habitabant.*" The Latin word *uti* seems to be typographical mistake for *ubi* ("where").

[35] See Augustine, *De consensv evangelistarvm* in CSEL xliii, p. 363. Bonaventure's citation is verbatim.

[36] Bonaventure cites what is a variant reading of Luke 11:8a. See Vulgate, p. 1629 and note.

him because he is his friend, nonetheless he will get up and give to him as many loaves as he needs because of his persistence." Colossians 4:2 reads: "Be constant in prayer, be vigilant in it," etc. *Weeping.* Augustine comments: "The eyes that had searched for the Lord and had not found him, were now ready for tears, and the woman wept more that the Lord had been taken away from the tomb than that he had been killed on the wood of the cross."[37]

It should be noted that in Luke 7:38 Mary wept out of *compunction.*[38] She wept out of *compassion* where John 11:33 says: "Jesus, when he saw her weeping."[39] She wept out of *devoted love* as in this passage. About this Psalm 41:4 states: "My tears have been my bread day and night, while it was said to me daily: Where is your God?"

So, as she wept. Here *consolation is offered* the desolate one both through *sight* and through *speech.* Through *sight* she is consoled by seeing angels. Thus the text continues: *So as she wept,* as one desolate, *she stooped down and looked into the tomb,* so that she might at least get some small consolation from looking at the place. But she received great consolation. *She stooped down,* through humility. Job 22:29 reads: "The person who has been humbled will be in glory and the one who has bowed down his eyes will be saved." Thus:

20. (Verse 12). *And she saw two angels in white sitting. In white they were sitting,* because they had come to announce the splendor of our solemnity, that is, of the resur-

---

[37] See Augustine, Tractate 121 n. 1 in CCSL xxxvi, p. 664. The citation is virtually verbatim.

[38] I remind readers that nowhere in Luke 7:36-50 is the woman named.

[39] The "Mary" of the Martha-Mary-Lazarus story of John 11:1-44 is not called Mary Magdalene.

rection.[40] *One at the head and another*[41] *at the feet where the body of Jesus had been laid.* Gregory explains why they positioned themselves in this manner: "From his passion the message was to go out that he who was God before all ages is a human being at its end. An angel was sitting at the head, so to speak, when through the Apostle John it is proclaimed that 'in the beginning was the Word, etc.' And an angel is sitting at his feet, so to speak, when it is said: 'the Word became flesh.'"[42] And so there was consolation for her from what she saw. Luke 24:22-23 says: "Some women of our company, who were at the tomb before it was light, astounded us, and not finding his body, they came, saying that they had seen a vision of angels, who said that he was alive."

21. (Verse 13). Not only did the Lord console her through the vision of the angels, but also through the speech of the angels. So the text continues: *They said to her: Woman, why are you weeping?* as if they were saying: Don't weep, for now is not the time for weeping, but for rejoicing, since the Lord has risen. But she refused to be con-

---

[40] Bonaventure seems to be alluding to an interpretation found in Homily 21 n. 2 of GGHG. See CCSL cxli, p. 175 and Hurst, pp. 158-159: "The angel appeared clothed in a white robe to proclaim the joy of our festival day, since the whiteness of the garment declared the splendor of the solemnity.... Our Redeemer's resurrection was our festival day because it led us back to immortality, and also a festival day of the angels, because by recalling us to the things of heaven it completed their number."

[41] On p. 508 n. 2 QuarEd rightly notice that the Vulgate reads *unum* ("one") while Bonaventure has *alium* ("another").

[42] Bonaventure has adapted Homily 25 n. 3 of GGHG. See CCSL cxli, p. 208 and Hurst, pp. 190-191. One of Gregory's key points is: "In Latin the word 'angel' means 'messenger.'" The references are to John 1:1 and 1:14.

soled, as she recalled the reason for her grief. *Because*[43] *they have taken away my Lord*, that is, his body which is said by synecdoche. *And I do not know where they have laid him*. Augustine notes: "This was the greater cause for her grief, since she did not know where to go to express her sorrow."[44] Thus she could say with Psalm 76:3: "My soul refused to be consoled," etc. Lamentations 1:16 reads: "For this reason do I weep and tears[45] run down from my eyes, because my consoler, the relief of my soul, has left me."[46]

22. (Verse 14). *When they had said this*. Now Christ's manifestation takes place for the one who does not want to be consoled. And first he manifests himself to the senses of the flesh, then of the mind. To the senses of the body, namely, by sight through seeing and by hearing through conversation. – So she first saw Jesus. Thus the text states: *When they had said this*, through which she had shown that she would not be consoled, *she turned around and saw Jesus standing there*. So she turned around, since love did not allow her to stay in one place, but rather now she looked in one direction and then in another. Another interpretation is that of Chrysostom: "Christ, silently appearing behind her, startled the angels, and by their movements and signs they showed her that they had seen something great. And this turned the woman

---

[43] On p. 508 n. 4 QuarEd accurately indicate that the Vulgate reads *Dicit eis: Quia* ("She said to them: Because") while Bonaventure has simply *Quia* ("Because").

[44] See Tractate 121 n. 1 in CCSL xxxvi, p. 665. The quotation is verbatim.

[45] The Vulgate reads *aquam* ("water") while Bonaventure has *lacrymas* ("tears").

[46] The Vulgate reads *longe factus est a me* ("is far from me") whilst Bonaventure has *recessit a me* ("has left me").

around."[47] *And she saw Jesus*[48] with the eyes of her body, but not of her heart. Thus: *And she did not know that it was Jesus.*

23. (Verse 15). In this way he had manifested himself through sight. Now he also manifests himself through conversation. So the text states: *Jesus said to her: Woman, why are you weeping?* As if he were saying: Do not weep. *Whom are you seeking?* She was seeking him, whom the spouse of The Song of Songs 3:1 was also seeking: "In my bed at night I sought him whom my soul loved." As if he were saying: You must not seek him among the dead, since Romans 6:9 states: "Having risen from the dead, he dies now no more. Death will no longer have dominion over him." But she did not yet recognize him through their conversation together. So the text continues: *She, thinking that*[49] *he was the gardener,* because he had come so early to the garden, *said to him: Sir, if you have taken him away,* that is, Jesus. She had not made mention of Jesus himself, but when she spoke of him, she only said "him," since, as Gregory maintains: "The force of love customarily brings it about that a heart believes everyone else is aware of the one about whom it is always thinking."[50] *Tell me where you have laid him, and I will take him away.* Seeing was not sufficient for her; she had to take him away according to The Song of Songs 3:4: "I held him, will not let him go till I bring him into my mother's

---

[47] Bonaventure has adapted Homily 86 n. 1. See PG 59:468. Hugh of St. Cher, p. 396i also cites Chrysostom, but has a version that is different from both that of PG 59 and of Bonaventure.

[48] On p. 508 n. 8 QuarEd correctly mention that the Vulgate reads *Iesum stantem* ("Jesus standing").

[49] On p. 508 n. 10 QuarEd accurately notice that the Vulgate reads *quia* ("that") whereas Bonaventure has *quod* ("that").

[50] See Homily 25 n. 5 of GGHG in CCSL cxli, p. 210 and Hurst, p. 192. Bonaventure's citation is virtually verbatim.

house and into the chamber of the one who bore me."[51] So she wanted to take him away.

24. (Verse 16). *Jesus said to her*. Previously he had manifested himself to her via an exterior sense. Now he manifests himself interiorly by calling her by name. Thus: *Jesus said to her: Mary*. Gregory comments: "After he had called her by the common word for her sex and was unknown, he calls her by name, so that she might recognize him by whom she was recognized."[52] *She turned*, that is, through the captivity of her mind.[53] Revelation 1:12 reads: "I turned to see the voice that was speaking with me." *She said to him: Rabboni, that is interpreted Master.*[54] *She turned*, not by means of her body, since she was already turned in body, but by means of her heart. Wherefore, Augustine states: "Then, he says, having turned with her body, she supposed what was not, but now having turned with her heart, she recognized what was."[55] Now that she recognizes him, she calls him "Master," because that was her customary title for him. In John 11:28 above Martha says to Mary: "The Master is here and is calling you."[56]

25. (Verse 17). *Jesus said to her*. Here *a publication of the manifestation* is imposed on Mary who now recognizes Jesus. And first he corrects her, and secondly sends her to

---

[51] Cant 3:4 begins: "When I had gone by them a little, I found him whom my soul loves...."

[52] Bonaventure adapts Homily 25 n. 5 of GGHG. See CCSL cxli, p. 210.

[53] Bonaventure alludes to 2 Cor 10:5: "... bringing every mind into captivity to the obedience of Christ."

[54] On p. 509 n. 2 QuarEd rightly notice that the Vulgate reads *quod dicitur* ("that is to say") while Bonaventure has *quod interpretatur* ("that is interpreted").

[55] Bonaventure adapts Tractate 121 n. 2. See CCSL xxxvi, p. 665 and FC 92, p. 58.

[56] The Mary of John 11:28, however, is not Mary Magdalene.

make the announcement. And he provides the reason: "I have not yet ascended to my Father."

26. But this verse seems to smack of falsehood and doubt:[57] – 1. Since other evangelists say that "the women came up and embraced his feet."[58] – 2. Furthermore, what reason is this: "For I have not yet ascended to my Father"? Indeed, this is the reason why she should touch him, since, once he has ascended, it would be impossible to touch him.[59]

Because of these problems there are multiple interpretations of this verse. Augustine interprets the touch to be that of the heart or of faith. For he observes: "*Do not touch me,* that is, do not believe in me in such a way as you still perceive things.... For how was she not still believing in him in a carnal way, when she was weeping for him as a human being? And the following sentence says this: *For I have not yet ascended to my Father,* that is, to equality with the Father in your heart."[60] – According to Gregory the touch is understood as bodily, but the Lord does not prohibit this as Gregory says "because he shunned the touch of women, for it was written: 'The women came up and embraced his feet.'[61] But in this he wanted to show her that she would be unworthy to touch him unless she

---

[57] Bonaventure anticipates his *quaestiones* style. See n. 28 below.

[58] See Matt 28:9: "And behold, Jesus met them (the women) and said: Hail. And they came up and embraced his feet and worshipped him."

[59] See Augustine, Tractate 121 n. 3 in FC 92, p. 58: "What is this? If, standing on earth, he is not touched, how would he, sitting in heaven, be touched by men?"

[60] Bonaventure adapts Tractate 121 n. 3. See CCSL xxxvi, p. 666 and FC 92, p. 59. The last sentence from Augustine, paraphrased by Bonaventure, reads: "There you will touch me when you have believed that I am God not unequal with the Father." Hugh of St. Cher, p. 396v,bc provides this Augustinian interpretation.

[61] See Matt 28:9.

believed rightly or completely. And he demonstrates this by the following sentence: 'For I have not yet ascended to my Father.' Jesus ascends to the Father in our hearts when he is believed to be equal to the Father."[62] – According to Chrysostom it is understood as bodily touch. And the Lord did not forbid touching, but signaled that he was to be touched with reverence more than he was when he was capable of feeling. And the following sentence indicates this. The Lord says: "I have not yet ascended," but nevertheless, I am preparing myself to ascend, and therefore I am not among you as I was previously.[63] – This verse can also be explained in another way. Since Mary was burning in a special way to see the Lord and therefore sought him with the greatest love, she wanted to rain kisses on his feet and not to let him go. But the Lord admonished her, showing that here is not the place of eternal enjoyment and the touching of Christ, but with the Father. Therefore, he says: "Do not touch me," that is, by touching me you want to experience eternal enjoyment here. "For I have not yet ascended," where the place of eternal enjoyment is and where you will never be frustrated. But now there must be bodily separation.

But go and tell my brothers, that is, the Apostles, about whom Psalm 21:23 says: "I will declare your name to my

---

[62] Bonaventure adapts Homily 25 n. 5-6 of GGHG. See CCSL cxli, pp. 210-211.

[63] See Homily 86 n. 2 in PG 59:469 and FC 41, pp. 449-450: "It seems to me that she wished to enjoy His presence still, in the same way as before.... Thus, to lead her to abandon this notion and to refrain from addressing Him too familiarly ... He elevated her thoughts so that she would treat Him with a more reverential attitude.... By saying 'I have not yet ascended' He meant that He was going to do so without delay; and that, because He was on the point of departing and of ceasing to be among men any longer, she ought not to regard Him in the same way as before." Hugh of St. Cher, p. 396v,bc cites other interpretations of Chrysostom.

brothers. *In the midst of the church I will praise you."* *And say to them*, proclaim the reality of the risen Christ, which consists in the dignity of glorification, through which he was now fit to journey to heaven. So the text says: *Say to them: I ascend*. Ephesians 4:10 reads: "The one who descended is the one who[64] ascended above all the heavens." The reality of the resurrection also consists in the excellence of divinity. For the text reads: *To my Father and your Father*, but God is not my Father in the same sense that God is your Father. Thus Gregory observes: "My Father by nature, your Father by grace."[65] The reality of Christ's resurrection also consists in the excellence of humanity, and the text touches on this when it says: "My God and your God." Augustine notes: "'My God' under whom I also am a human being; 'your God' because between you and him I am the Mediator."[66]

27. (Verse 18). *So*[67] *Mary Magdalene came*. This verse presents the fifth point, that is, announcement of the manifestation made by the Magdalene. So the text continues: *Announced to the disciples: I have seen the Lord, and he said these things to me*. Supply: Which had been foretold. Chrysostom observes: "She announced both the vision and the words, so that they might be instructed by both."[68]

---

[64] The Vulgate reads *et* ("also").

[65] Bonaventure adapts Homily 25 n. 6 of GGHG. See CCSL cxli, p. 212.

[66] See Tractate 121 n. 3 in CCSL xxxvi, p. 667 and FC 92, p. 60. This quotation is verbatim.

[67] On p. 510 n. 4 QuarEd accurately indicate that the Vulgate does not have *ergo* ("So").

[68] See Homily 86 n. 2 in PG 59:470: "Now Mary announced both the vision and the words, which could console them."

QUESTIONS

28. Question 1 revolves around the order of this manifestation. – For if the disciples were more worthy, it would seem that the Lord should have appeared first to them, and then the disciples would teach the women rather than have the women teach the disciples. – I answer that it has to be maintained that this was done according to the order of divine dispensation and the merit of human loving care. For this reason Gregory comments: "Since in paradise woman had set death before man, woman announces from the tomb life to men, and she, who had proclaimed the words of the death-dealing serpent, proclaims the words of the one who gives life."[69] The merit of human loving care, because, while the disciples went away, the woman remained, in affliction and desolation. And therefore, she merited consolation and refreshment more quickly through an apparition of the Lord.

29. Question 2 asks: Since Peter loved the Lord so ardently, why didn't he remain at the tomb weeping like Mary, but left? – And Chrysostom responds: "In a certain way it is the nature of womankind to be compassionate." And therefore, do not wonder that Mary wept bitterly at the tomb, while Peter experienced no such compassion.[70] – Others find the reason on the level of faith, since the woman hoped less in the resurrection and therefore was more sorrowful about the removal of the body whereas

---

[69] See Homily 25 n. 6 of GGHG in CCSL cxli, p. 212. The citation is virtually verbatim.

[70] See Homily 86 n. 1 in PG 59:467: "Womankind is inclined to mercy. Now I say this lest you wonder why Mary weeps bitterly at the tomb while Peter does not do likewise." Hugh of St. Cher, p. 395v,a comments: "Chrysostom solves the problem in this way. This women stayed for a longer time weeping, for in a certain way womankind is more compassionate and more apt for an appearance."

Peter, even if not fully, nonetheless in some way had faith. For it is said in Luke 24:12: "He went away, wondering to himself."[71] – Some find the reason on the level of love, that is, at that time she was more fervent and burned more ardently with love than the disciples and thereby showed herself to be more caring.[72]

30. Question 3 focuses on John 20:11: "So, as she wept, she stooped down and looked into the tomb." – What was she looking at that led her to know that he was not there? – Gregory gives the answer: "For the person who loves one glance is not enough, because the power of love intensifies the need to search."[73] And Augustine observes: "Since she loved so intensely, she did not think it easy to believe her own eyes or those of others."[74]

31. Question 4 considers John 20:12: Mary Magdalene saw the angels after the disciples had departed. But it is said in Luke 24:4-12 that the women related to the apostles that they had seen angels, and then the text says

---

[71] See Chrysostom, Homily 86 n. 1 in PG 59:467 and FC 41, p. 446: "… while she remained standing there.' She did this because she was by nature very easily discouraged, and she did not yet understand clearly the doctrine of the Resurrection as the others did."

[72] See Homily 25 n. 1 of GGHG in CCSL cxli, p. 205 and Hurst, p. 188: "When even the disciples departed from the sepulcher, she did not depart. She sought for him whom she had not found, weeping as she searched. Being inflamed with the fire of her love, she burned with desire for him who she believed had been taken away. So it happened that she who stayed behind to seek him was the only one who saw him."

[73] See Homily 25 n. 2 of GGHG in CCSL, cxli, p. 205. The quotation is virtually verbatim.

[74] Bonaventure adapts Tractate 121 n. 1. See CCSL xxxvi, p. 664 and FC 92, p. 56: "Can it be that, because she was grieving exceedingly, she thought that ready belief ought not be given either her own or their eyes? Or rather was her decision to look produced in her mind by a divine impulse?"

that the disciples went to the tomb. – I respond that in the third book of his *Harmony of the Gospels* Augustine says: "Luke says this by way of recapitulation, for they ran to the tomb when the announcement was made that contained only the news that the body had been taken away. And after this there was a vision of angels that they subsequently related."[75]

32. Question 5 raises two doubts. First, because Mark 16:5 mentions only one angel: "On entering the tomb, they saw a young man sitting at the right side, clothed in white robes." Second, Mark 16:5 states that Mary entered the tomb[76] whereas John 20:11 that she looked into the tomb. – Augustine handles these doubts in Book III of his *Harmony of the Gospels*: "On the first day of the week, that is, the Lord's Day, the women went very early to the tomb, as all the evangelists narrate.... And when they saw that the stone had been removed and before they had more carefully investigated ... they ran and told Peter and John ... who ran to the tomb and ... afterwards returned home. Now Mary with the others was standing outside the tomb weeping, that is, before the place of the stone tomb, but nonetheless within that area that they had already entered. Then they saw the angel sitting on the right hand upon the stone that had been rolled back from the tomb. Matthew 28:2 and Mark 16:5 tell of this angel. Then he said to them: 'Do not be afraid,' etc., which is what Matthew and Mark have. At these words Mary, as she was weeping, stooped down and look into the tomb, which is what the passage under discussion in John says. There she saw two angels in white sitting there ... who

---

[75] Bonaventure greatly adapts Book III, c. 25 n. 70. See CSEL xliii, pp. 368-369.

[76] In Mark the women who enter the tomb are: Mary Magdalene, Mary the mother of James, and Salome.

said to her: Woman why are you crying? ... And thus it is to be understood that the angels got up and ... stood, as Luke 24:4 says: 'Two men stood by them in dazzling raiment.'"[77] – So the contradictions are solved in this wise, for what one says the other omits. And whereas Mark calls "the tomb" the space before the sepulcher that had been enclosed by a wall, John calls "the tomb" the very place where the body of Jesus was.

33. Question 6 raises the issue of why the Lord did not immediately manifest himself to a woman in his proper form, but was perceived as a gardener. – Gregory answers that the reason for this was in Mary's manner of searching, "for since she loved and doubted, she saw and did not recognize him."[78] – But Bernard gives the reason that this happened to further enkindle her heart. For he states: "O delightful spectacle of love! The one who is sought and desired conceals himself and then is manifested. He conceals himself, so that he may be sought with greater ardor, and once sought after, be found with joy, and once found, to be held with care, and once held, not to be let go."[79]

34. Question 7 asks whether Mary believed that Christ was God. – And it seems that she did, since Martha said in John 11:27 above: "You are the Christ, the Son of the living God." – And further, how would her sins have been

---

[77] Bonaventure greatly modifies Book III, c. 24. n. 69. See CSEL xliii, pp. 362-363.

[78] See Homily 25 n. 4 of GGHG in CCSL, cxli, p, 209. The citation is virtually identical. See Hurst, p. 192 for Gregory's next sentence: "Her love revealed him to her, and her doubt prevented her from knowing him."

[79] See Pseudo-Bernard, *Meditatio in passionem et resurrectionem Domini* in PL 184:766AB.

forgiven her if she didn't have right faith?[80] – But Gregory and Augustine seem to be against this viewpoint in their interpretations of John 20:17 above: "For I have not yet ascended to my Father."[81] – The answer must be given that before his passion Mary believed that Christ was God, but loved him very dearly in the flesh. And so during the passion she conceived so great a sorrow and was so immersed in it that she could think of nothing but his humanity and death and did not recall his works of Majesty, but only the pains he suffered in his humanity.

35. Question 8 inquires after the meaning of John 20:17: "I ascend to the Father," since the Father is everywhere. – The answer has to be that this is understood causally, since he was making or was about to make them believe that he was equal to the Father in all things. Therefore, the word "to ascend," is used, etc.[82] – Another interpretation is: To the place where the Father is greatly manifested through his works, for he is said "to sit at the right hand,"[83] that is, where the higher goods are.[84]

---

[80] Again Bonaventure mistakenly identifies Mary Magdalene with the unnamed sinner of Luke 7:36-50.

[81] See John 20:17 n. 26.

[82] See Book III, d. 22. dubium 4 in Bonaventure's *Sentence Commentary* in Omnia Opera 3:465: "Now with regard to the ascension into the heaven of the Trinity. And this ascension is not an ascension to a place, but rather to the dignity and equality of the Father. It is not about Christ's acquiring a new dignity, but deals with his revelation of what he possessed from eternity."

[83] See Ps 109:1 and Mark 16:19-20: "So then the Lord, after he had spoken to them, was taken up into heaven and sits at the right hand of God. But they went forth and preached everywhere, while the Lord worked with them and confirmed the preaching by the signs that followed."

[84] See Book III, d. 18. dubium 3 in Bonaventure's *Sentence Commentary* in Omnia Opera 3:395: "But now that exaltation has a twofold meaning relative to Christ: either according to reality or according to our understanding. The exaltation of Christ according to reality is the elevation of Christ from the status of present life to the right hand of

John 20:19-21:23
Manifestation of the Lord to the disciples

36. *So when it was late that same day*, etc. In the previous section the Evangelist treated the manifestation of the Lord made to the women. Here he considers the Lord's manifestation made to *the disciples*. And this section consists of three parts according to the three manifestations involved, which are different with regard to *the manner* of the manifestation and *the reason* for the manifestation. So with regard to the manner: the first deals with *sight*, the second with *touch*, the third with *taste*. For in the first the Lord manifests himself. In the second he reveals himself as touchable. Third he offers food. – With respect to *the reason* for the manifestation. The first is *to remove the disbelief of all the disciples*. The second is *to remove the disbelief of Thomas*. The third is *to confirm love in Peter*. The second manifestation commences in verse 26: "And after eight days." The third begins in John 21:1: "Afterwards he manifested himself."

John 20:19-25
The Lord's manifestation to all the disciples

In the first manifestation three matters are determined. The first is the manifestation itself. The second is the mission of the disciples subsequent to the manifestation

---

the Father, and this happened in the ascension. And this exaltation is fitting for him according to his human nature, which was elevated into heaven. And thus to be exalted to the right hand of the Father is to be elevated to the higher goods of the Father. The other way is exaltation according to our human understanding. And so Christ is said to be exalted in our hearts when we believe that he is equal to the Father. And thus to be exalted to the right hand of the Father is to be exalted to equality with the Father."

where verse 21 reads: "So he said to them again: Peace to you." The third is the occasion that led to another manifestation, namely, Thomas's absence, where verse 24 states: "Now Thomas," etc. – So the manifestation itself is described in this order, for there are components that make this manifestation clear, namely, the gathering of the disciples, Christ's apparition, the words of the one appearing, the showing of his hands and feet after he had spoken, the rejoicing of the disciples at the Lord showing his wounds.

37. (Verse 19). So the first point touched upon is the gathering of the disciples. This took place both on account of the time, because it was late, and on account of the Jews, who were persecuting them. So the text reads: *So when it was late that same day*, namely, the Lord's Day, on which he had appeared to the Magdalene, *the first day of the week*, because on those days the Jews rested and ate unleavened bread. *And the doors had been closed*, for their protection. Thus *where the disciples had gathered for fear of the Jews*. So they had gathered together in one place, and by this they were worthy that the Lord might appear to them, according to what Matthew 18:20 says: "Where two or three are gathered in my name, there I am in their midst."

38. When the situation was set up this way, the text says, *Jesus came and stood in the middle*. Here is the second point, namely, the apparition of the Lord. So "he stood in the middle," so that he might be seen by all. So "he stood in the middle," so that he might show himself to be the mediator and the reconciler. In John 1:26 it is said to the Jews: "But in the midst of you has stood one whom you do not know." For he, as it is said in Ephesians 2:14, "is our peace, who has made both one."

39. So the text continues: *And he said to them: Peace be to you*. Here the third point is noted, namely, his gracious words, through which he comforts them. Thus Luke 24:36 says: "He said to them: Peace be to you. It is I. Do not be afraid." So Chrysostom comments: "With his voice he strengthened their agitated minds, saying: *Peace be with you*, that is, do not be troubled."[85] Philippians 4:7 reads: "May the peace of God, that surpasses all understanding, guard your hearts."

40. (Verse 20). *And when he had said these things,*[86] *he showed them his hand and his side*. Here the fourth point is noted, namely, Christ's showing of his wounds, by which he shows not only in spirit, but also in body that he was the same one who had suffered. And so he showed them his hands and his side, where there were wounds, and scars had remained. Thus Luke 24:39 reads: "Look at my hands and my feet that it is I myself."

41. *So the disciples rejoiced at the sight of the Lord*. Here is the fifth point, namely, the rejoicing of the disciples at the sight of the Lord. The Lord had promised them this joy in John 16:22 above: "Again I will see you, and your hearts will rejoice."

42. (Verse 21). *So he said to them again*. The second major point surfaces here, namely, the sending of the disciples which is consequent to the Lord's manifestation. The Evangelist intimates three things here, which the Lord conferred on the disciples to be sent, namely, fitness, authority, and power. Fitness, since he gave them peace.

---

[85] See Homily 86 n. 2 in PG 59:170: "And at the same time he quieted their agitated thoughts with his voice, saying: *Peace be to you*, that it, do not be troubled."

[86] On p. 512 n. 8 QuarEd accurately indicate that the Vulgate reads *hoc* ("this") whilst Bonaventure has *haec* ("these things").

Thus the text states: *So he said to them again: Peace be to you*, that is, the tranquility without which no one is fit to be sent toward persecutions. Thus Chrysostom observes: "Since they would have an unconquerable battle with the Jews, he again says: *Peace be to you*, giving them a consolation equal to the battle."[87] – He also bestowed authority on them, as he sends them, for the text states: *As the Father has sent me, I also send you*, that is, as I did not come on the basis of my own authority, but was sent and so came with authority. So too I am sending you, giving you authority. For Romans 10:15 says: "How will they preach, unless they are sent?" For in Isaiah 6:8 Isaiah also asked for this authority when he said: "Behold, here I am, Lord,[88] send me." Against the evil prophets Jeremiah 23:21 reads: "They were running, and I did not send them. I did not speak to them," etc. – He also gave them power, when he conferred the Holy Spirit. For he also says:

43. (Verse 22). *When he had said these things, he breathed on them.*[89] Augustine writes: "Through his breathing on them he signified that the Holy Spirit is not of the Father alone, but also of him."[90] *And he said to them: Receive the Holy Spirit*, that is, the gift of the Holy Spirit, not with

---

[87] See Homily 86 n. 2 in PG 59:470 and FC 41, p. 452: "For, since they had to wage unending warfare against the Jews, he often repeated the words: 'Peace be to you,' to give them consolation proportionate to the strife." Hugh of St. Cher, p. 397d comments: "Chrysostom gives two reasons why he said: [Peace be to you]. The first is since they had to wage unending warfare against the Jews, he says not once, but twice: Peace be to you, giving them consolation in the face of the strife."

[88] The Vulgate does not read *Domine* ("Lord").

[89] On p. 513 n. 2 QuarEd correctly mention that the Vulgate does not read *in eos* ("on them").

[90] See Tractate 121 n. 4 in CCSL xxxvi, p. 667 and FC 92, p. 60: "By his breathing [on them] he signified that the Holy Spirit is not the Spirit of the Father alone but also of him."

respect to all things, but for the remission of sins. And through this he conferred the power of the keys. Therefore, the text continues:

44. (Verse 23). *Whose sins you shall forgive, they are forgiven them*, that is, whom you shall loose, they are loosed, *and whose sins you shall retain, they shall be retained*,[91] that is, whom you shall bind, they are bound. Matthew 16:19 says: "What you shall bind on earth shall also be bound in heaven, and whatever you shall loose on earth shall also[92] be loosed in heaven."

45. *Now Thomas, one of the Twelve.* The third point occurs here, namely, the occasion for the third manifestation which is depicted here from three aspects: Thomas's absence, the report of the disciples, and his stubbornness.

46. (Verse 24). Thomas's absence is touched upon: *Now Thomas, one of the Twelve*, that is, one of those specially elected. John 6:71 above states: "Have I not chosen you, the Twelve?" Luke 6:13 reads: "He chose Twelve ... whom he also named Apostles." *Who is called the Twin*, because he was in doubt,[93] *was not with them when Jesus came.*

---

[91] On p. 513 n. 3 QuarEd rightly notice that the Vulgate reads *retenta sunt* "(are retained)" whereas Bonaventure has *retenta erunt* ("shall be retained").

[92] The Vulgate does not read *et* ("also") which occurs twice in Bonaventure's citation: "also ... in heaven."

[93] In his commentary on John 11:16 n. 26 above Bonaventure writes: "So the text states: *So Thomas, who is called the Twin, said*, as if he had been in doubt for a long time: *Let us also go that we may die with him.*" On p. 513 n. 5 QuarEd cite Blessed Albert's commentary on John 20:24: "But Blessed Bernard says that the reason he did not see the Lord when he appeared to the others was that he was outside the community of the Saints. And these are his words: You are mistaken, Holy Thomas, if you think that you will find Jesus outside the community of the Saints...." See Bernard of Clairvaux, Sermon VI n. 13 "In Ascensione" in SBOp 5.158: "You are mistaken, Holy Thomas, you are

And so he did not see the Lord when he came, since he had departed from the community.

47. (Verse 25). *So the other disciples said to him.* Here is the second point, namely, the report of the disciples. For they relate what they had seen: *We have seen the Lord.* They were telling him this, so that once he had heard the testimony of those who had seen the Lord he would believe in the resurrection. But what happened was a verification of what is written in John 3:11 above: "We testify to what we have seen, but you do not accept our testimony."

48. So the third point follows, namely, Thomas's stubbornness. *But he said to them: Unless I see in his hands*, etc. Hardheartedness is shown in this that he did not believe through hearing. He will not believe unless he himself sees, namely, *the print of the nails in his hands.* He further shows his hardness in this that he refuses to believe not only through hearing, but also through sight, unless touch is involved. Therefore, the text continues: *And I put my finger into the place of the nails and put my hand into his side*, namely, which had been perforated by the lance, *I will not believe.* In saying this, he was obstinate. Thus Chrysostom maintains: "Just as it is a sign of a lazy mind to believe simply that something happened, so too it is a sign of a most thick mind to investigate a matter endlessly from all sides."[94] But this hardness in the Apostle was permitted by divine dispensation to remove our obstinacy. For Gregory observes: "Mary of Magdala, who be-

---

mistaken if you hope to see the Lord while you are separated from the college of the Apostles."

[94] Bonaventure adapts Homily 87 n. 1. See PG 59:473. Hugh of St. Cher, p. 397y also cites this passage from Chrysostom, but in the middle of his citation he quotes Sir 19:4: "The person who is hasty to believe is light of heart."

lieved quickly, is of less benefit to me than Thomas, who doubted for a long time. For when he touched the wounds in the flesh of the Master, he healed the wounds of disbelief in us."[95]

QUESTIONS

49. Question 1 asks about John 20:23: "Whose sins you shall forgive, they are forgiven them," etc. – Contrary 1. Isaiah 43:25 says: "I am, I am the one who blots out your iniquities for my own sake."[96] Therefore, it is solely the Lord's prerogative to forgive sins. – 2. Furthermore, Matthew 9:6 reads: "But that you may know that the Son of Man has power on earth to forgive sins, he said to the paralytic: Arise," etc. Therefore, to forgive sins and to heal the incurable belongs to the same power. But such healing pertains to divine power and to the Christ-man and God alone. Thus it is the same with regard to forgiving sins. So the question is raised: How are God, the Christ-man, and the priest different? – 3. Moreover, concerning the ending of John 20:23, "Whose sins you shall retain, they are retained," it would seem that priests can prevent us from entering the kingdom.

I answer that it has to be said that there are two things to be considered in the matter of sin, namely, guilt and the guilty state of punishment. To forgive guilt pertains to God only in an effective sense, because God alone gives grace, which removes guilt. To forgive guilt pertains to the Christ-man in a meritorious sense. To forgive guilt

---

[95] Bonaventure adapts Homily 29 n. 1 of GGHG. See CCSL cxli, p. 245.

[96] Hugh of St. Cher, p. 397m also cites Isa 43:25 as he addresses an aspect of this question.

pertains to the priest in a dispositive sense, since once he has conferred the Sacraments and disposed a person, God forgives.[97] – Now there is another forgiveness with regard to punishment, and over this the priest has power, and the Christ-man, once there has been forgiveness of guilt, but the power of the Christ-man is superior and universal whereas the power of the priest is ministerial and particular. And these powers are ordained, because the priest does not have effective power in forgiving punishment except through the passion of Christ nor again is the passion of Christ conferred on any person except upon him whom God forgives guilt.

3. With regard to the objection that our salvation is in the hand of a priest, it has to be maintained that this power is to be understood in accordance with the principle: the key does not err.[98] Now the key does err when the priest looses someone whom God has not vivified or when he binds someone to a lesser extent than he should be bound. Thus Gregory says: "The disciples loosed one … living, whom the Master had raised when he was dead. For if the disciples were to loose … a dead person, they would display a fetid odor rather than power."[99]

50. Question 2 concerns John 20:22: "Receive the Holy Spirit." – It seems that he should not yet be giving them the Holy Spirit, since it is said in John 16:7: "If I do not go,

---

[97] See Book IV d. 5. a. 3. q. 1-2 and d. 18. p.1. a.2.q. 1 of Bonaventure's *Sentence Commentary* for greater detail and clarity.

[98] In Latin the phrase is *clave non errante* and refers to Christ's giving to Peter the power of the keys in Matt 16:19.

[99] Bonaventure adapts Homily 26 n. 6 by dropping out the name of Lazarus. See GGHG in CCSL cxli, p. 223 and Hurst, p. 205: "The raising of a man who had been four days dead well illustrates this. It shows the Lord first calling forth the dead man and restoring him to life … and then the one who had come forth living was loosed by the disciples."

the Paraclete will not come to you." Therefore, if he had not yet ascended, he should not yet be giving the Holy Spirit. – I respond that it has to be said that the Holy Spirit is said to be received or to be given, not by reason of essence, but by reason of effect. So the disciples had the Holy Spirit before the passion, but for the work of their salvation which is by grace. They had the Holy Spirit after the passion, but before the ascension for the forgiveness of sins. They had the Holy Spirit after the ascension for the preaching of our faith. So they were confirmed when the Holy Spirit descended in tongues of fire.[100]

51. Question 3 asks further about John 20:22: "Receive the Holy Spirit." To whom is this said? It seems that it was said to many. – Contrary is what the Lord said to Peter in Matthew 16:19 has: "I will give you the keys of the kingdom of the heavens." Wherefore, it seems that the power of releasing sins was specially given to Peter, but here it seems that it was given to all. – And it has to be said that the power of forgiving and the power of loosing were given to all the Apostles. Nonetheless, the plenitude of power was given in a most special way to Peter and to his successors, as the leader and head of all the Apostles. So since he was the head, it is said in Matthew 16:9: "I will give you." Now since the others were participants in his power, it is said here: "Receive," etc.[101]

---

[100] See Bonaventure's commentary on John 7 n. 57 and John 14 n. 34 above.

[101] In question 4 a. 3 ad 5-6 of his *Quaestiones de perfectione evangelica* Bonaventure addresses a similar question. See Omnia Opera 5:196: "For it was said to Peter in a separate and singular way, since in him the plenitude of power was principally and singularly granted, but it was said to the others all together.... Wherefore, although they had similar power, they did not have equal power."

52. Question 4 finds another issue in John 20:22-23. Since the Lord spoke these words to the eleven only: "Receive the Holy Spirit, whose sins you shall forgive," etc., it seems that not all priests have this power, but only those who take the place of the Apostles, such as Bishops, and not simple priests. – Furthermore, Gregory seems to say: "Those who obtain the position of governing receive authority to loose and to bind."[102] – It has to be said to this problem that to bind and to loose have a twofold meaning: either in the penitential forum or in the judicial forum. The first manner is fitting for presbyters by reason of orders. The second manner is fitting for bishops and other superiors by reason of dignity. Thus Hugh of St. Victor says: "There is one binding by which the ministers of the Church truly bind penitents with the debt of satisfaction that is enjoined. There is another binding by which those who are intolerable transgressors are bound with the bond of anathema."[103]

53. Question 5 addresses the objection of the heretics[104] concerning John 20:22: "Receive the Holy Spirit" and John 20:23: "Whose sins you shall forgive," etc. They say that no priest has the power of binding and loosing unless he has the Holy Spirit dwelling within him. Therefore, bad priests do not absolve, and not even the Pope, if he is evil. But if this is the case, then our salvation is in danger.

To this problematic there are many answers. – For some say that first the Holy Spirit is given, and afterwards the exercise of the power of loosing, since loosing or forgiving only take place in the love of the Church. Wherefore, they

---

[102] Bonaventure adapts Homily 26 n. 5 of GGHG. See CCSL cxli, p. 222 and Hurst, p. 204.

[103] This reference is actually to Richard of St. Victor. Bonaventure adapts *De potestate ligandi et solvendi*, c. 9. See PL 196:1165D.

[104] Perhaps, Bonaventure refers to the Waldensians.

say that it is not necessary that the priest have love, but it is sufficient that love is at least present in the Church.[105] – Another answer is that to loose has two meanings: by merit and office and by office alone. With respect to loosing by merit or worthily, it is necessary that he have the Holy Spirit, but with regard to loosing by office it is not necessary that he have the Holy Spirit. So when the Lord first gave the Holy Spirit, this is that it may be exercised worthily, or to signify that without the grace of the Holy Spirit forgiveness of sins is not given. But it is not necessary that that grace be in the priest, but in the Sacraments.

Now there can be yet another answer: The Holy Spirit is said to be given when his gifts are given. So there are certain gifts that are from the Holy Sprit and with the Holy Spirit and never without the Holy Spirit, such as love. And there are other gifts that are from the Holy Spirit and never with the Holy Spirit such as servile fear. And there are other gifts that are also from the Holy Spirit and can be with the Holy Spirit and without the Holy Spirit, and such are the characters. And since the power of confecting and binding and loosing are such powers, they remain both in the just and in the unjust. And this

---

[105] On p. 515 n. 4 QuarEd cite Bl. Albert's postill on John 20:22. Albert takes the heretics to be Manichees: "To this problem Master Wilhelm answers that the preceding gift of the Holy Spirit does not signify the sanctity of the minister, through whose sanctity sins are forgiven, but rather the sanctity of the Church, whose minister the priest himself is, for it is only in the sanctity of the Church that sins are forgiven. And this solution is true. And so, when it is said 'Receive the Holy Spirit,' this is not said to those men as if they were singular individual men, but it is said to them, as ministers of the Church, who on behalf of the Church and not for their own sakes receive what they receive...."

was done by divine dispensation, so that the sin of the prelate may not be injurious to the subject.[106]

54. Question 6 looks at John 20:24: "Thomas ... was not with the disciples when Jesus came." Now it is said in Luke 24:33 about the two disciples journeying to Emmaus: "They returned to Jerusalem and found the Eleven gathered together." And while they were narrating what they had seen, the text says: "Jesus stood in their midst."[107] So if the Eleven could only be constituted by Thomas' presence, it seems that Thomas was present there at that time. – To this question Augustine responds in Book III of his *Harmony of the Gospels*: "It is to be understood, it says, that Thomas had gone out from there before the Lord had appeared to them as they spoke."[108] So it is true that those two disciples found Thomas, but while they were prolonging their story, Thomas went out, and the Lord came in.

JOHN 20:26-31
THE LORD'S SECOND MANIFESTATION IS TO THOMAS

55. *And after eight days.* This section is concerned with the Lord's second manifestation, one made to remove the disbelief of Thomas. Two things are noted in this section. First is *the manifestation*, and second is *the building up of faith* consequent to the manifestation where verse 28

---

[106] See Book III. d. 34. p. II. a. 1. q. 1. ad 1 of Bonaventure's *Sentence Commentary*.

[107] Luke 24:36.

[108] Bonaventure gives the gist of Book III, c. 25 n. 74. See CSEL xliii, p. 376 and NPNF1, Volume 6, p. 219: "... it admits of little doubt that we must suppose Thomas simply to have left the company before the Lord showed Himself to the brethren when they were talking in the terms noticed above."

reads: "Thomas answered." – In the manifestation a number of things are suggested to us, namely, the gathering together of the disciples, the apparition of the Lord, his words to them, and his offering of himself to be touched or his perfect openness to be touched by Thomas.

Verse 26. The gathering together of the disciples is touched upon when it is said: *After eight days*, namely, after the resurrection and the first apparition. *His disciples were again inside*, in the same house, quiet and away from the din. *And Thomas was with them*. And so, since they were together and were inside, they were disposed to see the Lord, according to what Matthew 18:20 says: "Where two or three are gathered together in my name, there am I in their midst."

56. *Jesus came, the doors being closed, and stood in their midst*. This is the second point, namely, the apparition of the Lord. So he came and stood in the middle of them, so that all would see him. *And he said to them:*[109] *Peace be to you*. Here is the third point, namely, the Lord's words. Through this manner of speaking he manifested himself, because he was accustomed to greet people in this way, by wishing them peace, and had taught his disciples to give this salutation. Matthew 10:12 reads: "Into whatever house you enter, first say: Peace be to this house."

57. (Verse 27). *Then he said to Thomas*. The fourth point occurs here, namely, the showing of his wounds to be touched. For since Thomas had said, "Unless I put my finger into the place of the nails," etc., the Lord said to him: *Bring here your finger and see my hands*. Since he had also said, "Unless I put my hand into his side," the

---

[109] On p. 516 n. 2 QuarEd rightly notice that the Vulgate does not read *eis* ("to them").

Lord said to him: *And bring your hand and put it into my side*. And since he had said: Unless I do this, "I will not believe," the Lord said: *And do not be unbelieving, but believing*. Through all this I have done everything to satisfy what you wanted. Thus Gregory observes: "It was done by divine dispensation, so that a chosen disciple would be absent at that time when the Lord appeared to the others. Now on coming later, he heard. Upon hearing, he doubted. In his doubting, he touched. Having touched, he believed."[110] Habakkuk 2:4 states: "Now the person who is unbelieving, his soul will be right in himself, but my just one lives by faith."[111]

58. *Thomas answered*. Here is noted the building up of faith that proceeds from the Lord's manifestation. Now our faith is built up in a threefold way from the divine manifestation: by presence or vision, by absence or hearing, by the testimony of the Scripture. So according to the first way faith is built up in Thomas, who believed. According to the second way faith is built up in others who had believed those telling about these matters. According to the third way faith is built up in those who were to believe the Scriptures. So first is the faith of Thomas who believes through a vision of the Lord. Second the faith of others who believe through hearing. Third is the faith of those who were to believe through the testimony of Scripture.

59. (Verse 28). So the faith of Thomas is shown and is intimated in his right confession, for the text states: *Thomas answered and said*, after so great a manifestation, *My*

---

[110] Bonaventure adapts Homily 26 n. 7 of GGHG. See CCSL cxli, p. 224 and Hurst, p. 206.

[111] I translate the Vulgate: "Behold, the person who is unbelieving will not have his soul right in himself, but the just person will live by his faith."

Lord, with regard to his humanity, *and My God* with respect to his divinity. For he is God, because he created. He is Lord, since he has made us his servants. 1 Peter 1:18-19 says: "You were redeemed not with perishable things, with gold or silver[112]... but with the precious blood of Christ Jesus,[113] as of a lamb without blemish and without spot."

60. (Verse 29). *Jesus said to him.* Here there is a commendation of the faith of those who have been built up through hearing. This faith is preferable to that of Thomas, which was through presence and vision. And so the text states: *Since you have seen me, Thomas, you have believed. Blessed are those who have not seen and have believed*, because such a faith was of greater freedom and involved more of the individual. Chrysostom comments: "When someone says: Now I would like to have been there at that time and to have seen the Lord working miracles, let him think of 'Blessed are those who have not seen and believed.'"[114] 1 Peter 1:8 reads: "Though you have not seen him, you love him. You believe in him whom you also do not see now."[115]

61. (Verse 30). *Many other signs.* This verse touches on the faith of those who believe through what is written in the Scripture of such manifestations. So the text says that manifestations of this kind have been written down to build up the faith of those who could not see them. And so not all things have been written down, but those

---

[112] I translate the Vulgate: "with silver or gold."

[113] The Vulgate does not read *Iesu* ("Jesus").

[114] See Homily 87 n. 1 in PG 59:474. Bonaventure's citation is virtually verbatim.

[115] Bonaventure adjusts 1 Peter 1:8: "Though you have not seen him, you love. In him, though you do not see him, yet believing, you exult with joy unspeakable and triumphant."

that are sufficient for our faith. Thus the text continues: *Many other signs Jesus also worked in the sight of the disciples,*[116] that were not written in this book, for it is not beneficial to us to narrate all things, but to build up faith. So he adds:

62. (Verse 31). *But these have been written, so that you may believe.* Romans 15:4 reads: "Whatever things have been written, have been written for our instruction." *That you may believe*, the text says, *that Jesus is the Son of God,*[117] that is, believe the humanity and divinity in Christ. Luke 1:31-32 states: "You will call his name Jesus. He will be great and will be called the Son of the Most High." 1 John 5:5 has: "Now who is there who overcomes the world, but the person who believes that Jesus is the Son of God?" And since there is no status in faith, it ordains its goal to this end: *And that believing, you may have life*, since, as it is said in Hebrews 11:6: "Without faith it is impossible to please God," but by believing you possess life. 1 Peter 1:8-9 reads: "In your believing, you will exult with an unspeakable and triumphant joy, receiving, as the final issue of your faith, the salvation of your souls." *In his name*, that is, in faith in his name. Acts 4:12 states: "There is no other name given to men and women under heaven, through which we must be saved." 1 John 5:13 reads: "These things I am writing to you that you may know that you have eternal life, you who believe in the name of the Son of God."

---

[116] On p. 516 n. 12 QuarEd correctly indicate that the Vulgate reads *discipulorum suorum* ("his disciples").

[117] On p. 516 n. 13 QuarEd accurately mention that the Vulgate reads *Iesus est Christus Filius Dei* ("Jesus is the Christ, the Son of God").

Questions

63. Question 1 inquires about John 20:26: "Jesus came while the doors were closed." – For if he came for the purpose that he make himself known to Thomas through touch, it seems that he was weakening this way of coming to faith which he was trying to inculcate. For, just as a spirit cannot be touched, so too something that can be touched cannot enter through closed doors. And therefore, the entire event could be seen as an illusion. – Some respond that Christ had to show not only that he had a body, in which he had suffered, but also a divine body, that is, one united to divinity. And in order to show that he was divine, he came when the doors were closed. Thus Augustine comments: "Where divinity was present, closed doors did not obstruct the mass of the body. Indeed he could enter even though they were not opened at whose birth the virginity of his mother remained inviolate."[118] – But others answer that he did not show by this that he had a divine body, but a glorious one, because he showed that his glorious state was not just his, but that of all glorified bodies. And the opinion of Augustine is to be interpreted as an argument from a minor premise, and this is how Gregory explains it: "What is wonderful if the one, who had come earlier ... when the womb of the Virgin was closed, should come now after his resurrection ... when the doors are closed?"[119] And such is the argument from

---

[118] See Tractate 121 n. 4 in CCSL xxxvi, p. 667 and FC 92, p. 60. The citation is virtually verbatim.

[119] Bonaventure abbreviates Homily 26 n. 1 of GGHG. See CCSL cxli, p. 218 and Hurst, p. 201: "The Lord's body which made its entrance to the disciples through closed doors was the same as that which issued before the eyes of men from the Virgin's closed womb at his birth. Is it surprising if he who was now going to live for ever made his entrance through closed doors after his resurrection, who on his coming in order to die made his appearance from the unopened womb of a virgin?"

the minor premise. So this should also supply the reason why he had to prove that it was the same body which he would also manifest as glorious.

64. Question 2 deals with John 20:27: "Bring here your finger ... and put your hand into my side."[120] – 1. From what this verse says it seems that the body of Christ was wounded. But if this is so, it was not glorious. – 2. Moreover, if you say that the scars remained, it seems that he did not have full glory where there would be complete healing and no vestige of imperfection would remain. Wherefore, it seems that the body of Christ was not completely glorified. – If you say that they had remained only for the disciples' sake, then it seems that they would not be genuine, but counterfeit scars.

Augustine answers in his writing *Six Questions Answered for Pagans*: "Let those who have proposed these questions know that Christ did not show wounds, but scars to his disciples.... These scars would then have been counterfeit if no wounds have occurred beforehand.... They are not marks of powerlessness, but have been left through divine dispensation and the art of the most skilled physician." Augustine gives the example of the soldier who has been wounded, but who does not want to be healed by a physician, so that the signs of his wounds might remain.[121] – Now as Victor states, there was a threefold rea-

---

[120] John 20:27 reads: "Then he said to Thomas: Bring here your finger and see my hands; and bring here your hand and put it into my side and be not unbelieving, but believing."

[121] Bonaventure has abbreviated q. 1 n. 7 of Letter 102 or *Sex quaestiones contra paganos expositae*. See *S. Avreli Avgvstini Hipponiensis Episcopi Epistvlae*. Edited by Al. Goldbacher. CSEL xxxiiii; Prague: Tempsky, 1891, pp. 550-551. See further *Saint Augustine Letters*, Volume II (83-130). Translated by Wilfrid Parsons. FC 18 (New York: Fathers of the Church, 1953), pp. 152-153: "Let the man who proposed these questions know that after His resurrection Christ showed

son why the scars were preserved: "So he preserved the scars from his wounds not because he was incapable of healing them, but that he might bear for eternity the triumph of his victory; also that he might bolster faith in his resurrection since he was demonstrating that the same body that had died had been raised; and that he might indicate, by clear and manifest signs of the same death, to those redeemed by his death with what great mercy they had been aided."[122] A fourth reason could be ventured: For the shame of the damned, for Revelation 1:7 states: "And every eye will see him and they who pierced him."[123]

65. Question 3 addresses John 20:27: "And put your hand into my side," etc. – Therefore, the body of Christ was touchable, but, as Gregory says: "Whatever is touch-

---

scars, not wounds, as a proof to doubters.... He willed to show to those whom He was strengthening in unfeigned faith that it was not another body, but the same one which they had seen crucified, that had risen again.... If some brave man, fighting for his country and receiving many deep wounds, should tell a very skilled doctor, who could cure them so completely that no scars remained, that he preferred to be cured so as to leave the traces of his wounds as badges of honor, would you say that the doctor had counterfeited the scars because he used his skill – for a good reason – to leave them, although he could have used it to obliterate them? As I said above, they could only be proved counterfeit scars if there had been no wounds to heal."

[122] This citation is from Bishop Victor of Capua. See the previous note on Augustine and how some of his reasons overlap with those of Victor. See Sermon 242 n. 3 in *Sermons*. Translated by Edmund Hill. WSA III/7 (Hyde Park, NY: New City Press, 1993), p. 79: "And we're asked, 'So why did the Lord rise again with the scars of his wounds?' What are we to say to this, but that this too was a matter of power, not of need? He wished to rise like that, he wished to present himself like that to some people who had doubts. The scars of the wounds in that flesh healed the wounds of unbelief."

[123] The four reasons that Bonaventure adduces are found almost verbatim in the Glossa Ordinaria on Luke 24:40 without attribution to Bishop Victor. See PL 114:353D-354A

able is corruptible."[124] Wherefore, that body was corruptible. – If you say, as Chrysostom does, "this happened by way of condescension,"[125] then it is objected that if to be touched is contrary to the nature of a glorified body, then it is manifest in this that he did not show that he had a glorified body, but rather a non-glorified one.

And it may be answered that this reasoning is not valid, because by entering while the doors were closed he manifested his glorious body, but by being touched he showed that it was the same body that had suffered. – Now the answer can be given in another way. Just as something is visible in a twofold way: in first way, once the object is seen it cannot be hidden. That is the case with a rock. In the second way since it can be hidden, it can also change. The first way is in a certain sense the way of weakness and is not in the glorious body. The second way is that of strength and is in the glorious body. It is the same way with touch, for since what has been touched cannot escape and since this stems from weakness in a certain way, it does not belong to the glorified body. But to be touched, since it limits the thrust of the hand on something solid, although it could penetrate that very hand by its own power, this is an action of great strength. And this was in the glorious body, and especially in the body of Christ.[126]

---

[124] Bonaventure paraphrases Homily 26 n. 1 of GGHG. See CCSL xxxvi, p. 219 and Hurst, p. 201: "It cannot be otherwise then that what is touched is corruptible, and what is not corruptible cannot be touched."

[125] Bonaventure gives the gist of Homily 87 n. 1. See PG 59:474 and FC 41, p. 460: "But, one might understandably be puzzled as to how an incorruptible body could show marks of the nails and be capable of being touched by a mortal hand. However, do not be disturbed, for the phenomenon was an evidence of Christ's condescension."

[126] See Book IV d. 49 p. II, sect. 2. a. 3. q. 2 of Bonaventure's *Sentence Commentary* in Omnia Opera 4:1020-1021 where he discusses the sensory capacities of the glorified body. It must be confessed that

66. Question 4.asks about John 20:27: "Be not unbelieving, but believing." – Gregory raises this objection: "When Paul says in Hebrews 11:1, 'faith is the evidence of things not seen,' it is faith in those things that cannot be seen. For the things that are seen do not require faith, but recognition. Therefore, when Thomas saw the Lord, he did not yet have faith, but recognition."[127] – Gregory and Augustine[128] answer: "He saw one thing; he confessed another. He saw a human being and professed him to be God, for he said: 'My Lord and my God.'"[129]

67. But then it is objected: 1. Since he at the very least saw the one whom he had previously seen as dead, he knew about the resurrection, but did not believe. 2. Likewise, Thomas would not believe unless he saw. Therefore, "human reason provided the proof for his faith." So "his faith did not have merit."[130]

Bonaventure's thought in this question is dense. Does John actually say that Thomas touched the body of the risen Lord? See Glenn W. Most, *Doubting Thomas* (Cambridge: Harvard University Press, 2005), esp. p. 141.

[127] Bonaventure adapts Homily 26 n. 8 of GGHG. See CCSL cxli, pp. 224-225 and Hurst, p. 207: "When the apostle Paul says that *faith is the ground of things to be hoped for, the proof of things that are not evident*, it is clear that faith is the proof of those things which cannot be made evident: things that are evident no longer involve faith but recognition. Why then, when Thomas saw, when he touched, was it said to him: '*Because you have seen me, you have believed?*' He saw one thing, and he believed another. Divinity could not be seen by a mortal person. He saw a human being, and he confessed him as God, saying: '*My Lord and my God.*'"

[128] See Tractate 121 n. 5 in CCSL xxxvi, p. 667: "He saw and touched a human being and confessed the God whom he did not see or touch. Through what he saw and touched, once his doubt had now been removed, he believed...."

[129] The quotation is from Homily 26 n. 8 of GGHG. See CCSL cxli, p. 219 and the previous note.

[130] Bonaventure adapts Homily 26 n. 1 of GGHG. See CCSL cxli, p. 218 and Hurst, pp. 200-201: "But we must be certain that if a divine

I answer that it has to be maintained that since the Apostles knew about the mocking schemes of the demons, they could consider all that Christ was doing to be the work of some spirit in an assumed body. And so it was that some were still in doubt. And therefore, I say that through Thomas's seeing there was no certain knowledge nor did these manifestations produce cogent reasons that would take away the merit of faith. Rather these manifestations were only leading them to the gate of faith as they helped the weak soul that was not yet firm in faith.

68. Question 5 focuses on John 20:29: "Thomas, because you have seen me, you have believed." – It seems that he should have said: Because you have touched me, since it had not been sufficient for him to see. – To this Augustine gives a twofold response: Either "seeing" is understood to include touch, for "seeing" is the more common sense or Thomas did not dare to touch. So Augustine comments: "He did not say 'you have touched me,' but 'you have seen me,' since in a certain way seeing is the general sense.... Though it can be said that the disciple did not dare to touch."[131]

---

work is understood by reason it is not wonderful, nor does our faith have any merit when human reason provides a proof."

[131] Bonaventure abbreviates Tractate 121 n. 5. See CCSL xxxvi, pp. 667-668 and FC 92, p. 61. Hugh of St. Cher, p. 397v,m cites this passage from Augustine in almost the same abbreviated way that Bonaventure does. See also Most, *Doubting Thomas*, pp. 122-154, esp. p. 139.

CHAPTER TWENTY-ONE

1. *After these things Jesus manifested*, etc. This section deals with the third manifestation that was made *to confirm Peter*. It is divided into two parts, the first of which considers *the manifestation* while the second focuses on *Peter's confirmation* where verse 15 says: "So when they had breakfasted," etc.

JOHN 21:1-14
THE MANIFESTATION ITSELF

In the first part there are two components, since it is necessary to set the scene of the manifestation by describing the circumstances. So first the Evangelist treats these, and then in the second place he deals with the manifestation itself where verse 4 reads: "But when day was breaking," etc.

JOHN 21:1-8
MANIFESTATION OF HIS DIVINITY
BY A WONDROUS CATCH OF FISH

2. (Verse 1). The circumstances surrounding the manifestation are the place in which he was manifested, the

people to whom he was manifested, and the action or business the persons were engaged in.[1] – So first is the description of the place, in which this manifestation took place. The text says: *After these things Jesus manifested himself again, at the Sea of Tiberias.* Relative to place: "The Sea of Tiberias is the same as Lake Gennesareth and the Sea of Galilee."[2] It was also called the Sea of Tiberias, because this city was situated near this sea. It was also called Sea of Galilee from the region in which it was located. It is called Lake Gennesareth because of the natural properties of the lake itself. Thus it is called Gennesareth or generating breezes.[3] – *Now he manifested himself in this way.* The text now considers the persons to whom he is manifested and says:

3. (Verse 2). *There were together Simon Peter and Thomas, called the Twin, and Nathanael, from Cana in Galilee, and the sons of Zebedee, and two others of his disciples.* And so there were seven persons, since such a number is fitting and sufficient for every kind of testimony. And in this the sevenfold gift of the Holy Spirit is commended, which should be in those who go about fishing, that is, gathering in people for God.[4] About this sevenfold it is said in Isaiah 4:1: "Seven women will take hold of one

---

[1] On p. 519 n. 3 QuarEd cite Cicero's teaching that there are two types of circumstances: those of persons and those of the actions or the business the persons are engaged in.

[2] Bonaventure is quoting the Glossa Interlinearis.

[3] See Bonaventure's commentary on Luke 5:1 (n. 3) in *Bonaventure on Luke 1- 8*, p. 380: "And because there are waves and breezes come up there, it is therefore called *Lake Gennesaret*, that is, generating breezes." This interpretation ultimately goes back to Bede's commentary on Luke 5:1. See CCSL cxx, p. 113. Hugh of St. Cher, p. 398b has a very similar explanation of Sea of Tiberias, Sea of Galilee, and Lake Gennesareth.

[4] See Homily 24 n. 6 of GGHG in Hurst, p. 184: "We must also note that the Lord is described as having had his final banquet with seven disciples.... Why did he do this if not to declare that only those filled

man" – without these women there is no spiritual propagation – and Isaiah 11:2-3: "The spirit of the Lord will rest upon him, the spirit of wisdom and of understanding, the spirit of counsel and fortitude, the spirit of knowledge and piety, and he will be filled with the spirit of the fear of the Lord."

4. (Verse 3). *Simon Peter said to them*. Here is the action or task that offers the occasion for the manifestation. And this was the act of fishing for which all have gathered together. But Peter was the principal actor, since this manifestation occurred specially for him. Thus the text continues: *Peter said to them: I am going fishing*, as the leader, since he was a fisherman. Matthew 4:18 states: "As Jesus was walking by the sea of Galilee, he saw two brothers, Simon, who is called Peter, and his brother, Andrew, casting a net into the sea, for they were fishermen." And others joined. Thus the text says: *They said to him: We also are going with you. And*, in agreement with one another, *they went out and boarded the boat*,[5] so that they might fish. *And during that night*[6] *they caught nothing*, and so they had labored in vain. Luke 5:5 states: "Master, the whole night we have labored and have caught nothing." Gregory observes: "The disciples had great difficulty in their fishing, in order that, when their master came, great glory and triumph might be his."[7]

---

with the sevenfold grace of the Holy Spirit would be with him at his eternal meal?"

[5] On p. 519 n. 8 QuarEd rightly notice that the Vulgate reads *ascenderunt in navim* ("got into the boat").

[6] On p. 519 n. 8 QuarEd correctly indicate that the Vulgate reads *illa nocte* ("that night") while Bonaventure has *in illa nocte* ("during that night").

[7] This is a verbatim citation from Homily 24 n. 3 of GGHG. See CCSL cxli, p. 198 and Hurst, p. 181.

5. (Verse 4). *But when day was breaking.* Now the Evangelist describes the Lord's manifestation in two parts. First the manifestation itself is depicted. Then it is compared to the previous manifestations where verse 14 reads: "This is now the third time," etc. – In the manifestation itself he manifests himself twice. First with regard to his divine nature by working the miracle. Second with respect to his human nature by eating. So there are two smaller sections here. In the first the manifestation made by the catch of fish is described. In the second there is the manifestation of eating where verse 9 says: "So when they had landed," etc. – So the manifestation relative to the miraculous catch of fish is depicted in this order. First the apparition of Christ is noted. Second, what he says. Third, the miraculous catch of fish. Fourth, recognition of the Lord. Fifth, Peter's fervent love.

6. So the apparition of the Lord is touched upon when it is said: *But when day was breaking, Jesus stood on the shore.* According to the literal sense "when day was breaking, he was standing," for they could not see him at night. According to the spiritual understanding, "the breaking of day" signifies the time of grace, during which Christ has appeared. Romans 13:12 reads: "The night is far advanced. The day is at hand. Therefore, let us lay aside the works of darkness and put on the armor of light." And although he appeared, nevertheless, the disciples did not recognize him. Thus the text continues: *Yet the disciples did not know that it was Jesus.* Chrysostom comments: "He did not manifest himself to them right away, so that through the miracle he was able to perform they might recognize him."[8]

---

[8] This is a paraphrase of Homily 87 n. 2. See PG 59:475 and FC 41, p. 463: "When they were weary and discouraged, then Jesus appeared to them, yet refrained from making His identity clear at once, so that

7. (Verse 5). *So Jesus said to them.* Here the second point occurs, namely, the Lord's address. And he asks them the reason behind their great effort: *Children, have you anything to eat?* The Latin, *pulmentarium* ("anything to eat") refers here to everything by which bread is enhanced, whether this is fish or anything else. It is what we commonly call *pulmentum* ("pottage"). It is as if the Lord is asking them whether they have fish or have caught fish, from which they could enhance and flavor their food, so that the bread, flavored by this *pulmentarium,* might taste better.[9] But *they answered him: No*, as if they were saying: We are still at work, for we have not yet caught anything.

8. (Verse 6). *He said*[10] *to them: Cast the net to the right of the boat, and you will find.* Here the third point is noted, namely, the wonderful catch of fish. And it was wonderful, since, although they could catch nothing, they caught so many by obeying the divine command. So the text states: *So they cast their net,*[11] at the command of the Lord, *and now they were unable to draw it up on account of the great number of fish*. Something similar happened in Luke 5:6: "When they had done so, they caught[12] a huge number of fish." And so this results in a huge catch, so that divine largess might be shown, which according to James 1:5, "gives abundantly to all and does not reprove."

He might enter into conversation with them...." Hugh of St. Cher, p. 398k also cites part of Homily 87 n. 2.

[9] Hugh of St. Cher, p. 398m explains *pulmentarium* much the same way.

[10] On p. 520 n. 7 QuarEd correctly indicate that the Vulgate reads *dicit* ("he said") whereas Bonaventure has *dixit* ("he said").

[11] On p. 520 n. 8 QuarEd accurately mention that the Vulgate does not read *rete* ("net").

[12] The Vulgate reads *concluserunt* ("enclosed") while Bonaventure has *comprehenderunt* ("caught").

9. (Verse 7). *So the disciple said*, etc. This verse contains the fourth point, namely, John's recognition of the Lord. Thus: *So the disciple, whom Jesus loved*, that is, John, *said to Peter: It is the Lord.* So he calls him "Lord," since he had shown himself to be powerful, and the one whom all things obey, even fish. And therefore, he is to be feared, according to what Malachi 1:6 states: "If I am the Lord, where is my fear?" For the disciples called him Lord. John 13:13 above reads: "You call me Master and Lord."

10. *So*[13] *Simon Peter*. This verse surfaces the fifth point, namely, Peter's fervent love, which shows itself in that he could not contain himself, but had to act immediately. And so the text continues: *But Simon Peter, when he had heard that it was the Lord, girt his tunic about him*, lest he appear naked before the Lord, *for he was naked, and threw himself into the sea*, namely, to swim.[14] He did something similar in Matthew 14:28: "Lord, if it is you, command me to come to you over the water."

11. (Verse 8). *But the other disciples came with the boat.* Since they were not so fervent, they did not dare to cast themselves into the sea. Wisdom 14:5 says: "Men and women entrust their lives to a little wood," etc.[15] And there is another reason: *For they were not far from land*, and therefore could quickly get there, *but about two hundred cubits off, dragging the net full of fish.*

---

[13] On p. 520 n. 11 QuarEd rightly notice that the Vulgate does not read *ergo* ("So").

[14] See Chrysostom, Homily 87 n. 2 in FC 41, p. 463: "As soon as Peter recognized Him, then, he cast everything aside – fish and nets – and girded himself. Do you see both his respect and his love? Even though they were only two hundred cubits away, he did not even wait for the boat to get to Him, but came to Him, swimming."

[15] Wis 14:5 says: "... men and women also entrust their lives to a little wood, and passing over the sea by ship are saved."

12. The spiritual understanding is this. Fishing through-out the night, the fishermen catch nothing. But when it is morning, Jesus appeared, and they filled their nets. And being a distance of two hundred cubits from shore, they hauled in their nets. – The fishers are the preachers. Jeremiah 16:16 states: "Behold, I will send many fishers ... and they will fish them." And Matthew 4:19 reads: "Come after me, and I will make you fishers of human beings." – Night time is the time of the Law on account of the shadow of the letters of the figures of the Law. Hebrews 10:1 says: "The Law, having but a shadow of the good things to come, not the exact image of the objects." – When it was morning is the time of grace when Christ appeared. 2 Corinthians 3:15-18 states: "Down to today ... the veil is over their hearts...."[16] But we ... with faces unveiled, reflecting as in a mirror the glory of the Lord, are being transformed into his very image, from glory to glory, as through the Spirit of the Lord." – Then the nets are filled, since after the coming of Christ in the flesh truth is revealed, and fish are caught in the net of the Church. For this reason the Lord said in John 12:32 above: "If I am lifted up from the earth, I will draw all things to myself." – These fish, namely, the faithful, the preachers draw, for through their good example they lead them to life. About the manner of drawing them it is said in The Song of Songs 1:3: "Draw me after you. We will run in the odor of your ointment." – And the words, two hundred cubits away, refer to the double perfection that should be in the preacher, namely of life and of teaching. About these Matthew 5:19 states: "Whoever does and teaches them to

---

[16] 2 Cor 3:15 reads: "Yes, down to this very day, when Moses is read, the veil covers their hearts."

men and women[17] will be called great in the kingdom of the heavens."[18]

Questions

13. Question 1 addresses John 21:1: Since Lake Gennesareth has sweet water and is tiny in comparison with a sea, why does the Evangelist call it a sea? – It is to be said that this was done in accordance with the custom of the Jews who call a great gathering together of waters a sea, according to what Genesis 1:10 has: "And the gathering together of the waters he called seas."

14. Question 2 raises the objection that since it is written in Luke 9:62, "No one who puts his hand to the plow and turns back is fit for the kingdom of God," why is it that Peter, who had abandoned his nets, again returns to fishing? – Gregory responds: "After his conversion it was no sin to return to his occupation that had no sin attached to it before his conversion."[19] Thus Augustine comments: "It has to be understood that the disciples were not forbidden to seek necessary subsistence by their art, a licit and

---

[17] The Vulgate does not read *homines* ("men and women").

[18] See Theophylactus's commentary on John 21:9-14 in PG 124:307B: "Understand the things that have been said above by means of allegory. For the night was the time when the darkness of idolatry ruled, before the coming of Christ the sun, when the prophets labored and caught nothing.... But when the dawn of the sun of justice shone and the apostolic net was cast forth on the right side of teaching for which the Law and the prophets had prepared ... then the net is hauled in and not only Gentiles, whom we count as a hundred, but also Israelites, who can be understood to be fifty.... The remaining three signifies faith in the Blessed Trinity."

[19] See Homily 24 n. 1 of GGHG in CCSL cxli, p. 197. The quotation is virtually verbatim.

permissible one ... if they did not have anything else on which to live."[20]

15. Question 3 asks about the meaning of John 21:4: "Jesus was standing on the shore." Gregory queries: Since the Lord "before his passion walked upon the waves of the sea in the presence of his disciples in John 6:19, why is it that after his resurrection he was standing on the shore while his disciples were laboring away on the sea?"[21] – Gregory responds: "Through 'sea' is signified the present age.... Through the solid nature of the shore is signified the perpetuity of eternal rest.... So since our Redeemer had already moved beyond the corruption of the flesh, he was standing on the shore after his resurrection."[22]

16. Question 4 focuses on John 21:6 and asks: Why is it that after his resurrection the Lord commands that they cast their nets on the right side of the boat when before his passion in Luke 5:4 he gave the command to cast their nets into the sea without distinguishing which side of the boat? – Gregory answers: "The earlier catch, in which no particular order was given as to the side where the net should be cast, designated the present Church, which gathers the good along with the wicked.... But the later catch ... takes place only on the right side, because only the Church of the elect, which will have nothing of the works of the left side, will come to see the glory of his brightness."[23]

---

[20] Bonaventure adapts Tractate 122 n. 3. See CCSL xxxvi, p. 669 and FC 92, pp. 63-64.

[21] Bonaventure adapts Homily 24 n. 2 of GGHG. See CCSL cxli, p. 197.

[22] Bonaventure abbreviates Homily 24 n. 2 of GGHG. See CCSL cxli, p. 198.

[23] Bonaventure adapts Homily 24 n. 3 of GGHG. See CCSL cxli, p. 199 and Hurst, p. 181. Fundamental to this interpretation is what

17. Question 5 investigates John 21:7: Why is it that John is described as teaching Peter here when he says to Peter: "It is the Lord"? Didn't Peter know the Lord better than John? – Chrysostom observes: "Peter was more fervent while John was mentally superior and more insightful. While he recognized him more quickly, he did not hasten to him more quickly."[24]

John 21:9-14
Manifestation of the truth of his humanity by eating

18. *So when they had landed.* Now that the majesty of his divinity has been manifested in the miraculous catch of fish, here he manifests the truth of his humanity by eating. The order of this section is as follows. First is noted *the Lord's providence* in providing food. Second is *his graciousness* in inviting them. Third is *the enlightenment of the disciples* to recognize him. Fourth is *the Lord's munificence* in distributing food.

19. (Verse 9). So his providence in preparing food is intimated by the preparation of foodstuffs that were miraculously provided. Thus the text says: *So when they had landed, they saw a fire ready and a fish laid upon it, and bread,* and so a banquet had been prepared to which he was inviting them. Matthew 22:4 reads: "Behold, I have prepared my banquet, and everything is ready." And this indeed was miraculous. Thus Chrysostom observes: "No longer does he work from material provided, as he did be-

---

Gregory says: "Everybody knows that the good are designated by the right side and the wicked on the left...."

[24] Bonaventure modifies Homily 87 n. 2. See PG 59:475. Hugh of St. Cher, p. 398v,b also cites Chrysostom in a modified and expanded version.

fore the cross, but now that he might more miraculously show signs that what he did at that time from material provided he was doing according to a certain dispensation."²⁵ He wants to say that this fish was made from nothing. Not only did he prepare this meal miraculously, but also this preparation was done by means of Peter's ministry at the divine command. Thus the text continues:

20. (Verse 10). *Jesus said to them: Bring here some of the fish which you have just now caught*, so the truth might be proven by a miracle.

21. (Verse 11). *Now²⁶ Simon Peter went aboard*, as more diligent than the others, *and hauled the net onto the land. It was full of large fish, one hundred fifty-three in number.* Through this the magnitude of the miracle is shown both in number and quantity. By "large fish" we understand the blessed, who are great by charity. Matthew 11:11 states: "The person who is least in the kingdom of the heavens is greater than he."²⁷ And to add to the greatness of the miracle the text adds a fact about the net. Thus it reads: *And although there were so many, the net was not torn.* On the contrary it is said in Luke 5:6: "They caught²⁸ a great number of fish, and their net was tearing." Therefore, *although there were so many*, namely, "in number and quantity,"²⁹ they were in such number for the sake of

---

²⁵ Bonaventure adapts Homily 87 n. 2. See PG 59:475 and FC 41, p. 463: "For He now did not start from something already existing in making these, as He had done before the crucifixion [in making the loaves and fishes] according to some design of divine Providence."

²⁶ On p. 522 n. 5 QuarEd accurately indicate that the Vulgate does not read *autem* ("Now").

²⁷ Augustine, Tractate 122 n. 9 also interprets John 21:11 by Matt 11:11.

²⁸ The Vulgate reads *concluserunt* ("enclosed") while Bonaventure has *comprehenderunt* ("caught").

²⁹ Bonaventure cites the Glossa Interlinearis.

what they were signifying. That number signified perfection, taking numerical proportion into consideration.[30] Or that number signified universality, since, as Jerome says, "one reads in descriptions of the philosophers that there are that many kinds of fish in the sea."[31]

22. (Verse 12). *Jesus said to them*. Here the second point is noted, namely, the Lord's graciousness in inviting the disciples to partake of food. So the text continues: *Jesus said to them: Come and eat*. He is inviting them to breakfast, but in the future resurrection he will invite them to a feast, according to what Revelation 19:9 says: "Blessed are those who have been invited to the marriage feast of

---

[30] See Augustine, Tractate 122 n. 8 in FC 92, pp. 70-71: "And so when to the number ten of the Law the Holy Spirit is added through the number seven, there come to be seventeen, and this number, increasing by computing all the numbers from one up to itself, reaches one hundred and fifty-three. For if to one you should add two, there come to be, of course, three.... Then if you should add all the numbers which follow up to seventeen, the total arrived at is the above-mentioned number.... And this number also contains the number fifty three times, and in addition three itself, in regard to the mystery of the Trinity." On p. 522 n. 8 QuarEd cite Cyril of Alexandria who teaches that "one hundred designates the fullness of the Gentiles, fifty the remnant of the Jewish people to be saved, three the Trinity through whom and to whose glory the faithful are called and saved." Rupert of Deutz in CCCM ix, p. 781 maintains that the one hundred fifty-three are different types of believers: "Some are married; some are widows or continent and some lead a virginal life."

[31] This is not exactly what Jerome says. See Jerome's commentary on Ez 47:6 in PL 25:474C: "Those who have written about the nature and properties of animals say ... among whom is Oppianus Cilix, a most learned poet, that there are 153 kinds of fish and that all of them were caught by the apostles, and none remained uncaught, whether noble or ignoble, rich or poor, and every kind of human being was taken from the sea of this world for salvation." Hugh of St. Cher, p. 398v,q comments: "As is clear in the Glossa of Isidore: Of all the fish that live in the water; the philosophers count 153 kinds." See Book XII, c. 6 n. 63 of Isidore, *Etymologiarvm*: "Pliny says that the names of all the 143 animals living in the waters...."

the Lamb." He is inviting them now to bodily food, in order to intimate that he is inviting them to spiritual food. The Song of Songs 5:1 states: "Eat, my friends, and drink and become intoxicated, my dearly beloved." And Isaiah 55:1 reads: "All you who thirst, come to the waters. And you, who have no money, hasten, buy, and eat. Come, buy wine and milk without money and free of charge."

23. *And none of those reclining*. Here the third point occurs, namely, the enlightenment of the disciples to recognize the Lord. So the text says: *And none of those reclining*, that is, sitting back to eat, *dared to ask: Who are you?* Thus Chrysostom comments: "In silence and with great reverence they were sitting, attentive to him."[32] *Knowing that it was the Lord*, that is, since they were not asking him: Who are you? Hebrews 12:28 states: "Let us offer pleasing service to God with fear and reverence." Philippians 2:12 has: "Work out your salvation with fear and trembling."

24. (Verse 13). *And Jesus came*. This verse introduces the fourth point, namely, the munificence of the Lord in distributing food. So the text states: *And he took bread and gave it to them*[33] *and likewise the fish*, he gave to them, so that they might eat. And at the same time it is to be understood that he himself eat with them. For Chrysostom comments: "Indeed the text does not say that he ate with them. But Luke says in Luke 24:43: When he had eaten in their presence, he took up what remained and gave it

---

[32] See Homily 87 n. 2 in PG 59:475: "But in silence and fear and with great reverence they were sitting, attentive to him."
[33] The Vulgate reads *dat eis* ("gave it to them") while Bonaventure has *dabat illis* ("gave it to them").

to them."[34] So Gregory writes: "The Lord ate broiled fish and bread."[35] Christ gave. Through this action he signified that he was the most gracious distributor of all graces. Matthew 25:15 states: "He gave to each one according to his particular ability."

25. (Verse 14). *This is now the third time.* Having detailed the manifestation, the Evangelist now compares it to previous manifestations. Compared to the preceding it is the third, not because there were not many more, but because it is sufficient to write about these three to build up faith, according to what Deuteronomy 19:15 says: "In the mouth of two or three witnesses every word stands." So the text continues: *This is now the third time that Jesus was manifested to his disciples after he had risen from the dead,* as if the threefold manifestation was a sufficient explanation. Acts 10:40-41 states: "God caused him to be plainly seen, not by all the people, but by witnesses designated beforehand by God, that is, by us, who ate and drank with him after he had been raised from the dead."

QUESTIONS

26. Question 1 deals with John 21:11: "Although there were so many, the net was not torn." – But in the first catch of fish it is said in Luke 5:6 that the net was torn because of the great number of fish. Why is it that now the net is preserved intact? – Gregory answers: "In the earlier catch because of the great number of the fish the net is torn, because ... reprobates now enter with the

---

[34] See Homily 87 n. 2 in PG 59:476 and FC 41, p. 464: "Here, however, John did not say that He partook of food with them, though Luke said elsewhere of him: 'He was eating with them.'" See Acts 1:4.

[35] See Homily 24 n. 5 of GGHG in CCSL cxli, p. 201. The quotation is virtually verbatim.

elect in confessing the faith and they ... tear the Church apart with their heresies. But in the second catch of fish ... the net is not torn, because the holy Church of the elect, resting in continual peace ... is torn apart ... by no dissensions."[36]

27. Question 2 asks about the Lord's eating fish and bread according to what is said in Luke 24:42-43.[37] Since this activity pertains solely to an animal body, it follows that either Christ had an animal body or it was a phantom eating. – I respond that there is an eating that issues from necessity and that pertains solely to an animal body. And there is eating that issues from one's capacity, and that pertains not only to an animal body, but also to a glorious and spiritual body that purely has the power to eat. For the capacity to eat is not taken away from glorified bodies, but the necessity to eat.[38]

28. Question 3 asks: What happened to the food Christ consumed? For since the glorified body will not be nourished, it seems that it would be eliminated in nature's customary way. – I answer that just as water thrown in a fire is immediately absorbed by the fire, so too the food taken by the glorified body is immediately consumed by a

---

[36] Bonaventure adapts Homily 24 n. 3 of GGHG. See CCSL cxli, p. 199.

[37] I translate the Vulgate of Luke 24:42-43: "And they offered him a piece of broiled fish and a honeycomb. And when he had eaten in their presence, he took what remained and gave it to them."

[38] This interpretation is paralleled in Bonaventure's postill on Luke 24:42-43 (n. 54) in *Bonaventure on Luke 17-24*, pp. 2235-2236: "Now the Lord ate not out of need, but out of capacity. For just as 'the rays of the sun absorb water differently than the earth, which does so out of need while the sun does so out of power,' so too Christ, before his resurrection, ate food out of need, but after his resurrection he consumed food because he had the power to do so. And therefore, Augustine in Book XIII of his *De Civitate Dei* observes: 'Not the capacity, but the need to eat and drink are removed from glorified bodies.'"

certain spiritual power. Thus Augustine in his *On the Six Questions Answered for Pagans* maintains: "The thirsty earth drinks in water in a far different way from that of the sun's shining ray – the earth acts through need; the sun, through power. So, then, the happiness of the body after the resurrection will be as incomplete if it needs food as it will be if it cannot take food."[39] And the reason for this is that in the first it is needy while in the second it is powerless.

29. Question 4 concerns John 21:14: "This is now the third time that Jesus appeared," etc. – Why did the Lord appear to his disciples in such an interrupted way and was continuously with them until his ascension? – And Chrysostom maintains: "He withdrew from their sight sometimes, so that he might be sought more ardently, and have being sought, he might be loved, and having been loved he might be venerated more specially and more devotedly."[40] – Another reason is that the disciples, no matter how long the Lord was with them, loved him in a carnal way. He wanted to dispose them to spiritual love and by means of this prepare them for the reception of the Holy Spirit. Therefore he withdrew his bodily presence from their eyes for a short while until he would withdraw from them completely in the ascension and at that time their love would be entirely spiritual. So it was written in John 16:7 above: "If I do not depart, the Paraclete will not come to you," etc.

---

[39] Bonaventure adapts Letter 102 q. 1 n. 6. See CSEL xxxiv, p. 549 and FC 18, p. 152.

[40] See Homily 87 n. 2 in PG 59:475 and FC 41, p. 462: "Do you see that He was not continuously with them, or as He had been previously?" See also Chrysostom, Homily 1 n. 4 on Acts in PG 60:18-19: "*Through forty days*, for he came, and again disappeared. Why? That he might lead their souls to higher matters."

John 21:15-23
Confirmation of Peter in the love of Christ

30. *So when they had eaten, he said*, etc. Earlier the appearance of the risen Christ had been described. Now is the depiction of *the confirmation of Peter in love of Christ*. And since what is confirmed tends to perfection, this section is divided into two parts. For in the first part *Peter is made firm in his love for Christ*. In the second *he is invited to the consummation of love* which is through suffering where verse 18 has: "Amen, amen I say to you," etc.

John 21:15-17
Confirmation of Peter

So the confirmation of Peter in love of Christ takes place via a threefold interrogation. Thus there are three components in this first part according to the three questions. First, where verse 15 reads: "So when they had eaten." The second occurs where verse 16 states: "He said to him a second time: Simon," etc. The third is found in verse 17: "A third time he said to him: Simon," etc. – So the first question proceeds in this order. First is *Christ's question*. Second is *Peter's answer*, to which the Lord adds *an exhortation*. – Christ's questioning took place during the revelation that was the meal. So the text states:

31. (Verse 15). *So when they had eaten*. One should pay attention to the fact that during the meal he did not ask about his love, since, as it is said in Sirach 6:10: "There is a friend who is a companion at table, and he will not remain in the day of distress." But afterwards he asks: *Jesus said to Simon Peter: Simon, son of John, do you love me more than these do*? So he is asking about love, since he wanted to commit his flock only to a person who loves.

So he asks about a greater love, for he wants to commit his flock to one who loves more. Thus Gregory observes: "The person who does not have love ... should never accept the office of preaching."[41] Certainly, much less must he take on the office of a prelate, because, as it is said in John 10:11: "The good shepherd lays down his life for his sheep."

32. *He said to him: Yes, Lord.* Peter's answer occurs here. In it he answers that he loves, but not that he loves more, since he did not know the love of the others. Thus Augustine maintains: "In his response ... 'I love you,' Peter did not add 'more than these do.' He answered what he knew about himself, for he could not know to what extent Christ was loved by another ... since he could not see the heart of the other."[42] *You know that I love you.* In this answer Peter shows that he is not responding in a flatteringly way, but in a truthful way. For Chrysostom comments: "He is calling as witness the one who knows one's secrets."[43] In Jeremiah 17:16 Jeremiah made this invocation: "You know that I have not desired the day of human beings."[44]

33. *He said to him.* Here the text indicates that after Peter's answer there is an exhortation to action, since "the

---

[41] Bonaventure adapts Homily 17 n. 1 of GGHG. See CCSL cxli, p. 117.

[42] Bonaventure adapts Tractate 124 n. 4. See CCSL xxxvi, p. 683.

[43] See Homily 88 n. 1 in PG 59:479 and FC 41, pp. 470-471: "Then, after being questioned about his love for Christ once, and again a second time, when he had called on Christ as a witness who knew the secrets of his heart, he was thereupon questioned a third time also, and so was greatly disturbed."

[44] Jer 17:16 reads: "And I am not troubled, following you as my shepherd, and you know that I have not desired the day of human beings. What went forth from my lips has been right in your sight."

proof of love is its manifestation in deeds."[45] Therefore, he says: *Feed my lambs.* In this the wondrous love of Christ for his sheep is expressed, since he shows this to be the principal sign, among others, of his love. And indeed Peter fulfilled this and commanded that it be fulfilled. 1 Peter 5:1-2 reads: "Elders, ... tend the flock of God that is among you," etc.[46]

34. (Verse 16). *He said to him again.* The second question occurs here. It proceeds in a similar manner as the first, for first is Christ's question, then Peter's response, and Christ's exhortation. – So the Lord asks, as he did earlier, about love: *Simon, son of John, do you love me?* He is called "Simon, son of John," because he was a son of John. – and Peter answered: *He said to him: Lord, you know that I love you."* Bede observes: "Oh, what a faithful and pure soul, that did not fear to say to its creator, in whose eyes all things are naked and open: 'Lord, you know that I love you.'"[47] – *He said to him.* The exhortation occurs here, as it did earlier: *Feed my lambs.* He repeats the earlier exhortation. As Bede comments: "This is the sole and genuine proof of integral love towards God: if you strive to exercise diligent care for the brothers."[48] *Feed,* namely,

---

[45] See Homily 30 n. 1 of GGHG in CCSL cxli, p. 256 and Hurst, p. 236. The citation is virtually verbatim.

[46] Hugh of St. Cher, p. 399a cites 1 Peter 5:2.

[47] See Book II, Homily 22 for the Feast of Sts. Peter and Paul in *Bedae Venerabilis Homeliarvm Evangelii Libri II* in *Bedae Venerabilis Opera: Pars III Opera Homiletica, Pars IV Opera Rhythmica.* Edited by D. Hurst. CCSL cxx (Turnhout: Brepols, 1955), p. 344: "Oh, what a happy and pure conscience, that did not fear to say to its creator, in whose eyes are things are naked and open: 'Lord, you know that I love you.'" Bede alludes to Hebr 4:13: "And there is no creature hidden from his sight, but all things are naked and open to the eyes of him to whom we have to give account."

[48] This is a verbatim quotation from Book II, Homily 22. See CCSL cxx, p. 342.

by example, as the one about whom Psalm 77:72 says: "He fed them in the innocence of his heart."

35. (Verse 17). *A third time he said to him.* The third questioning occurs here and follows the same order as before, namely, question, answer, exhortation. – So the Lord asks about the same matter: *Simon, son of John, do you love me?* From this verse it is clear that *amare* ("to love") is taken in a good sense, just as *diligere* ("to love") is.[49] – And *Peter was saddened.* Here Peter's answer is noted, but he responds with sadness, since, as Chrysostom says,[50] he feared lest something similar happen to him as happened when he said: "I will lay down my life for you."[51] And so he was saddened *because he said to him for the third time: Do you love me?* But nevertheless, he did not despair, but rather responded with fidelity. *He said to him* and adds to his response: *Lord, you know all things,* as God, for he knew that he was the one who said in Jeremiah 17:10: "I am the Lord who searches hearts and innards," that is, thoughts and affections. – *He said to him: Feed my sheep.* Note the exhortation. And by "sheep" are understood the

---

[49] Bonaventure seems to be referring to Book XIV, c. 7 n. 1-2 of Augustine, *The City of God.* See FC 14, p. 359: "However, the Lord had not used the verb *amas* three times but only once, for twice He had used *diligis.* From all this we conclude that when our Lord used *diligis* He meant precisely the same as when He used *amas....* The reason why it seems to me that this point should be mentioned is that there are some who think that *dilectio* or *caritas* is one thing and *amor* is another. They maintain that *dilectio* is understood in a good sense and *amor* in a bad sense. Yet it is quite clear that not even the authors of secular literature make this distinction."

[50] See Homily 88 n. 1 in FC 41, p. 487: "... he was thereupon questioned a third time also, and so was greatly disturbed. Fearing a repetition of what had happened before (for, because he was overconfident at that time, he afterwards was overcome), he therefore once more turned to Him for support."

[51] See John 13:37.

more perfect subjects.[52] – It should be noted that the Lord commanded him to feed the sheep, not to shear them, not to eat them, because a shepherd is not commanded to feed himself out of love of Christ, but the sheep. Ezekiel 34:2-3 reads: "Woe to the shepherds of Israel, who fed themselves. Should not the sheep be fed by the shepherds? You ate the milk and clothed yourselves with the wool."

QUESTIONS

36. Question 1 asks: Since the other Apostles, who loved the Lord, were standing around, why was the question about love addressed solely to Peter? – One answer is that since the care of the flock had been specially committed to him among the others, he was asked especially about love. Thus Chrysostom comments: "Peter was the chosen one of the Apostles and the mouthpiece of the disciples and the head of the college."[53] Therefore, bypassing and skipping over the others, he spoke to him about these matters. – Another reason can also be assigned. Since Peter had notoriously denied him and therefore seemed not to be worthy to be over the rest of the Apostles, the Lord asked, so that he might show that his love exceeded that of the rest and to confirm the pastoral office that he had given him.[54]

---

[52] See Theophylactus on John 21:17 in PG 124:311C: "If perhaps the lambs are said to be more simple and are easily brought in, the sheep, on the other hand, are the more perfect."

[53] See Homily 88 n. 1 in PG 59:478 and FC 41, p. 470: "Now, why in the world did He pass over the other Apostles, and speak to this one about these matters? He was the chosen one of the Apostles, the mouthpiece of the disciples, and the head of the band."

[54] On p. 526 n. 4 QuarEd cite Cyril of Alexandria's commentary on John 21:15-17: "Now from the fact that the Lord said, 'Feed my lambs,' it is thought that there was a certain renewal of the apostolate already entrusted to him."

37. Question 2 asks: Since Peter could not respond to the question of John 21:15, "Do you love me more than these do?" because he didn't know about the others, why did the Lord ask the question? – I answer that it has to be maintained that the Lord asked this to show Peter's outstanding character in the asking and provide a correction in the answering. For Augustine notes: "That Peter loved the Lord more than the others appears evident where he questions him and says: 'Do you love me more than these do?' Although he knew what the situation was, he nevertheless asked so that we too might know Peter's love towards the Lord."[55] And Peter's correction is shown in this that he did not dare to put himself above the others, as he had done before the passion when he had said: "Even though all will be scandalized, yet not I."[56]

38. But then the question arises: Why does the Lord ask so often: Peter, do you love me? – Augustine answers: "So he asked three times, in order that a triple confession is paid back to the triple denial, so that his tongue may not give less service to love than to fear."[57] – Another reason is given. Since he is asking so that he might commend his flock to Peter and since he wanted to commend his flock three times, so he asks about Peter's love three times.[58]

39. But then the question surfaces: Why did he say to him thrice: Feed? – And the answer is that Christ's sheep have

---

[55] Bonaventure adapts Tractate 124 n. 4. See CCSL xxxvi, pp. 682-683.

[56] See Mark 14:29.

[57] Bonaventure modifies Tractate 123 n. 5. See CCSL xxxvi, p. 678 and FC 92, p. 77.

[58] See Chrysostom, Homily 88 n. 1 in FC 41, p. 471: "Moreover, three times Christ asked the question and three times gave the same injunction, to show how greatly He esteemed the office of carrying for His own lambs, and that to perform this task was most of all a proof of his love for Him."

to be fed in a threefold way, namely, by word, example, and temporal aid. For Bede notes: "The care of the pastoral office demands that the rector of the Church must diligently provide that his people are not bereft of temporal aid. He must give an example of virtue to them and dutifully provide them with the word of preaching."[59]

40. But then the question comes up: Why did he twice say to feed the lambs and once to feed the sheep? – "The lambs" are understood as the imperfect and very delicate in the faith, and these need more ample pastures, that is, more solicitous care. But "the sheep" are understood to be fully grown, who are capable of ruling themselves, and these do not require great care.

John 21:18-23
Peter is invited to the consummation of his love

41. *Amen, amen I say to you.* After detailing Peter's confirmation in love, there follows *his invitation to the consummation of his love.* Now the consummation of love is that a person lay down his life for Christ. And so this becomes an invitation to imitate his passion. The text follows this order. First, Peter is invited and made certain of the type of his death. Second, he seeks to be assured of the type of death John will have. Third, the answer is given him that

---

[59] Bonaventure adapts Book II, Homily 15 on the Feast of Sts. Peter and Paul. See CCSL cxx, p. 345. See Bernard of Clairvaux, Second Sermon n. 3 *In Resurrectione Domini* in SBOp 5.96: "So the three women bought their spices: mind, tongue, hands. For concerning these, in my opinion, Peter received the threefold command to feed the Lord's flock: feed them with your mind, feed them with your mouth, feed them with your works. Feed them with prayer from your soul, with exhortation by word, by a display of good conduct."

John will not suffer. Fourth, the understanding of believers that John was not going to die is corrected.

42. (Verse 18). So Peter is made certain by the Lord of the kind of death he would experience, namely, by passion and cross. And in order to make him certain, the text states: *Amen, amen I say to you*. And this is the passion that in his old age he would be crucified for Christ's sake. So the text says: *When you were young, you girded yourself and walked where you wished*, that is, you followed your own will. Sirach 18:30: "Son, do not pursue your lusts and turn away from your will."[60] *But when you are old, you will stretch forth your hands*, namely, on the cross,[61] *and another will gird you*, "namely, with chains,"[62] such as Nero, *and lead you where you do not want*, "that is, to death."[63] For as it is said in 2 Corinthians 5:4: "We do not wish to be unclothed, but rather clothed over." And the reason for this is given in Ephesians 5:29: "For no one ever hated his own flesh." Peter will be girded with chains. Acts 12:6 reads: "Peter was sleeping between two soldiers, bound by two chains." And since they have stretched these words to mean something other than the letter, the interpretation made by the Evangelist is set forth.

43. (Verse 19). *Now this*, namely, the stretching forth of his hands, *he said to signify by what manner of death he would glorify God*, for death on the cross, although it had been vilified before Christ, afterwards became glorious. And by this Peter became glorious. So Augustine observes: "... that denier ... elated by presuming, prostrate by denying, cleansed after weeping, proven by confessing,

---

[60] The Vulgate does not read *Fili* ("Son").

[61] See Augustine, Tractate 123 n. 5 in FC 92, p. 80: "'You will stretch forth,' he said, 'your hands,' that is, you will be crucified."

[62] This is the Glossa Interlinearis.

[63] This is the Glossa Interlinearis.

is crowned by suffering."[64] By this death Peter glorified the Lord, as Paul said in Philippians 1:20: "Christ will be glorified in my body, whether through life or through death." And since suffering is not good unless it is undergone willingly, he exhorts Peter to suffer willing. And so he says: *And when he had said this, he said to him*, that is, to Peter: *Follow me*. I came to the passion of the cross willingly, according to what Peter himself says in 1 Peter 2:21: "Christ suffered for us, leaving you an example, that you may follow his footsteps." About this following or walking in his footsteps the Lord said to Peter in John 13:36 above: "Where I am going, you cannot come now, but you will follow later."

44. (Verse 20). *Turning around, Peter saw the disciple*, etc. This verse introduces the second point: Peter, knowing about his death, asks about the death of John, for he wanted to be joined by a similar death to the one he had been joined in life through great love. And since Peter knew that the Lord loved John, he wanted to know by what death he wanted him to die. So the text reads: *Turning around, Peter saw following them the disciple*[65] *whom Jesus loved*, namely, John. And a sign of special love is shown when he continues: *the one who, at the supper, had leaned back upon his breast*, in John 13:23 above, *and said: Lord, who is it that will betray you?* He sought from him what had been secret, and this was a sign of love, and it had been revealed to him, as is said in John 13:26 above. And this was a sign of friendship, as is said in John 15:15 above: "I have called you friends, because

---

[64] Bonaventure adapts Tractate 123 n. 4. See CCSL xxxvi, p. 677 and FC 92, p. 76.

[65] On p. 527 n. 6 QuarEd rightly notice that the Vulgate reads *illum discipulum* ("that disciple").

everything that I have heard from my Father, I have made known to you."

45. (Verse 21). *So when Peter had seen him*, who he knew to be specially loved, *he said to Jesus*:[66] *Lord, what about this one?* Supply: will he suffer and thus come to you? Chrysostom notes: "Peter loved John very much. Therefore, since the Lord had foretold great things for Peter, he wanted him to participate with him[67] and said: 'Lord, what about this one?'"[68]

46. (Verse 22) *Jesus said to him.* Here in a third point Peter is made certain that John would not suffer, through the Lord's answer, in which he reveals the truth so that he might give a satisfactory answer to the question and rebuke curiosity as he corrects the inquirer. He reveals the truth where the text says: *Jesus said to him: So*[69] *I want him to remain until I come.* Bede interprets: "'So,' that is, to wait for the last day without the violence of persecution."[70] This is his answer to the inquirer. – When

---

[66] On p. 527 n. 8 QuarEd accurately indicate that the Vulgate reads *dixit Iesu* ("said to Jesus") whilst Bonaventure has *dicit ad Iesum* ("said to Jesus").

[67] "To participate with him" is my rendering of *communicator*.

[68] Bonaventure adapts Homily 88 n.2. See PG 59:480 and FC 41, pp. 473-474: "Moreover, here he showed the affection he had for the other, for Peter loved John very much.... Since Christ had predicted great things of him ... in the desire to have John share in all this, Peter said: 'What of this man?'" Hugh of St. Cher, p. 399v,a quotes from Chrysostom without attribution and has Peter ask for John "as a companion and participant."

[69] On p. 527 n. 9 QuarEd correctly mention that the Vulgate reads *si sic* ("if so") while Bonaventure has *sic* ("so"). Augustine and Hugh of St. Cher also read *sic*.

[70] See Book I, Homily 9 for "St. John the Evangelist" in CCSL cxx, p. 63: "'So' ... I do not want him to be consumed by the passion of martyrdom, but to wait for the last day without the violence of persecution. When it comes, I will receive him into the mansion of eternal beatitude."

he says: *What is it to you? You, follow me*, he rebukes him for the curiosity behind his question. Thus Chrysostom states: "What is it to you if I want him to remain? You, attend to your own matters and be solicitous concerning them."[71] Sirach 3:22 reads: "In many of his works be not curious, but always think about the matters that he has commanded you."[72] And therefore he repeats: *You, follow me*, as if he were saying: Think about this and exercise your concern about this.

47. (Verse 23). *So this saying went abroad among the brothers and sisters.* Here is the fourth point: the correction of the interpretation of the faithful that John was not going to simply die. So the text continues: *That*[73] *that disciple was not to die*, contrary to Psalm 88:49: "Who is the human being that will live and will not see death?" *But Jesus had not said.*[74] Here is the correction of that understanding, since Jesus had not said this, namely, that he would not die. *He had not said: He is not to die*, for, as it is said in Qoheleth 9:4: "There is no one who lives forever." *But rather: So I want him to remain until I come. What is that to you?* So the text is to be read and explained as a assertion as it was above.[75]

---

[71] Bonaventure adapts Homily 88 n. 2. See PG 59:480 and FC 41, pp. 474-475: "Therefore, He was saying to him (Peter): 'You have been entrusted with a mission; look after it, perform it, fight and struggle for it. What if I do indeed wish for him to remain here? You look after, and take care of, your own affairs."

[72] Sir 3:22 states: "... but the things that God has commanded you, think on them always, and in many of his works be not curious."

[73] On p. 527 n. 11 QuarEd rightly notice that the Vulgate reads *quia* ("that") while Bonaventure has *quod* ("that").

[74] On p. 528 n. 1 QuarEd accurately indicate that the Vulgate reads *dixit ei* ("said to him").

[75] See John 21:22 (n. 46) above.

Questions

48. Question 1 asks about John 21:18: "Another will gird you and lead you where you do not want to go." – It seems from this that Peter's suffering was involuntary and therefore not meritorious. – I respond that there is a twofold will: one of reason and one of nature. To will to suffer comes from the will of reason, but not willing to suffer issues from the will of nature or sensuality. Do not be amazed, since it was thus in the Head, for Matthew 26:39 states: "Father, if it be possible, let this cup pass by me, but not as I will, but as you will." Thus Augustine observes: "Peter unwillingly came to death, but willingly conquered death. And he left behind this feeling of weakness by which no one wishes to die, a feeling so exceedingly natural that not even old age could take it away from blessed Peter."[76]

49. Question 2 deals with John 20:19: "Signifying by what manner of death he would glorify God," for John 5:41 above says: "I do not receive glory from human beings." Therefore, since Peter was a human being, he did not glorify God. – I answer that although God might not be glorified in himself, nonetheless he is glorified for us in his saints who are suffering for his glory, since through this it is made known to us how many things are to be suffered for the love of God through the example of the saints for us.[77]

---

[76] See Tractate 124 n. 5 in CCSL xxxvi, p. 679 and FC 92, p. 80. The citation is virtually verbatim.

[77] This complicated sentence seems based on Chrysostom, Homily 88 n. 1. See FC 41, p. 473: "He did not say 'he should die,' but 'he should glorify God,' that you might learn that to suffer for Christ is glory and honor for the sufferer."

50. Question 3 asks why the Lord said in a special way to Peter in John 21:22: "You, follow me," since, if this is understood of the way of perfection, then many others have followed. The same would hold true if it is said about the way of suffering. If this saying deals with the type of death, Andrew also followed in this way.[78] – And the answer should be, according to some, that "you" is not to be read here in distinction from everyone, but only from John, with whom this passage also deals. – Another interpretation is that "you" refers here more to significance than to distinction, for since Peter was head of the Church and the principal leader and just as he excelled in leadership, so too he had to excel in imitation.[79]

51. Question 4 concerns John 21:20: "That disciple whom Jesus loved." – 1. How did he dare to say this since it is said in Ecclesiastes 9:1: "Men and women do not know whether they are worthy of love or hatred"? – 2. Furthermore, since Christ loves all, why did John attribute this to

---

[78] This question comes from Augustine, Tractate 124 n. 1. See FC 92, p. 82: "For why is 'Follow me' said to Peter and is not said to the others who were present at the same time? And surely they were following him as disciples [follow] their master. But if it must be understood with reference to suffering, did Peter alone suffer for Christ's truth? Was there not among those seven another son of Zebedee, John's brother, who after his ascension is disclosed to have been killed by Herod? But someone may say that, because James was not crucified, it was rightly said to Peter, 'Follow me,' as he experienced not only death but also the death of the cross, as Christ [did]."

[79] See Chrysostom, Homily 88 n. 1 in FC 41, p. 473: "And, if someone should say: 'How is it, then, that it was James who received the bishop's chair in Jerusalem?' I would make this reply: that Christ appointed this man, not merely to a chair, but as teacher of the world." On p. 528 n. 8 QuarEd cite Cyril of Alexandria on John 21:19: "'Follow me,' these words, if we follow the common opinion, can be understood of the following of disciples. But it seems that there is an enigmatic subtext: Follow the footsteps of my perils, insisting in a certain manner in word and deed on the same way, aiding the souls of those called in the faith...."

himself, namely, that he was more beloved? – This seems false, since Peter loved more. Wherefore, he was better and God has greater love towards those who are better. Therefore, he loved Peter more than John. – The first point can be answered in this manner: John knew that he was loved by revelation or by certain signs.[80] Relative to the second point, Augustine seems to say that John was more greatly loved whereas Peter loved more. And therefore, he asks: who was better? And he responds that Peter was better, but John was happier. And he twists these words into an allegory, saying, that John represents the contemplative life whereas the active life is signified by Peter. – But this raises other questions. Wherefore, Augustine himself says that justice lies hidden here, and mercy is manifest.[81] – So it has to be said that "to love more" has a twofold meaning. First is "to love more" with regard to a greater reward. And thus Jesus loved Peter more, with this understood that Peter would always love the Lord more. Second is "to love more" with respect to a greater display of love, since he showed many signs of love. And in this way he loved John more.[82]

---

[80] Bonaventure discusses this point in his commentary on Ecclesiastes 9:1. See *Commentary on Ecclesiastes*. Translation and Notes by Campion Murray and Robert J. Karris. WSB VII (St. Bonaventure, NY: Franciscan Institute Publications, 2005), pp. 319, 323-326.

[81] Bonaventure is summarizing Tractate 124 n. 4-5. I quote from the end of n. 4 and the beginning of n. 5 as found in FC 92, p. 87: "But as far as I understand it, I would easily answer that he who loves Christ more is better, but he whom Christ loves more is happier, if I could fully see how I might defend the justice of our Liberator who loves less him by whom he is loved more and [loves] more him by whom he is loved less. Therefore, in the manifest mercy of him whose justice is hidden I shall approach the discussion of the solution of this so immense question in accordance with the strength which he himself will bestow."

[82] For further explanations see Book III, d. 32 q. 6 of Bonaventure's *Sentence Commentary*.

52. Question 5 continues: But then there is a further question: Why did he show greater affections of love towards John, since he loved Peter more than John? – It seems that there was playacting on the Lord's part. – It can be responded to this that although Peter would merit a great reward, it, nevertheless, was fitting for Christ to show greater intimacy to John, since he was young and was a virgin and innocent. And these are the things, which in an admirable way make a person lovable and highly regarded both in the eyes of God and human beings. For Bede says: "This is John, who was found worthy to be honored by the Lord more than all the rest by a special privilege of love.[83] And his special gift of purity had made him worthy of a greater love."[84] And the Glossa says: "John was on more friendly terms with the Lord, because he was younger."[85]

53. Question 6 concerns John 21:22: "So I want him to remain, until I come." – So it seems that at least once before the coming of the Lord there was a soul that was not separated from the body. For "until I come" has not taken place. Therefore, it seems that John has not yet died, and an argument for this is that his body has not been found.

---

[83] See the responsory in the Roman Breviary for the third reading of the First Nocturn at Matins for the Feast of St. John the Evangelist on December 27.

[84] See the responsory in the Roman Breviary for the fifth reading of the Second Nocturn at Matins for the Feast of St. John the Evangelist. Both the responsory in n. 83 and this one ultimately go back to Book II, Homily 9 of Bede on The Feast of St. John the Evangelist. See CCSL cxx, pp. 61-62. See further Augustine, Tractate 124 n. 7 in FC 92, p. 93: "There are those who have felt, and these indeed no contemptible expounders of the Sacred Word, that the Apostle John was more loved by Christ precisely because he did not take a wife and lived most chastely from the beginning of his childhood."

[85] On p. 529 n. 2 QuarEd provide some passages from the Glossa Interlinearis that approximate the point Bonaventure's citation is making.

– I answer that it has to be maintained that besides the interpretation provided first by the disciples and which the Evangelist himself censures, namely, that he would not die, there are three other interpretations. The first is that he has not died, but will die at the coming of the Lord. But now he resides asleep under the earth, and therefore, his body has not been found. But this opinion is improbable, since it is incredible that the Lord would delay for so long a time in showing to the disciple whom he loved his glory which the Apostle longed for in Philippians 1:23: "I long[86] to depart and be with Christ." – There is another opinion that the Lord assumed him body and soul, and during that assumption he died and came back to life. – Even though this cannot be disproved, nevertheless, since it does not have authority, it is debunked with the same ease with which it was set forth as probative. – The third opinion maintains that John died and asserts nothing about his body, because nothing certain has been found. But this opinion provides this interpretation of what had been said, "So I want him to remain, until I come," that is, "to wait for the last day, not of the world, but of his death. When it comes, I will receive him into the mansion of eternal beatitude."[87]

John 21:24-25
Reason for our faith to be confirmed

54. *This is the disciple who,* etc. Previous treatments concerned the anxious care of the disciples and the revelation of Christ. Now the text presents a consideration of

---

[86] The Vulgate reads *desiderium habens* ("I desire") while Bonaventure has *cupio* ("I long").

[87] This quotation modifies Bede's interpretation in CCSL cxx, p. 63. See John 21:22 n. 46 above.

the *reason for our faith to be confirmed*. The Evangelist confirms this in us in a twofold manner: by certifying it in truth and by basing it in humility. He certifies it in the truth when he says that he is a true and reliable witness. He grounds it in humility when he shows that he could not write all things completely where verse 25 says: "Now there are many other things," etc.

55. (Verse 24). So the Evangelist states: *This is the disciple who bears witness concerning these things and who has written these things*. He is to be believed, and every doubt is to be pushed aside, since *and we know that his witness is true*. Chrysostom comments: "Since he wrote with great certainty, he did not hesitate to cite his own testimony, challenging his audience to examine the items, one by one, and to test what had happened. It is customary for us, when we think that we are telling something very true, not to reject our own testimony…. Thus the apostles said in Acts 5: 'We are witnesses of these words.'"[88]

56. (Verse 25). *Now there are many other things that Jesus did*. He shows that he did not write everything down completely. In this he humbles our intellect, lest we think that we are capable of knowing all things. Wherefore, he states that he did not write.[89] So the text says: *But if every one of these would be written, not even the world itself, I think, could hold them, the books that would have to be written*. This verse should be construed in this manner: "to hold those books that must be written," for our capability is tiny. Thus John 16:12 above has: "I have many things to say to you, but you cannot bear them now."

---

[88] Bonaventure adapts Homily 88 n. 2. See PG 59:481 and FC 41, p. 476. The citation at the end of Chrysostom's text is Acts 5:32.

[89] One can complete this sentence with: "he did not write down *everything*."

Question

57. But what is this that Christ's signs could not be held in the entire world, since the world would contain the books not only for his deeds, but for everything that has been done from the beginning of the world, if they were written down? – And it has to be said that there is a dual meaning to capability: bodily and spiritual, which happens through the intellect. If the text is understood in a bodily sense, then it was spoken through hyperbole, as in other places of Scripture such as Psalm 72:9: "They have set their mouth against heaven"[90] and concerning Solomon that he accumulated such a huge amount of silver that it was as plentiful as the stones in Jerusalem according to 1 Kings 10:27.[91] But if the text is spoken and taken on the level of the holding of understanding, then the text is true, for Augustine observes: "We know that our understanding would not hold what could be written about Christ. Let us take care to understand by right faith what he wrote, to put into practice by right action what he taught and come to the eternal gifts that the Lord himself has promised,"[92] with his help, who lives and reigns forever and ever. Amen.

---

[90] Hugh of St. Cher, p. 399n states that the Latins interpret this verse as hyperbole and cites Ps 72:9 in its entirety, and with that citation concludes his commentary on John's Gospel.

[91] 1 Kings 10:27 states: "And he (Solomon) made silver to be as plentiful in Jerusalem as stones...."

[92] On p. 530 n. 4 QuarEd indicate that they have not found these exact words in Augustine's writings and go on to quote Bl. Albert's postill on John 21:25: "For Augustine states: we know that our understanding would not hold what could be written about Christ. Let us take care to believe and understand with right faith what he wrote, to put into practice by right action and so fulfill what he taught, so that we can come to the eternal gifts that the Lord has promised."

INDICES

SCRIPTURE INDEX

OLD TESTAMENT

7:6	179	5:12-13	302
8:20	535	6:3	587, 587n5,
9:11	180		930
11:17	179	6:7	149n36, 517
14:4	458n37,	8:3	651, 209
	521n31	9:11	587
14:12	304	9:16	628,
14:15	608		628n132
15:3	492	10:6	665, 791n21
17:2	522	13:3	418
21:12	808	15:2	312, 522n36
22:29	953	15:4	591
24:13	196, 528	15:5	689
24:15	705	15:10	713, 937
24:17	861	16:8	841
24:25	196	16:12	915
26:12	407	17:14	357n81
26:14	865	17:45	433
27:19	486,	18:5	336
	486n131,	18:7	817
	599	18:9	519
29:16	444	20:13	335
30:4	485n123	21:2	819
30:25	612	21:12	274
33:19	278	21:13	571, 571n64
36:17	304, 887	21:14	902
41:25	492, 672,	21:16	761
	751	21:19	920
		21:23	402, 855,
Psalms			959
2:6	917	21:28	786
2:8	360	22:6	739
3:6	166, 166n85	24:8	455n22
4:3	320, 492	25:2	332, 333
4:7	67	26:1	342
4:9	15, 266	26:4	773

Qoheleth (Ecclesiastes)

Song of Songs(Canticle)

27:14	904	3:14-16	122
27:18	924	3:16	118n199,
27:24	925		123,
27:25	925		123n209,
27:26	911		123n211
27:27-31	910	4:40	620
27:32	924	5:25-29	735n49
27:35	925	5:43	638
27:37	917	6:37	330
27:45	912	6:38	331n10
27:46	478, 934n98	6:45	346
27:48	927	6:49	342
27:52	621	7:4	142
27:57	936n102	7:17	879n67
27:63	406	9:22	261, 610
27:64	939n112	9:27-28	611, 611n82
27:66	950n23	9:41	225n27
28:1	948, 948n18,	11:9	767n35
	949n21	13:32	224n24
28:2	963	14:3	595n32,
28:9	958n58,		595n34, 638
	958n61	14:8	646
28:18	687, 827,	14:12	691n16
	831	14:29	1010n56
28:19	185, 185n30	14:44	869
28:20	602, 811	14:54	875
Mark		14:68	885
1	149n38	15:24	925
1:8	109, 200	15:25	912
1:12	133	15:27	916
1:14	133	15:34	934n98
1:22	441,	15:43	939,
	441n125		939n110
1:28	259	16:1	642
3	123	16:2	949
		16:5	963

	700	14	12, 578, 685,
13:21	11, 23,		974n100
	397n168,	14:1	60, 722,
	685, 701,		737n57,
	705		812n78
13:21-30	701	14:1-14	25, 722
13:22	701	14:1-16:33	25, 721
13:23	34n3, 702,	14:2	723, 856
	1013	14:2-3	432
13:24	702	14:3	723, 724n12,
13:25	702		750, 807
13:26	703, 708,	14:4	725, 731
	1013	14:5	725, 731,
13:27	169, 704,		800n46
	709	14:6	16n31, 303,
13:28	704		478n102,
13:29	331n11, 704		556, 725,
13:30	705		732, 732n40,
13:31	686n1, 712,		893,
	717		893n106
13:31-38	712	14:7	727
13:32	713	14:8	728, 731
13:33	471, 686,	14:9	470n79, 678,
	713, 717		728, 732,
13:34	714, 718,		733, 733n41,
	770, 774		835n23
13:35	715, 850	14:10	313, 380,
13:36	715, 800,		513, 578n86,
	801n48, 873,		578n87,
	1013		678n111,
13:37	662, 665,		728, 835
	716, 874,	14:11	58, 475, 729,
	1008n51		734
13:38	716, 719,	14:12	8, 316n85,
	719n105,		578n87, 729,
	883		734, 734n46,

INDEX OF ECCLESIASTICAL AUTHORS

310v,a	259n118	330e-g	381n130
310v,e	260n119	330m	381n129
311c	261n121	331r-s	397n169
311d	269n142	332b	401n2
311m	13n24, 263n126, 263n127	332v,h	406n18
		332v,l	405n16
311v	272n3	332v,q	404n12
312b	276n12, 276n13, 276n14, 277n15, 277n16	333k	415n41
		333s	415n42
		333t	418n48
312f	277n18	333v,g	423n62
312h	277n20	333v,n	420n54
312v,a	279n22, 279n24	333z	419n49
313b	278n21	334	426n72
313i	284n33	334f	424n67
314a	282n30	334h	425n69
314v,a	285n37	334v,ab	432n92
314v,b	285n38	335d	434n99
314v,h	286n40	335f	435n100, 436n102
319v,c	316n83		
319v,h	311n75	335m	438n108
320b	312n76, 312n77	335pq	438n111
320v,f	317n87	335v,c	439n116
320v,l	312n76	335v,g	440n117
322v,c	326n2	335v,o	441n125, 443n128, 446n140
323c	331n12		
323v,a-324d			
	330n8	335v,u	442n127
323v,c	338n28	336m	445n137
325k	344n48	336s	450n7
327	359n82	336v,a	455n25
327d	357n79	336v,k	451n10
327f	352n65	336v,q	453n16
327m	357n81	337a	457n31, 457n32, 458n34
327o	354n69		
329v,x	377n126	337l	454n18, 456n43

XXXII.368713n84

Homily 6 621n111

Homily 11.1
(on Leviticus 19:2)
        844n45

Paul the Deacon
Homiliarius
        621n111

Pelagius, 124, 124n213

Peter Comestor,
        151n46
Historia evangelica
39   191n48

Historia scholastica,
        162n74
In evangelia
XXXVII   149n38
81   279n22
117   655n55
151   710n71
168   900n3
177   933n95

Peter Lombard
1 Cor 2:8 788n10
Gal 1:19   922n65

Sententiae
II.V.1   790n20
III.20.5   190n47
IV.V.3   113n189

Praepositivus
Summa   634n150

Prosper of Aquitane
*Liber Sententiarum ex
operibus S. Augustini
delibatarum*
I.7   715n91
364   856n80

Pseudo-Augustine
*De praedestinatione et
gratia*
c. 4   545n109

De spiritu et anima
54   856n78

Pseudo-Bernard
*Meditatio in passionem et
resurrectionem Domini*
        964n79

Pseudo-Dionysius,
        68
De divinis nominibus,
303n66
4.19   496n161
4.19-35   68n84

Mystical Theology
1.3   91, 91n138

Rabanus Maurus
*Commentaria in Libros IV
Regum*
2Kgs 16:18 467n69

INDEX OF PHILOSOPHERS, GRAMMARIANS, AUTHORS, AND PLAYWRIGHTS